D1570990

The Political Economy of Transnational Tax Reform

The Shoup Mission to Japan in Historical Context

This volume explores the history of the United States tax mission to Japan during the occupation following World War II. Under General MacArthur, economist Carl S. Shoup led the mission with the charge of framing a tax system for Japan designed to strengthen democracy and accelerate economic recovery. The volume examines the sources, conduct, and effects of the mission, and situates the mission within the history of international financial and fiscal reform. The book begins by establishing the context of progressive social investigations of taxation, including Shoup's earlier tax missions to France and Cuba. It then goes on to explore the Japanese background to the Shoup mission and the process by which American and Japanese tax experts shaped their recommendations. The book then assesses and explains the mission's accomplishments in the context of the political economies of the United States and Japan. It concludes by analyzing the global implications of the mission, which became iconic among international tax reformers.

W. Elliot Brownlee is professor emeritus at the University of California, Santa Barbara. Among his most recent books are *Federal Taxation in America: A Short History*, 2nd ed. (Cambridge University Press and Woodrow Wilson Center Press, 2004); *The Reagan Presidency: Pragmatic Conservatism and Its Legacies*, coedited with Hugh Davis Graham (2003); and *Funding the Modern American State: The Rise and Fall of the Era of Easy Finance, 1941–1995* (Cambridge University Press and Woodrow Wilson Center Press, 1996). His articles on the history of taxation and public finance have appeared in various scholarly volumes and in journals and periodicals, including *American Nineteenth Century History*, the *Asia-Pacific Journal*, *Explorations in Economic History*, *Keio Economic Studies*, *The National Tax Journal*, *Proceedings of the American Philosophical Society*, *The Quarterly Review of Economics and Business*, *Rikkyo Economic Review*, *Sekai (The World)*, *Social Philosophy and Policy*, *Tax Notes*, *The Wilson Quarterly*, and *The Wisconsin Magazine of History*.

Eisaku Ide is professor in the faculty of economics at Keio University, Japan. He has served on many governmental commissions and committees for agencies of the Japanese government, including the Cabinet Office; the Ministry of Internal Affairs and Communications; the Ministry of Agriculture, Forestry and Fisheries; and the National Governor's Association. His major field of scholarly emphasis is fiscal history, and he has published several books and numerous articles on the history of Japanese budgetary and monetary policy during the 1930s, 1940s, and 1950s. He recently published two articles in English: "The End of the Strong State?: On the Evolution of Japanese Tax Policy," with Sven Steinmo (in *The New Fiscal Sociology: Comparative and Historical Perspective*, Cambridge University Press 2009) and "The Origins of Macro-Budgeting and the Foundations of Japanese Public Finance: Drastic Fiscal Reform in Occupation Era" (in *Keio Economic Studies* 2011, vol. 47). He has received the Susumu Sato Award from the Japanese Association of Local Public Finance and the Sozei Siryokan Award from the Institute of Tax Research and Literature.

Yasunori Fukagai is professor in the faculty of economics at Yokohama National University. His field of scholarly emphasis is the history of economic thought, and his research has focused on British utilitarian thinkers. He has published numerous scholarly articles and two edited books, *Inspecting the Market Society: From Smith to Keynes* (in Japanese) and *British Empire, Social Integration and the History of Economic Thought* (forthcoming, with Martin Daunton and Junichi Himeno). He has organized many conferences and lectured widely in the United Kingdom, the United States, Canada, and Portugal, as well as Japan. He has received numerous major research grants, including a current one from the Japan Society for the Promotion of Science to support "The Organic View of the Society and the Designing of Economic Governance: Comparative Research on Economic Thought from the Fin-de-Siècle to the Inter-War Period." He is director of the developmental plan for the Carl S. Shoup Collection, which is held at the University Library of Yokohama National University.

The Political Economy of Transnational Tax Reform

The Shoup Mission to Japan in Historical Context

Edited by

W. ELLIOT BROWNLEE
University of California, Santa Barbara, United States

EISAKU IDE
Keio University, Japan

YASUNORI FUKAGAI
Yokohama National University, Japan

CAMBRIDGE
UNIVERSITY PRESS

CAMBRIDGE UNIVERSITY PRESS
Cambridge, New York, Melbourne, Madrid, Cape Town,
Singapore, São Paulo, Delhi, Mexico City

Cambridge University Press
32 Avenue of the Americas, New York, NY 10013-2473, USA

www.cambridge.org
Information on this title: www.cambridge.org/9781107033160

First published 2013

Printed in the United States of America

A catalog record for this publication is available from the British Library.

Library of Congress Cataloging in Publication Data

The political economy of transnational tax reform : the Shoup mission to Japan in
historical context / [edited by] W. Elliot Brownlee, University of California, Santa Barbara,
Eisaku Ide, Keio University, Japan, Yasunori Fukagai Yokohama National University,
Japan.
pages cm
Includes bibliographical references and index.
ISBN 978-1-107-03316-0 (hardback : alk. paper)
1. Taxation – Japan – History – 20th century. 2. Fiscal policy – Japan – History – 20th
century. 3. Japan – Economic conditions – 1945–1989. 4. Japan – Foreign economic
relations – United States. 5. United States – Foreign economic relations – Japan.
I. Brownlee, W. Elliot, 1941– II. Ide, Eisaku. III. Fukagai, Yasunori, 1954–
HJ2971.P65 2013
336.200952′09044–dc23 2012051628

ISBN 978-1-107-03316-0 Hardback

Contents

v

Contributors

Michael R. Adamson is an Independent Historian and Lecturer, California State University, Sacramento.

Takatsugu Akaishi is Professor of Economics, Nagasaki University.

W. Elliot Brownlee is Professor Emeritus of History, University of California, Santa Barbara.

Martin Daunton is Professor of Economic History, University of Cambridge.

Yasunori Fukagai is Professor of Economics, Yokohama National University.

Laura Hein is Professor of History, Northwestern University.

Eisaku Ide is Professor of Economics, Keio University.

Frances Lynch is Reader in French Studies, University of Westminster.

Ajay K. Mehrotra is Associate Professor of Law and History, Indiana University.

Mark Metzler is Associate Professor of History and Asian Studies, University of Texas, Austin.

Ryo Muramatsu is a PhD Candidate in Economics, Keio University.

Monica Prasad is Associate Professor of Sociology and Faculty Fellow at the Institute for Policy Research, Northwestern University.

Satoshi Sekiguchi is Associate Professor of Economics, Rikkyo University.

Joseph J. Thorndike is Director of the Tax History Project at Tax Analysts and Visiting Scholar in History, University of Virginia.

Preface

Each of the editors of this book took a different route to the collaboration that has culminated in this volume. In Japan, the mission of Carl Shoup has played an important role in narratives of the nation's post–World War II development, and, consequently, Eisaku Ide and Yasunori Fukagai learned about the mission very early on in their educations, during secondary school. In graduate school at the University of Tokyo, they deepened their interests as Fukagai specialized in the history of economic thought and Ide in the fiscal and financial history of Japan during the twentieth century. W. Elliot Brownlee did not encounter the mission until graduate school at the University of Wisconsin, when he was enrolled in a seminar, "Philosophers and Philosophies of Taxation," conducted by economist Harold Groves, a contemporary of Shoup's. Later, in 1979, at the annual meeting of the National Tax Association, Brownlee had the privilege of a long conversation with Carl Shoup during the plenary lunch. In 2002, while visiting the University of Tokyo, Brownlee launched a study of the Shoup mission as a significant episode in American efforts to export tax and economic ideas.

During 2007 and 2008, our research careers converged. Ide, who was teaching in the Economics Faculty at Yokohama National University (YNU), introduced Brownlee, who had returned to the University of Tokyo as a Visiting Professor, to the collection of Carl Shoup's papers and books in the YNU Library. It turned out that after Shoup's death in 2000, his family and YNU had arranged for the transfer of his books and papers from his barn in rural New Hampshire. The archive was vast, containing more than 700 boxes, and very few scholars had consulted it.

Subsequently, Ide moved from YNU to Keio University and at YNU Fukagai assumed responsibility for oversight of the Shoup Collection. In 2008–2009, the three of us began organizing an international conference. We were eager to mark the 60th anniversary of the tax mission of Carl Shoup in Japan and to deepen our understanding of both the Japanese and American contexts of the mission and its aftermath. More generally, the conference promised to be a useful occasion for stimulating inter-disciplinary and collaborative scholarship on the international history of public finance. In 2009–2010 Brownlee returned to Japan as a Visiting Professor at YNU and in December 2009 we convened the conference, jointly sponsored by YNU and Keio University. The chapters in this col-lection are either substantially revised versions of papers presented at the conference or papers that the discussions in Yokohama and Tokyo inspired.

A great many individuals assisted with the work that led to this volume. Beginning with the earliest phases of this project, Naohiko Jinno, Andrew DeWit, Iju Morinao, Ryo Muramatsu, and Satoshi Sekiguchi provided especially important guidance and support.[1] At various points, each of the authors who contributed to the volume provided ideas, sage advice, and other support that advanced the project as a whole. We are grateful as well to Robin Einhorn, Carolyn Jones, Isaac William Martin, Gene Park, and Dennis Ventry for their comments on various chapters in the volume. We are grateful as well to Dale Shoup Mayer for sharing recollections of her father, and to Douglas M. Moss for locating and sharing with us a copy of the unfinished memoir written by his father, Harold Moss, as well as other documents. Two anonymous readers for Cambridge University Press provided perceptive advice regarding the framework, structure, and scope of the book. At Cambridge University Press, Eric Crahan and Scott Parris provided welcome encouragement and suggested significant improvements in the volume, and Kristin Purdy efficiently and creatively expedited its editing.

We owe debts of gratitude to various individuals and groups at YNU and Keio University. At YNU, the following provided support and encour-aged the development of both the Shoup Collection and the December 2009 conference: Kunio Suzuki, the president of YNU; Yasuo Kokubun

[1] In this volume, with a few exceptions, we observe the convention of listing a Japanese surname before the given name. The exceptions include names mentioned in this preface, the names of the contributors to this volume, and the names of individuals cited, using the Western name-order convention, as the authors of publications or as correspondents.

and Shuji Mizoguchi, the vice presidents of YNU; Hiroshi Fukutomi and Osamu Yamaguchi, the former and the present director of the University Library; all the members of the Economics Faculty; and the Alumni Association for the Social Sciences (Fukyu-kai). For their conscientious and efficient stewardship of the Shoup Collection, including their support of our ongoing research within the Collection, we are grateful to the librarians of the YNU Library, Toshiaki Yokohama and Midori Morioka. In addition, Tomoari Matsunaga, Ken Kato, and Norikazu Chihara have played important roles in organizing the Shoup Collection and making it accessible to the scholarly community. At Keio University, we received significant financial support for organizing the December 2009 conference from the Keio Economic Society. Also, in its journal, *Keio Economic Studies*, the society published two papers that Brownlee and Ide had presented at the conference.[2]

Librarians of other manuscript collections have greatly eased our path. In the United States, these collections include the National Archives at College Park, Maryland; the Harry S. Truman Presidential Library; the Howard Gottlieb Archival Research Center at Boston University; the Rare Book and Manuscript Library at Columbia University; the Burton Historical Collection of the Detroit Public Library; the David M. Rubinstein Rare Book and Manuscript Library of Duke University; Special Collections of the Harvard University Law Library and the Department of Special Collections at Stanford University; and the State Historical Society of Wisconsin. In Japan, the collections include those at National Diet Library, the Policy Research Institute of the Ministry of Finance, and the Research Department of the Local Autonomy College.

We hope that our collaboration has produced a volume that will live up to the high standards Carl Shoup and his collaborators in the United States and Japan brought to the international and interdisciplinary study of the political economy of fiscal policy.

W. Elliot Brownlee, Eisaku Ide, and Yasunori Fukagai
Santa Barbara, Tokyo, and Yokohama
November 2012

---

[2] W. Elliot Brownlee, "Shoup vs. Dodge: Conflict over Tax Reform in Japan, 1947–1951," *Keio Economic Studies* 47 (2011), 91–122; and Eisaku Ide, "The Origins of Macro-Budgeting and the Foundations of Japanese Public Finance: Drastic Fiscal Reform in Occupation Era," *Keio Economic Studies* 47 (2011), 123–151. These essays do not appear in this volume.

Introduction

Global Tax Reform and an Iconic Mission

Tax reform is now a global preoccupation. Almost everywhere severe financial crises, with their attendant fiscal stresses, and the drive to maintain or increase global competitiveness have led to intensifying, and often conflicting, demands for reforms of tax systems. Many reformers emphasize the need to reduce tax burdens on mobile capital and labor; others focus on increasing government revenues. Some believe that tax reform can simultaneously advance both international competitiveness and tax capacity. Others see conflict between these objectives, and look for taxation to help strike a balance between the homogenizing forces of globalization, on one hand, and the maintenance of distinctive economic, social, and cultural orders, on the other. Meanwhile, the severe underperformance of the global economy has led to widely differing diagnoses, which have dictated conflicting approaches to taxes and tax reform. Regardless of their concerns and strategies for change, tax reformers now intently seek out useful models and analogies, both rigorous and casual, in the experiences of other nations. This volume represents an effort to advance this learning process by exploring the history of the United States tax mission to Japan in 1949–50, during the American occupation (1945–52).

OVERVIEW OF THE SHOUP MISSION

General Douglas MacArthur, as Supreme Commander for the Allied Powers (SCAP) – in effect, proconsul of Japan – delegated public finance economist Carl S. Shoup (1902–2000), a professor at Columbia University, to head a mission to undertake a huge task – nothing less than a thoroughgoing reform of taxation in Japan.[1] Shoup's specific charge was to frame a tax system that both strengthened a democratic state and helped accelerate the pace of capital investment and economic development in that industrial nation.

The enormous challenge and opportunity attracted exceptional talent to the mission. Shoup was one of the most prominent public finance economists of his generation. MacArthur gave him great latitude in appointing the rest of the mission, and by the time he arrived in Tokyo in May 1949 he had recruited a stellar assemblage of interdisciplinary analysts of public finance. Shoup's key colleagues on the mission included economist William Vickrey, who went on to win the Nobel Prize in economics; Stanley Surrey, whose later career included service as assistant secretary of the U.S. Treasury for Tax Policy and over three decades at Harvard Law School; William Warren, who was a professor at Columbia Law School and later the school's dean; and Howard Bowen, an economist who later served as president of Grinnell College and the University of Iowa. At the same time, Shoup and the Japanese government recruited three gifted public finance economists from Japanese universities to collaborate with Shoup – Ito Hanya, Shiomi Sabaru, and Tsuru Shigeto. Ito and Shiomi were two of the most distinguished students of public finance in Japan, and Tsuru, who was the most junior of the three, went on to become one of Japan's foremost development economists and a powerful intellectual force in advancing global understanding of the Japanese economy. After the mission's members returned to the United States, Martin Bronfenbrenner, who was to become the leading American expert on Japanese economic development, arrived in Japan to help implement the Shoup recommendations. MacArthur assigned Harold Moss, a talented Internal Revenue Agent on loan from the U.S. Treasury, to lead in expediting the implementation of Shoup's program. Moss went on later in his career to create the Foreign Assistance Office of the U.S. Treasury Department.

During the summer of 1949, Shoup and his exceptional team spent about three months investigating tax in Japan. They continued their work, largely at home, for another year. From their Columbia University headquarters, the Americans provided advice to the occupation and the Japanese government, and then returned to Japan during the summer of 1950. After each of their two visits, Shoup and his colleagues filed extensive reports, the first of which, accompanied by a Japanese translation, become foundational in the knowledge base of the postwar tax community in Japan.[2] SCAP translated the first Shoup report into Japanese, and circulated thousands of copies within Japan as part of an even larger public relations effort to sell Shoup's reform program to the Japanese public. In its two reports, the Shoup mission emphasized sweeping, fundamental reform based on the adoption of comprehensive income taxation at the national level, some capital-favoring reforms at the same level, and greater fiscal autonomy at the local level. The central goal was to increase the fiscal capacity of Japanese democracy by increasing popular confidence in its tax system. In 1950, the Japanese government implemented most of the changes that the mission had proposed in its first report.

THE SIGNIFICANCE OF THE MISSION

The recommendations made by the Shoup mission and the subsequent reforms may well have constituted the most dramatic tax reform program ever launched in a modern industrial nation. For this reason alone, Shoup's mission is worthy of close study in the contemporary search for approaches to fundamental global tax reform. In addition, the work of the mission was distinctly transnational in character. As such, its history was part of the global exchange of tax ideas within what historians Holger Nehring and Florian Shui describe as the larger story of the development of "the processes of social and political self-observation which have characterized modern societies."[3] The work of the mission included a close, transnational collaboration between a group of both American and Japanese tax experts.

By 1949 the Japanese government had succeeded in expanding its power within the structure of the occupation, and during 1949 the government proved itself able to shape the contours of the process of tax reform that MacArthur and Shoup initiated. Japanese tax reformers, both inside and outside the government, used the Shoup mission, and the ideas of Shoup and his American colleagues, to advance their own intellectual and political agendas, which had their origins in the period before World War II. Thus, the mission's history may well be important for shedding light on the possibilities for international collaboration in fiscal reform.

The Shoup mission may have incorporated collaborative elements, but it was fundamentally, within the context of the American occupation, an instrument of reform designed to advance distinctly American goals for Japan's future. As such, it represented what was no doubt the most ambitious intervention ever by one industrial nation in another on behalf of fiscal reconstruction. This distinctly top-down aspect of the Shoup mission also makes its history important to the study of contemporary transnational reform. As a government-sponsored – more accurately, perhaps, government-owned – project, the Shoup mission was one of the many transnational efforts at tax reform that governments, quasigovernmental agencies, and influential private entities had begun organizing earlier in the modern industrial era and would continue to organize into the twenty-first century. Arguably, it has been the work of these tax missions that has dominated the history of transnational tax reform since at least World War II.

During the early twentieth century, international tax investigations had become largely the province of representatives of powerful nations seeking in various ways to consolidate their financial spheres of influence. Often the sponsors of these investigations, which provided "tax assistance" or "technical assistance," called the investigations "missions," thereby trying to cloak them in an aura of public service. Many such missions were only subsidiary components of larger missions, whose scope extended beyond tax reform to encompass wholesale restructuring of financial systems.[4] After World War I, the interest of the United States in such missions intensified. Its huge and largely successful financial effort during the war, the great competitive strength of the American economy, and the wartime transformation of the financial stake of Americans in the world motivated the U.S. government and American financial experts to increase their export of advice, and to focus that advice on strengthening international capital markets. During the 1920s, these financial missions focused on countries that were in debt to the United States – especially Latin American nations that were the recipients of huge inflows of American capital, and American trading partners, such as France, that had became vulnerable as a consequence of the U.S. policies of high tariffs, rapid return to the gold standard, and repayment of World War I debts. Tax reform often became an integral part of the financial advising, which became known as "money doctoring." The most prominent of the "money doctors" was Edwin Kemmerer of Princeton University. He and most of these "money doctors" represented American financial interests, and they often sought to strengthen tax systems in order to expedite the repayment of creditors. Within the financial missions, however, the Americans who were tax experts often used their training in institutional economics to seek reform that addressed problems of inequitable tax distribution, monopoly power, and flawed democracy. To them, redistribution of economic power could be a desirable objective of fiscal and tax policy. They believed that "tax doctoring" had a legitimate political as well as an economic purpose, and often they believed that promoting equity and fiscal capacity could work together. Greater tax equity and a government more committed to social justice, they believed, could increase public confidence in government and, thereby, strengthen the fiscal capacity, in turn strengthening the borrowing capacity of governments.

Stress during periods of international financial crisis usually increased the level of interest in financial missions, but this pattern did not hold during the 1930s. The collapse of international monetary arrangements became so severe during the global depression of the 1930s that the frequency and scale of financial missions declined. Meanwhile, American tax experts interested in international tax reform were paying increasing attention to long-run structural problems and the promotion of progressive social reform abroad. During the late 1930s, these tax experts began to develop an interest in helping the nations they studied to use their fiscal systems, including taxation, to employ Keynesian countercyclical policies. In so doing, reinforced by the international collapse, they set the stage for a shift in the conventional emphasis of financial missions from the imposition of conventional gold-standard globalism to the encouragement of Keynesian-style financial autonomy. Scholars have appropriately labeled the later shift as "embedded liberalism," and identified its most important locus as resting in the early post-1945 years. The shift, however, began before World War II. In light of this chronology, and the wider goals of many of the tax experts involved in these missions, we might reasonably take liberties with the useful concept of "embedded liberalism," expanding its reach and describing the overall orientation of the dual emphasis on progressive social policy and Keynesianism that emerged during the 1930s among tax experts as a kind "embedded progressivism."[5] Shoup went on his first tax mission (to France) during the late 1920s, and then participated in two more, both in Cuba, during the 1930s. This aspect of his career provided significant examples of the "embedded progressivism," at least of the social justice variety, and in the Japan mission Shoup and his colleagues embraced both elements of the expanded approach to tax reform.

Shoup's earlier experience on tax missions, coupled with the familiarity of Harold Moss (the U.S. Treasury official who was the dominant tax expert on MacArthur's staff) with prewar financial missions, contributed to the designation of Shoup's investigations as a "mission." MacArthur had described numerous groups of his advisors as working on missions. The international financial community did not have a monopoly on the "mission" rubric, however, and the Shoup mission differed in a fundamental way from many of the financial missions of the prewar years. It was by no means part and parcel of a financial mission. It took up only the reform of taxation and therefore its work was not "money doctoring." The Truman administration, however, did attempt to coordinate Shoup's work with that of another mission that had general financial reform as its central responsibility. In this other mission – the so-called "Dodge mission" – a powerful Detroit banker, Joseph Dodge, led an effort to restructure Japan's financial system. These two independent missions, Shoup's and Dodge's, engaged in some of the same debates that had taken place earlier within financial missions over issues of social justice and Keynesian economics. These debates became exceptionally intense because they operated under separate and often conflicting authorities – Shoup under General Douglas MacArthur as Supreme Commander for the Allied Powers and Dodge under President Harry Truman and the Joint Chiefs of Staff.

The strength of the Dodge mission complicated the implementation of Shoup's recommendations and contributed to the reform program falling significantly short of Shoup's aspirations in both 1950 and the final two years of the occupation. The accomplishments of the mission were sufficiently impressive, however, to inspire the community of international tax experts. For them, the Shoup mission acquired a kind of iconic significance, demonstrating, many believed, what the best and brightest public finance specialists could accomplish abroad. In 1991, Malcom Gillis, an economist and tax-mission veteran himself, honored Carl Shoup along with another distinguished economist of public finance, Richard Musgrave. Gillis declared that their legacies "may be found not only in tax laws actually enacted, most notably in Japan (Shoup) and Colombia (Musgrave), but also in the residue of theoretical and applied insights where the proposals of their missions were stillborn, as in Liberia (Shoup) and Bolivia (Musgrave), in the impact of their missions in developing greater tax sophistication among the public in almost every instance, and finally, in the influence of all the Shoup and Musgrave missions upon tax reform programs initiated on all continents in the past four decades." Gillis added: "The Shoup mission to Japan was . . . the prototypical study, and the focus of that mission foreshadowed his approach to tax reform not only in later missions to Venezuela (1958), Brazil (1964), and Liberia, led by Shoup, but in missions organized for other countries, including Indonesia, in 1981–84" (a mission that Gillis led). He went on: "The Shoup mission to Japan was the first example wherein a group of distinguished American analysts had the opportunity to apply their formal skills to the problem of reforming an entire tax system."[6] Recently, public finance economists Roy W. Bahl and Richard M. Bird, who themselves led significant tax missions, correctly noted the influence of Shoup on the community of foreign tax advisors. Bahl and Bird pointed out that, while bilateral arrangements, international agencies such as the International Monetary Fund and the World Bank, and regional development banks eventually dominated in the mobilization of foreign expertise, "the path-breaking missions led by Carl Shoup to Japan in 1949–50 and by Richard Musgrave to Colombia in 1968 and Bolivia in 1976 created models on which future tax studies would build."[7] Indeed, of all the international tax investigations before and since the Shoup mission, along with Musgrave's Columbia mission, may well have been the most influential in shaping subsequent tax missions.

SCHOLARS AND THE SHOUP MISSION

Despite the potential significance of the Shoup mission, almost the entire body of historical analysis of it in English is of "first-generation" nature, contributed by scholars who participated directly in the creation and implementation of the mission's recommendations.[8] The numerous and accomplished historians in the United States who have studied the occupation of Japan have paid almost no attention to the Shoup mission.[9] The historians who have begun exploring the history of financial missions in a very productive way have had little to say about tax missions and have written nothing about Shoup's.[10] Public finance economists with an interest in economic development have made important contributions to understanding the legacy of the Shoup mission for international tax assistance, but they have tended to rely heavily on "first-generation" accounts.[11] A few American public finance economists have analyzed the effects of the Shoup mission on the Japanese tax system, but they have also tended to rely heavily on "first-generation" research.[12] Scholars in a wide variety of disciplines in the field of international political economy have made important contributions to the study of the recent history of financial missions, but they have rarely mentioned the Shoup mission or, for that matter, any of the tax missions of the early post-World War II era.[13]

Beginning with the Japanese economists who advised the Shoup mission, Japanese scholars have made much greater contributions to an understanding of the Shoup mission than American scholars. A great many social scientists and members of various policy communities in Japan have written about it. In fact, virtually all serious discussions of tax reform in Japan have reckoned with the Shoup recommendations, and authors usually take the recommendations as the starting point for their analysis.[14] Only a small fraction of the work by Japanese scholars on the Shoup mission has appeared in English. The literature has focused on the important question of the effects of the Shoup mission on the Japan's tax system and the development of the Japan's economy, but its examination of important issues of political economy has been limited. In addition, Japanese scholars have had difficulties in utilizing the historical archives in the United States.

This volume seeks to bring together and expand the two national streams of scholarly discussion relevant to the Shoup mission through an interdisciplinary collaboration of scholars. The contributors to this volume are united by their common interest in the study of political economy, their desire to apply it to transnational history, and their conviction that these interests applied to the history of fiscal development bring substantial rewards by way of understanding contemporary policy choices. In their chapters, the authors attempt to establish the history of the Shoup mission within a nuanced understanding of the interplay among politics, economics, and society in both Japan and the United States.[15]

The volume consists of four parts. Part One sets the origins of Shoup mission within the context of the multifaceted social investigations associated with the progressive movement, the New Deal, and mobilization for World War II. In addition, it analyzes the missions in which Shoup participated before travelling to Japan. Part Two of this volume explores the Japanese background to the Shoup mission and the process by which American and Japanese tax experts and their governments shaped the recommendations of the Shoup mission and their initial implementation. It also assesses the mission's short-run accomplishments (those through the end of the occupation in 1952) in the context of the configuration of economic and political interests in both the United States and Japan. The chapters in Part Three examine the long-running legacy of the Shoup recommendations for Japan. In the process, the chapters of Part Three contribute to the ongoing debate in Japan over the long-term effects of the Shoup mission on that nation's fiscal system, and to the development of a broader historical understanding of the forces that have shaped tax policy in Japan. The first three parts establish the Shoup mission as a major milestone within the history of tax missions through the early post-World War II years. Part Four examines the significance of the mission within the context of global fiscal reform since World War II. It suggests the importance of thinking about the policy debates that surrounded the mission as part of wider debates about international financial policy following

World War II. In addition, Part Four examines the post-1950 career of Carl Shoup to help assess the influence of the Japan mission on subsequent tax missions, and the extent to which Shoup and other tax economists learned from his experience in Japan. In the process, this section of the book evaluates the development of global tax missions since 1950 from the perspective of the ideals that Shoup and his colleagues espoused during the mission to Japan. The result is a critique of the direction of tax missions, often described as "neo-liberal," since the 1980s.

The contributors to this volume hope that the history of the Shoup mission may provide an opening and an opportunity not only to evaluate the work of tax missions over the past few decades, but also to assist Japan and the United States in addressing the fiscal challenges of the early twenty-first century. Both nations face looming crises in public finance – crises set up by global financial conditions and by characteristics of the political economies of Japan and the United States. There are broad similarities in the scale and structure of many of the fiscal problems in both nations, and the history of the Shoup mission, with its transnational dimensions, may help identify the possibilities for fundamental or comprehensive tax and fiscal reform in both. Many of the scholars who have contributed to this volume share the esteem Shoup and his colleagues held for base-broadening tax reforms because of the ways in which those reforms can promote horizontal equity, economic efficiency, trust in government, and a vibrant public sector. At the same time, however, Japan's lack of success in following through on the base-broadening recommendations of the Shoup mission illustrates the severe political problems that confront reformers who take that approach in seeking a resolution to today's fiscal crisis. Even so, the history of the Shoup mission might bring some guidance to today's reformers. This history suggests that certain procedural elements may be vital to fundamental tax reform in many societies. These elements include building a democratic consensus in support of modern tax systems, balancing a principled approach to reform at the same time as recognizing the force of historically contingent institutional constraints, extending collaborations of tax experts and political leaders across national boundaries, and establishing processes of social learning that have the capacity to sustain reform over several generations.

Notes

1. During the occupation, SCAP become commonly used as an acronym to refer not only to MacArthur, the Supreme Commander for the Allied

Powers, but also to his massive administrative bureaucracy in Japan. The acronym GHQ, standing for General Headquarters, also referred to this bureaucracy.

2. Shoup Mission, *Report on Japanese Taxation by the Shoup Mission*, Volumes I–IV (Tokyo: Supreme Commander for the Allied Powers, 1949).

3. Nehring, H., Schui, F., *Global Debates about Taxation* (New York: Palgrave Macmillan, 2007), 11.

4. Emily Rosenberg has written the best surveys of the history of the pre-1945 financial missions based in the United States. She discusses tariff reform at length, but she only mentions in passing American interest in reforming the internal tax systems of other nations. See Rosenberg, E. S., *Spreading the American Dream: American Economic and Cultural Expansion, 1890–1945* (New York: Hill and Wang, 1982) and *Financial Missionaries to the World: The Politics and Culture of Dollar Diplomacy, 1900–1930* (Durham: Duke University Press, 2003). In the latter book, see pages 87, 89, 222, and 238 for references to tax reform. The following sources are also very valuable for understanding the early twentieth-century financial missions based in the United States: Drake, P. W., *The Money Doctor in the Andes: The Kemmerer Missions, 1923–1933* (Durham: Duke University Press, 1989); and Schuker, S. A., "Money Doctors between the Wars" in Flandreau, M., ed., *Money Doctors: The Experience of International Financial Advising, 1850–2000* (New York: Routledge, 2003). These studies, however, like Rosenberg's, provide little information regarding any components of tax reform embedded in the earlier financial missions. The same is true of the histories of the financial missions of the early post-World War II years. For example, Michele Alacevich's excellent history of the Currie Mission to Columbia, 1949–53, never mentions the work of the mission or its chief economist, Richard Musgrave, on taxation. See Alacevich, M., *The Political Economy of the World Bank: The Early Years* (Palo Alto and Washington, D.C.: Stanford University Press and The World Bank, 2009), 11–63. The most helpful of the essays on the early postwar period is Helleiner, E., "The Southern Side of 'Embedded Liberalism:' America's Unorthodox Money Doctoring during the Early Post-1945 Years," in Flandreau, M., ed., *Money Doctors*, 249–75. Japan also has an important history of "money doctoring" before World War II. Michael Schiltz describes this as an effort "to establish a 'yen bloc' and a more or less self-sufficient Asian economic zone," and he discusses the activities of money doctors in Taiwan, Korea, China, and Manchuria. However, he does not discuss the role of the Ministry of Finance in restructuring tax systems within Japan's sphere of influence. See Schiltz, M., *The Money Doctors from Japan: Finance, Imperialism, and the Building of the Yen Bloc, 1895–1937* (Cambridge, MA: Harvard University Press, 2012). See p. 3 for the quotation.

5. For the most important usages of "embedded liberalism," see Ruggie, J., "International Regimes, Transactions and Change," *International Organization* 1983, vol. 36 (2), pp. 379–405; and Helleiner, E., "The Southern Side of 'Embedded Liberalism.'"

6. Gillis, M., "Legacies from the Shoup Tax Missions: Asia, Africa, and Latin America," in Eden, L. ed., *Retrospectives on Public Finance* (Durham: Duke University Press, 1991), 31–2.

7. Bahl, R. W., Bird, R. M., "Tax Policy in Developing Countries: Looking Back – and Forward," *National Tax Journal* 2008, vol. 61, p. 285. For other excellent discussions of foreign tax missions, see Gillis, M., ed., *Tax Reform in Developing Countries* (Durham: Duke University Press, 1989), and Tanzi, V., "A Review of Major Tax Policy Missions in Developing Countries," in van de Kar, H. M., Wolfe, B. L., eds., *The Relevance of Public Finance for Policy-Making* (Detroit: Wayne State University Press, 1987), 225–36. Of particular interest in the volume edited by Malcolm Gills are Carl Shoup's history of his mission (see footnote 8); his "Retrospectives on Tax Missions to Venezuela (1959), Brazil (1964), and Liberia (1970)," 252–314; and Gillis, M., "Tax Reform: Lessons from Postwar Experience in Developing Nations," 492–520.

8. The first, and best, history was Bronfenbrenner, M., Kogiku, K., "The Aftermath of the Shoup Tax Reforms, (Parts I and II)," *The National Tax Journal* 1957, vol. 10, pp. 236–54 and 345–60. In 1988, in preparation for the celebration of the fortieth anniversary of the Shoup mission, Shoup finally told his own story. This was published as Shoup, C. S., "The Tax Mission to Japan, 1949–1950," in Gillis, M., ed., *Tax Reform in Developing Countries*, 177–232. For that same celebration, Martin Bronfenbrenner somewhat updated his 1957 assessment; see Bronfenbrenner, M., "Dr. Shoup Revisits Japan – The Shoup Tax Mission Forty Years Later," typescript, Box #2 of three boxes at the "third location," Martin Bronfenbrenner Papers, Rare Book, Manuscript, and Special Collections Library, Duke University. Japanese experts who advised Shoup also made important "first-generation" contributions to understanding the Shoup mission and published some of their work in English. See Shiomi, S., *Japan's Finance and Taxation, 1940–1956* (New York: Columbia University Press, 1957); Tsuru, S., *Japan's Capitalism: Creative Defeat and Beyond* (Cambridge: Cambridge University Press, 1993), especially 52–4; and Ito, H., "Direct Taxes in Japan and the Shoup Report," *Public Finance* 1953, vol. 8, pp. 357–83. An important exception to the scholarship of the nonparticipating authors was an unpublished undergraduate honors dissertation: James, J. C., "Japanese Tax Policy in the Wake of the Shoup Mission," Dissertation for Part Two of the Tripos in Oriental Studies: Japanese Studies, King's College, Cambridge University, 1987. James consulted Japanese sources and for the first time provided Carl Shoup with a translation of an important assessment of the mission by Japanese Finance Minister Ikeda Hayato. See Shoup, C. S., ibid., 206, 211–16, and 220. In addition, see Chapter 16 of this volume. For recent scholarship, see Brownlee, W. E., "The Shoup Mission to Japan: Two Political Economies Intersect," in Martin, I. W., Mehrotra, A. K., Prasad, M., eds., *The New Fiscal Sociology: Taxation in Comparative and Historical Perspective* (New York: Cambridge University Press, 2009), 237–55.

9. Two notable exceptions are Dower, J. W., *Empire and Aftermath: Yoshida Shigeru and the Japanese Experience, 1878–1954* (Cambridge: Harvard University Press, 1988), 360–1; and Schonberger, H., *Aftermath of War: Americans and the Remaking of Japan, 1945–1952* (Kent, Ohio: Kent State University Press, 1989), 223. American historians, however, have paid a great deal of attention to the financial mission of Detroit banker Joseph Dodge. The best account is that of Schonberger, H., *Aftermath of War*, 198–235. An influential history of the Dodge mission by a participant in the occupation is Cohen, T., *Remaking Japan: The Occupation as New Deal* (New York: Macmillan, 1987), 429–42.

10. See footnote 4 for examples of this important literature and see Chapter 16 of this volume for a discussion of the significant literature on financial missions in the early post-World War II era.

11. See, for example, the scholarship cited in notes 6 and 7.

12. See, for example, Pechman, J. A., Kaizuka, K., "Taxation," in Patrick, H., Rosovsky, H., eds., *Asia's New Giant: How the Japanese Economy Works* (Washington, D.C.: The Brookings Institution, 1976), 320–2. Pechman and Kaizuka relied on Bronfenbrenner, M., Kogiku, K., "The Aftermath of the Shoup Tax Reforms."

13. See Chapter 16 of this volume for leading examples of this literature.

14. See the introduction to Part Three of this volume for a survey of the analysis of the Shoup mission by Japanese scholars, particularly the mission's effects on the development of the Japanese tax system and its contributions to capital formation and economic growth.

15. In doing so, the contributors are the first scholars to have made extensive use of certain archival sources in the United States and Japan, including the archives of the Japanese Ministry of Finance and Shoup Collection at Yokohama National University.

PART ONE

THE AMERICAN BACKGROUND

Introduction to Part One

This volume is a study of the political economies of the United States and Japan, of their intersection during the American occupation, and of the global significance of that intersection. In such a study individuals sometimes vanish from sight. We do not want this to happen in ours. The contributors to this volume believe that historical change is highly contingent, endowing individuals and ideas with the power to shape economic forces. In the history examined in this volume, various individuals and ideas made significant differences; however, one person – Carl Shoup – and his ideas played an exceptionally important role. His professional life provides a thread that helps connect the various episodes and topics within this volume's political economy framework, and his career – especially his ideas and political strategies – provides a window into the interior workings of the transnational political economy.

The essays that follow in Part One analyze the career of Carl Shoup from his graduate-student days at Columbia University through to launching the mission to Japan in 1949. During this twenty-year period, as these chapters detail, the economic institutionalism that thrived at Columbia University helped Shoup build a career that put him in the middle of national and international debates over tax policy and public finance. As a member of a multigenerational group of Columbia University social scientists, Shoup created and applied systematic economic knowledge to problems of public finance in the United States and an array of other nations. In this effort, Shoup demonstrated skills in social organization that often amplified the force of his policy ideas. As a policy entrepreneur, he proved effective in reaching consensus among experts, in seeing ways to help contending politicians reach agreement, and in communicating with broad-based communities of interest. The essays in Part One help identify the ideas and strategies that Shoup and his colleagues employed to understand the Japanese fiscal system and help reform it on behalf of both democracy and economic well-being.

Chapter 1, by W. Elliot Brownlee, suggests the connections between Shoup's early life and his later professional career. It focuses, in particular, on his important relationship with his father, Paul Shoup, a powerful business executive and lobbyist. The chapter, together with Chapter 2, "From Seligman to Shoup: The Columbia School of Taxation and Development," by Ajay Mehrotra, suggests that Carl Shoup was well positioned to work in a liberal way within the contradictions of American society. This was in part because his family history helped him to understand and value the workings of corporate capitalism and in part because his formal education gave him an understanding of capitalism's conflicts with democracy and its potential for increasing social inequity. In his professional life he struggled to reconcile the contradictions.

Mehrotra's chapter sets Shoup and his Columbia University mentors, particularly Robert Murray Haig, within a tradition of the analysis of public finance launched by Haig's mentor, Edwin R. A. Seligman. Mehrotra uses a wide analytical lens. He discusses the connections Seligman and Haig had with the progressive movement, assesses the importance of the efforts by Seligman, Haig, and Shoup to connect their scholarship with efforts to reform public finance, outlines the international scope of their scholarship and public service interests, and traces the intellectual history of their concepts of tax equity, which became recognized later in the creation of the rubric of "Haig–Simons" taxation. In addition to this, Mehrotra underscores the extended influence of Shoup's approaches to public finance, noting the influence of *Public Finance*, Shoup's *magnum opus* that appeared in 1969, two decades after the mission to Japan. Economist Martin Feldstein would agree. Almost four decades after the mission, at a National Bureau of Economic Research function in 1988 honoring Shoup and the other economists who had been the participants in the first Conference on Income and Wealth in 1937–8, Feldstein declared: "I think of myself as a bit of a student of Carl Shoup's, although I never sat in his classroom." He explained that "I had his big book on public finance on my shelf, I read through it, and I considered it a very critical part of my education as a public finance economist."[1]

Throughout *Public Finance*, the reader finds discussion and examples that Shoup extracted from the research he and others conducted during their tax missions around the globe. He launched this career-long research in a study of post-World War I France and continued it in Cuba, within the American sphere of influence in the Caribbean. These early missions, at one level, concerned attempts to strengthen foreign fiscal systems in order to repay American creditors. Frances Lynch's chapter explores in a critical fashion the sources and nature of Shoup's mission to France, in 1926 and 1927, as an assistant to Haig. Lynch assesses the principles that structured the mission to France, describes the French fiscal system, documents the difficulty Haig and Shoup faced in understanding the French tax system, and suggests important points of contrast between the political economy of France and the United States in the 1920s.

Lynch argues that the French investigation played a pivotal role in Shoup establishing some distance from the model of ideal tax reform he had developed as a student of Seligman and Haig. Shoup had to confront the reality that France had chosen a general sales taxation over income taxation through democratic processes. In the process of examining the Columbia model in the context of the French institution, Shoup came to see how the general sales tax was more progressive than he and Haig had imagined, and came to appreciate that the assumption that the modern triumph of democracy would inevitably lead to progressive income taxation was too facile, ignoring significant differences among nations' political economies and institutional arrangements. Shoup's emphasis, Lynch stresses, was on comprehending the reasons for France's adoption of a sales tax and explaining the way it worked, rather than on condemning it for falling short of the ideals of Seligman and Haig.

Chapter 4, by Michael Adamson, takes up Shoup's next two missions, both of which were conducted in Cuba in 1931 and 1938. He undertook these in collaboration with Seligman and then Roswell Magill, a law professor at Columbia University and former undersecretary of the U.S. Treasury. Shoup worked with Magill at the Treasury in 1937. Adamson's chapter parallels Lynch's in structure by analyzing both the Cuban political economy and the Shoup mission. The Shoup archives provide detailed documentation of the Cuban missions, and Adamson is able to explicate Shoup's motives, framework of economic principles, and research methodology, and suggest the effects of the two formal reports he and his collaborators produced. In addition, Adamson places the Shoup missions within the intensifying struggles inside the U.S. government, particularly between the departments of State and Treasury, over international monetary and financial policy during the Great Depression. Adamson emphasizes how Shoup adapted his recommendations to "a specific milieu in which a progressive income tax would have been nearly impossible to administer." Thus, both Lynch and Adamson discuss the ways in which

Shoup attempted to balance the universalist principles of the Columbia school of tax reform with an understanding of the economic, social, and political conditions in the countries whose fiscal systems he sought to reform. The experiences of balancing of tax principles and social conditions in France and Cuba prepared Shoup for his international missions which followed World War II.

Joseph Thorndike, in Chapter 5, then turns to the domestic side of Shoup's career as tax advisor to the U.S. government. Thorndike focuses on Shoup's extensive career within the Treasury during the New Deal and World War II. Thorndike is in agreement with Mehrotra with regard to Shoup's intellectual and institutional background, going on to develop this topic by describing and explaining how Shoup adapted his agenda for taxation to the exigencies of the Great Depression, New Deal policy debates, and the mobilization for World War II. Thorndike shows how Shoup emerged from an intense period of policy ferment with a strong commitment to much of the New Deal's tax program, although he maintained his attachment to the ideal of horizontal equity. This attachment led him to favor moderate alternatives to the most radical New Deal taxes, and to exercise a major influence as the 1934 coordinator of the "Viner Recommendations" (the product of a project led by University of Chicago economist Jacob Viner) over the mass-based income tax of World War II.

Through his participation in tax missions to France and Cuba and the advice he gave the federal government on tax policy during the New Deal, Shoup demonstrated his entrepreneurial skill and his capacity for social learning as well as his intellectual acumen and versatility. By the early years of the post-World War II era, Shoup had become one of the most renowned American students of public finance. With his 1949 selection as the leader of the tax mission to Japan, he was on the verge of the most significant opportunity of his career to expand the influence of the scholarly study of public finance.

Note

1. Martin Feldstein and Carl Shoup comments in Roy Blough et al., "Luncheon in Honor of Individuals and Institutions Participating in the First Income and Wealth Conference (December 1936-January 1937)," in Berndt, E. R., Triplett, J. E., eds., *Fifty Years of Economic Measurement: The Jubilee of the Conference on Research in Income and Wealth* (Chicago: University of Chicago Press, 1991), reprinted by the National Bureau of Research, http://www.nber.org/books/bern91-1.

Carl S. Shoup

Formative Influences

W. Elliot Brownlee

There is always more to a professional life than ideas and strategies. To have a better understanding of Carl Shoup's career and the political economy in which he thrived, it would be useful to know more about how his temperament, personality, background, and social experience equipped him for his role as both scholar and policy entrepreneur. The answers to such questions may rest partly in the history of Shoup's youth and early professional career. Unfortunately, the archival sources on this topic are not as abundant as for the topics that are the focus of the other chapters in this book. Despite this, the holdings of the Shoup Collection at Yokohama National University are sufficient to illuminate some of the formative influences on his career.

Carl Shoup was born in San Jose, California in 1902 and grew up within the affluent family of his father, Paul Shoup (1874–1946), a Southern Pacific Railroad executive. Paul had left school in San Bernardino at age 18 to became an agent and freight clerk for the railroad, quickly acquiring skills in shorthand and Morse code. Economic pressures diverted him from his early ambition to become a professional writer; however, he nonetheless succeeded, even in his early career, in writing articles for the *Los Angeles Evening Express* and publishing his short stories. Many of his stories appeared in *Sunset*, a Southern Pacific promotional magazine that was the precursor of today's *Sunset Magazine*.[1] Paul's ability to express himself clearly may well have helped him in his sustained rise through Southern Pacific, which had the largest transportation network and one of the most complex corporate bureaucracies in the world. He developed an intense involvement in Southern Pacific's historic role as a community builder. In 1907, as part of an elaborate property transaction, Paul led in founding Los Altos, which neighbored Menlo Park and was where he finally settled his family in 1918. In 1910, he took charge of Southern Pacific's municipal and interurban electric lines, and two years later the company made him president of the Pacific Electric Railway Company, which was an affiliate of Southern Pacific.

Paul's interest in local and regional economic development deepened, and he reinforced his business role with popular writing and speeches aimed at demonstrating the social contributions of the railroad. Paul had become one of the powerful boosters who integrated business and political careers in the swiftly growing towns of the Pacific Slope. The economic strategies of these boosters often depended on control of land (of which Southern Pacific was the largest owner in California), oil, and water. During World War I, Southern Pacific elevated Paul to a vice presidency in charge of all its property interests, including extensive oil holdings owned through small subsidiary corporations. Building human capital and cultivating community good-will were other key ingredients in the development strategy of this cadre of community leaders. Paul, being disappointed that he had to miss college, believed deeply in higher education. For example, during the 1920s he eagerly took the lead in organizing a joint effort by Southern Pacific and the University of California to enhance the reputations of their institutions among California's farmers.[2] In 1922, despite his lack of a college degree, he headed a major endowment campaign for Stanford University's medical school and the next year he became a trustee of the University. Subsequently, he played a fundraising role in Herbert Hoover's successful effort to establish the Stanford Graduate School of Business. In his Stanford roles, and in his career-long involvement in public relations, he sought to demonstrate Southern Pacific's sense of community responsibility.[3]

In 1929 Paul became President of Southern Pacific. In August, only a few weeks before the stock market crash, his picture made the cover of *Time* magazine. The inside story hyped efficiency gains in railroading and described Paul as the "man most responsible for Southern Pacific's present scope and vigor." *Time* gushed that "when seven members of California's Bohemian Club [whose annual Bohemian Grove meetings he regularly attended] were asked to write on a slip of paper the name of the most potent westerner of the present generation, five of the ballots bore the name of Paul Shoup."[4] The year before, Paul had worked vigorously to elect Herbert Hoover (his very close friend, fellow Stanford trustee, and fellow member of the Bohemian Club) to the presidency. With Hoover's election, Paul's business lobbying became increasingly national in scope, and Hoover aggressively sought Paul's business advice in the immediate wake of the Great Crash.[5]

In 1929 Paul's son Carl neared the completion of his graduate work (PhD, 1930), had already travelled to France with Robert Murray Haig, and had begun to teach at Columbia. He had always been an exceptional student. In 1920, after Palo Alto High School, he entered nearby Stanford. Carl graduated Phi Beta Kappa with a BA in law in 1924, the last year that Stanford allowed undergraduates in its law school. In the October after graduation, Carl married Ruth Snedden (1905–1998), another Stanford undergraduate, in New York city and the young couple remained there, even though she had not yet completed her BA. In his marriage and move to New York city, Carl hoped to broaden his career opportunities and at the same time create a greater degree of independence from his parents. He had displayed his writing and organization skills as both editor of the news department of the Stanford student newspaper (*The Daily Palo Alto*) and editor of the yearbook (1924 *Quad*), and he hoped to find work in journalism at the same time as trying his hand at creative writing.[6] In addition, the move brought Ruth close to her New York family. The Sneddens thought of themselves as Southern Californians, having grown up in Ventura County ranching families, but Ruth's father had become a prominent professor of education at Columbia. After earning a Stanford BA, he had taken a PhD at Columbia, pursued a teaching career in California and become the first commissioner of education in Massachusetts. In 1916 he returned to Columbia, which became the venue for his debates with John Dewey and Snedden's platform for national leadership of the "social efficiency" faction of the progressive education movement until his retirement in 1935.[7]

Despite Carl's search for more independence in New York city, he maintained a warm, close relationship with his father. Carl had learned how to be straightforward with him at the same time as going his own way, and his father generously supported the marriage and cross-country move.[8] In the move, Carl was grateful for the exercise of his father's business influence, which reached easily to New York city. In the summer of 1924, before the wedding, his father wrote letters of introduction to his friends in major banks, perhaps hoping to pave the way for Carl in banking if a job in journalism did not materialize. Paul remembered his own youthful interest in journalism, however, and was pleased to write letters to the New York *World* as well. He wrote to William Baisell (the managing editor), Herbert Bayard Swope (a renowned reporter who was the brother of Paul's friend Gerard Swope), and Joseph Pulitzer himself.[9]

The *World* hired Carl in early 1925, delaying his start date to give him time to take a European honeymoon that lasted several months. Carl worked at the paper less than a year. Most notably, he wrote an opinion piece that the *World* syndicated, titled "Mother Earth's New Heat Blanket May Transform World's Climate."[10]

Perhaps it was his prescience that led Carl to decide that returning to school for a professional education offered a better route to finding intellectual challenges and independence. In any case, his father-in-law provided an appealing model of accomplishment in a life that integrated scholarship with public affairs. Carl recalled that "contact with some Columbia University people," one of whom was no doubt his father-in-law, led him to decide in the spring of 1925 to enroll. During the winter semester of 1925–6, he began taking courses in law and economics.[11] This venture may have resulted in part from his long exposure to his father's absorption in the policy issues surrounding transportation, land, oil, and economic development.

At the same time as Carl reimmersed himself in education, Ruth returned briefly to Stanford, graduating in the class of 1926.[12] Carl made extremely swift progress at Columbia and in 1927 Carl and Ruth, along with their first child, all travelled to France with Robert Murray Haig. The next year Carl began his teaching career at Columbia in the School of Business. In early 1929, the family moved into a house in Riverdale, which his mentor Haig helped them select, and where they remained throughout Carl's career at Columbia.[13]

In the early phase of Carl's career, his father believed his son was wasting his talents. He soon changed his mind, however. When exactly is not clear. One possibility is that this occurred in early 1928. Haig had a leave from Columbia, just after his research sojourn in France, to direct research for the California Tax Commission and the governor of California. In the process of considering comprehensive reform of the state's corporate tax system, Haig had enlisted Paul Shoup, with Carl's assistance, to help him analyze the taxation of oil companies and banks.[14] In June, Haig wrote to Paul saying: "I have just received a letter from Professor Seligman, which contains a paragraph reading as follows: 'Shoup passed a brilliant examination and has already been helping me in reading some of the doctor's dissertations. He is a fine fellow.' I know that you will be interested in this report and I fear that Carl's modesty will prevent it from reaching you through him."[15] If that was not the occasion, in might been after Paul met Nicholas Murray Butler, Columbia University's president, at a social event in April 1931. Carl had just won tenure at Columbia and when he wrote to Butler to thank him for the promotion, Butler wrote back: "When in San Francisco a few weeks ago, I had the great pleasure of meeting your father at dinner, and I told him with what pride and satisfaction we were following your work on Morningside and what sort of a future of repute and distinguished service we predicted for you." Carl responded: "My father wrote to me concerning your conversation with him in San Francisco and I know that he appreciates very greatly the remarks which you were kind enough to make to him concerning my position here."[16] The elite worlds of Morningside Heights and Nob Hill had intersected.

In light of Paul Shoup's political activism and influence in the 1920s, and his close relationship with his son, it would be enlightening to know more about his early influence on Carl's politics. We can speculate that in 1930, at the time Carl completed his graduate work, he may well have identified himself with the progressive wing of the Republican party, which his father supported. Progressive Republican approaches to taxation fit quite comfortably with those of Carl's mentors at Columbia, particularly Seligman's, because Seligman and Haig tried to adopt postures that were either nonpartisan or bipartisan. Seligman and Haig fully recognized the importance of maintaining the strength of the private sector in order to keep what Schumpeter called the "tax state" strong. Although Seligman, and especially Haig, parted company with Secretary of the Treasury Andrew Mellon over certain of his proposed tax loopholes, Seligman warmly endorsed Mellon's program to preserve some progressive income taxation rather than replace it by a national sales tax. In 1924 Seligman embraced Mellon's income-tax reduction plan. Seligman commended Mellon for proposing the lowering of income tax rates, which Seligman claimed would increase tax revenues in a supply side fashion and initiate a chain of desirable events: enlargement of "the investment fund," an increase in "enterprise," increases in wages, and a reduction in interest rates. Although the plan would entail some sacrifice of "the principle of individual ability to pay," it would result in "maximum social advantage," Seligman wrote to Mellon. In addition, Seligman joined a lobbying group, The National Citizens Committee in Support of the Mellon Tax Reduction Proposal, organized by the Institute of American Business.[17] Seligman and Haig had significant Republican connections at the state level as well. In 1928, Haig helped progressive Republican Seabury C. Mastick organize the bipartisan New York State Tax Association, and in 1930 he became executive secretary and research director of the tax reform commission that the New York legislature created and Mastick chaired. Seligman was a member of the Mastick Commission, and after the completion of his dissertation Carl coauthored sections of the commission's staff report, which appeared along with the main report in 1932. The core strategy of the Columbia group was to seek bipartisan cooperation behind a base-broadening set of reforms of income taxation. In his contribution to the report, Carl articulated a critique, on the basis of his dissertation research, of sales taxation on the basis of its regressivity and its tendency to obscure the true cost of government. Although New York Governor Franklin Roosevelt had proposed the creation of the Mastick Commission originally, he ended up supporting a gasoline tax and proposing raising income tax rates and rejecting the commission's central recommendation – reducing income tax exemptions – in favor of raising income tax rates and making them more progressive.[18]

Seligman and Paul Shoup had close mutual friends who were powerful Republicans. Among them was Ogden Mills, New York businessman and Republican congressman who became Mellon's undersecretary in 1927. It is entirely possible that Paul, as well as Professor Snedden, had helped arrange Carl's introduction to Seligman, just as Paul had arranged introductions to other leading figures in New York City.[19] Seligman would play the same kind of role in Carl's professional life. In 1931, Seligman did so when helping to arrange the mission to Cuba (see Chapter 4). He wrote to Harry F. Guggenheim, an old New York friend and the U.S. ambassador to Cuba, and asked him to help Carl "in any way that you can. Perhaps also Mrs. Guggenheim will be willing to be of assistance to Mrs. Shoup in getting settled. Professor Shoup, as you perhaps know, is the son of the President of the Southern Pacific Railway."[20] From the beginning of their relationship with Carl, Seligman and Haig recognized and appreciated his gifts of intellect. In addition to this, they understood and saw value in his familial context and its expression in his charm, character, and connections. Although Carl had to work hard to live up to the intellectual expectations of Haig and Seligman, he had little trouble, on a personal level, in transferring his primary dependency for mentoring from his father to his Columbia professors.

Before Franklin Roosevelt's first term, father and son had already taken divergent policy paths. At the same time as Carl promoted broad-based taxation in his work for the Mastick Commission, Paul lobbied his friend Herbert Hoover to stimulate economic recovery by offering corporations generous investment tax credits for the 1931 tax year.[21] In 1932, while Carl and many of his colleagues at Columbia shifted toward Roosevelt, his father worked vigorously on behalf of Hoover's reelection, and then staked out vigorous opposition to aspects of the New Deal. Paul's opposition became especially intense after 1932, when his business roles became much more overtly political. In 1932, Paul left the presidency of the company when Southern Pacific's board of directors rejected a policy to protect jobs by spreading wage and salary cuts broadly among Southern Pacific's workforce.[22] He was kicked upstairs, to the position of vice chairman of the board, although he remained powerful as a member of the board's executive committee and as director of some thirty-four different railroad, oil, and water companies associated with Southern Pacific. At the same time, the parent company moved his office to New York city to enable him to head a major public relations and lobbying operation.[23]

From that base, Paul Shoup participated in the 1932 presidential campaign, and pushed his ideas about taxation.[24] A month before the election he addressed the American Bankers Association on the topic of "Over-Taxation: A Business Viewpoint." He described the dilemma that taxes were "a necessary evil" but "take the heart out of thrift." He declared that "The question then is how far we are justified collectively in picking the pockets of each other individually because of our collective necessities," and added: "that we have run riot in that direction goes without saying." He argued that Hoover, however, would control public expenditures by a combination of "careful thought and persuasion in action" and by resisting the "organized minorities" that "have a direct interest in the expenditure of money." He concluded by asserting that "it is wholly possible by reduction in taxes in this country – national, state and local, within five years to increase the value of private property in the United States as measured by earnings therefrom at least 25 per cent."[25]

Paul Shoup remained in his national political role until 1938, applying his connections and literary talents to oppose using Reconstruction Finance Corporation funds for unemployment relief, to campaign for Republican candidate Alf Landon in 1936, to condemn labor and Social Security legislation (including its tax provisions), and rail against other New Deal tax initiatives, particularly in the corporate realm.[26] In 1938, perhaps to push antilabor initiatives more aggressively without embarrassing Southern Pacific, he resigned his positions at Southern Pacific and took over the presidency of a group called Southern Californians, Inc. The Merchants and Manufacturers Association of Los Angeles had founded the group the year before to use mass media to persuade "Californians that unions were vicious, un-American, foreign dominated," in the words of historian Kevin Starr.[27] Later, in the last years of his life, he served as president of the Merchants and Manufacturers Association of Los Angeles, although he moved away from labor issues toward the problems of reconversion to a peacetime economy. On those problems, he and Carl had more to discuss.[28]

Carl and his father maintained a strong personal relationship that they insulated from their political differences. In fact, they seemed to grow closer during the 1930s and 1940s. Carl had proven himself a professional success. His marriage and family life flourished. Paul found himself in a more comfortable corporate role. Each was more relaxed and secure. Their relationship continued to have professional as well as the normal personal dimensions. Between 1932 and 1938, father and son both worked in Manhattan, only a subway ride away (with a train change at Times Square). Each had an exceptionally busy professional life and spent large chunks of time away from the city. Carl had his consulting work in Washington and Paul travelled extensively to Chicago, Washington, and California. Paul often spent August on the Pacific coast, Carl on Lake Winnipesaukee where Ruth's family summered.[29] Nonetheless, father and son kept in close contact, drew on each other for favors, and regularly discussed tax issues. Occasionally Carl would provide his father with personal tax advice or help one of his father's associates at Southern Pacific on a corporate tax problem.[30] Father and son each felt comfortable asking the other to check out someone who had asked for a favor.[31] Carl might break away from Columbia routines to pitch in with "an emergency down at my father's office," and Paul would routinely connect Carl with powerful friends who could help Carl with his research program.[32] For example, when Carl was working on the Twentieth Century Fund studies (discussed in Chapter 5), Paul arranged for Carl to meet Albert Lasker, the Chicago advertising mogul who had designed Warren G. Harding's presidential campaign, and Hale Holdren, the chairman of the board at Southern Pacific. Consequently, Carl was able to get their answers to an elaborate set of questions regarding the effects of income and estate taxation on business investment.[33] When the first of the Twentieth Century Fund books appeared, Paul Shoup asked for copies to be sent to Lasker, Holden, other powerful business friends, and Ray Lyman Wilbur, the president of Stanford University. Carl insisted on paying.[34]

Father and son kept in touch with each other's views on taxation, although they avoided political discussions that might lead to arguments. During the 1930s, because of their extensive personal contact, their prolific scholarly writing (Carl) and speech-making (Paul), and their busy schedules and professional/business correspondence, they rarely felt a need to put their views on taxes or economic issues in letters to each other. Consequently, it is difficult to know exactly how their exchanges affected their thinking about taxation and public finance. It may well have had a moderating effect on both. It seems likely that Carl may have acquired his preference for moderation in corporate taxation, particularly in the forms of excess profits and undistributed profits taxation, and his concern for the disincentive effects of high marginal rates of income taxation from his apprenticeship with Seligman and Haig and from taking his father's ideas seriously.

Carl's long and close relationship with his supportive father may have had an even more significant impact on his professional behavior and relationships. In part through the relationship with his father, Carl learned key elements of his professional persona – self-control in the midst of contention, respect for differing points of view, tactful avoidance of partisan labels (including "New Dealer" attached to himself) and rhetoric, and strategic searching for cooperation across political lines. In addition, Carl had learned something from his relationship with his father about how to cultivate his elders – such as Seligman and Haig early on, Jacob Viner and Roswell Magill a bit later, and then Douglas MacArthur. He never found an opportunity, however, as discussed in Chapter 10, to charm the formidable Detroit banker, Joseph Dodge. Throughout his career, Carl Shoup displayed all of these qualities in his efforts to merge the worlds of scholarship and policy and to nurture a political consensus that advanced the progressive ideals of his Columbia mentors. He had moved far beyond his father's stress on promoting the health and responsibilities of corporations. Carl Shoup had become a champion of republican hostility to special privilege in taxation and of using taxation as a social instrument for fostering democracy and state-building.

Notes

1. Four of the short stories appeared in *The Black Cat*, one of which won a prize in the magazine's 1900 story contest. The prize winner was "The Funeral at Paradise Bar," *The Black Cat* 7 (June 1902), pp. 27–38.
2. Orsi, R. J., *Sunset Limited: Southern Pacific Railroad and the Development of the American West, 1850–1930* (Berkeley: University of California Press, 2005), 299.
3. Mitchell, J. P., *Stanford University 1916–1941* (Stanford: Stanford University Press, 1958), 28 and 79–80; Shoup, C. S., ed., *1924 Quad* (Palo Alto: Stanford Class of 1924, June 1923), 48.

4. Douglas, J., "Paul Shoup: Naglee Park Railroad Man," *The Advisor*, 2006, vol. 32, p.7; McDonald, D., "Literary Harvests in Old Los Altos," in *Under the Oaks* (Association for the Los Altos History Museum, 2005); "Revived Rails," *Time*, August 12, 1929.

5. Paul Shoup to Herbert Hoover, November 7, 1929, Papers of Paul Shoup, M057, Department of Special Collections, Stanford University, Stanford, California. In his letter, Shoup reported to Hoover that he had conveyed the president's questions regarding post-Crash policy to a New York city meeting of businessmen, including Owen D. Young and Cleveland Dodge and, via telephone, to many other businessmen across the nation, including Thomas Lamont, Julius Rosenwald, A. D. Lasker, and Cyrus McCormick.

6. Shoup, C. S., ed., *1924 Quad*, 83.

7. Drost, W. H., *David Snedden and Education for Social Efficiency* (Madison: University of Wisconsin, 1967); Snedden, G. S., *Mountain Cattle and Frontier People: Stories of the Snedden Family, 1867 to 1947* (Center Sandwich, N.H.: The Intervale Publishing Company, 1989).

8. Paul Shoup to Carl Shoup, September 2, 1924, "Uncategorized" correspondence, Shoup Papers, Yokohama National University (hereafter YNU).

9. W. W. Woods, Vice President of The National City Bank to Paul Shoup, August 19, 1924; J. L. Alexander, Chairman of the Board, National Bank of Commerce, August 21, 1924; Challon Parker, Vice President of Guaranty Trust Company, August 24, 1924; Paul Shoup to Challon Parker, August 25, 1924; Paul Shoup to W. W. Woods, August 25, 1924; Paul Shoup to Carl Shoup, August 25, 1924; Paul Shoup to J. J. Hanauer, Kuhn, Loeb, August 25, 1924; Paul Shoup to J. L. Alexander, August 27, 1924; Paul Shoup to Carl Shoup, telegram, September 8, 1924; W. W. Woods to Paul Shoup, September 16, 1924, "Uncategorized" correspondence, Shoup Papers, YNU. On August 19, Woods wrote: "Through our friendships and connections all along the line there will undoubtedly be some satisfactory way of handling the matter, and I will give it my personal attention." On September 16 he provided an update: He had met Carl and "I feel quite sure there will be little difficulty in meeting your son's wishes when he returns" from his honeymoon.

10. Shoup, C. S., "Mother Earth's New Heat Blanket May Transform World's Climate," *Atlanta Constitution*, June 28, 1925.

11. Carl Shoup to R. C. McCrea, Dean of the School of Business, Columbia University, April 15, 1938, Box 390–3, Envelope #25, Shoup Papers, YNU.

12. Ruth Shoup subsequently earned an MA degree in education at Columbia and went on to serve as a member of the Board of Higher Education of New York city for an extraordinary forty-four years, from 1936 to 1970. She received appointments by mayors from Fiorello LaGuardia to John Lindsay. In her obituary, the *New York Times* wrote that "she gained a reputation as one of the board's most active and outspoken members, quite capable of scolding City Hall when it trespassed on the body's mandate to run the municipal colleges." See "Ruth Shoup, 94, City Educator," *New York Times*, July 18, 1998.

13. Carl Shoup to Robert Murray Haig, May 1, 1928, ALL, S-file; Carl Shoup to Robert Murray Haig, February 27, 1929, Uncategorized Correspondence, Shoup Papers, YNU.
14. Robert Murray Haig to C. C. Young, September 28, 1928 and December 15, 1928, Uncategorized Correspondence, Shoup Papers, YNU.
15. Robert Murray Haig to Paul Shoup, June 14, 1928, and July 6, 1928, Uncategorized Correspondence, Shoup Papers, YNU.
16. Carl Shoup to Nicholas Murray Butler, April 8, 1931; Butler to C. Shoup, April 10, 1931; C. Shoup to Butler, April 14, 1931, Box 380–1, Shoup Papers, YNU.
17. Edwin R. A. Seligman to Andrew W. Mellon, February 2, 1924, Edwin R. A. Seligman Papers, Butler Library, Columbia University; Bronson Batchelor to Otto H. Kahn, December 26, 1923, Otto H. Kahn Papers, William Seymour Theater Collection, Princeton University Library. In addition see Brownlee, W. E., "Economists and the formation of the modern tax system in the United States: the World War I crisis," in Furner, M. O., Supple, B., eds., *The State and Economic Knowledge: The American and British Experiences* (Washington D.C. and Cambridge, U.K.: Woodrow Wilson Center Press and Cambridge University Press, 1990), 429–32.
18. Thorndike, J. T., "The Depression and Reform: FDR's Search for Tax Revision in N.Y.," November 26, 2003, http://www.taxhistory.org/thp/readings.nsf/ArtWeb/44DC64199FBB0ED885256DFE005981FE?OpenDocument.
19. See their extensive correspondence including, for example, Ogden Mills to Paul Shoup, November 22, 1932, March 6, 1933, and April 15, 1936; Paul Shoup to Ogden Mills, September 15, 1932, October 27, 1932, Papers of Paul Shoup.
20. Seligman to Guggenheim, May 29, 1931, Box 37, Edwin R. A. Seligman Papers, Butler Library, Columbia University.
21. Barber, W. J., *From New Era to New Deal: Herbert Hoover, the Economists, and American Economic Policy, 1921–1933* (Cambridge: Cambridge University Press, 1985), 97.
22. "Southern Pacific in Sudden Shake-up," *New York Times*, July 15, 1932.
23. For a list of the companies in which Shoup participated, see "Corporate Connections: Paul Shoup," January 1, 1934, Box 10, Folder 121, Papers of Paul Shoup.
24. Paul Shoup to Herbert Hoover, September 19, 1932 and September 19, 1932; Paul Shoup to Ogden Mills, October 27, 1932, October 28, 1932.
25. Paul Shoup, "Over-Taxation: A Business Viewpoint," Talk before American Bankers Association Convention, Los Angeles, October 6, 1932, Papers of Paul Shoup.
26. On the RFC, see Paul Shoup to Herbert Hoover, July 1, 1932; on the 1935 reforms, see Paul Shoup to Harry Chandler, May 20, 1935; on the 1936 election, extensive correspondence with Alf Landon in Box 1, Folder 13 and Box 3, Folders 43–45; on the undistributed profits tax, Paul Shoup, "The New Tax Proposal of the President," Box 9, Folder 111; Papers of Paul Shoup.

27. Starr, K., *Endangered Dreams: The Great Depression in California* (New York: Oxford University Press, 1996), 192–3. In addition, see "Shoup Takes Post Here," *Los Angeles Times*, May 16, 1938.

28. See, for example, Paul Shoup to Carl Shoup, June 19, 1942, 2 Series No. 35; Carl Shoup to Paul Shoup, December 21, 1944; Paul Shoup to Carl Shoup, December 28, 1944; Uncategorized Shoup Papers, YNU. In addition, see Shoup, P., "The Role of Management in Postwar Transition," *Annals of the American Academy of Political and Social Science*, 1942, vol. 222, pp. 184–8.

29. During 1937 he spent only about a week per month in New York city. "Itinerary – Mr. Paul Shoup – 1937," Box 10, Folder 129, Papers of Paul Shoup.

30. George T. Holbrook, Assistant Controller, Southern Pacific Company, 165 Broadway, NY, to Carl Shoup, October 17, 1935, Box 392–3, Shoup papers.

31. Carl Shoup to Paul Shoup, 165 Broadway, NYC, August 20, 1934, Box 392–3, Envelope #25, Shoup Papers, YNU.

32. Carl Shoup explained that "An insurance agent had calculated some figures for him without taking into consideration the deduction allowed for state income taxes in the Federal return, with the result that the figures were off about 25% in the upper brackets. As the agent had not the time to re-compute the figures before they were wanted for printing, I was pressed into service to make the corrections." Carl Shoup to Susan Burr, June 10, 1936, Box 380–1, Shoup Papers, YNU.

33. Carl Shoup to Albert Lasker, October 30, 1935, Box 380–1, Envelope #5; Carl Shoup to Hale Holdren, October 30, 1935; Hale Holdren to Carl Shoup, October 31, 1935, Box 392–3, Envelope #24, Shoup Papers, YNU. Another example of this frequent help: In 1934, Paul introduced Carl to Julius H. Parmelee, Director, Bureau of Railway Economics, Transportation Bldg, Washington, D.C., July 2, 1934. He told Parmelee that Carl "won't want anything except to make your good acquaintance except as you may develop some research ideas in common." Paul Shoup to Doctor Julius H. Parmelee, Director, Bureau of Railway Economics, Transportation Building, Washington, D.C., July 2, 1934. Box 383–1, Envelope #2, Shoup Papers. YNU.

34. Paul Shoup to Carl Shoup, February 17, 1937; Carl Shoup to Raymond Rich, Twentieth Century Fund, February 18, 1937, Shoup Papers, Box 385–2, YNU.

2

From Seligman to Shoup

The Early Columbia School of Taxation and Development

Ajay K. Mehrotra

When Carl Sumner Shoup arrived in Japan in 1949 as part of the post–World War II American mission to reconstruct the Japanese fiscal system, he brought with him not only his experience as an academic economist and a longtime advisor to the U.S. Treasury Department, but also his deep intellectual commitment to fundamental tax reform. Improving tax systems to make them more rational, equitable, and democratic had long been part of Shoup's vision of institutional change and comprehensive fiscal reform. From his early doctoral research on the post–World War I French sales tax, to his work on reforming the Cuban tax system, to his 1930s scholarship on American subnational sales taxes and his contributions to New Deal tax policy, Shoup maintained much more than just a passing research interest in the links between taxation and economic and political development. Throughout his career he was committed to applying economic ideas about public finance to the practical issues of improving political and administrative institutions in redeveloping and lesser-developed nation states.

Shoup's commitment to pragmatic tax reform was an integral part of his professional identity. His belief in melding theory with practice

Earlier versions of this chapter were presented at the annual meetings of the International Institute of Public Finance, the Law & Society Association, the Social Science History Association, the Policy History Conference, and the Politics, Economy, and Culture Workshop at Indiana University, Bloomington. The author gratefully acknowledges participants at these venues for their assistance, as well as comments and suggestions from Tim Bartley, Richard Bird, Lisa Fahey, Mary Lou Fellows, Luis Fuentes-Rohwer, Morinao Iju, Greg Jensen, Marianne Johnson, Carolyn Jones, Isaac Martin, Steve Medema, Christy Ochoa, Scott Ritter, Malcolm Rutherford, Dennis Ventry, Jr., Tim Waters, and the editors of this volume.

had been cultivated during his years at Columbia University, where he received his doctorate in economics in 1930, and where he was a member of the faculty throughout his long and distinguished academic career. In many ways, Shoup was the culmination of a multigenerational tradition of research, scholarship, and policy guidance that can be described loosely as the Columbia school of taxation and development. This chapter seeks to unearth the intellectual history of this "school." More specifically, this chapter traces the genealogical connection between the type of economic institutionalism that was prominent at Columbia in the early twentieth century and Shoup's specific ideas about taxation and development. The aim is to provide some historical perspective on the principles and proposals that were central to the many Shoup tax missions and to his overall vision of a "prescriptive" or "political economy" branch of public finance.[1]

Although public finance scholars have long recognized that Shoup was "following in the grand tradition of his illustrious predecessors at Columbia,"[2] few have attempted to analyze the historical antecedents of Shoup's ideas and actions. Economic historians, by contrast, have identified the social sciences at Columbia as a hotbed of early twentieth-century institutionalism, but they have overlooked how this distinctive strand of American economic thought may have shaped ideas about taxation and development.[3] As a result, we know little about the intellectual environment and institutional conditions from which Shoup and his particular ideas about public finance emerged. This chapter attempts to delve deeper into the links between the early Columbia institutionalist strand of taxation and development and Shoup's political economy of public finance. It chronicles how Shoup's efforts to improve and reconstruct fiscal systems stemmed mainly from this Columbia training, and particularly from his interactions with his two leading mentors Robert Murray Haig and Edwin R. A. Seligman. This chapter aims to show how the intellectual orientation of the Shoup mission – particularly its commitment to tax justice and its self-confidence in exporting American economic ideas – emanated from a long Columbia tradition of using tax policy to guide economic and political development.

AMERICAN INSTITUTIONALISM AND THE COLUMBIA STRAND OF TAXATION AND DEVELOPMENT

Historians of economic thought in America have long debated the meanings and legacy of the "old institutionalism," which began in the late nineteenth century and arguably reached its zenith during the interwar period. Whereas an older historiography generally depicted institutionalism as a binary contrast with neoclassicism, current scholars seem to agree that turn-of-the-century American economic institutionalism was a diverse and eclectic intellectual movement. In fact, given the pluralism of the pre–World War II American economics profession, scholars with institutionalist leanings did not align themselves with just one camp but spread themselves along an intellectual spectrum. "Institutionalists as a group had no one method to defend and no one economic theory to peddle," Mary S. Morgan and Malcolm Rutherford have observed. "What they did have was a commitment to serious scientific investigation, detailed empirical work (though with no one method), serious theory building (which eschewed simple assumptions), and a commitment to understand the importance of economic institutions in determining economic outcomes."[4]

In addition to an allegiance to empirical inductive methods of economic analysis, institutionalist scholars had a strong faith in state action and legal reform as a means toward social change, although they frequently disagreed about the extent of government intervention in the economy and society. Unlike an older generation of laissez-faire economic thinkers, members of the early cohort of institutionalists were not opposed to considering public responses to prominent social problems.[5] Many early institutionalists were active members of American progressivism. They supported the use of state power to address the growing social ills of modern industrial capitalism. The use of public power to structure private incentives and reform fiscal systems would, over time, become an important part of the fledgling field of American public finance. These two central elements of institutionalism – a commitment to empirical inductive methods and a faith in state action and social reform – would be hallmarks of the early Columbia school of taxation and development, and subsequently the education of Carl Shoup.

Interdisciplinary Institutionalism at Columbia

Columbia became a leader in the nascent field of public finance mainly because of its large concentration of interdisciplinary scholars with institutionalist interests. Thorstein Veblen and John R. Commons are often hailed today as canonical examples of American institutionalism, but

there were numerous social scientists at Columbia who were also key figures in the early twentieth-century institutionalist movement. Economists
John Bates Clark, Henry R. Seager, Edwin R. A. Seligman, Wesley C.
Mitchell, Rexford G. Tugwell, and Robert Hale, among many others, all
fell within the broad ambit of institutionalism. Scholars in other departments at Columbia such as Karl Llewellyn, Adolf Berle, and Gardiner
Means in the law school; William Ogburn and Frank H. Giddings in
sociology; Charles Beard and James Harvey Robinson in history; and
John Dewey in philosophy were also linked to the general tenor of
institutionalism.[6]

Given its concentration of interdisciplinary institutionalists, Columbia
became one of the leading factories of social science research, with the
economics department leading the way. Along with the University of
Chicago, the University of Wisconsin, and Harvard University, Columbia
ran one of the leading graduate programs in economics. During the first
third of the century, it produced by far the most PhDs in the discipline.[7]
In terms of scholarly output, Columbia faculty members and those
economists who received their graduate training at Columbia wrote articles that frequently appeared in the discipline's flagship journal, the *American Economic Review*.[8] Columbia economists were also adept at securing research funding. The Rockefeller Foundation, the Twentieth-Century
Fund, and the Columbia Council for Research in the Social Sciences were
all significant benefactors of research conducted by Columbia's broad
Faculty of Political Science, of which the economics department was an
integral part.[9]

Columbia's leading position in economics was related to its geographical location. Much of the scholarship produced by its faculty was fueled
by and directed at the prominent social issues that consumed the residents
of one of the world's largest and leading global cities during a period of
rapid industrialization. Political economists such as Seligman and Seager
not only deployed their expertise to assist local agencies such as the New
York Bureau of Municipal Research, but they also viewed New York
City as a natural laboratory for the social sciences. Columbia University
consequently attracted socially engaged individuals such as Shoup, who
left an early career in New York City journalism to become a graduate
student in economics. Columbia's location in Manhattan, and the overall
intellectual and social reform ferment of the city thus provided faculty
members and graduate students with a unique, and highly fruitful, kind
of education outside the halls of the university.[10]

Of the various strands of Columbia's socially engaged economic research, among the best known was the quantitative work of Wesley Mitchell, who dedicated his career to the statistical study of business cycles.[11] Because institutionalism was often identified with empirical inductive methods, it is no coincidence that Columbia was pioneering the use of statistics among the social sciences at this time. Mitchell followed in the footsteps of an earlier generation of interdisciplinary Columbia social scientists who had begun the initial boundary work of legitimating statistical analysis in several different fields. Frank H. Giddings in sociology, Richard Mayo-Smith in political science, and Henry L. Moore in economics – to name just a few – all paved the way for other scholars to build on their initial interdisciplinary forays into statistics.[12]

The Fiscal Science Strand of Columbia's Economic Institutionalism

Another, less well-recognized, institutionalist element at Columbia had an equally formative influence on Shoup and his ideas: the focus on public finance and American political and economic development evident in the research carried out by Seligman and Haig. In fact, because the economics department emerged in the early twentieth century from its roots in Columbia's School of Political Science, many of the early economic institutionalists were truly *political* economists. Thus, well before Shoup arrived at Columbia in 1925 to begin his doctoral work with Haig, Columbia had already established itself as a leading center for the interdisciplinary study of public finance and development.[13]

There had been a focus on institutional development and the melding of theory and practice in Columbia's social sciences from the very beginning. When the German-trained John W. Burgess first founded the School of Political Science in 1880, he sought to import the European seminary style of education to American graduate students. This meant a rigorous three-year curriculum aimed at original and systematic research that would prepare graduate students for academic careers as well as public service. This proto-institutionalist blending of scholarship and service would inform future generations of students, including Shoup and his mentors, who eagerly applied their public finance ideas to the practical reconstruction of fiscal systems.[14]

What was most distinctive about Burgess and his vision of the Columbia School of Political Science was less its focus on public service, which other graduate programs at the time also emphasized, and more its attempts to make the study of American politics more "scientific."[15] A scientific study of politics entailed more empirical inductive research. For Burgess, this meant turning to comparative qualitative history to understand America's unique place in the world. In his first major treatise, *Political Science and Comparative Constitutional Law* (1898), Burgess exhibited the grand historical theorizing that was common in the late nineteenth century, but he did so by grounding his findings in the details of comparative constitutional law. By placing the U.S. Constitution within a broader comparative matrix, Burgess argued that the American republic with its separation of powers and strong executive and federalist structure was "many stages in advance of all the rest in this line of progress."[16]

Although he acknowledged that America's superior position in the advancement of Western civilization was not preordained and that several contingent events, particularly the Civil War, had propelled America to its dominant position, Burgess was quite confident "that the destiny of history is clearly pointing to the United States as the great world organ for the modern solution of the problem of government as well as of liberty."[17] The use of comparative analysis to illustrate the seeming superiority of American political, economic, and legal institutions would be passed along to other Columbia scholars, who self-confidently used the American fiscal system as a baseline for their linear visions of progressive tax reform. Indeed, the use of the United States as a model, as a "city on a hill," for other developing nation states became a dominant trope during the second half of the twentieth century, when American advisors actively began to export U.S. ideas and institutions.[18]

Burgess may have begun the Columbia tradition of investigating the causes and consequences of U.S. political and economic development, and imbuing such development with a hubristic American exceptionalism, but it was one of his most gifted students, Seligman, who integrated the scientific study of comparative historical change directly into the realm of public finance. Although Burgess was well aware of the importance of taxation to the American republic, it was Seligman who dedicated his entire career to exploring the practical variation in tax systems across place and time. The son of a prominent New York City, German-Jewish banking family, Seligman spent nearly his entire life at Columbia. After attending the Columbia Grammar School, he matriculated at Columbia College at the age of 14 and graduated in 1879. Throughout his early studies, Seligman traveled frequently with his family, learning several different European languages along the way. During college, Seligman was marked as a future colleague by Burges and Mayo-Smith.[19]

Like Burgess and Mayo-Smith, Seligman continued his education in Germany after college. There he studied with some of the leading figures of the German Historical School of economics, from whom he learned more about the historical institutionalism that undergirded the distinctively German tradition of *finanzwissenschaft*. Upon his return to Morningside Heights in 1882, Seligman enrolled in the School of Political Science and, with Burgess's encouragement, Columbia's law school. He earned his law degree in 1884 and his doctorate the following year. Seligman began teaching almost immediately at Columbia and never left. He became the first John McVickar Professor of Political Economy in 1904 (a chair later held by Haig and then Shoup), was head of the economics department for many years, and finally retired in 1931. With his facility for foreign languages and his cosmopolitan background, Seligman was a natural apprentice for Burgess's interests in comparative law and political economy and the fledgling Columbia school's emerging focus on international development.[20]

Seligman revered Burgess. He did a great deal to continue his mentor's efforts to empirically ground the study of political, legal, and economic institutions, and to use that knowledge to shape public policy. From the start, Seligman melded Mayo-Smith's use of quantitative data with Burgess's emphasis on qualitative comparative evidence to explore the historical specificity of various fiscal systems. Together with Mayo-Smith, Seligman helped start and run the *Political Science Quarterly* (*PSQ*), which was established in 1886. The journal was published by Columbia's Academy of Political Science, a research unit created in 1880 to link the law school with the new Graduate School in Political Science. Seligman would later edit and use the *PSQ* as a platform for the comparative historical study of public finance.[21]

In his countless articles and essays (many of which appeared in the *PSQ*) and his numerous treatises, Seligman set out to place comparative taxation into a broader historical perspective. To place economic ideas on a "truly scientific basis," Seligman proclaimed that an individual must understand "the necessity of treating economics from the historical stand point." This meant discarding the "exclusive use of deductive methods," and turning instead to "the necessity of historical and statistical treatment." Seligman claimed that he and his generation of early institutionalist economists were eschewing "the existence of immutable natural laws in economics," and "calling attention to the interdependence of theories and institutions, and showing that different epochs or countries require different systems."[22]

Columbia political economists such as Seligman did not just espouse ideas in an academic setting; they also set out to use their research to inform public policy. As the leading tax expert of his generation, Seligman became a sought-after advisor to all levels of government, serving as an economic expert to New York State and City, the U.S. federal government, and the League of Nations, as well as several private organizations.[23] Haig later recalled that Seligman's "zeal for progress and reform was militant and contagious." For Seligman, Haig observed, "it was immensely important that the student should be definitely instructed as to what ought to be and that he be fired with the zeal to bring it to pass in this day and generation."[24] The attention to historical specificity and political context and the application of economic ideas to practical reforms would become two central components in Shoup's own political economy of public finance.

Seligman's specific ideas about the importance of fiscal administration, which he handed down to Haig and Shoup, could also be attributed to Burgess's influence. Like Burgess, Seligman was educated as a lawyer and thus the legal and administrative details of tax systems were never completely divorced from his views about the broad architecture of public finance. Whereas Burgess was more concerned about the formal parchment institutions that structured American statecraft, especially written constitutions, Seligman understood that law as an institution could best be comprehended by how it conditioned individual and group behavior. In the same way as his legal realist colleagues on the Columbia law faculty, Seligman believed that the "law in action" was more important than the "law on the books."[25]

Attention to legal administration and the application of empirical academic research to practical policies were just two of the main components of the early Columbia strand of public finance. The third and perhaps most important element was a sanguine belief in democratic progress. Whereas Burgess privileged American constitutionalism as the ideal form of republican government, Seligman seemed more cautious in embracing a teleological view of progress; certainly his German historicist training should have guarded him against such linear and transhistorical thinking. Seligman and his intellectual heirs nonetheless firmly believed that properly formulated tax policy – devised by experts like themselves, of course – could facilitate the progressive development of egalitarian ideals and democratic institutions. This was most evident in Seligman's support for an income tax based on the principle of taxpaying capacity or "ability to pay."

Throughout his career, Seligman was a staunch supporter of what he referred to as the "faculty" theory of taxation. This principle was derived loosely from John Stuart Mill's concept of "ability to pay," but whereas Mill used the term to denote the equal economic sacrifice that ought to be part of an effective and equitable tax system, Seligman used the term "faculty" to refer to the equal taxation of economic power. The subtle distinction between "equal economic sacrifice" and "equal economic power" had significant implications for the practical aspects of tax policy. In Seligman's terms, taxation based on the principle of faculty meant that those with greater power to produce and consume wealth also had a larger responsibility to contribute to the common-wealth. Thus, those who earned more had an obligation to pay more in taxes to support the state – not just proportionally more but progressively more.[26]

Although Seligman held out the ability to pay principle as a universal criterion for tax fairness, he contended that varying stages of economic development would lead to different types of taxes aimed at capturing taxpaying capacity. Thus, a property tax might be suitable for a period of "primitive industry and commerce," but such a levy was wholly unwork-able for a modern urban-industrial society such as the late nineteenth-century United States. For his time and place, Seligman believed a broad-based, progressive income tax was one of the best ways to tap a citizen's faculty or tax-paying ability.

There was a latent tension in Seligman's philosophy of fiscal history. On one hand, he held out the principle of faculty or ability to pay as an aspirational aim – as an ideal type that could not be achieved in practice but could be a useful lodestar for policymakers struggling to cope with political tensions and changing circumstances. On the other hand, he contended that the historical evolution of tax systems suggested that social concerns about distributive justice ultimately drove fiscal reforms along a linear and teleological path. "Amid the clashing of divergent interests and the endeavor of each social class to roll off the burden of taxation on some other class we discern the slow and laborious growth of standards of justice in taxation, and the attempt on the part of the community as a whole to realize this justice," wrote Seligman. "The history of finance, in other words, shows the evolution of the principle of faculty or ability to pay – the principle that each individual should be held to help the state in proportion to his ability to help himself."[27] This apparent paradox would become a central component of the Columbia strand of taxation and development. It would also become a fundamental premise of the mid-century social science of development.

Robert Murray Haig and the Economic Definition of Income

Among his many students, Haig was undoubtedly the Seligman disciple who most clearly imbibed his mentor's teachings about taxation and development, including the latent tension in his philosophy of history. Contemporaries described Haig as Seligman's "intellectual heir" and as a person that Seligman "loved like a son."[28] After completing a dissertation on the history of the Illinois property tax under Seligman's supervision, Haig assisted his teacher by conducting field research on the single tax and other property levies in Canada.[29] Seligman provided critical guidance and assistance throughout Haig's graduate training and early career, securing fellowships for his best student, helping him navigate the academic job market, and even lending him money on occasion. Writing to a Columbia colleague, Seligman heaped high praise on Haig, indicating that "he stands first in the minds of the department and of myself."[30] In 1914, Haig joined Seligman as a Columbia colleague and he eventually succeeded Seligman as the holder of the McVickar chair in political economy when Seligman retired in 1931.[31]

Haig is perhaps best remembered today among public finance scholars and policymakers for his attempts to provide a comprehensive economic definition of income – a definition that elaborated on Seligman's notion of faculty. In a 1921 essay, "The Concept of Income," Haig credited Seligman and other intellectual predecessors for constructing the theoretical foundation for a systematic model of economic income. Haig's main objective was to apply "fundamental economics and equity" to the foundation he inherited from Seligman. Building on Seligman's notion that faculty reflected economic power, Haig defined income more precisely as "the money value of the net accretion to economic power between two points in time."[32]

This conceptual definition of income would soon become a trademark of tax reformers who sought to implement broad-based income taxes as a means to achieving greater social equity and economic efficiency. Although the 1921 essay did not directly address the normative issue of appropriate income tax rates or whether the tax system should be used to encourage economic growth, Haig's resolute belief in using a comprehensive definition of income as an ideal-typical base suggested that any deviation from such a base, including deviations used to promote capital accumulation, ought to be viewed with skepticism.

Haig's essay was part of a 1920 series of lectures delivered at Columbia by a group of leading tax experts. The lectures were aimed at a general audience, and their publication helped propel Haig (who edited the collection) to the heights of the profession. The conference and the subsequent volume also helped establish Columbia as a leading center for the study of public finance. More importantly, Haig's brief essay illustrated the central elements of the growing Columbia branch of taxation and development. In exalting broad-based income taxes, the essay's theoretical findings were supported by comparative historical evidence and inductive analysis. Haig's definition of income attended to the contemporary legal and administrative challenges confronting the income tax. And Haig used the essay to show how even a theoretical definition of economic income was a product of changing democratic values and economic conditions.

Although the essay was intended to be a theoretical exercise, Haig did not limit himself to the fanciful ideas of academics. He blended his conceptual analysis with a practical knowledge of income taxes in several jurisdictions and his own experience in helping draft the 1918 Revenue Act. Similarly, Haig did not side-step the legal and administrative difficulties facing the implementation of his theoretical notion of income, or what he referred to as "the imperfections of our present economic environment." Nor did he lose sight of the need to apply his research findings to practical tax reform. He held firmly to the view that the *legal* definition of taxable income ought to adhere as closely as possible to the *economic* definition of income. Haig's focus on the virtues of a comprehensive income tax with presumably low marginal rates was not lost on his students. Shoup continued his mentor's theoretical and practical engagement with the modern income tax by advancing the notion of a broad-based income tax – what Shoup referred to as a "unified type of income tax" – to his many tax missions.[33]

Finally, Haig acknowledged that the pragmatic, legal definition of taxable income was itself an evolving concept; one that was shaped by changing social and historical contexts: "The concept of *taxable* income is a living mutable concept which has varied widely from time to time and from country to country with the conditions under which it has had to operate."[34] Despite this gesture to the contingency of tax law and policy, Haig shared with Burgess and Seligman the nationalistic and whiggish view that the United States could be a beacon for other nation states as they paved their own paths to economic and political development.

The American income tax concept, he proudly proclaimed, "is probably the closest approach to true economic income yet achieved by any country."[35]

By the turn of the twentieth century, the United States was among the world's leading industrial powers, but its national administrative capacity was more akin to a developing nation. Unlike many European industrial democracies with strong civil service traditions, the United States lacked the bureaucratic capacity to implement the type of comprehensive income tax that Haig and other institutionally inclined economists had in mind. The adoption of a comprehensive income tax brought with it unique administrative challenges that other nations, which relied on scheduler or categorized taxation, did not face. Thus, Shoup came of age intellectually at a time when the United States itself was gradually developing the practical capabilities to implement an equitable, broad-based income tax. Molding a just and fair tax system in accordance with limited administrative capacity became an important element of Shoup's fiscal thinking, especially when he began participating in international tax missions.

Ultimately, Seligman, Haig and the entire Columbia tradition imbued in Shoup several important lessons about the relationship between taxation and development.

First, Shoup learned that equity and tax justice required an adherence to a comprehensive, broad-based tax system that treated all accretions of economic power equally. Haig had labeled this approach toward taxation "fundamental economics and equity." Shoup and others would later refer to this principle as "horizontal equity," the notion that similarly situated taxpayers ought to be treated similarly.

Second, allegiance to a comprehensive tax base meant that tax policy should remain neutral with regard to economic development. Whereas a later generation of public finance experts would advocate using tax incentives to increase savings and investment as a means to spur economic growth, Shoup and his mentors believed that departures from a comprehensive tax base would only distort economic decision-making and impede economic growth. They seemed to believe that the market, rather than the state, might be more effective in allocating scare resources. Instead of viewing tax policy as a tool of economic growth, they saw changing economic conditions, or what they referred to as "stages" of economic development, as one of the key factors that determined the type of tax system that was actually viable.

Third, Shoup came to understand that a society's level of development shaped the legal and administrative framework in which tax policy operated, and this framework, in turn, determined how close a tax system could come to the economic ideal. For the Columbia scholars, tax policy was not meant to be an effective tool to promote economic growth; taxes were contingent on a broader context. They were integral parts of a more complex matrix of economic, political, and social conditions. In short, Shoup believed, as did his mentors Seligman and Haig, that a comprehensive income tax was an aspirational ideal that could serve as a benchmark for lawmakers and policy analysts, but would remain unattainable because of practical circumstances and limitations. It was this tempered idealism that Shoup carried with him throughout his career.

SHOUP'S POLITICAL ECONOMY OF PUBLIC FINANCE

Shoup entered Columbia University when institutionalism was at its height. From the beginning, Shoup was attracted to the work of his two most formative mentors, Haig and Seligman. As a student and junior colleague, he solicited the guidance of both men, and each selected Shoup for important reform projects. Haig, who was the chair of Shoup's dissertation committee, recruited his top students to help investigate the redevelopment of French public finance in the wake of World War I. This study formed the basis of Shoup's own doctoral research on the origins and early development of the French turnover tax, a crude forerunner of the value-added tax (VAT).[36]

In 1930, Shoup's dissertation was published as a monograph. The study displayed the young scholar's Columbia training and his desire to balance the ideals of tax equity with practical realities. Echoing Seligman's linear view of fiscal development, Shoup "condemned" the French turnover tax as regressive, "as more unfavorable to the poorer classes than is an income tax." Similarly to Haig, however, Shoup seemed open to understanding why France had turned to a sales tax. He took into consideration local administrative conditions and the changing economic and political context of postwar French society to conclude that the turn to a consumption tax was seemingly inevitable. "Given the background of French public finance, with its powerfully established and many-branched system of indirect taxes, and with the still influential hostility of important taxpaying classes to the income tax," he wrote, "it is difficult to see how the situation could be otherwise." This early experience in France sparked Shoup's lifelong interest in sales taxes and the VAT, and also taught him about the role that political power and historical forces could play in shaping tax policymaking.[37]

Early Experiences as an Economic Advisor

Soon after Shoup's book on France was published, Seligman recruited him for an early tax mission to Cuba where Shoup received his first taste of exporting economic ideas. The 1931–32 Cuba mission differed dramatically from the work that Shoup had done with Haig in France. The French study took a detached, academic approach, and hence the authors were cautious and ambivalent about making strong normative judgments. By contrast, the Cuba project was filled with American hubris. It included the bold recommendation that the comprehensive and radical reforms recommended by American experts ought to be adopted whole-sale, without modification, so as to create a "firm foundation that would last for years to come." Thus, from the start – well before Shoup became a full member of the Columbia faculty – the school's orientation toward using American-centered tax expertise to assist redeveloping nation states and lesser developed regions had a formative influence on the young tax scholar.[38]

Although Shoup was exposed at an early stage to the international focus developing at Columbia, it was in his role as a domestic advisor that Shoup began to learn about the possibilities and limits of melding theory with practice. Soon after he was appointed to the Columbia Business School faculty, Shoup began turning his attention to the social realities of the Great Depression's effect on American public finance. He began by exploring subnational fiscal issues. In 1934, Shoup coauthored with Haig a path-breaking and exhaustive study of the rise of state sales taxes during the early 1930s. Filled with the teachings of the Columbia school, the book's central analytical question addressed who ultimately paid a sales tax. This had been a perennial puzzle among economists. Seligman, himself, had written one of the first American treatises on the topic.[39]

Studying the incidence of sales taxes was a first step in getting to Haig and Shoup's central concern, which was the distributional impact of the new state levies. The authors acknowledged that state sales taxes could yield substantial revenue, especially amidst an economic crisis. Harking back to the Columbia tradition's focus on distributional equity, however, they questioned whether such increased revenues ought to be generated at the expense of fairness and tax justice. They thus concluded that: "The sales tax as an emergency form of revenue, and certainly as the permanent part of any state's tax system, marks an unnecessary and backward step in taxation."[40] Over time, Shoup would temper his views on sales taxes, but for the time being concern for the distributional impact of sales taxes dominated his thinking and that of the Columbia school.

The success of the sales tax study brought Shoup to the attention of other leading tax experts, and gave the young scholar an opportunity to engage with national-level policymaking. In 1934, through his Columbia connections, Shoup began working with Roswell Magill, a Columbia law professor, in the U.S. Treasury Department. As part of an elite group of tax experts, Shoup developed proposals that corresponded with Seligman's general faculty theory and Haig's economic definition of income. At the same time, this initial experience with lawmaking taught him once again about the political powers that could constrain ideal policymaking. Many of the Magill group's recommendations reflected the leading ideas of contemporary public finance experts, including how a comprehensive income tax base with low exemption levels and moderately graduated rates could enhance "conscious interest in government," and hence foster greater civic participation. Nevertheless, the thrust of these proposals went unheeded by New Deal lawmakers, who seemed preoccupied with attempting to use tax policy instrumentally to "soak the rich."[41]

Despite the limited success of his initial Treasury Department service, Shoup's reputation soared among the tax policy community as he continued to impart the lessons of the Columbia school. As Shoup broadened his research interests and the audience for his work, he continued to rely on the guidance of his Columbia mentors. In the mid-1930s, Shoup was research director for a broad-based study on current tax problems sponsored by the Twentieth Century Fund, a New York-based nonpartisan research foundation. The influence of Shoup's mentors was evident. The foundation's Special Committee on Taxation, which supervised and approved the study's research agenda, consisted of leading businessmen and tax experts such as Haig, Magill, and Eustace Seligman, Edwin R. A. Seligman's son, who at the time was a leading tax and corporate attorney at the Wall Street law firm of Sullivan and Cromwell. As Shoup shared drafts of the study with Haig and the senior Seligman, he acknowledged their abilities to provide a breadth of knowledge and broad perspective. "I want you to know that you have spurred me on to new endeavors," Shoup wrote to Seligman. "If little of value on the fundamentals shows up in the finished study, it will not be because I have neglected to try to think about them. I am more indebted to you than I can well express, for the opportunity to get from you counsel and inspiration and a breadth of view that are too easy to lose in every-day work."[42]

The Shoup-led study culminated with the 1937 publication of the aptly titled *Facing the Tax Problem: A Survey of Taxation in the United States and a Program for the Future*. The book was a blend of detached, systematic economic analysis and highly detailed, normative recommendations for improving nearly every aspect of the existing fiscal order, from national income and wealth-transfer taxes, to subnational property and sales taxes, to intergovernmental fiscal relations. At first glance, the book's organization suggested that issues such as "tax justice," "ease of administration," and "tax consciousness" were "secondary aims" behind the primary goals of raising revenue and influencing social behavior.[43]

A closer look at the study's recommendations, however, indicates that the Columbia allegiance to a broad-based, moderately progressive income tax loomed large over the book's central proposals. The study conceded that abstract notions of ability to pay, including Seligman's faculty theory, were difficult to apply to concrete situations. Despite this, many of the detailed recommendations expressed attempts to move the existing tax base closer to Haig's economic definition of income, or what the authors referred to as a "unified type of income tax."[44] As part of their base-broadening suggestions, Shoup and his colleagues advised eliminating both the deduction for charitable donations and the tax-exemption of interest from state and local government securities – two seemingly sacred provisions of the income tax system that had been in existence since the adoption of the federal income tax in 1913. The most radical, and perhaps the most controversial, proposal, however, was the recommendation that "capital gains be taxed as part of the income tax base . . . computed annually on an accrual basis."[45]

The last recommendation rankled tax practitioners. As a result, Shoup found himself defending not only the study's conclusions, but also the ideas and reputation of Haig, his mentor and friend. In a series of correspondence between Shoup, Eustace Seligman, and George O. May, a leading tax accountant, Shoup felt compelled to explain the reasoning behind the proposal to tax unrealized capital gains.[46] In the process, Shoup explained how the recommendation was derived from an economic definition of income that was itself based on the notion of ability to pay. In an April 1937 letter to Eustace Seligman, May claimed that the taxation of unrealized capital gains was administratively infeasible and that it was based on an erroneous notion of accounting theory perpetuated by Haig's economic definition of income.[47] Shoup responded to May's letter by explaining Haig's intentions: "Professor Haig has advanced theoretical ideas on" the topic of taxing accrued capital gains, Shoup wrote, "not as 'accounting theories,' but as standards for a personal tax designed to measure ability to pay."

In other words, he was trying to discover a definition of "income" that would be most suitable for use in connection with the phrase "income tax," it being understood that the purpose of such tax was to tax people according to their relative "ability to pay." He was not, I believe, trying to discover the definition of income that would be suitable for all accounting purposes whatsoever.[48]

Shoup's letter did little to assuage May. Days later, May published a stinging critique of the Shoup-led study and its recommendations in the *New York Times*.[49] Consequently, the Twentieth Century Fund report, similar to the earlier Magill group's study, did not gain much traction with many lawmakers, although it did provide a comprehensive blueprint for subsequent generations of tax scholars and reformers.

The Shoup-led study was still a significant achievement for the growing Columbia school and its institutionalist perspective on public finance. With Haig and Magill on the Twentieth Century Fund's special committee and Shoup as Research Director, *Facing the Tax Problem* had the conspicuous imprimatur of some of Columbia's leading tax experts. The study's associate directors were also from the same intellectual lineage. Mabel Newcomer, a Vassar professor, was a Columbia graduate (PhD, 1917) and Seligman student who carried on the department's tradition of comparative fiscal research by becoming an expert on subnational taxation in the United States, Germany, and England.[50] The study's other associate director, Roy Blough, was a Wisconsin graduate (PhD, 1929) and John Commons student. Blough was teaching at the University of Cincinnati when he began working for Shoup. Soon thereafter he became a regular fixture in the New Deal Treasury Department. Afterwards, Blough became head of President Truman's Council of Economic Advisors. In 1955, he joined the Columbia Business School faculty.[51] Through his advisory work and his continued contact with his mentors, Shoup gradually became a central node in a growing international network of professional tax scholars and policy advisors. His participation in the 1949 Japanese tax mission came about because of his work with Haig and others in the New Deal Treasury Department.[52]

Shoup often welcomed foreign graduate students and scholars into his classroom, usually after an introduction from one of his mentors or colleagues. He frequently remained in touch with many of these foreign students, several of whom went on to become prominent academics and policymakers in their home countries. Even before he arrived in Japan, Shoup was in contact, via E.R.A. Seligman, with Japanese scholars such as Dr. Matsushita Shutaro of Kansei Gakuin University in Hyogo.[53] Shoup, like Seligman and Haig before him, essentially operated as an intellectual ambassador between American academics and foreign public finance scholars, often informing his colleagues about the latest scholarship emerging from abroad.[54]

Although Shoup was eager to learn from the experience of other countries and to export American economic ideas, he did not lose sight of the limits of his knowledge. When Seligman contacted Shoup in 1936 with an opportunity to assist Chinese officials and scholars with their evolving income tax regulations, Shoup diffidently demurred. Shoup informed Seligman that he would write to the Chinese "at great length if you wish it, but I find it somewhat difficult to prescribe for Chinese conditions."[55] If Shoup had learned anything early in his career, it was that the political tensions and practical realities of a given time and place could frequently constrain even the most noble of ideas and proposals.

Developing and Maintaining the Columbia Tradition

In addition to learning from his mentors and working with them to meld theory with practice, Shoup did a great deal to develop and maintain the Columbia tradition of taxation and development. Similar to Burgess, Seligman, and Haig, Shoup was not only an institutionalist, but also an institution builder. Just as he had been marked by his teachers as a promising student and scholar, Shoup singled out other budding tax experts at Columbia as future colleagues. C. Lowell Harriss and William S. Vickrey were among the first generation of students who worked closely with Shoup and Haig, and carried on the Columbia tradition as lifetime faculty members.

Harriss arrived at Columbia in the mid-1930s, after earning an undergraduate economics degree at Harvard and traveling throughout Europe and Northern Africa on an academic fellowship. His international interests no doubt led him to Shoup, who identified Harriss as one of Columbia's "best students" when he hired him as an assistant at the Treasury Department. Harriss's research interests gradually moved beyond taxation and development. He wrote on a variety of public finance topics including land valuation and local taxes, but early in his career Hariss was a faithful Shoup disciple, accompanying his mentor on several foreign tax missions.[56]

Similar to his close friend and contemporary Harriss, Vickrey's research interests covered a variety of topics, from public finance to urban economics to auction theory to inflation and unemployment. The son of a Protestant minister active in international relief work, Vickrey was educated abroad and received his undergraduate training in mathematics and engineering at Yale University. During college, he worked with the neoclassical economist Irving Fisher, a leading proponent of consumption taxes. Vickrey interrupted his graduate training at Columbia to work extensively in Washington, D.C., for the National Resources Planning Board and the Treasury Department. This early and extended hands-on experience blended well with Columbia's commitment to combining theory with practice, and "undoubtedly contributed to [Vickrey's] lifelong concern with details of taxation." When he returned to Morningside Heights in 1946, Vickrey completed a brash public finance dissertation in taxation, supervised by Haig and Shoup. The dissertation became his first book, in 1947, and was boldly titled *Agenda for Progressive Taxation*.[57]

Although some scholars have contended that Vickrey was influenced more by the neoclassicism of Irving Fisher than the institutionalism of Haig and Shoup,[58] the body of his work on public finance suggests that Vickrey relied on both neoclassical theory and certain aspects of institutionalism. In that sense, he was a key transition figure in Columbia's gradual, long-term shift in focus from eclectic institutionalism to a more conventional neoclassicism.[59]

In his efforts to maintain the Columbia tradition of taxation and development, Vickrey was instrumental in refining the Seligman–Haig–Shoup message that a comprehensive income tax could be both equitable and efficient. For example, his consistent support for the taxation of capital gains and his work on lifetime income averaging, or what he referred to as "cumulative averaging," suggested that Vickrey recognized that "practical politics" dictated the "retention of the income tax in approximately its present form."[60] Although he was in many ways more of a theorist than an empiricist, Vickrey believed throughout his long and illustrious career, which included the 1996 Nobel Prize, that "economic knowledge could help human beings get more out of life."[61] Other Shoup students followed in the footsteps of Harriss and Vickrey. Lorraine Eden, one of Shoup's last doctoral students, has focused her scholarship on the taxation of international business. Meanwhile, Richard M. Bird, perhaps more than any other Shoup student, has continued the Columbia tradition by dedicating his entire professional career to the specific topic of taxation and international development.[62]

In addition to mentoring a new generation of public finance economists, Shoup attempted to further Columbia's focus on taxation and development in other ways. As an institutional leader at Columbia, Shoup believed in preserving the Economics Department's history and building the library's collection of economic materials. Decades earlier, Seligman had taken important steps in the same direction. Seligman had actively participated in commemorating the university's 150-year anniversary. Toward the end of his career, he was the living institutional memory of the Economics Department. After he retired, Seligman sold his vast private library, which included numerous valuable economic pamphlets, to the Columbia University library.[63] Shoup followed Seligman's example. When Seligman passed way, Shoup assisted Haig and Eli Ginzberg (Columbia PhD, 1934) in organizing a memorial and a volume of essays honoring Seligman's career at Columbia.[64] Shoup did something similar for Haig, working with colleagues to collect Haig's "fugitive papers on public finance" and by gathering some of Haig's personal papers and archiving them in the Columbia library.[65]

Shoup realized that preserving the works of an older generation of colleagues was critical to maintaining and preserving the Columbia tradition. In the late 1950s, when Shoup was the department chair, he helped the Columbia library secure the personal papers and private library of one of his former teachers, Henry L. Moore. At the time, Moore's pioneering work in statistics was increasingly appealing to neoclassical University of Chicago economists such as George J. Stigler, who was contemplating writing an intellectual biography of Moore, whom he identified as "perhaps the most important American economist in the first half of the twentieth century." Shoup himself had hoped that one of his colleagues at Columbia (Stigler had left Columbia for Chicago in 1958) would take up the task of chronicling Moore's life and achievements. He prodded Joseph Dorfman by suggesting he could have exclusive access to the Moore papers.[66] In the end, neither Dorfman nor any of the other Columbia economists took up Shoup's call, but Stigler soon thereafter published a brief and critical essay on Moore's role in initiating the study of "statistical economics."[67]

Research and Scholarship

Institution-building and formulation of tax policies were both central aspects of Shoup's career. The greatest example of how Columbia molded the tax scholar, however, was in his overall research and scholarship, especially in his focus on taxation and development. Among the many things he learned from his mentors, one of the most important was the notion that a society's development was, at bottom, a historical process, one that was conditioned by changing social, political, and economic circumstances. The broader context frequently determined the direction of fiscal reforms.

Seligman's influence in this regard was unmistakable. The elder colleague was one of the leading economic historians of his generation. His *Economic Interpretation of History* (1902) was a well-received foray into the philosophy of history that critically analyzed European theories of dialectical materialism. The book was translated into several languages, including Japanese, and became a seminal text for other scholars such as Charles A. Beard.[68] Throughout his career, Seligman spent a great deal of time researching and writing about the history of economic thought with particular reference to taxation. At his death in 1939, he was hard at work on a multivolume *History of Fiscal Science* that remained unfinished and unpublished.[69] Shoup was well aware of Seligman's historicist leanings and he emulated his mentor to a certain degree. In the late 1950s, Shoup embarked on his own book project on the history of economic thought and taxation. His *Ricardo on Taxation* (1960) was a rich study of classical economic ideas informed by archival research and an extensive use of secondary sources. Shoup also shared his historical knowledge with others. He worked closely with graduates of Columbia's history program, such as Sidney Ratner who wrote a doctoral thesis on "The Political History of the Federal Income Tax" under the supervision of Allen Nevins.[70]

The history of taxation, however, was a minor interest for Shoup compared to his theoretical fascination with a comprehensive income tax. If one of Haig's career goals had been to apply Seligman's criterion of faculty or ability to pay to the modern American income tax, Shoup seemed equally focused on refining and popularizing Haig's economic definition of income. Throughout the 1930s, while Shoup was working for the U.S. Treasury Department, teaching business school classes, and assisting with tax missions to Cuba, he was also working on a large book project about the concept of income. It appears that the book was initially conceived as another collaborative project between Haig and Shoup, but over time it became one of Shoup's main academic endeavors.

The book was designed to be a comparative and extensive exploration of the economic definition of income in all its facets. In this sense, it was to be a comprehensive elaboration of Haig's classic 1921 article and a continuation of Columbia's institutionalist commitments to using inductive, empirical methods to inform policymaking. Shoup researched what economists in England and the continent had written on the topic, and he began to compose a manuscript that would examine nearly every aspect of the concept of income, from the appropriate taxable unit (the individual or the family) to the treatment of imputed income and capital gains, to the distinction between gross and net income, and the proper line between deductible business expenses and nondeductible personal spending. Throughout his early research and writing, he shared drafts of his growing chapters with Haig and Seligman and solicited their guidance on the scope and findings of his study.[71]

Shoup was not the only scholar interested in furthering Haig's ideas. As Shoup was working on his book, a junior economics professor at the University of Chicago, Henry Simons, was embarked on a nearly identical research project. Simons began his graduate training at Columbia in 1922, but followed his main mentor, Frank Knight, from Iowa to Chicago in the late 1920s.[72] Jacob Viner – who taught at Chicago and worked alongside Haig and Shoup in the New Deal Treasury Department – notified Simons about Haig and Shoup's fledgling book. Simons contacted Haig in 1936 and offered to send the senior scholar a copy of his own "crude and incomplete manuscript." Initially, Simons had little faith in his nascent tract. "I have little proprietary interest in the stuff," he wrote in reference to his manuscript. "It's unlikely ever to seem like a good book to me." By contrast, Simons believed that the Haig (and Shoup) book on the concept of income "is likely to be a major influence in the future of income taxation."[73]

In the end, Shoup did not complete his *magnum opus* on the economic concept of income. His ongoing commitments to the Treasury Department and his teaching distracted him. The 1938 publication of Simons's manifesto, *Personal Income Taxation: The Definition of Income as a Problem of Fiscal Policy*, no doubt gave him pause about the originality of his own work.[74] Nonetheless, with funding support from the Columbia Council for Research in the Social Sciences, Shoup continued to research continental theories of income taxation well into the early 1940s, when the outbreak of World War II compelled nearly all tax experts to focus on more pressing practical issues.[75] During and after the war, Shoup continued to serve the Treasury Department, advancing the cause of broad-based income taxation whenever he could. In 1949, on the mission to Japan, he had perhaps his most significant opportunity to advance the core reform of the tax program that Haig had pioneered.

The Legacy of Tax Missions

Shoup had been active in tax missions well before his 1949 visit to Japan. From his experiences working with Haig in France and Seligman in Cuba, he had learned the importance of tax reforms aimed at greater fairness and neutrality. Some aspects of Shoup's later missionary work, however, seemed to veer from the Columbia school's emphasis on using a broad-based income tax as a means of furthering tax equity and efficiency. The innovative suggestion of using a VAT for Japanese local governments was one proposal that conflicted with Shoup's (and the Columbia school's) allegiance to a comprehensive income tax base. It also demonstrated that Shoup was attempting to break free of the linear view of fiscal progress that had dominated the thinking of his mentors. Even though a VAT was not adopted in Japan until 1989, the novelty of Shoup's recommendation earned him the moniker of being "the intellectual father of the value-added tax," a label he accepted only ambivalently – perhaps because he had been so thoroughly imbued to be skeptical of the distributional impact of a consumption-based tax.[76]

Still, if the greatest legacy of the Shoup missions was their ability to set the agenda for future tax reform, as some scholars have suggested,[77] the overall vision for such fiscal reform was shaped by a particular branch of Columbia school institutionalism. There was perhaps no better evidence of this than the similarity between the ways in which Shoup and Seligman approached the process of designing tax systems. In 1991, Shoup reflected back on his missionary work to identify the three vital tasks of any tax mission. They formed a hierarchy. "Tax architecture" formed the top tier, followed by "tax engineering," and then "tax administration." The "three tasks," he concluded, "must be accomplished almost simultaneously."[78]

Roughly seven decades earlier, Seligman had made remarkably similar observations about the importance of the "three stages" of "every new fiscal project." In the introduction to Haig's 1921 volume on the income tax, Seligman contended that each of these phases taken together were vital to the design and execution of comprehensive tax reform. The first stage consisted of settling the "fundamental principles" on which a tax system could be built. These were "primarily economic in character," and included issues such as the proper definition of income – a question that dominated Haig's career. The second stage related to "the legal and constitutional aspects" of tax laws, their "precise legal effect." The third, which Seligman singled out as "perhaps the most significant of all," was "the administrative aspect," the interpretation of tax laws and the mediation of conflicting views held by taxpayers and the treasury.[79] That Seligman's overarching ideas anticipated Shoup's later assessment of tax missions should come as no surprise. After all, Shoup's first experience with exporting fiscal ideas and policies came from his work relating to Seligman's 1931 mission to Cuba.

More importantly, the resonance between Shoup's recollections and those of Seligman show how both were products of an institutional culture that valued broad, contextual, and empirically grounded perspectives on tax reform – a culture that by the 1950s began to fade as the Columbia Economics Department gradually abandoned its institutionalist orientation to embrace neoclassicism.[80] Unlike their neoclassicist colleagues, members of the early Columbia school of taxation and development did not exalt theory or ideology over practical results. Nor did they seek merely to quantify the dead-weight loss created by tax distortions using formal models. This group of scholars and reformers was committed to "melding" – a word that Shoup particularly liked – inductive empirical analysis with broad economic principles to develop pragmatic ways to improve the everyday lives of people living in the developing world. Shoup and his colleagues were not always successful in implementing their reform proposals, but they remained true to their conviction that fiscal science was a means toward social progress and improvement.[81]

Coda: Shoup's "Public Finance" – a Life's Work

Carl Shoup's career was the apex of a multigenerational Columbia tradition of public finance research, scholarship, teaching, and missionary work that stretched back to the turn of the twentieth century. The impact of his ideas and actions continued to reverberate not only through a subsequent generation of scholars interested in taxation and development, some of whom were Shoup's students, but also through his last major scholarly endeavor, his path-breaking 1969 textbook, *Public Finance*.

In a foreword to the first edition, the eclectic economist Harry G. Johnson noted that Shoup, along with Richard Musgrave, was "the dean of contemporary public finance experts."[82] Written just two years before his retirement, Shoup's textbook represented the breadth and depth of a life's work, as well as the most current thinking in the field. The book reflected the main tenets of the early Columbia strand of taxation and development: the empirical grounded research in various tax systems across space and time; the application of such research to practical concerns with administrative challenges in mind; the desire to reduce economic inefficiencies of certain taxes (including income and sales taxes); and, perhaps most importantly, the overriding concern with the equitable distribution of tax burdens as a fundamental aspect of public finance.

From this perspective, Shoup's *Public Finance* provides a stark contrast with the reigning orthodoxy in present-day American public finance. As Steve Medema, in an introduction to a recently republished edition of Shoup's textbook, has explained: "When set against today's ahistorical, a-institutional texts, Shoup's myriad references to world tax systems and his generalist (rather than U.S.-specific) approach to issues of tax policy is at once startlingly and refreshingly distinctive."[83] Where did Shoup receive this distinctive view on taxation? To answer this essential question, we need only look to the textbook's dedication, where the memory of Shoup's Columbia teachers Haig and Seligman are honored, or to the book's acknowledgements, where Shoup expressed his "greatest indebtedness" to his two mentors, who introduced him to "the field of public finance and supplied the stimulation and the standards that are the prerequisites to any endeavor of this kind."[84]

Notes

1. Lorraine Eden has identified Shoup, along with Richard Musgrave, as "leading world figures" of the "prescriptive" or "political economy" school of public finance – a school that "combines rigorous theory with practical policy advice. Eden, L., "Retrospectives on Public Finance: An Introduction to the Issues," in Eden, L., ed. *Retrospectives on Public Finance* (Durham and London: Duke University Press, 1991), 3–4.
2. Bird, R. M., Head, J. G., eds. *Modern Fiscal Issues: Essays in Honor of Carl S. Shoup* (Toronto: University of Toronto Press, 1972), vii.
3. Rutherford, M., *The Institutionalist Movement in American Economics, 1918–1947: Science and Social Control* (New York: Cambridge University Press, 2011), 223–56; Biddle, J., "Social Science and the Making of Social Policy: Wesley Mitchell's Vision," in Backhouse, R., Creedy, J., eds. *The Economic Mind in America: Essays in Honour of D.P. O'Brien* (Aldershot: Edwar Elgar, 1999), 257–80; Ginzberg, E., "Economics at Columbia: Recollections of the Early 1930s," *American Economist*, 2009, vol. 34 (2), 14–19; Dorfman, J., "The Department of Economics," in Hoxie, R. G., ed., *A History of the Faculty of Political Science, Columbia University* (New York: Columbia University Press, 1955), 161–206.
4. Morgan, M. S., Rutherford, M., eds. *From Interwar Pluralism to Postwar Neoclassicism* (Durham, N.C.: Duke University Press, 1998), 3.
5. Ross, D., *The Origins of American Social Science* (New York: Cambridge University Press, 1992), 411–15; Fourcade, M., *Economists and Societies: Discipline and Profession in the United States, Britain and France, 1890s–1990s* (Princeton: Princeton University Press, 2009), 82–3.

6. Rutherford, M., *The Institutionalist Movement in American Economics, 1918–1947: Science and Social Control*, 223–26.

7. Froman, L. A., "Graduate Students in Economics, 1904–1940," *American Economic Review* 1942, vol. 32 (4), pp. 817–26. Although Wisconsin was a leading center of institutionalism, it did not develop the dominant position in public finance that Columbia commanded. Johnson, M., "Public Finance and Wisconsin Institutionalism, 1892–1929," *Journal of Economic Issues* 2011, vol. 45 (4), pp. 965–83, 980.

8. Backhouse, R. E., "The Transformation of U.S. Economics, 1920–1960, Viewed Through a Survey of Journal Articles," in Morgan, M. S., Rutherford, M., eds., *From Interwar Pluralism to Postwar Neoclassicism* (Duke University Press, 1991), 100–4; Hoxie, R. G., ed., *A History of the Faculty of Political Science, Columbia University* (New York: Columbia University Press, 1955), 159.

9. Dorfman, J., "The Department of Economics," in Hoxie, R. G., ed., *A History of the Faculty of Political Science, Columbia University* (New York: Columbia University Press, 1955), 161–206.

10. Bender, T., *Intellect and Public Life: Essays on the Social History of Academic Intellectuals in the United States* (Baltimore: Johns Hopkins University Press, 1997), 49–77; "Shoup, Carl (Sumner)," in: Rothe, A., ed., *Current Biography*, Vol. 10 (H.W. Wilson Co. 1949), 569–71; Ricchiuti, J. L., *Civic Engagement: Social Science and Progressive-Era Reform in New York City* (Philadelphia: University of Pennsylvania Press, 2007).

11. Mitchell, W. C., *Business Cycles* (Berkeley: University of California Press, 1913); National Bureau of Economic Research, *Business Cycles: The Problem and Its Setting* (New York, National Bureau of Economic Research, 1927); Biddle, J., "Social Science and the Making of Social Policy: Wesley Mitchell's Vision," in Backhouse, R., Creedy, J., eds. *The Economic Mind in America: Essays in Honour of D.P. O'Brien* (Aldershot, Edwar Elgar, 1999), 257–80.

12. Camic, C. Xie, Y., "The Statistical Turn in American Social Science: Columbia University, 1890–1915," *American Sociological Review* 1994, vol. 59 (5), pp. 773–805; Gieryn, T. F., "Boundary-work and the Demarcation of Science from Non-science: Strains and Interests in Professional Ideologies of Scientists," *American Sociological Review* 1983, vol. 48, pp. 781–95.

13. Rozwadowski, F., "From Recitation Room to Research Seminar: Political Economy at Columbia University" in William J. Barber, W. J., ed., *Economists and Higher Learning in the Nineteenth Century* (New Brunswick, NJ: Transaction Publishers, 1993), 169–202.

14. Ibid.; Dorfman, J., "Department of Economics," 172.

15. "In all the convulsions of political history, described as advance and reaction," Burgess boldly proclaimed, "the scientific student of history is able to discover that the zigzags of progress are ever bearing in the general direction which the combined impulses toward nationalism and humanism compel." Burgess, J. W., *The Middle Period, 1817–1858* (New York: Charles Scribner's Sons, 1897), 243.

16. Burgess, J. W., *Political Science and Comparative Constitutional Law* (Boston: Ginn & Company, 1898), 39.
17. Ibid., 40.
18. Latham, M. E., *The Right Kind of Revolution: Modernization, Development, and U.S. Foreign Policy from the Cold War to the Present* (Ithaca, NY: Cornell University Press, 2011), 58–61.
19. Rozwadowski, "From Recitation Room to Research Seminar," 196–7; "Edwin Robert Anderson Seligman. Autobiography (1929)," in Asso, P. S., Fiorito, I. Samuels, J. W., eds., *Documents From and On Economic Thought* (Boston: Elsevier, 2006).
20. Mehrotra, A. K., "From Berlin to Baltimore: German Historicism and the American Income Tax, 1877–1913," in: Nuetzenadel, A., Strupp, C., eds., *Taxation, State and Civil Society in Germany and the United States from the 18th to the 20th Century* (Baden-Baden: Nomos Publishers, 2007), 167–84. On the contrast between Anglo-Saxon public finance and German *finanzwissenschaft*, see Musgrave, R. A., "Public Finance and Finanzwissenshaft Traditions Compared," *FinanzArhiv/Public Finance Analysis* 1996–7, vol. 53 (2), pp. 145–93.
21. *A History of Columbia University, 1754–1904* (New York: Columbia University Press, 1904), 274–5.
22. Seligman, "Change in the Tenets of Political Economy with Time," *Science – Supplement*, April 23, 1886, 381.
23. Dorfman, J., "Department of Economics," 175.
24. "The Teacher. An Address by Robert Murray Haig," in *Edwin Robert Anderson Seligman, 1861–1939* (Stamford, CT: Overlook Press, 1942), 16–17.
25. For more on legal realism at Columbia during this period, see Schlegel, J. H., *American Legal Realism and Empirical Social Science* (Chapel Hill: University of North Carolina Press, 1995), 50–5; Duxbury, N., *Patterns of American Jurisprudence* (New York: Oxford University Press, 1997), 83–8.
26. Seligman, E. R. A., "The Theory of Progressive Taxation," *Political Science Quarterly* 1893, vol. 8 (2), pp. 220–51, 245.
27. Seligman, E. R. A., *The Income Tax: A Study of the History, Theory, and Practice of Income Taxation at Home and Abroad*, 2nd ed. (New York: Macmillan Co., 1914), 4.
28. H. S. Bloch to R. M. Haig, July 23, 1939; E. Seligman Jr. to R. M. Haig, July 28, 1939, Carl S. Shoup Papers, Yokohama National University Library, Yokohama, Japan [hereinafter CSSP].
29. Haig, R. M., *A History of the General Property Tax in Illinois* (Champaign, IL: University of Illinois Studies in the Social Sciences, 1914); R. M. Haig to E. R. A. Seligman, July 22, 1914, Edwin R. A. Seligman Papers, Cataloged Correspondence, Butler Library Rare Book and Manuscript Collections, Columbia University, New York, NY [hereinafter ERASP]; Haig, R. M., *The Exemption of Improvements from Taxation in Canada and the United States: A Report Prepared for the Committee on Taxation of the City of New York* (New York: City Press, 1915).
30. E. R. A. Seligman to A. E. Chandler, August 22, 1915; E. R. A. Seligman to R. M. Haig, April 13, 1911; August 18, 1915; October 29, 1917,

Correspondence: Seligman, 1908–1922, Robert M. Haig Papers, Butler Library Rare Book and Manuscript Collections, Columbia University, New York, NY [hereinafter RMHP].

31. "Robert Murray Haig," *Political Science Quarterly* 1953, vol. 68 (3), pp. 479–80.
32. Haig, R. M., "The Concept of Income – Economic and Legal Aspects," in Haig, R. M., ed., *The Federal Income Tax* (New York: Columbia University Press, 1921), 2, 27.
33. Haig, R. M., "The Concept of Income – Economic and Legal Aspects," 16. Shoup, C. S., Blough, R., Newcomer, M., *Facing the Tax Problem: A Survey of Taxation in the United States and Program for the Future* (New York: The Twentieth Century Fund, 1937).
34. Haig, R. M., "The Concept of Income – Economic and Legal Aspects," 27 (emphasis in the original).
35. Ibid.
36. Haig, R. M., Shoup, C. S., Werth, A., Molodovsky, N., *The Public Finances of Post-war France* (New York: Columbia University Press, 1929).
37. Shoup, C. S., *The Sales Tax in France* (New York: Columbia University Press, 1930), 353. For more on Shoup's work in France, see Chapter 3 of this volume.
38. "Seligman Outlines New Cuban Tax Code," *New York Times*, February 13, 1932, 24; "Professor Aiding Cuba in Finance," *Washington Post*, July 5, 1931, R4. For more on the Cuba mission, see Chapter 4 of this volume.
39. Haig, R. M. and Shoup, C. S., *The Sales Tax in the American States* (New York: Columbia University Press, 1934); Seligman, E. R. A., *The Shifting and Incidence of Taxation* (Baltimore: American Economic Association, 1892).
40. Haig and Shoup, *Sales Tax in the American States*, 108.
41. Brownlee, W. E., "Shoup Mission to Japan: Two Political Economies Intersect," in: Martin, I. W., Mehrotra, A. K., Prasad, M., eds., *The New Fiscal Sociology: Taxation in Comparative and Historical Perspective* (New York: Cambridge University Press, 2009) 243–4; Thorndike, J. J. "'The Unfair Advantage of the Few': The New Deal Origins of 'Soak the Rich' Taxation" in: *The New Fiscal Sociology: Taxation in Comparative and Historical Perspective*, 29–47.
42. C. S. Shoup to E. R. A. Seligman, November 26, 1935, ERASP.
43. Shoup, C. S., Blough, R., Newcomer, M., *Facing the Tax Problem: A Survey of Taxation in the United States and Program for the Future*.
44. Ibid., 320–1, 412.
45. Ibid., 413.
46. G. O. May to E. Seligman, April 26, 1937; C. S. Shoup to G. O. May, April 29, 1937; E. Seligman to C. S. Shoup, July 30, 1937, Box No. 392–2, CSSP.
47. G. O. May to E. Seligman, April 26, 1937, Box No. 392–2, CSSP.
48. C. S. Shoup to G. O. May, April 29, 1937, Box No. 392–2, CSSP.
49. George O. May, "An Analysis of the Problem of Taxation," *New York Times*, May 9, 1937, E8.

50. Shackelford, J., "Newcomer, Mabel (1891–1983)," in: Emmett, R., *Biographical Dictionary of American Economists* (London: Thoemmes, 2006), 660–65.
51. Roy Blough," in: *Current Biography 1950* (New York: H.W. Wilson Co., 1951), 57–9. Blough went on to write his own seminal textbook on tax policy and tax administration. Blough, R., *The Federal Taxing Process* (New York: Prentice-Hall, 1952). The Twentieth-Century Fund project was also an important incubator. Two of Shoup's best students, C. Lowell Harriss and William Vickrey, were on the study's research staff. Shoup, C. S., Blough, R., Newcomer, M., *Facing the Tax Problem: A Survey of Taxation in the United States and Program for the Future*, vii.
52. Brownlee, W. E., "Shoup Mission to Japan: Two Political Economies Intersect."
53. C. S. Shoup to E. R. A. Seligman, January 4, 1937, ERASP.
54. C. S. Shoup to E. R. A. Seligman, December 2, 1936, ERASP; C. S. Shoup to R. G. Blakey, October 29, 1934, CSSP.
55. C. S. Shoup to E. R. A. Seligman, December 9, 1936, ERASP. In his letter to Shen Li-ren of China, Shoup provided some rather detailed comments about how to classify different types of taxpayers; the administrative challenges of the excess profits tax; and the importance of accounting systems that "clearly reflect income." C. S. Shoup to Shen Li-ren, December 9, 1936, ERASP.
56. Wright, M. N., "Dr. C. Lowell Harriss, Expert in Economics, Land Policy" *Boston Globe*, January 19, 2010; C. S. Shoup to E. R. A. Seligman, January 31, 1938, ERASP.
57. Harriss, C. L., "William Spencer Vickrey, 1914–1996, Nobel Laureate in Economics," *Economic Journal*, 2000, vol. 110, pp. F708–19; Koehn, R. H., "Vickrey, William Spencer" in: *Biographical Dictionary of American Economists*, 853–59.
58. Dimand, R. W., Koehn, R. H., "From Edgeworth to Fisher to Vickrey: A Comment on Michael J. Boskin's Vickrey lecture" *Atlantic Economic Journal*, 2002, vol. 30 (2), pp. 205–8; Boskin, M. J., "From Edgeworth to Vickrey to Mirlees: The Vickrey Lecture," *Atlantic Economic Journal*, 2000, vol. 28 (1), pp. 14–22.
59. Rutherford, M., *The Institutionalist Movement in American Economics, 1918–1947: Science and Social Control*, 252.
60. Vickrey, W., *Agenda for Progressive Taxation*, 381; Vickrey, W., Shoup, C. S., "Need for Gains Tax Reform," *New York Times*, December 13, 1964, E8.
61. Harriss, C. L., "Nobel Laureate William Vickrey: Stockholm Seminar," *American Journal of Economics and Sociology*, 1998, vol. 57 (2), pp. 239–42.
62. See, for example, Eden, L., *Multinationals in North America* (Calgary: University of Calgary Press, 1994); Eden, L., *Retrospectives on Public Finance*; Bird, R. M., *Taxing Agricultural Land in Developing Countries* (Cambridge, Harvard University Press, 1974). Shoup also influenced a generation of public finance students with his scholarship. Martin Feldstein once noted that he thought of himself as "a bit of a student of Carl Shoup's," even though he did not formally study with him, mainly because Shoup's "big book on

public finance" was "a very critical part" of Feldstein's "education as a public finance economist." Feldstein, M., "Luncheon in Honor of Individuals and Institutions Participating in the First Income and Wealth Conference" in: Berndt, E. R., Triplett, J. E., eds. *Fifty Years of Economic Measurement: The Jubilee of the Conference on Research in Income and Wealth* (Chicago: University of Chicago Press, 1990), 9.

63. Columbia Library to Seligman [n.d.], Box #54 – Miscellaneous, 1932–7, ERASP; Dorfman, J. "Edwin R.A. Seligman," in: *Dictionary of American Biography* 1958, vol. 12, supp. 2, pp. 606–609.

64. W. Withers to R. M. Haig, December 4, 1939; R. M. Haig to A. E. Holcomb, December 4, 1939; Memo "Suggestions for the Seligman Memorial," [n.d.]; Memo "Memorial Meeting in Honor of Edwin Robert Anderson Seligman, 1861–1939, Low Memorial Library, Columbia University, December 22, 1939," Box 386–1, Letter File Box (1938–40), CSSP. The memorial essays were eventually published in *Edwin Robert Anderson Seligman, 1861–1939* (Stamford, Conn.: Overbrook Press, 1942).

65. H. H. Wiggins to C. S. Shoup, September 15, 1954; "In Memoriam, Robert Murray Haig, 1887–53," C-file, Correspondence 1955, No. 16, CSSP.

66. C. S. Shoup to the Heirs of Professor Henry L. Moore, June 21, 1956; C. S. Shoup to J. Dorfman, March 14, 1957; G. J. Stigler to C. S. Shoup, March 31, 1959, CSSP.

67. Stigler, G. J., "Henry L. Moore and Statistical Economics," *Econometrica* 1962, vol. 30 (1) pp. 1–21.

68. Barrow, C. W., "From Marx to Madison: The Seligman Connection in Charles Beard's Constitutional Theory," *Polity* 1992, vol. 24 (3), pp. 379–97.

69. R. M. Haig to E. Seligman, November 28, 1939; R. M. Haig to F. K. Mann, January 2, 1940; F. K. Mann to R. M. Haig, January 24, 1940; E. Seligman to R. M. Haig, February 16, 1940, CSSP.

70. A. Nevins to C. S. Shoup, et al. December 17, 1941; C. S. Shoup to S. Ratner, January 2, 1942; January 3, 1942; January 6, 1942, CSSP.

71. See the many letters and drafts from C. S. Shoup to R. M. Haig and E.R.A. Seligman contained in Boxes 26–31, The Concept of Income, especially Box. 29, Folder 4: "Carl's Outlines – Research Project," RMHP.

72. Stigler, G. J., "Henry Calvert Simons," *Journal of Law & Economics* 1974, vol. 17 (1), pp. 1–5.

73. H. C. Simons to R. M. Haig, October 22, 1936, Henry C. Simons Papers, Box 3, Folder 22, Special Collections Research Center, University of Chicago Library [hereinafter HCSP]. Haig continued to correspond with Simons, complementing him on his manuscript and putting him in touch with Shoup, who by then was well into his own book manuscript. In one letter, Haig informed Simons that "you and Shoup ought to have a talk and inform each other of accomplishments, plans, and hopes." R. M. Haig to H. C. Simons, December 22, 1938, HCSP.

74. Shoup read a copy of Simon's thesis in 1937 and recommended *Facing the Tax Problem* to him. He also provided detailed notes on the dissertation at the same time expressing his admiration for what he called "a significant contribution to the tax literature." C. S. Shoup to H. C. Simons, March 20,

1937, HCSP; Brownlee, W. E., "Shoup Mission to Japan: Two Political Economies Intersect," 244–5.

75. C. S. Shoup to R. M. Haig, July 1942, Box 31– Concept of Income, Folder 4, RMHP. The book manuscript on the concept of income evolved from a collaborative project with Haig to a single-authored manuscript that spent a great deal of space taking on Irving Fisher's arguments about the difference between using income and consumption as the proper tax base. As this manuscript developed, Shoup corresponded regularly with Seligman about "the Fisher chapter." C. S. Shoup to E. R. A. Seligman, August 11, 1938; Octctober 11, 1938, ERASP.

76. Thirsk, W., "Intellectual Foundations of the VAT in North America and Japan," in: Eden, L., ed., *Retrospectives on Public Finance*, 133–48. Despite being the intellectual fountainhead of the VAT, Shoup is supposed to have said that he "didn't go to bat for the VAT." Johnston, D. C., "Carl S. Shoup, 97; Shaped Japan's Tax Code," *New York Times*, March 31, 2000, A25.

77. Gillis, M., "Legacies from the Shoup Tax Missions: Asia, Africa, and Latin America," in: Eden, L., ed., *Retrospectives on Public Finance*, 50; Medema, S. G., "Shoup, Carl Sumner (1902–2000)" in: Emmett, R. B., ed., *The Biographical Dictionary of American Economists, Vol. 2* (London: Thoemmes Continuum, 2006), 766–73, 770.

78. Shoup, C. S., "Melding Architecture and Engineering: a Personal Retrospective on Designing Tax Systems," in: Eden, L., *Retrospectives on Public Finance* (Duke University Press, 1991). Also, see Chapter 16 of this volume.

79. Seligman, E. R. A., "Introduction: The Problem in General" in: Haig, R. M., ed., *The Federal Income Tax* (New York: Columbia University Press, 1921), vii–ix.

80. Rutherford, M., *The Institutionalist Movement in American Economics, 1918–1947: Science and Social Control*, 223–256, 255–60.

81. Shoup, C. S., "Melding Architecture and Engineering: a Personal Retrospective on Designing Tax Systems," 19.

82. Johnson, H. G., "Forward" in: Shoup, C. S., *Public Finance* (Chicago: Aldine Publishing, 1969), xi–xii.

83. Medema, S. G., "AldineTransaction Introduction," in Shoup, C. S. *Public Finance* (2009 [1969]); Medema, S. G., "Shoup, Carl Sumner (1902–2000)."

84. Shoup, C. S. *Public Finance* (1969), iv.

3

The Haig–Shoup Mission to France in the 1920s

Frances Lynch

INTRODUCTION

Carl Shoup had barely begun his graduate studies in economics at Columbia University under the supervision of Professor Robert Murray Haig before he found himself spending seven months in France as a research assistant to Haig.[1] The two formed part of a larger interdisciplinary team of fifty researchers, mainly from Columbia University, who were embarking on a major study of the social and economic conditions of postwar France.

Although a victorious country in the First World War, it had taken France at least six years to repair the damage caused to the country's social and economic infrastructure. The one striking aspect from an American perspective was that the political system of the Third Republic had survived the trauma of the war and postwar years intact. As Carlton J. H. Hayes, Professor of History at Columbia University and overall editor of the seven-volume study, explained, France had in per capita terms suffered the greatest losses and shouldered the biggest burden during the war. The postwar years had, however, been "characterised by no cataclysm, by no striking revolution, by not even a serious threat of revolution."[2] It was the French currency that had suffered, losing 80 percent of its prewar value when it was eventually stabilized. In comparison with the complete collapse of the currencies of Germany and other defeated countries this was not a serious loss. For a victorious ally, however, it was neither expected nor fully understood.

Although the Columbia project was academic rather than sponsored by the American government (unlike many missions subsequently undertaken by Shoup), it came at a critical time in Franco-American relations. Eight years after the end of the First World War, a war that had transformed the United States from an international debtor into the world's largest creditor and industrial power, Americans were, in Haig's words, "observing Europe with cold and disillusioned eyes."[3] France, as the second largest debtor to the United States with debts of greater than U.S. $4,000 million (only very slightly lower than those of Britain), had been subjected to particular criticism during the months and years that it spent negotiating a settlement of its debt.[4] The British government was seen to be taking action to increase taxes and cut expenditure in order to restore the convertibility of sterling at the prewar rate and signed an agreement with the United States on June 19, 1923 in which it undertook to repay all of its loans with interest in sixty-two annual installments. In contrast, it was not until April 29, 1926 that the French government finally agreed to a repayment schedule for its loans from the United States.[5] In the intervening years, rather than stabilize its domestic finances, restore the value of the franc, and repay its wartime loans, France had allowed inflation to erode the value of the franc, thereby reducing the value of its domestic debts but making repayment of its external debt very much harder. As the major creditor of France, the United States was particularly critical of French policy. In the words of Haig, "the French, confronted with a great financial problem, showed an incapacity to tax themselves with the courage and resourcefulness displayed by the English and Americans."[6]

The main issue of contention between the two countries, and one on which the French government ultimately had to concede, was whether France's ability to repay its war debts should be linked to its receipt of reparations from Germany.[7] For the American taxpayer, the issue was whether the French should pay more in taxes to enable American taxes to be cut. French public finances were therefore an issue of immediate relevance to Americans because, as Haig put it, "anything salvaged from the doubtful paper of . . . France lying in the strong-box of the federal Treasury meant that much more off the federal income tax."[8] It is interesting to note that such criticism of France was not shared outside the United States. The British economist, John Maynard Keynes, who had publicly denounced French policy on reparations during the international negotiations leading to the Treaty of Versailles, the peace treaty with Germany, nonetheless wrote in early 1926 that "France was one of the most heavily taxed countries in the world" with a marginal rate on the general income tax of 60 percent compared with a marginal rate of income tax in the United States of 23 percent.[9]

THE AMERICAN VIEWPOINT

Exactly what the French paid in tax and how they levied their taxes had thus become an issue of concern far beyond the confines of the French tax inspectorate and the French taxpayer. Within the United States, Edwin Seligman, professor of political economy at Columbia University, was an important contributor to the debates about public finance in the United States and had written extensively about France before Haig and Shoup embarked on their research. Haig, Seligman's former student, had written that "it seems probable that no academic economist, by voice or pen, has ever reached and influenced so many of his [Seligman's] contemporaries."[10] In Seligman's view, it was the failure of the French government to raise more in taxation during the war that was the main source of the problems of inflation and financial instability afterward. Furthermore, when the country's government did face up to the need to increase taxes after the war, he criticized it for choosing to raise more through an indirect sales tax, which was generally seen to be regressive, rather than through more progressive income taxes. Although critical of the French government in its domestic political choices, Seligman sympathized with its demands for reparations from Germany and saw the American insistence on recovering its war loans made to countries such as France as impractical and morally reprehensible.[11]

On the issue of whether the war should have been financed through loans or taxes, many American economists had argued that taxation was the more appropriate method of financing. Seligman disagreed, partly because it was the case that every government – including that of the United States – had chosen to borrow initially, and partly because he thought that it would have been "suicidal" to attempt to finance a war exclusively through taxation. He did, however, consider that "as the war proceeds a continuously larger amount can and should be raised by taxation, although at no time will the government be free from the necessity of relying to a considerable extent upon the issue of public credit."[12] In the case of France, he felt that the government had shown an "unwarrantable timidity" in raising taxes to pay for the war.[13] According to Seligman's calculations, on the eve of the war the tax burden in France was very similar to that in the United States and the United Kingdom.

TABLE 1. *Tax Per Capita (in US dollars)*

	France	USA	UK
1913–14	25.12	22.95	26.89
1918–19	30.74	63.84	96.45

Source: Seligman, E. R. A., *Studies in Public Finance*, 35.

Whereas both of these countries had greatly increased taxes during the war years (almost quadrupling in Britain and almost tripling in the United States), however, France had made little effort to do so; see Table 1. As a result, at the end of the war the per capita tax burden in France was only very slightly higher than in 1914.

When measured as a proportion of total national revenue rather than per capita income, taxes – as Brownlee points out – accounted for a larger share in the United States than in any of the other countries involved in fighting the First World War.[14]

It is nonetheless important to note that Seligman criticized the French government for its "timidity" in raising taxes rather than for its policy of expecting a great deal of the cost of the war and postwar reconstruction to be covered by reparations from Germany. Indeed, he had gone into print denouncing Commerce Secretary Herbert Hoover's demands for the repayment of war loans. "Can we blame France [he argued] for saying that, if the United States and Great Britain demand payment in full of the indebtedness, she will certainly not be overgenerous in her demands for reparations from Germany."[15] If the Americans had a legal right to their repayment, he claimed that they had no moral right to what were in effect excessive war profits, earned only because the United States had entered the war at such a late stage. Had the United States participated in the war from its outset, then – as Seligman argued – it would have emerged as impoverished as France and the other victors at its close. In 1922 he wrote that "Reparations and allied debt payments are for the present inextricably intertwined."[16]

Seligman was most critical of the French government when it finally faced up to increasing its taxes in 1920 in order to try to balance its "normal" expenditure. It did so by introducing a sales tax that was to cover almost half of the deficit in the ordinary budget, with direct taxes contributing less than one-third to closing the gap. Throughout his life's work on taxation and in opposing the introduction of a federal sales tax in the United States after the First World War, Seligman argued that "direct taxation ... generally forms the last steps in the historical development of public revenues."[17] In addition, he drew a clear link between income taxes on the basis of people's ability to pay and democracy, arguing that "in democratic communities, where the legislation is influenced by the mass of the people, we commonly discern a tendency to oppose indirect taxes on consumption."[18] At the same time he conceded that the theories of taxation and the forms taxation took in practice in different societies were heavily influenced by the economic basis of that society.[19]

The main criticism of sales taxes found in standard public finance textbooks at the time was that they were "extremely prejudicial to the development of industry, irksome, inconvenient to the payers, and very costly in collection."[20] It was somewhat surprising, therefore, that the American business community actually campaigned vigorously for the introduction of a sales tax in the United States after the First World War. This was an instance where the context in which the tax was debated explained more than the theory. As far as the American business community was concerned, the sales tax was a lesser evil than the excess profits tax that had provided the bulk of wartime federal taxation.[21] Dismissing the academic economists' criticisms of the tax, the business community claimed that it would be simple to manage, highly productive in terms of revenue, and fair to everyone. The only uncertainty was over whether it would be borne by business or be passed on to the consumer. In the end, as the rates of surtax and excess profits tax came down after the end of the war, the support for the sales tax among businesses declined.[22] At the same time, strong opposition to the sales tax from farm and labor groups in particular convinced the American Congress that the sales tax was unpopular and unnecessary.[23]

The American debate doubtless influenced Seligman's view of the sales tax when it was introduced in France in 1920. He was to condemn it unequivocally as "a discredited remnant of an outworn system ... essentially undemocratic in its nature."[24] He went on to argue that the sales tax was unsatisfactory in a number of respects. The yield, he maintained, would be uncertain because there would be no way of accurately predicting what it would be as it would depend on the number of transactions and on whether the tax was passed on to the consumer, and if that were the case, its yield would depend on the elasticity of demand for the product. Furthermore, if the tax was passed on to the consumer this might lead to a fall in sales. If it was not passed on, it would become a tax on gross receipts rather than on profits and thereby be unfair. Other criticisms of the inequity of the tax were that it would favor large integrated concerns over small specialist producers. In addition, Seligman argued that on a purely practical level it would be difficult to collect, because both buyers and sellers would have an incentive to avoid the tax. His greatest criticism was that a general sales tax would be impossible to apply progressively.[25] As we saw in Chapter 2, Seligman was a great believer in the role that tax policy could play in developing egalitarian ideals and institutions. For this reason, he argued that an income tax charged on the basis of the taxpayer's ability or "faculty" to pay was fairer than a sales tax that was unrelated to individual income.

Although he conceded that the forms taxation took in practice in different societies were heavily influenced by the economic basis of that society, it was clear that he did not consider that the structure of the French tax system – with its overreliance on indirect taxes – reflected the underlying economic structure of the country. He viewed it as "the last resort of countries which find themselves in such fiscal difficulties that they must subordinate all other principles of taxation to that of adequacy."[26] Gabriel Ardant, writing many years later, was to argue that in economies such as France at that time, where there were vast numbers of people employed in small-scale production and distribution, it was very difficult to raise revenue through income tax.[27]

Other explanations for the lack of support for income taxes in France and a preference for taxes on expenditure focus on the deeply rooted suspicion of the majority of French people toward an inquisitorial state. This is due in part to the fact that the growth of the state predated industrialization in France rather than coinciding with it, as occurred in the United States.[28]

THE HAIG–SHOUP "MISSION" TO FRANCE

When Haig and Shoup arrived in Paris to carry out their research, they would have been influenced by the critical attitude held in the United States and underpinned by economic theory toward how the French managed or mismanaged their public finances. It was hardly surprising that they were not welcome visitors in the French Ministry of Finance. As Haig confided to his friend and one-time governor of the Bank of England, Sir Joshua Stamp, he had been "submitted to every variety of insult" in the process of trying to access and understand the details of French public finance. "I find the French accounts to be much worse than anyone could possibly imagine. Errors running up to billions of francs creep up almost daily to be dismissed with a shrug of the shoulder by the dejecting and hopeless functionaries at the Ministry."[29] His findings did not fundamentally challenge the views of Seligman that the sales tax could not be justified on the grounds of economic theory. In explaining why democratically elected governments in France on both the left and right had chosen to stabilize their country's public finances in such an apparently regressive way, however, both Haig and Shoup became much more sympathetic to the ways in which the French government had restored financial stability in practice.

In his analysis of French public finances, Haig shared Seligman's view that the French approach to taxation and public finance was "backward" but he was much less critical than Seligman of the French tax policy during the war and up to and including the introduction of the sales tax in 1920. He felt that it was only in understanding "the political war waged in France over the reform of the system of direct taxes" that culminated in the passage of the bill to introduce a system of income taxation on the eve of the war, that the postwar changes could be understood.[30] In view of the French history of tax reform, he considered that the French wartime government was to be commended for its decision – in the face of considerable domestic criticism – to replace the inelastic taxes inherited from the French Revolution, known as *les quatre vieilles*, with a modern system of income taxes despite the administrative difficulties of changing the tax system in wartime.[31] Overall, Haig concluded that French governments had made a serious effort, particularly in the last two years of the war, to cover the normal needs of the budget at the same time as relying on loans to finance the specific needs of war and reconstruction.

The "political war" to which Haig referred had been waged for seven years by the parties that were to govern France in coalition (the *union sacrée*) during the war.[32] Since France's defeat in 1870, which resulted in it becoming the most heavily taxed country in Europe, the Radical party had been trying to introduce changes into the fiscal system initiated by Napoleon Bonaparte first following the revolution of 1789.[33] With the wealthiest 10 percent paying no more than 2 percent of their income in taxes, there was some support in the country for reforming the system to make the rich pay more.[34] Although the Radical leader, Joseph Caillaux, managed to bring a reform bill before the chamber of deputies in 1907 on the basis of a two-stage income tax (a general tax on incomes above a certain threshold, and a second tax levied on different sources of income), he did not have the full support of his party. In fact the Radicals in the

Senate gave their support to the Conservatives in order to block the bill repeatedly until 1914.

Haig's understanding of the reasons for the final acceptance of the bill in 1914 was that it was not due primarily to the needs of financing the war or any acceptance that the wealthy should pay more in tax. Instead it actually represented a pragmatic acknowledgement that loans and indirect taxes alone could no longer cover normal public expenditure. Haig thought that it was the size of the projected budget deficit for "normal" expenditure in 1914, quite irrespective of the extra demands of preparing for an imminent war, which led the government to push through the first part of Caillaux's tax reform. Under the law of March 29, 1914, the three traditional "objective revenue taxes" (the building tax, land tax, and tax on incomes from securities) were restructured and on July 15, 1914, just a couple of weeks before the declaration of war, a new general tax on total income was introduced.[35]

For several reasons, however, the law of March 29, 1914 was to be of more symbolic than real importance. First, although it was a progressive tax, the rates were so low – ranging from 0.4 percent to a top marginal rate of 2 percent – that it did not represent any greater tax on incomes than had previously been implemented. Second, because it was a tax on total income but did not include taxes on each source of income, it made it very difficult for the state to assess total income.[36] Third, the total disruption caused by the outbreak of war led to its implementation being postponed.

Alexandre Ribot, the new Conservative minister of finance in the wartime coalition government, was a life-long opponent of the income tax and, indeed, of any tax increase to pay for the war. This view was on the grounds that either Germany should pay for it or that its cost should be shared with future generations in France.[37] With the war lasting longer than predicted, however, in 1916 Ribot reluctantly raised the 2 percent rate of the general tax on total income to 10 percent and introduced a war excess profits tax designed to ensure that those who had profited most from the war should help pay for it. This necessitated a declaration of the profits made during the war and enough trained inspectors to assess and collect the tax, although it was never the intention to begin collecting the tax during the war. In the depressed conditions of 1919–20, however, many businesses that had made profits during the war lost them. Furthermore, given the low interest rates and the depreciation of the franc, it made financial sense for businesses to postpone paying the tax for as long as possible.

TABLE 2. *Yield from Direct Taxes in France between 1916 and 1919*

Year	Direct Taxes (Yield in millions of francs)	Expenditure (in millions of francs)	Direct Taxes (as a percentage of expenditure)
1916	32.5	28,113	0.1
1917	201.0	35,320	0.6
1918	512.0	41,897	1.2
1919	869.0	30,688	2.8

Source: INSEE, *Annuaire Statistique. Résumé Rétrospectif* (Paris, 1951), 303, 316.

In spite of many complaints of enforced bankruptcy, about two-thirds of the 16.4 million francs due had actually been paid by 1924.[38] It was only when Ribot was replaced in 1917 by Joseph Thierry, described as "the rare Third Republic politician who was qualified to deal with financial and commercial questions," that a serious effort was made to raise more revenue from taxation.[39] For the first time during the war years, Thierry actually drew up a budget for "ordinary" nonwar expenditure.[40] Following further increases in the top marginal rate of tax from 10 percent to 12.5 percent and then to 20 percent, Thierry was to introduce five new schedular taxes on different sources of income, along the lines initially proposed by Caillaux in 1907.[41] These taxes were to be levied on income from business, on agricultural incomes, earned income, incomes from professions, and particular revenues from capital.[42] The entrenched opposition to official intrusion into private affairs meant that it was agreed that taxpayers, apart from those earning "professional" incomes, did not have to declare their total income if they preferred to let the authorities estimate it and calculate the tax due. The rate of tax on business income was set at 4.5 percent; on agricultural incomes it was 3.75 percent (although this tax usually had to be estimated, and because the estimate was made on the basis of the rental value of the land rather than the actual value, the tax demanded was artificially low); the tax on workers' and employees' incomes above a certain threshold was 3.75 percent (in practice workers, particularly if they were married, did not pay any tax); the tax on professional incomes was 3.75 percent, but with fewer permissible deductions; and the tax on revenue from capital was 4 percent.[43] The new income tax was seen to be a progressive tax on the rich, so it was generally very popular.[44] The yield, which can be seen in Table 2, increased rapidly, albeit from a very low base in 1916, but it fell far short of expenditure.

As Haig was to show, Thierry did not stop there. He now wanted to complete the income tax reform by reorganizing the system of indirect taxation. For this he envisaged setting three different rates for a new tax on expenditure: a basic rate of 0.1 percent would be levied on all transactions at both wholesale and retail levels, with a rate of 5 percent levied on all individual retail purchases of nonessentials, and a 10 percent rate levied on the purchase of luxury goods. Haig was quite favorable to the sales tax as proposed by Thierry on the grounds that it would raise much-needed revenue immediately and would provide a tax yield that kept pace with inflation. In contrast to what he and his colleagues argued in opposing a federal sales tax in the United States, Haig did not disagree with Thierry's claim that the French sales tax would be progressive. What mattered was that three different rates were to be set depending on the degree of necessity of the good, with a zero rate for basic necessities.[45] It was when the proposal was watered down by Thierry's successor, Louis Lucien Klotz, in order to reduce the burden on the consumer that its yield fell far short of expectations. Only two rates were included, which were levied at the retail but not at the wholesale stage: a small stamp duty on retail sales of over ten francs, and a 10 percent rate on the purchase of luxury goods.[46] In 1918, only 160 million francs were raised compared to the 1,150 million francs predicted.[47]

With the wartime tax measures targeted at the rich, revenue from taxation covered no more than 18 percent of the cost of the war (compared with 28 percent in the United Kingdom). Most of the cost of the war – 54 percent – was raised through domestic loans, as the French middle classes happily invested in short-term bonds and longer-term securities rather than paying taxes.[48] This meant that the vast majority of peasants and working class families were exempt from paying any income tax. Of the remaining expenditure during the war years, 16 percent came from foreign borrowing and more than 12 percent from advances from the Bank of France.

The unwillingness of Klotz to raise more in taxation before 1920 has been explained, not by his poor grasp of public finances or by a foolish naivety that Germany would pay France for the full cost of the war and reconstruction, but because he was waiting to see how much Germany would be asked to pay in reparations before turning to the French taxpayer for funds to cover the public deficit. Prominent economists, such as Charles Rist and Charles Gide, were opposed to the payment of large reparations from Germany because of the disruption that it would cause to international trade. Their preferred solution was an international one whereby the cost of the war and reconstruction would be borne by many countries rather than by Germany alone.[49] Official French policy was to fix the size of the German financial reparations at a modest figure that could be mobilized immediately (with American investors buying the reparation bonds).[50] After months of Allied wrangling, however, the Treaty of Versailles did not actually specify a sum for reparations.

As far as Haig was concerned, the question of Germany's payment was "only subsidiary."[51] The shortfall in the budget for "normal" expenditure due to the low yield from direct taxes was not surprising in view of the complicated nature of the new fiscal laws and their need for detailed legal explanations. In addition, he recognized that the new tax on war profits presented a diminished number of officials with a whole set of new problems and investigative tasks to which they were not accustomed. Recently demobilized tax inspectors in effect had to learn their old jobs all over again. It was not at all surprising, he felt, that in the difficult circumstances of postwar France the tax yield was much lower than it might have been.[52]

The complete reform of the tax system in 1920 was a surprising way for the French Ministry of Finance to cover the budget deficit. As well as the shortage of skilled personnel able to understand and implement the new tax legislation, there was continued uncertainty over how much money the French needed to raise in taxation because of the failure to reach an international agreement over reparations. For some commentators, the most unexpected aspect was that a right-wing government in the most right-wing parliament since 1876, which included parties opposed to the introduction of the income tax in 1914, now raised the marginal rate of the general income tax from 20 percent to 50 percent, at the same time as continuing to exempt 70 percent of the total labor force. Those individuals on lower incomes working as manual laborers or in agriculture were exempt from paying income taxes altogether.[53] Haig, however, hardly referred to the increase in direct tax rates at all, focusing instead on the new sales tax or turnover tax introduced at the same time. In fact Haig was so favorable toward the sales tax, describing it as "the most interesting chapter in the history [of the French] tax system since the war," that he decided that Shoup should make it the subject of his doctoral thesis.[54]

Notwithstanding Haig's views, the French government's preference for raising more revenue through indirect taxation was seen by the international community as a regressive step taken by a government desperate for an immediate source of income. Opinion inside France was broadly sympathetic to the fiscal measures, however, considering them to be fair, progressive, and workable.[55] The new turnover tax was a general tax levied on the gross receipts from all business transactions – wholesale as well as retail – in the extractive as well as the manufacturing sector, and on many commercial payments including interest and commissions. Sales of agricultural products from the farm were exempt, as were sales for export and from a few public utilities.

The tax was initially set at the low rate of 1.1 percent. The luxury tax, which had been introduced in 1918 at a rate of 10 percent on retail sales of luxury articles as well as on receipts from luxury hotels and restaurants, was incorporated into the turnover tax at the rate of 10 percent and with an intermediary rate of 3 percent.[56] As far as Haig was concerned, the sales tax responded perfectly to the inflationary situation in France because its yield increased with the rise in prices unlike that of other taxes, including income tax.[57] The National Assembly that approved the tax made it clear that it was not to be a tax on business, because it was to be shifted onto the consumer in its entirety. This, as Haig remarked, was quite unlike the situation in the United States where, in the debate over the proposed sales tax, there was considerable uncertainty as to whether it was to be a tax on business or a tax on consumption. The main mistake of French governments, he thought, was not that they had introduced a sales tax but that they had concluded that the tax reforms, up to and including those of 1920, were the last sacrifice that they would have to make. When foreign and then domestic lending dried up after 1921 creating an immediate budget deficit, rather than increase taxes again – which according to Haig was the obvious thing to have done – the French government made another effort to extract reparations from Germany, this time through the physical occupation of the Ruhr coalmines.[58]

CARL SHOUP AND THE SALES TAX IN FRANCE

It was in assisting Haig to research and write *The Public Finances of Post-War France* and then writing his thesis, which was subsequently published as a book, that Shoup first examined many of the fiscal issues that were to absorb him throughout his very long and productive life as an academic and advisor to many governments throughout the world. Shoup's ability, which he was to demonstrate from the very beginning of his career, was to analyze any change in a country's tax system in terms of the historical, political, and economic context in which it was implemented, rather than assessing it solely in the light of the prevailing economic theory. It was his willingness to understand the reasons why the French had introduced a sales tax and to explore how it operated in practice rather than to condemn it as backward and regressive that helps explain why his first book was to become such a classic in the field of taxation.

Initially Shoup was more critical of the French sales tax than Haig. However much he saw it as a second-best solution to the problems of French finances, he was to develop an understanding of the reasons for its adoption and success in France. This led his book to be seen as "the first exhaustive study of any sales tax published in the United States and is to this day one of the most complete studies of this type ever undertaken."[59] Following the subsequent development of Shoup's ideas of public finance and of how he applied those ideas to real-world problems he encountered in his tax missions in Cuba, Venezuela, and Japan, to mention just a few, it is interesting to focus on exactly how Shoup analyzed the sales tax. He initially sought to understand the forces operating in French society that caused the nation to accept a new tax that was rejected by other democratic countries, particularly the United States and the United Kingdom, on the grounds that an expansion of income taxes was a fairer method of raising revenue. In addition to addressing what is now termed the "fiscal sociology" of the sales tax, he focused on the political context in which the tax was introduced as well as the capacity of the French tax administration to cope with the government's greatly expanded need for revenue.

Fiscal Sociology

One of the most interesting questions for Shoup was why the French adopted a new tax that was not seen by any group in society in France or elsewhere as an advance in taxation policy. Any explanation must, he decided, involve an understanding of why all other taxes were rejected and why a complete monetary collapse was rejected. France, he asserted, had won the war and the French people were not prepared to accept a monetary collapse as they might have done had they been defeated. At the same time, the scale of the human and physical damage suffered during the war meant that it was not an option to cut public spending after the war in order to stabilize public finances. There was therefore public support for increasing taxation not in order to redistribute wealth, but to be able to pay the interest on the bonds needed to finance reconstruction and pay war pensions.

In addition to this, Shoup showed how little support there was for increasing the revenue from income taxes. The Conservatives were unwilling to see any further rises in the marginal rates of income tax and there was little support for widening the tax base to include all those who had never previously paid any income tax. In the inflationary conditions of postwar France this could easily have happened by default if not by design. Shoup would have been aware that, far from being seen as a progressive tax charged on the basis of ability to pay, income taxes were seen by many as falling most heavily on those least able to pay because it was argued that everyone else could find ways, either legal or illegal, to avoid paying them.

In the collective memory, one of the most popular measures of the French Revolution had been to abolish income taxes and replace them with indirect taxes.[60] As long as income tax was seen as a tax on the rich it was acceptable; however, as soon as more people became liable to pay as a result of inflation – which in the absence of a satisfactory settlement of the reparations/war debts issue was likely to continue – it was clear to the government that it would be rejected by the bulk of the labor force.

Given the large number of people who were exempt from paying income tax, its yield was not expected to fill the 8.5 billion franc gap in the ordinary budget predicted for 1921. The case for the sales tax, as Shoup saw it, was that no other existing tax would have generated sufficient revenue to close the budget deficit. As Table 3 shows, the total number of individuals paying each of the schedular income taxes was low, as was the yield, with most of the revenue coming from the general income tax.

Whether the sales tax discriminated against the poor, Shoup was less certain. "To some, the most severe criticism of all against the tax is that it may discriminate against the poor, for if it is largely shifted, it becomes a tax on expenditures, and as such inversely progressive – the rich man paying in tax a smaller percentage of his income than the poor, as his expenditures amount to a smaller percentage."[61] He showed that the French deputies who supported and passed the tax expected that it would be regressive, and for that reason agreed to exempt a number of necessities from it as well as applying a higher rate of tax on luxury goods. "The chances are strong," he concluded, "that it is more unfavorable to the poorer classes than is an income tax." He could not, however, see what the alternative to the sales tax would have been in France at that time.[62]

Writing in 1969, Shoup argued that "the criterion of progressivity by income or wealth is commonly but erroneously applied in judging the

TABLE 3. *French Income Tax from 1920 to 1924*

Year	1920	1921	1922	1923	1924
General income tax					
Number of contributors	541	977	1,119	1,027	1,201
Revenue	1,143.0	1,504.0	1,272.0	1,524.0	2,352.0
Schedular taxes:					
Wages and pensions					
Number of contributors	1,093	2407	2754	731	855
Revenue	131.0	299.0	332.0	166.0	254.0
Industrial and commercial profits					
Number of contributors	1,260	1,369	1,475	1,604	1,589
Revenue	755.0	996.0	942.0	1,170.0	1,660.0
Agricultural profits					
Number of contributors	190	247	240	276	328
Revenue	18.2	28.5	19.4	25.1	44.9
Income from noncommercial professions					
Number of contributors	42	65	73	71	74
Revenue	24.6	46.9	51.4	58.1	80.4
Total revenue from income tax	2,072	2,874	2,617	5,803	4,391

Note: Number of contributors in thousands; revenue in millions of francs.
Source: INSEE, *Annuaire Statistique. Résumé Rétrospectif* (Paris, 1951), 246–7.

turnover tax alone, without comparison with some other tax.... The only legitimate questions are the following: is the turn-over tax progressive relative to, say, an equal-yield value-added tax? Is a destination–principle turnover tax progressive relative to an origin–principle turnover tax? Does exemption of food stuffs coupled with a correspondingly higher rate on the remaining taxable goods produce a tax that is more progressive than the one without the food exemption? What of exemption of farmers? Of small retailers?"[63] Indeed, he admitted that forty years after the introduction of the turnover tax in France almost no research had been done to gather answers to these questions. Where he did consider the sales tax as it was applied in France to be unfair was in the exemption of farmers. In addition to this, he considered the exemption of farmers from paying any direct tax on the value of their land and property to have been inequitable.

We have seen in Chapter 2 of this volume how important the issue of "horizontal equity" was to become to Shoup. As it applied to the sales tax in France, it turned on the question of whether the tax was passed on to the consumer, resulting in higher prices, or was borne by business. The nature of the debate in France at the time was over whether or not the turnover tax was inflationary. In introducing the tax, the Minister of Finance argued that the tax was necessary to reduce the size of the budget deficit, whereas critics on the left argued that the tax itself, because it was passed on to the consumer, would be inflationary and should be replaced by a tax on capital and higher taxes on income. The tax on capital, commonly called a capital levy, was firmly rejected by French economists in the 1920s. As Edgar Allix explained, not only would a capital levy reduce the amount of revenue that could subsequently be raised from income tax but – with very little of French capital being held in liquid assets – it would be unworkable in practice. Those same economists, however, could not deny the evidence that after the introduction of the sales tax, prices in France continued to rise. Shoup acknowledged that "the most important question of all concerning the turnover tax is, who finally pays it? Important as this question is, no answer can be given here. [. . .] If France had not levied the turnover tax she would have had to levy some other tax, or let inflation grow more rapidly than it did."[64]

Unable to settle the matter, Shoup simply analyzed how the French themselves understood the question. Politicians in France thought of the sales tax as a tax that would be passed on until it finally rested with the consumer. The National Assembly that passed the tax made it clear that it did not want it to be a tax on business. Indeed, as Shoup pointed out, the continuing rise in prices in 1920 gave the appearance of a strong "sellers' market," with production unable to keep up with demand. This was coupled with the universality of the tax as proof that capital could not shift to a nontaxed field. Opinion changed in 1921–2 as the economic crisis of those years brought businessmen losses for which they blamed the turnover tax in part. With the return of better times, however, the belief in shifting seems to have returned. Shoup himself said in a footnote that: "it is the writer's belief that in both a strong seller's market and a buyer's market the tax is apt to remain on the business man. When prices are changing rapidly, 10 per cent or more at a time, in periods of serious inflation or deflation, the sale price actually arrived at may be largely a matter of chance, and might well be exactly the same as if there were no tax. A stable price level, on the contrary, promotes more careful consideration of the tax as an item of expense that must be covered."[65] Authorities who have studied the problem most closely have concentrated on the degree of elasticity of demand and on whether the commodity in question is produced under increasing, decreasing, or constant cost.

Maurice Bokanowski, the rapporteur général of the Chamber of Deputies, argued that although increasing the rate of turnover tax might lead to a rise in prices, not to increase it would lead to further depreciation in the value of the franc and a much greater rise in prices.[66] With no resolution of the argument and the size of the public deficit increasing from 9,000 million francs in 1922 to 12,000 million in 1923, Poincaré's government opted to increase all taxes – and not only the turnover tax – by 20 percent in 1924.[67] It was not a measure that worked financially or politically. Inflation continued to rise and the government fell. When Poincaré was returned to power in 1926, however, he decided to take the fiscal issue out of the political debate by appointing a committee of experts to recommend which taxes contributed most to inflation. To the astonishment of the American observers, the committee concluded that it was income tax that led to higher prices and called for an increase in the rates of the turnover tax.[68]

The debate about whether or not a sales tax would add to inflation or would curb it continued throughout the interwar period. As late as 1939, Harry Gunnison Brown remarked on the popular assumption that a general sales tax must necessarily raise all prices on the grounds that a tax on the output of a particular commodity would increase the price of that commodity by reducing its supply. This assumption was quite erroneous, he argued, because a general sales tax on all goods and services would not reduce total output unless workers were prepared to remain idle and owners of capital were prepared to see their capital depreciate unused. He argued that there was no basis in monetary theory for supposing that a general tax on all goods would make average prices permanently higher. "To raise the general level of prices there must be either a decrease of supply of goods in general or an increase of demand (as through an increased volume of money). If a tax on the output of all goods neither decreases supply nor increases demand, on what basis is it to be argued that such a tax will raise prices? If a tax on all goods does not raise prices, it must lower the money incomes of . . . workers, capitalists, and landowners. Such a tax on all output will reduce the income of the capitalist and of the landowner in the same proportion that it reduces the income of the worker, but not in any greater proportion. And since wages are a much larger part of the total product of industry than is either interest on capital or rent of land, a general output tax takes more from the wages of labor than it takes from interest or rent."[69]

Shoup was to return to this issue during the Second World War when he wrote a book with Milton Friedman and Ruth P. Mack in which he argued that "while there is only one type of income tax that promises effective control of inflation, there are several types of sales tax available: a general sales tax, or turnover tax, on all transactions, as in Germany; a manufacturer's sales tax, as in Canada; a wholesale sales tax, as in Great Britain and Australia; or a retail sales tax, as in several states of the United States."[70] He went on to say: "The only major advantage of the turnover tax is that for a given amount of revenue a smaller rate is needed, and consequently the inducement to evasion of the tax at any one point is somewhat smaller. But there are many more taxpayers, hence many more points of potential evasion.... Unless farmers are effectively included, the turnover tax also favors the kind of finished product that, dollar for dollar of finished value, is produced with less than average processing and marketing costs (and with more than average farm cost)."[71]

Historical Contingency

For Shoup, the main reason for the introduction and support in France for sales tax lay in the political composition of the French National Assembly. The Radical Socialists and Revolutionary Socialists, who had campaigned for a more comprehensive income tax and a wealth tax instead of a sales tax, had lost seats in the 1919 elections to the National Assembly, holding only 168 out of 626 seats. Furthermore, only fifty deputies were from the manufacturing sector compared with more than twice that number who were landowners or farmers. This explained why the tax did not include the transactions of the agricultural sector – a mistake in his view.

Given that the rural population at that time numbered 21 million, compared with 18 million urban dwellers, the turnover tax was an example of an agricultural majority discriminating against an urban minority. The argument that had the sales tax been imposed on the sale of farm products it would have been passed on to the consumer in the form of higher food prices, hitting those on lower incomes hardest (because the National Assembly had made it clear that it intended the tax to be passed on to the consumer), was, he felt, simply used to disguise the political bias of the National Assembly. Not only was the exclusion of farm products used to silence left-wing opposition to the tax, but he thought that it was also a deliberate way to keep farmers on the land and stop them drifting into towns and joining in the wave of political protests sweeping France at that time. The revenue lost each year through the exemption of agriculture, estimated at about 145 million francs, was seen as a small price to pay for social and political stability.[72]

The tax won the support of all political parties in the National Assembly apart from the Socialists. With the marginal rate of income tax set at 50 percent (compared with 2 percent in 1914), the Conservatives, as representatives of the wealthy, thought the tax was the only one possible. In general the majority of big businesses supported the turnover tax on the grounds that they would merely collect the tax before passing it on to the consumer. In addition, surprisingly the Radicals – who represented small businesses and traders – gave it their support, being seduced by the idea that it would be the least painful of all taxes in terms of collection and would produce a large yield.[73]

ADMINISTRATIVE CAPACITY

Reflecting many years later on the reasons for the adoption of the turnover tax in France and elsewhere after the First World War, Shoup explained it as "an attempt to collect large amounts of revenue with tax administrative machines that had been crippled by war, in countries struggling with inflation."[74] The problem of high rates of evasion could be made nearly equal, as could the costs of compliance, if the tax was collected by business firms rather than households and set at a sufficiently low rate so "that few firms would find it worth while to risk incurring the penalties of evasion."[75]

What Shoup found particularly surprising was that the Radicals, who represented consumers and small businesses, were in favor of the tax. In addition, their argument that it would be easy to collect was an argument frequently put forward in the American debate in defense of the sales tax. Shoup found no evidence to support this in France. In proposing the new tax in 1920, Klotz had argued that all taxpayers were to keep a special register in which they recorded all their purchases and sales that were subject to the tax for a period of three years. Although the Senate subsequently ruled that records of purchases did not need to be kept, the turnover tax nonetheless constituted a huge intrusion into the lives of French businesses. According to a calculation in 1922, it was estimated that 78 percent of those paying the turnover tax could have been entirely exempted with a loss of only 10 percent in total revenue. Although no such exemption was granted, smaller businesses were offered the option of paying the turnover tax on the basis of an estimate or *forfait* that removed much of the burden of keeping records.[76] Nonetheless, the argument that the sales tax was favored because of the fears of fiscal inquisition that the income tax necessitated is not tenable because both taxes involved unwelcome inquisition and both offered the option of allowing the state to make estimates of the tax owed instead.

Another aspect of the sales tax that Shoup identified as stretching France's administrative capacity to implement it was in the top rate for luxury goods and services. Opponents of the tax advanced several arguments against it, namely that it would destroy the luxury trade in Paris; that, because exports were exempt, it would be easy to evade by arranging the delivery of luxury goods in neighboring countries such as Belgium or Switzerland; and that if luxury goods were defined mainly by their price, in times of inflation an increasing number of products would be subject to the luxury tax. The main criticism of the luxury tax as it applied to cafés, restaurants, and hotels concerned inconsistencies between departments in standards of classification. Shoup explained that one measure that was taken to address the issue of the impact of inflation on the definition of a luxury product was to fix the price by decree rather than by law, which allowed for more frequent adjustments. This, however, added to the administrative burden of the tax. In spite of all the criticism of the luxury tax, he pointed out that during the period between 1921 and 1925 it brought in between 14 percent and 17 percent of the total turnover tax revenue. Another positive indicator was that the number of hotels with the highest classification that were subject to the 13 percent as opposed to the 4 percent luxury tax increased fivefold, whereas second-rate ones increased by only 42 percent in the same period, between 1920 and 1927.[77]

Another issue that he discussed at length was why the left-wing government, the *Cartel des gauches*, that was in power between 1924 and 1926 did not abolish the sales tax as it had promised. Rather than replace it by introducing a capital levy or increasing rates of income tax, the left-wing coalition had called for the sales tax to be replaced with a production tax on several products including meat, coal, coffee, tea, cocoa, sugar, rice, and fertilizers. In explaining why the National Assembly accepted a replacement tax on only two of these products, coal and slaughtered meat, Shoup offered a further justification for the turnover tax. Unless the state was prepared to lose revenue as a result of the change, a new production tax levied at only one stage of a product's economic life would have to be at a considerably higher rate than that of the turnover tax. A high rate levied only once would provide a much greater incentive for evasion than a low rate levied several times. A replacement tax levied on suitable products, such as coal, did however offer a number of advantages or eliminate some of the disadvantages of the turnover tax. First, a single

TABLE 4. *Main Sources of Government Revenue between 1921 and 1929 and 1938 (in millions of francs)*

	Income Taxes	Turnover Tax	Total Budgetary Receipts	Expenditure
1921	2,821	1,915	23,119	32,846
1922	2,632	2,295	23,888	45,187
1923	3,796	3,030	26,224	38,293
1924	4,942	4,100	30,568	42,511
1925	6,477	4,563	33,455	36,275
1926	6,064	7,495	41,902	41,976
1927	7,808	8,621	45,746	45,361
1928	7,678	9,295	48,177	44,248
1929	8,709	12,373	64,268	58,850
1938	8,574	9,848	54,606	82,345

Source: INSEE, *Annuaire Statistique 1951* (Paris, 1952), 305–6, 316.

production tax reduced the number of taxpayers whom the tax inspectors had to control. Second, if they were large businesses they would be known to the authorities and, as in the case of coal, would probably have taken steps to avoid paying the turnover tax through vertical integration or becoming commission merchants and paying the tax on gross commissions rather than on the value of the coal. In the event, the replacement tax on coal was set at a low rate of 1.8 percent.[78]

CONCLUSION

The way in which the French stabilized their public finances in the 1920s challenged much of what Seligman had written and predicted. France remained a democracy with a developed economy; however, it showed a distinct preference for raising more revenue from sales taxes than from income taxes. Far from having an uncertain yield, the turnover tax generated a steady increase in revenue from its inception, as can be seen in Table 4.

It was not replaced by higher income taxes and a capital levy by the left-wing coalition government, as they had promised, but was replaced in some instances by a single tax on production. Each year the list of goods liable to the production tax instead of the sales tax was extended, greatly complicating the system. The turnover tax was finally abolished by the left-wing Popular Front government in 1936, only to be reintroduced in 1939 when the production tax that replaced it failed to meet the financial needs of a government rearming for war.[79]

In his study of the sales tax in France, Shoup shared Seligman's criticism that the turnover tax gave priority to horizontal equity over vertical equity. He did not consider that the exemption of foodstuffs from the tax necessarily made it less regressive because it was, in his view, introduced simply as a result of the domination of the right-wing agricultural sector in the National Assembly rather than a wish to ease the burden on poorer families in a progressive manner. If he felt that the sales tax imposed a greater burden on the poor than an income tax, however, he could see that in 1920s France for a variety of historical and administrative reasons the sales tax met the primary purpose of a tax better than any other: "some kind of general sales tax it seems there was bound to be."[80] His main criticisms were that it was not as easy to collect as had been predicted and that it changed the methods of business by favoring the vertical integration of firms.

Shoup's early work on sales taxes in France meant that he was exposed to a country and a fiscal reform that directly challenged the teachings and political preferences of his mentors at Columbia University. At the same time, however, it enabled him to put into practice the methodology that Seligman in particular advocated. If Seligman had devoted his academic life to the study of the differences in national tax systems on the basis of empirical evidence rather than fiscal and political theory, Shoup's research demonstrated the value of detailed empirical research in undermining conventional wisdom. He showed conclusively that where Seligman regarded income taxes to be the most democratic and progressive form of taxation, in the political and economic context of postwar France a majority of people actually preferred indirect taxes. What he showed was that it was the political context even more than the economic one that determined the nature of the French tax system in the 1920s. In what was described by Seligman as "a brilliant examination," he defended his thesis on the sales tax in France at Columbia University in 1928.[81] If their time spent in France had reduced Haig to the state of a "nervous wreck," the meticulous research into the social, political, and economic contexts in which the French had introduced a sales tax, was to launch Shoup's career.[82]

Notes

1. Brownlee, W. E., 'The Shoup Mission to Japan: Two political economies intersect,' in Martin, I. W., Mehrotra, A. K., Prasad, M., eds., *The New Fiscal Sociology. Taxation in Comparative and Historical Perspective* (Cambridge and New York: Cambridge University Press, 2009), 241.

2. Haig, R. M. (with the assistance of Carl S. Shoup, Alexander Werth and Nathalie Molodovsky), *The Public Finances of Post-War France* (New York: Columbia University Press, 1929), v.

3. Ibid., 114.

4. Moulton, H. G., Pasvolsky, L., *War debts and World Prosperity* (Washington D.C.: The Brookings Institute, 1932), 91.

5. Ibid, 84.

6. Haig, R. M., op cit, 3.

7. Ibid, 88.

8. Ibid, 114.

9. Johnson, H. C., *Gold, France and the Great Depression 1919–1932* (New Haven and London: Yale University Press, 1997), 76.

10. Hoxie, R. G., *A History of the Faculty of Political Science, Columbia University* (New York: Columbia University Press, 1955), 117.

11. Seligman, E. R. A., *Lectures in Public Finance, 1927–28* (New York: Reprinted Warren J. Samuels, 2001), 55.

12. Seligman, E. R. A., *Essays in Taxation, 1931* (New York: Augustus M. Kelley, 1969), 747 (reprint).

13. Ibid., 761.

14. Brownlee, W. E., *Federal Taxation in America. A Short History*, 2nd ed. (Cambridge and New York: Cambridge University Press, 2004), 65.

15. Seligman, E. R. A., *Studies in Public Finance, 1925*, 53.

16. Ibid., 55.

17. Seligman, E. R. A., *Essays in Taxation, 1931*, 6.

18. Ibid., 7.

19. Ibid., 1.

20. Due, J. F., 'The evolution of sales taxation, 1915–1972' in Bird, R. M., Head, J. G., eds., *Modern Fiscal Issues. Essays in Honor of Carl S. Shoup* (Toronto: University of Toronto Press, 1972), 319.

21. Brownlee, W. E., *Federal Taxation in America. A Short History*, op cit, 65.

22. Due, J. F., op cit, 322.

23. Haig, R. M., Shoup, C. S., *The Sales Tax in the American States* (New York: Columbia University Press, 1934), 6.

24. Seligman, E. R. A., *Studies in Public Finance*, op cit, 131.

25. Ibid.

26. Seligman, E. R. A., *Studies in Public Finance*, op cit, 131.

27. Ardant, G., *Histoire de l'impôt*. Volume 2 (Paris: Fayard, 1972), 41.

28. Morgan, K. J., Prasad, M., 'The Origins of Tax Systems: A French-U.S. Comparison,' *American Journal of Sociology* 2009, vol. 114 (5), pp. 1350–94.

29. Robert M. Haig to Joshua Stamp, 5 September 1927, Carl S. Shoup Papers, Yokohama National University Library [hereinafter CSSP].

30. Haig, R. M., *The Public Finances of Post-War France*, op cit, 5.

31. Ibid, 33.

32. Delalande, N., *Les Batailles de l'Impôt. Consentement et Résistances de 1789 à nos Jours* (Paris: Éditions du Seuil, 2011), 215–42.

33. Ardant, G., *Histoire de l'impôt*, op cit, 339.

34. Piketty, T., *Les Hauts Revenus en France au XXe Siècle* (Paris: Grasset, 2001), 255.
35. Piketty, T., op cit, 246–54.
36. Morgan, K. J., Prasad, M., 'The Origins of Tax Systems: A French-U.S. Comparison,' op cit.
37. Horn, M., *Britain, France and the Financing of the First World War* (Montreal: McGill-Queen's University Press, 2002), 81–2.
38. Schuker, S. A., *The End of French Predominance in Europe* (Chapel Hill: The University of North Carolina Press, 1976), 65.
39. Horn, M., *Britain, France and the Financing of the First World War*, op cit, 167–8.
40. Haig, R. M., op cit, 51.
41. Piketty, T., op cit, 254–9.
42. Schremmer, D. E., 'Taxation and Public Finance: Britain, France and Germany' in Mathias, P., Pollard, S., eds., *The Cambridge Economic History of Europe* (Cambridge: Cambridge University Press, 1989), 393.
43. Lynch, F. M. B., 'A Tax for Europe. The Introduction of Value Added Tax in France,' *Journal of European Integration History* 1998, vol. 4 (2), pp. 70.
44. Dauzat, A., 'Les conditions d'application de l'impôt sur le revenu en France', *Revue Politique et Parlementaire* 1920, vol. 3, pp. 80.
45. Haig, R. M., op cit, 38.
46. Trachtenberg, M., *Reparation in World Politics: France and European Economic Diplomacy 1916–1923* (New York: Columbia University Press, 1980), 41; Haig, R. M., op cit, 37–9.
47. Lynch, F. M. B., op cit, 71.
48. Mouré, M., *The Gold Standard Illusion* (Oxford: Oxford University Press, 2002), 31.
49. Trachtenberg, M., op cit, 41–5.
50. Ibid, 56.
51. Haig, R. M., 58.
52. Haig, R. M., op cit, 59.
53. McMillan, J. F., *Twentieth Century France. Politics and Society 1898–1991* (London: Edward Arnold, 2001), 92; Piketty, T., op cit, 259–62.
54. Haig, R. M., op cit, 350.
55. Schuker, S. A., op cit, 58.
56. Shoup, C. S., op cit, 3–25.
57. Haig, R. M., op cit, 350.
58. Ibid., 79.
59. Due, J. F., op cit, 231.
60. Dauzat, A., op cit, 74.
61. Shoup, C. S., *Sales Tax*, op cit, 353.
62. Ibid, 353.
63. Shoup, C. S., *Public Finance* (New Brunswick, N.J: Transaction Publishers, 2006), 224.
64. Shoup, C. S., *The Sales Tax*, op cit, 322.
65. Shoup, C. S., 324.
66. Schuker, op cit, 65.

67. Sirinelli, J.-F., Vandenbussche, R., Vavasseur-Desperriers, J., *La France de 1914 à nos Jours* (Paris: Presses Universitaires de France, 1993), 60.
68. Haig, R. M., op cit, 151.
69. Brown, H. G., 'The Incidence of a General Output or a General Sales Tax' in American Economic Association, *Readings in the Economics of Taxation* (London: Allen, Second edition, 1966), 330–9.
70. Friedman, M., Mack, R. P., *Taxing to Prevent Inflation* (New York: Columbia University Press 1943), 87.
71. Ibid, 88.
72. Shoup, C. S., *The Sales Tax* op cit, 90–4.
73. Ibid, 21.
74. Shoup, C. S., *Public Finance*, op cit, 207.
75. Ibid., 208.
76. Shoup, C. S., *The Sales Tax*, op cit, 71.
77. Ibid., 157–79.
78. Shoup, C. S., op cit, 121–56.
79. Ibid.
80. Ibid., 351.
81. E. R. A. Seligman to Robert M. Haig, June 4, 1928, CSSP.
82. Robert M. Haig to Joshua Stamp, November 7, 1927, CSSP.

4

The Shoup Missions to Cuba

Michael R. Adamson

When Carl Shoup arrived in Havana in June 1931 on behalf of a con-
valescing Edwin R. A. Seligman to study the Cuban revenue system and
make recommendations to reform it, "financial collapse was imminent,"
as U.S. Ambassador Harry F. Guggenheim had warned President Gerardo
Machado. Cuba was sinking under the weight of massive external debt,
much of which Machado contracted to fund the massive public works
program that he had launched after his election in November 1924. The
means by which Machado was maintaining full service on those debts
was fueling political unrest, which had been on the rise ever since he
extended his rule through a dubious reengineering of the constitution
in 1927 and a carefully orchestrated reelection in 1928. The collapse in
sugar prices and the drop in Cuba's share of the U.S. market in the wake
of the Hawley–Smoot Tariff Act were wreaking havoc on the economy.
Unemployment was rampant, thousands of businesses lay in ruins, and
hundreds of thousands of people were living on the brink of starvation.

Notwithstanding Seligman's narrow brief to "modernize" the tax system according to "scientific" principles, of which he was the leading the-
oretician, Wall Street and Washington linked the mission to short-term
debt repayment and avoidance of default. Seligman and Shoup studied
the Cuban tax system with a view to making it more equitable as well
as more efficient, consistent with their belief that social justice was an
integral component of public finance. The unwillingness of private creditors to renegotiate loan contracts that pledged for their repayment tax
revenues from many of the indirect taxes that the financial missionaries found objectionable, however, would limit the extent to which their
recommendations might be implemented. Civil insurrection fueled by

Machado's debt-servicing austerity measures, and its suppression, would prevent their recommendations from even being considered by the Cuban Congress.[1]

When Shoup arrived in Havana with Columbia University law professor Roswell Magill more than seven years later on a second mission, much had changed politically, as Machado had been ousted in the early days of the Roosevelt administration.[2] As was the case with the earlier operation, however, the mission took place only because of unresolved external debt issues. In 1934 Cuba had defaulted on its public works debt. Although the government had resolved some, but not all, of these debts in default, the U.S. State Department was conditioning its financial and trade assistance to all of Latin America on recipient government consideration on behalf of U.S. business and investor interests. In the case of Cuba, the department was holding up a possible export–import (Exim) bank loan until Havana passed legislation authorizing payments on debts outstanding to the American contractors who had built the central highway and the capitol. Indeed, Shoup's second mission was prompted by an exasperated Treasury Secretary Henry Morgenthau, who was anxious to aid Cuba over State Department objections. Shoup and Magill would offer recommendations for tax and administrative reform similar to those of the earlier mission, but only the reforms that satisfied State Department conditionality would be implemented.[3]

This chapter shows that Shoup's missions to Cuba went forward in the interest of American capital and its official representatives. At the same time, the missions presented Shoup with the opportunity to offer tax and fiscal advice on the basis of his understanding and analysis of the economic, political, and social conditions that he encountered. As was the case with his earlier experiences in France, Shoup was willing to temper Seligman's theory-driven advocacy of an income tax by adjusting his recommendations to a specific milieu in which a progressive income tax would have been nearly impossible to administer. It should be noted that Shoup's missions to Havana stand in contrast to the work of his dollar diplomacy predecessors, Edwin W. Kemmerer in particular.

SETTING THE STAGE FOR THE 1931–2 MISSION

The State Department's close relationship with Wall Street forms the essential backdrop to the first Shoup mission to Cuba. It was a product of America's development as an industrial power from 1870 to 1914 and the professionalism–managerialism of the public and private administration that accompanied it. Specifically, it involved a public–private partnership, dubbed "dollar diplomacy," that supported American expansionism in the wake of the 1898 war with Spain.

During the first two decades of the twentieth century, Wall Street became increasingly able and willing to float sovereign loans in New York on a market basis. Despite this, in a number of instances – most notably involving Cuba and the other republics of the Caribbean basin – official guarantees of repayment, in the form of customs receiverships, financial advisers, and military occupations, enticed bankers to lend. As Emily Rosenberg writes, "dollar diplomacy" was paternalistic, involving bankers seeking new business, government officials interested in America dominating a sphere of influence, and financial experts, dubbed "money doctors," consulting foreign clients. "Controlled loans" that refunded debts and restored the financial solvency of borrowers promised regional peace, stability, and development, as well as the displacement of European financiers and traders.[4]

In the case of Cuba, President McKinley appointed General Leonard Wood in the wake of the 1898 war as military governor and charged him with establishing political stability and social order. Before the occupation ended in May 1902, Secretary of State Elihu Root and Republican Senator Orville Platt of Connecticut devised the so-called Platt Amendment and attached it to the Army Appropriations Bill of 1901. Article I prohibited Cuba from making any treaty that impaired its "independence." Article II limited Cuba's ability to borrow from foreign sources by requiring the government to service external debts out of ordinary revenues; Washington sought to minimize the possibility that governments of creditors could use force to collect payment. Article III gave Washington the right to intervene as it wished to protect Cuba's independence. Overall, the amendment provided the means by which Washington might informally control Cuba without having to annex its racially inferior population, which American officials deemed incapable of independence.[5]

Time and again, Washington invoked the Platt Amendment to intervene to suppress political revolts and labor disturbances that threatened direct U.S. investments, the value of which increased from $50 million in 1896 to $1.3 billion in 1924. Louis A. Pérez, Jr. argues that: "The Platt Amendment therefore stood for more than a guarantee of political stability. It also represented a commitment to the defense of foreign capital."[6]

A series of Wall Street loans, often linked to the withdrawal of the marines, played a critical supporting role in relations between Washington and Havana. In 1904 Speyer & Co. floated a $35 million loan, in part to meet obligations to the army arising from the 1898 war. In 1909 Speyer issued a $16.5 million loan to retire loans outstanding from the colonial period and fund infrastructure projects. In 1914 and 1923, J. P. Morgan issued loans of $10 million and $50 million, respectively. Customs receipts secured each of the loans, with priority determined by the order in which they were issued. The 1904 issue, for instance, had a claim on 15 percent of total customs receipts, a percentage that the government promised to increase should it prove to be insufficient to meet its debt service obligations.[7]

Over time, however, the Platt Amendment became an uncertain means by which to accomplish the ends of U.S. foreign policy. As a tool of hegemony, Pérez concludes, it "gradually weakened from overuse, and because the object of intervention included everything, the means of intervention included nothing." By the mid-1920s, the mere threat of intervention had increased domestic political instability and economic insecurity. Actual intervention in the Dominican Republic, Haiti, Nicaragua, and Panama fomented regional hostility. Growing condemnation of U.S. interventionism across Latin America prompted Secretary of State Henry L. Stimson to declare a regional policy of "nonintervention" soon after his appointment in 1929. Even as Washington's interest in sending in the marines under the Platt Amendment waned, however, the bankers who extended loans and other credits to Cuba after 1923 (and the investors who bought them) continued to base their decision-making on the expectation that Washington would, in fact, intervene directly should Havana ever threaten to default on its external obligations.[8]

Gerardo Machado initiated a public works program that set the Cuban government on the road to financial insolvency. Machado, a businessman who became head of the Liberal Party, leveraged nationalist sentiment by supporting the revision of the Platt Amendment during his successful 1924 presidential campaign. In addition, he promised social and administrative reforms. Once in power, however, public works commanded his attention. Under a July 15, 1925 law, the government constructed a 700-mile central highway, roads, aqueducts, sanitation projects, bridges, and buildings. To complete the program, Machado incurred substantial external debt, despite the fact that the July 15 law created a special public works fund to finance the program on a pay-as-you-go basis and Machado had pledged to fund it from internal sources.[9]

Declining sugar prices prompted Machado to rethink his pledge. Some 80 percent of the government's revenues derived from the sugar industry. Persistent global overproduction led to the value of Cuba's crop plummeting, from $400.1 million in the fiscal year (FY) 1922–3 to $198.3 million in FY 1927–8. Public revenues fell more gradually, from their peak of $91.3 million in FY 1923–4 to $81.0 million in FY 1927–8. After 1929, the sugar industry collapsed, with devastating consequences for the government's accounts. The Hawley–Smoot Tariff Act, reflecting the lobbying of American beet sugar producers, exacerbated the crisis. Cuban producers saw their prices plummet to half of that received by their American competitors. In response, Cuba and six other nations signed on to the Chadbourne Plan, a scheme to limit output. Cuba cut production by 36 percent, but the other members actually increased their output. The plan, devised by Thomas L. Chadbourne, a New York corporate lawyer who had invested in two Cuban sugar mills, spelled disaster for laborers and small growers. Cuba's share of the U.S. market fell from 49.4 percent in 1930 to 25.3 percent in 1933. Overall, exports to America fell from $434 million in 1924 to $80 million in 1932. Government revenues collapsed in line with the fall in commodity prices and exports, to $47 million in FY 1931–2.[10]

Despite this, Machado strove to complete the public works program, claiming that it would enable Cuba to lower its dependence on American investment and trade. With his consolidation of power into a de facto dictatorship following his 1928 reelection, Machado paid increasingly less heed to the political pressures that had prompted him to promise to fund the public works program on a cash basis in the first place.

Machado contracted loans "with almost casual abandon" to fund public works projects and cover budget deficits. To accelerate the program beyond the country's ability to pay for it out of current revenues and existing surpluses, the government issued deferred payment certificates to contractors Warren Brothers and Purdy & Henderson from the extra-budgetary public works fund. The contractors, in turn, presented them for cash payment at the Chase National Bank branch in Havana. In February 1927, Machado contracted $10 million credit with Chase, which the bank used to purchase outstanding certificates. Cuba's deteriorating finances prompted the alarmed bankers at J. P. Morgan to issue a "stopgap" $9 million loan in July 1927. Almost immediately, Machado sought to borrow another $60 million to accelerate the completion of the 700-mile central highway. To sidestep J. P. Morgan's bankers, Machado again turned to Chase to tie any new loan to legislation and secure it with a first lien on the public works taxes. In July 1928, the bank agreed to discount $50 million in deferred payment certificates held by the contractors. With the government's revenues in decline, however, Chase was unwilling to keep the entire credit on its books. In October 1928 and January 1929, it offered 40 percent of it to investors as public works certificates. In the fall of 1929, Machado secured an agreement from Chase to convert $40 million in public works certificates into fifteen-year bonds and extend a new, short-term $20 million credit to complete the central highway.[11]

Despite the concerns of the U.S. State Department's representatives in Havana, it all but ignored Article II of the Platt Amendment. For instance, the department sat on its hands when Harry Guggenheim, who became ambassador in 1929, reported that public works lending in general was characterized by "crass stupidity" on the part of bankers who were lending excessively to protect Machado and their exposed positions. Subsequently, the department refused to intervene when Guggenheim urged it to prevent Machado from borrowing additional funds. Only the collapse of the New York bond market, owing to global debt crisis, ended Machado's ambitions.[12]

The U.S. State Department recognized the dictatorial characteristics of the *Machadato*, but concluded that the opposition was too weak to protect American investments and property, should it gain power. It relied on the fear that default would invite intervention by the United States. Apparently it sufficed. Machado adopted draconian measures to balance the budget and service Cuba's Wall Street loans in full. In doing so, he created economic, political, and social conditions that made it virtually impossible for the government to act on the advice of the Seligman–Shoup mission.[13]

Cuba enjoyed excellent credit despite this because bankers and investors believed that Washington would invoke the Platt Amendment to protect their interests. Cuba's bonds, as Ambassador Guggenheim reflected, sold "on a like basis with those of Denmark and very much higher than those of most Latin American republics."[14] As the *New York Times* put it, the Platt Amendment made Cuba "economically almost as much a part of the Union as is New York State."[15] The illusion on the part of bankers and investors that the Amendment underwrote Cuban credit enabled Machado to borrow beyond Cuba's means. As of FY 1931–2, Cuba's debt topped $150 million, two-thirds of which was due within ten years. The floating debt, that is the debt that required ongoing financing, was estimated to be as high as $26.5 million. Federal spending, including the servicing of debt, was expected to reach $60 million, however revenues were expected to reach $55 million at most.[16]

The invitation to Seligman to advise his regime was part of a desperate scramble on Machado's part to avoid default. He had slashed public salaries by as much as 60 percent, laid off civil servants, closed post offices, hospitals, schools, and other public facilities, and, reluctantly, suspended heavy construction projects. This had not been enough. In early 1931, as Seligman was entering into contract discussions with Cuba's Treasury Department, Machado approached Ambassador Guggenheim and asked him to support his decision to postpone repayment of the $20 million short-term credit for six months. The request marked the beginning of a decade of effort on the part of bankers, bondholder associations, and the U.S. government to address Cuba's external debt problems. Guggenheim explained dryly that it was "a very inopportune time to discuss Cuban finances with the bankers," given the debt crisis that was now engulfing all of Latin America and shuttering the New York bond market. In the interest of protecting its commitments, however, Chase initiated a series of ninety-day extensions on the $20 million short-term credit. At the same time, Guggenheim and Chase Vice-President Shepard Morgan called for direct U.S. financial supervision. In keeping his policy of "nonintervention," Secretary of State Stimson refused to consider their pleas.[17]

THE SELIGMAN–SHOUP MISSION OF 1931–2

In the summer of 1931, Carl Shoup studied Cuba's finances and its tax system from his post in the offices of the National Economic Commission. As the presidential decree that authorized the mission put it, the government recognized that its fiscal system was not in accord with "economic science." On the recommendation of the commission, Cuba's Treasury Department invited Seligman to advise the government. Renowned for his work on public finance, the Columbia University professor had advised the U.S. Treasury Department during World War I and, during 1922–3, had served on the League of Nations Committee on Economics and Finance, which had studied double taxation.[18] Seligman could not travel, however, for he had suffered a heart attack in 1930. The commission nominated his Columbia University colleague, Robert Murray Haig, to conduct the study under Seligman's supervision. Haig, however, was unavailable owing to a prior commitment to the New York State Commission for the Revision of the Revenue Laws. Seligman suggested Shoup.[19]

The scope of the mission to Cuba was officially limited to a study of the "unscientific and inadequate" revenue system but, unsurprisingly, political and business leaders in Cuba looked to Seligman – who advised Shoup from New York – for solutions to a broad range of economic and financial problems, including external debts. Ambassador Guggenheim warned Shoup to make his brief clear, as both government and opposition leaders were poised to use the mission to political advantage. On his arrival, therefore, Shoup stated publicly that the scope of the mission was restricted to "an examination of the revenue system of the national and local governments.... a survey of taxes, fees, and prices of government services." United States and Cuban officials understood that implementation of the mission's recommendations would occur over years rather than months. At the same time, Shoup appreciated the immediate need of the government to service its debts and pay its employees "decent wages," and so hoped that his work might have an appreciable short-term impact.[20]

Pressure to expand the scope of the study reached the highest levels of government. In August, Treasury Secretary Mario Ruiz Mesa surprised Shoup by telling him that he expected the final report to address the debt problem and, if Shoup had time to make a study of it, the spending side of the budget. The Cuban Treasury was not considering a debt consolidation because without the explicit support of the State Department it could not obtain terms as favorable as those on its outstanding loans. With the government "living from hand to mouth, day by day," as Shoup put it, however, the Cuban officials "were eager to get advice from any responsible source." Shoup wanted to "try to get together something on the debt situation" before the end of the mission. Seligman welcomed the opportunity "to do certain things in the debt matter, and perhaps later in the matter of expenses of the budget." When it came time to publishing his report, however, Seligman restated the narrow scope of the mission. "The details of this program are interconnected," Seligman intoned, "and we can take no responsibility for any one of the recommendations unless it is considered in its proper connection with all the others." He slammed the door on any suggestion that *El Plan Seligman* would solve the economic crisis. Rather, the goal of the mission was "to shape a firm foundation that would last for years to come."[21]

Seligman and Shoup confronted a Cuban tax system that was based largely on various forms of sales taxation, the burden of which fell on the lowest classes. From Spanish rule, Cuba inherited customs duties, transfer taxes, a real estate tax, and a tax on industry and commerce. Direct taxation remained light. The lack of income and land taxes allowed the wealthy to escape taxation almost entirely. The substantial class of absentee owners paid virtually no tax. Customs duties constituted the main source of revenue for the ordinary budget; however, receipts from this source declined as a percentage of total revenues with the decline in sugar and, secondarily, tobacco prices and production. Customs revenues accounted for two-thirds of total revenues in FY 1913–14, but this dropped to only 48.4 percent in FY 1928–9. Rather than impose direct taxes, the government raised revenues by increasing taxes or creating new ones, such as a stamp tax and 1 percent gross sales tax. The means of financing the Public Works Fund under the July 15, 1925 law "could not [have been] more deplorable." The law allotted to the fund a 0.5 percent tax on sales and gross receipts, a mortgage tax, a surcharge on customs duties, a gasoline import tax, a vehicle license fee, a tax on the export of money and goods, a tax on the rental value of land and buildings, and half of the excess territorial tax. An emergency law of January 29, 1931 expanded the scope of the sales tax and added 2 percent to the tax on mortgage loan interest.[22]

Pledges of revenues to service loans limited the scope of tax reform. Excise taxes on alcoholic beverages, bottled soft drinks, tobacco products, matches, and playing cards had been imposed by a February 27, 1903 law, which was modified to tie these taxes to the first Speyer loan. "By strict interpretation of the contract," the tax rates could not be increased without the consent of the bankers, leaving relatively prosperous distillers and brewers "grossly undertaxed." The January 29, 1931 emergency law increased the Speyer loan excise taxes by an average of almost 100 percent. Overall, Cuban loan contracts provided for much more rapid amortization than was typically the case on foreign loans, so the government was paying 40 percent more each year toward retiring the debt than on interest payments.[23]

Bankers stood pat, however, when Seligman queried them on the possibility of stripping the pledges of specific revenues from their loan contracts. They had promised to assist Seligman in conducting the study, which is understandable given their interest – Chase National Bank in particular – in seeing to it that Havana improved its capacity to collect the revenues needed to service the loans that they had extended. They limited their cooperation, however, so there were absolutely no changes made to the security provisions of their loans. Seligman called a conference to solicit bankers' views on ways to minimize the chance that Cuba would default or declare a moratorium on its debts. The meeting produced nothing substantial by way of developing or implementing the recommendations of the mission. Seligman and Shoup assumed that there would be no loan contract revisions in the near future. Still, for their report they estimated revenues under two scenarios: "an ideal scheme," involving "the total abolition of the sales tax and many of the burden-some individual taxes" pledged to the Public Works Fund ("Proposal Number One"); and the status quo, which involved no changes to the Public Works Fund taxes ("Proposal Number Two").[24]

Shoup approached the reform of Cuba's tax system with a toolkit of progressive ideas and theories on public finance developed at Columbia University under Seligman. As he showed in his study of France's tax system, however, in addition to this Shoup believed that appropriate tax policy could only be devised after gaining a practical and thorough under-standing of both the historical context of the development of tax struc-tures and existing conditions and circumstances "on the ground," includ-ing a state's administrative capacity. Thus Shoup went to great lengths to gather comprehensive statistical information and develop additional empirical data through substantive, rather than perfunctory, interviews. In balancing principles and pragmatism, he distinguished himself from his more celebrated (and studied) counterpart at Princeton University, Edwin W. Kemmerer.

During the 1920s and early 1930s, Kemmerer consulted many govern-ments that were seeking external finance for economic development pur-poses. Invariably, he recommended an orthodox program that included currency stabilization through the restoration or establishment of the gold standard; the creation of an independent central bank with exclusive right to issue notes and the regulation of other banks in much the same manner as the Federal Reserve regulated its member banks in America; balanced budgets; and fiscal and tax reforms aimed at increasing revenues and enhancing economic efficiency and transparency. These recommen-dations were not at all controversial. They constituted the foundation of the liberal consensus that prevailed from 1880 to 1914, which del-egates to international financial conferences held at Brussels in 1920 and Genoa in 1922 reaffirmed. Moreover, the political and economic elites of the countries that Kemmerer consulted welcomed the financial orthodoxy that the money doctor peddled. In addition to this, they had often initiated the implementation of institutions such as central banks well before the Princeton professor's arrival.[25] Hence, as Paul W. Drake notes, "the transfer of technology was quite small." Despite this, the compatibility of vision and the promise of Wall Street finance meant that Kemmerer enjoyed "spectacular success" in having client governments adopt his program "without serious revisions."[26] Kemmerer's prescrip-tions remained constant over time, even when the cataclysm of depres-sion suggested that countercyclical measures were in order and many of his client governments rejected the financial orthodoxy.[27] In fact, Drake observes, Kemmerer could have mailed in his orthodox recommendations to his clients; the interviews that he conducted sought not to gather data to inform their advice, but to build support for program implementation. This is not surprising, given their grounding in neoclassical theory and elite consensus on how the international system ought to operate.[28]

To gain an understanding of the tax system and its impacts on individual economic behavior and business decision making, Shoup analyzed government documents, conducted surveys of various revenues, and interviewed dozens of people. He shared his findings with Seligman and together they developed recommendations that considered the institutional, sociological, and historically contingent realities of Cuba, as they understood them.[29]

On the basis of their investigation, Seligman and Shoup advocated a reform of the tax system that incorporated "the two great principles of universality and equality," which featured in the systems of the world's leading democracies. Their recommendations aimed "primarily to secure from a revised system of taxation about the same amount of revenue as can be secured normally from the present system" – with "normal" defined for the purposes of analysis as FY 1929–30. Their proposal retained the import duties that constituted the largest single source of revenue, but most of the government's revenue would come "from a centralized tax on real estate levied on rental value, from a personal income tax to be assessed on presumptive rather than actual income, from a tax on the net profits of business enterprises, chiefly corporate, and from an inheritance tax." Under the plan, the sales tax, most of the stamp and consumption taxes, the lottery, and all of the new taxes imposed by the emergency law of January 29, 1931 would be abolished. Taxes on business, real estate transfers, and mortgages would be reduced. Reflecting Seligman's instruction to Shoup that "our real efforts must be devoted to administrative reform," the report recommended several steps to rationalize revenue collection, including abolishing the municipal collection of national taxes and creating permanent, professional staff and a statistical bureau within the treasury.[30]

The design of the personal income tax, for one, illustrates how Shoup balanced progressive principles with pragmatism. For Shoup, a personal income tax was desirable because the current system was "relatively expensive to administer" and was "subject to frequent and wide fluctuations." In addition to this, it was inequitable. The system not did take into account "a person's wealth . . . or his family obligations." Moreover, relying on indirect taxation concealed the average citizen's role as a tax-payer, diminishing "his sense of civic responsibility." That is, it impaired the development of democratic values in society. A direct tax that took account of "the resident's relative economic situation" would improve both efficiency and equity in the tax system. Its exact nature might vary, however, depending on the circumstances: "Each country must develop its own system of taxation, suitable to it own history and present environment." On the basis of his statistical studies, surveys, and interviews, Shoup concluded that Cuba was not ready for a "comprehensive personal income tax." He was "more inclined to favor a dwelling-unit tax, as a presumptive income tax,"[31] for he did not believe "that the Cuban public would welcome [a complicated personal income tax] in the way it must be favored, in any country, if it is to be a success." Adopting such a tax would have required *Cubanos* to make abrupt changes in personal behavior, including keeping detailed records and interacting frequently with tax officials. In addition, comprehensive tax on the basis of actual income was not suitable for an unstable commodity-dependent economy such as Cuba's, Shoup concluded. This was because it would produce "wide fluctuations in yield," that would be "financially embarrassing to the government." Finally, devoting considerable resources to "obtain[ing] complete justice in the distribution of [the] burden of this tax" would be somewhat "wasted when the tax system as a whole contain[ed] many other taxes not distributed so meticulously." For these reasons, Shoup opted for a presumptive income tax on the basis of either paid rentals or the value of the dwelling used.[32]

Publication of the report set off, as one analyst described it, "an explosion of favorable and adverse commentaries" in the press, as Cubans vigorously debated their economic future. According to the Cuban Chamber of Commerce, impartial assessments of the report's technical merits were rare. Apparently even rarer were reviews by qualified economists. Reflecting the spectrum of particular interests that would be affected by their implementation, all of the report's recommendations were subjected to scrutiny. Several critics charged that the plan favored foreign investors. An interesting twist on this theme alleged that Seligman and Shoup recommended the personal tax on presumptive income to lessen the burden on foreign investment. Others alleged that the plan supported large landowners at the expense of urban property owners. Both supporters and opponents of *El Plan Seligman* questioned the assumption that FY 1929–30 was an appropriate baseline year and concluded that it would be impossible to generate the $122 million in revenues expected by Seligman and Shoup in "normal" years (the Cuban Treasury collected just $119 million in revenues in FY 1929–30). Owing to the disastrous economic situation, observers agreed that few *Cubanos* could bear the burden of higher direct taxes on their income and property, even if the government abolished indirect taxes, as recommended in the report. The growing number of vacant buildings and evictions for failing to pay rent undercut the assumption that taxes on income and real estate would increase revenue collections, critics argued.[33]

Even those who hailed its release conceded that *El Plan Seligman* was dead on arrival.[34] Political chaos determined its fate. An armed uprising in August 1931 ended any chance of Washington-induced political reform under Machado. Led by the principal moderate leaders, including Carlos Mendieta and former president Marion Garcia Menocal y Deop, the revolt quickly collapsed. Machado arrested dozens of political opponents, including Mendieta and Menocal. As Pérez writes, the failure of the "old-line opposition" to overthrow Machado "announced the political bankruptcy of the nineteenth-century political class." The unsuccessful uprising exposed traditional methods of opposition as "unworkable" and "summoned new political forces in the struggle against Machado," composed of intellectuals, professionals, students, workers, and Communist Party members. For his part, Machado retrenched and no longer heeded embassy or U.S. State Department officials. After 1931, government forces and insurgents fought openly. In this unsettled political environment and with the economy in free fall, it is little wonder that "absolutely nothing" was done to implement the recommendations of *El Plan Seligman*, as José E. Cortiñas, one of two employees seconded from the Cuban Treasury to assist Shoup, reported in April 1932.[35]

THE SHOUP–MAGILL MISSION OF 1938–9

Shoup traveled to Havana for a second time at the end of 1938. Now professor of economics at Columbia, he was accompanied by Roswell Magill, a Columbia University law professor and former undersecretary of the U.S. Treasury in the Roosevelt administration. This mission took place when an interdepartmental debate on American foreign economic policy was reaching its climax in the context of regional security concerns.

Franklin D. Roosevelt's victory in the November 1932 election created the basis for institutional challenges to the U.S. State Department's traditional authority over foreign economic policy. Many New Deal officials were eager to use public capital to promote overseas stabilization and development. Under the authority of and using the resources that Congress granted to the treasury secretary under the Gold Reserve and Silver Purchase Acts, officials in that department – director of monetary research Harry Dexter White in particular – promoted a direct role for the government as a manager of exchange rates and capital flows.[36]

With the creation of the Exim Bank in 1934, the administration acquired an additional means of promoting economic development abroad. President Roosevelt established Exim by Executive Order 6581 under the provisions of the National Industrial Recovery Act to finance trade with Russia. Soon thereafter, Roosevelt created a second Exim bank to handle silver coinage arrangements with Cuba. Its first operation, a $3.8 million credit, allowed the government to pay salaries in arrears of public employees and military personnel. Cuba tapped the bank repeatedly for this type of operation. The bank's brief soon expanded to include all countries except Russia. Warren Lee Pierson, Exim Bank's president from 1936–45, sought to establish Exim as a robust development bank that financed capital goods purchases and extended loans.[37]

The U.S. State Department frustrated Pierson's ambitions, however, by vetoing credits to governments that remained in default on their dollar debts. In the context of surging German fascism and Japanese militarism, Exim and treasury officials increased their pressure on the U.S. State Department to drop its objections. Several substantial loan applications pushed the institutional battle to a head, prompting an internal review of the department's Exim lending policy, the result of which was a moderate amount of development lending to Latin America. The U.S. State Department, however, still expected governments to show good faith in settling remaining debts in default – and they were the arbiters of what "good faith" entailed.[38]

In December 1933, four months after Sumner Welles, as special representative of the Roosevelt administration, orchestrated the end of the *Machadato*, Cuba defaulted on its public works debt and the $1.5 million in unsecured obligations that it owed to contractors Purdy & Henderson and Warren Brothers. Soon thereafter, it declared a moratorium on payments into the sinking funds of the J.P. Morgan and Speyer loans, although it continued to pay the interest on them.[39]

Initially Welles showed more interest in providing U.S. financial and economic assistance to Machado's successor than in the external debt situation. Once Cuba elected Miguel Mariano Gómez y Arias as its president of a permanent government, however, Welles did an about-face, instructing the American embassy to let the Cuban government know that the

U.S. State Department expected it to address the default. If it showed any reluctance to do so, Welles told the embassy to emphasize "somewhat forcefully that the policy of cooperation undertaken by this Government means 'cooperation' and not playing the role of Santa Claus."[40]

With such "encouragement" from Welles and the embassy, the Gómez government entered into negotiations with representatives from Chase National Bank and the contractors. A settlement reached in December 1937 called for an $85 million, forty-year refunding issue. The deal did not, however, address monies owed to the contractors. The U.S. State Department promised to block all financial assistance until Havana settled these debts.[41]

In the context of falling government revenues, owing to a disastrous sugar crop Exim now offered Cuba aid with no strings attached. Pierson traveled to Havana to discuss the financing of a $4.5 million public works program. On his return, however, U.S. State Department officials pressured him to pare down the proposal considerably. Despite this, Pierson recommended that Exim finance highway construction and the improvement of Havana's water works.[42]

The Exim offer was made in the context of heightened concern in Washington about the regional security threat posed by Germany and Japan. In the wake of the Munich conference, U.S. Treasury Secretary Henry Morgenthau instructed his staff to assist Latin America as part of a "financial Monroe Doctrine." In October, Harry Dexter White complained that the U.S. State Department was continuing to block the extension of essential financial aid. In December, an incensed Morgenthau castigated the department for its intransigence, telling officials that "when a quasi-governmental banking-lending agency is used as leverage to collect private debts – I personally would think twice about it." He wondered how "wise" it was to use Exim as a lever to collect private debts. Pierson echoed the treasury secretary, observing that the U.S. State Department had tried to use Exim "repeatedly" in this way without success.[43]

The U.S. State Department did not budge from its position. It saddled the prospective Cuban loan with additional conditions, namely that it reform the revenue system, reorganize its treasury department and, most importantly, reduce spending, which had topped 80 million pesos for the first time since the onset of the Depression in FY 1936–7. Welles, now undersecretary of state, told the Cuban ambassador that the administration was willing to send experts to conduct a study, if the government invited them. The offer quickly turned into a requirement. The U.S. State Department informed Morgenthau that any infrastructure funding was contingent on certain revisions of the tax system. Welles and Assistant Treasury Secretary Wayne Taylor arranged to send Magill and Shoup to assist Cuba in meeting the expectations of the U.S. State Department.[44]

From 1934–9, Shoup had worked steadily for the U.S. Treasury Department's Division of Tax Research. In 1934, Magill brought Shoup to Washington as one of seven consultants to study the federal revenue system. Shoup's work on sales taxation had impressed Magill, as had his work on the staff of the New York State Commission for the Revision of the Revenue Laws, which Shoup had joined after he returned from Havana. Shoup played a key role in organizing the project. He then participated in a two-year study of taxation in America, sponsored by the Twentieth Century Fund. This research was published as *Facing the Tax Problem: A Survey of Taxation in the United States and a Program for the Future*. In late 1937, Magill asked Shoup to consult the treasury on tax issues in the context of the deepening recession in the United States.[45]

The two experts arrived in Havana with a brief to recommend "immediate measures to assure the balancing of the budget and adequate guarantees for loan or financing operations." For FY 1939 – the first in which the fiscal and calendar years were aligned – Cuban officials expected a budget deficit of 5 million to 10 million pesos. As they explained in their report, Shoup and Magill "were not asked to investigate and analyze government expenditures," and so they were not in a position to assess "whether expenditures can and should be curtailed, or whether they should be expended." Nevertheless, the U.S. State Department's insistence that Havana find ways to cut spending set the parameters of the mission. On reading the reports produced by the missions, a person might conclude that Shoup's assignment in 1938 had not changed since 1931. The scope of the second mission, however, was broader. Magill and Shoup hinted at the expectations of U.S. officials when they wrote: "The accomplishment of the desired results appear to require either a reduction in expenditures," although holding revenues constant, or increasing revenues of a similar amount and keeping spending at its current level. At the same time, the experts left it to the Cuban government to work out spending cuts, if the latter were to take their cue from the U.S. State Department and balance the budget through that approach.[46]

Shoup and Magill had far less time to conduct their investigation than Shoup enjoyed in 1931. They relied on the Cuban Treasury Department to supply them with information on revenue collections and statistics on industry and commerce. They found that official data on the latter in particular were lacking. With the assistance of Emilio Collado from the U.S. State Department, Shoup and Magill interviewed officials and representatives of leading corporations to determine productive capacity across sectors and gather views on modifying the fiscal system.[47]

Shoup found that little had changed in either the economic or tax structures since 1932, and his recommendations varied little from those of *El Plan Seligman*. They included shifting the tax system away from sales taxes and customs duties toward taxes on "invested wealth," incomes, and inheritances, that is, the taxes "generally accepted as the most refined instruments for taxing individuals according to prevailing standards of ability to pay" and that "probably have on the whole less unfavorable effects than most other taxes on production and consumption." Recognizing the need to shift the tax burden away from those who continued to suffer within the commodity-based economy, Shoup recommended centralizing property tax collections; expanding the existing tax on profits, interest, and dividends into a comprehensive income tax; replacing a retail sales tax and various consumption taxes with a manufacturer's sales tax; reducing customs duties; and repealing myriad minor taxes. He returned to the central issue of the first mission, namely taxes pledged for loans, whose elimination he urged through refunding issues. These reforms would be part of a program to strengthen the government's fiscal powers. The treasury secretary would acquire more authority, introduce professional civil service procedures to tax administration, and crack down on evasion. Distributional equity was important to Shoup, but as a means to an end. Greater fairness would increase confidence in government, reduce tax cheating, promote economic efficiency, and strengthen revenue flows, all of which would link public finance and democratic citizenship.[48]

Little was apparently done, however, to implement the Magill–Shoup prescriptions for structural reform. There was no material shift in the percentage of total tax revenues that Havana collected from import duties and sales taxes to taxes on income and profits. By 1942, the national government was relying more than ever on customs revenues to fund its budget. At the same time, the percentage of tax revenues derived from sales taxes remained essentially unchanged from FY 1937–8, which Magill and Shoup used as a baseline. Revenues derived from the growth in trade generated by World War II did, however, alleviate the immediate need for the national government to undertake structural reform. The value of Cuba's sugar trade with America, for instance, more than tripled, from $53 million in 1940 to $170 million in 1944.[49]

In September 1940, a bill that provided funds to settle the contractors' claims became law. The U.S. State Department quickly approved "a broad program of cooperation," including Exim financing of a "moderate and largely self-liquidating program of public works." A Cuban economic mission met with American officials from a number of agencies. From those discussions came an agreement on the outline of a program that included a $4 million Exim revolving credit to be devoted to infrastructure rehabilitation and up to $10 million in funds for agricultural development. The scope of the program included "a thoroughgoing reorganization of the fiscal administration and reform of the tax system," to be undertaken by a joint United States–Cuban committee. Undersecretary Welles instructed the committee to use the reports from both Shoup missions to assist it in its work. In addition, the department insisted that the government cut its spending by 10 percent, which it believed could be done without laying off public employees.[50]

For Washington, mobilizing a united regional response to the perceived security threat posed by Germany and Japan limited the extent to which U.S. officials prodded Havana to act. In April 1941, in the absence of any evidence of structural tax reform, Havana secured the blessing of the U.S. State Department for $30 million in Exim assistance: $25 million for development projects and the balance for the creation of a central bank.[51]

CONCLUSION

Cuba did not present Seligman, Shoup, and Magill with the ideal laboratory for harnessing tax reform to enable financial stabilization or to strengthen democracy. Machado was a dictator in all but name by the time that Shoup arrived in Havana. Moreover, the means by which Welles maneuvered the de facto dictator from power had unintended consequences. As Philip Dur and Christopher Gilcrease show, in the process of encouraging politicians and army officers to oust Machado, the Cuban military "cast off its constitutional moorings." Soldiers soon mutinied and Fulgencio Batista, their leader, eventually seized power. Throughout the 1930s, ineptitude and inaction on the part of executive and legislative leaders redounded to Batista's benefit. At the time of the second Shoup mission, Batista was the dominant factor in Cuban domestic affairs.[52]

Debt crises limited the efficacy of Shoup's first mission to Cuba, even as resolving sovereign debt issues served as its proximate cause. Bankers refused to renegotiate their loan contracts; although Cuba had yet to default, conditions in the New York bond market did not permit the country to liquidate its obligations with a new loan that removed the pledges for repayment that Shoup and Seligman found objectionable. Thus, the financial missionaries failed to persuade creditors to accept a fundamental revision of the Cuban tax system, and insurgency blocked the implementation of a more modest version of *El Plan Seligman*.

On his second mission, Shoup made similar recommendations for revision of the tax structure and for administration reform to those that he had offered in 1931. The only reforms that Cuba implemented, however, were those insisted on by the U.S. State Department as conditions of a proposed Exim loan.

Circumstances in Cuba did permit Seligman, Shoup, and Magill to be "much less restrained in giving advice," as W. Elliot Brownlee observes, than Haig and Shoup had been in France.[53] As a result, the missions to Cuba afforded the Columbia University financial experts the opportunity to propose a tax system that they believed to be appropriate for the island nation. In this respect, the missions were significant moments in the history of exporting ideas on public finance.

Notes

1. Guggenheim quoted in Pérez, L. A., Jr., *Cuba under the Platt Amendment, 1902–1934* (Pittsburgh, PA: University of Pittsburgh Press, 1986), 285; Anderson, G. E., "The Taxation Muddle in Cuba; American Loans Obstruct Needed Reforms," *The Annalist*, May 22, 1931, pp. 933, 941; Benjamin, J. R., "The *Machadato* and Cuban Nationalism, 1928–1932," *Hispanic American Historical Review* 1975, vol. 55, pp. 66–9; Brownlee, W. E., "The Shoup Mission to Japan: Two Political Economies Intersect," in Martin, I. W., Mehrotra, A. K., Prasad, M., eds., *The New Fiscal Sociology: Taxation in Comparative and Historical Perspective* (New York: Cambridge University Press, 2009), 242–3; Whitney R. W., *State and Revolution in Cuba: Mass Mobilization and Political Change, 1920–1940* (Durham, NC: University of North Carolina Press, 2001), 57–8.
2. Benjamin, J. R., "The *Machadato* and Cuban Nationalism," 86–91; Dur, P., Gilcrease, P., "U.S. Diplomacy and the Downfall of a Cuban Dictator: Machado in 1933," *Journal of Latin American Studies* 2002, vol. 34, pp. 255–82.
3. Benjamin, J. R., "The New Deal, Cuba, and the Rise of a Global Foreign Economic Policy," *Business History Review* 1977, vol. 51, pp. 69–70; Pollitt, B. H., "The Cuban Sugar Economy in the 1930s," in *The World Sugar Economy in War and Depression, 1914–1940* (London: Routledge, 1988), 100–3; Pollitt, B. H., "The Rise and Fall of the Cuban Sugar Economy," *Journal of Latin American Studies* 2004, vol. 36, pp. 320–1; Whitney, R. W., *State and Revolution in Cuba*, 59–61.

4. Rosenberg, E. S., *Financial Missionaries to the World: The Politics and Culture of Dollar Diplomacy* (Cambridge, MA: Harvard University Press, 1999), esp. 56–60; Veeser, C., *A World Safe for Capitalism: Dollar Diplomacy and America's Rise to Global Power* (New York: Columbia University Press, 2002); Plummer, B. G., *Haiti and the Great Powers, 1902–1915* (Baton Rouge, LA: Louisiana State University Press, 1988), 140–79.

5. LaFeber, W., *The American Age: United States Foreign Policy at Home and Abroad: 1750 to the Present*, 2d ed. (New York: W. W. Norton & Company, 1994): 209–10; Pérez, L. A., *Cuba under the Platt Amendment*, xvi–xvii, 29–55.

6. Pérez, L. A., *Cuba under the Platt Amendment*, 155 (quoted), 88–166; O'Brien, T. F., *The Revolutionary Mission: American Enterprise in Latin America, 1900–1945* (New York: Cambridge University Press, 1996), 205–33.

7. Porter, J. S., ed., *Moody's Manual of Investments and Security Rating Service: Foreign and American Government Securities* [hereafter *Moody's*] (New York: Moody's Investor Service, 1927), 449–51; O'Brien, T. F., *The Revolutionary Mission*, 214–33.

8. Pérez, L. A., *Cuba under the Platt Amendment*, 248–55, 249 (quoted). On "nonintervention," see Wood, B., *The Making of the Good Neighbor Policy* (New York: Columbia University Press, 1961), 13–47.

9. Sherwell, G. B., "Future Loans to Latin America," *American Bankers Association Journal* 1926, vol. 19, p. 130; Curtis to the Secretary of State, May 3, 1928, *Foreign Relations of the United States* [hereafter *FRUS*], *1928*, II: 646.

10. Hunt, J. L., *Relationship Banker: Eugene W. Stetson, Wall Street, and American Business, 1916–1959* (Macon, GA: Mercer University Press, 2009); McAvoy, M., *Sugar Baron: Manuel Rionda and the Fortunes of Pre-Castro Cuba* (Gainesville, FL: University Press of Florida, 2003), 159–231; Pérez, L. A., *Cuba Under the Platt Amendment*, 279–82; Pollitt, B. H., "The Cuban Sugar Economy in the 1930s," 100–3; Whitney, R. W., *State and Revolution in Cuba*, 58–61.

11. Chase National Bank, "Cuban Public Works Financing," undated [1935], Francis White Papers, Ferdinand Hamburger, Jr. Archives, Milton S. Eisenhower Library, Johns Hopkins University, Baltimore, MD, series IV, box 20; Chase National Bank, Foreign Department, "Cuban Government Indebtedness," Winthrop W. Aldrich Papers, Baker Library, Harvard Business School, Boston, MA, box 110; *Moody's* (New York: Moody's Investor Service, 1928), 449–51; *Moody's* (New York: Moody's Investor Service, 1930), 552–4; *Moody's* (New York: Moody's Investor Service, 1931), 580–6; Pérez, L. A., *Cuba Under the Platt Amendment*, 284 (quoted); Smith, R. F., *The United States and Cuba: Business and Diplomacy, 1917–1960* (New York: New College & University Press, 1960), 125.

12. Curtis to the Secretary of State, May 3, 1928, *FRUS, 1928*, II: 645; Judah to the Secretary of State, June 25, 1928, *FRUS, 1928*, II: 654; Guggenheim, H. F., *The United States and Cuba: A Study in International Relations* (New York: New College & University Press, 1934), 124 (quoted); Pérez, L. A., *Cuba under the Platt Amendment*, 284–5.

13. Pérez, L. A., *Cuba under the Platt Amendment*, 284–9, Whitney, R. W., *State and Revolution in Cuba*, 57.

14. Guggenheim to the Acting Secretary of State, January 29, 1930, *FRUS, 1930*, II: 687 (quoted).

15. Denny, H. N., "Cuba Working Hard to Maintain Credit," *New York Times* [hereafter *NYT*], June 14, 1931.

16. "Financial Situation of the Government," Memorandum of Conversation with Luis E. Aizcorbe, July 27, 1931, Edwin R. A. Seligman Papers, Butler Library, Columbia University, box 37; Shoup to Seligman, July 27, 1931, Seligman Papers, box 37; "Funded Debt of Cuba Is Put at $153,754,000," *NYT*, August 5, 1932.

17. Guggenheim to the Secretary of State, January 20, 1931, *FRUS, 1931*, II: 46 (quoted); Guggenheim, Memorandum, April 23, 1931, *FRUS, 1931*, II: 57–8; "Loan Strengthens Cuba's Finances," *NYT*, June 28, 1932; "$20,000,000 Cuban Credit Extended," *NYT*, July 14, 1932; "Funded Debt of Cuba Is Put at $153,754,000"; Guggenheim, H. R., *The United States and Cuba*, 128–9; Pérez, L. A., *Cuba under the Platt Amendment*, 281–2; Smith, R. F., *The United States and Cuba*, 127–33.

18. Seligman discussed his work for the League of Nations in his book, *Double Taxation and International Fiscal Cooperation* (New York: The Macmillan Co., 1928). The work of the relevant committees was published in the League of Nations, Economic and Financial Commission, *Report on Double Taxation* (Geneva: Imp. Atar, 1923); League of Nations, Committee of Technical Experts on Double Taxation and Tax Evasion, *Double Taxation and Tax Evasion* (Geneva: The League, 1927).

19. Oscar Garcia Montes to Seligman, letters of February 17, 1931, March 2, 1931, March 28, 1931, April 28, 1931, and May 14, 1931; Mario Ruiz Mesa to Seligman, letters of May 22, 1931 and May 29, 1931; Martel to Seligman, May 29, 1931 (all found in Seligman Papers, box 37); Seligman to Garcia Montes, letters of March 2, 1931 and April 6, 1931 (all found in Seligman Papers, box 38).

20. Shoup, press statement, n.d. [June 1931], Carl S. Shoup Papers, Yokohama National University Library, Cuba Series, box 2, no. 17 (quoted); Guggenheim to Seligman, June 10, 1931; Shoup to Seligman, June 11, 1931; Shoup to Seligman, July 24, 1931 (quoted) (all found in Seligman Papers, box 37). Critics closely identified the mission and its recommendations with Seligman, and faulted him for sending someone in his place. They wondered how he could make his prognostications without ever having set foot on the island. See "La Incognitade Mr. Seligman," *Informacion*, January 7, 1932; Morini, C. R., *Contra El Plan Seligman* (Havana: Cultural, S. A., 1932).

21. Shoup to Seligman, August 8, 1931 (quoted); Shoup to Seligman, August 8, 1932; Guggenheim to Seligman, January 12, 1932 (all found in Seligman Papers, box 37); Seligman to Shoup, August 13, 1931, Seligman Papers, box 38 (quoted); Seligman quoted in "Seligman Outlines New Cuban Tax Code," *NYT*, February 12, 1932.

22. "To the Technical Commission for the Study of Tex Reform," n.d. [1937], Shoup Papers, Cuba Series, box 2, no. 17 (quoted); Shoup to Seligman, letters

of June 15, 1931 and June 26, 1931, Seligman Papers, box 37; Anderson,
G. E., "The Taxation Muddle in Cuba"; Seligman, E. R. A., Shoup, C. S.,
A Report on the Revenue System of Cuba (Havana: Talleres tipográficos de
Carasa y cía., s. en c., 1932), 351–6.

23. Anderson, G. E., "The Taxation Muddle in Cuba" (quoted); Seligman, E. R.
A., Shoup, C. S., *A Report on the Revenue System of Cuba*, 169 (quoted),
351–6; *Moody's, 1930*, 552–4.

24. Morgan to Seligman, January 7, 1931; Wiggin to Seligman, June 3, 1931;
Speyer to Seligman, June 3, 1931; Batcheider to Seligman, August 22, 1931;
Speyer & Co. to Seligman, August 18, 1931; Shoup to Seligman, October 9,
1931 (all found in Seligman Papers, box 37); Seligman to Shoup, August 1,
1931; Seligman to Anderson, August 14, 1931; Seligman to Speyer & Co.,
August 14, 1931; Seligman to Speyer & Co., August 20, 1931; Seligman
to Guggenheim, January 6, 1932 (all found in Seligman Papers, box 38);
Seligman, E. R. A., Shoup, C. S., *A Report on the Revenue System of Cuba*,
21–8.

25. See Jaramillo, M., *Esteban Jaramillo: Indicador de la Economia Colombiana*
(Bogotá: Taurus, 2006), 66–74, 89–128.

26. Drake, P. W., *The Money Doctor in the Andes: The Kemmerer Mission,
1923–1933* (Durham, NC: Duke University Press, 1989), 250 (quoted), 249
(quoted).

27. On the countercyclical measures introduced by Colombian finance minister
Esteban Jaramillo, see Jaramillo, E., *Esteban Jaramillo*, 208–36.

28. Drake, P. W., *The Money Doctor in the Andes*; Eichengreen, B., "House
Calls of the Money Doctor: The Kemmerer Missions to Latin America, 1917–
1931," in Drake, P. W., ed., *Money Doctors, Foreign Debts, and Economic
Reforms in Latin America from the 1890s to the Present* (Wilmington, DE:
SR Books, 1994), 110–32; Seidel, R. N., "American Reformers Abroad: The
Kemmerer Missions in South America, 1923–1931," *Journal of Economic
History* 1972, vol. 32, pp. 520–45.

29. Seligman to Shoup, June 9, 1931, Seligman Papers, box 38; Shoup to Seligman, June 19, 1931; Shoup to Seligman, July 9, 1931; Shoup to Seligman,
August 13, 1931 (all found in Seligman Papers, box 37).

30. Seligman, E. R. A., Shoup, C. S., *A Report on the Revenue System of Cuba*,
9–12, 8 (quoted), 9 (quoted), 87–93; Seligman to Garcia Montes, January
11, 1932, Seligman Papers, box 38 (quoted); Seligman to Shoup, June 24,
1931, Seligman Papers, box 38 (quoted).

31. Shoup to Seligman, August 13, 1931, Seligman Papers, box 37 (quoted).

32. Seligman, E. R. A., Shoup, C. S., *A Report on the Revenue System of Cuba*,
401 (quoted), 402 (quoted), 403 (quoted), 404–11.

33. Andres, F., "La Propiedad Urbana y Rustica Lo Que Necesita Es la Rebaja
de sus Obligaciones en un 50 por 100," *Diario de la Marina*, February 17,
1932, p. 3; Bango, R. G., "El Plan Seligman Grava al Propietario Cubano
y Beneficia al Extranjero," *Diario de la Marina*, February 18, 1932, p. 2;
Morini, C. R., "La Propiedad Cubana Sufriría un Terremoto Peor Que el de
Oriente con el Plan Fiscal de Seligman," *Diario de la Marina*, February 14,
1932, p. 1; Ortega, A. A., "Apreciaciones acerca del informe sobre el sistema

tributario de Cuba que presentó el Professor Edwin R. A. Seligman," *Boletin Oficial de la Cámara de Comercio de la República de Cuba* 1932, vol. 27, pp. 217–8; Rodriquez, M. G., "El Informe del Profesor Seligman," *Diario de la Marina*, February 14, 1932, p. 4; Rodriquez, M. G., "Las Criticas del Plan Seligman," *Cuba Importatora e Industrial* 1932, vol. 8 (quoted in translation), p. 9.

34. See "El Gobierno de Cuba Ofrecio Ayer un Almuerzo-Homenaje al Profesor Seligman," *Diario de la Marina*, February 14, 1932, p. 3; "Los Industriales Han Ofrecido un Homenaje al Profesor Seligman," *Diario de la Marina*, February 17, 1932, p. 8.

35. Shoup to Seligman, August 13, 1931, Seligman Papers, box 37; Cortiñas to Seligman, April 8, 1932, Seligman Papers, box 37 (quoted); Pérez, L. A., *Cuba under the Platt Amendment*, 289–95, 289 (quoted).

36. Adamson, M. R., "'Must We Overlook All Impairment of Our Interests?': Debating the Foreign Aid Role of the Export-Import Bank, 1934–1941," *Diplomatic History* 2005, vol. 29, pp. 600–4.

37. Adams, F. C., *Economic Diplomacy: The Export-Import Bank and American Foreign Policy, 1934–1939* (Columbia, MO: University of Missouri Press, 1976), 68–73.

38. Adamson, M. R., "Must We Overlook All Impairment of Our Interests?," 604–8.

39. "Cuba Will Default on $4,718,000 Bonds," *NYT*, December 28, 1933; Cuba in Default on $4,718,860 Debt," *NYT*, January 1, 1934; "Cuba to Suspend Debt Amortizing," *NYT*, April 11, 1934; Benjamin, J. R., "The New Deal, Cuba, and the Rise of a Global Foreign Economic Policy," 73–6.

40. Welles to Caffery, February 15, 1936, Sumner Welles Papers, Franklin D. Roosevelt Presidential Library, Hyde Park, NY, box 145.

41. Adamson, M. R., "The Failure of the Foreign Bondholders Protective Council Experiment, 1934–1940," *Business History Review* 2002, vol. 76, pp. 479–514.

42. Meeting in the Treasury Department, December 14, 1938, Henry Morgenthau, Jr., Diary, Franklin D. Roosevelt Presidential Library, Hyde Park, NY (hereafter HMD), vol. 156: 117–21; Wright to Welles, January 11, 1939, Welles Papers, box 57; Gellman, I. F., *Roosevelt and Batista: Good Neighbor Diplomacy in Cuba, 1933–1945* (Albuquerque, NM: University of New Mexico Press, 1973), 163–8.

43. Meeting in the Treasury Department, December 14, 1938, HMD 156: 117–21 (quoted); Morgenthau to Roosevelt, October 10, 1938, draft of letter, not sent, Harry Dexter White papers, Seeley G. Mudd Manuscript Library, Princeton University Library, box 1; Meeting in Morgenthau's office, October 11, 1938, HMD 145: 259–93; Morgenthau to Roosevelt, October 17, 1938, Record Group 56, Chronological File of Harry Dexter White, November 1934–April 1946, (National Archives, College Park, MD [hereafter NAII]), box 2.

44. Briggs, Memorandum of Conversation, August 29, 1938 (837.51/2151), Record Group 59, Decimal File, 1930–1939, NAII; Welles to Beaulac

October 13, 1938, *FRUS, 1938*, V: 483–5; Welles, Memorandum of Conversation, October 18, 1938, Welles Papers, box 170; Wright to Welles, January 11, 1939; Wright to Welles, January 23, 1939; Wright to Welles, January 30, 1939; Wright to Welles, March 6, 1939 (all found in Welles Papers, box 57); Meeting in the Treasury Department, December 14, 1938, HMD 156: 117–21; Wright, Memorandum of Conversation, February 25, 1939, *FRUS, 1939*, V: 522–4; Casanova y Diviño, J. M., *Presupuestos de la Nación* (Havana: Molina y cía, 1939), tables facing page 16; Magill, R., Shoup, C. S., *The Cuban Fiscal System, 1939: A Study Made at the Request of the Secretary of the Treasury* (New York: privately printed, 1939), tables on pages 3–7.

45. Brownlee, W. E., "The Shoup Mission to Japan," 243–5; Blum, J. M., *From the Morgenthau Diaries: Years of Crisis, 1928–1938* (Boston: Houghton Mifflin Company, 1959), 439–51.

46. Magill, R., Shoup, C. S., *The Cuban Fiscal System*, 7–8.

47. "Ningún Sistema Tributario Puede se Bueno si los Encargados de su Aplicación no Tienen la Debida Garantía y Establidad en sus Cargos," *Noticiero Mercantil*, December 31, 1938; "Volveran Magill y Shoup Cuando Hayan Clasificado y Preparado su Informe," *El Mundo*, January 6, 1939.

48. Magill, R., Shoup, C. S., *The Cuban Fiscal System*, 10, 15–17, 68.

49. Ibid., table 5, page 10; "Decreto No. 1," *Boletin Oficial de la Secretaria de Hacienda* 50 1940, vol. 50, pp. 30–7; "Decreto No. 3571," *Boletin Oficial de la Secretaria de Hacienda* 1940, vol. 50, pp. 254–67; "Decreto No. 67," *Boletin Oficial de la Secretaria de Hacienda* 1942, vol.52, pp. 185–95; Pérez-López, J. F., *The Economics of Cuban Sugar* (Pittsburgh, PA: University of Pittsburgh Press, 1991), table 31 on page 136.

50. Martínez Fraga to the Department of State, translation, August 29, 1940, 772; Beaulac to the Secretary of State, September 13, 1940, 762; Welles to Morgenthau, September 14, 1940, 778–9; Beaulac to the Secretary of State, September 19, 1940, 780; Hull to Morgenthau, October 4, 1940, 780–1; Welles to Morgenthau, October 10, 1940, 782–3; Welles to Martínez Fraga, December 4, 1940, with enclosure, "A Program of Economic Cooperation Between the United States and Cuba," December 3, 1940, 784–8 (all found in *FRUS, 1940*, V); George Messersmith, Memorandum, January 8, 1941, *FRUS, 1941*, VII: 127–9.

51. George Messersmith, Memorandum, January 8, 1941, 130; Hull to Messersmith, January 11, 1941, 133–4; Cortina to Messersmith, translation, April 15, 1941, 146–7; Cortina to Messersmith, translation, April 15, 1941, 148–53; Secretary of State to Jones, April 28, 1941, 155; Memorandum of Conversation, April 28, 1941, 156–7; Memorandum handed to the Cuban Ambassador, May 5, 1941, 157 (all found in *FRUS, 1941*, vol. 7); Smith, R. F., *The United States and Cuba*, 174–5.

52. Dur, P., Gilcrease, C., "U.S. Diplomacy and the Downfall of a Cuban Dictator," 256.

53. Brownlee, W. E., "The Shoup Mission to Japan," 242.

5

Mr. Shoup Goes to Washington

Carl Shoup and His Tax Advice to the U.S. Treasury

Joseph J. Thorndike

When Carl Shoup organized his tax mission to Japan in 1949, it was not his first venture into public service. Since the early 1930s, he had been almost continually employed by the U.S. Treasury Department as a consultant. Although never willing to leave academia for a permanent slot place on the New Deal payroll, Shoup was a charter member of the treasury "Sub-Brain Trust:" a group of academic experts recruited to advise the Roosevelt administration on economic matters.[1]

Although episodic and usually hidden from public view, Shoup's sojourns in the treasury – which extended throughout the pivotal years of World War II – were instrumental in shaping midcentury fiscal policy. Initially, his recommendations only met with limited success; for the first half of the 1930s, political realities made hard truths a hard sell in Washington. Over the course of a decade, however, Shoup's ideas on tax reform made their way from the margins to the center of the policy process.

Shoup's ideas – which he developed with a cohort of like-minded economists working in the treasury – guided federal policymakers through the fiscal watershed of World War II. In particular, his understanding of tax fairness bolstered efforts to transform the federal levy on personal income from a "class tax" to a "mass tax." This change, which had sweeping implications for federal finance in the postwar world, was not simply an improvised solution to exigent realities. It reflected more than ten years of careful thought within the treasury about how to improve and modernize the nation's fiscal infrastructure. Shoup was a leader in developing this agenda, and his contributions – including a series of major reports in 1934 and a briefer but influential study in 1937 – paved the way for a new and highly durable tax regime.

AN AGENDA FOR TAX REFORM

Soon after he took the reigns at U.S. Treasury Department, Secretary Henry Morgenthau recruited a team of experts to develop plans for sweeping tax reform. To lead the effort, he picked Roswell Magill, a law professor from Columbia University, and Jacob Viner, an economist from the University of Chicago. Both were distinguished experts, but neither was much of a liberal. Left-leaning commentators grumbled,[2] but Morgenthau was unrepentant. "These people have been recommended to me as being intellectually honest," he told reporters, "and that is all I have required."[3]

Viner's interest in fiscal policy – especially as an instrument of economic recovery – was deep, profound, and provocative. He was among the earliest and most influential advocates of using fiscal policy to jumpstart the economy, and he argued for innovative tax reforms that might help pull the nation from its deep economic slump.[4] Viner was not a technical tax expert, however, and he hired someone else to help him develop the treasury's nascent tax program: Carl Shoup, a young but promising economist from Columbia University.[5]

Shoup was a veteran of the Roosevelt tax policy, having served on the staff of the New York State Commission for the Revision of the Revenue Laws during Franklin D. Roosevelt's tenure as governor. Although independent, the revenue commission figured prominently in several fiery tax debates, including Roosevelt's dramatic proposal to hike state income taxes in 1931 and 1932.

Shoup was never a New Deal loyalist, however, and he was hard to characterize politically. In general terms, he supported many of Roosevelt's economic goals but he jealously guarded his reputation for evenhanded analysis, even to the point of antagonizing patrons in the administration. He was, in fact, an economist's economist – deeply engaged in the scholarly debates of his profession and disinclined to sully himself with partisan entanglements. In addition, he was enamored of his faculty position at Columbia, and although agreeing to join the treasury for a limited engagement in the summer of 1934, he declined a regular staff position.

Shoup's team at the treasury focused on four key issues: (1) administrative revision and simplification of the tax system; (2) the distribution of the tax burden; (3) the relationship between the federal, state, and local revenue systems; and (4) the use of taxation to stabilize the business cycle. This was a sweeping research agenda, but the group completed it in just three months.[6]

By and large, the treasury experts worked alone. Neither Shoup nor his colleagues relied on extensive help from congressional staff to prepare the studies, although relations with Capitol Hill were warm. The group enjoyed a particularly collegial relationship with the professional staff of the Joint Committee on Internal Revenue Taxation. Footnotes to the Viner studies, as the final set of recommendations were known, are filled with respectful but not uncritical citations to Joint Committee publications. Despite this, Morgenthau was determined to develop his own source of expertise within the treasury. Shoup and his colleagues tried to give him what he wanted, pursuing their tax studies independent of fiscal experts outside the treasury, including those in congress, other administration departments and the private sector.

The Viner Recommendations

Shoup's team delivered its final recommendations in September 1934. "We find ourselves," Shoup reported, "in substantial agreement on the use that should be made of the various taxing instruments available."[7] The reports covered enormous ground, containing volumes on everything from alcohol taxation to tobacco duties. Two topics, however, got particularly intensive consideration: individual income taxes and federal consumption taxes. In addition to this, the group explored other topics in depth, including estate taxes, business income taxes, excess profits taxes, and the use of taxation to stem inflation. Some of these issues would prove politically salient in the years to come, especially estate taxes and the taxation of business profits. The group's most important – and enduring – recommendations, however, focused on the relative merits of taxing income and consumption.

The Viner studies began with a stern warning about debt. "The situation calls for more than merely drifting with the tide of expenditure," Shoup warned in his summary memo. Debt was useful, perhaps even necessary, when used to encourage recovery but it should never become a substitute for long-term fiscal discipline. Debt shifted the fiscal burden forward, saddling future generations with the cost of current expenditures. "Viewed narrowly as a matter of tax technique, hidden taxation of this type is the worst kind of tax," Shoup wrote. The distribution of its burden was almost impossible to predict, and it tended to penalize certain sectors of the economy more than others. In general, excessive debt could lead "with disquieting swiftness" to unjust distributions of the fiscal burden.[8]

Even more important, debt had a corrosive effect on the American polity. It encouraged taxpayers to expect more for less, fostering self-indulgence and weakening "tax morale:" the willingness of people to impose taxes on themselves (through representative government) and to pay those taxes once they were in place. Once a nation got used to debt, Shoup contended, it quickly became a bad habit. Accordingly, Shoup and his colleagues were willing to accept any tax increase – even one they found objectionable for reasons of fairness or administrative practicality – if the only alternative were unrestrained debt.[9]

In fact, debt had already become a national habit, albeit through necessity. The country had been running a deficit since 1931, caught between plummeting tax revenue and rising relief expenditures.[10] The Viner team acknowledged that trying to balance the budget over the short term was unrealistic and unwise; debt financing might actually spur recovery, although fiscal austerity threatened to nip it in the bud. Along with many other officials in the Roosevelt administration, they still believed in the need for fiscal balance. Not immediately and not every year but someday, they maintained, the federal government must return to paying its bills. This strain of fiscal conservatism had a powerful appeal in the treasury, especially in the secretary's office, but it was shared by many of the department's tax experts, too.[11]

Clearly, the tenets of fiscal Keynesianism had not at that point established much of a foothold in the treasury. Although most of the department's economists believed that deficits were tolerable, and perhaps even desirable, in the depths of depression they were by no means advocates of countercyclical tax policy. In retrospect, it can be hard to fathom their innate fiscal conservatism. If they understood that tax hikes could prolong the depression, then why did they not more vigorously question the orthodoxy of balanced budgets? As economist Herbert Stein later pointed out, "there was not then in the country enough sophistication – or sophistry – to generate such questions."[12] The Viner economists, in fact, were acutely aware of their ignorance and technical limitation. They believed that the state of economic knowledge was too humble to support the creative, countercyclical use of the federal taxing power, even if it seemed theoretically appealing.

"The tax system, so the argument runs, may be employed to eliminate business cycles," Shoup observed, "or at least to lessen their severity, by penalizing 'over-saving' and encouraging consumption, by checking speculation, by favoring certain geographical or social classes at the expense of others, by encouraging business initiative, by discouraging 'unwise' business expansion, and so on." Although tempting, such tax activism was dangerous. No one understood taxes well enough to predict macroeconomic effects with any certainty. "There is a heavy burden of proof to be borne by those who would attempt to use the tax system to influence decidedly the major economic currents of the country," Shoup concluded.[13]

INDIVIDUAL INCOME TAX

The most important recommendations to emerge from the Viner studies concerned individual income tax. Shoup's team called for a broader, steeper levy on personal income, and it urged lawmakers to make better use of this fair and efficient tax. To raise additional revenue, the team recommended higher rates for every bracket, as well as a broad reduction in personal exemptions. By adding more people to the tax rolls, lower exemptions would make the income tax more productive and reliable. Lower exemptions would, in addition, foster tax awareness, "increasing the number of direct taxpayers and thereby the number of persons having a conscious interest in government."[14]

The income tax had been a salutary addition to the nation's revenue system, according to Louis Shere, author of the volume on distribution of the tax burden. "It is probably safe to conclude that before the enactment of the individual income tax law the Federal tax system was regressive, and thereafter it became progressive," he wrote. He believed that future reforms should add to this progressivity. Higher rates in the upper brackets would help, but lower exemptions were the key. Reduced exemptions would add millions of middle class taxpayers to the rolls, producing lots of new revenue. This revenue, in turn, could be used to pay for cuts in more regressive consumption taxes. When evaluating progressivity, Shere explained, it was vital to assess the combined burden of direct taxes, such as the income tax, and indirect levies, such as excise taxes on consumer goods.[15]

Historically, Democrats had been unmoved by such arguments. During the Hoover administration, Andrew Mellon had repeatedly suggested exemption cuts, both as a means to close revenue shortfalls and to help boost tax consciousness among lower income groups. Most Democrats, however, insisted that the income tax should remain narrow – a burden targeted squarely at the rich. During the revenue-buoyant 1920s, party leaders had even championed increases in the already-high exemptions. In 1924, they managed to win passage for a major exemption

hike, ignoring objections from Mellon and many Republican legislators.[16]

The depression forced Democrats to backtrack, at least partially. In
1932, Congress had lowered exemptions to help raise revenue, adding
1.7 million people to the tax rolls. As Ogden Mills, Mellon's successor
at the treasury, was quick to point out, however, that there were still
just 3.6 million taxpayers in a nation of 120 million people.[17] In early
1933, President-elect Roosevelt had briefly considered further reductions
to help shrink the deficit, and a few party stalwarts swallowed hard and
signed on for the plan but most Democrats howled in protest and so the
idea was dropped.[18]

Tax experts, such as those writing the Viner studies, were broadly sympathetic to lower exemptions, especially when combined with a rollback
in consumption taxes. As one economist noted in early 1935: "A readjust-
ment that would base our entire tax program quite definitely on the principle of ability to pay rather than on convenience and opportunism would
receive the commendation of practically every person whose opinions on
the subject of taxation I have read."[19] In 1934, the Tax Policy League sur-
veyed public finance professors at 52 of the nation's 100 largest universities, seeking their opinions on various tax policy issues. Unanimously, the
respondents endorsed a graduated income tax. By contrast, only 12 percent supported a federal sales tax. Tobacco and gasoline excises won more
support, but respondents believed that consumption taxes should remain
a secondary source of federal revenue. The economists were not asked
specifically about personal exemptions, but their overwhelming support
for income taxation implied the possibility of a broader levy. In addition, the group supported taxing "unearned" income from investments
at higher rates that "earned" income from wages and salaries.[20] Such preferential treatment was intended to benefit middle- and lower-income taxpayers, who presumably worked hard for their money. If the income tax
was paid solely by the rich, there would have been no equity argument to
justify such a preference. The earned income distinction only made sense
as part of a broader income tax. Treasury economists agreed with their
professional colleagues. In a volume written by Roy Blakey, an economist
from the University of Michigan, the Viner team proposed that the individual income tax supply 50–75 percent of total federal revenue during
prosperous years. Even during recessions, they maintained, it could still
provide 25–50 percent. As currently structured, the tax could never meet
these goals, at least not reliably.[21] In 1934 fiscal year, for example, the
individual tax supplied just 14.2 percent of total revenue expenditures.[22]

High exemptions were at the root of the problem. In a slump, the income of a rich person tends to fall faster than the income of a poor person, causing the tax base to shrink more rapidly than overall national income.[23] The early years of the Great Depression had demonstrated this effect. Critics of the income tax seized on the revenue decline, using it to justify reduction, or even repeal, of the individual income tax. A vocal minority even suggested replacing the levy with a new federal sales tax.[24]

If the income tax is to be rescued from its depression-borne inconstancy, then it must be broadened, Blakey maintained. He was not suggesting some sort of cosmetic extension of the income tax, a symbolic effort to assess small amounts against modest incomes, chiefly as a means of promoting tax awareness. Instead, Blakey sought a dramatic extension of the tax into the middle classes. A broad-based income tax could be the nation's principal, and most reliable, revenue source, he argued.

In one convoluted sentence, Blakey invoked two distinct fairness arguments to justify income tax generally and a broader tax more specifically: "It raises most of the taxes for ordinary and emergency purposes from the most prosperous businesses and the individuals who have the most ability and who profit most from the opportunities which society and governmental protection afford them."[25] The first half of this statement rests on the "ability to pay" argument for progressive taxation. Taxes, Blakey was suggesting, should take account of the differing economic circumstances of various taxpayers; those with the greatest resources should be asked to pay the most. Economists of Blakey's generation generally regarded ability to pay as the best benchmark for tax fairness. The standard was, however, notoriously problematic: it was hard to define and easy to manipulate. On a practical level, it required policymakers to make a series of arbitrary decisions about exemptions and rates. Political leaders could invoke "ability" standards to defend just about any tax reform they might choose, and experts struggled vainly to reconcile real-world tax policy with this nebulous ideal.[26]

For all its faults, ability to pay was a better standard than Blakey's second stab at defending the income tax. Raising revenue from people who "profit the most" from governmental services had once been a popular idea among economists. "Benefit" theories tried to distribute the tax burden according to the benefits that individual taxpayers received from the public sector. In the latter years of the nineteenth century, however, critics had begun to complain that such a standard was impractical; many benefits were simply impossible to measure. With the impact of most government services spread broadly and variously throughout the population, benefit was too vague to serve as a practical guide. As a result, benefit theories had given way to "ability" theories, at least among experts.[27]

In any case, Blakey remained committed to the fairness of an income tax. It was, he declared, a bulwark against the inherent injustice of a modern economy. Its adoption in 1913 had been a triumph for political and economic democracy. "The masses of people and their representatives have seen the phenomenal growth of industry, of cities, with their large corporations, trusts, incomes, and other numerous evidences of wealth," he wrote. The people would never abandon the income tax – "one for which they struggled hard and long and one which serves perhaps to mitigate rather than to exaggerate the harsh injustices of fortune and the even more irritating injustices of those who have controlled industry and government in the modern economic regime."[28]

Equity, however, was only part of Blakey's case for income taxation. In addition to this, expedience figured prominently. The levy was a fine revenue tool that was productive and resilient. In good years, it could yield large surpluses for the federal treasury. If allowed to accumulate, extra revenue might even carry the government through lean times, staving off economic turbulence by correcting for imbalances in the economy. "They may check the overextension of plant and unbalanced production that would follow unduly large profits and surpluses, and they may help to build up industrial and government insurance reserves that may steady purchasing power and decrease tax drains for relief purposes in bad times," he wrote.[29] These were attractive possibilities, especially as economists debated the possibility that business miscalculation, over-investment, and underconsumption had been root causes of the Great Depression. In addition, such thinking ran perilously close to the sort of macroeconomic regulatory taxation that the Viner economists had warned against in their general recommendations. In Blakey's case, however, it was simply too tempting a possibility to ignore.

When it came to specifics, Blakey urged that exemptions be dramatically reduced. Broadening the income tax would "lessen its narrow class, or undemocratic character;" millions of new taxpayers would join the system, diluting complaints that the levy was designed to "soak the rich." Policymakers should be bold. "It probably is not politically feasible to lower them as much as should be done," Blakey conceded, but major reductions were vital. Exemptions might reasonably be cut from $2,500 to $2,000 for married couples and heads of household. Even better, they could be slashed to $1,600. Individuals, meanwhile, should see their exemption fall from $1,000 to $800.[30] Contemporary estimates put the

mean family income for 1935 at $1,631, with 21 percent of families
making more than $2,000 annually. Blakey's suggestion, then, implied
a dramatic expansion of the income tax. In 1935, Americans filed 4.5
million returns, out of a total of more than 38.4 million households and
single individuals. Of these returns, roughly 4 million showed that some
tax was due. If rates were reduced according to Blakey's more conservative goal, it seems likely that the income tax would have doubled its
reach.[31]

Although calling for lower exemptions, Blakey suggested an increase in
rates. It was important, he said, to raise rates across the board, including
the lowest brackets. Under the Revenue Act of 1934, the "normal" income
tax was levied at 4 percent.[32] By comparison, Great Britain imposed a
normal rate of 22 percent. Blakey urged a modest move in the British
direction. The bulk of personal income, he pointed out, was found in
the middle and lower regions of the income scale. As a result, modest
rate hikes could raise enormous revenue. Each increase of 1 percent, he
predicted, would bring in roughly $50 million in depression years and
perhaps $100 million in more prosperous times. Of course, increases in
the normal rate would raise the burden on the lowest brackets, but this
was no reason to hold back. Such increases, Blakey said, "may not be
necessary in prosperous times, but, if large revenues from the income
tax are absolutely essential in times like these in order to provide for
emergency relief and also in order to avoid large general sales taxes which
are regressive, it is necessary to call on these income classes."[33]

Higher rates, of course, would be unpopular – even more so when
combined with lower exemptions – but lawmakers could not bend to the
winds of popular opinion. "This revision should be within the bounds of
political expediency but there should be no shrinking from a courageous
tax policy for the maintenance of STRONG public credit even in the face
of contemporary unpopularity," Blakey declared. "Such taxes as these
are not popular and never will be popular, but real statesmen must face
realities and, if necessary leave popular acclaim to history."[34]

CONSUMPTION TAXES

Consumption taxes were not popular with the Viner economists, and
especially not with Shoup. Whether structured as excise, sales or processing taxes, they were regressive and undesirable. They were extremely popular with legislators, however, who depended on them to raise roughly
50 percent of total revenue. Given the nation's fiscal crisis, the Viner

team had to walk a fine line. Although calling for an eventual rollback in consumption taxes, the team made room for their temporary role as emergency levies. It was a grudging concession, but one necessitated by economic and political realities.

In fiscal 1934, excise taxes provided 45.8 percent of total federal revenue. When combined with the processing tax levied under the Agricultural Adjustment Act, consumption taxes were supplying roughly half of the government's annual receipts. By contrast, individual income taxes contributed just 14.2 percent, and corporate income taxes another 12.3 percent.[35] As a result, major cuts in consumption taxes were simply not realistic, at least over the short term. They were a necessary, if distasteful, expedient.

Some consumption taxes were less distasteful than others. The best were user fees, especially automotive taxes on gasoline and related products. These were the only excises worth keeping, argued Shoup, who wrote the Viner study on excise taxes. Paid principally by drivers and roughly correlated with benefits derived from government-built roads, these taxes had some claim to fairness. Policymakers clearly agreed, and they made good use of them; in fiscal 1933, automotive taxes raised $174 million, of which $125 million came from the gasoline tax. Shoup warned policymakers to avoid temptation, as claims to fairness depended on the earmarking of associated revenue.[36]

Although defensible, user fees were a distinctly secondary source of federal revenue. Other consumption taxes, most notably excises on alcohol and tobacco, dwarfed the automotive levies. They were, in fact, pillars of the revenue system. Alcohol taxes raised $259 million in 1934 – more than twice as much as estate and gift taxes combined. Tobacco brought in even more. Raising $425 million in 1934, its revenue bested the $420 million brought in by the individual income tax.[37] This was big money and it posed a dilemma for the Viner economists. Their proposed expansion of other, more progressive taxes would not raise sufficient revenue to eliminate excise taxes. Even reducing them would be prohibitively expensive, especially in the current fiscal climate. How, then, could revenue needs be reconciled with standards of tax fairness?

Fairness clearly demanded the elimination of most consumption taxes. "On the whole," wrote Shoup, "they do not form a desirable part of a fiscal system in normal times."[38] Since World War I, most economists had endorsed cuts in excise taxation, arguing that such levies were regressive and economically inefficient. They fell heavily on the poor, although discriminating in almost random fashion among products and taxpayers.

The Great Depression had unfortunately made selective excises more important, not less. Receipts from income taxes had fallen precipitously along with the nation's economic fortunes. Many excises, by contrast, were less sensitive to economic conditions, depending on the elasticity of demand associated with the taxed product. During the depression, excise taxes had generally held up well. The growing importance of excise revenue, however, was not an automatic function of the sinking economy; it reflected a conscious decision by federal lawmakers to lean more heavily on this reliable revenue tool. The Revenue Act of 1932 had imposed a slew of new excises, at the same time as raising rates on many that already existed.[39]

Taxes on tobacco and alcohol were among the most familiar revenue tools of the American government. They had been levied in some form for most of the nation's history. The early history of the American nation placed consumption taxes front and center, from the revolutionary era through the early republic.[40] Of course, excise taxes had often played the villain in American historical dramas. They had a starring role in the Whiskey Rebellion of the 1790s.[41] George Washington's ride through the Pennsylvania frontier had silenced critics temporarily, but the taxation of alcohol, tobacco, and other consumer goods remained a subject of spirited debate for most of the nation's early history. For all the controversy surrounding excise taxes, however, they had been a fixture of American taxation since at least the Civil War. Alcohol even remained a taxed (albeit illicit) product during Prohibition. Given this familiarity – not to mention enormous productivity – the Viner economists were willing swallow hard and endorse the retention of alcohol and tobacco taxes.

Tobacco taxes were such a vital source of revenue that the Viner team devoted an entire volume to the subject. Columbia University economist Reavis Cox, who was author of the volume, did not like the tobacco taxes. They were too steep, he declared, and they discriminated among different kinds of tobacco products without rhyme or reason. Despite this, he acknowledged they were here to stay. "The fiscal situation necessitates high taxes," he conceded, "and the tobacco taxes are too reliable and too productive to be reduced at this critical juncture."[42]

Cox expended considerable effort in trying to compare the relative burden imposed by tobacco and income taxes. In general, the tobacco taxes were far too heavy. At current rates, he noted, someone smoking a pack a day would pay $21.90 annually in federal cigarette taxes. That was the same amount that a single man earning $1,568 annually would pay in income taxes; a family of four could earn $3,868 before paying that much. With contemporary estimates putting the mean family income for 1935 at $1,631, tobacco taxes were clearly regressive. Paid at the same rate by every smoker, they imposed a much higher burden on the poor than the rich.[43]

Tobacco levies might be justified as luxury taxes as smoking was a choice, however, not a biological imperative. "Life can be sustained without the use of tobacco," Cox conceded. He quickly dismissed the argument, however, pointing out that notions of "luxury" were socially determined, dependent on custom and the standard of living. Efforts to impose taxes on the basis of "luxury" status were necessarily arbitrary, unfair, and inconsistent. Moreover, if popular opinion and consumption patterns were any indication, tobacco did not seem to be much of a luxury. The inelasticity of demand for tobacco products suggested that many people considered them necessities. If tobacco taxes were intended to be sumptuary duties, it was even more offensive. Cox declared: "Why the judgment of a few that tobacco is at best a waste and at worst pernicious should be permitted to outweigh the contrary judgment of the vast majority remains a mystery."[44]

If the tobacco taxes were bad, most other excises were worse. Narrow consumption taxes were an easy refuge for lazy politicians. Without political considerations, excise taxes would be reduced to "an almost insignificant role" in the tax system, the Viner team concluded. Even during depression, when revenue was scarce and alternative taxes unproductive, excise levies were properly consigned to a supporting role. More progressive levies could achieve any legitimate economic goal currently assigned to excise taxes.[45]

In a detailed memo on "miscellaneous" taxes – a rubric the Viner team used to describe excises other than those on alcohol, tobacco, and automotive products – Shoup outlined the nation's convoluted system of consumption taxes. In general, he explained, excises could be divided into four groups. The first group of excises was levied on items consumed almost exclusively by the rich: works of art, yachts, high-priced clothing, club dues, jewelry, and such other desirable items. The second group taxed articles and services used by the middle class as well as by the wealthy, but almost never by the poor: cameras, checks, telegraph messages, phone calls, electricity, electric fans, firearms, and insurance, for instance. A third group focused on items used by a broad array of people except the very poorest of the poor, including items such as candy, meat, chewing gum, public transportation, playing cards, soft drinks, and toiletries. The last group of excises was imposed on necessities consumed by almost everyone: things such as butter, candles, coal, coffee, and cotton – all "deemed necessities at least by those who use them," Shoup noted.

In general, taxes in the first group yielded relatively little revenue. Using projections for 1935, Shoup predicted that excises on luxurious goods would increase by just under $207 million, or roughly 0.5 percent of total federal revenue. Excises on the poor and middle classes, by contrast, would bring in more than $1.8 billion. Lawmakers, Shoup concluded, were using excise taxes to reach taxpayers near the bottom of the income scale – people who were not currently earning enough to pay income taxes. In other words, excise taxes were imposed *because* they were regressive, not despite that fact.[46]

Regressivity did not necessarily mean that all excises were inherently unfair, Shoup pointed out. Some could, in fact, be defended as luxury taxes. When imposed on unnecessary or superfluous items of consumption, they were in some sense optional – people could choose to avoid them by shifting their consumption patterns away from taxed goods. The extent of their continued consumption was an indication that they had some ability, or at least willingness, to pay. "Consider the tax on admissions," Shoup suggested. "Why are admissions taxed, and not salt? Obviously, one answers, because the latter is a necessity that even the poverty-stricken must have, whereas purchase of the former is evidence, if not of luxury, at least of a well-being that forms a basis for equitable taxation."[47]

If ability to pay was the standard, Shoup complained, other taxes were better suited to the task of raising revenue fairly. "Luxury" was hard to define and impossible to administer as a standard of tax policymaking. The entire effort was haphazard, producing a set of taxes with no internal and extrinsic logic. "The 'non-necessity' concept, logically applied, would involve a much wider range of taxes than exist at present," Shoup wrote. "If radios are taxed, ask the radio manufacturers, why not household oil burners, washing machines, electric waffle irons, fans, etc., also?" Indeed, makers of taxed goods complained bitterly – and legitimately – that they were being singled out.

Consumers as well as manufacturers suffered from the piecemeal approach to excise taxation. In trying to identify and codify the items of taxation, Congress often missed its intended target. Or it hit the target, but brought down a variety of similar goods as well. One ostensible luxury tax targeted "articles made of, or ornamented, mounted or fitted with, precious metals" that sold for $3 or more. In trying to tax jewelry, however, lawmakers had inadvertently taxed most fountain pens as well.[48]

Luxury, then, was an elusive concept that was easy to grasp in general terms but hard to define with precision. Most excise taxes were implemented only loosely on the basis of the notion of luxury, if at all. Instead, lawmakers were often guided by a keen sense for political vulnerability. Industries with mediocre representation in Washington often found their goods saddled with taxes. The tax legislative process frequently degenerated into a mad scramble among manufacturers, with every business trying to shield itself from the tax system. When the going got rough, there was no "business community;" it was every industry for itself.[49]

Some excise taxes were designed to protect narrow business interests from competition. The oleomargarine tax was the most famous example. First imposed in 1886, it raised the price of margarine relative to butter. It originally taxed yellow margarine more heavily than white margarine, on the presumption that consumers might be fooled into thinking the item was, in fact, butter. Supporters defended the tax as a blow for consumer rights. It was, however, was a blight on the tax system, representing a triumph of special interests.[50]

Finally, Shoup outlined the myriad administrative problems that plagued excise taxes. Even when lawmakers managed to define items narrowly, they could not anticipate all the attendant complexities involved in trying to make the tax work. As a result, the Bureau of Internal Revenue fought an endless battle to bring order out of chaos, promulgating one regulation after another. The agency was forced to make delicate and dubious distinctions. The toiletry tax, for instance, did not apply to "permanent wave solutions," but did apply to substances producing "finger waves" or "wave sets." "Fur" taxes applied to all kinds of fur, including mink, sable, and even sheepskin (assuming, that is, that the sheepskin was dyed, and therefore more fur-like; regular sheepskin was exempt). A clock included in a car was an "automobile accessory" instead of a clock and therefore taxable at 2 percent instead of 10 percent but a clock built into a thermostat was, in fact, a clock and therefore taxable as such.

Such tortured interpretations were inevitable when trying to tax certain items and not others. Similar problems surrounded income taxation, where definitions of income were notoriously subject to interpretation. Excise duties were regressive, casting doubt on the entire enterprise, as why spend so much time trying to make an unfair tax somewhat less unfair?

General sales taxes avoided some of the problems inherent in the patchwork excise system. By taxing almost all items, they were at least consistent. To Shoup, however, that made general sales taxes even more distasteful: they were consistently unfair. "A sales tax should not be used to replace any of the tax revenue now being received by the Federal Government," Shoup concluded. "Even if revenue needs should force an increase in taxation, it would be preferable to rely first on increases in income and estate taxes, and possibly on some of the temporary excises, before levying a sales tax."[51]

Although some excises could be dubiously defended as luxury taxes, a general sales levy lacked even that fig leaf of fairness. Luxuries were hard to define but necessities were easier, and a sales tax would fall on many. Shoup evaluated several kinds of sales taxation, including a retail sales tax imposed directly on the consumer at the point of sale. He focused, however, on a manufacturer's tax. When levied at this earlier stage in the economic cycle, a sales tax involved fewer taxpayers and, consequently, fewer administrative problems. A manufacturer's sales tax, moreover, promised to raise substantial revenue. A 1 percent levy would yield between $240 million and $290 million annually.[52] In addition, its yield would be fairly reliable, Shoup predicted. "To those in search of a 'stable' tax base, the manufacturers' sales tax offers far more than either the personal or corporation income tax," he wrote.[53]

The sales tax was undesirable for any number of reasons. First, it would undermine relief efforts, forcing the government "to hand out relief payments with one hand and with the other take back part of the money through a tax on necessities." Although exemptions for food and clothing might ameliorate that problem, the tax would still be highly regressive. Second, the sales tax would be hidden from consumers; paid by manufacturers, who would then presumably pass it on in the form of higher prices, it would remain invisible to most Americans. Hidden taxes were bad taxes as they ran counter to the ideals of a democratic society, and they made people careless about the cost and functions of government.[54]

A Tepid Reception

Taken as a whole, the Viner studies provided a comprehensive, largely dispassionate assessment of the federal tax system. The memos were careful, closely reasoned documents filled with detailed analysis of highly technical issues, as befitted an arcane subject such as taxation. Despite this, the studies were animated by a lively commitment to progressive ideals. The economists recruited to the treasury proved to be strong supporters of a progressive federal tax system, and they were particularly fond of the individual income tax, a levy they regarded as the best overall tool for raising national revenue.

The Viner studies were not simply intellectual underpinning for Democratic Party dogma; although the overwhelming majority of Democrats supported the income tax, most wanted a narrow version of the levy. For the Democratic majority, the income tax was best kept steep and narrow. It was established to exact a fair contribution from the rich, serving as a counterbalance to regressive but remunerative excise taxes on consumption.

The Viner economists challenged this view. The income tax would best serve the cause of progressive taxation if it was dramatically broadened, they argued. It should tax the middle class, not just the wealthy. Although rates on the rich should remain fairly steep, they were not the place to look for additional revenue. Raising rates on wealthy taxpayers promised to raise little revenue but cause substantial economic harm. The best reform would extend the tax downward into the heart of the middle class.

This was not a popular message in Democratic circles, including the White House. President Roosevelt would soon propose a major tax bill, but this central recommendation of the Viner team was nowhere to be found in the new legislation. The Revenue Acts of 1935 and 1936 – which together form the high-water mark for New Deal legislative tax reform – owed little to the Viner recommendations. These laws, which focused on raising tax burdens for the rich and revamping the basis of corporate income taxation (with an eye toward raising tax burdens on wealthy shareholders as well), sprang from a different intellectual and bureaucratic tradition. This tradition was dominated not by economists, such as Shoup and Viner, but by New Deal lawyers, such as Herman Oliphant and Robert Jackson.[55]

SHOUP'S RETURN

Although the Viner–Shoup recommendations from 1934 lacked political traction among elected officials, they continued to influence tax experts in the Roosevelt administration. The treasury repeatedly called on Viner's economic consultants to analyze federal tax policy in both broad and narrow terms. One particularly important request came in 1937, when Roswell Magill asked Shoup to prepare a new, more concise evaluation of the federal revenue system (Magill himself had left the treasury in November 1934, just a few months after the completion of the Viner reports, but had returned to the department in January 1937). Shoup agreed, this time enlisting the aid of economist Roy Blough to help prepare the study.

In most respects, Shoup's 1937 conclusions mirror his thoughts from three years earlier. He endorsed a reduction in income tax exemptions, with the hope that broader income taxes would raise much-needed revenue at the same time as permitting a reduction in excise taxes. Indeed, for those just above the new exemptions, Shoup and Blough recommended that substantially *all* new income tax liabilities be offset by reductions in less desirable levies, including tariff duties.[56]

On the subject of rates, the authors supported modest increases in most of the middle brackets. Notably, in addition they recommended a reduction in rates for the nation's richest taxpayers. "The federal personal income tax rates are very low at the bottom and very high at the top," they observed. "They are probably higher at the top than they should be, in view of the incentives to avoidance and evasion that they create, and the consequent administrative troubles, and in view, also, of the danger of stifling the willingness to take risks."[57] By suggesting a cut in high-end rates, Shoup was again challenging the dominant ethos of New Deal taxation, at least to that point. In addition, his proposals were consistent with new political realities, as Roosevelt and his advisers began to confront a powerful revolt among conservative Democrats unhappy with New Deal tax reforms.

Old political realities, however, were still a factor in reform. Liberal and moderate Democrats had not lost their taste for soaking the rich, and Shoup recognized the political utility of high rates. "To the present writers, it seems most important to make the income tax a tax that will appeal to the community's sense of justice, even at the cost of having a higher rate scale," he and Blough concluded.[58] If the income tax was to play the central role in federal finance that they envisioned, its rate structure would have to accommodate popular – and politicized – notions of tax fairness. Politics, for Shoup, was an integral part of policymaking.

The soak-the-rich ideology was still shaping official treasury views on tax reform. At the time Shoup and Blough were finishing their report, the treasury's internal tax staff was completing another round of major tax revision studies. These reports, modeled on the Viner studies from three years earlier, echoed many of Shoup's recommendations, especially regarding a cut in exemptions. Despite this the treasury's tax staff was unwilling to embrace calls for moderation in upper brackets, instead recommending further rate hikes for the nation's richest taxpayers.[59]

After completing his 1937 study with Blough, Shoup remained a consultant to the treasury, offering Magill occasional memos on salient tax issues. In 1938, for instance, he analyzed various ways that the government might raise an additional $500 million to $1 billion in tax revenue. Echoing his earlier work, Shoup called for higher taxes on individual incomes and estate. Again, however, he declined to recommend that wealthy taxpayers be made to bear the entire additional burden. In fact, he restated his call for a reduction in upper bracket rates.

These speculations are too vague to show just where the rates might best be raised, but I think they indicate that somewhere in the middle or lower-middle brackets rather than in the upper-middle or higher brackets is the place. It might even be advisable to lower, at the same time, the very highest surtax rates.[60]

Two years later, in a memo ruminating on tax changes that might spur economic growth, Shoup again stressed the utility of high-end rate cuts. Although tax cuts directed at consumers might succeed in bolstering the economy, upper-bracket cuts aimed at investors promised even greater rewards. "The stimulation of investment by changes in the tax system requires much bolder moves and more patience than the stimulation of consumption, but the rewards are probably much greater," he concluded.[61]

Shoup's commitment to progressive taxation was not faltering in these memos from the late 1930s. He remained a steadfast opponent of most taxes on consumption, and a proponent of levies, such as the income and estate taxes, that allocated burdens according to a person's ability to pay. Shoup was dubious – as he had been for years – about politically driven efforts to soak the rich *exclusively*. In general, tax revenue was destined to rise, he believed, if only to support a large and growing federal welfare state (and later to help pay for national defense). That revenue must necessarily come from a broad cross-section of the population, not a tiny sliver of the nation's economic elite. Excessively high income tax rates – Roosevelt's favorite tool for recasting the incidence of the federal tax system – were of dubious efficacy, especially given the rising incentive for tax avoidance that accompanied any rate increase. Such policies were even more problematic given the overriding need to encourage economic recovery. Shoup never lost sight of principal aim: designing a tax system that allocated burdens fairly at the same time as allowing for investment and economic growth.

As the decade of the Great Depression gave way to war mobilization, Shoup continued to offer advice to treasury officials. The need for new revenue to support this mobilization dominated treasury tax analysis in the late 1930s and early 1940s. At the request of department officials, Shoup continued to offer his guidance, and he repeatedly made the case for broader income taxation, arguing that it was the best way to raise revenue and control the powerful inflationary forces unleashed by wartime spending. In 1941, Shoup joined two other economists, Milton Friedman and Ruth P. Mack, in a major study on the use of taxation to control inflation, including an examination of withholding techniques designed to withdraw purchasing power from consumers on a current basis (rather than waiting for end-of-year tax return filing).[62] In 1942, Shoup passed the group's conclusions along to treasury officials, who were already deeply enmeshed in developing plans for wartime taxation.[63]

In addition to this, Shoup continued to argue for tax reforms that would encourage investment. Although many economists were calling for tax reforms designed to boost consumption, Shoup emphasized the importance of increased business investment. "The stimulation of investment by changes in the tax system requires much bolder moves and more patience than the stimulation of consumption," he acknowledged, "but the rewards are probably much greater."[64] Although the economic boost for consumption was more or less limited by the amount of money left in the hands of consumers (through low-end tax cuts, for instance), the upside of investment incentives was unlimited. "While investment may be more difficult to stimulate than consumption by changes in the tax system, it does not face the same narrow limits of expansion that consumption does," he wrote. "The increase in consumption varies (directly) within limits set by the amount of money released to the consumer; the increase in investments has no such limit."[65] As a result, Shoup continued to extol the growth potential of "a drastic decrease in the upper brackets of the income tax;" although expensive in the short-term, such cuts might prove enormously valuable in the medium to long run.[66]

Throughout the early 1940s, Shoup continued advising the treasury, even though he resisted repeated requests that he join the department full time. His friend and frequent collaborator, Blough, was by then heading the treasury tax staff, and the two maintained a running correspondence on various tax issues.[67] In early 1941, for instance, Blough asked Shoup for his thoughts on various means of raising an additional $1 billion in federal revenue. In addition, he sought Shoup's advice on excess profits taxation, a red-hot issue in the run-up to war, and a subject to which Shoup was already devoting considerable attention.[68] Blough credited

Shoup with improving the profits legislation then pending in Congress (and soon to become law).[69] "The bill still contains some of the features which you particularly disliked but, I think, has been substantially improved," he wrote in February 1941. "In my opinion your trip to Washington last week has had very useful results."[70]

Later that year, Shoup offered advice to Morgenthau on how to present anti-inflation tax proposals to the public, counseling the treasury secretary to keep his explanations simple.[71] During the remaining years of the war, he returned to the treasury for extended periods, helping direct research on a numerous tax issues. As policymakers set about their much-noted transformation of the income tax from a "class tax" to a "mass tax" – chiefly through the adoption of lower exemptions, much as Shoup had long counseled – he was offering near-constant advice to his past and future colleagues, especially Blough.

CONCLUSION

During his long affiliation with the New Deal Treasury, Shoup played a central role in crafting midcentury tax reforms. His leadership of the 1934 Viner studies did not bear immediate fruit; suggestions for a broad-based income tax remained anathema in Democratic circles until at least the late 1930s. Political events eventually caught up with Shoup's economic analysis, however, and by the early 1940s his plans for middle class income taxes were starting to find a real audience.

Shoup's intellectual work on behalf of fundamental tax reform – and comprehensive income taxation, in particular – had a subtle but enduring influence. After its first official articulation in the Viner studies, the work became a touchstone for New Deal tax experts. Later work by Shoup and treasury staff economists allowed for the gradual refinement and elaboration of these ideas. By the time World War II came along and recast the terms of fiscal debate, Shoup's ideas offered a practical blueprint for wholesale reform.

Wartime tax policy deviated frequently from the careful design laid out by Shoup and his colleagues, and tax politics were different during the war, but not absent. Despite this, the treasury plans for broader income taxation helped guide the wartime debate, strengthening the hand of those who opposed using a general sales tax to finance the war. Indeed, the most enduring legacy of Shoup's treasury service may well have been the defeat of the sales tax and the adoption of a mass income tax: both key elements in the Shoupian fiscal framework.

Notes

1. Anon, "Treasury Orders Bank, Tax Studies," *New York Times*, June 27, 1934, pp. 19.
2. Ward, P. W., "Henry Morgenthau and His Friends," *Nation*, August 14, 1935, pp. 182.
3. Ibid.; Waltman, F., Jr., "14 Are Named To Check All U.S. Finances," *Washington Post*, June 27, 1934.
4. For more on Viner and his views of fiscal policy, see Thorndike, J. T., "The Fiscal Revolution and Taxation: The Rise of Compensatory Taxation, 1929–1938," *Law and Contemporary Problems* 2010, vol. 73 (1), pp. 95–122.
5. "Treasury Orders Bank, Tax Studies," p. 19; Blum, J. M., *From the Morgenthau Diaries*, Vol. 1 (Boston: Houghton Mifflin, 1959–1969) 298; U.S. Department of the Treasury, "Press Service No. 2–7," June 24, 1934, Box 62; Tax Reform Programs and Studies; Records of the Office of Tax Analysis/Division of Tax Research; General Records of the Department of the Treasury, Record Group 56; National Archives, College Park, MD.
6. Waltman, F., Jr., "14 Are Named To Check All U.S. Finances"; U.S. Treasury, "Press Service No. 2–7"; Carl Shoup, September 16, 1996.
7. Shoup, C. S., "The Federal Revenue System: Forward and Summary of Recommendations," September 20, 1934, Records of the Office of Tax Analysis; Box 62; Tax Reform Programs and Studies; Records of the Office of Tax Analysis/Division of Tax Research; General Records of the Department of the Treasury, Record Group 56; National Archives, College Park, MD; full text reproduction available at http://taxhistory.tax.org/Civilization/Documents/Surveys/hst23735/23735-1.htm.
8. Ibid.
9. Ibid.
10. U.S. Office of Management and Budget, *Historical Tables, Budget of the United States Government for Fiscal Year 2005* (Washington, DC: Executive Office of the President Office of Management and Budget, 2004), 21, available at: http://www.whitehouse.gov/sites/default/files/omb/budget/fy2005/pdf/hist.pdf, accessed October 8, 2012.
11. On fiscal conservatism in the Roosevelt administration, see Zelizer, J. E., "The Forgotten Legacy of the New Deal: Fiscal Conservatism and the Roosevelt Administration, 1933–1938," *Presidential Studies Quarterly* 2000, vol. 30 (2), pp. 331–58.
12. Herbert Stein, *Presidential Economics: The Making of Economic Policy from Roosevelt to Clinton* (Washington, DC: American Enterprise Institute for Public Policy Research, 1994), 31.
13. Shoup, C. S., "The Federal Revenue System: Forward and Summary of Recommendations."
14. Ibid.
15. Louis Shere, The Distribution of Federal Taxes, 1934, Box 62; Tax Reform Programs and Studies; Records of the Office of Tax Analysis/Division of Tax Research; General Records of the Department of the Treasury, Record Group 56; National Archives, College Park, MD.

16. Exemptions increased from $1,000 to $1,500 for individuals and from $2,500 to $3,500 for married couples. See U.S. Department of the Treasury Internal Revenue Service, Wilson, R. A., "Personal Exemptions and Individual Income Tax Rates, 1913–2002," *Statistics of Income Bulletin* Spring 2002, pp. 216–25. Available at: http://www.irs.gov/pub/irs-soi/02inpetr.pdf, accessed October 8, 2012.

17. U.S. Treasury, *Annual Report of the Secretary for 1932* (Washington, DC: Government Printing Office), 29.

18. Mark Leff has argued that certain influential Democrats were attracted to the notion of a broader income tax, making the idea politically viable. See Leff, M. H., *The Limits of Symbolic Reform: The New Deal and Taxation, 1933–1939* (New York and Cambridge [UK]: Cambridge University Press, 1984), 102–19.

19. Gerstenberg, C. W., "Exemptions Under the Income Tax," *Bulletin of the National Tax Association* 1935, vol. 20 (6), pp. 176.

20. Slemrod, J. B., "Professional Opinions About Tax Policy: 1994 and 1934," *National Tax Journal* 1995, vol. 48 (1), pp. 121–47.

21. Blakey, R. G., Federal Revenue System: Federal Income Tax (Certain Phases), September 20, 1934, Tax Reform Programs and Studies; Records of the Office of Tax Analysis/Division of Tax Research; General Records of the Department of the Treasury, Record Group 56; National Archives and records Administration, College Park, MD. Full text reproduction available at http://www.taxhistory.org/Civilization/Documents/Surveys/hst23737/23737-1.htm

22. U.S. Office of Management and Budget, *Historical Tables, Budget of the U.S. Government*, Fiscal Year 2011 (Washington: U.S. Government Printing Office, 2010), 32.

23. Blakey, R. G., Federal Revenue System: Federal Income Tax (Certain Phases).

24. Ibid.

25. Ibid.

26. Buehler, A. G., "The Principles of Expediency and Justice in Taxation," *Bulletin of the National Tax Association* 1936, vol. 21 (5), pp. 131.

27. For an influential critique of benefit theories, and a defense of ability standards, see Seligman, E. R. A., "Progressive Taxation in Theory and Practice," *Publications of the American Economic Association* 1894, vol. 9 (1–2), pp. 7-222. In addition, see Buehler, A. G., "The Principles of Expediency and Justice in Taxation," 131.

28. Blakey, "Federal Revenue System: Federal Income Tax (Certain Phases)."

29. Ibid.

30. Ibid.

31. Income estimates for the years before World War II are notoriously unreliable, but these numbers are drawn from the best source available: National Resources Committee, *Family Expenditures in the United States* (Washington, DC: Government Printing Office, 1941). See also ibid. For data on the number of returns filed, see 1998 IRS Data Book, September 2000 and IRS Statistics of Income Bulletin, Fall 2002. For information on the number of households and individuals, see U.S. Dept. of Commerce, Bureau of the

Census, Historical Statistics of the United States: Colonial Times to 1970 (Washington, DC: GPO, 1975), 299; George Thomas Kurian, Datapedia of the United States, 1790–2000: American Year by Year (Latham, MD: Bernan Press, 1994). On the number of returns showing tax due, see Gerstenberg, "Exemptions Under the Income Tax."

32. The normal rate applied to all income above the exemption level. In addition, many well-to-do taxpayers also paid a surtax according to a steeper, progressive rate schedule.

33. Blakey, R. G., "Federal Revenue System: Federal Income Tax (Certain Phases)."

34. Blakey, R. G., "Federal Revenue System: Federal Income Tax (Certain Phases)," emphasis in the original.

35. U.S. Office of Management and Budget, *Historical Tables, Budget of the United States Government for Fiscal Year* 2005, 31.

36. Shoup, C. S., "The Federal Revenue System: Forward and Summary of Recommendations."

37. Wallis, J. J., "Federal government internal tax revenue, by source: 1863–1940." Table Ea594-608 in Historical Statistics of the United States, Earliest Times to the Present: Millennial Edition, edited by Susan B. Carter, Scott Sigmund Gartner, Michael R. Haines, Alan L. Olmstead, Richard Sutch, and Gavin Wright. New York: Cambridge University Press, 2006. http://dx.doi.org.proxy.its.virginia.edu/10.1017/ISBN-9780511132971. Ea584-678.

38. Shoup, C. S., "The Federal Revenue System: Forward and Summary of Recommendations."

39. Lawmakers had opted for excise taxes in lieu of general sales taxation. See Schwarz, J. A., "John Nance Garner and the Sales Tax Rebellion of 1932," *Journal of Southern History* 1964, vol. 30 (2), pp. 162–80.

40. For a neoconservative critique of excise taxes, and a history of their imposition in the United States, see the various essays in Shughart, W. F., *Taxing Choice : The Predatory Politics of Fiscal Discrimination, Independent studies in political economy* (New Brunswick, NJ: Transaction Publishers, 1997).

41. See, for example, Slaughter, T. P., *The Whiskey Rebellion: Frontier Epilogue to the American Revolution* (New York: Oxford University Press, 1986).

42. Reavis Cox, The Federal Revenue System: The Tobacco Taxes, September 20, 1934, Box 62; Tax Reform Programs and Studies; Records of the Office of Tax Analysis/Division of Tax Research; General Records of the Department of the Treasury, Record Group 56; National Archives, College Park, MD.

43. Ibid.

44. Ibid., 116–17.

45. Carl Shoup, The Federal Revenue System: Manufacturers' Excise and Special Taxes, 1934, Tax Revision Studies; Tax Reform Programs and Studies; General Records of the Department of the Treasury, Record Group 56; National Archives and Records Administration at College Park, MD.

46. Ibid.

47. Ibid.

48. Carl Summer Shoup, Excise Taxes, June 1, 1934, Records of the Office of Tax Analysis, Box 1: Excise and Sales Taxes in General, General Records of the Department of the Treasury, Record Group 56; National Archives, College Park, MD.
49. Leff, M. H., *The Limits of Symbolic Reform*, 19–30.
50. Shoup, C. S., "Excise Taxes."; Shoup, C. S., "The Federal Revenue System: Manufacturers' Excise and Special Taxes."
51. Carl Shoup, The Federal Revenue System: The Sales Tax, September 20, 1934, Box 62; Tax Reform Programs and Studies; Records of the Office of Tax Analysis/Division of Tax Research; General Records of the Department of the Treasury, Record Group 56; National Archives, College Park, MD.
52. If food and clothing were exempted, as fairness almost certainly demanded, then the yield would drop to $160 million to $170 million, respectively.
53. Shoup, C. S. "The Federal Revenue System: The Sales Tax."
54. Ibid.
55. For more on the Revenue Act of 1935, see Thorndike, J. J., ""The Unfair Advantage of the Few": The New Deal Origins of "Soak the Rich" Taxation," in Martin, I. W., Mehrotra, A. K., Prasad, M., eds, *The New Fiscal Sociology: Taxation in Comparative and Historical Perspective* (Cambridge; New York: Cambridge University Press, 2009).
56. Shoup, C. S., Blough, R., "A Report on the Federal Revenue System Submitted to Undersecretary of the Treasury Roswell Magill, (September 20, 1937)" *Tax Notes - Arlington 1996*, vol. 70 (9), pp. 1071–90. http://taxhistory.org/thp/readings.nsf/cf7c9c870b600b9585256df80075b9dd/7555c9d686d69ae785256e430078dbfe?OpenDocument.
57. Ibid.
58. Ibid.
59. United States Department of the Treasury, "Tax Revision Studies: Income, Capital Stock, and Excess-Profits Taxes, 1937" *Tax Revision Studies, 1937*; *Tax Reform Programs and Studies*; Records of the Office of Tax Analysis/Division of Tax Research; General Records of the Department of the Treasury, Record Group 56; National Archives at College Park, MD.
60. Carl Shoup, Plans for Additional Revenue, 1938, Records of the Office of Tax Analysis; Box 43; Methods of Raising Additional Revenue; Records of the Office of Tax Analysis/Division of Tax Research; General Records of the Department of the Treasury, Record Group 56; National Archives, College Park, MD.
61. Carl Shoup, Effects of Taxation on National Income, 1940, Box 34; Economy in General; Records of the Office of Tax Analysis/Division of Tax Research; General Records of the Department of the Treasury, Record Group 56; National Archives, College Park, MD.
62. Shoup, C. S., Friedman, M., Mack, R. P., *Taxing to Prevent Inflation: Techniques for Estimating Revenue Requirements* (New York: Columbia University Press, 1943).
63. See Brownlee, W. E., "The Shoup Mission to Japan: Two Political Economies Intersect," in Martin, I., Mehrotra, A., Prasad, M., *The New Fiscal Sociology:*

Taxation in Comparative and Historical Perspective (Cambridge: Cambridge University Press, 2009), 245–6.

64. Carl Shoup, Effects of Taxation on National Income, 1940, Box 34; Economy in General; Records of the Office of Tax Analysis/Division of Tax Research; General Records of the Department of the Treasury, Record Group 56; National Archives, College Park, MD, full text reproduction available at http://taxhistory.tax.org/Civilization/Documents/Fiscal/HST29013/hst29013(a).htm.

65. Ibid.

66. Ibid.

67. I am indebted to Elliot Brownlee for his generous sharing of unpublished research on the Shoup–Blough correspondence.

68. See, for example, Shoup, C. S., "The Taxation of Excess Profits I," *Political Science Quarterly* 1940, vol. 55 (4), pp. 535–555; Shoup, C. S., "The Taxation of Excess Profits II," *Political Science Quarterly* 1941, vol. 56 (1), pp. 84–106; Shoup, C. S., "The Taxation of Excess Profits III," *Political Science Quarterly* 1941, vol., 56 (2), pp. 226–249; Shoup, C. S., "The Concept of Excess Profits under the Revenue Acts of 1940–42," *Law and Contemporary Problems* 1943, vol. 10 (1), pp. 28–42.

69. On excess profits laws passed in 1940 and 1941, see Bank, S. A., Stark, K. J., Thorndike, J. J., *War and taxes* (Washington, DC: Urban Institute Press, 2008), 87–91.

70. Roy Blough to Carl Shoup, February 26, 1941, Papers of Carl Shoup, Yokohama National University.

71. Carl Shoup to Henry Morgenthau, Jr., November 4, 1941, Papers of Carl Shoup, Yokohama National University.

PART TWO

SHOUP IN JAPAN: THE ENCOUNTER

Introduction to Part Two

Part Two of this volume examines the encounter between the Shoup mission and Japanese society. The chapters that follow examine the conditions within Japan – intellectual, political, and economic – that shaped both the framing of the *Report on Japanese Taxation* (1949) and the reception of its recommendations.[1] These chapters also consider the role of the changing objectives of the American occupation and the related disagreements within the occupation over tax reform and its objectives of social democratization, recovery from war, and economic development.

The recommendations for tax reform that emerged from the transnational encounter encompassed a broad range of reforms across the entire spectrum of tax instruments and levels of government. At the heart of the recommendations was an effort to place a greater emphasis within the Japanese tax system on horizontal equity – "equal treatment of those equally circumstanced," as Shoup defined it two decades later.[2] The base-broadening would, the mission's members believed, increase public trust in the fairness of the tax system, taxpayer compliance, and, in turn, revenue capacity. At the same time, Shoup and his colleagues proposed reducing the marginal rates of personal income taxation, including a cut of the top rate from 85 percent to 55 percent. To encourage compliance with the personal income tax by small and medium-sized businesses, Shoup recommended limiting the deduction of depreciation only to those unincorporated nonfarm business filers who maintained good records. Such filers would submit special returns (the "blue return" system) and would be reassessed only after examination of their books. The mission also recommended two new national taxes: (1) a net worth tax to offset partially the regressive effects of the rate cuts, and (2) an accessions tax, which would replace all estate and gift taxes with a tax on the total of gifts or bequests received over a beneficiary's lifetime. In the realm of corporate taxation, the mission proposed a variety of changes. The most important was a revaluation of assets to take account of wartime and postwar inflation. The intent was to allow corporations to build up depreciation reserves and avoid paying huge capital gains taxes. In addition, the mission recommended reducing the normal rate of corporate income taxation to 35 percent, taking some modest steps toward integrating personal and corporate income taxation (including reduction of the taxation of dividends under the personal income tax), and adopting a modest undistributed profits tax to encourage payment of dividends. In addition, the mission proposed to repeal excess-profits taxation and an unpopular transactions tax that the Japanese government had recently adopted.[3]

The most ambitious of the Shoup proposals for fiscal reform were those that called for the reorganization of public finance at the local level. Shoup recommended creating a Local Finance Commission that would have considerable powers, including determining central government grants, extending emergency taxing authority to localities, and adjusting property tax rates across localities. In addition, Shoup recommended the transformation of local taxation. Under the Shoup program, all localities would move away from dependence on funding from the central government and develop their own revenue sources. Local governments would rely increasingly on the real estate tax, which would be decided on the basis of capital value, including the new valuations on business assets. Prefectures would rely primarily on an existing local tax on business income. This tax, called the "enterprise tax," would be transformed into a value-added tax (VAT).[4]

The chapters in Part Two develop the history of the transnational encounter surrounding the adoption and transformation of these recommendations. In Chapter 6, Yasunori Fukagai explores the history of the systematic economic analysis of taxation in Japan prior to the arrival of the Shoup mission in 1949. Fukagai assesses, in particular, the influence of both European and American political economists on Japanese intellectuals after the beginning of the Meiji era. He discusses the extent of the influence in Japan of the leading American political economists of the late nineteenth and early twentieth centuries, especially Richard T. Ely and Edwin R. A. Seligman. Seligman's ideas, as developed by Robert Murray Haig and Carl Shoup, were quite familiar to scholars of public finance in Japan. In the process, Fukagai considers the relative importance on

Japanese thought and tax practices of the German historicists (a point traditionally emphasized by historians of economic thought in Japan), the American political economists, and innovative Japanese economists. In the process, he locates Japanese tax experts within the international exchange of ideas that intensified during the late nineteenth century, and demonstrates that by the time of Shoup's arrival in Japan, those experts had acquired a familiarity with political economists in Europe and the United States, and had already adapted their ideas to social conditions in Japan.

Chapter 7, by Professors Laura Hein and Mark Metzler, takes up the history of the tax community and the policy environment in Japan during the decades of the 1940s and 1950s. Hein and Metzler identify and analyze the competing strands of economic thought and development strategies within this community and show how these strands shaped debates over taxation during the period of the Shoup mission. At the same time, they explore the overlapping missions of Joseph Dodge and Carl Shoup. Hein and Metzler emphasize significant differences in their approaches to financial reform in Japan, and show how the alliances that Dodge and Shoup formed in Japan diverged. The authors highlight the close but tangled relationship between Dodge and Finance Minister Ikeda Hayato, and Shoup's friendship with Tsuru Shigeto and other economists who were often critical of the financial policies of Prime Minister Yoshida Shigeru's government. Hein and Metzler argue that in Japan the Shoup mission played only a marginal role in what was an ongoing policy conversation in that nation – a conversation that had its roots in the period prior to the Pacific War. In the process, they point to the resilience and vitality of the Japanese policy community and suggest that its own interests shaped the outcome of the Shoup mission.

The next two chapters in this part, "Shoup and the Japan Mission: Organizing for Investigation" and "Shoup in the 'Social Laboratory,'" by W. Elliot Brownlee and Eisaku Ide, discuss how Shoup's mission addressed the challenge of investigating and understanding fiscal and economic conditions in Japan. Chapters 8 and 9 explain how and why General Douglas MacArthur selected Shoup for the tax mission to Japan; how Shoup, in turn, assembled his team; and how Shoup conducted his investigation during his first visit to Japan. Brownlee and Ide detail how Shoup – even before the arrival of the mission in Japan – sought to build bridges with the community of tax experts in Japan. Shoup's organizational work for the mission to Japan and his conduct within Japan demonstrated that Shoup had drawn effectively on his experiences in France, Cuba, and Washington D.C. Chapter 10, "Tax Reform and the American Occupation of Japan: Who Killed Shoup?," shifts to the analysis of the successes and failures of the Shoup mission during the occupation and its immediate aftermath.

In this chapter, Ryo Muramatsu and Brownlee undertake a close analysis of the implementation in 1950, and then the almost immediate roll-back, of a central element of the Shoup recommendations – the taxation of interest income and capital gains at the same rate as regular income. This was a key component of the base-broadening reforms that Shoup promoted to establish horizontal equity and thereby win the trust of the Japanese public for income taxation. The authors examine the contests within both the Japanese government and the American occupation, and the forces that led to its ultimate defeat. This chapter pays particular attention to the role of the conflicting strategy, embraced by both the Japanese government and Joseph Dodge, to accelerate private capital investment through a set of special incentives for the mobilization of savings within the banking system. In what was a crucial defeat for Shoup, Muramatsu and Brownlee see a victory for the capital-formation strategy that the Japanese government had taken up after the Meiji restoration, and that Dodge had favored as well. In part because of Dodge's support, the Japanese government was able to return to the strategy even before the end of the American occupation. Thus, Muramatsu and Brownlee emphasize the strength of hostility both within the Japanese government and business interests and within elements of the American occupation. The authors suggest that the conflicts inside the American occupation over tax policy paralleled similar conflicts over tax policy within the United States at home, and produced similar failures with regard to the adoption of comprehensive income taxation.

Elsewhere, Brownlee has emphasized the central role of Dodge in the failures of the comprehensive program of reform that Shoup and his colleagues had recommended.[5] In this article, Brownlee identified a major fracture within the occupation – the conflict between the democratizing and base-broadening program of Shoup, who received vigorous support from General MacArthur until the Korean War, and the corporatist approach of Dodge. Brownlee found that both Shoup and Dodge sought some of the same economic goals – the economic recovery of Japan, the integration of Japan within the postwar trading world, the expansion of Japanese production in new export industries, and price stabilization. But they sharply disagreed over the best policies by which to pursue those goals and over the meaning of economic recovery. Shoup believed, from

a Keynesian perspective, that Dodge's policies were excessively deflationary. Shoup also attached more importance to a robust public sector.
Under his commission from Douglas MacArthur, Shoup placed far more
emphasis on the social goal of democratization. Shoup skillfully used
his standing with both Harold Moss and MacArthur to advance his tax
reform agenda, but on virtually every one of their disagreements Dodge
ultimately prevailed.

In 1950, the Korean War and increasing pressure for a separate peace
treaty with Japan diverted MacArthur from tax reform. Consequently,
Dodge was able to succeed in preventing Shoup from extending his recommendations into the expenditure side of the budget and thereby linking
taxing and spending in ways that might have built popular support for
both a larger government and a more robust tax system. In addition
to this, Dodge deliberately failed to use his influence over the Japanese
government to bargain for the adoption of local tax reform and base-
broadening reform.

This volume does not deal in a comprehensive way with the successes
and failures in enacting the Shoup recommendations during the occupation. The chapters in Part Two, however, provide enough evidence
to construct a preliminary overview of the reasons for the outcomes in
1950–1. Also, the chapters in Part Three go on to examine the long-term
fate of some reforms – those in the areas of local taxation, corporate
taxation, and administrative reform – that enjoyed some initial success
during the occupation.

For those recommendations the Japanese government either failed to
enact or reversed early on (sometimes even during the occupation itself),
the chapters in this section find some truth to the suggestion, which some
contemporary Japanese critics advanced, that Shoup and his colleagues
were too far removed from Japanese reality and had relied too heavily
on a theoretical model of taxation. For example, Shoup may well have
underestimated the strength of support inside and outside the government for Japan's capital-formation strategy. In addition, he may have
underestimated the resistance of the Japanese public, and Japan's government, to the new, experimental taxes, especially a VAT, which the
mission had recommended as an independent revenue source for prefectures. The Japanese government inserted a VAT in the tax code in 1950
but then failed to implement it. In recommending a VAT, the mission had
seemingly ignored earlier public hostility to another regressive consumption tax (the transactions tax). Moreover, the mission had not recognized

the time that the Japanese government would require to work through a wide variety of technical problems. The mission itself had in fact only just begun to understand the complexities inherent in a VAT.

The mission's members may have relied too heavily on ideal tax theory in certain areas of tax policy, but in other areas it attempted to apply tax principles in a way that respected historical and social realities and took seriously the opinions of the Japanese government, particularly the tax specialists within the Ministry of Finance (MOF) and Japanese economists. In making some of their recommendations, such as the revaluation of corporate assets, Shoup and his colleagues accepted departures from the Haig-Simons ideals and demonstrated clear respect for the opinions of Japanese experts. Shoup found significant support from representatives of local governments, some Socialist politicians, and Japanese economists for some of the mission's theoretically driven reforms of local finance. In addition, before emphasizing the view that the mission ran roughshod over Japanese institutional reality and history, we ought to take into account the significant array of contingencies that worked against Shoup's success. The timing of the consideration of the Shoup recommendations was unlucky, coming after the support for MacArthur's democratization program had waned within both Japan and the U.S. government, after support in Washington had grown for the conservative program of the Yoshida administration, and after the Japanese public had come to blame the occupation for a variety of significant economic problems. In addition, powerful members of the leadership of the occupation, especially Dodge, and the occupation staff (including technicians in both the Internal Revenue and Finance Divisions of the Supreme Commander for the Allied Powers) opposed and undermined key reforms. In short, the vagaries of historical contingency worked against the mission.

Notes

1. *Report on Japanese Taxation by the Shoup Mission* (Tokyo: Supreme Commander for the Allied Powers, 1949).
2. Shoup, C. S., *Public Finance* (New York: Aldine, 1969), 23.
3. *Report on Japanese Taxation by the Shoup Mission* (Tokyo: Supreme Commander for the Allied Powers, 1949), Volume I, 51–5, 83, 105–12; and Volume II, 123–31; 165–7; 224.
4. C. S. Shoup, to SCAP, August 12, 1949, enclosed in Radiogram, SCAP to Vorhees, "Taxation Progress Report," August 12, 1949, Box 6369, file folder: unmarked, RG 331, National Archives and Record Administration.

5. Brownlee, W. E., "Shoup vs. Dodge: Conflict over Tax Reform in Japan, 1947–1951," *Keio Economic Studies* 2011, vol. 47, pp. 91–122. This essay was originally presented in December 2009 as a paper at the Political Economy of Taxation in Japan and the United States: A Symposium on the Occasion of the 60th Anniversary of the 1949 Mission of Carl S. Shoup in Japan, at Keio University and Yokohama National University.

6

Political Languages of Land and Taxation

European and American Influences on Japan, 1880s to 1920s

Yasunori Fukagai

INTRODUCTION

When the mission of Carl S. Shoup arrived in Japan in 1949, the Japanese framework of taxation had already developed within a tradition dating from the land tax reform in 1872. In a long history under a feudal system, provincial domains had collected taxes mostly in the forms of the rice tribute and compulsory labor. During the 1870s, the newly established Meiji Government reformed the land tax paid in cash at a uniform nationwide rate. This meant that the financial base for that period consisted mainly of land taxation.[1] Following this, the Meiji Government promoted a new scheme of taxation by combining the land tax with other taxes, including the income tax established in 1887. Even during the early 1890s, however, the land tax share of national revenues remained at more than half. Around the time of the Chinese-Japanese war in the mid-1890s, Japanese public finance gradually diversified because of expenditures. The Japanese government turned to a combination of direct and indirect taxation and increasing public debt. The debt grew as a consequence of the warfare that culminated in World War II, leading to the final stage of the tax reform in 1940.

Throughout the period until the end of WWII, some important parts of national revenue were still supported by the land tax. The condition of national revenue was therefore tightly linked to the relationship between landlords, including absentee owners and the peasantry.[2] In the liberal reform of the post-WWII era, the traditional land tax was abolished through the land reform scheme of 1946, transforming peasants into farmers who owned their own land. This ending of the traditional landlord-peasantry relationship produced a radical change in the basis of national finance, and this provided an important context for the mission of Shoup and his colleagues in 1949.

In its beginning phase, the Meiji Government invited *oyatoi gaikokujin*, that is, intellectuals and engineers from the West, to Japan. In the decades between the late 1860s and mid-1880s, these foreigners supplied ideas, culture, and practical knowledge to Japanese public sectors and to academics in various dimensions. Japanese members learned Western ideas via variety of methods, including importing volumes from the West and sending ambitious youths abroad. Concerning taxation, the idea of the land tax reform in 1872 was inspired by a volume by British author William Ellis.

In the early 1880s, some *oyatoi gaikokujin* assumed the dominant role in diffusing ideas about public finance and taxation. From the mid-1880s, however, Japanese scholars gradually started to take the core role in introducing contemporary ideas from Europe and America. By the early 1900s, some Japanese academics were ready to produce systematic descriptions of tax systems, mostly in textbook form.

By the time the Shoup mission arrived in Japan, the Japanese framework of public finance and taxation had been formulated as a blend of ideas from the West adapted to the Japanese context. The blend was composed of British and French ideas until the early 1880s; however, later on it shifted to German ideas including some bypasses. The ideas of Edwin R. A. Seligman, who was trained in Germany, had gained acceptance among Japanese academics since the 1910s, so Shoup encountered familiar ideas when he reached Japan in 1949.

After reviewing how the Western idea of finance and taxation entered into Japan up to the 1890s, this chapter focuses on the variety of American ideas around the turn of the century and their influence on Japan. In addition, it discusses the appearance of the Japanese discussion of taxation during the first three decades of the twentieth century.

THE FORMATION OF THE IDEA OF TAXATION IN MODERN JAPAN: LATE 1860s TO 1880s

Japan Met with the West: Transition of the Exemplar

For more than two centuries, during the closed system of Japanese society, transmission via the Dutch was the only route to receive ideas from the West. After the arrival of the American navy in Japan in 1853, which forced Japan to open its closed system, many Japanese intellectuals utilized their knowledge of the Dutch language to grasp the other languages and culture of the West. In this way, from the late 1860s many volumes – especially those by English and French authors – were rapidly translated into Japanese.

Since the beginning of the Meiji regime, Japanese society had accepted the style of the West on various levels. Japan made a transition in exemplars from Britain and France to Germany beginning in the early 1880s. The civil law code and the commercial law in Japan were formulated along the lines of the Napoleonic civil laws. The popular economic journalism in that decade advocated free trade, partly imitating the Manchester school. Modern political ideas, both British ideas represented by John Stuart Mill and French ones represented by Jean-Jacques Rousseau, were translated and introduced no later than the early 1880s.[3] The exemplar for Japan, however, dramatically shifted especially after the coup d'état in 1881. The German Union became regarded as a good example of how to accomplish national unity. In imitating the German style during the 1880s, Japan enacted the Constitution of the Empire of Japan and established the Imperial Parliament in 1890.[4] Academically, many Japanese youth who dared to take the chance to study abroad chose to go Germany beginning in the mid-1880s. The Shakai Seisaku Gakkai (the Society for the Study Social Policy) was established in 1897, aspiring to become the equivalent to the German Sozialpolitik association.[5]

During the 1870s to 1890s, the newly established Meiji Government gradually formulated the financial basis of the state. The land tax reform in 1872 provided the nationwide scheme of taxation under a uniform rate. The rate of 3 percent in the beginning was slightly higher than that of the average in the Edo period and was too heavy a burden for the peasant, so many political controversies and riots occurred.[6] The rate of land tax was reduced to 2.5 percent in 1876. Until the 1880s, the land tax and the tax on alcohol accounted for most of the national revenue. In accordance with the increasing necessity of annual expenditure, especially for the navy, the government adopted the income tax in 1887. Under this tax, Japanese citizens with annual incomes of 300 yen and more had the obligation to pay income taxes. The law declared that all of the incomes from family members should be summed up under the head of family (*koshu*), who was defined as the person responsible for paying the income tax.

The Key Ideas of Public Finance and Taxation Entered into Japan from the West

Following the collapse of the ancient regime of Tokugawa in 1867, the newly launched regime of the Meiji Government attempted to set up a political and economic system that imitated that of the West. The earliest translation of economic literature was the small British volume, Ellis's *Outlines of Social Economy* (1846), which was retranslated from a Dutch translation into Japanese by Kanda Takahira as *Keizai-Shogaku* in 1867.[7] Owing to this understanding, Kanda wrote *Denso Kaikaku Kengi (Proposal of Land Tax Reform)* in 1870.[8]

Since the seventeenth century, under the Tokugawa regime, local finance had mostly been managed in a divided fashion by the local state (*Han*) under the general inspection of the Edo Shogunate (central commanding government). During the peaceful regime of Tokugawa, many intellectuals of the school of Confucianism provided a variety of ideas for managing the local states.[9] For the newly formed Meiji regime, the major financial task was to provide nationwide uniformity as well as to generate the necessary amount of national revenue. Following the proposal by Kanda, the Meiji Government promoted the scheme of land tax reform in 1872, and enacted it in 1873.

For the purposes of high learning, by the late 1860s *Elements of Political Economy* by Francis Wayland, an American author, was already being utilized as a textbook at Keio Gijuku.[10] Economic journalism began to develop in the mid-1870s and the most influential organ became *Tokyo Keizai Zasshi (Economic Journal of Tokyo)*, directed by Taguchi Ukichi, which favored the line of the Manchester school. Some of the major classical texts in political economy were introduced during the same period. The first Japanese translation of John Stuart Mill's *Principles of Political Economy* (1848), by Hayashi Tadasu and Suzuki Shigetaka, appeared between 1875 and 1885 in twenty-nine subvolumes.

Some portions of Mill's *Principles* relative to finance and taxation were translated into Japanese in two other publications around 1880: *Shuzei-Yoron (Elements of Collecting Taxation)* by Waku Masatatsu (1879) and *Kanmin Keizai-Ron (The Inquiry on the Public and Private Economy)* by Watanabe Tsunekichi (three volumes published in 1879–1880).[11]

During the same period, portions of Paul Leroy-Beaulieu's *Traité de la science des finances* (two volumes published in 1877) on tariff, local taxation, and paper money were translated into Japanese under the title of *Zaisei-Ron (Treatise of Public Finance,* 1880). The translator was

Tajiri Inajiro, who had graduated from Yale University and undertook the responsibilities of the public officer at the Ministry of Finance. Under his organization, the tax branch of the Ministry of Finance continued to translate some parts of Leroy-Beaulieu's work, including the *Sozei-Ron* (*Treatise of Taxation*), in 1883 to 1885. In addition to these lists of translations, there was a unique publication by a Japanese author that demonstrated the importance of liberty relative to the egalitarian distribution of property. It was by Harada Sen, one of the translators of Jean-Jacques Rousseau's *Social Contract*, titled *Jiyu-Teiko: Zaisan-Heikin-Ron* (*The Elements of Liberty: On the Average of Property*) in 1882.

In the early 1880s, the acceptance of ideas from the West, including public finance and taxation, entered a new stage. It was the combination of two elements: the start of the course for political economy at the University of Tokyo, which was soon transformed into the Imperial University, and the shift of the standard knowledge of this field from British and French to German and partly American sources.

In 1880, at the University of Humanity of the University of Tokyo,[12] a young American, Ernest Francisco Fenollosa, assumed the first lectureship for the fields of philosophy, sociology, politics, and political economy. Fenollosa, who was esteemed as *oyatoi gaikokujin*, was the same person who later recognized the uniqueness and excellence of Japanese traditional fine arts and assembled the huge collection that now forms the core of the Japanese collection of the Museum of Fine Arts, Boston.

The basic discipline for Fenollosa at Harvard had been philosophy, so he was obliged to catch up immediately with the ideas of various fields after his arrival in Toyko.[13] The students of the University of Humanity in that period were required either to take a course in history or literature or to take two courses from among philosophy, politics, and political economy. For the political economy class, Fenollosa utilized some volumes including the *Principles of Political Economy* by Mill. Some other staff members joined him to teach the courses on politics and political economy. Among them was another *oyatoi gaikokujin*, Karl Rathgen from Germany, who gave the lectures on public administration, administrative law, and industrial and commercial policy.[14] Tajiri Inajiro also joined as a professor and gave some lectures on the field of monetary issues.

Among the first graduates of the course on political economy, Wadagaki Kenzo was appointed to conduct research abroad, and he studied at King's College London, Cambridge, and Berlin. During his stay abroad, he became the first professor of political economy at the University of Tokyo, and because of the change in the status of the university, his position became that of a professor at Imperial University.[15] After his return, Wadagaki conveyed the German idea of *Finanzwissenschaft* to Japanese students. When the *Kokka-Gakkai Zasshi* (*Journal of the Society for the Science of State*) started in 1887, Wadagaki contributed an article titled "Zaisei-Gaku Taii" (the elements of public finance) to its first volume.[16] In this article, Wadagaki emphasized the importance of German ideas (especially those of Wagner and von Stein), and conveyed the essence of these ideas by relying heavily on the writing of Luigi Cossa.

The noteworthy issue here is that the introduction of German ideas around 1890 was mostly provided via the Italian author Cossa. Cossa took his graduate course under Lorenz von Stein and Wilhelm G. F. Roscher in Germany, and occupied the first chair of professorship for finance in Italy at the University of Pavia. Among his many publications, *Primi Elementi di Scienza delle Finanze* (1876) was translated into Japanese under the title *Zaisei-Gaku* in 1889 through the medium of an American translation.[17] Machida Chuji, who translated this work into Japanese, was a journalist who graduated from the subcourse of Imperial University and published his own book, called *Chokuzei Oyobi Kanzei* (*Direct and Indirect Tax*), in 1889. In this volume, Machida pointed out that the Japanese budget had been mostly based on the direct tax on land, and argued that Japanese taxation should be reformed by combining direct and indirect taxation for the purpose of sustaining the development of Japanese society.[18] In addition to the translation by Machida, there was another route for the transmission of the German idea via Cossa. Karl Theodor von Eheberg translated Cossa into German many times.[19] The second edition of *Grundriß* (translated by Eheberg) was retranslated into Japanese twice: as *Zaisei-Genron* (*The Principles of Public Finance*) by Terada Yukichi and Hiratsuka Sadajiro in 1891 and as *Zaisei-Gaku* (*Public Finance*) by Wadagaki Kenzo in 1902.[20] Alongside the translation of the Cossa's volumes, the American author Richard T. Ely provided a conduit for the transfer of German ideas to Japan. Some Japanese youths joined his classes at Johns Hopkins, and later on, around 1890, translated some of his works.

Meanwhile, some branches of the Meiji Government tried to grasp the new ideas being transmitted from Germany. The works by contemporary authors von Stein and Roscher were translated during the 1880s. The writings of Adolph Wagner were translated in 1890s, albeit as very limited parts of his analysis of tax administration.[21]

The highlight of the discourse over public finance and taxation in Japan before the mid-1890s was the writing of Sagane Fujiro. He was one of the individuals attending the class of Wadagaki Kenzo, and enrolled in the graduate program of Imperial University. Until 1890, most of the Japanese publications in this field had been translations or abridgements of Western literature. Sagane produced the inclusive volume of *Zaisei-Gaku* (*Public Finance*) in 1889, which was the first substantial volume in this field written by a Japanese author. Later, Sagane was appointed to the position of professor at Gakushu-in. Much was expected of him; however, he died prematurely at the age of 28.

AMERICAN DISCUSSION OF TAXATION AND ITS ACCEPTANCE IN JAPAN IN THE 1880s TO 1910s

American Background for Ely, Seligman, and the Single Tax Movement

After the Civil War in the 1860s, American society engaged in an extended process of reforming its public institutions in order to adapt to the tide of social and industrial change. Meanwhile, social movements that carried labels such as populism, the social gospel, and socialism brought pressure for economic and political reform. Among these, Henry George's campaign gained popularity.

Beginning in the 1870s, the impulse for reform reshaped academic life. Many ambitious students decided to pursue graduate education in Germany, where the new academic research area of *Sozialwissenschaft* flourished. The American connections with research on economics in Germany were perhaps tighter than in any other discipline.[22] Among them, the figures of Richard T. Ely and Edwin R. A. Seligman emerged to become influential in conveying German ideas to the United States between the late 1880s and 1930s. Ely turned out to be one of the leading advocates for social progressivism and had a career sometimes wrapped in controversy. Seligman was a steady promoter of the discourses in public finance and taxation and in the history of economic thought.

Ely: Textbook and Social Progressivism

After completing a course in philosophy at Columbia College in 1876, Richard Theodore Ely enrolled in the University of Halle to continue his work in philosophy, and then switched to political economy under Karl Knies at the University of Heidelberg. He completed his PhD in 1879, and continued to study in Berlin. In 1881, he was invited to be an associate

professor at The Johns Hopkins University, which had been founded in
Baltimore in 1876 as the first research university in the United States.[23]

In the early stage of his carrier at Johns Hopkins, Ely produced an
article titled "The Past and the Present of Political Economy" (1884), in
which he placed himself in the line of a new school of economic thought.
Ely energetically produced textbooks in political economy, and many
volumes relative to contemporary issues. His approach was unique in
several ways. First, as a scholar who was trained in the German historical school, Ely produced *An Introduction of Political Economy* (1889),
which explained the economic reasoning behind the historical development of modern capitalism. Second, he had a powerful interest in evaluating society with reference to socialism and Christianity, which yielded
French and German Socialism in Modern Times (1883), *Recent American Socialism* (1885), and *Social Aspects of Christianity* (1889). This
interest placed him in the mainstream of the social gospel movement and
progressivism. Third, he was committed to the practical analysis of taxation. In Baltimore, he began to study taxation with both the Baltimore
Tax Commission and the Maryland Tax Commission, and continuously
contributed the articles to *The Baltimore Sun*. This project culminated in
the volumes of *Problems of To-day: a Discussion of Protective Tariffs,
Taxation, and Monopolies* (1888), and *Taxation in American States and
Cities* (1888). In part III of the latter, titled "Taxation as it Should Be,"
Ely proposed the idea of the exemption of real estate from state taxation,
urging the creation of an independent revenue base for Baltimore and
the other rapidly growing local governments. Some years later, Seligman
described this volume by Ely as being "well-known."[24]

His commitment to progressive social causes and the spread of the
rumor that he was a socialist led Ely to recognize that he had no chance
of being promoted to the rank of professor at Johns Hopkins. In 1892,
Ely moved to a professorship at the University of Wisconsin, where he
developed his ideas, applying the German style of social analysis within
the setting of the state of Wisconsin. His analysis ranged widely over
various issues, including the importance of municipal management, theoretical analysis of the development of monopoly, and the legal foundation
of contracts. These issues led to the creation of many volumes, including
The Coming City (1902), *Monopoly and Trusts* (1903), and *Property and
Contract in their Relations to the Distribution of Wealth* (two volumes
published in 1914).

Ely, together with his colleague John R. Commons, established the
University of Wisconsin as a major center for the academic field of the

analysis of social policy. In this way, at the turn of the century Ely was one of the major promoters of American progressivism.[25] During the first two decades of the twentieth century, however, Ely moved away from the field of taxation.

Single Tax Movement: Its Influence and Popularity, and Its Relationship with Seligman and Ely

Henry George, a journalist based in California, published *Progress and Poverty* in 1879, which achieved a high reputation, including a highly celebrated campaign in Britain and Ireland that began in 1882. The publication of *Progress and Poverty* won support for the idea of establishing a single tax on land, and regional organizations emerged to advocate its adoption within the United States. In 1901, the periodical *The Single Tax Review: A Record of the Progress of Single Tax and Tax Reform Throughout the World* was founded to advance this movement. The advocates of single tax were not unanimous, however, and there were two distinct streams: those who supported the original idea of George and his early followers, who were inclined to socialism, and the promoters of free trade, especially free internal trade.

George transformed the idea of the Ricardian labor theory of value, which had originally showed the inverse relationship between wages and profit, and the tendency of profits to decline in the long run. In his transformed idea of the inverse relationship between rent and wages, George demonstrated the conflict of the interest between landlords and peasantry. This theorizing led to the radical reform of land tenure as a solution, so the advocacy of the single tax was often regarded as a form of socialism.[26]

The representative of the other stream of single taxation was Thomas G. Shearman, who published a volume called *Natural Taxation: An Inquiry into the Practicability, Justice and Effects of a Scientific and Natural Method of Taxation* in 1895. In contrast with George, who logically applied the reasoning of David Ricardo, Shearman defined the ground rent in the light of price formation, and showed that the landlords ought to be taxed. In 1883, Shearman had already demonstrated before the American Free Trade League that free trade without indirect taxation was "the only road to the manufacturing prosperity and high wages." In 1892, he delivered a lecture titled "Taxation and Revenue: the Free-trade View" at the meeting of the Brooklyn Ethical Association.[27] In this way, some of the advocates of a single tax on land were free-traders or, rather, were inclined to reject the control of market and trade by government, including through indirect taxation.

From the 1890s to the 1910s, the idea and the movement of a single tax grew in popularity. These two streams sometimes merged into the writings of eager authors such as Louis F. Post.[28] Beginning in the 1890s, many local associations for single tax were established. The activities of these associations included many publications, and sometimes discussions involving professional academics.[29] After 1901, *The Single Tax Review* sometimes included contributions by Leo Tolstoy, and it published an annual version, *The Single Tax Yearbook*, in the mid-1910s. At the end of the 1890s, *Japanese Notions of European Political Economy* was published (2nd edition, 1899). The book's cover identified the author as Tentearo Makato, and its subtitle as "Being a Summary of a Voluminous Report upon that Subject Forwarded to the Japanese Government." Apparently, Tentearo Makato was a pseudonym, and the true author was James Love, a single taxer from New Jersey.[30] During the 1910s, the single tax movement became the subject of academic research and some dissertations appeared on the topic.[31]

In early writings, including *On the Shifting and Incidence of Taxation* (1892) and *Essays in Taxation* (1895), Seligman incorporated discussions of single taxation.[32] The style of his analysis was that of an historian of economic thought. In part 1 of *Shifting and Incidence*, he dealt with the ideas of single tax along with the other styles of general excise taxation, general property tax, and more eclectic tax systems. According to him, there were three types of single taxation: the single tax on luxuries, the single tax on houses, and the single tax on land. Seligman's style of historical analysis of the idea was neutral, lacking any connotation of criticism of the contemporary single tax movement. In his discussion of the single tax as a form of classified taxation of real estate, Seligman identified that the tax would be "levied on the ground owner alone," and he added that "this would correspond to Henry George's single tax."[33]

In chapter 3 of his *Essays in Taxation*, Seligman concentrated on the idea of the single tax. Contrary to Isaac Sherman, who proposed to levy state and local taxes on real estate, Seligman grasped that the discussion by George was correct on one key point. In Seligman's summary, Sherman asserted that "the tax ought to be borne by the whole community . . . and the taxation of land would be shifted from the landowner to the consumer;" however, "Mr. George says that the tax on land values will stay on landowner."[34] Although Seligman agreed with George on this point, his agreement did not extend any further. Seligman cautiously examined the idea of single tax on land in terms of its fiscal, political, ethical, and economic defects. In his opinion, "the remedy for social maladjustments does not lie in any such lopsided idea; the only cure is the slow, gradual evolution of the moral conscience of mankind."[35]

In the first decade of the twentieth century, Seligman occasionally spoke at meetings of single taxers[36] or joined in discussions with them at such meetings.[37] Although Seligman made the critical examination on the idea of single tax, he had never had the experience of being the target of attack from the single tax movement.

The situation for Ely was very different than for Seligman. In his *Recent American Socialism* (1885), Ely placed George's argument in the context of the beginning of revolutionary socialism in the United States. In the latter stages of his career, however, Ely had a very difficult and complex relationship with the single tax movement. This issue is partly related to the ideas that led him to participate in the social gospel movement, but had more to do with his ideas regarding land economics. Around 1920, Ely developed a new interest in the field of land economics and he established the Institute for Research in Land Economics at the University of Wisconsin.[38] In the process, Ely abrogated the reasoning of classical political economy, which had treated rent as economic surplus, and analyzed rent on land from the viewpoint of utility.[39]

Some of the single taxers regarded Ely's new idea of land economics to imply the rejection of the idea of single tax. They found two reasons as to why this might be the case. First, the emphasis of land economics on the use of the marginal utility theory meant departure from the classical political economy, from which George had derived the basis of his reasoning. Second, Ely's discussion seemed to be in conflict with the practical interest of manufactures and traders. Following this second point, the Manufacturers and Merchants Federal Tax League, which was based in Chicago, conducted a harsh and obstinate campaign against Ely. Its director, Emil Oliver Jorgensen, repeatedly claimed that the University of Wisconsin was improperly using public funds to support a political organization. Although Jorgensen was a single taxer, his position differed from that of George, and followed the line of Shearman.[40] Under pressure exerted by these campaigns, Ely – who was then around seventy years old – decided to leave the University of Wisconsin, where he had been for more than thirty years, and move to Northwestern University, which agreed to accept Ely's institute. The campaign by Jorgensen relentlessly continued;[41] however, Ely was able to develop his research on land economics and publish a very challenging volume called *Land Economics* with George S. Wehrwein (1940).[42]

Acceptance of the Single Tax Movement, Ely and Seligman in Japan: 1890s–1910s

As a result of its war with China in 1894–5, Japan started to shift from agricultural society toward industrialization. There were some issues to be resolved, however, and tasks to be accomplished. First, the economic situation of the peasantry was becoming severe because of the diffusion of market transactions into rural areas. The necessity of engaging in these transactions often caused farmers to become peasants under the burden of loans. Second, the government had to establish an adequate financial basis for the system by combining various schemes of taxation and debt, which meant that the government had to seek out new ideas relating to public finance and taxation. For the former, the idea of a single tax had some limited influence during the 1890s. The major discussion in Japan, however, gradually shifted to the German stream of *Sozialpolitik* and Marxian analysis, which turned out to be influential at the beginning of the 1920s.[43]

Translations of Ely in Japan. Beginning in 1881, Japanese students joined Ely's classes at Johns Hopkins. After their return to Japan, some of these PhD students translated volumes written by him. Among his earlier publications, *An Introduction to Political Economy* (1889) was translated into Japanese under the title *Ishi Keizai-Gaku* (*Mr. Ely's Political Economy*) in 1890 by Sato Shosuke, and most chapters in *Taxation of American States and Cities* (1888) were translated as *Beikoku Shu-Shi Sozei-Ron* in 1893 by Iyenaga Toyokichi and Shiozawa Masasada.[44] In the translator's preface to the former, Ely was identified as representing the new trends of political economy. In advance of these translations by his students, Sagane Fujiro had already translated "The Past and Present of Political Economy" under the title *Shin-Kyu-Ryo-Ha Keizai-Gaku Yoryo* (1888).

The Influence of George and the Single Tax in Japan. Since the late 1880s, some of the writings by George had been introduced to Japanese audiences through reviews and translations. For example, *Social Problems* (1883) was translated by Eguchi Sansei under the title *Shakai Mondai* (1892). The influence of George in Japan was primarily on socialist and/or

Christian inclined groups, and secondarily on advocates of free trade. Despite this, there were few who grasped and transformed the single-tax idea in a way that might be applicable to Japanese society. Among these rare individuals, two are noteworthy: Jyo Sentaro and Tanzei-Taro Garusuto.[45]

After the civil war in Japan in 1867, Jyo Sentaro, a teenager from the soldier class in the defeated province of Nagaoka, decided to enroll at Keio Gijuku. His performance as a student was remarkable and he was admitted to Keio at the age of nineteen. He devoted several years to working in some local institutions of higher learning including Tokushima Branch of Keio, followed by Risshisha at Kochi, and Nagaoka Gakko. In his classes, contemporary tomes such as Mill's *Representative Government* and Henry Thomas Buckle's *History of Civilisation in England* were utilized. When Jyo decided to build a career in journalism and commentary on social issues, he differed from the popular journalists who utilized the new terms from the West in a superficial fashion to carp or ridicule, often employing cartoons. Jyo's intellectual goals were ambitious. In the 1880s, he read the writings of George, including *Progress and Poverty* and *Social Problems*, and from these readings published a combined and abridged translation, *Saisei Kigen: Fuzei Zenpai*, in 1891.[46] In addition, Jyo produced an anonymous political novel, pretending to be a British author. In his novel, in which Japanese troops defeated China, in suppressing the confused situation of anarchy a revolutionary government adopted a nationwide scheme of finance on the basis of the single tax. This novel was called *Shin-Cho Metsubo: Shina no Daitoryo* (*The Collapse of Qing: The President of China*) and remained unpublished for long time.[47]

In the late 1880s, one of the missionaries of the Disciples of Christ in Yokohama, Charles E. Garst, spent a great deal of time in the northeast area of Japan, and grasped the severe conditions of daily life among peasants.[48] On a visit to the United States, he discovered the discourses of George and, after returning to Japan, he turned to the analysis of Japanese poverty on the basis of George's insights.[49] He published *Tanzei* (*Single Tax*, 1897) and *Tanzei-Keizai-Gaku* (*The Political Economy of Single Tax*, 1899) in Japanese under the pen name Tanzei-Taro Garusuto.[50] Adding to these writings in Japanese, Garst published a brief volume in English titled *Great Economic Equation: Co-ordination of Individualism and Socialism, the Theory of the Economic Millennium* (Tokyo, 1898). Although it has been totally neglected, it shows that Garst grasped the essence of George under the transformed theory of rent devised by Ricardo.

Garst's argument that conditions of land tenure caused the miserable situation of peasants won some popularity in Japan. Nikaido Kahei was among those inspired by Garst's campaign. Nikaido Kahei conducted a political campaign on the basis of single tax advocacy during the general election in 1902.[51] Under the name Tanzei-Shugi-Sha Nikaido Kahei (The Single Taxer Nikaido Kahei), he published a volume called *Keikoku Saimin: Tanzei Ho-Gi* (*Managing the State and Securing the People: The Principles of Single Tax*) in the same year.[52] He argued that the product of labor and the earnings from movable property should belong to individuals because the product results from their efforts, but that the product from the land should be held communally. On the principles of single taxation, Nikaido argued that the burden of national budget should rest on land tenure in order to promote national industry, particularly manufacturing and trade.

Although the idea of single taxation won some followers in Japan around the turn of century, its influence was very limited. In 1910, a volume appeared with the title *Tanzei-Ron* (*Single Tax*) by Hashimoto Masajiro. It demonstrated the merit of a single tax on income, however, instead of one on land.

The Acceptance of Seligman in Japan. In contrast with some volumes by Ely that were translated into Japanese during 1890s, those of Edwin R. A. Seligman's works came fairly late. The earliest introduction of his ideas was in *Seriguman-Shi Ruishin-Kazei-Ron* (*Mr. Seligman on Cumulative Taxation*) by Kanbe Masao, presumably in 1901. In 1909, part of the latter half of *Shifting and Incidence* was translated as *Sozei-Tenka-Ron* by Sekiguchi Kenichiro. In 1910, Mikami Masashi, a graduate from Yale University, published *Sozei-Ron*, which was a translation of the majority of *Essays in Taxation*. Since the 1910s, passages by Seligman in these volumes had been frequently referred to by Japanese authors, especially historical descriptions of the idea of taxation and on the contrast between single and double taxation.[53]

FORMATION OF THE SYSTEMATIC DISCUSSION OF TAXATION IN JAPAN

Starting near the end of the 1890s, some German writings on public finance were translated directly into Japanese. First, Amano Tameyuki produced *Zaisei-Gaku* (*Public Finance*) in 1899, which was the translation of Gustav Cohn's *Finanzwissenschaft* (1889), namely the second volume of *System der Nationalökonomie*.[54] Although a very small portion of the writings of Adolph Wagner had been translated into Japanese during the 1890s, the substantial introduction of his writings to Japanese academics was delayed until 1904. In that year, Takimoto Yoshio, a professor at Tokyo College of Commerce, published *Waguna-Shi no Zaisei-Gaku* (Mr. *Wagner on Public Finance*, two volumes), which contained the introductory explanation and abridged translation of Wagner's *Finanzwissenschaft*.

Although Sagane Fujio had published *Zaisei-Gaku* (*Public Finance*) in 1889, after his premature death at the age of 28 there was a long absence of any publication of volumes in this field by Japanese authors. In the early 1900s, some volumes appeared that were based around lectures at various universities and colleges. In contrast with the early stages of the Meiji reformation, when most of the printing was on the basis wood-cuts, these new publications used Gutenberg printing and reached a larger audience. In 1906, one of the founding members of the Japanese Society for the Study of Social Policy, Takano Iwasaburo, published *Zaisei Genron* (*Principles of Public Finance*). Following this, a number of full-scale publications appeared, including works by Horie Kiichi, Matsuzaki Kuranosuke, and Ogawa Gotaro.

In 1909, Horie Kiichi at Keio University published a volume on public finance. In utilizing Francesco S. Nitti's argument, Horie showed the tendency of public expense to increase because of the growth of military expenses, the expansion of public sectors, the increase of public debts, the enlargement of the police force, and the adaptation of social policy.[55] Three years later, Matsuzaki Kuranosuke at the Imperial University of Tokyo published *Saishin Zaisei-Gaku* (*Modern Public Finance*). Matsuzaki suggested that the principles of taxation in France and the United States differed from those in Japan, and consequently warned against the thoughtless introduction of foreign systems of taxation. He defined taxation as the compulsory means for maintaining the expense of the economy of the state, and warned that the political action of the state might not be in the interest of the Japanese people. In his view, the people of Britain should be happy because the statesmen of contemporary Britain respected the national interest and people's happiness in the same way as they respected their own lives. In this line, Matsuzaki critically examined the four principles of taxation of Adam Smith while mentioning the single principle of morality proposed by Emil Sax and the nine principles of Adolph Wagner.[56]

Beginning with the close of World War I, Ogawa Gotaro at the Imperial University of Kyoto produced many volumes in this field.[57] When considering the relationship between taxation and social policy, Ogawa

examined the arguments of Wagner and Seligman. First, for the definition of taxation Ogawa summarized Wagner's view that public finance
is designed to secure the necessary expense of the state by imposing a
compulsory burden, and that social policy aims to correct the deficiencies of social distribution. In grasping Wagner's logic, Ogawa challenged
the latter part of this, and showed that taxation on behalf of social policy could be compatible with the aim of garnering revenues.[58] Second,
Ogawa examined Seligman's criticism of Wagner's remark on the validity
of proportional and progressive taxation. In Ogawa's summary, Wagner
declares that taxation should be proportional from the purely financial
point of view; however, progressive taxation was possible from the viewpoint of social policy. In using Seligman as the representative critic of
Wagner, Ogawa summarized Seligman's views as denying the applicabil-
ity of taxation for the purpose of social policy, and identified social policy with socialism. Under this simplified summary of Seligman's beliefs,
Ogawa criticized both Wagner and Seligman. In Ogawa's view, taxation
for financial purposes, even without the purpose of redistribution, could
bring about redistribution of wealth and progressive taxation for financial purposes could produce results similar to taxation for the purpose of
social policy. In addition, he believed that progressive taxation for social
policy could be the remedy to inequality without implying communism.
Thus, Ogawa showed that the progressive taxation for social policy could
be compatible with the aim of raising necessary revenues without carrying
a socialist connotation.[59]

Ogawa, later published some monographs on Japanese issues in
English.[60] In 1932, Ogawa rewrote *Zaisei-Gaku* in collaboration with his
successor to the chair of public finance at Imperial University of Kyoto,
Shiomi Saburo. In 1949, when Nihon Sozei Kenkyu Kyokai (the Japan
Society for the Study of Taxation) was organized following the suggestion
by Carl S. Shoup, Shiomi was the person who became its first president.[61]

The works of Horie, Matsuzaki, Ogawa, and Ogawa and Shiomi
tended to accept the German ideas of the inevitable tendency for national
budgets to grow. Japanese authors got the German idea from various
sources, including Karl Theodor Eheberg (originally developed from
Cossa), Francesco Saverio Nitti (Italian), and Seligman (American). Many
Japanese authors utilized Seligman's argument in their description of the
classification of tax, on the history of the idea of single and double tax,
and on the contrast between direct and indirect taxes.

In 1930 and 1931, Ouchi Hyoe, who was a professor in the field of public finance at Imperial University of Tokyo, published the volumes making

up *Zaisei-Gaku Taiko* (*Elements of Public Finance*).[62] Two issues related to these volumes should be noted here. First, although Ouchi's explanations of the nature of finance and taxation for the existing system in Japan did not differ extensively from those that other experts in public finance had offered since 1920, Ouchi was unique in situating the meaning of historical changes of this field within the broader context of social conditions.[63] Second, Ouchi adopted a Marxian approach, as had many academics in other fields of social science during the late 1920s. Among Marxian-inclined intellectuals, there were two streams of understanding of the Meiji reformation in the late 1860s and the character of existing Japanese capitalism. Under this *Nihon-Shihonshugi-Ronso* (the Controversy of Japanese Capitalism), one of the two streams was the *Rono* faction, which viewed the Meiji reformation as the revolution from feudalism to capitalism, and described the existing social order in Japan as modern capitalism. The other was the *Koza* faction, which saw the Meiji reformation as constituting only half of the revolution, and described Japanese society to be half-feudal and half-military in character.[64] Among these two factions, Ouchi took the line of the *Rono* faction.

CONCLUSION

There were certain stages in the story of the formation and development of modern ideas of taxation. From the late 1860s to the beginning of the 1880s, the discussion of finance from the West had been brought into Japan either via volumes of British writings on political economy or through the French work of Leroy-Beaulieu. In utilizing the British idea derived from Ellis, land tax reform was accomplished as the first step in modernizing Japanese public finance. Following the program of *oyatoi gaikokujin*, the Japanese university system gradually increased its capacity to cover the discipline of political economy.

Beginning with the coup d'état in 1881, the exemplar for Japan turned to Germany instead of Britain and France, and the basic approach to public finance and taxation started to shift to the application of German ideas. Before Japanese academics began to grasp Wagner's ideas, however, the ideas of the Italian Cossa and the American Ely were introduced during the late 1880s and 1890s.

In the United States between the 1880s and 1920s, George's idea won popularity and stimulated the spread of the single tax movement. Within the academic discussion, Ely committed to the social gospel movement and became a target of criticism by the single taxers. In contrast, Seligman steadily formulated the full-scale discipline of taxation in an academic way, and never experienced a similar attack. In Japan during the 1890s there were some figures, including the American missionary Garst, who advocated the idea of single tax as a way of alleviating the miserable situation of peasants. The influence of this idea, however, was very limited.

During the early 1900s, Japanese academics began to produce systematic monographs in the field of public finance. Alongside the influence of German ideas, especially Wagner's, were those of Seligman, who was often referred to by Japanese authors during the late 1910s. In the process, many Japanese academics in this field adopted the new political languages of taxation, and departed from an emphasis on the traditional land tax. This shift reflected the historical transition of Japanese society from an agrarian base to the combination of industrial and agrarian bases in the mid-1890s. For ten centuries or more, the Japanese system of taxation had been based mainly on the land tax, which had originated from the combination of So, Yo, and Cho. Even the land tax reform in 1873 provided a high degree of continuity with the traditional land tax. The challenge for the Japanese government was therefore to enlarge the basis of public finance by including indirect taxation, increasing reliance on public debt, and by demonstrating the reasons for doing so.

From around 1930, Ouchi Hyoe analyzed Japanese public finance from the perspective of one of the Marxian schools, called the *Rono*. In the same period the scholar Ogawa Gotaro shifted his career to politics, and in 1932 Shiomi Saburo became a co-author with Ogawa. In 1949, when Shoup directed his mission's analysis of Japanese taxation, both Ouchi Hyoe and Shiomi Saburo played influential roles. Ouchi and his group provided an intellectual framework within which the Japanese public could understand tax reform, and Shiomi took the lead in organizing Japanese tax experts to respond to the recommendations of the Shoup mission.

Notes

1. Although the Japanese framework of taxation in the 1870s had included a variety of indirect taxes adapted from those of the previous Tokugawa regime, around 80 percent of the national revenue came from the land tax.
2. Land taxes were the largest revenue source until the late 1890s, when indirect taxes, particularly the tax on alcohol, became more important. Among direct taxes, the land tax remained more important than income taxation until World War I.

3. The first Japanese translation of John Stuart Mill's *On Liberty* (translated by Nakamura Masanao) had appeared in 1871, when Mill was still alive. Jean-Jacques Rousseau's *The Social Contract* was translated at least three times in this period by Hattori Toku (1877), Nakae Chomin (1882–5), and Harada Sen (1883).

4. The political and cultural scheme of Japan until the end of World War II was very complex. The political regime and economic performance followed the style of the West, and the widespread sense and morality of social and family values was mainly based on Confucianism, and the traditional belief in Japanese identity originated from, or rather recalled, the ancient myth in Shintoism.

5. For general information of the evolution of economic ideas in Japan, see Morris-Suzuki, T., *A History of Japanese Economic Thought* (London: Routledge, 1989) and Sugihara, S., Tanaka, T., eds., *Economic Thought and Modernization in Japan* (Cheltenham: Edward Elgar, 1998).

6. These political controversies were accompanied by discontent and political disputes among the newly established Meiji Government, which culminated in the South-West civil war in 1877.

7. Kanda had served in the *Bansho-Shirabe-Sho* (the Research Institute of the Foreign Writings) at the closing of the Tokugawa regime.

8. The nationwide financial system in Japan had long history that started in the seventh century with the public ownership of land. The subsystem of private ownership had gradually merged since the tenth century. In 1582, after the long civil war during the fifteenth and sixteenth centuries, the nationwide examination of land (*Taiko-Kenchi*) was introduced to check land tenure and fertility.

9. The tradition of Japanese Confucianism formed the stream of the political and economic ideas in Japan, see Maruyama, M., *Studies in the Intellectual History of Tokugawa Japan*, translated by Mikiso Hane (Princeton: Princeton University Press, 1974), originally published in Japanese in 1952.

10. Fukuzawa Yukichi had visited the United States in 1860 and 1867, and Europe in 1862–3 as a member of missions. After his return, Fukuzawa endeavored to develop the Keio Gijuku, which had begun in 1858 as a school for Dutch learning.

11. Their publication preceded the first translation of *The Wealth of Nations* (1776) by Adam Smith into Japanese by Ishikawa Eisaku and Saga Shosaku in 1884–8.

12. Under the combination of various institutions since the end of the Edo period, the Imperial university system in Japan was gradually formulated. Until the end of 1870s, the University of Tokyo had subdivisions consisting of the Universities of Law, Physics, Natural Science, Humanity, and Technology. The fields of politics and political economy came under the University of Humanity.

13. In the field of philosophy of the West, the knowledge among students was mostly built on a superficial understanding of Herbert Spencer, so Fenollosa's lectures on Descartes, Kant, and others, were highly regarded by the students. With regard to other disciplines, especially political economy, however, his

coverage was rather accidental, based mostly on whatever volumes he happened to have at hand.

14. From November 1888 to March 1889, Rathgen made a series of lectures on local finance at the workshop of self-government and administration. These were published as *Chiho-Zaisei-Gaku* [*Local Finance*], aurally translated by Nakane Juichi, 1889.

15. In 1886, the regulation of Imperial University was proclaimed, and the University of Tokyo was reformed accordingly. With the establishment of the Imperial University of Kyoto in 1897, it was renamed the Imperial University of Tokyo.

16. Although the courses of politics and political economy had belonged to the University of Humanity of the University of Tokyo until 1885, both were transferred to the University of Law when Imperial University started. These courses jointly established the Kokka Gakkai.

17. Cossa's *Primi Elementi* (1876) was translated into English in 1888 based on its third edition (1882) with a change of title, namely *Taxation: Its Principles and Methods*. Horace White provided an introduction and notes to it. The Japanese translation by Machida Chuji in 1889 was from the English one, however the title was returned to its original meaning, *Zaisei-Gaku* [*Public Finance*].

18. Later, in 1895, Machida established the economic journal *Toyo Keizai Shinpo Sha*, which continues to this day. After his resignation, he joined the Bank of Japan. After becoming a member of parliament in 1912, he assumed the positions of ministers of agriculture, commerce, and industry and finance.

19. The first German translation by Eheberg was *Grundriß der Finanzwissenschaft* (1882). In publishing new editions of the translation, Eheberg enlarged Cossa's original discussion to reflect the German context and include the German ideas of Roscher, Sax, Wagner, and so on. Until the second edition of *Grundriß* published in 1888, Eheberg kept Cossa's name on the title. In the later editions, however, he put his own name as the author without indicating Cossa.

20. For the latter translation on 1902, Wadagaki listed Cossa as the author, Eheberg as the translator, and himself as the re-translator. In addition to these translations, one of the latter editions of Eheberg was translated into Japanese by Otake Torao (1924).

21. Lorenz von Stein's *Handbuch der Verwaltungslehre* (1876) was translated into Japanese by Arakawa Kunizo in 1882 under the title of *Kokuri-Ron* [*Theory of the State*]. The translation of Adolph Wagner was delayed until the 1890s. The recording branch of the Home Office translated *Kanri-Hokyu-Ron* [*On the Salary of the Governmental Official*] in 1893; the secretariat of the Upper House produced the abridged translation of banking from the economic writings of Wagner in 1894; and the Agricultural and Commercial Office translated *On Public Finance Concerning the Prussian French War in 1870–1871* in 1895.

22. Rogers, D. T., *Atlantic Crossings: Social Politics in a Progressive Age* (Cambridge: Belknap Press, 1998), 84. For the broader context of the location of

American social sciences in the late nineteenth century, see Ross, D., *The Origins of American Social Sciences* (Cambridge: Cambridge University Press, 1991), part II.

23. For the biographical aspects of Ely, see Ely, R. T., *Ground Under Our Feet: An Autobiography* (New York: MacMillan, 1938), and Rader, B. G., *The Academic Mind and Reform: The Influence of Richard T. Ely in American Life* (Kentucky: University of Kentucky Press, 1966).

24. Seligman, E. R. A., *Essays in Taxation* (New York: MacMillan, 1895), 404.

25. Schäfer, A. R., *American Progressives and German Social Reform, 1875–1920: Social Ethics, Moral Control, and the Regulatory State in a Transatlantic Context* (Stuttgart: Franz Steiner Verlag, 2000), 79.

26. Ely regarded George as "the beginning of revolutionary socialism in the United States." Ely, R. T., *Recent American Socialism* (Baltimore: Johns Hopkins University, 1885), pp. 16f.

27. Shearman's address appeared in Brooklyn Ethical Association, *Man and the State, Studies in Applied Sociology: Popular Lectures and Discussions before the Brooklyn Ethical Association* (New York: D. Appleton and Company, 1892).

28. See Post, L. F., *Outlines of Louis F. Post's Lectures on the Single Tax, Absolute Free Trade, the Labor Question, Progress and Poverty, the Land Question, &c.* (New York: The Sterling Library, 1894).

29. For example, Love, J. Plehn, C. C., De Witt, T. H. B., *A Correspondence between an Amateur and a Professor of Political Economy* (Philadelphia: J. B. Lippincott and Co, 1898). In this pamphlet, the amateur James Love corresponded with Professor Carl C. Plehn at the University of California, Berkeley.

30. The pseudonymous author is identified as James Love; see *The Single Tax Review*, 1901, vol. 1 (1), 12.

31. Young, A. N., *The Single Tax Movement in the United States* (New Jersey: Princeton University Press, 1916). Speek, P. A., *The Single Tax and the Labor Movement*, a *Bulletin of the University of Wisconsin*, 1917, No. 878, pp. 247–426. During the 1890s, before these works had appeared, under Seligman's encouragement, Stephen F. Weston had taken up the single tax and its implications for social justice in his graduate work at Columbia University. Weston, S. F., "Principles of Justice in Taxation," *Studies in History, Economics and Public Law*, 1903, vol. 17 (2), pp. 1–299.

32. Seligman, E. R. A., *On the Shifting and Incidence of Taxation, Publications of the American Economic Association* (Baltimore: American Economic Association, 1892), vol. 7 (2–3); and Seligman, E.R.A., *Essays in Taxation* (New York: Macmillan, 1895).

33. Seligman, E. R. A., *Shifting and Incidence*, 2nd ed. (New York: Macmillan, 1899), 236.

34. Seligman, E. R. A., *Essays in Taxation* (New York: Macmillan, 1895), 65–6. The volume that Seligman examined is Sherman, I., *Exclusive Taxation of Real Estate, and the Franchises of a Few Specified Moneyed Corporations and Gas Companies. Remarks of Isaac Sherman before the Assembly Committee on Ways and Means of the State of New York, October, 1874* (New York:

M. B. Brown, 1875). In addition, Seligman examined Sherman's ideas in *Shifting and Incidence*, 2nd ed. (New York: Macmillan, 1899), 133.

35. Seligman, E. R. A., *Essays in Taxation* (New York: MacMillan, 1895), 94.
36. For example, Seligman delivered an address on "Agreements in Political Economy in their Relations to Tax Reform." He concluded that "as the next step of tax reform is concerned, the reduction and final abolition of the local tax on personal property, there is a substantial agreement between the economists and the single taxers." The Massachusetts Single Tax League, *The Massachusetts Single Tax League Banquet to College Professors and Political Economists* (Boston: The Massachusetts Single Tax League, 1902), 8.
37. For example, on the occasion of the dinner discussion of the Economic Club of Boston on April 27, 1905, C. B. Fillebrown (President of the Massachusetts Single Tax League) delivered an introduction, followed by a Seligman's address titled "The Taxation of Ground Rent Resolved."
38. For the aim of this institution, see Ely, R. T., Shine, M. L., "The Institute for Research in Land Economics and Public Utilities," *The Sewanee Review: Language and International Affairs*, 1924, vol. 32 (3), 313–6.
39. In his analysis of land economics, Ely utilized the concept of the margin of utilization of land, see Shine, M. L., Wehrwein, G. S., Ely, R. T., *Cost and Income in Land Utilization: Volume II of the Outlines of Land Economics* (Michigan: Edwards Brothers, 1922).
40. Emil Oliver Jorgensen published some pamphlets to attack the institute and Ely himself. The most straightforward one was the volume titled *Prof. Richard T. Ely Exposed!: Showing how a Gigantic Nation-wide Scheme, Financed by Special Interests, Engineered by Prof. Ely of Wisconsin University, and Masquerading under the Guise of "Research"* (Chicago: Manufacturers and Merchants Federal Tax League, 1924).
41. After Ely's move to Northwestern University, Jorgensen published the larger-scale volume of *False Education in our Colleges and Universities; an Expose of Prof. Richard T. Ely and his "Institute for Research in Land Economics and Public Utilities" Showing how a Gigantic Nation-wide Scheme, Financed by Special Interests, Engineered by Prof. Ely of Wisconsin University, and Masquerading under the Guise of "Research," has been set on Foot in our Educational Institutions to Lead People, not Towards the Right Solution of our Economic Problems but Away from it* (Chicago: Manufacturers and Merchants Federal Tax League, 1925).
42. In his autobiography, *Ground Under Our Feet* (1938), Ely never mentioned the hard experience of Jorgensen's campaigns. For Ely's concentration on land economics, the attack on him by Jorgensen, and his decision to move to Northwestern University, see Rader, B. G., *The Academic Mind and Reform* (Lexington: University of Kentucky Press), 209; Cord, S. B., Andelson, R. V., "Ely: A Liberal Economist Defends Landlordism," *American Journal of Economics and Sociology* 2004, vol. 63 (2), 361–79.
43. Throughout the decades between 1890s and 1920s, Christian-based ideas and movements were influential to some extent in Japan, especially in the style of settlement.

44. Sato and Iyenaga had enrolled in Ely's classes and completed their PhD dissertations under the supervision of Herbert B. Adams. Sato's dissertation was on the "History of Land Questions in United States," which was published in *The Johns Hopkins University Series in Historical and Political Science*, fourth series, 1886. Iyenaga's dissertation was on the "Constitutional Development of Japan, 1853–1881," which appeared in the ninth series of the same journal in 1891. With the exception of the writings of George and his followers, Sato's dissertation was one of the first academic analyses of American land questions. Later, Sato held an appointment at the Sapporo College of Agriculture, and was the first president of the Imperial University of Hokkaido. Iyenaga took the position of lecturer at Tokyo Senmon Gakko, followed by that of professor at Keio University. In 1901, he returned to the United States and devoted himself to the extension branch of the University of Chicago until 1911. Shiozawa enrolled in Iyenaga's class at Tokyo Senmon Gakko, and joined as the cotranslator of Ely's *Outline*. Later, Shiozawa enrolled in graduate work at the University of Wisconsin under the supervision of Ely, and went on to become the second president of Waseda University.

45. On the acceptance of George's idea in Japan, see Yamazaki, Y., *Henri Jyoji no Tochi-Seido Kaikaku-Ron* [*Henry George's Idea on the Reform of Land Tenure*] (Osaka: Izumiya Publishers, 1961), chapter 12 and appendix II (pp. 178–200, 268–81).

46. Literally, the title of this translation/adaptation meant *Ambitious Remarks on Securing Society: Abolishing All Taxation*.

47. Although this novel was written during 1892–4, it was not published until 1968. It is now available in *Jyo Sentaro Chosaku-shu* [*The Works of Sentato Jyo*], edited by Yamashita, S. and Kobayashi, H., *Nagaoka Shi-Shi* [*The Series of History of Nagaoka City*], no. 37, 1998.

48. Charles E. Garst (1853–1898) was a graduate from the military academy at West Point in 1876. He was baptized as a Disciple in his birthplace, Dayton, Ohio. After leaving the army in 1883, he became a missionary in Japan.

49. His widow discussed Garst's knowledge of George's volume and the idea of single tax. Garst, L. D., *A West-Pointer in the Land of the Mikado* (New York: Flemming H. Revell Company, 1913), 184–5, 239, 288.

50. After the death of Garst in 1898 *Tanzei-Keizai-Gaku* was edited by Ogawa Kinji. His pen name meant the combination of the single (*Tan*) – tax (*Zei*), the first son (*Taro*) and the Japanized pronunciation of Garst (*Garusuto*).

51. Nikaido Kahei had been the village chief of Kananari, a rural area of Miyagi prefecture in North-East Japan, and attended Haristos Orthodox Church. For information regarding Nikaido, see Goto, A., "The Thinker of Miyagi, no.5, Nikaido Kahei," Gallery Talk at Tohoku Historical Museum, Tagajyo, April 2004.

52. This volume was published by an organization called *Teikoku Tanzei-Kai* (the Imperial Society for Single Tax).

53. After World War II, both parts of *Shifting and Incidence* were fully translated into Japanese in two volumes by Ide Fumio: *Sozei-Tenka-Gakusetsu-Shi* in 1950 and *Sozei-Tenka-Riron* in 1951.

54. Amano was one of the students in Wadagaki's class at Imperial University, becoming a professor at Tokyo Senmon Gakko, and later at Waseda University.

55. Horie, K., *Zaisei-Gaku* [*Public Finance*] Tokyo: Hobunkan, (1909), 96. In the early twentieth century in Japan, Nitti's *Principi di Scienza delle Finanze* (1903) was read via its 1904 French translation titled *Principes de science des finances*.

56. Matsuzaki compared the definition of principle of taxation given by Adam Smith, Adolph Wagner, and Emil Sax in *Saishin Zaisei-Gaku* [*Modern Public Finance*], fourth edition, Tokyo: Yuhikaku-Shobo, (1912), 282–6, 292–3, 334–50.

57. The publications of Ogawa Gotaro include *Kosai-Ron* [*Public Debts*], 1918; *Zaisei-Soron* [*Outline of Public Finance*], 1919; *Shakai-Mondai to Zaisei* [*Social Problems and Public Finance*], 1920; *Sozei-Ron: Sozei-Soron* [*Taxation: Outline of Taxation*], 1922; and *Sozei-Seiri-Ron* [*Disposition of Taxation*], 1923. In 1917, during his professorship at the Imperial University of Kyoto, Ogawa stood as a candidate for a member of parliament and won election. In 1924, he resigned from his professorship and devoted his career to politics. In 1929, he assumed the position of vice minister for finance in the Hamaguchi cabinet, and became minister of commerce and manufacturing later.

58. Ogawa, G., *Sozei-Ron: Sozei-Soron* (Kyoto: Naigai-Shuppan, 1922), 27.

59. Ogawa, G., *Sozei-Ron: Sozei-Soron*, 428, focused on Seligman, E. R. A., *Progressive Taxation in Theory and Practice,* 2nd edition (*American Economic Association Quarterly, third series* Volume 9, no. 4), Princeton, NJ: Princeton University Press, (1908), 130–4. For the volume of Wagner, Ogawa referred to Wagner A., *Finanzwissenschaft*, II, Teil. 2 Aufl., mentioning sections 159 and 185.

60. For example, Ogawa, G., "Expenditures of the Russo-Japanese War," in: Sakatani, Y., ed., *Publications of the Carnegie Endowment for International Peace*, (New York: Carnegie Endowment for International Peace, 1923).

61. The society was more commonly known in the United States as the Japan Tax Association, which was how Shoup referred to the organization in order to suggest a direct parallel with the National Tax Association in the United States. See Chapter 16 of this volume.

62. The volumes of *Zaisei-Gaku Taiko* by Ouchi Hyoe appeared with the expression of Jo and Chu, which implied that the third one, Ge, was scheduled although it never appeared.

63. For example, Ouchi showed the transition from Smith's four principles on taxation to Wagner's nine in light of dynamic historical change. Ouchi, H., *op. cit.*, vol. 2, pp. 326, 341, and 345–6.

64. The *Rono* faction was named after the journal of *Rono*, which referred to a movement drawn from both laborers (*Ro*) and peasants (*No*). The *Koza* faction was named after *Nihon Shihonshugi Hattatsu-shi Koza* [*The Series of History of the Development of Japanese Capitalism*] published by Iwanami (1932–3).

7

Raising Taxes for Democracy

The Japanese Policy Environment of the Shoup Mission

Laura Hein and Mark Metzler

When the Shoup mission members arrived in Tokyo in May 1949, they entered a highly politicized arena where Japanese protagonists, acting under the authority of the occupation supergovernment, battled each other for control over fundamental economic decisions. This is not a story of Americans unilaterally imposing their views on Japanese. The American fiscal experts not only entered a complicated field of Japanese economic and political opinions, but they disagreed among themselves. Their recommendations and the effects of their reforms on the tax structure were understood through the ideas and institutions already in place. Nor did the Americans provide levels of fiscal expertise that Japan lacked. As Finance Minister Ikeda Hayato stated shortly after the end of the occupation – proudly and accurately – "as for our country's tax system as a system, we had deeply researched the examples of various continental European countries and had advanced the tax system's theoretical grounding to a relatively high level, so in that domain we did not particularly need to ask for foreign guidance." Rather, he said, the reason for welcoming the foreign experts' mission was political.[1]

Taking a cue from Ikeda, this chapter addresses the Japanese policy environment encountered by the Shoup mission and discusses some basic questions concerning money and taxation in modern times. We focus on three points.

The first point relates to the context of the great postwar inflation. Inflation was itself a kind of taxation, or social "forced savings," as was widely understood during the occupation. By the time the Shoup mission arrived, the fiscal battle over inflation was being concluded, setting new parameters for future policy action. This was a three-way fight, partly about different views of the economy but fundamentally about political power. The dispute over inflation set the stage anew, establishing a political and economic context very different from conditions prevailing only two years earlier. Connected to this is a conceptual question: in an age when states can create money at will, why do they need to resort to taxation at all? This too came down to the need to control inflation, and it demonstrates how taxation had become essential to the constitution of money itself.

Second, Japanese progressives and conservatives each welcomed the Shoup mission, albeit for different reasons. This unusual congruence highlights another theme of this chapter, that the Shoup mission members responded to the discursive context already created by Japanese fiscal experts. Despite the recent war, American and Japanese experts could work easily together because they shared basic common understandings. The Shoup mission's recommendations harmonized with the concerns of both progressive economists and conservative Ministry of Finance officials because of these shared understandings. Their experience explains one source of the fundamental, quietly successful compromises that made postwar Japan a "newly born Japan" (*shinsei Nihon*), as even conservatives such as Ikeda Hayato boasted.[2]

At the same time – our third point – great political differences remained among Japanese. These included basic questions about the social allocation of resources, the use of the tax system to favor the political base of the ruling party, the fiscal independence of local governments, and the democratic awareness and agency of citizen taxpayers themselves. "Taxes," as academic economist Ōuchi Hyōe declared, "are a fundamental principle of democratic politics."[3] We conclude that the Shoup mission altered the conditions under which Japanese fought out these issues, but it both arrived and went home in the middle of the contest, making its members supporting actors in a drama with Japanese protagonists.

THE POSTWAR JAPANESE FISCAL DEBATE, 1945–8

When Japanese remember the first three postwar years, they often emphasize the economic difficulties created by high inflation and the black market. U.S. occupation officials also feared the effects of "the great inflation that hung over Japan like some immense, brooding presence."[4] Despite price controls, inflation had already become a problem in the last year of the war, when wholesale prices crept up to 3.5 times the 1934–6 average.

Prices climbed more rapidly after the war ended: by 365% in 1946, 196% in 1947, and 165% in 1948.[5]

The high inflation of the first three postwar years was deliberately fueled by the Japanese government's funding of industrial production through the direct creation of money and credit. This policy, described as "forced saving" by means of inflation, succeeded in preventing a complete economic collapse, but it provoked intense popular criticism.[6]

Broadly speaking, postwar Japanese experts can be divided into three positions on inflation and fiscal policy.[7] The first group, self-identified as political progressives, blamed Japanese authorities for the war and saw inflation as a mechanism for financing it. In peacetime, too, they thought inflation was antidemocratic. Political progressives were committed to using fiscal policy to redistribute income and strengthen the power of local governments. Here we focus on Tokyo University professor Ōuchi Hyōe (1888–1980), who was postwar Japan's most prominent authority on fiscal matters. Members of this progressive group, such as Ōuchi and Tsuru Shigeto (1912–2006), had close ties to the government's Economic Stabilization Board, although by 1949 they were mainly outside of government. The second group, self-identified as probusiness moderates, was willing to tolerate inflation in the interests of industrial recovery and development. This position is exemplified by the future prime minister Ishibashi Tanzan (1884–1973) who, as finance minister in 1946–7, was the architect of the inflationary policies of the early postwar years. The third group consisted of probusiness conservatives who believed in low taxes and balanced budgets and were relatively unconcerned about poverty. The key individual here was the 1949 finance minister and future prime minister, Ikeda Hayato (1899–1965).

Ōuchi Hyōe

Ōuchi, a professor, Ishibashi, a journalist-politician, and Ikeda, a bureaucrat, differed in their policy preferences but fundamentally shared an economically oriented view of the world. Who were they, and why did they differ on inflation? Although he only worked as a government bureaucrat as a young man, Ōuchi served on many official committees and functioned as an important public intellectual after World War II. He made his opposition to inflation known soon after the end of the war.

Ōuchi began life as a smart boy from an elite provincial family on the island of Awaji, on the Inland Sea. After graduating from Tokyo Imperial University in 1913, he took a job at the Ministry of Finance's bank division. One of his early assignments was to study how the combatant countries in World War I financed the war. Ōuchi left the ministry in 1919 when Tokyo Imperial University offered him a professorship in the newly established economics department. Tokyo Imperial University was not only the apex of the national educational hierarchy, but was itself a critically important part of the state structure, designed from the beginning to train the administrative elite governing the country.

Within this context of power and privilege, Ōuchi repeatedly ran up against the strictures of state authority. He edited the economics department's journal but was suspended from the university in 1920 because he published Morito Tatsuo's translation of an anarchist text by Peter Kropotkin. Ōuchi used the opportunity to study in Heidelberg, where he read Marxist texts unavailable at home and experienced first-hand the years of German hyperinflation, an experience that would profoundly influence his later thinking about his own country after World War II. After returning to Tokyo University in 1923, Ōuchi enjoyed a distinguished career as the country's leading public finance authority, training dozens of young men for careers in the economic bureaucracy and in business.

In 1938, Ōuchi's leftist political views again involved him in conflict with state authorities, who had him arrested and imprisoned. Released in 1939, he spent most of the war years dealing with his legal problems until he was finally acquitted in 1944. This history only enhanced Ōuchi's prestige after the war, and he returned to Tokyo University, then served as president of Hōsei University, and published over fifty books.[8]

The main lesson Ōuchi learned from German history was that inflation was a pernicious force, because it destabilized society in several ways. First, it caused great anxiety among the population. Second, it weakened democratic government by hampering effective tax collection, as the Weimar government discovered in the early 1920s. Third, this combination of widespread anxiety and ineffective government convinced enough Germans that radical change was needed for the Nazis to seize power. Thus the "complete atrophy of the fiscal system" was a major reason for the later fascist takeover.[9] Ōuchi thought that in Japan, as in Germany, "monopoly capitalism" had gained control in the 1930s. He further identified inflation as the monopoly capitalists' main technique for shifting costs from big business to the population as a whole.[10] He also thought the Japanese government had privileged industry at the expense of consumers, both during and after World War II. In short, the fiscal questions of inflation and taxation were, in Ōuchi's view, vital to the survival of democracy.

Ishibashi Tanzan

Ishibashi Tanzan had a more sanguine view of inflation. The son of a Nichiren priest, Ishibashi as a young man graduated from Waseda University and then served as a volunteer soldier. He was quite liberal, democratic, and internationalist in his ideas. Ishibashi was one of only a few Japanese to argue publicly that his country should not have an empire at all and to point out the folly of taking over Manchuria in the 1930s. Instead, he advocated an economy based on international trade and free markets.

Ishibashi was Japan's most prominent Keynesian. As a journalist in the 1920s, he had read the English economist's writings, particularly Keynes' critique of the British government's deflation policy, which informed Ishibashi's critique of the deflation policies pursued by the Japanese government in 1949.[11] Having advanced to the position of publisher of the *Oriental Economist* (*Tōyō keizai shinpō*), the country's most influential business newsweekly, Ishibashi was himself an entrepreneur and a strong supporter of big business. His policy as finance minister in 1946–7 was to fund business recovery via the inflationary creation of money and credit.

Ishibashi, like Ōuchi, based his postwar diagnosis on his understanding of the economic consequences of World War I. But he drew nearly opposite lessons. For Ōuchi, the German hyperinflation served as the great historical warning. For Ishibashi (and for many other Japanese), the key lesson came out of Japan's own experience: the danger of depression, which had been induced in the 1920s by the government's mistaken deflation policies, culminating in the disastrous decision to restore the gold standard in 1930 (something Ōuchi had supported at the time).[12] Ishibashi had been one of the loudest critics of the deflation policy. He later described the unnecessary depression that resulted from it as the ideal environment for nurturing ultranationalists in both Japan and Germany.[13] Although both men opposed fascism, one blamed postwar inflation and the other postwar deflation for its advance.

Ikeda Hayato

Ikeda managed to be both a follower of Ishibashi and a strict anti-inflationist, as political and economic circumstances seemed to dictate. In Ikeda's "half lifetime before becoming a politician," as he explained it in 1952, he was a career tax official. Accordingly, he had "a mountain of things to say on the subject" of taxation.[14]

After graduating from the law department of Kyoto Imperial University (1925), Ikeda entered the Ministry of Finance. His elite but "provincial" education placed him at a disadvantage there, however, because "if you were not from Tokyo University you were not a person." His career in the Tax Bureau also kept him off the main ladder that led to the top ministry positions (the Budget Bureau was the place to be).[15]

Until 1932, Ikeda served in various prefectural tax offices but then contracted a terrible skin disease and could not work again until 1937. His first wife (who was a cousin of the emperor's adviser Kido Kōichi) died during this trying time. After his recovery, Ikeda was transferred to the Tokyo tax office, where he became a section chief in 1937 and pushed hard to make up for lost time.

According to journalistic accounts, it was in 1940, when Ikeda headed the Tokyo District Tax Office and was known to be an ambitious and unforgiving "tax ogre," that he first came to the attention of the *zaikai*, the politically organized business world. At that time, Ikeda imposed an enormous inheritance tax on the estate of Nezu Kaichirō, founder of the Tōbu Railway and a prominent business leader. Ikeda's friend Yamamoto Tamesaburō, the managing director of the Dai Nippon Beer Company (later Asahi Brewing), interceded and convinced Ikeda to cut the levy to less than one-quarter of the original assessment. This individualized tax cut turned out to be smart politics. Zaikai "godfather" Miyajima Seijirō (1897–1963), chairman of the Japan Industrial Club and afterward a leader in the postwar Keidanren (Federation of Economic Organizations), was an executor of the Nezu estate.[16] Apparently impressed with Ikeda's decisive handling of matters touching on the interests of the rich and well-connected, Miyajima took a liking to him. Zaikai backing would later propel Ikeda to the top of the political world.

In 1945, Ikeda was appointed chief of the Ministry of Finance Tax Bureau, making him the country's highest tax official. A newspaper headline highlighted his achievement in becoming the "first bureau chief from Kyoto University."[17] In 1946, Ikeda reached the pinnacle of the bureaucratic hierarchy when he was named administrative vice-minister of finance. He thus served as vice-minister under Ishibashi Tanzan in 1946–7.

In this context, the position of the Ministry of Finance itself deserves comment. The ministry enjoyed tremendous prestige and administrative power, which encompassed authority over the national budget, with all that implies, and over taxation, combined with oversight of the central bank, monetary policy, and private financial institutions. (This is only a partial list of its reach.) For political leaders, an appointment as finance minister was routinely the last stop before becoming prime minister, and many prime ministers, like Ikeda, had careers as Ministry of Finance officials before entering politics. In addition to this, the ministry emerged from war and defeat administratively intact, at a time when other powerful institutions were in disarray or were eliminated altogether. Only nine Ministry of Finance officials were purged during the occupation; with the exception of the director of the Budget Bureau, most were younger functionaries who had handled foreign assets that the Japanese government had appropriated during the war.[18] By contrast, the occupation's personnel purge of military, political, and industrial leaders, and the abolition of the House of Peers created an opportunity for career bureaucrats to move into top political positions.[19]

It was apparently Miyajima Seijirō who first brought Ikeda to the attention of Prime Minister Yoshida Shigeru. Miyajima, an old classmate and intimate friend of Yoshida's, financed Yoshida's political career and arranged strong business backing for him. Yoshida, himself an elite government official in the Ministry of Foreign Affairs before entering politics, recruited Ikeda to his Liberal Party in July 1948. Yoshida took advantage of the many retirements and forced retirements of politicians to recruit twenty-five high-level bureaucrats into politics. This was the famous "Yoshida school," of which Ikeda became known as the star pupil.[20]

When Yoshida formed his third cabinet in 1949, he appointed Ikeda as minister of finance. According to *Asahi* newspaper reporter Shioguchi Kiichi, Miyajima Seijirō conducted the final job interview, at Yoshida's request summoning Ikeda to his office, quizzing him on his economic views, and then telephoning Yoshida to tell him that Ikeda would do. Miyajima then, the story goes, turned to a surprised Ikeda and told him, "You are now Finance Minister" (*"Kimi, Ōkura-daijin da"*).[21] Ikeda would serve repeated terms as finance minister, also inheriting the leadership of Yoshida's political faction. He became prime minister in 1960, when he became famous for his tax cuts and "positive" spending policy.

The Harmonization of Different Views

The views of these three men harmonized in complicated ways. Ōuchi's fear of inflation aligned him with Ikeda against Ishibashi, even though politically he was far closer to Ishibashi. In 1949 Ikeda rejected the inflationary policies of his former boss, Ishibashi, and became the more-or-less willing executor of Joseph Dodge's deflation policy. Then in 1956, when Ishibashi became prime minister, Ikeda served as his minister of finance, rejoining Ishibashi in his promotion of "positive" policies.

The three men also differed in their attitudes toward the Cold War. Ikeda's anticommunism aligned him with U.S. concerns, whereas Ōuchi and Tsuru were leaders in the very large anti-Cold War political protest movement in 1950s Japan. Both Ōuchi and Tsuru were interested in the Soviet model of a modern, rationally planned economy. Ishibashi disagreed with socialism but shared Ōuchi's pacifism and was equally opposed to American Cold War priorities. Later he led a Japanese friendship mission to Communist China, hoping to establish better diplomatic and trading relations. Fiscally, the views of the ideas of the Shoup group were closest to those of the leftwing economists, such as Ōuchi and Tsuru.

POSTWAR INFLATION AS UNJUST TAXATION

When the war ended, so did many of the authoritarian controls that had kept inflation under increasingly shaky control. Inflation then became severe, as early postwar government leaders tolerated it in the interests of industrial recovery. Furthermore, U.S. occupation authorities, surprisingly, permitted the Japanese state to retain its command over the creation of money and credit. (By contrast, the Japanese military had quickly seized control of this aspect of government in the areas they had occupied during the war.)[22] Thus, the Japanese authorities did not lack for means of funding after the war. Japan did lack almost everything else, however, and the imbalance between the abundance of money and the dearth of goods meant inflation. The initial short-lived postwar cabinet, in which Shibusawa Keizō was minister of finance, made this problem worse by issuing huge subsidies to reimburse and protect the industrial firms that had worked closely with the wartime state. Wartime industrial financing had been conducted through the highly centralized banking system, therefore these subsidies also bailed out the banks.

One of the first and most outspoken critics of this inflationary finance was Ōuchi, who emphasized the problems that inflation created for the daily life of consumers and criticized the government for not putting their plight first.[23] In November 1945 in a national radio address, he famously scolded the minister of finance for using inflation rather than effective tax collection to resolve the country's debts. "I tremble at the foolhardiness of your inflation policy," Ōuchi told Minister Shibusawa

Keizō.[24] To Ōuchi's delight, Shibusawa stopped paying the government's wartime debts to munitions companies, the main focus of Ōuchi's criticism, and implemented a variety of new policies that Ōuchi supported, including a one-time wealth levy implemented in conjunction with the "new yen" reform of February–March 1946.[25] SCAP (Supreme Commander for the Allied Powers) at that time concurred with Ōuchi, meaning that Shibusawa could not refuse these reforms. Later in 1946, Ōuchi, writing together with four of his former students, argued that the government should institute higher taxes to meet revenue needs rather than printing new money, an activity that he considered "the most traditional and unjust form of taxation."[26]

As Ōuchi explained, taxation and inflation were alternative ways for governments to pay for war. In World War I, Ōuchi noted, all the major combatants had issued large volumes of public bonds, in effect creating new money to pay for their wartime purchases. Britain raised taxes before and during the war, leaving its economy in much better shape after 1918 than Germany's. This finding buttressed his argument that the German hyperinflation was more the result of German actions than of reparations imposed on it. (This debate was highly relevant to Japan after World War II – from his side Ishibashi, adapting Keynes' critique, blamed reparations for German hyperinflation.)

In World War II, as well as World War I, the Allies had relied on taxation far more than the Axis, Ōuchi noted. (Britain covered 29 percent of its war costs through taxation, and the United States 37 percent.) By contrast, Germany and Japan both kept taxes too low to even cover the increased interest on the higher public debt caused by war expenditures. Undertaxation and slashed production levels were the two major causes of postwar inflation in both Germany and Japan, Ōuchi thought.[27]

These well-publicized arguments, and Ōuchi's willingness to stake out the performative space of democracy, made him famous in postwar Japan. In the June 1946 book on inflation that Ōuchi published with his students, the economists jokingly depicted the government as a mediocre college student, answering exam questions on fiscal policy set by the patient but slightly exasperated professors, who doubted their dim student's capabilities. Their confident, didactic tone about the arcane subject of public finance was at least as appealing to their readers as the content of their comments.[28]

Ōuchi himself had just turned down the opportunity to join the government as minister of finance. The Shidehara cabinet lasted less than eight months, until the Liberal Party won the first postwar election in May

1946. The new prime minister, Yoshida Shigeru, first offered the position of finance minister to the ardently anti-inflationary Ōuchi.[29] One reason Ōuchi refused was because he assumed, probably correctly, that he would be undercut by the career officials (such as Ikeda) who were nominally under him. Yoshida's own policy position was evidently not at all fixed at this point, for he subsequently offered the post to Ishibashi.

Ishibashi was convinced that the great danger was not inflation but rather postwar deflation and depression. Citing Keynes, he argued that true inflation could happen only during periods of full employment – which clearly did not apply to postwar Japan, with its millions of displaced and underemployed people. The current wave of price increases, he contended, was not inflation but "famine prices," a reflection of shortages and chronically low production levels.[30] Ishibashi, who favored economic decontrol in general, deliberately abolished price controls. He directed the establishment of the Reconstruction Finance Bank, a parastatal agency that in effect created and lent vast sums of money to priority industries, mainly coal mining, iron and steel, electric power, and fertilizer production.

Ishibashi's system benefited entrepreneurs who received governmental or bank subsidies, dispensed mainly in the forms of low-interest loans. The real repayment burden of these loans, in a time of high inflation, diminished daily. The immediate losers in this process were the general public, whose purchasing power shrank when prices rose faster than wages. The inflationary financing of industry was thus a form of *social* forced investment, which transferred purchasing power to favored industries. In justification of this policy, Ishibashi argued that that net social effect was general economic reconstruction – a benefit to all. Industrialists liked the subsidy system, quietly expressing their support in the form of briefcases full of cash delivered to politicians and officials, as came to light in the 1948 Shōwa Electric scandal that helped discredit the Reconstruction Finance Bank-centered subsidy system as a whole.[31]

Although inflation was problematic, it offered a great opportunity to tenant farmers under the occupation-sponsored land reform program. Postwar inflation made the land reform far more effective than would otherwise have been the case. In Ronald P. Dore's memorable comment, fixing land purchase prices during a time of high inflation, combined with low-cost loans, meant that the final cost of a *tan* of rice land equaled a few packs of cigarettes.[32] This great redistribution of wealth to the most poverty-ridden area of the economy happened without the need for any explicit political battles.

SCAP was critical of the inflation policy and purged Ishibashi from public office in May 1947. Its public justification was the unfounded charge that Ishibashi had supported the war. The purge silenced Ishibashi politically until the occupation ended, but the next two cabinets continued the inflationary subsidy policy, making it clear that the motivation for this policy was the ongoing weakness of the recovery and cabinets' tenuous hold on power rather than Ishibashi's personal inclination.[33]

To summarize, postwar inflation in part reflected basic shortages of goods. In part, it reflected more money chasing these scarce goods, and this inflationary creation of money and credit functioned as a kind of taxation. From this point of view, the people paid, and the government and its clients received: this is the essential relationship that constitutes taxation. There were, however, practical limits to this ability to tax via inflation. The government, acting via the banking system, could create money easily enough. The problem was in absorbing the "excess" purchasing power generated by that new money once it reached the hands of consumers. Taxation in the strict sense was needed in these circumstances not to "get money" as such but to *regulate* its value. In this way, taxation under a system of inflationary financing was essential to the social constitution of money itself.

Both Japanese and American economists intended taxation to absorb purchasing power. Carl Shoup himself did a study in 1941 on "the amount of taxation needed to avert inflation," showing that he thought along these lines.[34] After Ishibashi's purge, the Ministry of Finance used taxation to achieve monetary control, with some success by 1948. As SCAP economist and Shoup mission advisor Martin Bronfenbrenner described it, this absorption of purchasing power in the hands of the public had actually "checked a rampant inflation" before Dodge's arrival in February 1949. (Or at least it moderated inflation significantly.) Bronfenbrenner applauded that goal but considered it an unfinished project because inflation control was accomplished "with a patchwork tax system," held together with "chewing gum and baling wire." Reliance on taxes to control inflation pushed this system to its limits.

THE SPECTRE OF TAX REVOLT

As the pressure on the tax system increased, it seemed to authorities, including Ikeda, that the nation faced a potential tax revolt with a dangerously revolutionary edge. In a post-occupation memoir published in 1952, Ikeda frankly acknowledged the truth of the popular postwar understanding that "if you pay your taxes honestly, you'll be hung out to dry."[35] (The Japanese metaphor might suggest, more than putting out the laundry, the image of a line of gutted fish or squid.) Ikeda explained that taxpayers and officials were caught in a "vicious circle," as, under the pressure of inflation, tax collectors needed to deliver more taxes, squeezing taxpayers harder, provoking more evasion and resistance, leading to arbitrary mass reassessments and ever more resistance.

In the first place, taxation had become incredibly complicated. "To raise the aggregate amounts required to check inflation," Bronfenbrenner wrote, "a bewildering multitude of direct and indirect taxes were in force." Second, taxes were heavy. Inflation had made people's incomes appear to swell in monetary terms, as Ikeda explained, making more lower-income earners subject to the income tax. Materially, however, people's living standards in 1947 had been reduced to about half the level of the mid-1930s. Many formerly comfortable people pursued a "bamboo shoot lifestyle," meaning they peeled off family possessions one layer at a time, selling them in order to fend off starvation. Ikeda estimated that citizens paid the government 24 percent of their income in 1948 and 26 percent in 1949.[36] This statistic does not even begin to convey how hard it was to make ends meet. In 1948, some two-thirds of household spending went to food alone – and many people were still hungry. Of the one-third of household income that remained after necessary food expenses, taxes took almost 60 percent. Relative to actual consumption levels, Japanese taxes were outstandingly high in international comparison.[37] In these circumstances, tax resistance could take on a desperate edge.

A third problem was that enforcement became more uneven, arbitrary, and corrupt, creating anger at its unfairness. At the center of the national tax system was the income tax, which relied on self-assessment. The self-reporting system was first adopted in April 1945 but evasion was widespread. All the tax experts – American and Japanese – saw popular acceptance of taxation as crucial, and believed that the government risked its legitimacy if enforcement seemed capricious. Shoup mission members thought that encouraging compliance was one of the most important aspects of their task. This issue was treated very seriously by occupation officials too. General William F. Marquat, head of SCAP's Economic and Science Section, at one point demanded a report on the number of Japanese indicted for tax evasion every ten days and expressed his displeasure when the list seemed too short.[38] In Ikeda's view, it was only natural that if taxes were excessive, people would do their best not to pay. This is why he wanted to lower taxes, reasoning that the perception of fairness would induce greater voluntary compliance and actually result in higher returns. Ikeda had approved the self-reporting system in 1945, and claimed that it had worked until wartime discipline broke down. After the defeat, he thought, "it was as if politics, society, economy, and culture all lost their way," and "all morality and discipline was loosened."[39] From a less bureaucratic and more democratic standpoint, we could say that the Japanese people, having contributed so much to the imperial state, were not inclined to fund it further.

Bronfenbrenner concurred with Ikeda, commenting that, in this environment of ubiquitous underreporting, "arbitrary mass reassessments were carried out periodically . . . as each local tax office strove to meet or exceed its quota of collections. . . . ":

> Honest and dishonest suffered alike, and taxes were collected in the presence of armed Occupation troops, almost literally at gun-point. Widespread evasion was met with widespread extortion, and accompanied by widespread corruption of the underpaid tax personnel. The tax collector had replaced the policeman as the nation's bogey; "bad taxes" were a main economic talking point of the Japanese Communist Party. Capital accumulation, either individual or corporate, required tax evasion almost as a *sine qua non*.[40]

From a tax collector's standpoint, as represented by Ikeda, taxation turned into "a fight with the people as a whole." Sometimes these were actually physical fights, both attacks on tax offices and ad hoc people's courts (*tsurushi-agé*) where individual tax collectors were "tried" by groups of angry taxpayers. Like Bronfenbrenner, Ikeda correctly feared that the Japan Communist Party was benefiting from this situation.[41]

THE SHOUP MISSION'S WELCOME

Ikeda and Ōuchi both welcomed the Shoup mission, but for different reasons. Ōuchi wanted a high-tax and high-public service welfare state based on the British Beveridge Plan. Ikeda wanted to cut taxes, calm popular anger, and erect an elite mutual support system for the big banks, industry, the Ministry of Finance, and his own political party.

The Shoup mission itself was one of a flurry of American expert missions sent overseas. As part of this activity, Shoup, with his wide experience as a taxation consultant in various countries (recounted in Chapters 3 and 4), is well described as an international "fiscal doctor." The reference here is to the widespread practice of U.S. "money doctoring," which goes back to the beginning of the twentieth century. American "money doctors," the most prominent of whom was Dr. Edwin Kemmerer of Princeton University, led expert missions to other, often subordinate or semi-subordinate countries, in order to redesign their fiscal, monetary, and central banking institutions. These missions began as an overtly empire-building project.[42] Most of these "money doctors" had a conservative, Wall Street orientation, unlike the more progressive bent of the Shoup reforms. Nor was the United States the only twentieth century power to advance its interests in this manner. Before 1945, Japanese experts had led their own official or semiofficial missions to redesign fiscal and monetary institutions in places where Japan enjoyed financial influence, and many of these individuals contributed to Japan's postwar economic plans.[43]

Joseph M. Dodge fit the money-doctor mold. Already a veteran bank executive, Dodge in 1945–6 headed the finance division in the U.S. Military Government in occupied Germany and participated in the 1946 Colm-Dodge-Goldsmith monetary reform plan there, before being appointed to oversee Japanese government finances. Dodge's high-level and authoritative mission arrived in Tokyo in February 1949. His prime directive was to stop inflation. It was Ōuchi who dubbed this new policy the "Dodge Line," and the name persisted.[44] Dodge immediately took command of Japanese government finances, establishing a critical context for the reception of the lower-level advisory mission led by Shoup, who came to Japan two months later.

The Dodge Line, which coincided with Yoshida's new Liberal Party government, meant a great change of course. It was also a grand simplification. Dodge ordered the government's many special accounts to be combined into a single consolidated budget, which was required to balance revenues and expenditures. He demanded year-to-year balance in what the Japanese government considered to be capital-investment accounts, which resulted in a deflationary "super-balanced budget," as it was dubbed. In addition to this, Dodge also instituted a single exchange rate – the famous ¥360/$1 rate – in place of an ultracomplex system of multiple foreign-exchange rates (which varied depending on the good in question and the foreign source or market). This action helped dismantle the elaborate system of emergency administrative controls that had begun in 1937, of which the occupation-era Economic Stabilization Board system now formed the latest layer. Simultaneously, the occupation's *zaibatsu*-busting program was ended.

In many respects, the Dodge Line was a case of deflationary overkill. It was certainly perceived that way, with dismay, by nearly all of the Japanese involved (as well as by Shoup and many SCAP officials; see Chapters 8 and 10). Despite this, by the spring of 1949, inflation had been considerably reduced owing to increased production, price and wage controls, and stepped-up taxation. The two short-lived coalition governments formed by the Socialist Party, the Democratic Party, and the National Cooperative Party had worked hard to achieve this outcome. Arisawa Hiromi, Tsuru Shigeto, and the Economic Stabilization Board took leading roles in shaping these policies.[45] As Ishibashi had anticipated, the much harsher Dodge Line also induced an economic depression, euphemistically referred to by both Dodge and Ikeda as a "stabilization crisis."

Ikeda expected to find an ally in Dodge but was soon disappointed. After the seventeen-month interval of coalition government, Yoshida Shigeru returned to office as prime minister, first forming a caretaker cabinet and then, as a result of the January 1949 elections, gaining a strong majority in the Diet. As part of this electoral sweep, Ikeda won a Diet seat from Hiroshima Prefecture. During the campaign, the Liberal Party had promised both big tax cuts and ¥100 billion in public spending. After becoming finance minister on February 16, however, Ikeda immediately faced the thankless task of negotiating an austerity budget with the unbending Joseph Dodge.

Initially, Ikeda and other finance ministry officials thought Dodge's arrival would end what they considered the ridiculous meddling of SCAP's reformist New Dealers, who had been very active in arenas such as land reform and protection for industrial workers. Ikeda agreed with Dodge on the desirability of controlling inflation and balancing the national budget, which is why they quickly shut down Ishibashi's Reconstruction Finance Bank. In addition, Yoshida and Ikeda shared American alarm about Communism and the recent military victories by the Chinese Communists, although they resisted pressure from the United States to rapidly remilitarize Japan. Ikeda and ministry officials were, however, greatly disappointed to discover that Dodge would subject them to much tighter fiscal control. Ikeda found it trying to deal with "stubborn old grandpa" Dodge, as recorded by Ikeda's personal secretary Miyazawa Kiichi (another future prime minister).[46] Ikeda thus appeared in public as the executor of Dodge's unpopular deflation policy, in many ways still acting as the underling rather than the executive minister of finance. Moreover, like Ishibashi, Ikeda was committed to steering scarce resources to industry – as was everyone from Arisawa Hiromi to Bank of Japan governor Ichimada Hisato. Ikeda thought the American banker was taking the austerity plan much too far.

This is why, although Ikeda had initially welcomed Dodge as a counter to American New Dealers, he welcomed Shoup to counterbalance Dodge. Ikeda even suggested that the idea of inviting the Shoup mission arose from his own talks with Dodge, which Ikeda described as "tax reduction negotiations."[47] Dodge did not see these talks as negotiations, nor were tax cuts on the table. Ikeda nevertheless pleaded for a tax cut, even if only a token one for public relations purposes. The Japanese "patient" was certainly ill and needed treatment, Ikeda told money-doctor Dodge, but a minor tax reduction would serve as a sedative. If the medicine were "sugar-coated," it would go down more easily.[48] Dodge would not budge. This was the political context in which Shoup was welcomed.

There was also an intellectual context, consisting of a shared culture and ethos of expertise. The late 1940s was a heyday for transnational technocratic ideas and approaches to policy. The Shoup mission's rapport with likeminded Japanese experts was not unusual. When dealing with complex technical subjects, Japanese and American experts frequently sat down together and amicably worked out new systems, as happened with the Richard Rice mission on statistics and the William H. Wandell mission on social security.[49] In all these cases, both Japanese and American economic experts believed that their recommended reforms would make Japan more democratic.

Tax experts found they had much in common even when their economic philosophies differed. Although Ikeda called Shoup's approach excessively theoretical, on the whole he welcomed Shoup's expertise and praised his professionalism. Comparing it to Dodge's top-down and authoritarian approach, Ikeda and Tsuru both praised the thoroughness of Shoup's research into Japan's actual social conditions.[50] Shoup also clearly respected Ikeda's team. In a retrospective essay about the mission, he opened by commenting that the officials who came from the Ministry of Finance "were of very high quality" and that their command of English and their "knowledge of the Japanese fiscal system made them invaluable colleagues."[51] The Americans felt even more comfortable with Japanese academic economists. They went surprisingly far in their efforts to make this collaboration formal with three such individuals. As W. Elliot Brownlee reports, Shoup and the man who originally recommended him, L. Harold Moss, both wanted to include Tsuru, Shiomi Saburō, and Ito Hanya on the mission, but their more politically minded bosses in SCAP preferred to have an all-American team.[52]

Regardless of their fluency in English, these men spoke the same professional language as their American counterparts. Despite the recent war between their two nations, they had read the same books and learned from the same events, particularly the economic problems of interwar Europe. Just as Shoup brought his knowledge of tax systems and experience as a "tax doctor" in post-World War I France and Cuba to his analysis of Japan, Japanese tax economists brought to the table expertise on the interwar German, Italian, British, Soviet, and American tax systems, not to mention their own national experience over the past century. For this reason, the Japanese government swiftly passed "a set of rationally structured tax laws" based on the Shoup mission's recommendations that eliminated the confusing maze of surcharges and special taxes.[53]

Typically, the Japanese knew precisely when the Americans were proposing something that was unique to American practice or was not yet in place anywhere in the world. For example, when a different American commission – staffed by businessmen rather than technocrats – recommended in 1949 that the government privatize electric power generation facilities, almost every Japanese individual involved complained that the proposal followed idiosyncratic American practice rather than considering European systems.[54] Similarly, Ikeda Hayato complained that the value-added tax advocated by Shoup was not an established practice in other countries.[55]

TAXATION FOR DEMOCRACY

This shared culture of expertise meant that these tax experts all recognized that their differences were expressions of their divergent political visions. "Public finance is the way that political organizations administer and distribute wealth," as Ōuchi explained.[56] Three aspects of fiscal democracy in particular absorbed their attention: the social allocation of resources, local fiscal autonomy, and public understanding of and commitment to the system of taxation.

The Social Allocation of Resources

Ōuchi and other progressives thought that the government should choose a high-tax, high-service strategy and use the tax system to allocate resources more fairly among the population. By contrast, Ikeda rejected both high taxes and the goal of equalizing incomes. For this reason, Ikeda also put far less value than Ōuchi did on making the tax system progressive or taxing various sources of income equally. The Shoup mission took a position closer to Ōuchi's than to Ikeda's.

To put it another way, this fight was over the proper size of government, and the extent to which the state should ensure a minimum livelihood to all its citizens. In contrast to Prime Minister Yoshida's pledge to keep taxes low, Ōuchi wanted to follow Great Britain's example and institute "cradle to grave" social services that would provide health care, schooling, unemployment insurance, and old-age pensions for all. Beginning in late 1949, Ōuchi chaired the government's Social Insurance Commission (Shakai Hoshō Seidō Shingikai). Its final report on October 16, 1950, based on the British Beveridge Plan, advocated a long-term, comprehensive social insurance system for the whole population.[57] Ōuchi wanted to provide a solid fiscal basis for those services and sought to mobilize public opinion to that end through his many books and college lectures. In a 1953 popular-press book, *Economics for Ladies*, Ōuchi explained that taxes enabled the state to provide households with necessary services, such as subsidized health insurance and schooling.[58] In addition, he reminded his reading public in 1965 that higher taxes could support social democracy only when taxes focused on civilian needs. Prewar governments had directed "rarely less than 30% of government spending" to the military, Ōuchi explained, much to the detriment of civilian standards of living.[59] In other words, the state was the appropriate institution to provide a minimum standard of living for all its citizens, and taxes were the best mechanism for funding this, provided they were not diverted to military spending. Ōuchi's expansive approach to public finance, as opposed to a narrow technical focus on the mechanisms for implementing fiscal policy, was his signal contribution to postwar debate on the subject.[60]

The Shoup reformers shared Ōuchi's comprehensiveness of vision as well as his assumptions that fiscal education, transparent, streamlined rules, and a progressive tax structure all reinforced democracy. As Jerome B. Cohen, who provided staff support to the Shoup mission, put it: "The purpose... is to effect permanent reforms which will provide Japan with a more efficient, a more scientific, and above all a more equitable system of taxation than she has hitherto possessed."[61]

Although the Shoup mission did not publicly weigh in on the issue of the proper size of the state, it shared Ōuchi's preferences for both a more progressive income tax and for increasing reliance on the tax. Here too, the Shoup mission's position contrasts more sharply with that of Ikeda. Ikeda was not particularly concerned with making the tax system more progressive in 1949, and he thought taxation needed an overhaul mainly in the sense that it should shrink. He approached the Shoup mission as if its mandate was to make recommendations about tax cuts rather than to assess the tax structure, and he ignored this section of the mission's recommendations.[62] Ikeda strategically misrepresented the Americans, claiming that although Shoup did not at first understand the need for tax cuts, by the time Shoup visited Japan on a second trip in 1950, "he almost completely accepted my point of view."[63]

Shoup and Ōuchi agreed that emphasizing a more progressive income tax was the best tactic to make the tax system fairer. Ōuchi had argued in 1946 that property taxes were preferable to income taxes because poor people typically owned no property, but by 1949, after the agricultural land reform, he had changed his thinking.[64] He concurred with Shoup that Japan should rely most heavily on the income tax, because it was structured in a way that assigned the heaviest burden to those who could best afford it. After the Shoup reforms, Ōuchi continued to insist that the government place even more weight on the income tax, and complained that too much revenue came from excise taxes, which were disproportionately paid by the poor.[65]

Similarly, Ōuchi strongly supported Shoup's effort to reform the tax system comprehensively, both out of a desire for greater fairness and out of recognition that piecemeal reforms would change economic behavior in unintended ways. Changes in one tax would affect many other decisions throughout the economy; therefore, all changes should be integrated into a coherent system. As part of this effort, both men wanted to equalize taxes from assets as well as wages.

Local Fiscal Autonomy

The Shoup mission did reintroduce one important issue – independent local government financing. Occupation officials thought that one institutional barrier to democratization in Japan was the inability of localities to protect themselves from national government power. At the end of 1947 they abolished the Home Ministry, which had control over local governments, and oversaw the enactment of the new Local Administration Law. That reform had a major missing piece, because the Ministry of Finance collected most taxes nationally and then doled out subsidies to prefectural and municipal authorities. The Ministry of Finance thus still controlled local governments' access to revenue. After December 31, 1947, that ministry accordingly became the main enforcer of local government subordination to national priorities.[66]

The Shoup mission attempted to change this fiscal dependence by giving local governments an independent revenue stream, on the basis of sales taxes at the prefectural level and property taxes at the local level, as in the United States. The mission members calculated that this would increase local revenues by at least ¥40 billion. Jerome Cohen summarized the mission's position:

> In order to reduce the highly centralized power of the national government and develop a grass-roots democracy, the occupation has been working toward greater local autonomy, to some degree in prefectures but principally in cities, towns, and villages. This program is in danger of collapse, however, because localities have not received adequate fiscal powers to pay for carrying out new responsibilities. The Mission's recommendations were designed to remedy this omission.[67]

These policy efforts were welcomed by Ōuchi and his circle and rejected by the ruling political party. Ōuchi had actually published a short article in English on local and municipal finance as early as 1917, but then moved on to other issues.[68] After the war, Ōuchi headed the National Research Group for Regional Survey Research (Chihō Chōsa Kikan Zenkoku Kyōgikai), which carried out economic analysis for local governments on such topics as overpopulation, depopulation, declining natural resources, and pollution. The organization contracted with local and national government bodies and also published the resulting data.[69] One of Ōuchi's students, Takahashi Masao, who worked for the Economic and Scientific Section of the occupation and later with Ōuchi on some of these projects, said that his interest in local government financing was first sparked by conversations with occupation personnel.[70] The Liberal Party government directed by Yoshida and Ikeda, however, either truncated these reforms or repealed them almost as soon as the occupation personnel had left for home. In this way, and in others, as Miyamoto Ken'ichi put it, Shoup's reforms were "only half-realized."[71] Although progressive governments in many of Japan's major cities and a few prefectures pushed for greater fiscal autonomy in the 1960s and 1970s, these efforts only gained significant legal ground in May 1995 with the passage of the Law for the Promotion of Decentralization and the "Trinity Reform" of subsidies, local taxes, and allocation formulas that began in 2002.[72]

Democratizing Fiscal Consciousness

Although everyone involved thought that building support for paying taxes was important, both Ōuchi and Shoup saw their task as vital to the constitution of democracy. Ōuchi thought citizens should understand the way the tax system favored some groups over others and insist on participating in those decisions. By the end of the occupation, as Ōuchi noted with approval, unlike the prewar era, income taxes were being collected from farmers and small businessmen, rather than from employees alone. Employees' taxes had actually declined, although compliance was still far greater for people whose taxes were withheld by their employers.[73]

Efforts to collect taxes equally across the whole population soon halted, however. After Japan regained sovereignty, government leaders seemed far less concerned with equitable tax compliance than were Ōuchi or Shoup. Officials of the Liberal Party and then the Liberal Democratic Party undermined this aspect of tax reform. They deliberately structured enforcement policy to favor farmers and other self-employed people, who provided the Liberal Democratic Party with loyal votes, at the same time that they enforced withholding from wage-workers' paychecks, since urban industrial workers were more likely to vote Socialist. Tsuru asserted that the Ministry of Finance "deliberately underestimated the income of the self-assessed group" in order to sabotage Socialist prime minister Katayama Tetsu's attempt to pay a "living-cost subsidy" to government employees in 1947. Later Ikeda conspicuously praised the mechanism of the self-assessment system as an expression of citizen participation "as members of a democratic state," even though it encouraged illegal action by a favored segment of the population.[74]

Farmers and small businessmen responded with massive tax evasion and unswerving support for the Liberal Democratic Party. Nor was this political manipulation of the revenue system secret. The resulting tax situation was popularly expressed as "*ku-ro-yon*" (9–6–4) or "*tō-gō-san*" (10–5–3), meaning that employees paid 90 or 100 percent of their income tax obligations, small business owners paid 50 or 60 percent of theirs, and farmers paid only 30 or 40 percent.[75] The Ministry of Finance never policed this kind of tax evasion systematically, notwithstanding the humorous depiction of their zeal in Itami Jūzō's film, *A Taxing Woman* (*Marusa no onna*), further rewarding rural voters at the expense of urban ones.

To return to 1949, Shoup's thinking on this point was again closer to Ōuchi's than to Ikeda's. Both men saw voluntary compliance as only one aspect of well-informed citizen activism; one that should be balanced by popular monitoring of government priorities. They wanted to help citizens use their new economic knowledge to challenge and redirect state authority. Their priorities were shaped in part by their common assumption that during the war Japan's leaders had imposed dangerously irrational policies on their own people, so their priorities were to make the system both more scientific and fairer. Ōuchi was at his most scathing when he rejected wartime arguments that "when the Japanese people offer their taxes to the state, they are offering the first fruits of the harvest to the gods."[76] Taxes were not "first fruits" offered up to the gods, but public money to be used for public purposes. Their shared distaste for that worldview brought technically minded Japanese and Americans together during the occupation years.[77]

Ōuchi and Shoup had each articulated the need for transparent rules and clearly stated policies long before 1949. Brownlee tells us that Professors Edwin R. A. Seligman and Robert Murray Haig, both of whom taught Shoup, believed that democracy required an economically literate public, showing that Shoup and Ōuchi enjoyed a meeting of minds on this point.[78] In addition to this, Brownlee notes that Shoup was particularly critical of arguments that confused people: "an intelligent democracy cannot be erected on a basis of long-continued ignorance with respect to taxation."[79]

This concern for education explains why Ōuchi wrote for popular audiences, as did Shoup himself. For example, Ōuchi explained in a handbook that introduced public-finance statistics to a popular audience in 1965 that, "We Japanese, who are capitalists and workers on the one hand, are on the other national citizens (kokumin) and citizens (shimin) of local organizations, that is, cities, towns, and villages." As such, citizens have the responsibility to pay taxes, and "the modern state – both socialist and capitalist" has a responsibility to improve standards of living for them. Ōuchi went on to explain that unlike government publications on the same subject, "this book looks hard at how public finance affects the standards of living of the citizens. In particular it assesses the extent to which the huge increase in revenues over the last decade has improved living standards."[80]

Shoup also evoked the "tax atmosphere" as a crucial component of what would now be called "building capacity" for democracy. This concern explains his recommendation that the government create incentives for tax compliance. Creating a good "tax atmosphere" meant giving citizens ammunition to prevent the government from financing its activities in an undemocratic manner. Shoup not only advocated popular monitoring of fiscal policy; he conducted his own mission in ways that made it more likely. When his work was completed, Shoup deliberately announced his recommendations to the public before he submitted them to the Japanese government. Shoup – and his Japanese collaborators – hoped to build popular support for his ideas, knowing that the Japanese government would dislike some of the proposals, such as greater fiscal autonomy for local governments.[81] It is possible that he released the report first on the advice of Tsuru Shigeto. Tsuru had discovered the power of public opinion in 1947 after writing the first white paper on the economy, which revealed official assessments of the national economy to the public for the first time ever and became a surprise best-seller.

What, then, was the effect of the Shoup mission? The cross-cutting affinities explored in this chapter explain why the core elements of Shoup's tax reform remained in place after the Americans left, and why some specific elements were quickly abandoned. The same could be said of the persistence of Dodge's balanced-budget principle, but not most of his other restrictions. Together these changes established an enduring social-fiscal settlement. Inflation after 1949 was moderated and balanced by taxation. Taxation itself was made somewhat fairer, simpler, and less disruptive. It was reshaped to protect the interests of some Japanese at the expense of others. The postwar debate over tax structure and tax policy never divided neatly along national lines. In the end, Shoup was more a supporting actor than a major player in what was essentially a Japanese drama.

Notes

1. Ikeda, H., *Kinkō zaisei [Balanced Public Finance]* (Tokyo: Jitsugyō no Nihon Sha, 1952), 291 and Chapter 6 of this volume.
2. See, for example, Ikeda, H., *Kinkō zaisei*, 91.
3. Ōuchi, H., *Fujin no keizaigaku [Economics for Ladies]* (1953, revised ed. 1955), reprinted in volume 8 of *Ōuchi Hyōe chosakushū* (Tokyo: Iwanami, 1975), 509.
4. Cohen, T., *Remaking Japan: The American Occupation as New Deal* (New York: The Free Press, 1987), 171. Cohen was chief of SCAP's labor division.
5. Tsuru, S., *Japan's Capitalism: Creative Defeat and Beyond* (Cambridge: Cambridge University Press, 1993), 45.
6. Metzler, M., *Capital as Will and Imagination: Schumpeter's Guide to the Postwar Japanese Miracle* (Ithaca, NY: Cornell University Press, 2013).
7. See Bronfenbrenner, M., "Four Positions on Japanese Finance," *Journal of Political Economy* 1950, vol. 58 (4), pp. 281–8.
8. Hein, L., *Reasonable Men, Powerful Words: The Ōuchi Group and Political Culture in 20th Century Japan* (Washington, DC, and Berkeley, CA: University of California Press, The Woodrow Wilson Center Press, 2004). Japanese edition 理性ある人びと力ある言葉:大内兵衛グループの思想と行動、東京: 岩波書店、2007年7月; Ōuchi H., *Keizaigaku gojūnen [50 Years of Economics]* (Tokyo: Tōkyō Daigaku Shuppankai, 1959).
9. Ōuchi, H., Arisawa, H., Wakimura, Y., Takahashi, M., and Minobe, R., *Nihon infureshyon no kenkyū* (Tokyo: Kōdōsha, 1946), 30.

10. Ōuchi, H., "Keizai," [Economics], in T., *Sengo Nihon shōshi* [*Short Post-war History of Japan*] (Tokyo: Tokyo Daigaku Shuppankai, 1958), 63–174, especially pp. 76–81. Ōuchi drew on Constantino Bresciani-Turroni's *The Economics of Inflation: A Study of Currency Depreciation in Post-War Germany* (London: Allen and Unwin, 1937), a book that Dodge also studied.

11. On Ishibashi, see Nolte, S. H., *Liberalism in Modern Japan: Ishibashi Tanzan and His Teachers, 1905–1960* (Berkeley: University of California Press, 1986); and Metzler, M., *Lever of Empire: The International Gold Standard and the Crisis of Liberalism in Prewar Japan* (Berkeley: University of California Press, 2006).

12. Ōuchi, H., "Kin yushutsu kinshi shiron" [Historiography of the gold export embargo] *Keizaigaku ronshū* (*Tōkyō Teikoku Daigaku*), 1927, vol. 5 (4), pp. 103–42.

13. Ishibashi T., October 1951, in Ishibashi Tanzan Zenshū Hensan Iinkai, ed., *Ishibashi Tanzan zenshū* [*Complete Works of Ishibashi Tanzan*] (Tokyo: Tōyō Keizai Shinposha, 1970–72), vol. 15, 203.

14. Ikeda, H., *Kinkō zaisei*, 91.

15. Shioguchi K., *Kikigaki: Ikeda Hayato* [*Reminiscences: Ikeda Hayato*] (Tokyo: Asahi Shinbunsha, 1975), 13–15.

16. For the *zaikai*, see Fletcher, W. M., *The Japanese Business Community and National Trade Policy, 1920–1942* (Chapel Hill: University of North Carolina Press, 1989); Yanaga, C., *Big Business in Japanese Politics* (New Haven, CT: Yale University Press, 1968); and Carlile, L. E., "Zaikai and the Politics of Production in Japan, 1940–1962," PhD dissertation, University of California, Berkeley, 1989.

17. Shioguchi K., *Kikigaki: Ikeda Hayato*, 13–15.

18. Calder, K. E., *Strategic Capitalism: Private Business and Public Purpose in Japanese Industrial Finance* (Princeton, NJ: Princeton University Press, 1993), 44, 301.

19. The Ministry of Finance was, however, physically dispersed when SCAP commandeered the ministry's headquarters in September 1945 and was not reassembled in the old headquarters until March 1956.

20. Masumi J., (trans. Carlile, L. E.) *Postwar Politics in Japan, 1945–1955* (Berkeley, CA: Institute of East Asian Studies and Center for Japanese Studies, 1985), 279.

21. Yanaga, C., *Big Business in Japanese Politics*, 141–3; Kumon, S., Koyama, K., Satō, S., *Postwar Politician: The Life of Masayoshi Ohira* (Kodansha America, Tokyo: 1990), 68, 92, 122; Kiichi, S., *Kikigaki: Ikeda Hayato*, 25. On Miyajima, see Fletcher, W. M., *The Japanese Business Community and National Trade Policy, 1920–1942*.

22. Ōuchi, H., "The World Monetary System and Japan's Economic Future." *Contemporary Japan* 1947, vol. 16 (4–6), pp. 117–33.

23. Ōuchi, H., "Keizai," pp. 84–5.

24. Reproduced in Arisawa Hiromi and Inaba Hidezō, eds., *Shiryō sengo nijūnenshi: Keizai* [*Postwar Twenty-year History in Documents: Economics*], vol. 2 (Tokyo: Nihon Hyōronsha, 1966).

25. Itō Mitsuharu confirms the speech's impact in Asahi Shinbun Henshūbu, ed., *Shōwa shi no shunkan* [*Key Moments of the Showa Era*] (Tokyo: Asahi Shinbunsha, 1966), 201.
26. Ōuchi, H., et al., *Nihon infureshyon no kenkyū*, 30.
27. Ōuchi, H., et al., *Nihon infureshyon no kenkyū*, 30. Other economists blamed inflation on the expected costs of Japan's reparations or on the costs of the occupation (which the Japanese government also bore); Hijikata S. and Kangyō Ginkō Keizai Kenkyūkai, *Nihon keizai no antei to kyōkai* [*Outlines of a Stable Japanese Economy*] (Tokyo: Kōbunsha, 1949), 13–22.
28. Takahashi Masao in his introduction to *Nihon infuresyon no kenkyū*; Hiraoka Toshio, "Kyōju gurūpu sannin otoko–Ōuchi Hyōe, Arisawa Hiromi, Takahashi Masao," in *Bungei shunjū*, 25.3 1947, pp. 40–7.
29. Hein, L., *Reasonable Men, Powerful Words: The Ōuchi Group and Political Culture in 20th Century Japan*, 88–89.
30. Ishibashi to Lower House, July 25, 1946, in *Ishibashi Tanzan zenshū*, 1946, vol. 13, pp. 186–202; *Oriental Economist*, August 19, 1946, pp. 518–23; Andō Yoshio interview with Ichimada Hisato, "Sengo no kinyū seisaku" [Postwar financial policy], in Andō, *Shōwa keizai shi e no shōgen* (Tokyo: Tokyo Mainichi Shinbunsha, 1966), 294–7.
31. According to Mrs. Ikeda, the president of Shōwa Electric personally brought a briefcase of money to Ikeda's house, but he refused it (Shioguchi, *Kikigaki*, 18).
32. Dore, R. P., *Land Reform in Japan* (London: Oxford University Press, 1959).
33. Ishibashi's purge is documented in SCAP, Government Section, Box 2275E, Files 8 and 9, U.S. National Archives (see also Kensei Shiryōshitsu, National Diet Library, Tokyo).
34. Quoted in Brownlee, W. E., "The Shoup Mission to Japan: Two Political Economies Intersect," in Martin, I. W., Mehrotra, A. K., Prasad, M., eds., *The New Fiscal Sociology: Taxation in Comparative and Historical Perspective* (Cambridge: Cambridge University Press, 2009), 245.
35. Ikeda, H., *Kinkō zaisei*, 92–3.
36. Ikeda, H., *Kinkō zaisei*, 92–4, 251. Dower, J. W., *Embracing Defeat: Japan in the Wake of World War II* (New York: W. W. Norton, 1999), 140–8.
37. Bronfenbrenner, M., "Four Positions on Japanese Finance," *Journal of Political Economy* 1950, vol. 58 (4), pp. 281–8.
38. Suzuki Gengo, in conference proceedings in *The Occupation of Japan: Economic Policy and Reform* (Norfolk, VA: General Douglas MacArthur Foundation, 1980), 81.
39. Ikeda, H., *Kinkō zaisei*, 92–3.
40. Bronfenbrenner, M., "Review of Report on Japanese Taxation by the Shoup Mission, Second Report on Japanese Taxation by the Shoup Mission by Carl S. Shoup," *American Economic Review*, 1951, vol. 41 (5), p. 983. Bronfenbrenner, J., Bronfenbrenner, U., Fitzgerald, B., et al., "Dr. Martin Bronfenbrenner (1914–1997): Scholar, Critic, Cynic, and Comrade-in-Arms," *American Journal of Economics and Sociology*, 1999, vol. 58

(3), pp. 491–522 and Ikeo, A., *The American Economist Martin Bron-fenbrenner (1914–1997) and the Reconstruction of the Japanese Economy (1947–1952)*, CHOPE Working Paper 2011–11 (Durham, NC: CHOPE, June 2011). Available at: http://hope.econ.duke.edu/sites/default/files/Ikeo20110616c-Letter-BronfenbrennerJapan.pdf, accessed September 27, 2012.

41. Ikeda, H., *Kinkō zaisei*, 93–4, 251; "Anti-Tax Activities of Japan Communist Party," February 2, 1948, Military Intelligence Section, General Staff, SCAP, 7497–6 (National Archives).

42. Thanks to Professor Katalin Ferber for her comments. See Drake, P. W., *The Money Doctor in the Andes: The Kemmerer Missions, 1923–1933* (Durham, NC: Duke University Press, 1989); Rosenberg, E. S., *Financial Missionaries to the World: The Politics and Culture of Dollar Diplomacy, 1900–1930* (Cambridge, MA: Harvard University Press, 1999); Flandreau, M., ed., *Money Doctors: The Experience of International Financial Advising, 1850–2000* (London and New York: Routledge, 2003).

43. Schiltz, M., *The Money Doctors from Japan* (Cambridge, MA: Harvard University Press, 2012), and Metzler, M., *Lever of Empire: The International Gold Standard and the Crisis of Liberalism in Prewar Japan*, (Berkeley: University of California Press, 2006), 14–90.

44. Tatsurō, U., *Japan's Postwar Economy: An Insider's View of Its History and Its Future* (Tokyo: Kodansha, 1983), 50.

45. Tsuru, S., *Japan's Capitalism: Creative Defeat and Beyond*, 47–8.

46. Miyazawa, K., *Tōkyō–Washinton no mitsudan* [*The Tokyo–Washington Secret Talks*] (Tokyo: Bingokai, reprint ed., 1975), 14–15; Ikeda, H., *Kinkō zaisei*, 215.

47. Ikeda, H., *Kinkō zaisei*, 95, 251–3.

48. Dodge memo of 3/25/1949 meeting, "Budget-Ikeda Interviews," Japan-1949–1, Joseph M. Dodge Papers, Burton Historical Collection, Detroit Public Library.

49. Hein, L., *Reasonable Men, Powerful Words: The Ōuchi Group and Political Culture in 20th Century Japan*, 87-113; see also, O'Bryan, S., *The Growth Idea: Purpose and Prosperity in Postwar Japan* (Honolulu: University of Hawaii Press, 2009).

50. Ikeda, H., *Kinkō zaisei*, 95, 106, 122, 252–4; Tsuru, S., *Japan's Capitalism: Creative Defeat and Beyond*, 52.

51. Shoup, C. S., "The Tax Mission to Japan, 1949–1950," in Gillis, M., ed., *Tax Reform in Developing Countries* (Durham, NC: Duke University Press, 1989), 177–8.

52. Brownlee, W. E., "The Transfer of Tax Ideas during the 'Reverse Course' of the U.S. Occupation of Japan," in Nehring, H., Schui, F., eds., *Global Debates about Taxation* (London: Palgrave-Macmillan, 2007), 177 n. 19.

53. Tsuru, S., *Japan's Capitalism: Creative Defeat and Beyond*, 52–4, 105.

54. Hein, L., *Fueling Growth: The Energy Revolution and Economic Policy in Postwar Japan* (Cambridge, MA: Harvard University Press, 1990), 188–202.

55. Ikeda, H., *Kinkō zaisei*, 256.
56. Tsuru, S., "Kaisetsu" [Analysis], in *Ōuchi Hyōe chosakushū*, vol. 7 (Tokyo: Iwanami Shoten, 1974–1975), 684–90.
57. Ōuchi, H., ed. *Sengo ni okeru shakai hoshō no tenkai* [*Overview of the Postwar Social Insurance System*] (Tokyo: Shiseidō, 1961), 3–26; Beveridge, W., *Social Insurance and Allied Services* (London: Her Majesty's Stationery Office, 1942).
58. Ōuchi, H., *Fujin no keizaigaku* [*Economics for Ladies*], 509.
59. Ōuchi, H., and Naitō, M., *Nihon zaisei zusetsu* [*Japanese Public Finance in Graphs*] (Tokyo: Iwanami Shinsho, 1965); Ōuchi, H., *Fujin no keizaigaku* [Economics for Ladies], 623–32.
60. Tsuru, S., "Kaisetsu" [Analysis].
61. Cohen, J. B., "Tax Reform in Japan," *Far Eastern Survey*, 1949, vol.18 (26), pp. 307–11, quotation p. 307.
62. Brownlee, W. E., "The Shoup Mission."
63. Ikeda, H., *Kinkō zaisei*, 96.
64. Ikeda, H., et al., *Nihon infureshyon no kenkyū*, 30.
65. Ikeda, H., *Fujin no keizagaku*, 524.
66. Akira, A., "The Making of the Postwar Local Government System," in Ward, R. E., Yoshikazu, S., eds., *Democratizing Japan: The Allied Occupation* (Honolulu: University of Hawaii Press, 1987), 253–83 esp. 274–5.
67. Cohen, J. B., "Tax Reform in Japan," 310.
68. Ouchi, H., "The Japanese Financial Department," in *Japanese Administration and Finance* (New York: Bureau of Municipal Research and Training School for Public Service, 1917), no. 83, 45–56.
69. Ōuchi, H. and Shin Chōsa Kikan Zenkoku Kyōgikai ed., *Chiiki to sangyō* [*Regional Economies and Industry*] (Tokyo: Shinhyōron, 1969).
70. Takahashi, M. sensei Beiju Kinen Kankōkai, ed., *Nijūseiki no gunzō: Takahashi Masao no shōgen* [*The Twentieth-century group: Takahashi Masao's Account*] (Tokyo: Daiichi Shorin, 1989), 133.
71. Hein Interview, Miyamoto Ken'ichi, May 18, 2009, Kyoto.
72. Mochida, N., *Fiscal Decentralization and Local Public Finance in Japan* (London: Routledge, 2008), 1, 9. Localities still have little autonomy in their spending decisions.
73. Ikeda, H., *Fujin no keizagaku*, 509, 524, 628–9.
74. Tsuru, S., *Japan's Capitalism: Creative Defeat and Beyond*, 242. Ikeda, H., *Kinkō zaisei*, 94; Kaizuka, K., "Japanese Public Finance since the Shoup Commission," *American Economics Association Papers and Proceedings*, 1992, vol. 82 (2), pp. 221–5.
75. weblio jisho, http://www.weblio.jp/content/964, accessed August 20, 2010; thanks to Professor Mario Ōshima for this information.
76. Ōuchi, H., *Keizaigaku gojūnen*, 308–9.
77. As many scholars have shown, Japanese leaders also mobilized much modern scientific expertise in the war effort. Mizuno, H., *Science for the Empire: Scientific Nationalism in Modern Japan* (Stanford, CA: Stanford University Press, 2009); Yamanouchi, Y., Koschmann, J. V., Narita, R., *Total War and 'Modernization'* (Ithaca, NY: Cornell East Asia Series, 1998).

78. Shoup, C. S., "The Tax Mission to Japan, 1949–1950,"
79. Brownlee, W. E. (2007) citing Shoup, C.S. et al., *The Sales Tax in the American States* (New York: Columbia University Press, 1934), 104–5.
80. Ōuchi, H., Naito, M., *Nihon zaisei zusetsu*, p. iv.
81. Brownlee, W. E., "The Transfer of Tax Ideas during the 'Reverse Course' of the U.S. Occupation of Japan," 168.

8

Shoup and the Japan Mission

Organizing for Investigation

W. Elliot Brownlee and Eisaku Ide

In the years immediately after World War II, Carl Shoup focused primarily on the reconstruction of the U.S. tax system, just as he had earlier. An unexpected opportunity arose, however, to undertake a major international tax mission – the mission to Japan during the American occupation. Shoup did not hesitate in seizing the opportunity. He recognized that the reform project would be of unprecedented scope and significance and might have the potential to influence the future of worldwide taxation.

Meeting the challenge, however, would require far more effort and organization than in Shoup's work in France and Cuba. The agenda would be much more robust; the mission's objectives were more ambitious and complicated. It seemed to have the primary goal of promoting democracy in Japan, rather than relieving American creditors or taxpayers. It would require attention to the changes that Keynesian ideas had made in the analysis and prescriptive advice of economists. To implement the objectives of the mission, he decided that he had to revise the organizational platform for reform that General Douglas MacArthur had built during the American occupation of Japan. In particular, Shoup had to strengthen the commitment of both occupation authorities and the Japanese government to principles of tax reform, and to enhance their ability to investigate economic and fiscal conditions within Japan.

GENERAL DOUGLAS MACARTHUR AND HAROLD MOSS

Well before the Shoup mission in 1949–50, MacArthur, as the Supreme Commander for the Allied Powers (SCAP) in Japan, had already launched a project of comprehensive tax reform. MacArthur intended it to be a central component of his effort to democratize Japanese society. In this early phase of tax reform, which began in early 1946, MacArthur and his jerry-rigged organization (referred to, in addition to MacArthur himself, as SCAP) worked closely with the Japanese government. The results, however, were incoherent and arbitrary, in large part because SCAP lacked any tax or fiscal experts. The early reforms raised significant revenues but increased popular resistance to the occupation and had the counterproductive effect of undermining the legitimacy of Japan's fiscal system.

In late 1947, the problems in both administering the Japanese tax system and planning for its future had grown sufficiently severe for MacArthur to borrow experts in tax administration from the U.S. Treasury. He jealously guarded his control of the occupation, and always disliked including officials in his government whose primary loyalties were either to President Truman or cabinet officials other than the Secretary of the Army. In recruiting U.S. Treasury experts, therefore, MacArthur began by finding an individual he could trust as a leader. He singled out L. Harold Moss, a young but accomplished agent within the Bureau of Internal Revenue (the BIR, which was renamed the Internal Revenue Service, or IRS in 1953), and appointed Moss head of SCAP's Internal Revenue Division.[1]

With a high-school education, some business courses, and experience as an IBM punch card operator in the Department of Agriculture, Moss had taken a clerical job at the BIR in 1932, at only 19 years of age. By 1935, he had become a collection agent in the office of the southern Manhattan District, which included Wall Street. Success in that hard-nosed arm of the BIR earned the precocious young man an opportunity to travel abroad, and in 1937 he joined a new collection office established in Manila. His youthful success in catching tax evaders and his skillful handling of the efforts of the American Chamber of Commerce of the Philippines to reduce retroactively taxes which had been owed to the U.S. government during World War I amazed MacArthur. Moss won MacArthur's trust and friendship, which no doubt contributed to his promotion as chief of the Far Eastern division of the BIR in 1940. Moss escaped the Philippines before its fall to Japan and in 1946, after wartime service in the Navy as an intelligence officer and aviator, he returned to the BIR, which in 1947 loaned him to the U.S. Army to serve as Tax Advisor and then Acting Budget Advsior as well to the South Korean Interim Government. In the process of revising Korean tax law, he later recalled, he acquired "a good knowledge and understanding of Japanese tax laws and administration" because Japan "had imposed" its "tax system upon

Korea" during their occupation. During the period of Moss's service in Korea, MacArthur summoned him twice to recruit him for service within SCAP. Moss, who took notes in shorthand, remembered that MacArthur told him that taxation was "the only firm and continuous link that exists between a government and every citizen of the country," and stressed the importance of introducing in Japan "a system of taxation which not only is fair and equitable to all citizens and taxpayers, but also is designed and operated in a manner which generates a feeling of mutual respect between the citizens and their government." MacArthur was confident that Moss would succeed in Japan. In the Philippines, he told Moss, "you were faced with a difficult, if not impossible situation..., and if you could do the impossible in Manila, you should be able to do it in Japan."[2] In November 1947 MacArthur wrote to the Commissioner of Internal Revenue requesting Moss' reassignment. MacArthur said that Moss had "a clear grasp both of past deficiencies and the broad concept underlying corrective measures," and he reported that he had "known Mr. Moss for a number of years" and had "great confidence in his maturity of judgment and professional qualifications." The reassignment of Moss, MacArthur concluded, "would materially re-inforce our position in the achievement of basic objectives, so many of which are dependent upon the adequacy of internal revenue."[3] Before accepting MacArthur's invitation, Moss conducted a preliminary investigation and decided that MacArthur needed to recruit experts in tax administration from the BIR and other U.S. agencies and to summon "on a short-term basis, top-flight tax economists and policy experts to conduct an overall study of the Japanese tax laws... and to prepare a report for a nation-wide system that should assure a sound tax system for the future." Moss arrived in Japan in early 1948 and quickly improved the capacity of SCAP to oversee tax collection and to collaborate effectively with tax experts in the Ministry of Finance (MOF). With MacArthur's support, his first step was to override the view of the military staff that "The Japanese come to us; we don't go to them." Moss began to promote improvements in tax administration within the Japanese government, and to think more generally about tax reform. He and other members of the BIR whom the U.S. Treasury loaned to SCAP focused on tax administration. In May 1949, at the urging of supportive officials within the MOF, after a year of futile persuasion, they forced the Japanese government, under a directive from MacArthur, to create a semiautonomous counterpart of the BIR, called the Tax Administration Agency.[4] Later that year Moss engineered a civilian takeover of the tax surveillance that the 8th Army (the military arm of the occupation) had been conducting since 1947 and the granting of greater autonomy for tax administration to the Tax Administration Agency of the Japanese government. In so doing Moss ignored the objections of both the 8th Army generals and Joseph Dodge. Moss regarded this as his greatest bureaucratic victory, and believed that MacArthur's support had been the key.[5]

In the spring of 1948, Moss and MacArthur overcame objections within SCAP and invited what Moss described as "a special mission of outstanding tax economists" who would "conduct a comprehensive survey of the national and local tax laws." The charge of the mission, consisting of what MacArthur hoped would be the "best brains in the world," was to submit, Moss wrote, "appropriate recommendations to bring about a more equitable distribution of the tax burden among the various groups of the economy; a reallocation of the revenue sources among the national, prefectural, and local governments; and such other modifications of the tax law as were considered necessary for the democratization of the tax system."[6]

THE RECRUITMENT OF CARL SHOUP

MacArthur, supported by the Department of the Army, gave Moss effective control over the appointment of the expert personnel for the mission. Moss focused, in particular, on the appointment of a leader for the mission, and organized an elaborate search process that took him to San Francisco, Chicago, New York, and Washington D.C., where he interviewed numerous U.S. Treasury officials and tax economists. He asked them: "Who was good?" In an interview Moss later recalled that "everyone said Shoup."[7]

This probably came as no surprise to Moss. In the postwar period, Shoup's scholarship and public service career had continued to flourish. He was in line to become president of the National Tax Association in 1949, and he had published an influential article on the incidence of the corporation income tax and a major text on national income accounting, *Principles of National Income Analysis*.[8] The latter demonstrated that he moved beyond the institutionalism that his mentors had helped pioneer, and was taking up the analysis of the relationship between taxation and levels of national income that the Keynesian revolution had pushed forward.[9] Meanwhile, his work as a consultant for the U.S. Treasury had expanded. Roy Blough, Shoup's collaborator on *Facing the Tax Burden* (1937) who had become director of tax research in 1938, stayed on in that position until 1946. Shoup consulted continuously with him on virtually all aspects of the transition of the nation's tax system from wartime to peacetime conditions.[10] After Blough left the treasury, Shoup worked directly with Undersecretary of the Treasury A. L. M. Wiggins until Wiggins returned to private life in July 1948.[11] In 1947 Wiggins invited Shoup to "draw up a report that would blueprint a permanent peacetime tax system." With the assistance of William Warren, a tax specialist in the Columbia law school and Shoup's closest personal friend at Columbia, and with the benefit of informal advice by Robert Murray Haig, Shoup proposed taking advantage of the postwar "peacetime dividend" to undertake a massive reform of the federal tax system along Haig-Simons lines. The elaborate set of reforms he recommended would have raised a number of key tax rates, but the overall revenue reductions he proposed would have reduced the potential for political backlash. Key provisions Shoup advocated included income averaging, treatment of capital gains as regular income, taxation of unrealized capital gains at death through an accessions tax, reduction of high progressive rates, and integration of personal and corporate income taxation. In early 1948, however, the Congress – over a veto by President Truman – reduced the peace dividend through across-the-board tax cutting. Without the peace dividend, the treasury had little leverage to bargain for support of the Haig-Simons tax reform. The treasury abandoned its project but thanked Shoup for the "valuable ground work" he had contributed for future comprehensive reform.[12]

By September 1948, Moss had a short-list for a leader of the mission consisting of "the three distinguished tax economists in the U.S."[13] He did not identify the three, but they included Shoup, Roy Blough, who in 1946 had left the Treasury for the University of Chicago, and Louis Shere, a professor at Indiana University who had been Blough's assistant during the war. (For a discussion of Shoup's collaboration with Blough, see Chapter 5 of this volume.) All three were public finance specialists who had cycled through academe, private foundations, and the tax research office of the U.S. Treasury. Moss asked Shere if he was available. He said that he was, but added that Moss also ought to consider either Roy Blough or Carl Shoup. He added that among the three (including Shere himself) his top choice would be Shoup. "If he could get" Carl Shoup to serve, Shere told Moss, he "should stop the search."[14] Moss evidently followed Shere's advice.

Moss also considered seriously Harold Groves, an economics professor at the University of Wisconsin. Groves, however, had withdrawn himself from consideration. The reasons for this help us to understand the intellectual and political strategies that shaped the Shoup mission's design of taxes for export.

Since the early 1930s, Groves had been influential in providing practical advice on tax reform to both the State of Wisconsin and the federal government. Similarly to Shoup, he had served in the U.S. Treasury during World War II. He strongly identified with the tradition of progressivism that was associated with the "Wisconsin idea" of Robert M. LaFollette and based heavily on the ideas of Groves's mentor at the University of Wisconsin, John R. Commons. He was the leading proponent of applying Commons's "institutionalism" to the study of taxation. As such, Groves's approach was distinct in an important way from that of Shoup and his mentors at Columbia, and from the other economists whom Moss is known to have considered. Groves believed even more strongly that tax reform – regardless of its objectives – required far more than an application of economic or public finance principles, however derived. Structural reform, he argued, required deep knowledge of the social setting of tax policy and the contending social forces that decisively shaped tax politics. This orientation led Groves to be deeply skeptical of the practicality, even under the best of institutional conditions, of the mission that Moss sought to organize. According to economist Martin Bronfenbrenner, a colleague of Groves at Wisconsin at the time, Groves "doubted that any outsider, ignorant of 'things Japanese,' could ever reform the Japanese tax system in any satisfactory or enduring way." Such "scruples," Bronfenbrenner reported later, led Groves to withdraw "his name from consideration."[15] After the completion of the Shoup mission, Groves reflected that the mission had been too prescriptive. A better approach, he suggested, would have been to outline several broad patterns of tax reform and allow Japan to choose among them (see Chapter 16).

Shoup agreed with Groves on the need to take local conditions into account as he pursued tax reform. He had learned that lesson more than a decade earlier, in France. Despite this, he had far greater confidence in the force of the ideals of Haig, harnessed with his own organizational capacities, to bring significant tax reform to Japan. Although Groves had demurred, Shoup was ready to accept Moss's invitation. Part of the reason was no doubt the persuasiveness of Moss, who was even more confident than Shoup in achieving comprehensive reform, on the basis of what he believed had been his own seemingly very successful year of work in Japan and cooperation with officials and experts within MOF. What Moss had learned about Shoup's tax philosophy and accomplishments led him to conclude that Shoup was the ideal person to advance the agenda that Moss, MacArthur, and the U.S. Treasury had in mind for reform in Japan. At the end of September 1948, Moss had an extended conversation with Shoup and on October 1 he wrote to the army indicating that "Dr. Carl Shoup will probably head the mission." A few days later, he travelled to New York, where he met with Shoup and sealed the deal.[16]

Thus, just a year after one door to reform closed on Shoup in Washington DC, another door opened. The invitation to devise a reform program for Japan was exhilarating. He had an agreement with both MacArthur and Moss regarding the general scope and nature of the reform program. Given what he believed to be the power of MacArthur and SCAP over the Japanese government, Shoup saw an opportunity to enact far more of his reform agenda than he, or the other disciples of Haig, had ever had in the United States or anywhere overseas. Moreover, he had the commitment of MacArthur and Moss to publish the results of the mission and circulate them widely. This promised to present an opportunity to disseminate his ideas for reform and strategy recommendations in the U.S. as well as in Japan.

THE RECRUITMENT OF SHOUP'S INNER CIRCLE

As part of his agreement with MacArthur and Moss, Shoup had, at least at first, complete discretion in choosing the other members of his mission. He considered fourteen candidates in a formal way.[17] He had already had decided on two of them – William Vickrey and William Warren – and had introduced them to Moss in October when he visited Columbia. Shoup and Haig had shared responsibilities for directing Vickrey's graduate studies, and had arranged a faculty appointment for him at Columbia. Warren was a member of the Columbia Law School faculty and Shoup's closest friend at Columbia. Shoup trusted both of them completely, used both of them to test his ideas on, and needed the combination of economic and legal creativity that the pair provided.

Shoup expected that Vickrey would play an especially important role in the mission. In various projects with Shoup and other economists, Vickrey had demonstrated a powerful capacity to think in original ways about institutional reform, and to generate ideas for colleagues who focused more on persuasion. Vickrey, with his powerful mathematical skills, had become far more facile than Shoup in working within the analytical frameworks of Keynesian economics. As early as 1936–7, he had worked with Shoup, assisting him in the study sponsored by the Twentieth Century Fund, and then moved to the staff of the Federal Reserve Board. During the war, Vickrey first assisted Shoup and Blough in the tax research division of the U.S. Treasury and then conducted research at the Department of Commerce, including an assignment with the Committee on Economic Development.[18] In all of these assignments, Vickrey worked creatively but very much within the approach to income taxation – and particularly the definition of taxable income – that Haig had pioneered and Shoup had worked to apply. In his dissertation, published in 1947 as *The Agenda for Progressive Taxation*, Vickrey had proposed exceptionally creative refinements of Haig's model by addressing in a comprehensive way the problems of timing in taxation (see Chapter 2).[19] On a much lower level of sophistication, Vickrey shared Haig and Shoup's worries about high marginal tax rates at the top of the progressive scale. Vickrey believed that such rates "merely drive more taxpayers to the use of . . . loopholes."[20] On a practical level, Vickrey had also already impressed Shoup by his service on a foreign tax mission, which, along with Shoup's missions to France and Cuba, served as preparation for the mission to Japan.

In 1945, Rexford G. Tugwell, then Governor of Puerto Rico, invited Haig – a former Columbia colleague and a trusted friend – to lead a tax mission that the territory's legislature had authorized. Tugwell knew that Haig had been single-handedly responsible for drafting the first income tax law in Puerto Rico in 1924–5, and wanted him back "to make an investigation of the complete tax system structure . . . , and to prepare a report thereon with recommendations for changes in the nature of the taxes, rates of taxes, levying of taxes, etc."[21]

Haig visited Puerto Rico in September 1945 but needed assistance to follow through with what turned out to be an extremely ambitious set of proposals for comprehensive reform. Tugwell authorized Haig to make Vickrey, whom Haig had described as a "ball of fire," the leader of Haig's team in Puerto Rico.[22] Haig arranged for Vickrey, who was a Quaker and a wartime conscientious objector, to be assigned to a Civilian Public Service Camp in Puerto Rico.[23] From December through September, Vickrey visited San Juan, crafted recommendations, drafted legislation, and negotiated with Puerto Rican Treasury officials. Haig gave Vickrey a great deal of latitude, at one point writing that "You are far away, and the sensible course, indeed the only course possible, is to leave everything to your discretion."[24]

Haig and Vickrey recommend a thoroughgoing reform of the Puerto Rican tax system. At the core was a broad-based income tax structured along Haig-Simons lines.[25] Vickrey refined Haig's ideas in the areas of capital gains taxation and income averaging and added an innovative element of his own: an accessions tax – a tax on the accumulated gifts, inheritances, and bequests of individuals.[26]

In March 1946, Puerto Rico's legislature passed a preliminary draft of Vickrey's accessions tax, prompting him to describe it to Haig as "the best inheritance tax law that I know anything about."[27] The combination of the broadening of the tax base and a progressive rate that sloped steeply up to 70 percent, however, touched on a popular protest. For having proposed the tax, Vickrey "received all the 'stones,'" as Puerto Rico's chief of the Bureau of Income Tax told Haig.[28] Haig and Vickrey stood firm on the accessions tax, focusing on improving it rather than repealing it, but the comprehensive reform program made little progress through Puerto Rico's legislature and then collapsed when Tugwell left the governorship in September.

Tugwell and Haig did not blame Vickrey for the failure of reform. They recognized that throughout the mission Vickrey had to cope with a Puerto Rican Treasury Department that had little enthusiasm for reducing the importance of consumption taxation. At the end of the process, Tugwell told Haig that "Vickrey has done an outstanding job which is recognized by all of us who know anything at all about the problems and the conditions under which he worked."[29] Despite the lack of results, Vickrey had learned a great deal from his struggles with recalcitrant bureaucrats, including the treasurer of Puerto Rico, about the practical problems that had to be faced in adapting Haig-Simons principles to the institutions and practices of taxation in an unfamiliar society.

Whereas Vickrey would provide economic insight to the mission, Warren would offer legal creativity, just as he had in collaborating with Shoup at the U.S. Treasury. Both Shoup and Warren wanted more support in the realm of legal analysis and drafting of specific proposals, and they agreed on adding Stanley Surrey, a young lawyer at the University of California, Berkeley, to the team. He had graduated from Columbia Law School in 1932, worked as legislative tax counsel in the Treasury from 1937 to 1947, collaborating with Shoup, served on a U.S. Treasury delegation in 1946 to negotiate tax treaties, and then worked with Warren on an income tax project of the American Law Institute in 1948.[30]

Similarly to Shoup and Warren, Surrey had already developed an intellectual commitment to closing loopholes in the income tax. In 1989, in response to an interviewer's question regarding his selection of Surrey for the mission, Shoup recalled how hostility to tax preferences shaped his choice of colleagues: "My own prejudices determined the selection of the members of the Tax Mission, and if Surrey had been an advocate of tax preferences, I might not have asked him to join the mission." Shoup went on to elaborate, explaining that he wanted "people I knew," and that Surrey, Warren, and Vickrey were his "professional friends." He "knew their thought processes." He said. "I was continually learning from them in shaping my own ideas."[31]

The last major organizational piece was the addition of a third economist who would give the economists a technical majority of the five-member mission. Shoup looked for someone who worked outside the tight Columbia circle. His first choice was his former colleague and boss at in the Office of Tax Research, Blough of the University of Chicago. Blough turned down Shoup's offer, however, citing commitments to teaching and to a possible tax mission to Turkey.[32] Shoup then turned to John Due, another close U.S. Treasury collaborator, who was then a professor of economics at the University of Illinois. Shoup had an important reason to select Due – his expertise on local taxation. In October, Shoup explained to Due that "there has already been a considerable reform of the Japanese tax system by the Occupation" but a major problem remained in that "the tax revenues are too centralized in the national government from the point of view of guaranteeing the necessary amount of local initiative and independence when the time comes for the occupation to be ended." Thus, "the entire problem of division of revenues, grants-in-aid and similar intergovernmental public finance questions needs to be examined and proposals for reform suggested." Due refused, reluctantly, because of health problems. Shoup then, perhaps on Due's advice, turned to Due's colleague at Illinois, economist Howard R. Bowen of the University of Illinois, who agreed to serve.[33]

Bowen had been chief economist for the House Ways and Means and Senate Finance Committees during World War II and then an economist with Irving Trust. He was not a close colleague of Shoup's, but Shoup knew him and, for the purposes of the mission, valued his expertise in two topics: intergovernmental fiscal relations and the social setting of public finance.[34] When Shoup wrote to Bowen to invite him to serve, he told him that "One of the biggest problems we shall have to advise on is that of the fiscal relations of the national government with the prefectures and the local units." He explained: "In view of your interest in this subject, as indicated by the work you did in Britain in 1938, I should like to suggest that you consider this as one of your special fields of interest in Japan." Shoup quickly added: "Each member of the commission will of course want to discuss and form his judgment on all of the major tax problems."

He went on, however, to say that "I think it will be helpful if each of us also has one or two major fields of interest for which he can be primarily responsible," and "this area of intergovernmental fiscal relationships is also one, it seems to me, to which could be profitably applied the kind of cultural analysis that you have so interestingly carried out in the opening chapters of your *Toward Social Economy*."[35]

Shoup referred to Bowen's research on English grants-in-aid (payments from the central government to local authorities), which he had published as a monograph in 1939.[36] Bowen's study looked to the English experience with grants-in-aid to derive lessons for American state governments, which were still struggling to reform the general property tax at the local level or augment local revenues from new statewide taxes. The lack of progress in local tax reform and intergovernmental transfers, Bowen wrote, means "that within almost any state in the country the local tax system is highly inequitable, the backwardness of many local authorities is unbelievable, and the differences between local areas in quality of service and in burden of local taxation is appallingly wide."[37] On the basis of the much more extensive English history in providing grants-in-aid, Bowen derived six lessons and argued for their greater use in the United States: (1) grants-in-aid are "a practicable device of local finance thoroughly capable of being efficiently and honestly administered," (2) "conditional grants-in-aid are effective in stimulating local authorities to extend and improve their services," (3) "large grants can be made without destroying local autonomy and without producing local mendicancy," (4) "a complicated formula can successfully be used in distributing the grants" among local governments, (5) "modern conditions call for an increasing emphasis on the problem of ironing out the differences between authorities in financial ability," and (6) there was a need "to consolidate" separate subventions for different purposes "into a system."[38]

Bowen's recommendations went beyond English experience. To implement the last three reform lessons, Bowen proposed a concrete equalization formula that would be new to England as well as the American states. The formula would, he claimed, more or less equalize services across local governments, taking into account both the financial need and the taxpaying ability of those governments.[39] He concluded by warning, however, that "the differences between England and America are such that it is not ordinarily advisable or possible to transplant English institutions bodily into the American environment." Nonetheless, Bowen concluded, "America has much to learn from English experience in local government finance. England has pointed the way to the solution of problems and has demonstrated the practicality of the solution, even though she herself has not yet fully exploited its potentialities."[40]

On a practical level, Bowen's program for reforming grants-in-aid appealed to Shoup as providing an approach that offered promise in helping to untangle the mind-numbing complexity of intergovernmental fiscal relations in Japan. To Shoup, Japan's federal system of government seemed more reminiscent of England's than of the United States, and in Japan, as in England, grants-in-aid seemed to have attained greater scale and significance than in the United States.

On a more philosophical level, Bowen's institutionalism appealed to Shoup. Bowen demonstrated in *Toward Social Economy* that he understood the extent to which economic development depended on its institutional environment, and the difficulty facing efforts to "substitute intelligence and planning for random collective behavior" in shaping institutions. He was pessimistic about the prospects. To some extent, Bowen may have shared the kind of pessimism that Groves expressed, although he gave greater weight to the role of historical contingency in reform by taking up the issue of when "important modifications" of fundamental institutions were "generally possible." Bowen declared that important modifications were possible: "Only when the institutions in question have become so thoroughly outmoded as to precipitate a virtual breakdown in the social order, and then only after serious (and usually bloody) conflict between the proponents of the new order and the guardians of the status quo."[41] Bowen perceived the wartime defeat of Japan and the empowerment of SCAP as circumstances that created an unusual opportunity for fundamental change. Similar to Shoup, Bowen was prepared to apply principles derived from historical experience, such as that of England with grants-in-aid, to restructure Japan's tax state in a fundamental way.

With Bowen's selection, Shoup completed the official membership of the tax mission to Japan – three economists, Shoup, Vickrey, and Bowen, and two lawyers, Warren and Surrey. As a team, they reflected the formidable capabilities of the professional tax expertise that had emerged from the American experience of institution building during the progressive era, the New Deal, and two world wars.

RECRUITMENT OF THE SUPPORTING CAST

Shoup was not entirely satisfied with the results of his recruitment effort. Although he had already defined his general approach to reforming Japan's tax system – an approach on the basis of the combination of

American experience and the principles of Haig – he believed that his group had to learn more about Japanese conditions to flesh out a reform program. He would need more intellectual capital to turn the mission's program into effective legislation and regulations.

Shoup saw three major lacunae in the mission's structure. The first problem was that none of the members had deep knowledge of European tax systems. Shoup believed that such knowledge would provide useful inspiration for the reform of a tax system based in part on European precedents. Shoup was seriously considering adding Fritz Neumark, "an early refugee from the Nazi regime in the 1930s," as a kind of junior member of the team. Shoup had met Neumark at a postwar conference, exchanged publications, and came to regard him as having "unparalleled knowledge of European tax systems, including a detailed knowledge of each type of tax." Shoup dropped the idea in the face of the "administrative difficulties," however, that would delay Neumark's appointment.[42] The two other problems were particularly severe. First, none of the five members was in any sense a Japanese specialist. None had studied or written about any aspect of Japanese life, and none read or even spoke Japanese. Second, none of the members of the mission were able to stay behind in Japan to follow up on the implementation of the mission's recommendations after the senior members had returned to their university positions. Shoup and his Columbia colleagues expected to have an ongoing role in overseeing aspects of their recommendations, but they would do so from a high-level point of view, far removed from daily operations in Tokyo. Moss would be on the scene, but Shoup was not entirely certain that he or his staff would fully or effectively support the sophisticated recommendations of the mission.

Neither of these last two problems – a lack of local expertise and follow-through capacity – was unusual for American missions to occupied Japan. A lack of Japanese expertise was typical of the occupation's expert missions. As historian John Dower has written, "One would be hard pressed to find a single Japan specialist" on "the advisory missions that regularly shuttled between Washington and Tokyo."[43] Many SCAP bureaucrats and army officers who reported to MacArthur were suspicious of experts who seemed too knowledgeable about Japan. They feared such experts had the potential for disloyalty. In addition, the SCAP bureaucracy played on MacArthur's ferocious independence to become increasingly adept at following its own course after missions had gone home.

Part of Shoup's solution to the mission's lack of Japanese expertise was to go beyond the appointment of the five official members of the mission by creating a tier of members whom he called "research associates." Shoup knew of no senior public finance economists in the United States who had any significant knowledge of Japan. He was, however, able to find several junior colleagues who not only did, but had some working knowledge of both written and spoken Japanese. Shoup's first appointee as research associate was Jerome B. Cohen, an economist trained by Haig at Columbia University.[44] He was a newly appointed faculty member at the City College of New York and a consultant in the Division of Research for Far East, Department of State, for which he wrote a classified report, "The Course of Inflation in Post-Surrender Japan." Moreover, Cohen had just completed a major survey of Japan's economy in which he stressed the need for balancing the budget to control inflation. He had concluded that "the productivity of the Japanese tax system is considerably less than is necessary for balancing the budget and is not in line with the economy's overall capacity to pay."[45]

Cohen had heard of the Shoup mission in Washington and nominated himself as an "economic assistant." He explained to Shoup that he was already slated to go to Japan for three months on behalf of the State Department, however he would prefer to work on the tax mission. Shoup obtained and read Cohen's report, and his references checked out.[46] In addition, Shoup noted that Cohen had served as a Japanese language officer in U.S. Naval Intelligence and that, in that capacity, he had participated in the bombing survey in Japan. In the process, he had honed his Japanese and acquired some experience in interrogating Japanese military officers and civilians.[47] Cohen's language skill may well have been the most important asset to Shoup, who wrote to Bowen saying that Cohen "speaks Japanese and I think it would be well for the mission to have at least one junior member who could talk with the Japanese, although SCAP will be ready to furnish us with all the translators we need."[48]

In hiring the second research assistant, Shoup made his only appointment outside the university world. He hired Rolland Hatfield, an economist who served as director of tax research for the state of Minnesota before the war and returned to that job afterwards. During the war he had served in the Army Air Corps and had learned some Japanese in the Army Language School. The clincher was that in 1945–6, Hatfield had finished his army service in the Public Finance Division of SCAP, where he had investigated the asset holdings of the emperor and worked on problems of Japanese local finance. Hatfield could reinforce Bowen in his vital study of local finance.[49]

Cohen was willing to go to Japan before Shoup to establish a liaison relationship with the public finance specialists in SCAP, prepare research materials, and set preliminary schedules. Neither Cohen nor Hatfield, however, was willing to stay on after the conclusion of the mission's work in September. The solution to Shoup's need arrived in early February in the form of an unsolicited letter from a junior economist at the University of Wisconsin, Martin Bronfenbrenner. He asked whether "there may exist next year a vacancy on your staff which I might conceivably fill."[50]

SPECIAL APPOINTMENT AND ASSIGNMENT
FOR BRONFENBRENNER

Bronfenbrenner was a macroeconomist, trained by Milton Friedman at the University of Chicago. He had learned Japanese during the war while serving in the navy, and was beginning to shift his research interests to Japan, despite the discouragement of senior scholars. At a Madison reception, Harvard's John K. Fairbank had told Bronfenbrenner "that the 'Japan field' was dead, and that I had best shift my interests to China." Friedman had warned his student that "'all that Japanese stuff' might ruin me as an economist," Bronfenbrenner later recalled.[51] Despite such comments, Bronfenbrenner ignored his elders and applied to the Social Science Research Council for a world area fellowship that would fund a year's study of Japan's postwar recovery program while he was on leave from the University of Wisconsin. Meanwhile, he took a trip to Washington "to investigate civilian jobs in the Occupation" but was disappointed to learn "that General MacArthur had all the economists and statisticians he needed, and that my knowledge of Japanese made no difference." He won the fellowship, which was contingent on his obtaining "permission to enter Japan for this purpose." Meanwhile, he had heard about the planning for the Shoup mission. In February he wrote to Shoup with a bright idea. Bronfenbrenner proposed that he would fund his own appointment to Shoup's staff. "There would be no financial drain on your tax reform project's meager resources," he told Shoup.[52]

In his letter, Bronfenbrenner reminded Shoup that "we have had cor-respondence" and "met briefly" at the American Economic Association convention in 1947. Shoup did, in fact, remember the correspondence because Bronfenbrenner, as a rather junior professor, had offered remark-ably sharp criticisms of Shoup's text on national income and product accounting. Bronfenbrenner had assigned the text in class but found that some of Shoup's suggestions for reforms were "either impractical or positively misleading." Shoup recalled that Bronfenbrenner's criticisms had been astute yet polite, and said he respected Bronfenbrenner's independence.[53]

In addition, Shoup found Bronfenbrenner's training and background compelling. Shoup liked the fact that although Bronfenbrenner had received rigorous training in Keynesian macroeconomics, he was not a slavish devotee of the structural variant championed by Alvin Hansen and some other American Keynesians. Bronfenbrenner was adept in statistics and had also acquired the practical experience in fiscal and monetary analysis that Shoup prized – two years in the U.S. Treasury, including one year as a revenue estimator, and two more years at the Federal Reserve Bank of Chicago as an economic forecaster. During the war, he served for three years in the navy as a language officer, including 15 months immersed in formal language instruction. (It turned out that he had been a classmate of Cohen's in language school.[54]) Bronfenbrenner's assignments during the war included reading undelivered letters from Japanese troops and reporting the contents to sociologists and historians interested in wartime morale, and after the war listening in on telephone calls to Korea to pick up information about the efforts of the *zaibatsu* to hide assets. He had acquired, he told Shoup, "a certain degree of competence in the Japanese language both spoken and written, which I should like to reinforce while I am in Japan."

Although public finance was not a "major field" for Bronfenbrenner, he had published three articles on taxation. These confirmed that he shared Shoup's dissent from the most extreme New Deal thinking on progressive taxation. Bronfenbrenner reinforced this particular point by making it clear to Shoup that there was some intellectual distance between himself and Groves, one of Bronfenbrenner's senior colleagues in Madison. Much later, in his unpublished autobiography, he described Groves as "personally genial and likeable, despite great zeal for tax progressivity as an end in itself."[55]

Two other qualities suited Bronfenbrenner for Shoup's team. The first was a profound fascination with Japanese society. In 1945, during his military service in Japan, he had caught what he later described as "the Japan bug." This "bug" remained in his system for the rest of his life, and it led him to make increasingly large intellectual and emotional investments in Japan. The second was that Bronfenbrenner fit poorly in the economics department of the University of Wisconsin, which he had joined in 1947. He was uncomfortable, in particular, with the distinctive institutionalism of the Wisconsin economics department. Bronfenbrenner found that after the death of John R. Commons in 1945, "the institutionalist position was apparently degenerating into the dogma that democratically-organized labor (or agriculture) 'could do no wrong' and should be 'above the law.'" He considered this "pernicious nonsense, as bad as the Republican 'what helps business helps you' distortion of economic orthodoxy." As a consequence, in the Wisconsin economics department, he wrote later, "I found myself in opposition from Day 1, given the inflationary situation and trade-union power prevailing in 1947." Shoup knew that he would have a teammate both devoted to understanding conditions in Japan and enthusiastic about Shoup's centrist approach to the study of fiscal policy.[56]

A month after receiving Bronfenbrenner's letter, Shoup sent a telegram proposing the possibility of a two-year appointment. "Your telegram," Bronfenbrenner responded, "was perhaps the most welcome which I have ever received."[57] The appointment would not be as an expert on the mission but as a tax economist – in a civil service appointment – within the Internal Revenue Division of SCAP. Shoup immediately passed on Moss's sketch of what they would expect of Bronfenbrenner. Ideally, he would "precede you by several weeks, after having been thoroughly briefed by you . . . as to the projects on which he could concentrate on arrival." Moss was willing to then "assign him exclusively to your mission while here." Most important, "after the mission departed he would be able to continue with our Division in the implementation of your recommendations." Shoup told him that he would have to do some additional reading in "standard tax material," including "Vickrey's *Agenda for Progressive Taxation*, if you have not done so recently."[58]

In making his arrangements to join the mission, Bronfenbrenner encountered what he later ironically called "the little problem of my security clearance."[59] This "little problem" dated from early wartime when an unfair accusation of "Communist sympathies" had led the Office of Naval Intelligence to force Bronfenbrenner to resign his commission and then to be discharged "under honorable conditions" (a discharge somewhat less honorable, however, than an "honorable discharge").[60] In 1949, Bronfenbrenner asked the U.S. Civil Service Commission to take the exceptional step of completing a formal investigation of his loyalty before he accepted his appointment abroad.[61] With Shoup's assistance, Bronfenbrenner obtained the exception and obtained his clearance.[62] There were, however, two unfortunate consequences. First, the clearance process delayed Bronfenbrenner's arrival in Japan until after the completion of Shoup's first visit. Second, in the process of demanding exceptional treatment in the clearance problem, Bronfenbrenner had alerted the army and, in turn, MacArthur's own intelligence service to his "little problem."[63] The problem would return to complicate the successful completion of Shoup's mission.

THE RECRUITMENT OF JAPANESE MEMBERS

Shoup not only recruited American research associates with knowledge of Japan and the Japanese language, but in addition searched for Japanese scholars with expertise in Japanese fiscal affairs. He intended to add them, somehow, to his team. Shoup regarded the need for the expertise of Japanese colleagues as a high priority. He was not entertaining the possibility that the mission would make major course corrections on the basis of Japanese advice. In forming the mission, however, he tried to take account of Japanese conditions, economic ideas, and politics in ways that no other head of an occupation mission had done.

As early as October 1948, he had discussed the appointment of Japanese experts as full members of the mission with Moss and told John Due that the mission "might develop into a Commission of say, seven or eight persons of whom two or three would be Japanese students of public finance."[64] Moss proposed the idea to Finance Minister Ikeda Hayato and Ikeda in turn consulted with his staff. The MOF and its Tax Bureau were enthusiastic and suggested three economists – Shiomi Saburo of Kyoto University, and Ito Hanya and Tsuru Shigeto, both based at Tokyo Shoka University.[65]

Shoup's request had dovetailed nicely with an effort by Yoshida Shigeru and Ikeda to plan in an innovative way forward for tax reform. During elections in January 1949, Yoshida promised to repeal an unpopular national consumption tax on transactions and to reduce income taxes through increasing exemptions. Keeping this promise, however, might mean causing trouble with banker Joseph Dodge, who had just begun to impose his regime of fiscal stringency. At the same time the MOF, under pressure from Yoshida supporters in the Diet from certain less developed areas of Japan, sought ways of working more flexibly with the regional goal, or quota, system for allocating income taxes. The MOF was acutely aware that on this issue it was caught between the Diet and the Japanese public, on one hand, and SCAP on the other.[66] In January, therefore, in an effort to find novel ways of solving both problems, Ikeda appointed his own tax commission. According to the *Mainichi Shimbun*, the new "Taxation Investigating Committee," which consisted of professors, businessmen, and other experts, would "study methods of improving the present taxation system and increasing tax collections."[67] At the same time, Yoshida and Ikeda were uncertain and apprehensive about what changes the Shoup mission might champion, although they hoped that Shoup would somehow provide cover for the tax cuts the Yoshida government had promised. Shiomi and Ito, both of whom had served as MOF consultants for many years, were members of the new tax commission, and Ikeda no doubt hoped that they would prove effective in shaping the work of the Shoup mission.[68]

Shiomi and Ito were senior and distinguished, however the third scholar whom Ikeda proposed, Tsuru Shigeto (1912–2006), was more than fifteen years younger, less well-known, and not a specialist in public finance and taxation. Also, much of his professional career had been outside Japan. He was the son of a wealthy industrialist from Nagoya who in the early 1930s sent his son to college in the United States. During 1929–30, as a high school student, Tsuru had criticized Japan's invasion of China and organized a campaign against Imperialism. He, along with many other students, was arrested under the Maintenance of Public Order Law, briefly imprisoned and then expelled from high school, making admission to a Japanese university impossible. In the United States, he attended Lawrence University, the University of Wisconsin, and Harvard University, where he received both his BA (1935) and PhD (1940) degrees in economics. At Harvard, Joseph Schumpeter supervised Tsuru's dissertation on business cycle theories and their application to Japan. Tsuru's graduate student colleagues included Paul Samuelson, John Kenneth Galbraith, and Richard A. Musgrave. Although Tsuru published articles on Marxian economic theory and helped found the journal *Science and Society: A Marxian Quarterly*, under Schumpeter's influence his economic research became increasingly eclectic.[69]

After Pearl Harbor, Tsuru was repatriated, and in 1944 he joined the Japanese Foreign Office. During this service he specialized in economic planning, joining a "Special Survey Committee" of professors. According to Tsuru, Schumpeter was crucial in initially connecting him with one of these professors, Nakayama Ichiro, who had also studied with Schumpeter (in Berlin during the 1920s) and in the 1930s had joined the faculty of Tokyo Shoka. In 1943, Nakayama assisted Tsuru in obtaining a part-time job at the East-Asian Economic Research Institute of Tokyo Shoka. On the "Special Survey Committee," Tsuru met the economists Wakimura Yoshitaro and Arisawa Hiromi, whose careers entwined with that of Ouichi Hyoe at the University of Tokyo. As historian Laura Hein has written, Tsuru and Wakimura "worked together on many projects that combined socialist principles, economic reasoning, and political relevance."[70] Their emphasis was on the internal development of Japanese resources rather than full-bore immersion in the international economy. Tsuru established a close relationship with the Socialist Democratic Party of Japan, but he was versatile in his approach to economic policy, applying both socialist principles and Keynesian categories of analysis within an overarching Schumpeterian framework. That framework, vigorously promoted by the economists at Hitotsubashi University, proved highly influential in reinforcing Japanese policy during the high-growth era of 1953–73.[71]

During the early occupation, Tsuru accepted an appointment as an economic advisor to the Economic and Scientific Section (ESS) in the Division of Statistics and Research. A condition of acceptance was the appointment of another economist, Takahashi Masao, who was a member of the circle surrounding Ouichi. Together, the two of them organized the collection and processing of modern macroeconomic data on Japan's economy.[72] In 1947 he left SCAP to take up the position of vice-minister for the Economic Stabilization Board – an instrument for coordinating planning for recovery – in the coalition Socialist government of Katayama Tetsu. In that role, he spearheaded the drafting of the "Economic White Paper of 1947," which represented, as Tsuru later wrote, "the first time in Japan that macroeconomic analysis was applied in the diagnosis of the economy as a whole."[73] As a Keynesian document, aspects of it riled Marxists to the left of Tsuru. Ultimately it had more influence on the Yoshida government than on the Katayama government. After the collapse of the Katayama government in February 1948, Tsuru returned to Tokyo Shoka University and waited in the wings for service in another government.[74]

From a political standpoint, Tsuru might have seemed the least reliable. Yoshida and Ikeda appreciated Tsuru's technical capacities, however, and his commitment to strengthening the Japanese economy. Yoshida and Ikeda were not particularly concerned about his moderate Marxism. Moreover, they understood that his U.S. education and fluency in English equipped him to be an effective liaison between Japanese and American experts. In addition, Ikeda trusted Tsuru because of a family connection between Ikeda's first wife and Tsuru's father-in-law, who was a member of a family descended from the "Three Architects of the Meiji Restoration." Consequently, Yoshida and Ikeda settled on the nomination of Tsuru for the Shoup project.

Shoup was indeed enthusiastic about Tsuru. In mid-April, Shoup wrote that "the more I hear about Dr. Tsuru the more strongly I favor appointing him as a member [of the mission]." Shoup admitted that "I am aware of his philosophical background which is far from conservative, to say the least." Despite this background, he went on to say that "this does not disturb me for the particular problem we have in mind." Shoup emphasized that "we need to have on the commission a Japanese member who is thoroughly trained in modern economics, and who talks English well, and who has a high degree of intelligence. And I understand that Dr. Tsuru fulfills all of these requirements." For emphasis, Shoup concluded: "A good deal of our tax problem is going to involve rather complex economic reasoning."[75] Ten days later, Moss wrote back that "Dr. Cohen [who had arrived early in Tokyo] and I had a long talk with Dr. Tsuru yesterday," and that he "will be pleased to render all the assistance possible to you and the other members of the Mission."[76] Although Shoup was unfamiliar with the other two nominees, he cheerfully embraced them as well. By April 20, Shoup had heard that SCAP had invited Shiomi to serve, and that he had accepted. Shoup quickly began an effort to read Shiomi's scholarly publications.[77]

To accommodate the Japanese economists, Moss proposed creating a four-member commission that would include two Americans (Shoup and probably Vickrey) and two Japanese experts (probably Tsuru and Shiomi). This group would formally make recommendations to the five-member Shoup mission, which would, in turn, technically make its own, independent recommendations. The two Japanese economists and their advisers would obviously have less influence because the Shoup mission could overrule them, but Shoup and Moss wanted genuine collaboration. They respected Japan's economists and wanted to involve them intimately in the work of planting American tax ideas in Japanese soil. The objectives were to take advantage of their expertise and to win their support for the mission's approach to reform. Shoup also liked the idea because he had had successful experiences in working within tiered approaches designed to mesh the work of experts with the advancement of political objectives. He had worked successfully under this model when he worked for the Twentieth Century Fund's Committee on Taxation and when he wrote *Facing the Tax Problem*. He had learned that the expertise at the bottom of the process often wound up playing a decisive role in crafting the final recommendations. In addition, he understood that the status of a "commission" might provide greater visibility and impact for his findings than a "mission," elevating them above those of the other missions that Washington was in the process of sending out to Japan. Furthermore, he and Moss may well have hoped that the tiered arrangement would enable their proposal of Japanese collaboration to escape a veto by skeptical SCAP bureaucrats.

The issue of the appointment of Japanese members dragged on longer than any other surrounding the composition of the mission. Ultimately, SCAP refused to give approval to awarding any high-status appointments to Tsuru and his two colleagues. The reasons for this almost certainly had to do with the vigilance of GHQ's security arm, G-2, commanded by Major General Charles A. Willoughby. Willoughby was a leading member of MacArthur's "Bataan Boys," and had been MacArthur's intelligence chief since Manila. With MacArthur's full support, Willoughby turned G-2 into what historian Takemae Eiji has correctly called "the most powerful agency inside MacArthur's headquarters." Willoughby consolidated both military and civilian intelligence operations under his command, conducted loyalty checks on occupation personnel through his loyalty desk, ran a domestic surveillance group composed of former Japanese intelligence officers, dabbled in Japanese politics, and – through his 441st Counter-Intelligence Corps – monitored, and often harassed, politicians and intellectuals on the left.[78] Willoughby's G-2 was able to exercise great influence over civilian personnel decisions in part because MacArthur had assigned no independent authority for personnel to SCAP. That authority rested entirely with the military in G-2 (personnel) under the command of another "Bataan Boy," Brigadier General William Biederlinden, who worked closely with the even more powerful Willoughby in vetting and policing civilian personnel through a loyalty desk in Willoughby's Public Safety Division.[79] Unsurprisingly, as Theodore Cohen, a labor specialist within the ESS, wrote: "In a country where Marxist terminology was the common coin of intellectual exchange.... Willoughby was out of his depth" and believed "Democratic socialists were not allies in the fight against the communists but subverters of the established order."[80]

The result was that Tsuru and his colleagues did not participate as formal members of the Shoup mission. Shoup worked around this problem by informally consulting with them, especially Tsuru, throughout his visit to Japan. Despite the obstacles that the military intelligence units of GHQ had thrown in his way, Shoup successfully arranged a high degree of collaboration with the community of Japanese economists.

While he struggled to arrange for the participation of Japanese experts in the mission, Shoup briefed his colleagues with regard to conditions in Japan. In late April 1949, with only days left before his departure for Japan, Shoup sent two letters to his mission colleagues. He was able to provide them with only limited guidance. Before Shoup launched into a report on what he had learned from officials in Tokyo and Washington, DC, he urged his colleagues to gain "some knowledge of Japanese history and customs before we get there." He based this advice, he said, on conversations he had been having with "those who have been in Japan recently." He did not mean the officials. He was referring to personal friends – a Columbia physics professor, the chaplain of Columbia University, and a psychiatrist. Part of the rationale for his advice was narrowly political: "I believe that the success of our mission will depend in part on the incidental impression that we make on the Japanese with respect to our knowledge of and interest in Japan." Another part was substantive, although expressed rather diffidently: "And, the more we know of this background material, the more apt we are, I suppose, to reach conclusions in the tax field that are appropriate to Japanese conditions." To help his colleagues deepen their "background" understanding of Japan, Shoup proposed a short-list of books: Edwin O. Reischauer's *Japan: Past and Present* (the 1946 edition), Ruth Benedict's *The Chrysanthemum and the Sword* (1946), George Sansom's *Japan: A Short Cultural History* (1932), and J. F. Embree's *Suye Mura: A Japanese Village* (1939). Shoup described Reischauer's and Benedict's books as ones that "can be read straight through with profit." His comments on the other two books were less inviting. Although he described Sansom's book as "the most substantial work in English on Japanese culture," he wrote that "it lavishes so much detail on periods so far back in time that I find myself reading it only in a selective manner." He described the book by anthropologist Embree as "an extremely detailed account of daily life in a remote Japanese rural community." He did not offer any guidance to discerning or understanding the key themes or problems that the four authors took up.[81]

The pressures of preparation for the mission probably prevented Shoup's colleagues from reading Sansom or Embree extensively. If they did, however, they would have certainly noticed the stress that those two scholars placed on what they believed was a unique culture, and might have decided to slow their rush to produce policy prescriptions. Shoup and his colleagues would have been apt to take particular note of

Embree's close attention to the vitality of village life and what he described as democratic practices at the local level of Japanese society. It is much more likely that Shoup's colleagues found the time to read Reischauer and Benedict, because their books were easy reading and had achieved a good deal of visibility since their appearance about two years earlier.[82]

What would Shoup and his colleagues have been most likely to glean from Benedict and Reischauer? The answer to this question is obviously speculative; however, Shoup and his colleagues could hardly have missed the central themes of the power of the group and of a "culture of shame" in Benedict's book. Benedict suggested that "the Japanese," in the words of historian John Dower, "behaved in accordance with situational or particularistic ethics, as opposed to so-called universal values as in the Western tradition."[83] On the basis of her belief that the Japanese are "not conditioned to pursue lost causes," and her assessment that MacArthur had avoided imposing "fresh symbols of humiliation" on the defeated nation, Benedict concluded that MacArthur had a strong likelihood of accomplishing his goal of democratizing Japanese society.[84] Reading Benedict might have both reinforced the natural optimism of Shoup and his reformist colleagues, and impressed on them the need for showing respect to the defeated people.

Digesting Reischauer's history would have almost certainly reinforced those attitudes. In thinking about the future possibilities of Japan, he described its people as "pragmatists" who "in the past have shown themselves capable of abandoning old customs and habits of thought when convinced that there was something better." Thus, he concluded, "remarkable progress has been made since the surrender toward the creation of a peaceful and democratic Japan." Historical examples of democratic innovation included the politics of the 1920s. Reischauer pointed to "thousands of bureaucrats, military leaders, business men, and intellectuals, all contending for control of the government." He added: "There was even a growing demand that all classes be allowed to participate in politics." He went on to note that in the 1920s Japanese businessmen, "influenced by the philosophies of the victorious Western democracies, tended to look with disfavor on the high taxes required for large naval and military establishments." Reischauer concluded that "Liberal elements at the time of the surrender were weaker than they had been in the 1920s, but among older political leaders and urban intellectuals and white collar workers there remained a solid core of liberal thinkers, who, freed from the restrictions and fears of the old regime, emerged as proponents of a new democratic order in Japan."[85]

Later in the memo, Shoup offered some modest help with regard to the history of Japan's tax institutions. After mentioning that SCAP had asked Shiomi Saburo "to serve on our Tax Commission," Shoup included his own notes on a 1929 article that Shiomi had written on Japanese taxation before 1912. In the notes, Shoup emphasized tax reforms and public finance during and after the Meiji Restoration, and paid closest attention to the reliance on deficit finance, and on new taxes "introduced without system" to fund the wars with China (1894–5) and Russia (1904–5), and defense spending afterward. The implicit message was that Japan had a long history of taxation characterized by the complications and disruptions of wartime mobilizations. This message supported Shoup's goal of cleaning up the distortions that war and inflation had produced in what he regarded as essentially a modern tax system.

Shoup devoted most of his briefing letters to an assessment of the political and policy environment in which the mission would operate. He outlined the opportunities and constraints created or imposed by SCAP, by the mission of Joseph Dodge, by the cabinet-level National Advisory Commission that coordinated economic policy in Japan, and by the Japanese government. He reported a "strong difference of opinion with SCAP, or at least within the group of Americans in Japan (including in that group Joseph Dodge, head of the mission recently sent over by the State Department to stabilize prices and clear up the money situation), as to whether tax rates should be increased, held constant, or decreased." In addition, he warned of "considerable pressure from the Japanese ... for an increase in the personal exemptions (which are indeed extremely low by our standards, in view of a general rise in wages, etc. under inflation) and for repeal of the transactions tax." Shoup did not take a position on tax cutting and urged his colleagues to "keep our minds wide open on this subject, and that, as we do make them up, we still keep our counsel to ourselves, until our report is finished." He expressed concern, however, that getting the "facts and figures" for their report might be difficult: "It is clear that the statistical basis for much of the information we shall want is extremely poor, and Japanese willingness to accept and elaborate highly imperfect data is pretty strong." Shoup set his remarks in a context of pessimism with regard to the prospects for postwar economic recovery. In addition, he noted "the definite policy of the Washington authorities to push for a self-sufficient Japan within a very few years," and, citing problems of trade, food production, raw materials, and unemployment, wrote that "It remains unclear, to me, however, just how this is to be achieved."[86] This issue turned out to be always in the background of the mission's work, and significant disputes over strategies of economic development between two groups – each of which contained both American and Japanese experts – would shape both the formulation and implementation of the Shoup recommendations.

Shoup had launched an investigation in which he assumed a responsibility for understanding the meaning of local circumstances and institutions – economic, social, and political – before proposing sweeping changes in the fundamental fiscal mechanisms of the Japanese tax state. More than forty years later, in 1993, Tsuru noted his role as an advisor to the mission and analyzed its work. He ignored the effects of the occupation's Red scare, and praised Shoup's efforts to investigate social realities in Japan. Tsuru wrote that "of all the missions sent by the United States to Japan during the Occupation period the Shoup Mission was the most conscientious." He explained that "all of the Mission members took great pain in trying to learn complexities, traditional and contemporaneous, of the local conditions before applying modern principles of taxation of which they were at the frontier."[87]

Notes

1. On tax reform early in the American occupation, including Leo Cherne's mission and the enactment of anti-*zaibatsu* taxation in 1946, the adoption of New Deal-style income taxation, the deployment of the 8th Army to supervise tax collection in 1947, and the Moss mission in 1948, see Brownlee, W. E., "The Transfer of Tax Ideas during the 'Reverse Course' of the U.S. Occupation of Japan," in Nehring, H., Schui, F., eds., *Global Debates About Taxation* (Houndsmills, UK: Palgrave Macmillan, 2007) 158–60; Brownlee, W. E., "The Shoup Mission to Japan: Two Political Economies Intersect," in Martin, I. W., Mehrotra, A. K., Prasad, M. eds., *The New Fiscal Sociology: Taxation in Comparative and Historical Perspective* (Cambridge: Cambridge University Press, 2009), 239–40; and Brownlee, W. E., "Shoup vs. Dodge: Conflict over Tax Reform in Japan, 1947–1951,' *Keio Economic Studies 2011*, vol. 47, pp. 94–6.
2. Harold Moss, "With MacArthur in the Far East and Japan, 1937-1951" (ca. 1990), typescript in possession of Douglas M. Moss, and used with his permission; Interview of Harold Moss by Dick K. Nanto, July 21, 1973, copy with corrections by Harold Moss in possession of Douglas M. Moss, and used with his permission; and Koyanagi Shunichiro, "The Creation of Post-War Tax Administration and GHQ; The Contribution of Harold Moss" ("Sengo Zeimu Gyosei no Keisei to GHQ"), in *Taxation as Low Culture [Ho Bunka to shite no Sozei]* Mori Seiichi, ed. (Tokyo: Kokusai Shoin, 2005), 120–4. This is an extended interview with Moss conducted in Pittsburgh in 2000 and 2001. We are grateful to Ryo Muramatsu for translating the Koyangi interview into English.

3. Douglas MacArthur to George J. Schoeneman, November 1, 1947; and Harold Moss, "Biographical Sketch." Copies of both are in the possession of Douglas M. Moss, and used with his permission.
4. For the MOF view of this issue, see "Testimony of Takahashi Mamoru: The MOF," in *Materials of the Postwar Financial History*, Part 2 [*Sengo Zaiseishi Koujyutsu Shiryo Dai 2 satsu*] (Ministry of Finance, July 24, 1952), 3–4, Library of Economics, University of Tokyo. For American perspectives, see H. Moss, "With MacArthur in the Far East and Japan, 1937–1951" and Harold Moss, "Historical Summary of the Japanese Tax System," June 30, 1951, Box 8377, file folder: "Historical Summary of the Japanese Tax System," RG 331, National Archives and Records Administration, Washington, DC. For the directive reorganizing tax administration, see R. M. Levy to the Japanese Government, "Reorganization of National Tax Administration of the Japanese Government," May 4, 1949, Box 6836, file folder: "Taxation," RG 331.
5. In the fight Moss submitted the crucial memoranda, "Tax Surveillance Program" and "Brief of Tax Surveillance Program Staff Study," to MacArthur's Chief of Staff on September 23, 1949. See File folder: "Taxation," Box 6836, RG 331. Also, See Harold Moss, "Historical Report for 1949 of Internal Revenue Division, ESS, January 20, 1950, File folder: "Taxation," Box 6836, RG 331. On MacArthur's role and the opposition by the generals, see Harold Moss, "With MacArthur in the Far East and Japan, 1937–1951." On Dodge's opposition to ending surveillance, see the interview of Harold Moss by Dick K. Nanto.
6. H. Moss "With MacArthur in the Far East and Japan, 1937–1951" and H. Moss, "Historical Summary of the Japanese Tax System," June 30, 1951, RG 331.
7. Koyanagi Shunichiro, "The Creation of Post-War Tax Administration and GHQ; The Contribution of Harold Moss," 142.
8. Shoup, C. S., "Incidence of the Corporation Income Tax: Capital Structure and Turnover Rates, *National Tax Journal* 1948, vol. 1, pp. 322–9, and Shoup, C. S., *Principles of National Income Analysis* (New York: Houghton Mifflin, 1947).
9. Shoup had begun this transition during the late 1930s. In 1988, Harvard economist Martin Feldstein, who was president of the National Bureau of Economic Research (NBER) at the time, noted Shoup's early transition. In an NBER occasion honoring Shoup and the other economists who had been the participants in the first Conference on Income and Wealth in 1937–8, Feldstein observed that at that time Shoup's research on the definition of taxable income paralleled research on national income. At the 1988 celebration Shoup concurred, noting that the 1937–8 conference led to the publication of his *Principles of National Income Analysis* and informed "a good deal of the work that I and my colleagues did," including "many of our tax reports." Martin Feldstein and Carl Shoup comments in Blough, R. et al., "Luncheon in Honor of Individuals and Institutions Participating in the First Income and Wealth Conference (December 1936–January 1937)," in Berndt, E. R., Triplett, J. E., eds., *Fifty Years of Economic Measurement: The Jubilee of the Conference*

on *Research in Income and Wealth* (Chicago: University of Chicago Press, 1991), reprinted by the National Bureau of Economic Research.

10. R. Blough, Minutes of Meetings with Consultants, May 2, 1945 through June 21, 1946, Papers of Roy Blough, Harry S. Truman Presidential Library.

11. A. L. M. Wiggins, "Daily Log File, 1947–1948," A. L. M. Wiggins Papers, Harry S. Truman Presidential Library.

12. C. S. Shoup to A. L. M. Wiggins, April 12, 1949 and A. L. M. Wiggins to C. S. Shoup, July 28, 1948, Shoup Papers, Box 391–3. See, also, C. S. Shoup and W. Warren, "A Suggested Outline for a Peace-Time Federal Tax System," December 24, 1947, Shoup Papers, F-file "Federal Tax Reform," Library of Yokohama National University (YNU).

13. L. Harold Moss "Special Mission to Conduct Survey of Japanese Tax Structure, December 7, 1948, Box 7637, file folder: "9 TR-60 Shoup Tax Mission," RG 331. Moss had settled on his choice in September; his December memo was for the army's personnel records. For some of Moss's recollections of the search, see H. Moss, "With MacArthur in the Far East and Japan, 1937–1951," RG 331.

14. Louis Shere to C.S. Shoup, March 26, 1949, C-file # 15, Shoup Papers, YNU.

15. Bronfenbrenner, M., "Marginal Economist," unpublished autobiography, Special Collections, Duke University Library, Chapter 14, 17.

16. L. Harold Moss to Mrs. Wells, OAB, CPED, OSA, "Tax Mission to Japan," October 1, 1948, Box 2144, file folder: "Taxes, Shoup Mission 1949," RG 331; and Koyanagi Shunichiro, "The Creation of Post-War Tax Administration and GHQ; The Contribution of Harold Moss," 142.

17. The lists of experts Shoup considered are in his handwritten notes, Shoup Papers, Series 4, No. 4, Envelope #113, YNU.

18. W. S. Vickrey to R. M. Haig, October 31, 1945, Box 54, Haig Papers; Vickrey, "Curriculum Vitae, 1960–1992," Box 43, Papers of William Vickrey, Columbia University Rare Book and Manuscript Library.

19. See also Vickrey, W. S., "Averaging of Income for Income Tax Purposes," *Journal of Political Economy* 1939, vol. 47, pp. 379–97, and Vickrey, W. S., *Agenda for Progressive Taxation* (New York: Ronald, 1947).

20. Vickrey, W. S., *Agenda for Progressive Taxation*, 14. Shoup strongly recommended the book to Moss. C. S. Shoup to H. Moss, September 30, 1949, Box 7637, file folder: "9 TR-60 Shoup Tax Mission," RG 331.

21. R. M. Haig, "A Proposed New Income Tax for Porto Rico: The First Step in a Plan for the Revision of the Revenue System of Porto Rico" and R. M. Haig to Governor H. M. Towner, Chairman, Tax and Revenue Commission of Porto Rico, February 9, 1925, Box 52, Haig Papers; R. M. Haig to R. G. Tugwell, March 21, 1945, Box 54, Haig Papers; R. G. Tugwell to R. M. Haig, April 24, 1945; Box 54, Haig Papers.

22. R. M. Haig to R. G. Tugwell, October 31, 1945, Box 54, Haig Papers.

23. R. M. Haig to R. G. Tugwell, December 7, 1945, Box 54, Haig Papers. For more detail on the Vickrey's conscientious objector status, see W. S. Vickrey to R. M. Haig, October 17, 1945, Box 54, Haig Papers. Vickrey received a regular appointment from Tugwell after he returned to civilian status in May 1946. R. M. Haig to R. G. Tugwell, May 22, 1946, Box 54, Haig Papers. In May 1946, Vickrey returned briefly to New York in order to defend his

doctoral dissertation, which he was simultaneously revising for publication. W. S. Vickrey to R. M. Haig, April 20, 1946 and May 22, 1946, Box 54, Haig Papers.

24. R. M. Haig to W. S. Vickrey, March 13, 1946, Box 54, Haig Papers.

25. For the elements of the program, see R. M. Haig, "The Proposed Revision of the Puerto Rico Revenue System: A General Statement," June 17, 1946 and R. M. Haig, "A Proposal for a New Income Tax Law for Puerto Rico Submitted to Governor Rexford Guy Tugwell (Report Number One)" February 8, 1946, Box 52, Haig Papers.

26. W. S. Vickrey, "Exposé des motifs: Vickrey," December 28, 1945, Box 51, Haig Papers; Haig, "Memorandum Regarding Death and Gift Taxes in Puerto Rico Submitted to Governor Rexford Guy Tugwell (Report Number Two)," June 17, 1946, Box 52, Haig Papers.

27. W. S. Vickrey to R. M. Haig, March 31, 1946, Box 54, Haig Papers.

28. S. G. Ramirez, Chief of the Bureau of Income Tax, to R. M. Haig, June 3, 1946, Box 51, Haig Papers. W. S. Vickrey, "Exposé des motifs: Vickrey," December 28, 1945.

29. R. G. Tugwell to R. M. Haig, September 12, 1946, Box 54, Haig Papers.

30. On the cooperation between Shoup and Surrey in the 1930s, see Ramseyer, M., Shoup, C. S., "Japanese Taxation: The Shoup Mission in Retrospect," *The Japan Foundation Newsletter* 1989, vol. 16, pp. 5. On the Warren and Surrey collaboration in 1948, see W. Warren to C. S. Shoup, July 18, 1948, Shoup Papers, C-file, Envelope 15, YNU.

31. Ramseyer, M., Shoup, C. S., "Japanese Taxation: The Shoup Mission in Retrospect: An Interview," *The Japan Foundation Newsletter* 1989, vol. 16 (4), pp. 5–6.

32. R. Blough to C. S. Shoup, October 25, 1948, Shoup Papers, C-file, Envelope 15, YNU.

33. C. S. Shoup to J. Due, October 27, 1948 and J. Due to C. S. Shoup, November 2, 1948, Shoup Papers, C-file, Envelope 15, YNU. After Shoup arrived in Tokyo in May, he learned that John Due's health had improved. Shoup quickly wrote to Due, asking him to take a year's leave from the University of Illinois and "help put into effect the recommendations that our Mission will make (or such of them as prove acceptable)." Due, however, could not arrange the leave. C. S. Shoup to J. Due, May 31, 1949 and J. Due to C. S. Shoup, Shoup Papers, June 8, 1949, C-file, Envelope 15, YNU.

34. See Ramseyer, M., Shoup, C. S., "Japanese Taxation: The Shoup Mission in Retrospect: An Interview," 6, and Bowen, H. R., *Toward Social Economy* (New York: Rinehart, 1948).

35. C. S. Shoup to H. R. Bowen, January 14, 1949, Bowen series, Shoup Mission, Mission Correspondence, Series 1 Box 1, Shoup Papers, YNU.

36. Bowen, H. R., *English Grants-in Aid: A Study in the Finance of Local Government* (Iowa City: University of Iowa, 1939).

37. Ibid., 139.

38. Ibid., 140.

39. Ibid., 93–121. The formula Bowen proposed provided, first, for a calculation of the need for the local provision for each category of service (education, housing, poor relief, highways, etc.) in each locality. This calculation would

be made on the basis of the "total expenditure of all local authorities for the service" allocated according to a demographic index (number of people served). Next, the formula estimated the taxpaying capacity of the various localities. Bowen determined the average tax rates levied and collected by local governments. The final step was to determine the size of the grants that the central government should pay to each locality in order to accomplish complete equalization. The amount of each grant to a locality was simply the difference between its financial need and its financial ability.

40. Ibid., 140.

41. Bowen, H. R., *Toward Social Economy*, 35.

42. F. Neumark to C. S. Shoup, December 17, 1947, C. S. Shoup to F. Neumark, January 12, 1948, N-File, Correspondence 1945–9; C. S. Shoup to H. Moss, December 10 and 30, 1948 and February 9, 1949, Mission Correspondence, Moss Series; C. S. Shoup to G. Colm, C-file, Council of Economic Advisors, February 2, 1949, Shoup Papers. Shoup Mission All No. 8, Envelope #16, Shoup Papers.

43. Dower, J. W. *Embracing Defeat: Japan in the Wake of World War II* (New York: W. W. Norton, 1999), 222.

44. In his dissertation work, Cohen began under Haig's direction and took up the topic of "The Finances of New York City." Cohen recalled that "I had bitten off far more than I could chew and dropped the whole thing when I went to Washington shortly before the outbreak of war." Cohen completed his graduate work under Carter Goodrich. Shoup and Haig began a major project on this same topic in 1950. See J. Cohen to C. S. Shoup, May 19, 1950 and November 21, 1948, Shoup Papers, Cohen Series, 1 No. 1, YNU.

45. Cohen, J. B., *Japan's Economy in War and Reconstruction* (Minneapolis: University of Minnesota Press, 1949), 453. Dower may have been unaware of Cohen's appointment, but membership of the Shoup mission does not contradict Dower's basic point about the lack of Japanese specialists on expert missions.

46. J. B. Cohen to C. S. Shoup, November 21, 1948; M. Gottschall to C. S. Shoup, December 1, 1949; R. Emerson to C. S. Shoup, 3 December 1948; J. B. Cohen to C. S. Shoup, 10 January 1949; Cohen series, Shoup Mission, Mission Correspondence, Series 1, Box 1. A copy of Cohen's State Department report, "The Course of Inflation in Post-Surrender Japan," is located in Envelope No. 123.

47. Cohen described his interviewing style as "firm and at times sharp." He wrote that "the thought that one should accurately reveal his real income to tax authorities was wholly alien to the oriental mind." Cohen tended to interrogate, rather than interview, Japanese taxpayers when Shoup's mission conducted its investigations. Shoup disliked Cohen's approach and did not ask him to return with the mission in 1950. See Cohen, J. B., "Fiscal Policy in Japan," *The Journal of Finance* 1950, vol. 5, 119 and 122; and J. B. Cohen to C. S. Shoup, August 9, 1949, Shoup Papers, Cohen Series 1, No. 1, YNU.

48. C. S. Shoup to H. R. Bowen, January 14, 1949, Envelope #30, Shoup Mission, Mission Correspondence, Series 1 Box 1, Shoup Papers, YNU.

49. R. Hatfield, "MEMORANDUM FOR: Dr. Carl S. Shoup," June 17, 1949, Shoup Mission, Mission Correspondence, Series 1 Box 1, Shoup Papers, YNU. In 1989, Shoup recalled that he did not know Cohen and Hatfield "but I had been told that they had some Japanese experience in Army Language School and elsewhere and that they knew something about Japan." Ramseyer, R., Shoup, C. S., "Japanese Taxation: The Shoup Mission in Retrospect," 6.
50. M. Bronfenbrenner to C. S. Shoup, February 7, 1949, Bronfenbrenner Series, 1 No. 1, Shoup Papers, YNU.
51. Bronfenbrenner, M., "Marginal Economist," Chapter 14, 15–17.
52. M. Bronfenbrenner to C. S. Shoup, February 7, 1949, Bronfenbrenner Series, 1 No. 1, YNU.
53. M. Bronfenbrenner to C. S. Shoup, February 7, 1949, Bronfenbrenner Series, 1 No. 1, YNU; Bronfenbrenner, M. "Marginal Economist," Chapter 14, 16.
54. Bronfenbrenner, M. "Marginal Economist," Chapter 14, 17.
55. M. Bronfenbrenner to C. S. Shoup, February 7, 1949, Bronfenbrenner Series, 1 No. 1, NYU; Bronfenbrenner, M., "Marginal Economist," Chapter 14, 13.
56. Bronfenbrenner, M., "Marginal Economist," Chapter 14, 10.
57. M. Bronfenbrenner to C. S. Shoup, March 9, 1949, Bronfenbrenner Series, 1 No., 1, YNU.
58. C. S. Shoup to M. Bronfenbrenner, March 10, 1949, Bronfenbrenner Series, 1 No. 1, YNU.
59. Bronfenbrenner, M., "Marginal Economist," Chapter 14, 17.
60. Bronfenbrenner, M., "Marginal Economist," Chapter 14, 6–7.
61. M. Bronfenbrenner to U.S. Civil Service Commission, April 28, 1949 and M. Bronfenbrenner to C. S. Shoup; April 28, 1949, Bronfenbrenner Series, 1 No. 1, YNU.
62. M. Bronfenbrenner to C. S. Shoup, May 15, 1949, Bronfenbrenner Series, 1 No. 1, YNU; Bronfenbrenner, M., "Marginal Economist," Chapter 14, 17.
63. M. Bronfenbrenner to R. R. West, Civil Affairs Division, Department of the Army, May 4, 1949, Bronfenbrenner Series 1, No. 1, YNU; Bronfenbrenner, M., "Marginal Economist," Chapter 14, 17.
64. C. S. Shoup to J. Due, October 27, 1948, Shoup Papers, C-file, Envelope 15, YNU.
65. In 1949, Tokyo Shoka University (in English, Tokyo University of Commerce) was renamed Hitotsubashi University.
66. "Testimony of Takahashi Mamoru: The Postwar Tax Administration," in *Materials of the Postwar Financial History*, Part 2 [*Sengo Zaiseishi Koujyutsu Shiryo Dai 2 satsu*] (Ministry of Finance, July 24, 1952), 3–4, Library of Economics, University of Tokyo.
67. Typescript, "Taxation Investigating Committee Appointed to Study Improvements in System," Box 7637, 9 TR-60 Shoup Tax Mission, RG 331.
68. On Shiomi's cooperation with the MOF, see Hirata, K., Chu, S., and Izumi, M., *Retrospect and Prospect of Taxation in the Showa Era*, Vol. 1 [*Showa Zeisei no Kaiko to Tenbo, Jyokan*] (Tokyo: Okura Zaimu Kyokai, 1971), 512.

69. McCraw, T. K., *Prophet of Innovation: Joseph Schumpeter and Creative Destruction* (Cambridge: Harvard University Press, 2007), 413–14.

70. Hein, L., *Reasonable Men, Powerful Words: Political Culture and Expertise in Twentieth-Century Japan* (Washington, D.C. and Berkeley: Woodrow Wilson Center Press and University of California Press, 2004), 251, n. 2. For more on the Ouichi group and its intellectual connections with the Shoup mission, see Chapter 7 of this volume.

71. For suggestions of this influence, see McCraw, T. K., *Prophet of Innovation: Joseph Schumpeter and Creative Destruction*, 578–9.

72. Hein, L., *Reasonable Men, Powerful Words: Political Culture and Expertise in Twentieth-Century Japan*, 101.

73. Tsuru, S., *Japan's Capitalism: Creative Defeat and Beyond* (Cambridge: Cambridge University Press, 1993), 16.

74. For sketches of Tsuru's life, see Hein, L., *Reasonable Men, Powerful Words: Political Culture and Expertise in Twentieth-Century Japan*, 251 n. 2; Perlman, M., "Series Editor's Note," in Tsuru, S., *Japan's Capitalism: Creative Defeat and Beyond*, 267–70; and Secchi, C., "Biographical Note," in Tsuru, S., *Institutional Economics Revisited* (Cambridge: Cambridge University Press, 1993), 173–81. On the immediate postwar years, see Tsuru Shigeto, *Looking Back on the Crossroads of My Life [Ikutsumo no Kiro wo Kaiko Shite: Tsuru Shigeto Jiden]* (Tokyo: Iwanami Shoten, 2001), 213–15.

75. C. S. Shoup to Moss, April 14, 1949, Box 7637, File folder: 9 TR-60 Shoup Tax Mission, RG 331.

76. H. Moss to C. S. Shoup, April 23, 1949, Box 7637, File folder: 9 TR-60 Shoup Tax Mission, RG 331.

77. C. S. Shoup to H. Bowen, R. Hatfield, S. Surrey, W. Vickrey, and W. Warren, April 20, 1949, in Shoup Papers, Series 4 No. 4, Envelope 117, YNU.

78. Takemae, E., *Inside GHQ: The Allied Occupation of Japan and its Legacy* (New York: Continuum, 2002), 161–168.

79. On Beiderlinden's role, see Cohen, T., *Remaking Japan: The American Occupation as New Deal* (New York: The Free Press, 1987), 127, 132–4. On the loyalty desk, see Takemae, E., *Inside GHQ: The Allied Occupation of Japan and its Legacy*, 164.

80. Cohen, T., *Remaking Japan: The American Occupation as New Deal*, 92.

81. C. S. Shoup to H. Bowen, R. Hatfield, S. Surrey, W. Vickrey, and W. Warren, April 20, 1949, in Shoup Papers, Series 4, No. 4, Envelope 117, YNU.

82. Thirty years later, Shoup singled out Benedict's book as one of the few books on Japan that the members of the mission had read before arriving. See Perry, J. C., *Beneath the Eagle's Wings, Americans in Occupied Japan* (New York: Dodd, Mead, 1980), 154.

83. Dower, J. W. *Embracing Defeat: Japan in the Wake of World War II*, 219.

84. Benedict, R., *The Chrysanthemum and the Sword: Patterns of Japanese Culture* (Boston: Houghton Mifflin, 1946), 305 and 309.

85. Reischauer, E. O., *Japan: Past and Present* (New York: Alfred A. Knopf, 1946), 145, 148, 187, 189, and 191.

86. C. S. Shoup to H. Bowen, R. Hatfield, S. Surrey, W. Vickrey, and W. Warren, April 20, 1949, in Shoup Papers, Series 4, No. 4, Envelope 117, YNU; "Memorandum to Howard Bowen, Rolland Hatfield, Stanley Surrey, William Vickrey, and William Warren," undated (but post-April 27 and April 28, 1949), Shoup Papers, Series 4, No. 4, Envelope 118, YNU.
87. Tsuru, S., *Japan's Capitalism: Creative Defeat and Beyond*, 52.

9

Shoup in the "Social Laboratory"

W. Elliot Brownlee and Eisaku Ide

THE "PRESSURE COOKER"

In May 1949, Shoup's mission arrived in Japan and began its investigation in what he later described as "a pressure cooker environment." He recalled that "the seven of us worked, ate, and slept Japan and its tax problems." When in Tokyo, residing in the Imperial Hotel, "we simply lived taxation at meal times and all through the day."[1] After two meetings with General Douglas MacArthur and a few days of discussions with Harold Moss and his Internal Revenue Division staff, Shoup was already entertaining strong views on the Japanese tax system. He seemed most preoccupied by tax evasion by the relatively wealthy. "We are learning of the enormous gap between the tax laws on paper and how taxes are actually assessed and collected," he wrote privately to his family. "It's more striking even than in France." In addition, he asserted that "Japanese firms either keep no books at all, or several sets of books (one for creditors, one for the tax collector, one for management purposes, etc.)."[2]

During the second week of his visit, Shoup and three of his colleagues became tax tourists. They took to the rails and visited the major cities of Osaka, Kyoto, and Nagoya as a central part of what Shoup described the "fact-finding" phase of their work. They had already read through the massive mountain of data that Moss and his staff had assembled, most of which came from the Ministry of Finance (MOF). Shoup and his colleagues had decided that they could not trust the data, however, and, in any case, needed their own first-hand impressions of how Japan's tax system actually worked. On the investigatory journey, and those that followed, Moss and Finance Minister Ikeda Hayato ensured that Shoup had all the support he wanted. Forty years later, Shoup remembered with particular gratitude the contributions of "several of the younger Japanese officials in the Finance Ministry" who "were assigned as interpreters. Their high level of general capability, including an excellent command of English and knowledge of the Japanese fiscal system, made them invaluable colleagues."[3]

On this first trip, Shoup was accompanied by Hara Sumio, chief of the Tax Systems Department of the MOF's Tax Bureau. He had spent several years in England before the war and spoke English well,[4] but Akagawa Genichi, an official from the Ministry of Foreign Affairs, accompanied the group as the official interpreter. Akagawa also had extensive knowledge of Japanese taxation. Hara and Akagawa had to travel separately, in the Japanese section of the trains. Shoup remarked to his family that "Segregation is strictly enforced in all travel; ordinary trains, street cars and buses and marked 'Off Limits to Occupation Personnel,' some of the trains carry an 'Allied Coach.'" In the cities, the segregation was de facto; Shoup and his party traveled by chauffeured automobile.

On this first major expedition, the Japanese press, probably encouraged by both Moss and the Japanese government, treated the members of the Shoup mission as celebrities. Shoup wrote home that "At the Osaka station there were the Governor of the Prefecture, the Mayor, and other assorted officials; about a dozen news photographers and another dozen news correspondents" as well as "the U.S. Internal Revenue man in charge, and one or two other Military Government Officials." At the hotel ("deluxe as usual") a news conference followed breakfast. "I almost got out of [it], but the Military Gov't man said the papers had helped in their drive for taxes and they wanted to keep on the good side of the press." Shoup told the press that "the problem regarding small and medium enterprises is the most important topic in Japanese tax reform." He added: "This is not only just Japan's problem but also a remarkable research topic in Cuba, France, and even the United States."[5] After the hoopla, Shoup and his colleagues turned to serious work. They spent "most of the day . . . talking with the Japanese tax officials in their offices." With the help of Hara and his assistant, "we dug into tax files, examining actual returns." They tried to continue their work that evening at dinner with "their Japanese hosts," despite the fact that "four geisha entertainers hovered around, pouring sake and later on doing tricks with matches." Shoup and his party "engaged chiefly in light conversation" but "we also got in some tax discussion," he reported to his family.[6]

In Kyoto, their next stop, they found it even more difficult to "fact-find." They traveled on a Sunday, and their Japanese hosts had scheduled sightseeing that included no less than eleven sites before a 6:30 PM dinner with the governor and the vice-mayor. They began what became an ongoing, but often futile, effort to contain the entertainment. That day they managed to delay their arrival until 3 PM, limiting their touring that day to a lacquer-ware workshop and a fine-arts and curio store.[7] At dinner, however, they found themselves in a local restaurant where they sat along one side of a large room while their Japanese hosts sat on the opposite side, thus preventing "all conversation between hosts and guests."

Monday was better, but not much. In the morning, Hatfield slipped away with Howard Bradshaw, an Internal Revenue Division expert on local taxation, to confer with local Kyoto tax officials. The other members of the mission endured "more courtesy calls" and "discussions with military Gov't men." The members of the mission then arranged a "session with heads of large Japanese manufacturing concerns and department stores" and a meeting with an economic development committee for the Kyoto area. The latter, however, proved to be "too formal to be very informative," including more than thirty people "around a large table" with "reporters and news photographers in the back of the room." That afternoon, the hunger of the investigators for informality prompted them, while wandering the "alley-ways of small shops," to pick "one out at random (a retail tea store)" and ask "the owner what his chief tax problems were." They were rewarded: "For nearly an hour he discussed the issues lucidly." Despite this, a private conversation proved impossible. "Just as we started talking with him," Shoup wrote home, "I noticed a young man grab the phone and talk earnestly for some minutes. Sure enough, the Kyoto paper next day carried a report on the interview. The reporter had been trailing us all afternoon."[8]

For the next two weeks, into mid-June, Shoup and colleagues found it more productive to stay close to their offices in Tokyo, conferring extensively with Moss and his staff, and Shoup's Japanese sources, including Hara and Hirata Keiichiro, director of the Central Tax Office.[9] During the initial weeks, they worked intently, benefiting from cool, clear weather. They slowed down only when William Vickrey was hospitalized for a week in an army infirmary for a "heavy" case of measles, and when the social demands were strenuous. Shoup still complained that "There is, if anything, somewhat too much social life," and reported to his family that one day they were "offered drinks at the formal opening of the new Japanese Internal Revenue Bureau (sake, beer, 3 p.m.), at the cocktail party for a visiting group of U.S. tax agents (cocktails, 5 p.m.), at a dinner given for us at a nearby club (7 p.m.), and in between the first and second parts of [a] movie (10 p.m.)." He added: "Can't say that I'm not keeping in practice. Next week we have only 3 dinner engagements." Lobbying was a not-too-subtle accompaniment of the social whirl. They viewed the movie that evening as a "pre-preview, given for our benefit, in the private projection room of the film company." The rhetorical question for his family: "Why the intense interest in our mission?" The answer: "There is a 150% (not 15% tax) on all movie admissions."[10]

During this period, Shoup and his colleagues welcomed occasional jaunts out of Tokyo, which were not devoted entirely to business. Shoup wrote to Haig that "we can take week-end trips in Army sedans for a very small charge to scenic points near Tokyo. There is some fine scenery around; much of it reminiscent of some of the mountains districts in New England. The finest deluxe hotels in Japan are all restricted for use by the Occupation Forces (including us civilians) at very reasonable prices." In addition to this, they occasionally got out of their hotels and stayed in Japanese homes. After returning from Kyoto and the Kansai area, Shoup told Moss that he wanted to stay in the home of a peasant. Hara was deeply impressed and tried to arrange the visit; however, he was worried about how Shoup would fare around the mosquito-infested rice fields and the lavatories that collected human waste for fertilizer. Hara talked frankly with Shoup, who responded: "I like mountain climbing and camping. I have experienced such a natural environment many times. There is no problem." Hara was relieved but then surprised when Shoup, frustrated when the MOF's preparations lagged, drove himself to nearby Chiba prefecture. A few days later, Shoup, Bowen, and Hara held their planned inspection of conditions in Chiba. Moss recalled that "we must have talked to fifteen farmers about their tax problems." They visited the home of a peasant, who turned out to be a single mother whose husband had died five years earlier, leaving her with five children. Moreover, a flood had recently swept away a wall of her house. Nonetheless, she had to pay what Shoup regarded as excessive income taxes. Shoup told Hara that the visit gave him "impressions beyond the theory," and after he returned to Tokyo he continued to be anxious about the future life of the peasant. Subsequently, he and Bowen returned to Chiba for an overnight visit with a farmer he described as "relatively well-do-to."[11]

In mid-June, only about six weeks after arriving, Shoup was ready to give Haig an assessment of the progress of the mission. Shoup wrote that the borders of the puzzle were beginning to take shape, despite the difficulties the investigators faced. "The general nature of the problem we are facing begins to be apparent," he told Haig. On one hand, "both in the law and as seen through the figures on tax collections, the Japanese tax system is one of the most modern in the world." The income tax, he explained, was "on a pay as you go basis, complete with withholding at source (including interest and dividends) and quarterly estimates of income not subject to withholding." On the other hand, "when we come to how the system works in practice, we find that 'self-assessment' is largely just a name for arbitrary assessment by the tax office." Shoup admitted that no one knew whether or not a more transparent process would produce more income "chiefly because the tax payers have no accurate accounting records." He was confident, however, that big business evaded taxes through "elaborate systems of books designed to conceal rather than reveal." In looking for solutions, Shoup rejected "moving into extensive indirect taxation" because he believed "evasion of the indirect taxes seems to be at least as extensive and maybe more so." He had decided that at the core of the problem was a vicious circle of excessively high rates and comparable levels of evasion. "How to break this circle is one of our first problems."

The political situation in Japan weighed on his mind, just as it did on an earlier mission. He told Haig that this situation "reminds me a good deal of the kind of thing we encountered in France." He meant two things. First, he was facing hostility from the Japanese government that resembled the hostility he and Haig had encountered in France. He acknowledged that "we are an occupying force whose 'recommendations' will be accepted while we are here;" however, they "will not necessarily endure after we are gone." Second, he was facing a powerful attachment to indirect taxation.[12]

Shoup, William Warren, Stanley Surrey, and Rolland Hatfield departed from Tokyo Station for their most ambitious journey on the day after Shoup wrote to Haig. Vickrey, who was still recovering from measles, and Bowen, who arrived late because of a stopover in Detroit to visit Joseph Dodge, joined the other four later.[13] Over two weeks they visited four cities in Kyushu and four more in central and western Honshu, including Hiroshima.[14] They continuously interviewed tax collectors, taxpayers, local government officials, and ordinary citizens. They accosted fishermen along the shore and miners deep in coal pits. On this trip they found a way to become more efficient in both their data gathering and their analysis. From their first tour around the countryside, they had learned how to reduce the social distractions and the limitations of segregation.

They had the Supreme Commander for the Allied Powers (SCAP, named after the title of its leader General MacArthur) requisition a private railroad car and attached it to scheduled trains and, on one leg of the trip, its own locomotive. The hotel-on-rails provided convenient sleeping accommodation and an office in which they could confer easily and at length among themselves, manage their growing piles of documents and notes, prepare for their interviews, and consult with Japanese informants. In the process, they reduced the pressures from their Japanese and SCAP hosts and the newspaper reporters. Despite this, they did not succeed in entirely eliminating the distractions. At the end of the trip, Shoup reported home: "I've been quite well all the trip, although pretty tired after some days of interviewing, especially when they were topped off by an official Japanese dinner." On a typical evening in their car, the investigators rehashed the day's interviews and prepared their approaches to the next. Although they now planned more carefully, they also retained their flexibility. At the end of June, Shoup told his family that "This morning Surrey, Takahashi [one of Shoup's translators] and I descended unannounced on the Communist headquarters at Nagano, this region being noted for Communist activity, and got their views on the tax problem. We came on them so suddenly they didn't even stick close to a party line – they weren't prepared." As the trip neared its end, Shoup wrote to his family saying "The trip has been successful in gathering information, and our group has gotten along without friction, altho packed pretty close in the private car for 10 days."[15]

The trip had made a very positive impression on Finance Minister Ikeda and his secretary, Miyazawa Kiichi (later finance minister and prime minister). Miyazawa recalled: "I had a strong impression with regard to the Shoup mission that all of the members were extremely respectful. Their language was polite, and they travelled all over Japan using trains possessed by the army of occupation, and they studied very deeply."[16]

CRAFTING THE RECOMMENDATIONS

In early July, the missionaries returned to Tokyo and moved simultaneously into the last phase of their "fact-finding" and the beginning of crafting recommendations. The mission engaged MOF officials in intense conversations over roughly twenty-five topics that Shoup had identified as significant. Beginning on Monday, July 4, they spent eight days working their way through a carefully constructed schedule of morning and afternoon conferences, alternating between the Forestry Building and Ikeda's official residence. They took a break only on Sunday. At the same time, to prepare for the writing of a report, Shoup drafted detailed questions and topics and assigned them to the members of the mission.[17] During this period, exchanges with Japanese economists became more intense. Shiomi Saburo provided Shoup with English drafts of three papers, "Contributions" ("dues" other than taxes), "Discrepancy between the Rich and Poor in Japan," and "Reform of the Tax System Involves Many Problems," as well as a complete set of the *Kyoto University Economic Review* for 1926–43.[18]

Shoup and Vickrey attended all but one of the sessions, whereas the others joined only those that took up their special assignments. Shoup had decisively taken charge of shaping the overall direction and structure of the mission and the report that would soon emerge. He had chosen Vickrey as his closest advisor, asking him to apply his acute economic analysis to all of the topics discussed and to help to develop a coherent set of recommendations. Shoup directly involved Tsuru Shigeto in the conversations. Tsuru later recalled the significant role played by Vickrey, emphasizing that Vickrey "had a very sharp theoretical sense." Consequently, Tsuru explained, "I was required to act as a mediator between him and the Japanese government."[19] On the especially sensitive issue of intergovernmental finance, Shoup and his colleagues met in two sessions, one with MOF officials only and another with just Ogita Tamotsu, the president of the Local Autonomy Agency, and Yasui Seiichiro, governor of the Tokyo metropolitan area.[20] To help Shoup prepare for this discussion, Shiomi arranged for a special trip by Warren to Kyoto in mid-July to meet with prefectural officers.[21]

After extensive consultations with occupation officials – Moss, other SCAP bureaucrats, Japanese consultants, MacArthur himself, and even Dodge and the members of the National Advisory Council (through a kind of teleconference) – Shoup and a few colleagues went into isolation. During the first week in August, Shoup, Vickrey, Warren, and Hatfield – the members of the mission who were still in Japan – packed up at the Imperial Hotel, left everyone behind in Tokyo, and traveled several hours into the interior mountains to the ancient town of Nikko. They checked into a hotel that had been constructed during the Meiji era. The hotel's angular Gothic lines gave it the appearance of a Black Forest retreat. "This is a very pleasant place," Shoup told his family, "4,000 ft. high, cool, quite away from the sweaty weather of Tokyo. The four of us have three rooms, and three typewriters, and we are using this chance, where it's cool and quiet to work morning noon and night getting the report written." Since his youthful trips to the Sierras, two of Shoup's favorite recreations were mountain climbing and fishing. There was no time for either here, however, or for more than six hours of sleep. The three Columbia professors typed away while Hatfield played the role of research assistant. They allowed no interruptions, even when "representatives of a coal miner's union showed up ... to present their views on the tax system." The missionaries "just accepted their written memorandum and wouldn't even go into the lobby to say hello." As they finished chapters, they sent them to Tokyo by messenger, and a week later they returned to Tokyo with a complete manuscript for the four-volume *Report on Taxation in Japan*. A few weeks later, Shoup noted that "although there is substantial agreement among the members of the mission on all major points, responsibility for the report in its final details attaches chiefly to Vickrey, Warren, and myself."[22] They were all exhausted, but four decades later Vickrey recalled: "As a team leader Shoup proved to be extraordinarily effective as a hard but scrupulously fair driver, coupled with a genuine concern for the welfare of his team members that brought out the best in their work."[23]

At the end of his mission in Japan, Shoup sent a summary of the *Report on Taxation in Japan* to Haig along with the comment: "I believe you will discern in the recommendations the pervasive influence of the teachings of Professor Robert M. Haig."[24] The mentor replied: "The program you have evolved seems to me to be intelligent, original and clever. Let me hope that they will put it into effect." He looked "forward eagerly to the opportunity to hear the full story from the lips of the chief actors."[25]

Shoup believed Haig's teachings and principles had enough intellectual power to lift the mission's proposals for innovative taxes above the level of risky experimentation. Consequently, he thought of the mission as advancing cautious reform rather than daring experimentation. "We have tried," Shoup wrote to the Department of the Army when he completed his report, "to keep a judicious balance between no undue experimentation and no slavish adherence to the past." He explained: "We are recommending for Japan a tax system that is dependable, but that is also modern." Shoup and his colleagues believed that if the Japanese government adopted the entire reform program, however, the result would be more than "modern." It would be unique and, in their view, uniquely superb. Shoup declared: "We believe that the Japanese people should have the opportunity to be able to say, within five or ten years, that they have the best tax system in the world – even better than the American tax system. We have formulated our recommendations with this aim in mind. The rest will be up to them" – the Japanese people.[26]

The experts from America believed they had presented Japan with the means for fiscal salvation, and welcomed the support of the occupation authorities to advance their agenda; however, they regarded the ultimate outcome as being dependent on the workings of Japanese democracy.

By the end of the mission, Shoup and his colleagues had discovered that they had moved beyond the situational analysis of Ruth Benedict to acquire a deeper respect for the strength of Japanese democracy. Their immersion in Japanese tax politics had, in fact, led them to become optimistic about the prospects for their recommendations, particularly when publicized by the wide distribution of the *Report on Japanese Taxation*. This optimism may well have resulted from Shoup's conversations with Tsuru. As Shoup told Martin Bronfenbrenner a few years later, he and his colleagues had held out hope for the election of a coalition government that included Socialists. This would have supported the mission's more innovative reforms, even though they had initially become law as a consequence of the uneven balance of power between SCAP and the Japanese government.[27]

The members of the Shoup mission hoped that through the contributions of Japan as a democratic "social laboratory," key parts of the Haig program would catch on elsewhere, including the United States. Less than a month after he returned from Japan, Shoup was installed as president of the National Tax Association, at the time the foremost organization for the exchange of ideas between economists and tax practitioners. The topic he chose for his presidential address was "Tax Reform in Japan." In it, he declared that "my aim is only partly that of describing and analyzing the Japanese system. It is," he went on, "also to consider whether any of the measures recommended for Japan might be applicable to the United States." He added: "As of the present moment, it appears likely the recommendations of the tax mission will be enacted into law in a special session of the Diet scheduled for the end of October or sometime in November."[28] Later chapters in this volume explore the outcomes of the subsequent legislative deliberations.

IMPLEMENTATION: A FOOTNOTE ON THE ROLE OF BRONFENBRENNER

While Shoup and his colleagues settled back into their Columbia routines, Moss managed the implementation of the mission's recommendations. In this process, he engaged in extended negotiations which involved General MacArthur, Joseph Dodge, Moss's own Internal Revenue Division (IRD), other divisions of SCAP, and the Japanese government. As other chapters in this part of the volume suggest, severe internal disagreements within the IRD, the rest of SCAP, and the Japanese government severely complicated Moss's work. In these negotiations Moss relied heavily on hard data and economic arguments. Ultimately, all parties praised his fairness and patience. In summarizing his experience with Moss, Finance Minster Ikeda Hayato reminded Secretary of the Treasury John Snyder that "in some cases the difference of opinion between the Occupation and the Government of Japan was such that there appeared to be strong pressures befalling upon him to take coercive measures in order th realize quick results." However, "this he resisted all the time, instead he took every pain to explain and persuade until a mutually acceptable solution was reached." In these negotiations Moss relied heavily on the services of Bronfenbrenner. In this work he provided a continuing link for Moss and Shoup with both the Japanese tax experts within government and the economists outside it who had worked informally with Shoup.[29]

In October 1949, about six weeks after his arrival in Tokyo, Bronfenbrenner finally travelled to Kyoto, where he met with Shiomi. In preparation, he wrote to Shiomi informing him that he had "read several of your articles with both pleasure and profit" and asking to meet with him to talk about "various aspects of the final Shoup Report on which you contributed preliminary versions." Following their meeting, Shiomi summarized his advice in a trenchant memorandum that Bronfenbrenner passed on to Shoup. Despite this, Bronfenbrenner regarded Shiomi's advice in general as too cautious and vague, and he clearly preferred his consultations with Tsuru.[30]

Tsuru was Bronfenbrenner's most important confidant. He had followed Tsuru's work since 1935 and, before joining Shoup during the summer of 1949, struck up a correspondence with Tsuru. In Japan, the two economists had quickly discovered that they had much to talk about. This relationship blossomed and became an important part of Bronfenbrenner's immersion in Japanese society. The relation encompassed more than consultation over tax policy. Tsuru proposed that they collaborate in teaching a graduate seminar on "Western macro-economics" at Hitotsubashi. "I accepted with alacrity," Bronfenbrenner recalled "after ascertaining that the seminar was held on Wednesday afternoons, when we were off duty." He "came to look forward to those Wednesday afternoons" when he drove his "little British Austin, which I named *Akaji-Zaisei* or 'Deficit Finance'" between downtown Tokyo and Kunitachi, the suburb where Hitotsubashi was located. Tsuru "was then working on a Marx-Keynes synthesis" and the seminar included "several young Hitotsubashi professors and students who would later achieve prominence in Japanese economic circles," including "the international economist Kojima Kiyoshi, the development economist Shinohara Miyohei, and the econometrician Yamada Isamu." The group was ideologically "a mixed bag... with Tsuru on the Left and Yamada on the Right, defining my own position as the middle."[31]

Bronfenbrenner's informal technical consultations with Tsuru helped considerably with his conscientious effort to reconcile differences between Shoup and the MOF over the mission's proposals – particularly the recommendations of value-added taxation and the reforms of local taxation. What Bronfenbrenner did not know, however, was that Tsuru was on Major General Willoughby's surveillance list, and military intelligence was about to intervene once again in the tax reform project. "In early 1950," Bronfenbrenner recalled, "the rumor seems to have started that these Hitotsubashi seminars were 'covers' for anti-Occupation political plots, or even for training in revolutionary tactics."[32] In April 1950, G-1 and G-2 launched a purge that led to the firing and expulsion from Japan of SCAP personnel, Bronfenbrenner recalled, "on suspicion of anything from 'dangerous thoughts' to high treason." In his autobiography, he described "this situation [being] as close to totalitarianism as I have ever come." Harold Moss, who had confidantes in the security arms of MacArthur's General Headquarters, called Bronfenbrenner into his office to tell him that "the process had started" in his case. Moss advised Bronfenbrenner that "since I had my Madison job to return to [... I should] best resign and return, breaking my two-year contract." Moss and Shavell, with Bronfenbrenner, went over the dossier that G-1 had assembled. It included his "'irregular' security clearance" a few months earlier, the Hitosubashi seminars with Tsuru, his "pro-Japanese" tax work, a scholarly article of his (on inflation-fighting in Japan) that the Public Information Office had dubbed "Leftish," and a letter that Bronfenbrenner had written on SCAP stationery to the editor of the *Nihon Keizai Shimbun* (the *Japan Economic Times*, today known in English as *The Nikkei*) defending the value-added tax. In the letter, Bronfenbrenner had attacked the American newspapers who opposed the value-added tax with an argument that he picked up, absent mindedly, from the American Communist Party. He wanted to visit G-1 and G-2 and clear up all of these issues; however, Moss convinced him not to on the grounds that this would prompt G-2 to identify and the cut off Moss's "networks" within G-sections. Bronfenbrenner agreed to resign and in August 1950 he returned home, just before Shoup returned for the mission's second visit. It is a powerful commentary on the competence of the American occupation that the only American scholar purged from the tax reform work in Japan was the one most knowledgeable about Japan and, in addition, the one who was the most conservative.

Apparently Bronfenbrenner did not expect either Shoup or Moss to do more on his behalf, and bore them no ill will. Bronfenbrenner and Shoup continued their friendship, and Bronfenbrenner remembered Moss as "the most competent and efficient non-academic boss I ever had."[33] At the time, however, Bronfenbrenner and Shoup both worried about whether the purge might disrupt the adoption of the Shoup recommendations. Perhaps it did, particularly with regard to the proposal of a value-added tax, but in retrospect Shoup regarded their joint accomplishments as substantial. Seven years later, in commenting on a draft of Bronfenbrenner's history of the mission, Shoup urged him "to let the reader know of the significant part that you yourself played, in 1949–50, in getting the system enacted and understood by the Japanese."[34]

Notes

1. C. S. Shoup to J. C. Perry, February 22, 1979. See the quotation by John Curtis Perry in *Americans in Occupied Japan* (New York: Dodd, Mead, 1980), 153.
2. C. S. Shoup to his family, May 12 and May 14, 1949, in Appendix B, "Extracts from letters by Shoup from Japan," in Shoup, C. S., "The Tax Mission to Japan, 1949–1950," in Gillis, M., ed., *Tax Reform in Developing Countries* (Durham: Duke University Press, 1989), 224. To the best of our knowledge, these family letters are not in the Shoup Papers at Yokohama National University (hereafter YNU).
3. Shoup, C. S., "The Tax Mission to Japan, 1949–1950," 179–80.
4. C. S. Shoup to H. M. Groves, May 25, 1950, Folder 9, Box 12, Harold M. Groves Papers, State Historical Society of Wisconsin.
5. Local Autonomy College, *Post War Autonomy History Vol. XIII* [*Sengo Jichi Shi 13kan*] (Tokyo: Jichi Daigakko, 1975), 46.
6. C. S. Shoup to his family, May 25, 1949, "Extracts," 224–5.
7. "Mr. Shoup and His Mission-Group's Schedules for Sight-seeing Tour in Kyoto Sunday," May 22, 1949, Shoup Papers, All No. 8, YNU.
8. C. S. Shoup to his family, May 25, 1949, "Extracts," 224–5.
9. Watanabe, T., *Recollections of Japanese Public Finance under the Occupation* [*Senryoka no Nihon Zaisei Oboegaki*] (Tokyo: Nihon Keizai Shinbunsha, 1966), 224.

10. Shoup to his family, "Extracts," June 11, 1949. Shoup also reported that we "were startled by [the] excellence" of the movie; C. S. Shoup to R. M. Haig, June 16, 1949, Robert M. Haig Papers, Butler Library, Columbia University.

11. Local Autonomy College, *Post War Autonomy History XIII*, 68; C. S. Shoup to R. M. Haig, June 16, 1949, Robert M. Haig Papers, Butler Library, Columbia University; Interview of Harold Moss by Dick K. Nanto, July 21, 1973, with corrections by Moss, in the possession of Douglas M. Moss, and used with his permission.

12. C. S. Shoup to R. M. Haig, June 16, 1949, Robert M. Haig Papers, Butler Library, Columbia University.

13. While Shoup and the others began their trip, Warren visited Nagoya and Osaka and then joined the group on their swing back to Tokyo from the western side of Japan. Cohen, who arrived in Japan earlier than the other members of the mission, had already visited the western part of Japan, so he investigated conditions in the Tohoku area and Hokkaido rather than join the main group.

14. For a schematic map of their travels, see Fukuda, Y., *Tax Recommendations by Carl S. Shoup* [*Shaupu no Zeisei Kankoku*] (Tokyo: Kasumi Shuppan-sha, 1985), 454. The map is part of the supplementary materials for this work, which is a modern translation of the two reports of the Shoup mission.

15. C. S. Shoup to his family, June 30, 1949, "Extracts," 225.

16. Mikuriya, T. and Nakamura, T., eds., *Retrospect of Miyazawa Kiichi* [*Miyazawa Kiichi Kaiko Roku*] (Tokyo: Iwanami Shoten, 2005), 111.

17. Undated notes by Shoup, Shoup Papers, Series 4 No. 4, Envelope 116, YNU.

18. S. Shiomi to C. S. Shoup, July 12, 1949, July 21, 1949, and August 12, 1949, and C. S. Shoup to S. Shiomi, July 27, 1949, "Japan Box 321," Shoup Papers, YNU.

19. *Retrospect and Prospect of Taxation in the Showa Era*, Vol. II [*Showa Zeisei no Kaiko to Tenbo, Gekan*] (Tokyo: Okura Zaimu Kyokai, 1979), 419.

20. "Suggested Schedule of Conferences with Finance Ministry," Shoup Papers, ALL No. 7, YNU.

21. S. Shiomi to C. S. Shoup, July 12, 1949 and July 21, 1949; "Japan Box 321," Shoup Papers, YNU.

22. C. S. Shoup to his family, July 27, August 2, August 3, and August 7, 1949, "Extracts," 226; Shoup, C. S., "Tax Reform in Japan," Presidential Address, National Tax Association, Wednesday, September 21, 1949, in *Proceedings of the Forty-second Annual Conference on Taxation Held under the Auspices of the National Tax Association* (Sacramento, CA: National Tax Association, 1950), 400.

23. Vickrey, W., "Carl Sumner Shoup," *The New Palgrave: A Dictionary of Economics, Volume 4*, Eatwell, J., Milgate, M. and Newman, P. eds. (London: Macmillan, 1987), 326.

24. C. S. Shoup to R. M. Haig, September 1, 1949, Haig Papers, Butler Library, Columbia University.

25. R. M. Haig to C. S. Shoup, September 9, 1949, Correspondence, 1945–9, "C-File" Series, Shoup Papers, YNU.

26. "To West from Shoup," August 24, 1949, Box 6836, file folder: "Taxation," RG 331, National Archives and Records Administration, Washington, DC.
27. Shoup told Bronfenbrenner this in an interview prior to the publication of Bronfenbrenner, M., Kogiku, K., "The Aftermath of the Shoup Tax Reforms, Part I," *The National Tax Journal* 1957, vol. 10, pp. 346–7. Prior to the publication of the article, Shoup reviewed a draft that reported this interview. He made no suggestions for correction. C. S. Shoup to M. Bronfenbrenner, May 27, 1959, Box 27, File: "Tax Mission 1950 (1)," The Papers of Stanley Surrey, Harvard University Law Library Special Collections.
28. Shoup, C. S., "Tax Reform in Japan," 400–13.
29. H. Ikeda, to John Snyder, July 10, 1951, letter in possession of Douglas M. Moss. For a discussion of Moss's negotiating role, see Brownlee, W.E., "The Transfer of Tax Ideas during the 'Reverse Course' of the U.S. Occupation of Japan," in Nehring, H. and Schui, F., *Global Debates About Taxation* (New York: Palgrave Macmillan, 2007), 169–72; and Brownlee, "Shoup vs. Dodge: Conflict over Tax Reform in Japan, 1947–1951," *Keio Economic Studies* 47 (2011), especially 102–14.
30. M. Bronfenbrenner to S. Shiomi, October 11, 1949, Box 7637, File fiolder: "9 TR-60 Shoup Tax Mission," RG 331; M. Bronfenbrenner to C. S. Shoup, January 21, 1950 with attachment of Shiomi's paper, "Criticism of the Shoup Report," No. 1, Bronfenbrenner Series, Shoup Papers, YNU.
31. Bronfenbrenner, M., "Marginal Economist," Chapter 15, 6, unpublished autobiography, Special Collections, Duke University.
32. M. Bronfenbrenner to C. S. Shoup, January 10, 1950, Bronfenbrenner Series 1, No. 1, Shoup Papers, YNU.
33. M. Bronfenbrenner to C. S. Shoup, May 5, 1950, Bronfenbrenner Series 1, No. 1, Shoup Papers, YNU; Bronfenbrenner, M., "Marginal Economist," Chapter 14, 4 n. 5.
34. C. S. Shoup to M. Bronfenbrenner, May 27, 1959, Bronfenbrenner Series 1, No. 1, Shoup Papers, YNU. See footnote 27.

10

Tax Reform during the American Occupation of Japan

Who Killed Shoup?

Ryo Muramatsu and W. Elliot Brownlee

In 1949, Carl S. Shoup, a public finance economist at Columbia University, led a group of distinguished tax experts on a mission to occupied Japan. During that mission, Shoup and his colleagues proposed a sweeping, fundamental reform of that nation's tax system. In 1950, in what may well have been the most dramatic tax reform program undertaken in a modern industrial nation during the twentieth century, the Japanese government implemented most of the changes that the mission had proposed. Over the next few years, however, starting even before the end of the occupation, the Japanese government significantly modified the central parts of the "Shoup" tax system.[1] Very few scholars outside Japan have written at length about the history of the Shoup mission, even though many American historians have written extensively, and powerfully, about the occupation.[2] In contrast to this, scholars in Japan have devoted a great deal of ink to the subject. There are two explanations that they have most commonly advanced to explain the collapse of the Shoup system. These reasons are often described as mutually reinforcing. The first is simply the end of the occupation in 1952, which freed the Japanese government to return to prewar patterns of taxation.[3] The second is a shift of economic goals toward "capital accumulation" that began during the occupation and continued after its conclusion.[4] None of these scholars has made an in-depth analysis of the reasons for the collapse. Most striking is the absence of analysis of the roles of various actors, such as Japanese bureaucracy, political parties, business, and the occupation bureaucracy – particularly the Supreme Command for the Allied Powers (SCAP) – in the collapse.[5] This chapter will augment analysis of the collapse of the Shoup system by concentrating on the taxation of interest income and capital gains on transactions in securities, which was an important focal point of the mission's recommendations, and by encompassing views from both Japanese and American sides of the occupation.

The Shoup mission regarded its most central recommendations to be those providing for expanded income taxation, the uniform taxation of all income (along Haig-Simons lines), suppression of special favors within the tax code, reduction of confiscatory rates of taxation at the highest rates of progressive income taxation, and the creation of a transparent tax code. To advance the uniform taxation of all income, the Shoup mission recommended that all forms of income, including interest income and realized capital gains, should be included in the income tax base and taxed at the same rate. Our focus in this chapter is on a particular historical episode – the taxation of interest income and realized capital gains of security transactions during the American occupation of Japan. In addition to this, we are interested in the prospects for broad-based taxation in Japan and elsewhere. The history of the Shoup recommendations might assist in reflections on the possibilities and limitations of such an approach to tax reform as modern nations struggle with the contemporary, international crisis in public finance.

TAXATION OF INTEREST INCOME AND CAPITAL GAINS ON SECURITY TRANSACTIONS BEFORE SHOUP

From the introduction of the progressive income tax during the early Meiji era, Japan provided favorable treatment of interest income and capital gains on transactions in securities. This policy was embedded organically in a broader, organized effort to get Japanese society behind national goals. During World War II, the Japanese government expanded this prosavings system to mobilize resources and contain inflation at the same time as minimizing tax increases. In a classic effort to "capitalize patriotism," the government engaged in aggressive savings campaigns where the Ministry of Finance (MOF) worked with the Home Ministry to establish reducing consumption and increasing savings as patriotic behavior. Among the tactics used was the organization of savings associations in all walks of life, reinforced by incentives for participation, including generous tax breaks. Within the income tax, the government introduced a particularly complex system of classifications of interest income that provided distinct advantages to interest earned on bank deposits. One of the advantages fell to depositors in the widespread system of postal savings banks, which the MOF controlled from within its Deposit Bureau.

Beginning in 1942, these depositors received the interest tax-free on accounts containing fewer than 5,000 yen. The MOF mobilized these savings for the purchase of government debt. The Bank of Japan remained the most important source of government borrowing throughout the war; however, the lending by postal savings banks grew even more rapidly, taking about one-third of Japan's war debt by the time of the surrender. The middle class made this possible. One estimate is that, by 1944, Japanese households saved 44 percent of their disposable income.[6]

Prior to the American occupation, the Japanese government privileged capital gains, excluding them from income taxation. Starting in 1937, however, the government imposed a modest tax on transfers of securities. During the wartime period, the government adopted various measures that constrained the development of equity markets and more than offset the benefits that stockholders enjoyed by virtue of the exclusion of their capital gains from income taxation. At the end of the war, the stock market was shut down, not to be reopened by General Douglas MacArthur until 1949. By the end of the war, investments had shifted heavily from equities toward deposits in the banking sector, which accounted for about 80 percent of all private sector assets. In the words of Takeo Hoshi and Anil K. Kashyap, banks had become "the dominant supplier of funds" for both public and private investment.[7]

In 1947, under the supervision of the American occupation, the Japanese government broadened the base of its progressive income tax, significantly reducing the privileges of both interest income and capital gains. The tax reforms of 1947 consolidated all forms of regular income, including interest income, and taxed it at the same, steeply progressive rates. Despite this, the reforms maintained the tax-free status of postal savings accounts. In 1946, the government had increased the ceiling from 5,000 yen to 10,000 yen, and in 1947 the government increased it again, this time to 30,000 yen. At the same time, the Japanese government introduced the taxation of capital gains, applying the progressive rate structure to 50 percent of capital gains although maintaining the old tax on transfers of securities. The income tax was self-assessed, but both banks and brokers were required to submit information to the Tax Bureau about their depositors and clients.

The regular savings banks reported on depositors to whom they had paid more than 300 yen in interest in a given year. The banks withheld taxes on interest income at the lowest rate in the progressive rate structure (20 percent). Despite this, the 1947 reforms included two provisions designed to continue to provide tax relief to recipients of interest and incentives for taxpayers to channel their savings into the banking system. These two provisions resulted from a compromise between the Banking Bureau and the Tax Bureau, both located within the MOF.

The first provision provided an incentive to large depositors related to paying taxes on their interest income. Under this provision, recipients of interest from accounts in regular savings banks could opt out of paying the self-assessed, progressive tax on that income if they accepted a flat rate of 60 percent on their interest income and agreed to submit to the withholding of that tax. Thus, recipients of bank interest who would have faced a tax rate above 60 percent if they consolidated their interest income with their labor income enjoyed special treatment under the 1947 system.

The second provision, championed by the Banking Bureau, allowed banks to create secret bank accounts for customers making time deposits. The customers who opened such accounts did not have to report their names and addresses to the bank. Instead, they used their name seals, and many of the accounts were held in the name of a fictitious person. The price for holding such time-deposit accounts in regular savings banks was automatic withholding of interest at the 60 percent tax rate. Under this system, owners of secret bank accounts could not escape paying the 60 percent tax rate. There was no tax-withholding "price" for maintaining secret accounts in postal banks, but exercising secrecy could enable individuals to evade the 30,000 yen limit on tax-free interest by spreading their savings across multiple banks in the national postal system.

The secret bank accounts quickly became an important element in Japan's financial structure. By the end of 1949, 58 percent of the funds held in time deposits and installment savings accounts (within commercial banks) were in secret accounts, and more than 15 percent of all deposits (again, within commercial banks) were in secret accounts. The share would grow to 58 percent by the end of the year.[8] By the 1950 fiscal year, deposits in postal savings banks had roughly tripled since the end of the war, and amounted to about 13 percent of deposits in commercial banks.[9]

THE SHOUP MISSION: THE FIRST VISIT AND RECOMMENDATIONS

Shoup and his colleagues arrived in Japan in May 1949. During their four-month investigation, they heard vigorous complaints about the system of taxing interest income from bankers who wanted even more favorable tax treatment of depositors. The bankers protested that the collection of information about depositors was too costly and wasteful, and that even the reduced taxes under the 60 percent withholding option discouraged customers. What most bankers wanted was a return to a straightforward classified income tax system, and the taxation of interest income at a flat rate of 20 percent (the minimum tax rate under the 1947 consolidated tax system). Banks would withhold the tax but not report any information about depositors to the MOF. The bankers claimed that the effect of reducing the rate of taxation on deposit income would lead to increasing bank deposits and thus, in turn, increasing tax revenues. The Bank Bureau of the MOF and the Bank of Japan supported the bankers in their recommendations.[10]

The Shoup mission also heard complaints from the securities brokers – complaints that they had made ever since the enactment of the 1947 reforms. The brokers protested that the taxation of capital gains even at the 50 percent level (1) privileged deposits in time accounts in commercial banks over the purchase of securities, and (2) required troublesome and costly administrative work by securities brokers. The firms and the Japanese Securities and Exchange Commission asked for repeal of the income tax on capital gains relating to stocks and reduction or repeal of the security transfer tax.[11]

In September 1949, the Shoup mission published its report with a hugely ambitious set of recommendations for reforming the Japanese tax system. With regard to the taxation of interest income and capital gains, the mission urged moving in the reverse direction to that desired by bankers and brokers. The mission proposed both abolishing secret bank accounts and taxing interest income at exactly the same rates as other forms of income. Shoup pointed out that the present "policy of allowing depositors to spread their deposits anonymously in large numbers of accounts" was designed to enable depositors to conceal "not only the interest income but also income from other sources." If such accounts were taxed lightly, Shoup argued, bank deposits would "become a haven of tax avoidance for the wealthy individual, and the principle of progressive income taxation could be completely vitiated." Shoup went on to assert that the "full taxation of bank deposits would have the beneficial effect of driving the wealthy investor out of bank deposits and into types of investment, such as the purchase of stocks and other equities, which the banks cannot well undertake themselves. This would provide more funds of the kind that can actually be used for capital expansion." Finally, Shoup noted the large variation in interest rates that borrowers were charged and those paid to depositors, and declared that they indicated "either excessive profits for the banks or great inefficiency in the handling of the banking operations." Thus Shoup, in a not so subtle fashion, pointed to the need for banking as well as tax reform.[12]

Under the reforms proposed by the Shoup mission, banks would have to collect information on all depositors and turn it over to the Tax Bureau, which would use it to enforce the payment of taxes on interest income through the self-assessed income tax. (Banks would continue to withhold taxes on interest income at the minimum level of 20 percent, whereas taxpayers who owed more would meet their obligation when they filed their self-assessed tax returns.)

A rigorous, literal interpretation of the Shoup recommendations with regard to the taxation of interest income earned on bank accounts would lead to the inference that the mission proposed eliminating the tax-exempt status of accounts in postal banks and abolishing secret accounts in those banks. The mission's 1949 report, however, made no specific references to postal banking or postal bank accounts, and no documentary evidence exists to suggest that the Shoup mission ever discussed postal banking issues in that year. It may well be that recognition of the widespread popularity of postal bank accounts led the mission to discretely avoid the topic, and leave its disposition to Japanese government.

For the taxation of capital gains, the Shoup mission again recommended moving in the opposite direction to that recommended by powerful financial entities. At the heart of the Haig-Simons definition of income was the interchangeability of labor income and capital gains as sources of economic power, and Shoup and his colleagues had developed a deep commitment to the ideal that Robert Murray Haig, Shoup's mentor at Columbia, had pioneered. Thus, the Shoup mission did not hesitate, or look closely at conditions in Japan, before deciding to recommend that the reformed income tax should fully include both capital gains and capital losses. The recommendation, however, was for far less than doubling the taxation of capital gains. The rate proposed for the top bracket of capital only increased from 42.5 percent to 55 percent because of the reductions in the highest marginal rates that the mission recommended (from 85 percent to 55 percent for the top bracket).

Far more important, and with greater implications for effective tax burden, were the mission's proposals for administrative reforms designed to prevent evasion of capital gains taxation. These included the requirement that transfers of stock shares, which included enrolling the names and addresses of the new owners on the books of the corporation, had to take place within a month of purchase or else the new owner would not be allowed to sell the stock. Purchasers of corporate bonds would be required to register their names and addresses or else they would not be able to demand interest payment.[13] With this system of name transfer and registration in place, "tax officials could ascertain who is or was the owner of any particular share or bond."[14] For a tax cheat, effective administration of the capital gains tax could mean an enormous increase in taxes.

Finally, the mission stopped short of recommending repeal of the trans fer tax. It did, however, express some reservations about the tax. The mission noted that the security transfer tax "is almost universally in use," but declared: "It is difficult to find a justification for it." The mission was tempted to recommend repeal but explained that it had "not had time to study [the tax] carefully."[15]

Shoup made his recommendations on the taxation of interest income and capital as part of a coherent program for strengthening the income tax as a social instrument. Special exemptions for interest and capital gains, Shoup believed, would foment tax resistance among wage and salary earners who paid their taxes largely through withholding, and tax avoidance among those who did not have taxes withheld but whose income was taxed at higher rates than interest and capital gains. (The secret bank accounts, Shoup and his colleagues were convinced, provided an important means for tax avoidance.) A horizontally equitable income tax, Shoup was equally confident, would persuade public to accept the income tax as fair and be willing to maintain it, avoiding the curses of deficit spending, inflation, and a starved public sector. With public confidence in income tax, the Japanese government would be able to achieve an adequate level of social investment. At the same time, taxing all income at the same rate would avoid privileging one or more form of income (wages, profits, interest, capital gains, and rent) over the others, and thus distorting the allocation of resources among the factors of pro- duction (labor, capital, and land). The result would be balanced economic growth – a growth in productivity across all factors of production. For Shoup, there was no trade-off between democracy and economic growth. Shoup's central goal was to win popular support for the income tax, and he was unwilling to jeopardize this effort by providing special favors to capital, and thus abandoning horizontal equity. Shoup rejected facile sug- gestions that there were conflicts inherent in tax policy between the goals of promoting equity and capital formation. In terms of these goals, Shoup recalled that he and his colleagues on the mission "were much more con- cerned with both equity, especially horizontal equity, and reduction of

excess burden (economic efficiency) and were willing to let capital formation reach whatever level the market would then call for."[16] This was a
matter of emphasis, however, rather than a search for theoretical purity.
Thus, within the income tax system, he was willing to offer the wealthiest
citizens lower rates of tax in the highest brackets. In the remainder of
the tax code, he was willing to provide some special encouragement for
investment through the abolition of excess-profits taxation provision for
a thoroughgoing revaluation of corporate assets, and the replacement of
a local income tax (the enterprise tax) with a sales tax (a value-added
tax).

IMPLEMENTING SHOUP'S RECOMMENDATIONS: TAXATION OF INTEREST INCOME

Implementation of Shoup's recommendations required action by the
Japanese government. General Douglas MacArthur, as the personal
embodiment of SCAP, had the power to issue directives and, in principle, warmly embraced the Shoup recommendations. Despite this, he
left the enactment of specific measures largely up to the Japanese government. (SCAP, however, retained the power to block the introduction of
legislation, or amendments to proposed legislation, in the Diet.) For its
part, the government, through Prime Minister Yoshida Shigaru, endorsed
the recommendations in principle, and the Tax Bureau within the MOF
supported many of the specific recommendations, including those for the
taxation of interest income and capital gains. Within SCAP, L. Harold
Moss, a U.S. Treasury expert on loan to the Internal Revenue Division
(IRD) within the Economic and Scientific Section (ESS) of SCAP, headed
the IRD, and managed negotiations with the MOF. He enthusiastically
supported almost all of the Shoup recommendations. Even after returning
home to Columbia, Shoup continued to consult actively with Moss and
IRD staffers, especially economist Martin Bronfenbrenner, over implementing the mission's recommendations.

In late 1949, a national debate ensued over Shoup's recommendations.
Among the participants were prominent public finance economists. They
had a great deal of respect for the professionalism of Shoup and his colleagues, often shared Shoup's attraction to Haig's ideal tax system, and
had little in common politically with the bankers and wealthy depositors. Their sophisticated assessments help put Shoup's proposals for the
taxation of interest income and capital gains in the context of Japanese
economic institutions. One of the economists was Shiomi Saburō of Kyoto

University, who had joined two other Japanese economists who acted as formal advisors to the mission. A month after Shoup had left Japan, Shiomi wrote to him, reporting various objections that had emerged within Japan's tax-policy community to the mission's recommendations, including the taxation of interest income. Shiomi began by noting that "it has been a long national custom that the people first deposit money in a bank who [*sic*] invests it." Shiomi went on to report agreement with Shoup, saying that "it is desirable that this practice should be corrected in future and the people should be educated to interest themselves in direct investment." This was seen as a long-term process, however. In the short-term, inflation threatened. Under this threat, "the secrecy of deposit is playing a helpful role for collecting deposits for banks and any drastic measure to stop this habit had better be avoided."[17]

The most influential economists who held such views clustered in a network centered at the University of Tokyo. A representative of this group's assessment of the Shoup reforms was Suzuki Takeo, who was a lecturer at the University of Tokyo and dean of economics at Musashi University. As early as November 1949, at the first meeting of the newly formed Japanese Tax Association, and then a few months later at a conference organized at the University of Tokyo, he analyzed the taxing of interest income in the context of the implications of the Shoup recommendations for capital accumulation. He recognized that the Shoup recommendations had to be considered together with those of another American, Joseph Dodge, president of the Detroit Bank, whose mission overlapped with, and took precedence over, Shoup's. Dodge came to Japan in February of 1949, earlier than Shoup, with greater authority than Shoup by virtue of holding an appointment made by President Harry S. Truman, and having received his charge in the form of a directive issued by the Joint Chiefs of Staff. That charge focused his mission on controlling inflation, and Dodge had great flexibility in pressuring the Japanese government to implement his nine-point program, which became known as the "Dodge Line." Suzuki correctly recognized that Shoup "did not stay within the scope of the Dodge-plan, which merely aimed at monetary stabilization, but tried to formulate a consistent and constructive economic policy that would overrun Mr. Dodge's plan."

Suzuki went on to explain that "Mr. Dodge intended to amortize national debts by the excess of income over appropriations," and then turned these "forced savings" over to the banks, "which held [*sic*] many national debts." Then, Dodge assumed, the banks would "invest in private business to accumulate their capital. This plan originated from the idea that private investment . . . was more efficient and productive than national investment." In contrast, Shoup's plan, Suzuki wrote, promoted both public investment and "spontaneous savings," which would be "invested directly in stocks by private citizens" who were primarily members "of the large income class." In Suzuki's view, "Dr. Shoup's accumulation method is more positive and concrete than Mr. Dodge's method," promising to promote "democracy" in capital markets. Suzuki added: "The Shoup Mission's recommendation marks a step forward as it will serve the purpose of restoring the accumulation of capital to its normal form under a stabilized economic [sic] condition." In Suzuki's view, the "removal of the privileged treatment of the taxation on the interest of bank deposits . . . is not only desirable but also . . . should be followed as the normal form of the accumulation of capital." Thus, Suzuki correctly understood Shoup's intentions with regard to the promotion of balanced economic growth through a horizontally equitable income tax, and was decidedly supportive of them in the long run. Despite this, however, Suzuki believed that Japan was not ready for this Shoup reform. Two "prerequisites" had to be established first: "(1) Our existing banking system should be reformed to the commercial banking system after the Anglo-American fashion," and "(2) The long-established custom of our general public to invest indirectly [i.e., through bank deposits] should be remedied." His concluded that Shoup's "recommendation may be an ideal one to be adopted as a permanent measure" eventually, but "it is doubtful whether such [a] measure is effective as one to be adopted immediately."[18]

Ironically, a Japanese banker reinforced Suzuki's second point about what he and Shiomi referred to as the power of "custom." A president of what his American intermediary described as "one of the large Japanese banks," wrote to Moss saying that "the economic history of Japan . . . shows that bank deposits have long been the main source of capital accumulation, and the growth of capital has been promoted by banks by means of the indirect investment of these deposits." This banker added a key point: "Due consideration has to be given that the tax law is more easily enforced on bank depositors than on others. The tax system must be free of discrepancies on inequity in its treatment, and must not be unjustly severe on depositors." The banker asserted what Moss and Shoup knew full well: the self-assessed income tax was poorly administered, resulting in inequities bearing harshly on individuals who paid relatively more of their taxes through withholding. The basic solution proposed by the banker was to abolish information at the source (the banks) and leave the reporting of interest income entirely to individuals. In addition, he proposed phasing-out secret accounts and replacing them with a system for registering fixed-income bank accounts. In contrast to Shiomi and Suzuki, however, he made no concession to Shoup's arguments on behalf of long-term restructuring of both the tax system and the banks. The American banker, L. W. Chamberlain, resident vice president in Tokyo of the National City Bank of New York, told Moss that "From conversations I have had with other bankers, I feel quite sure it represents the almost unanimous opinion of Japanese bankers."[19]

Shoup responded vigorously to such criticism, arguing that the inflation-fighting benefit of the secret bank accounts was modest, and that failure to establish the principle of horizontal equity in the short term would increase inflationary pressures in the long term. In Shoup's view, unless the principle of horizontal equity became bedrock in the tax system, the public would lose confidence in the fairness of the tax system and consequently resist taxes, leading to inflation or a starved public sector, or both. "As to [the] secrecy of deposit," he wrote to Shiomi, "this is much too high a price to pay for the relatively small contribution that it makes toward checking inflation. Unless everyone can be sure that all the major avenues of outright evasion under the tax law have been closed the confidence of the people in the tax system will deteriorate, and the ultimate result will be a far greater inflationary pressure."[20]

Shiomi continued to convey reservations, however, and at the same time sharpened his own views. In January 1950, Bronfenbrenner forwarded some "concrete proposals by Shiomi" to Shoup, including one to the effect that "Some method should be contrived to harmonize income tax administration with the requirements of banking and investment." Bronfenbrenner explained that Shiomi "has in mind here the problems raised by prohibiting anonymous or fictitious-name bank accounts, and requiring registration of security transfers." Shiomi meant, Bronfenbrenner added, that "these measures, essential to proper tax enforcement, may drive money into hoards and particularly decrease equity investments which Japan needs."[21] Apparently Shoup did not answer Bronfenbrenner, or correspond further with Shiomi, who had not altered Shoup's belief in the importance of even-handed, broad-based income taxation to a healthy investment climate and sound economic recovery in Japan.

In late 1949 and early 1950, the Japanese government agreed to adopt a major element of the fundamental Shoup recommendation regarding taxation of interest income. In April 1950, with the vigorous endorsement of the Taxation Bureau, the Diet enacted legislation taxing interest income on the same basis as all other income. In response to the complaints of powerful commercial banks, wealthy depositors, and the industrial partners of the banks, however, the Diet made some modifications to the Shoup-recommended system. One was to raise the threshold of interest income from 300 yen to 1,000 yen per year for reporting information for the purposes of tax collection. The intent was simply to adjust the old threshold to reflect the reality of inflation that had more than doubled price levels since the adoption of the original threshold in 1945.

Other modifications were more significant. One was to retain the tax exemption of interest on postal savings deposits of 30,000 yen or less. Another was to stop short of legislative prohibition of new or existing secret banking accounts. Instead, on April 11, 1950, the Banking Bureau issued an ordinance retroactively suspending new secret accounts, effective from December 31, 1949. At the same time, the Banking Bureau encouraged, but did not require, banks to suspend existing secret accounts. On July 19, 1950, in a move that paralleled that of the Banking Bureau, the Post Savings Bureau notified its post offices that they should require new depositors to verify their names and addresses and prevent them from opening multiple accounts. Similar to the Banking Bureau, however, the Post Savings Bureau did not require identification or suspension of multiple accounts that were already in existence.[22] The moment for adopting full – or at least close to full – taxation of interest income had stalled, as had the effort to provide the administrative apparatus required to tax interest. Moss probably would have preferred a complete prohibition on secret accounts imposed by legislation, however in the absence of a directive by MacArthur or the Joint Chiefs via Dodge, he lacked the means to compel the Japanese government to initiate such a measure. MacArthur was unwilling to go further in imposing tax reform on the Japanese government, and Dodge never had sufficient interest in comprehensive tax reform to advance it by using his power over the budgets of the Japanese government.[23]

IMPLEMENTING SHOUP'S RECOMMENDATIONS: TAXATION
OF CAPITAL GAINS ON SECURITIES

MacArthur probably supported the broadening of the base of income taxation to include capital gains. A prominent tax consultant to MacArthur recalled the General had declared that "The stock exchange, any stock exchange is purely an instrument for gambling. It's a device of the devil. It is evil. It has no economic function."[24] In any case, there was no doubt in the minds of the SCAP bureaucracy or the Yoshida government about the importance of approving this particular provision. Within the Japanese government, the Tax Bureau of the MOF supported this change, and Finance Minister Ikeda Hayato was willing to go along with it, at least for a time, because he liked other parts of the Shoup recommendations, particularly the abolition of the transactions tax and the cuts in income tax rates. Consequently, in December 1949, the government submitted a bill to the Diet, approved by SCAP, that would enact the reform and discontinue the tax on securities transfers. To enforce the capital gains tax, the bill followed the Shoup recommendations by providing a system of required name transfer (after two months rather than one month) and registration.[25]

The security brokers intensified their lobbying activity. They had objected to the 1947 changes and the Shoup recommendations, and now faced a new problem. The stock market, which MacArthur had only allowed to reopen in May 1949, slipped into a recession during the summer, just about the time at which Shoup left Japan. As a consequence of Dodge's decision to end new loans by the Reconversion Finance Bank and to prevent the government from using the Counterpart Funds to replace the bank's loans, companies had been forced to expand their stock issues dramatically, causing stock prices to plummet. Prices had fallen sharply from September 1949, and then in December 1949 the stock market decline turned into a panic-driven rout that extended into January 1950, when the Diet took up the base-broadening legislation.[26]

The government, meanwhile, recognized the severity of the crisis by adopting a variety of countermeasures to shore up stock prices. The government's efforts to modify the Shoup recommendations regarding the capital gains on security sales focused on the system of name transfer and registration. Brokers argued that both the one-month deadline for name transfer and the requirement for registration would cause a lot of troublesome work, discourage securities investment, and fail to help in verifying income. In an effort to reach a compromise, brokers proposed dropping the deadline and either creating new institutions to manage name transfers or establishing a requirement that owners endorse and register their stocks during every accounting period.[27]

In January 1950, the government abandoned the administrative reforms that the Shoup mission had proposed to enforce the capital gains taxation. The government announced that it had decided to postpone the establishment of a deadline for name transfers and, instead, was going to create an institution for easy name transfers, just as the brokers had recommended.[28] The government prepared two bills and the cabinet council approved them in February 1950. The bill authorizing name-transfer agencies cleared the Lower House in April, but it failed to pass the Upper House. The cabinet council then reversed its decision and decided not to submit the other bill, which would have authorized a deadline for name transfers. At the same time, with the vigorous endorsement of the Taxation Bureau, the Diet provided that the reformed system of consolidated income taxation would include full taxation of capital gains, including those on transactions in securities. Thus, the government had, in principle, embraced the full taxation of capital gains but, at the same time, had scrapped measures that would have provided the means of enforcement. The securities brokers won a major political victory that amounted to a reversal of the progress of the fundamental Shoup reforms.[29]

Moss's IRD decided, at least for the moment, not to press for the Japanese government to adopt any substitute, compromise legislation. Shoup received the news of this from Kenneth Sanow, one of Moss's key assistants. Sanow reported that the failure to adopt the registration of securities was an exception to the enactment of the mission's recommendations in "the national tax field." He explained that the Finance Division of the ESS had supported the Japanese government's position that "registration would destroy the freedom of transferring shares and would have a depressive effect on the market." This was "Presumably because shareholders could be taxed on their earnings." He advised Shoup that "Alternative solutions were suggested to replace the registration of securities, but all offered loopholes for tax evasion." Sanow added that "The opposition was quite strong." Rather than give in to it by adopting one of the compromises, "which would not obtain the desired objective," he explained that "it was felt advisable to await your return," which was anticipated to occur during the summer.[30] Unspoken in the letters from the cautious Sanow was the assumption that Dodge would back up the Finance Division in opposing effective detection of capital gains, and that Moss was unwilling to take on Dodge just yet. Moss had a great deal else on his plate, including a tangled negotiation over reform of local taxation, which was far more challenging than even the issue of capital gains taxation.

Shoup immediately reaffirmed his strong position on this issue. "If the opposition was indeed based on the thought that full taxation would have a depressive effect on the market," he told Moss, "I am prepared to take a firm stand against any such objection." Shoup stated the threat to the integrity of the nascent tax reforms with crystal clarity. "If we are to subsidize securities, let us do so by means other than tax evasion." Shoup added that he had asked William Warren, a Columbia University tax lawyer who was his closest friend on the mission, "to give special thought to this matter."[31] The Moss forces had not given up either, hoping to get MacArthur behind administrative reform when the Shoup mission returned to Japan. Later in May, Henry Shavell, deputy chief of the IRD, provided Shoup with the same assessment that Sanow had regarding the reasons for the outcome of the securities registration issue. "We were faced with strong opposition from both ESS and Japanese parties," he said. Despite this, Shavell and Harold Bradshaw, another Moss assistant, each told Shoup that they were ready to fight, using the same words: "I feel sure that such opposition can be over-ridden providing your mission reiterates its stand on this issue this summer."[32] As members of the IRD staff prepared for Shoup's second visit, they flagged "registration of securities" as an important issue for the mission to consider.[33] Shoup faced a huge challenge here. As with the taxation of interest income, his program to tax capital gains effectively had halted because of economic conditions in Japan, the influence of powerful interest groups, the desire of the Yoshida government to curry favor with these groups, and the unwillingness of either MacArthur or Dodge to force tax reform on the Japanese government.

THE SHOUP MISSION: THE SECOND VISIT

In 1950, MacArthur and Moss invited Shoup and his colleagues to return to Japan to follow up on the progress that SCAP and the Japanese government had made in implementing his recommendations. Shoup returned to Tokyo in August and focused on the areas in which the Japanese government had fallen short of the mission's expectations. In pressing SCAP and the Japanese government to adopt more of the mission's program, however, Shoup faced the problem that resistance to some of the key Shoup reforms was gathering force both inside and outside the Japanese government, and within the American occupation – led by Dodge and his close ally Eugene Reed, who was chief of the Public Finance Branch and a powerful force within the larger Finance Division in which Reed's branch was located. In fact, the influence of Dodge and Reed grew along with the economic problems created by the intensifying Korean War and its increasing demands on MacArthur's attention. Shoup and his colleagues realized they were running out of time to shape Japan's financial system in a fundamental and sustained way, and they were ready for a more direct confrontation with Dodge than they had been willing to make previously. At the same time, however, they were prepared to collaborate closely with Japanese tax officials in working out reasonable compromises.[34]

During what became known as the "second" Shoup mission, he and his colleagues devoted considerable attention to the taxation of interest income, the related issue of the enforcement of self-assessed income tax, and the income taxation of capital gains. Shoup had followed the development of these issues, and on the eve of his return to Japan the IRD had flagged them as important issues for him to analyze.[35] Shoup assigned the primary responsibility for studying these issues to his Columbia colleague Warren.

Warren spent much of his time during the second visit studying how to reform the system of secret bank accounts. He discovered that the data with regard to the effectiveness of the Banking Bureau in discontinuing "fictitious accounts" were limited. He took note, however, of a report from the Tax Bureau that there had been a significant decline in deposits in such accounts in commercial banks following the regulations issued by the Banking Bureau in April. On August 1, however, some 55 billion yen remained in secret accounts.[36] In addition, Warren noted that the increase in deposits in postal bank accounts had slowed in July, subsequent to the regulatory tightening.[37]

With regard to the taxation of capital gains from security transactions, Warren saw an opportunity to intervene in the political process as a kind of policy entrepreneur, hammering out a compromise that, with vigorous support from SCAP, might prove acceptable to the brokers. In September, Warren had several meetings with securities firms regarding the various means of verifying the capital gains reported by taxpayers. In a meeting with the brokers, Warren announced that the mission had dropped the idea of establishing deadlines for name transfer but was considering recommending simply that securities firms would report customers' purchases and sales to a tax office.[38] In subsequent meetings, some securities brokers responded positively to the idea but proposed that they should only file information for large transactions – purchases or sales of at least 500 shares of stock or with a value of at least 100,000 yen. Two key representatives of the Tokyo brokers indicated that in three years, assuming "the stabilization of our economy and particularly the completion of reorganization of the securities dealers," they would be willing to consider a more stringent system – one providing for the reporting of all daily transactions.[39] Warren agreed in principle with the idea of reporting just the largest transactions, but he made a counter-proposal – reporting the purchases or sales of at least 200,000 yen over a three-month period. The brokers, however, demurred, and the discussions ended without any agreement.

The primary means by which the mission sought to influence the Japanese government and SCAP was the publication of a second major report, which the mission would draft in the form of a press release. As had been the case a year earlier, Shoup hoped that the document would assist the Tax Bureau and Moss in mobilizing support for the reform program within the Japanese public and government, and make it more difficult for the Public Finance Division of SCAP to undermine his proposals.[40]

For the report, Warren drafted a powerful condemnation of what he described as "evasion practices." These, Warren explained, took the form of "fictitious or anonymous commercial or savings bank accounts, fictitious or anonymous postal savings accounts and fictitious or anonymous accounts with brokers for the purchase and sale of securities." These accounts "place an almost impossible burden on the administration of the self-assessed income tax because even a reasonable number of investigators would have great difficulty in detecting the true owners of the plethora of fictitious accounts." He went on to attach blame to the "brokers, bankers and even postal savings clerks" as well as their clients: "Taxpayers have been encouraged in many cases to open fictitious accounts to evade taxes by some brokers [and] bankers" and "where information reports are required to be filed with the Tax Administrative Agency, often only the fictitious names have been disclosed on the reports even when the true owners were known to the reporting agents." He added in no uncertain terms that: "An equitable administration of the self-assessed income tax requires that these practices cease immediately." Warren acknowledged that the ordinance by the Banking Bureau and the Postal Savings Bureau suspending secret accounts had been "helpful;" however, he viewed it as clearly inadequate. What was needed was "a law prohibiting the use of fictitious names and anonymous designations." This would apply "to the postal savings system, the banks, other financial institutions, brokerage houses, and the like." Warren, with his savvy legal eye, concluded with practical suggestions as to the construction of legislation that would cover both old and new accounts in the difficult period of transition.

Finally, with regard to securities transactions, Warren proposed the requirement for "identification and the recording of the account in the name of its true owner" when securities (including coupon bonds) were purchased or sold, and the creation of a system for phasing out existing accounts identical to the system proposed for secret bank accounts. Warren added that in addition to this it was "necessary to institute immediately a system of information returns from the financial institutions and brokerage houses. These returns will provide MOF with selected information on unusual transactions, the purchase and sale of securities of more than a certain number of shares or a minimum yen account."[41]

On September 18, three days before Shoup's scheduled press conference, Moss hand-delivered to the various divisions of the ESS the draft of the extended report that Shoup and his colleagues intended to release to the press. In the draft document they had retained most of Warren's analysis of the taxation of interest and capital gains. They had, however, dropped Warren's recommendations for toughening the regulation of postal banks, and for ending the exemption of interest on postal bank accounts. In circulating the draft, Moss asked the division heads to advise if "the proposed statement contains any references, conclusions or recommendations which might be considered contrary to SCAP policy or occupation objectives."[42] Various divisions raised objections and questions, and there also was "a difference of opinion" regarding the issuance of a press statement. The next day, to keep the press statement alive, Shoup agreed to modify it to take into account almost all of the negative responses, which included one by the Finance Division regarding Warren's statement on the secret bank accounts and security transactions. The division wanted Shoup to go even further in editing Warren's proposals. Shoup obliged by deleting that section altogether. He added, however, that he would make it "the subject of a separate memorandum."[43] On September 20, SCAP submitted the revised press release to the Japanese government, "in the hope that it will serve as a guide to the accomplishment of needed reforms in the Japanese national and local tax systems," and the release became public the next day.[44]

As promised, Shoup made no mention of the secret bank accounts and security transactions in the press statement, however he did allude to them in a "confidential report" that he submitted to SCAP at the same time to amplify the second report. In a section recommending a program of forgiveness of tax evaders, he declared that "evasion and underreporting of income remain today the most serious administrative problems in the new tax system." He went on to propose that, in the future, "areas of evasion" could be, and ought to be, limited by "information returns from brokers, bankers, and the like." Shoup warned, however, that if the government instituted a new information system without an adequate provision for forgiveness of prior tax evasion, either "cash withdrawals from the banks and brokerage houses" and damage to the economy would follow or brokers and bankers would sabotage the information system. Shoup had come to see a forgiveness system as the key to winning the support of some bankers and brokers on tax reform. "If the forgiveness principle is adopted, withdrawals are likely to be at a minimum, and the cooperation of the brokers and bankers in filing the information return is likely to be wholehearted."[45]

Shoup and Warren wrote an elaborate analysis of the issue of secret bank accounts and security transactions for a technical appendix on the topic of "Measures to Aid Enforcement." They provided a far more extensive discussion of security transactions than the one that they had included in their original press conference draft. In this appendix, they suggested that in order to detect tax evasion, brokers should make "an additional carbon copy of all orders to buy or sell shares of stock or debt instruments." Shoup and Warren explained that "The order pads would be serially numbered," and that "Monthly or quarterly the carbon copies of all customer transactions would be turned over to the processing division of the Tax Administrative Agency." This was in essence the proposal that Warren had informally made to the brokers – without the specification of a reporting threshold.

In this appendix, Shoup and Warren proposed stringent changes in the operations of postal banks, on the belief that the limitation on deposits in tax-free postal accounts "has been flagrantly violated." They concluded their discussion of the postal banks by calling for removal of the exemption from taxation of interest on postal savings accounts. They declared that "the facts" do not bear out the claim that "the accounts belong only to the low income groups." They asserted that "many belong to the higher income groups and in fact have been used to evade income taxes." They concluded that: "the exemption of the interest on such accounts from income tax seems unwarranted, arbitrary, and likely to lead to capricious results in the savings programs of the Japanese people." In the various memoranda and reports that the Shoup mission submitted during the eighteen months of its service, this was the only occasion when the mission called specifically and directly for abolition of the exemption of postal bank interest from taxation. This particular reform proposal was probably low on the agenda of the mission, despite the strong feelings of Shoup and Warren, because they knew it had no support from anywhere in the Japanese government, including the MOF.[46]

SCAP waited until November to release the appendices to the second Shoup report, and then entirely deleted the analysis and recommendations regarding secret bank accounts and security transactions. The recommendations of the second Shoup mission on this key matter had become a dead letter, never delivered to the Japanese government or public. SCAP never made public, or explained to Shoup, that Moss and the IRD had firmly rejected Shoup's last-ditch proposal of a system for forgiving tax evaders. As early as September 26, Moss wrote to General William Marquat, the chief of the ESS, saying that providing significant forgiveness might encourage taxpayers to expect additional forgiveness in the future. "The personnel of this Division, without exception," Moss told Marquat, "are opposed to any plan which, if adopted, would make it possible for an honest taxpayer to say: 'I have been a 'sucker' for filing an honest tax return'." Moss reported that "This Division feels that other techniques can be utilized for achieving Dr. Shoup's objective for the establishment of a workable and efficient information return system," and "the Division is therefore continuing discussions on this problem with Japanese tax authorities, brokers, bankers, and others concerned, with the view of working out a suitable alternative."[47]

In November, Moss wrote to Shoup to describe the political circumstances that, he said, explained the severe truncation of the appendices.[48] Moss pointed to SCAP's desire, while preparing for a peace treaty, to avoid recommendations that were "certain to raise further controversies" with the Japanese government. Moss also explained that the IRD was reluctant to support "release of material objected to by other parts of SCAP," and referred, in particular, to objections by Reed's Public Finance Branch.[49] Moss did not offer any details on the views of the ESS on the recommendations regarding secret bank accounts and security transactions, but in October Sanow had written to Shoup implying that the objections had not come from within the IRD. After Sanow had reviewed the offending appendix, he told Shoup: "From a tax standpoint there can be no objections to the recommendations in this section." He added that, "as to the recommendations on securities, the other interested parties in SCAP should be consulted as to the possible adverse effects on the stock market."[50]

Weakness in the stock market was, in fact, a major concern in both the Japanese government and the Finance Division of the ESS. Another concern was over what Japanese banks described as the "over-loan" problem: an increase of the loan-to-deposit ratio from slightly more than 70 percent in mid-1949 to more than 90 percent toward the end of

1950. To finance the rapid growth of loan activity that was unmatched by increases in deposits, banks had to borrow at increasingly high levels from the Bank of Japan. Dodge became concerned about this problem as early as April 1950. He told Marquat that "the banks are extremely overloaned. Their 85 per cent or more of assets in loans compares with 27.5 per cent for all of the banks in the United States." He admitted that the latter may be low, but "the former is outrageously high from the standpoint of either solvency or liquidity."[51] This had become "a dangerous situation, only stabilized by the ignorance of the mass of bank depositors." The pressure on banks grew even worse after the outbreak of the Korean War in June 1950, when a procurement boom took hold and Japanese companies increased their bank borrowings to meet American demands for strategic goods. At the same time, the combination of excess demand and monetary expansion by the Bank of Japan had produced a resumption of inflation.[52] Japanese bankers announced that they "could not accept the over-loan anymore," and the Finance Division was not prepared to put any additional pressure on either the bankers or the Japanese government.[53]

THE POST-SHOUP DENOUEMENT

After the conclusion of the work of the "second" Shoup mission, the Japanese government moved gradually but relentlessly to complete the burial of its recommendations regarding the taxation of interest income and capital gains. For the issue of interest income, the burial came as part of a larger program of action to resolve the banking crisis. At the same time that the Shoup mission completed its second visit, both the Banking Bureau of the MOF and Ichimada Hisato, governor of the Bank of Japan, concluded that they had to take action.[54] In September, Ichimada announced that he would like to correct the "over-loan" problem in a gradual fashion. In October he reduced the purchase of government bonds, and then in December 1950 and March 1951 he raised the interest rates charged to commercial banks when, in the Bank of Japan's judgment, their loan-to-deposit ratios became excessive.[55] In addition, the Banking Bureau and the Bank of Japan took steps to increase the flow of deposits into the banking system. In November 1950, they called on commercial banks to increase the interest rates they paid on time deposits. The commercial banks were inclined to comply; however, they urged the government to take other measures as well that would not put as much pressure on bank profits. Most important, they called on the government to restore the tax breaks that implementation of the Shoup recommendations had reduced. Representatives of the banks declared that they continued "to strongly urge the government to implement the withholding taxation and restore the secret bank accounts." They believed that "a tax break on interest should come first before the rise in the rate for the deposit augmentation."[56] The Banking Bureau agreed that tax incentives were "the first thing to do," declaring that the restoration of the secret accounts and a reintroduction of a low-rate withholding option were "the ultimate solutions."[57] In 1953, Banking Bureau officials recalled that in late 1950 they had regarded the Shoup recommendations as the central problem: "The new tax system based on the Shoup Recommendation had a remarkable tendency to prevent the deposit growth."[58]

The Tax Bureau, led by its director Hirata Keiichiroō, however, had a different perspective on the Shoup recommendations. The Tax Bureau attempted to stand by the horizontal equity that Shoup had advanced, even though it recognized the political obstacles to their implementation. In this instance, the Tax Bureau opposed the restoration of tax breaks for earners of interest income. Thus, the Tax Bureau turned out to be in agreement with Shoup, Moss, and his IRD of SCAP. In other words, this was a case in which the alignment of bureaucratic forces and contention on tax policy cut across the American-Japanese divide, with Moss's IRD, Shoup, and the Tax Bureau facing off against Reed's Public Finance Branch and the Finance Division as a whole, Dodge, and the Banking Bureau. In late 1950, the opposing sides within the MOF and SCAP produced inaction. Within SCAP, MacArthur and the ESS did not choose sides in the conflict between the Public Finance Division and the IRD, so although SCAP had buried the Shoup recommendations on secret bank accounts it did not advocate any change in the policies of the Japanese government.

In 1951, the Banking Bureau persuaded the Yoshida cabinet to embrace the Banking Bureau's position. Consequently, well before the end of the occupation, the government began to revert to overt pre-Shoup policies, and to do so in an extensive way, encompassing various aspects of income taxation.[59] Dodge and Reed, who took over the entire Finance Division in 1951, supported such moves; however, Moss and IRD could only watch with disappointment as the Japanese government and the Finance Division of SCAP cooperated in using the tax code as a tool to stimulate capital investment in a highly selective way, that is to say in particular sectors and industries rather than in the broad-based way Shoup favored.[60] In July 1951, the IRD was disbanded, and the much-depleted tax staff was transferred to the dominant Finance Division, where it had less influence over ESS and SCAP policy. The next month Moss returned to the Washington DC. No institutional advocate for the Shoup recommendations remained.[61]

Two subsequent steps in early 1951 established even more favored treatment of interest income. One step reduced the information banks were required to submit regarding their depositors. Banks would have to provide information only when depositors received more than 5,000 yen per year. A second step reintroduced a lower-rate withholding path for tax payment on interest income. Under this revision, taxpayers could choose to have banks withhold taxes on interest income at the rate of 50 percent, and thereby be relieved of paying any additional taxes. Thus, depositors who would have otherwise had to face a rate higher than 50 percent on their deposits received a tax break. This was not a huge break, however, in light of the facts that the top rate on personal income was 55 percent and the government was often unable to verify the interest income taxpayers reported on individuals' self-assessed forms. In fact, Hirata and the Tax Bureau had succeeded in limiting the damage to the Shoup recommendations regarding interest income.[62]

In addition to this, in early 1951 the Yoshida government began to move toward altogether abandoning the tax on gains from securities transactions. The cabinet was almost ready to take that step; however, the Tax Bureau was reluctant, despite the fact that capital gains taxation of securities had become little more than a hollowed-out, empty shell. In March 1951, Yoshida appointed a Commission for Tax Reform, which a month later recommended a return to taxation of only 50 percent of capital gains realized from security transactions. In June 1951, the Diet enacted legislation formally allowing security brokers to sell beneficiary certificates whose owners could hold them anonymously. In August, the Liberal Party's recommended budget included outright repeal of the capital gains tax on securities and its replacement by the revival of a new security transfer tax. Some legislators in the Diet stressed that actual revenue from the income tax on the capital gain of securities was very small as a consequence of the lack of a verification mechanism. In fact, by 1952 the revenue from the taxation on capital gains from securities had fallen to only 338 million yen and accounted for only 0.45 percent of self-assessed income tax revenues.[63] Although Hirata acknowledged the low revenue productivity, he still stood by the tax, arguing that it would be embarrassing to abandon such a key part of the Shoup recommendations without further study. Hirata, with some SCAP support, temporarily succeeded in his delaying tactics. Thus, the Tax Bureau had – at least for that moment – become a more effective proponent of the Shoup recommendations on the taxation of both interest income and capital gains than the tax unit within the ESS. Despite this the tide had turned, promising further erosion of the Shoup system of horizontal equity.

The commercial banks proceeded to intensify their lobbying, looking to go beyond the 50 percent withholding option to the unequivocal restoration of secret bank accounts.[64] They pointed to the fact that the over-loan problem had become more acute during 1951 as the loan-to-deposit ratio climbed to over 100 percent and stayed at that level into 1952 despite increases in the interest rates on time deposits. Moreover, inflation continued to rise, driven by foreign demand for Japanese textiles after American purchases of strategic material declined in the spring.[65]

In October 1951, the Bank of Japan took account of the inflation problem and the need to keep prices down to expand exports of armaments to the United States. The bank raised the official discount rate and stopped supplying funds through commercial banks to industry except for electricity, steel, and shipbuilding.[66] At the same time, the Banking Bureau asked commercial banks to control the size of loans to companies.[67] Both the Bank of Japan and the Banking Bureau called for restoration of the secret bank accounts. Ichimada complained to Dodge that, in Dodge's words, "one of the obstacles to deposit increases is not the interest rate on deposits but the way the tax office goes into the banks and examines the deposit accounts of taxpayers. If bank deposits are to increase this practice has to be eliminated."[68]

In advancing its case, the Banking Bureau pointed out that the Securities Investment Trust Act had already expanded the scope of secret transactions. The measure included a provision that enabled security brokers to sell beneficiary certificates that could be held anonymously. The Banking Bureau argued that this legislation gave security holders a tax advantage not available to bank depositors and destroyed the intellectual defense of the Shoup reform. In an internal document, the Banking Bureau declared: "Today, the prohibition of anonymous deposits is logically invalid."[69] Apparently Finance Minister Ikeda, who had supported the secret bank accounts in 1947, agreed; he overruled the objections of Hirata and the Tax Bureau.[70]

In January 1952, in response to the coordinated push by the Banking Bureau, the Bank of Japan, and the MOF, the Yoshida government asked for SCAP's approval to restore the secret accounts in commercial banks.

Reed, with prompting by Sanow, had to point out the obvious: that the measure was "contrary to basic SCAP policy" of "maintenance of the principles of equity and ability to pay with regard to taxation." He did not, however, recommend that SCAP act on that observation. SCAP did not block the proposal in the Diet.[71] Without objection from SCAP, the Diet enacted the authorizing legislation on February 11, 1952. Legislation finally clarified the status of secret bank accounts, albeit in a fashion that was completely at odds with the Shoup recommendations. In the same year, the Japanese government increased the tax-free ceiling on postal savings accounts from 30,000 to 100,000 yen. The argument was that merging multiple accounts to prevent tax evasion was very difficult but that if the limit was raised, the number of violations would decrease.[72]

In 1952, the Tax Bureau finally shifted its position on the taxation of capital gains, and the MOF recommended abolishing the tax on capital gains from securities and proposed restoration of the securities transfer tax. This step, however, was too obvious a violation of the Shoup recommendations and SCAP did not approve the proposal. In 1953, with the occupation having passed into history, the Diet enacted these recommendations.[73]

Meanwhile, commercial bankers welcomed the full restoration of secret bank accounts and heightened their demands by calling for the taxation of interest income to be capped at the minimum rate of 20 percent. Their specific proposal was for a dramatic shift from the taxation of interest income at progressive rates that topped out at 50 percent to taxation at a flat rate of 20 percent. The proposed measure became known as the "20% Separate Withholding Tax," meaning that the taxation of interest income would be "separate" from that of other income, and set at the rate of 20 percent, which would be automatically withheld for all taxpayers.[74] The Tax Bureau of the MOF held out against this dramatic change in the Shoup system longer than it did over capital taxation. Finally, however, in January 1953 the Tax Bureau agreed to recommend a reduction in the rate of taxation under the withholding option from 50 percent to 40 percent.[75] The Tax Bureau hoped this would mollify the bankers and quite possibly lead to increased revenues by reducing the incentive for taxpayers to cheat the MOF. The Yoshida government approved the ministry's recommendation.

The success of a no-confidence vote in the Diet (unrelated to the financial issues), however, led to the dissolution of the Lower House, a delay in approving the budget, and a general election that weakened the Liberal Party, and required it to compromise with other parties to win majorities in the Diet. Among those parties was the conservative "Reform" (*Kaishin-to*) party, which decided to compete with the Liberal Party by proposing an even larger cut in the tax on interest income – the adoption of a "10% Separate Withholding Tax."[76] The MOF vigorously opposed the idea, but found itself excluded from the negotiations with the Liberal and Reform Parties.[77] The Yoshida government decided that it had to accept the Reform Party's proposal to win passage for an acceptable budget. The result of this episode of interparty competitive rate cutting was the August 1953 enactment of the 10 percent "separate" withholding tax. The victory over Shoup was complete.

WHO OR WHAT KILLED SHOUP?

The posing of the question "who or what killed Shoup?" is based on the premise that the Shoup recommendations – as a package of measures for comprehensive, fundamental tax reform – died. In this chapter, we have not examined the validity of this premise in a comprehensive fashion, but the history we have presented regarding Shoup's central recommendations – the introduction of the Haig-Simons comprehensive taxation of income – supports the premise. Moreover, this history suggests that a significant part of the Shoup program was stillborn, never having been enacted into law, and that even more of importance did not survive until the end of the occupation. Most importantly, the Japanese government never effectively cut off the means to evade income taxes on interest income and capital gains from transactions in securities. In effect, throughout the occupation the Japanese government countenanced tax evasion as a means of continuing the traditional policy of taxing interest income and capital gains at favorable rates. In the wake of the Shoup mission's first visit to Japan, the government failed to enact its recommendations for administrative solutions to this problem, and then a year later SCAP buried the follow-up recommendations made by the mission during its second visit. During 1951–3, even before the end of the occupation, the Japanese government went on to altogether abandon any pretense of attempting to apply uniform tax rates to either interest income or capital gains.

In short, the end of the American occupation did not mark a significant line of demarcation, or even constitute the proximate cause, of the demise of the Shoup tax system, at least as gauged by the history of the Shoup recommendations regarding the taxation of interest income and capital gains. Thus, we do not find much evidence to support one of the two explanations – the end of the occupation – most commonly offered by scholars in Japan to account for the collapse of the Shoup system. The second such explanation – a shift of the occupation's economic goals toward capital formation – has much more to recommend it, but this, too, faces some difficulties. The first difficulty is that, when posed in too extreme a form, the explanation risks neglecting significant aspects of the Shoup system designed to promote capital formation. There are three points to be made with regard to this difficulty. First, Shoup made pragmatic concessions to concerns about the need to encourage capital formation. Horizontal equity was Shoup's foremost goal; however, his advocacy of lower marginal rates in the top brackets of income taxation, abolishing excess-profits taxation, revaluating corporate assets, and replacing the enterprise tax with value-added taxation all meant that he supported some use of tax vehicles to create incentives for private capital formation. Second, Shoup's political strategy for strengthening income taxation through enhancing horizontal equity was meant to enable the government to increase investments in human capital and social infrastructure. Third, Shoup worried that going too far by way of investment-favoring tax incentives might put economic recovery at risk. For him, the safest way to advance healthy investment and economic growth was through an even-handed, level playing field with across-the-board strengthening of markets.

The capital-formation explanation for the demise of the Shoup system does, nonetheless, accurately recognize that Japan's financial community, both private and public, wanted to go much further than Shoup was willing to go by way of market interventions designed to enhance private capital formation. They sought ad hoc, fragmented, highly selective encouragement of capital formation in particular sectors and industries, and their desire was the main driving force in defeating the Shoup income tax system. In addition, this explanation does not necessarily go far enough in explaining the death of the Shoup recommendations. In the search for explanations, it is necessary to answer two additional questions:

• Why did Japanese leaders favor the capital-formation strategy that prevailed?
• Why did the American occupation authorities decide to support this particular strategy?

Part of the answer to the first question lies in the patterns of the politics of taxation in democratic capitalistic societies – patterns that Shoup, over his long career, recognized and struggled against in the United

States, Japan, and elsewhere. In Shoup's view, such societies are drawn to progressive income taxation, although progressive rate structures ironically create powerful incentives for both economic and political elites to carve out loopholes within income tax. The history of taxation of interest income and capital gains from securities transactions during the period when Japan was occupied seems to provide evidence to support Shoup's interpretation.

In addition, the answer to the first question involves recognition of the broad consensus among Japanese economic elites (since the Meiji Restoration) in the strategic importance of promoting savings deposits and the aggressive deployment of these savings on behalf of rapid industrialization. Although the wartime financial regime shifted priorities to military mobilization, it also emphasized the strategic importance of savings. It helped lay down what became the bedrock of postwar finance in the form of both the "main bank" system of commercial development and the postal banking system for funding the Fiscal Investment and Loan Program (FILP) and thereby, through its lending to local governments and other agencies, supporting Japan's flourishing "construction state." Consistent with this history is the fact that during the occupation the Japanese government shaped tax policy according to the imperatives of both interest-group politics and a traditional emphasis by the government on using the banking system to increase and mobilize savings on behalf of national priorities.

Turning to the second question on the reason the American occupation shifted economic growth and capital formation strategies, we find part of the answer in the scholarly literature on the general history of the occupation period.[78] Quite simply, the politics of the Cold War, especially after the outbreak of the Korean war, weakened MacArthur and gave the anti-Communist Yoshida government greater leverage with the Truman administration to advance its tax agenda. An emphasis on Cold War politics, however, obscures what we would suggest was another important factor – one that was quite independent of this: the persistent hostility of Dodge toward the kind of tax reform that Shoup favored.

Dodge never supported comprehensive tax reform along the lines of the Shoup report, either in the United States or Japan. Dodge had no sympathy for the central goals of Shoup's tax program: establishing long-term public support for a robust system of income taxation and government social spending in both Japan and the United States. Dodge lacked enthusiasm for the growth of government, distrusted Keynesian economics, supported tax increases only when necessary to balance budgets and contain inflation, and never displayed any interest in promoting horizontal equity in taxation in either country. In addition, Dodge shared the preference of the Japanese government for the strategic use of the banking system on behalf of economic development.

Dodge's attitudes stymied Shoup's reforms in early 1949, by which time Dodge had acquired more power over economic policy than anyone else in the American occupation. The Truman administration had, in effect, granted Dodge the same kind of proconsul authority in economic matters that MacArthur had earlier enjoyed as the personification of SCAP. President Truman had provided Dodge with sufficient discretion to compel the Japanese government to adopt the full Shoup program, but at that crucial time he consistently refused to use his power in that way. Then, later that year, Dodge and his allies within SCAP played the dominant role in the failure of the occupation to embrace the whole of the Shoup program during budget negotiations with the Japanese government.

Even if Dodge had forced Finance Minister Ikeda and his prime minister to accept the unqualified, Shoup-style tax reform, their hostility to the key elements of the Shoup program probably would have eventually proved fatal to the program. Institutional change can, however, be highly contingent. Accordingly, Dodge's decision not to embrace the full Shoup program, particularly during critical budget deliberations in late 1949, may have made a significant difference. The early 1950 adoption of the entire Shoup package – including effective taxation of both interest income and capital gains – would have created more time for Shoup, Moss, and the economist Bronfenbrenner to engage in a process of mutual exchange and social learning in collaboration with Japanese experts.[79]

The history of the taxation of interest income and capital gains on security transactions reveals that Shoup and his colleagues within the mission and the IRD had much in common intellectually with experts in the Tax Bureau, and that the latter had significantly different approaches to social reform than the leadership of the nascent Liberal Party. Although Shoup and his colleagues were idealistic, they were willing and able to work cooperatively and flexibly with Japanese tax officials to hammer out meaningful compromises.

Dodge may have made an enormous difference not only during the occupation but also in the following decades. What if Shoup's tax experiments in Japan had had more time to prove themselves politically and economically, and then survived? The subsequent history of public finance in Japan might have been very different. If Shoup's reforms had survived,

Japan's tax system would have had a far greater measure of horizontal equity. If Shoup was correct, the system would have been more likely to achieve sustained public support and to enhance continued productivity than the loophole-riddled tax code that has fostered public cynicism, encouraged the institutionalization of tax-cutting politics, contributed to economic stagnation, and helped create the current fiscal crisis in the public sector.

Notes

1. In recent years, some scholars have concluded that the "Shoup" elements of the Japanese tax system were less important the "pre-Shoup" and "post-Shoup" elements. For the best statement of this point of view, see Jinno, N., "The 'Japanese-Model' Fiscal System," in Okazaki, T., Okuno-Fujiwara, M., *The Japanese Economic System and its Historical Origins* (Oxford: Oxford University Press, 1999), 208–38.
2. Among the American historians who have written in depth on the occupation, the only ones who reference the Shoup mission are Dower, J., *Empire and Aftermath: Yoshida Shigeru and the Japanese Experience, 1878–1954* (Cambridge: Harvard University Press, 1988), 360–1 and Schonberger, H., *Aftermath of War: Americans and the Remaking of Japan, 1945–1952* (Kent, Ohio: Kent State University Press, 1989), 223.
3. Sato, S., Miyajima, H., *Sengo Zeiseishi* (2nd revised ed.) (Tokyo: Zeimukeiri Kyōkai, 1990).
4. Hayashi, T., "Shoup Kankoku to Zeisei Kaikaku," in Tokyo Daigaku Shakaikagaku Kenkyūjo, ed. *Sengo Kaikaku 7* (Tokyo: University of Tokyo Press, 1974); Miyajima, H., *Sozeiron no Tenkai to Nihon no Zeisei* (Tokyo: Nihon Hyōron Sha, 1986).
5. A Japanese historian who has made a major, in-depth contribution to the understanding of the work of the American occupation is Takemae Eiji. See his *Inside GHQ: The Allied Occupation of Japan and its Legacy* (New York: Continuum, 2002). However, he discusses the Shoup mission in only a cursory fashion, see 143–4.
6. On the wartime savings campaigns, see Fujihira, S., "Conscripting Money: Total War and Fiscal Revolution in the Twentieth Century," PhD dissertation, Princeton University, 2000, 101–18; Garon, S., *Molding Japanese Minds: The State in Everyday Life* (Princeton, NJ: Princeton University Press, 1997), 8–15, and 154 (for the estimate of the savings rate). On early twentieth-century precedents, see Pyle, K. B., "The Technology of Japanese Nationalism: The Local Improvement Movement, 1900–1918," *Journal of Asian Studies* 1973, vol. 33, pp. 51–65.
7. Hoshi, T., Kashyap, A. K., *Corporate Finance and Governance in Japan: The Road to the Future* (Cambridge, MA: MIT Press, 2001), 66. For their discussion of the transformation of Japan's financial system during World War II, see ibid., 51–89.

8. Ōkura Daijin Kanbō Bunsho-ka, *Okura-sho Nenpō Shōwa25 Nen* (Tokyo: Ōkura Daijin Kanbo Bunsho-ka, 1953), 247.

9. Ōkurashō Zaiseishi-shitsu, ed., *Shōwa Zaiseishi –Shūsen kara Kōwa made* vol. 19 (Tokyo: Tōyō Keizai Shinpō Sha, 1978), 482–5, 583.

10. Ōkurashō Zaiseishi-shitsu, ed., *Shōwa Zaiseishi –Shūsen kara Kōwa made* vol. 18 (Tokyo: Tōyō Keizai Shinpō Sha, 1982), 193 ff., 201 ff., and 213, ff.; and Kokuritsu Kokkai Tosyokan Chōsa Rippō KōsaKyoku, *Zeisei Kaisei ni kansuru Shiryōshū(5)* (Tokyo: Kokuritsu Kokkai Tosyokan Chōsa Rippō Kōsa Kyoku, 1950), 52 ff.

11. Nihon Shōken Keizai Kenkyūjo , ed., *Nihon Shōkenshi Shiryō, Sengo-hen, 5.* (Tokyo: Nihon Shōken Keizai Kenkyūjo, 1985), 885 ff. and Nihon Shōken Keizai Kenkyūjo, ed., *Nihon Shōkensh Shiryō, Sengo-hen, 6* (Nihon Shōken Keizai, Kenkyūjo, 1987), 712.

12. Shoup Mission, *Report on Japanese Taxation by the Shoup Mission*, vol. 1 (Tokyo: Supreme Command for the Allied Powers, 1949). See "D – Interest on Bank Deposits and Other Loans," pages 98–101.

13. Shoup Mission, *Report on Japanese Taxation*, vol. 3, "F – Evasion and Enforcement of Tax on Capital Gains," pages B17–B18.

14. Shoup Mission, *Report on Japanese Taxation*, vol. 4, "C – Procedural Steps in the Administration of the Income Tax," page D 23.

15. Shoup Mission, *Report on Japanese Taxation*, vol. 2, "G – Other Indirect Taxes," page 177.

16. For Shoup's recollection on this point, see Shoup, C. S., "Melding Architecture and Engineering: A Personal Retrospective on Designing Tax Systems," in Eden, L., ed., *Retrospectives on Public Finance* (Durham, NC: Duke University Press, 1991), 24.

17. S. Shiomi to C. S. Shoup, October 15, 1949, Japan Box No.1, Shiomi file, Carl Shoup Collection, Yokohama National University (hereafter YNU).

18. Suzuki, T., "Summary of the Paper on the Reform of the Income Tax Recommended and its Relation to the Accumulation of Capital Read at the Sectional Meeting (November 24, 1949)," in ALL Series No. 7, Envelope #7; and Suzuki, T., "The Shoup Mission's Report and the Problem of Capital Accumulation," in Faculty Association of the Economics Department of Tokyo University, *Criticism of the Shoup Mission's Report on Japanese Taxation* (Tokyo: Yūhikaku, June and July, 1950), translated by Shibata Tokue, September 22, 1951, in 4, No. 4, Envelope #87, Shoup Collection (YNU).

19. L. W. Chamberlain to H. Moss, October 25, 1949 with unsigned memorandum, "Tax Revision Desired by Banks (Based on Dr. Shoup's Recommendations)," File folder 10 PE-80 Shoup Report and Recommendations, Box 7637, RG 331, National Archives and Records Administration, Washington, DC. Moss was circumspect in responding to Chamberlain. He wrote a sharp "No!" in the margin next to the Japanese banker's proposal to end the withholding system, however he diplomatically told the Chamberlain that "Your interest in this problem is appreciated and I shall be grateful for any further comment you may care to offer." H. Moss to L. W. Chamberlain, November 5, 1949, File folder 10 PE-80 Shoup Report and Recommendations, Box 7637, RG 331.

20. C. S. Shoup to S. Shiomi, November 25, 1949, Japan Box #1, Shiomi file, Shoup Collection (YNU).
21. M. Bronfenbrenner to C. S. Shoup, January 21, 1950 with Shiomi, S, "Criticism of the Shoup Report," attached, 1, No. 1, Bronfenbrenner Series, Shoup Collection (YNU).
22. Postal Savings Bureau, "Notice of Ministry of Postal Services No. 1122," July 19, 1950, All. No. 7, Shoup Collection (YNU).
23. Brownlee, W. E., "Shoup vs. Dodge: Conflict over Tax Reform in Japan, 1947–1952," *Keio Economic Studies* 2011, vol. 47, pp. 104–8.
24. Cherne, L., Oral History taken by Jerold Auerbach, December 23, 1961, 564–6, Box 129, Leo Cherne Collection, Howard Gotlieb Archival Research Center, Boston University.
25. Nihon Shōken Keizai Kenkyūjo, ed., *Nihon ShōkenshiShiryō, Sengo-hen, 6* (Tokyo: Nihon Shōken Keizai Kenkyūjo, 1987), 719ff.
26. The Tokyo Stock Exchange stock price index was 176.9 in September in 1949 and fell to 163.0 in October, to 138.9 in November, to 125.6 in December, and to 108.6 in January 1950. Tokyo Shōken Torihikijo, *Tokyo Shōken Torihikijo Ju-nenshi: Nenpyō Shohyō* (Tokyo: Tokyo Shōken Torihikijo, 1961), 10.
27. Nihon Shōken Keizai Kenkyūjo, ed., *Nihon Shōkenshi Shiryō, Sengo-hen, 6*, 22ff., 714ff, 717ff.
28. *The Nihon Keizai*, January 19, 1950.
29. Ōkurashō Zaiseishi-shitsu, ed., *Shōwa Zaiseishi – Shūsen kara Kōwa made*, vol. 14 (Tokyo: Tōyō Keizai Shinpō Sha, (1979), 482; Inoue, I., *Shoup no Dainiji Zeisei Kankoku* (Tokyo: Kasumi Shuppan-sha, 2004), 297; and *The Nihon Keizai*, May 3, 1950.
30. K. Sanow to C. S. Shoup, May 5, 1950, All No. 7, Shoup Collection (YNU). Moss was on an extended trip to the United States during this period.
31. C. S. Shoup to H. Moss, May 11, 1950, File folder: Shoup Projects, Box 7631, RG 331.
32. H. Shavell to C. S. Shoup, May 23, 1950, 4, No. 4, Shoup Papers (YNU); H. Bradshaw to C. S. Shoup, May 23, 1950, File folder: Memorandum for Shoup, Box 7507, RG 331.
33. K. Sanow, "Suggested National Revenue Topics for Presentation to Dr. Shoup."
34. Brownlee, W. E., "Shoup vs. Dodge: Conflict over Tax Reform in Japan, 1947–1952," *Keio Economic Studies* 2011, vol. 47, pp. 110–14.
35. Sanow, K., "Suggested National Revenue Topics for Presentation to Dr. Shoup," July 31, 1950," File folder: Shoup Recommendations, Box 7631, RG 331.
36. The report was from Hara Sumio of the Tax Bureau, see the Internal Revenue Division, "Memo for file: Information Report by Banks," September 15, 1950. Box 359, Shoup Collection (YNU).
37. "Measures to Aid Enforcement," Envelope # 6, Box 361, Shoup Collection (YNU).
38. *The Nihon Keizai*, September 9, 1950.
39. Kobayashi, M., president of the Tokyo Securities Exchange, and Toyama, G., president of the Tokyo Securities Dealers' Association to W. Warren,

September 14 and 15 (two letters), SM All No. 7, Shoup Collection (YNU). On the setting of a high threshold for reporting transactions, see also Okumura Tsunao, President of Nomura Securities Co. in Tokyo, to C. S. Shoup, August 23, 1950, Ibid.

40. Brownlee, W. E., "Shoup vs. Dodge: Conflict over Tax Reform in Japan, 1947–1952," *Keio Economic Studies* 2011, vol. 47, pp. 114–17.

41. For Warren's draft, see "Statement of Conclusions and Recommendations, Shoup Tax Mission," September 21, 1950, in File folder: Shoup Tax Report 1949, Box 5980, RG 331. This draft is dated September 21 but it is the version that was circulated within the ESS on September 18, 1950.

42. J. E. Monroe to C. S. Shoup and H. Moss, "Press Conference at Dr. Shoup's Departure," September 9, 1950, and H. Moss to ESS Division heads, "Dr. Shoup's Proposed Press Release," September 18, 1950, File folder: Shoup Recommendations, Box 7631, RG 331.

43. H. Moss to W. Marquat, "Mr. Shoup's Proposed Press Statement," September 19, 1950, File folder: Shoup Recommendations, Box 7631, RG 331.

44. W. Marquat to the Japanese Government via the Ministry of Foreign Affairs, September 20, 1950, File folder: Shoup Tax Report-1949, Box 5980, RG 331. For the final version of the press release, see "Press Statement of the Shoup Tax Mission, September 21, 1950," in File folder: Missions-Shoup, Dr. Carl S. – Tax Mission 1949 and 1950, Box 6740, RG 331.

45. C. S. Shoup to SCAP, September 21, 1950, File folder: Shoup Tax Report-1949, Box 5980, RG 331.

46. "Measures to Aid Enforcement," Envelope # 6, Box 361, Shoup Collection (YNU).

47. H. Moss to W. Marquat, September 26, 1950, File folder: Shoup Tax Report-1949, Box 5980, RG 331.

48. Brownlee, W. E., "Shoup vs. Dodge: Conflict over Tax Reform in Japan, 1947–1952," *Keio Economic Studies* 2011, vol. 47, pp. 117–20.

49. H. Moss to C. S. Shoup, November 14, 1950, Box No. 354, Shoup Collection (YNU). Two days later, Moss added more details. H. Moss to C. S. Shoup, November 16, 1950, ibid.

50. K. Sanow, "Comments on Recommendations of Shoup Technical Report 'Measures to Aid Enforcement,'" October 6, 1950, RG 331.

51. J. Dodge to W. Marquat, April 19, 1950, Box 3, Japan 1950 series, Joseph M. Dodge Papers, Detroit Public Library.

52. The wholesale price index increased 20.6 percent from June to December in 1950. Keizai Kikakuchō Sengo Keizaishi Hensan Shitsu, ed., *Sengo Keizaishi Sokan-hen* (Tokyo: Ōkurashō Insatsu-kyoku, 1957), 340.

53. Nihon GinkōHyakunen-shi Hensan Iinkai. *Nihon Ginkō Hyakunen-shi 5* (Tokyo: Nihon Ginkō, 1985), 575 ff. On the role of the Public Finance Division in suppressing the appendices, see ESS/PF to IRD, "Release of Appendix Material for Shoup Report," October 20, 1950, file folder: Shoup Report Local Government, Box 7604, RG 331.

54. On the position of the Banking Bureau, see Takamoto, M. ed., *Jitsuroku Sengo Kinyū Gyōseishi* (Tokyo: Kinyū Zaisei Jijō Kenkyūkai, 1985), 342.

55. Nihon Ginkō Hyakunen-shi Hensan Iinkai, *Nihon* Ginkō *Hyakunen-shi 5* (1985), 389ff.

56. *The Nihon Keizai*, December 8, 1950.

57. *The Nihon Keizai*, November 13, 1950.

58. Ōkura Daijin Kanbō Bunshoka, *Ōkurashō Nenpō Shōwa 25 Nen* (1953), 512.

59. In early 1951, other such measures included accelerated depreciation rates for various types of corporate assets, special treatment for depreciation of machinery used in various heavy industries, repeal of the undistributed profits tax on non-family corporations, and an extension of the deadline for corporate revaluation of assets. Later in the year there was another round of modifications, including the enactment of special exemptions for bad debts, retirement salaries, and reserves for price changes. For a summary of many of these changes, see H. Moss to W. Marquat, January 27, 1951 in Japan 1951, Box 7, Dodge Papers.

60. On the agreement of Dodge, Reed, and the Japanese government, and the disagreements between Reed and Moss, see E. Reed to W. Marquat, October 5, 1950, Japan 1950, Box 2, Dodge Papers; H. Moss to W. Marquat, October 18, Japan 1950, Box 10, Dodge Papers; H. Moss to W. Marquat, "Tax Measures to Encourage Japanese Production," January 27, 1951, Japan 1951, Box 7, Dodge Papers; and Kishimoto, K., "GHQ no Zeimu Gyōsei ni Oyoboshita Eikyō," *Sengo Zaiseishi Kōjutsu Shiryō No. 3*, 21–2.

61. H. Moss to C. S. Shoup, February 2, 1951, with enclosed "Weekly Tax Report, January 20, 1951," and H. Moss to C. S. Shoup, August 3, 1951, Harold Moss Series, Shoup Mission, Mission Correspondence, Box 2 (YNU).

62. Izumi Minomatsu in the Tax Bureau at the time remarked: "The rate of the withholding tax option was really high. Probably Mr. Hirata made efforts and it became 50%." See Hirata, K., Chu, S., Izumi, M., eds., *Shōwa Zeisei no Kaiko to Tenbō: Jōkan* (Tokyo: Ōkura Zaimu Kyōkai, 1979), 465. On the negotiations between the MOF and GHQ, *Watanabe Takeshi Nikki*, 1983, is useful. This is the diary of Watanabe Takeshi who was in charge of public relations in the MOF from 1946 to 1951. See, in particular, his entries for January 8, 10, 21, and 24, 1951.

63. Ōkurashō Zaiseishi-shitsu, ed., *ShōwaZaiseishi – Showa 27–48 Nendo* vol. 6 (Toyko: Tōyō Keizai Shinpō Sha, 1990), 36.

64. *The Nihon Keizai*, November 13, December 15, 1950 and January 18, 1951.

65. Nihon Ginkō Hyakunen-shi Hensan Iinkai, ed., *Nihon* Ginkō *Hyakunen-shi 5* (1985), 408.

66. Nihon Ginkō Hyakunen-shi Hensan Iinkai, ed., *Nihon* Ginkō *Hyakunen-shi 5* (1985), 410.

67. Ōkurashō Zaiseishi-shitsu, ed., *Shōwa Zaiseishi – Shusen kara Kowa made* vol. 12 (Tokyo: TōyōKeizai Shinpō Sha, 1976), 596.

68. J. Dodge, "Meeting with Mr. Ichimada, Thursday, 8 November," November 9, 1951, File folder: Dodge Mission – October–November 1951 Memoranda, Box 5977, RG 331.

69. Ōkurashō Zaiseishi-shitsu, *Showa Zaiseishi – Shusen kara Kowa made*, Vol. 12 (1976), 477 ff.

70. Takamoto, M. ed., *Jitsuroku Sengo Kinyū Gyōseishi* (1985), 284 ff.
71. E. Reed to W. Marquat, January 7, 1952, File folder: Local Taxation-Reform, Box 2144, RG 331.
72. *The Nihon Keizai*, January 20, 1952. For the argument justifying the 1952 increase in the tax-free ceiling for postal savings accounts, see Shirane, T., Chief of Postal Savings Bureau, Ministry of Postal Services, "As regards raising the maximum amount of postal savings and preventing deposits for tax-evasion," n.d., Box 359, Shoup Collection (YNU).
73. *The Nihon Keizai* on June 30, 1952, and November 8, 1952. On the IRD's position on the MOF's proposed reform of capital gains, see K. Sanow to C. S. Shoup, February 12, 1952, 4, No. 4, Shoup Papers, YNU. (In 1951, when Moss returned to the U.S. Treasury, Sanow became chief of the tax unit.) In 1953 the Diet also took the step of making the first 150,000 yen of other capital gains tax free and exempting 50 percent of other capital gains above the 150,000 yen level from income taxation. All capital losses on other capital gains, however, remained deductible in calculating taxable income.
74. Zenkoku Ginkō Kyōkai Rengōkai, *Zeisei ni kansuru Kenkyū* (Tokyo: Zenkoku Ginkō Kyōkai Rengōkai , 1953), 19. Under this proposal, banks could still offer secret accounts, but the incentive to use them for tax evasion would disappear because of the automatic withholding of 20 percent of the interest received.
75. *The Nihon Keizai*, January 20, 1953.
76. On the Kaishin-to's proposal, see Ōkurashō Zaiseishi-shitsu, ed., *Shōwa Zaiseishi –Shōwa 27–48 Nendo*, vol. 14, (Tokyo: Tōyō Keizai Shinpō Sha, 1990), 69 ff. On the MOF's criticism of the inflationary potential of the Kaishin-to's budget, see ibid., 73.
77. Ōkurashō, Shōwa 28 nendo Yosan ni taisuru Kaishin-to Syusei An ni taisuru Iken (MOF, Japan); *Mainichi Shinbun*, July 15, 1953.
78. For fine examples of this scholarshiup in English, see, for example, Dower, J., *Empire and Aftermath: Yoshida Shigeru and the Japanese Experience, 1878–1954* (Cambridge: Harvard University Press, 1988), Schonberger, H., *Aftermath of War: Americans and the Remaking of Japan, 1945–1952* (Kent, OH: Kent State University Press, 1989), and Takemae, E., *Inside GHQ: The Allied Occupation of Japan and its Legacy* (New York: Continuum, 2002).
79. See Brownlee, W. E., "Shoup vs. Dodge: Conflict over Tax Reform in Japan, 1947–1951," *Keio Economic Studies* 2011, vol. 47, pp. 104–110.

PART THREE

LEGACIES FOR JAPAN

Introduction to Part Three

After the end of the American occupation, Japanese governments generally found it convenient to ignore the question of the long-term legacy of the Shoup mission as a matter for serious inquiry. Japanese governments often postured on this issue. At times they saw advantages to blaming the occupation and the Shoup mission for fiscal problems. At other times – particularly when they sought to demonstrate their commitment to democratic taxation – they chose to espouse the ideals of Carl Shoup and his colleagues. One of earliest examples came in July 1951, when the occupation was winding down and Harold Moss was returning to the United States. The Minister of Finance Ikeda Hayato wrote to the powerful Secretary of the Treasury John Snyder, praising Moss' "service for the democracy of Japan" through changing "the Japanese tax system to a democratic basis."[1] Beneath the official rhetoric of Japanese governments, however, public finance economists continued to have a serious interest in analyzing the economic and fiscal effects of the mission – an interest that they had begun to pursue before the end of the occupation.

In 1950, a Japanese economist, Suzuki Takeo, launched the rigorous discussion of the economic effects of the Shoup recommendations. As Muramatsu and Brownlee discussed in Chapter 10, he focused on the stimulation of economic growth in a Japan recovering from the devastation of war. He distinguished between two ways in which capital formation, as advanced by architects of the economic policies of the American occupation, might contribute to economic growth. One way, which Suzuki and many other economic experts at the time preferred, was through one aspect of the tax reform that the Shoup mission had recommended and the Japanese government had implemented: tax cutting to

278

benefit corporations and wealthy individuals. The other way was through the program of budgetary retrenchment and financial reform, including the adoption of a unitary exchange rate, which Joseph Dodge brought to Japan.[2] Debate over the relative influence, and the manner of influence, of Shoup's approach as opposed to Dodge's on capital formation continued until the late 1950s and early 1960s, when signs of the Japanese "economic miracle" first appeared. Two Marxist economists, Hayashi Yoshio and Shima Yasuhiko, were very influential in persuading policymakers that Suzuki's views had been correct. As Marxists, however, Hayashi and Shima sharply criticized the Shoup recommendations for fostering economic inequality by cutting tax rates for wealthy individuals and allowing the revaluation of corporate assets.[3]

During the late 1960s and early 1970s, public finance economists began to reexamine the Shoup recommendations and recognize the extent to which they had embraced the ideals of promoting tax equity rather than capital formation. These economists also concluded that, to the extent that the Shoup mission attempted to advance economic growth, the mission did so less by providing incentives that favored capital formation and more by promoting neutral taxation that would remove barriers to growth. Miyajima Hiroshi, an economist at the University of Tokyo, powerfully advanced this line of interpretation. He was the first Japanese scholar to explore the prewar roots of Shoup's thinking about tax policy, and he attached great significance to the Twentieth Century Fund's 1937 study, *Facing the Tax Problem*, that Shoup had led in writing.[4] Miyajima criticized scholars such as Suzuki, Hayashi, and Shima for having neglected the role of Shoup's ideas and policy intentions.[5] Subsequently, other Japanese scholars, particularly Hayashi Takehisa and Sekiguchi Satoshi, supported and refined Miyajima's argument by studying other prewar projects in which Shoup, William Vickrey, and other members of the Shoup mission had taken part.[6] Despite this, Miyajima and those who followed in his footsteps did not resolve the question of what Shoup's real intentions had been because they did not have access to primary sources, particularly those from occupation or other U.S. sources.

At the same time, economists recognized the extent to which the Japanese government had fallen short of enacting the key recommendations that Shoup and his colleagues had designed to advance tax equity and improve the quality of Japanese democracy. A few Japanese economists had actually begun much earlier to emphasize the Shoup mission's concern with equity issues and the failure of the Japanese government to adopt the mission's democratizing recommendations. In

August 1951, Tsuru Shigeto told Shoup that "Many of the reforms advised by your mission and once incorporated into our law are now in the process of being whittled away."[7] In 1953, Ito Hanya wrote in a scholarly essay that "Judging from the development of tax reforms these last three years, Japanese taxation is showing a tendency to restore the old system which was in effect before the Shoup recommendations." Ito and other Japanese economists noted, for example, the many ways in which the Japanese tax code privileged capital income, and thus departed from Shoup's ideal of horizontal equity within a comprehensive income tax. Ito wrote that he understood the illogical aspects of and impracticality of challenging "the fiscal pattern based on a capitalistic order of economy." He went on, however, to assert that "there is, on the other hand, a limit to the policy which favours capital," and "the tax policy of the Japanese government of these past few years seems to have overstepped the limit."[8] Japanese scholars also noted the failure of the government to provide an independent tax base for local government through a value-added tax and the other means that Shoup had recommended. Thus, they began to deemphasize the significance of the Shoup recommendations in shaping the postwar history of the tax system. The Shoup recommendations still remained the starting point for historical analysis, however, and there was wide agreement on the general conclusion that the Shoup mission had been an influential force in the development of the tax system.

Economist Ishi Hiromitsu, who during the 1980s and 1990s was a member, and chair, of the Tax Advisory Commission, and the postwar financial history project in Japan's Ministry of Finance (MOF), tried to capture the consensus at that time regarding Shoup's influence. On the one hand, he identified areas in which the effect of Shoup's recommendations had proved to be limited. He stressed, in particular, the post-Shoup introduction of measures that were designed to encourage capital formation but ran against the grain of the Shoup recommendations. These measures included preferential taxation of capital gains from the sales of securities, reductions in the taxation of big business, and the abolition of net worth and accession taxes. On the other hand, he wrote that "the mission's contributions to reconstructing the post-war tax system in Japan are considerable." Part of the reason for this, he explained, was that "Had there been no Shoup Mission, Japan's tax system might have moved towards a different type of system with a greater share of indirect taxation." For Ishi – particularly during his service on the Tax Advisory Commission – his reification of the Shoup recommendations for horizontal equity went hand in hand with his goal of introducing or raising broad-based consumption taxes, such as the value-added tax.[9]

Another major scholar, Kaneko Hiroshi, who also became a member of the Tax Advisory Commission, similarly held up elements of the Shoup plan, particularly the Haig-Simons principles, as ideal guides to contemporary reform. He did so within the field of legal studies. Kaneko, who joined the law faculty at the University of Tokyo in the 1950s, occupied a chair established in 1951 in response to a recommendation by the Shoup mission to create courses in tax law in Japanese universities. In his subsequent career, he pioneered the introduction of the fields of policy analysis and economic theory into tax law. He interpreted the Shoup recommendations for the Japanese legal community, arguing that tax lawyers needed an understanding of the principles of Haig-Simons taxation in order to apply the reformed tax code.[10] Kaneko wrote: "The Shoup Report was a great experiment. It attempted to design a country's entire tax system according to a consistent theory. American tax theory was at the time the world's most advanced, and the *Report on Taxation* systematized that theory."[11] Kaneko spent time at the Harvard Law School in the early 1960s and mid-1970s and felt that he owed a significant intellectual debt to Stanley Surrey as well as to Shoup. In 1995, about a decade after Surrey's death, Kaneko and Hirata Keiichiro cochaired a committee that raised a half million U.S. dollars in Japan to fund an endowed chair at Harvard Law School honoring Surrey.[12] Kaneko's student, Nakazato Minoru, also closely studied the Shoup recommendations and admired their central concepts and the ideals they represented. He called for attention to be paid to "the Shoup Report's educational impact." He explained that "Even if the tax system based on the Shoup report was short lived, the Shoup report's intellectual impact was tremendous. It remains today an inspiration to many Japanese tax scholars."[13]

Ishi and Kaneko contributed to and accurately represented the formation of a new consensus in the 1980s. Japanese economists still disagreed, however, over many details associated with the complex story about how the comprehensive Shoup reforms had played out over the decades. The economists only rarely examined the history of taxation and public finance in Japan prior to the Shoup reforms in detail. This was true even of Ishi, who had noted that "when the Japanese government departed from the Shoup system" it "turned towards a return to prewar traditions and practices which it considered particularly suitable to the Japanese situation." Ishi was vague about what those "traditions and practices" might have been, and he also declared that "the foundations on which the Shoup Mission was to erect the new tax structure in Japan had experienced a complete break with the past by the events of the Second World War and postwar inflation. Prewar values had become irrelevant as a basis of postwar taxation."[14] Ishi and the other economists who had studied the Shoup mission still agreed, in effect, that modern Japanese tax history began with Shoup. The post-Shoup reforms may have harkened back, or even drawn on, pre-occupation precedents, but Japanese scholars still preferred not to remove the veil from that history.

During the 1990s, however, one scholar, University of Tokyo economist Jinno Naohiko, whose academic "grandfather" was Ōuchi Hyōe, did just that. Similarly to Ishi and Kaneko, Jinno admired the Shoup recommendations. Following in the footsteps of Ishi, Jinno would eventually serve as chair of the Tax Advisory Commission (actually, the successor to that commission). Jinno's interest in the recommendations, however, was less instrumental than Ishi's. He admired the theoretical, as opposed to the practical, content of the Shoup recommendations. Jinno did not struggle to make them relevant to contemporary policy issues. His scholarship set the Shoup mission in a larger, well-articulated historical context. In the process, Jinno cast greater doubt than other economists had on the overall importance of the effects of the Shoup recommendations. In a 1999 translation of work that first appeared in Japan in 1993, he declared: "The Shoup Report... served mainly to endorse the tax system formed during the war period." Jinno claimed that Shoup had added little that had survived, and to the extent that it did, the net effect of his reforms was to reinforce the tax regime that the Japanese government had established during World War II.[15] In describing this regime, Jinno emphasized the wartime tax reforms undertaken by the Japanese government in 1940. These reforms did not feature a comprehensive income tax along the lines that Shoup and his mission colleagues favored. Instead, they included an expanded personal income tax built on what Jinno described as "two planks, consolidated income tax levied with graduated rates, and classified income tax levied with proportional rates." To implement this system, Japan added a collection-at-the-source system (several years in advance of the United States and Great Britain) for normal tax liability on salary and wage income. These reforms sought to increase the tax burden, both absolute and relative, of the modernized sector of the economy. In the same year the central government undertook a complicated set of reforms relating to local taxation and intergovernmental transfers. These were designed to reinforce, in Jinno's words, "the capability of local communities to maintain order." In the process, however, these reforms increased the ability of the central government to control the way in which local governments provided public services. Through this tax reform, as Jinno has written, "a centralized-deconcentrated system operated by means of fiscal-resource control was formed in embryo."[16]

Even though some scholars in Japan disagreed with Jinno's weighing of the relative importance of the various Shoup recommendations, virtually all agreed that the most salient elements of the current Japanese tax system had more to do with the combination of developments before and after Shoup's visits than with the Shoup recommendations. Jinno agreed with Ishi and Kaneko that some of the Shoup recommendations that survived the post-1950 counterreformation – especially the encouragement of income taxation and containment of consumption taxation, the reform of tax administrative practices, the reform of property taxation, and the stimulation of tax education and professionalism – made significant contributions to Japan's tax system, even though the collective influence of earlier and subsequent reforms were greater. The authors of the current volume generally work within this consensus of Shoup's influence. They mostly conclude that although Shoup did not remake the Japanese tax and fiscal system, he did transform it in important ways. The chapters of Part Three do not, however, examine all of the post-1950 survivors in depth. They tend to focus on the fate of the Shoup recommendations that, if implemented, would have produced the most dramatic democratizing shifts in the Japanese tax system. These recommendations included imposing a genuinely comprehensive income tax, an integration of corporate and personal income taxation, and significant restructuring of local finance, including the fiscal relationships between central and local governments. Shoup accomplished less in these matters than he did in the areas of tax administration and others noted above, but he still had a significant impact in those areas that had the greatest potential for dramatic reform, even though the results were not what he sought.

The authors of the chapters in Part Three of this volume undertake to set the Shoup recommendations in a very long-term historical context that ranges from the period before World War II through the high-growth years after the war. Monica Prasad begins Part Three with a chapter titled "Avoiding the Aid Curse? Taxation and Development in Japan." Prasad broadens the discussion of the Japanese financial system by exploring the relationship between postwar fiscal reforms, including both Shoup's administrative reforms and the financial reforms that Dodge championed, and trends in American foreign aid to Japan. She suggests taking a more positive view than Muramatsu and Brownlee of the financial program favored by Dodge, and she places more emphasis than any of the other contributors on the importance of Shoup's administrative reforms. She regards these reforms, coupled with the "Dodge Line," as having strengthened Japan's tax capacity and helped it avoid excess reliance on foreign aid. Among the administrative reforms, Prasad stresses the importance of the "blue return," which enabled corporations to gain more certainty in taxation in exchange for their agreement to keep better records and submit to audit.

Chapters 12 to 14 explore the fate of other key Shoup recommendations in the areas of tax administration, local finance, and corporate taxation. In contrast to the immediate collapse of the recommendations for broad-based income taxation and the experimental taxes (value-added, accessions, and capital stock), the erosion of the other Shoup recommendations occurred in an unusually complicated and prolonged fashion. These chapters therefore adopt a long time frame, and the authors argue that the failure or at least weakening of these recommendations reveals a great deal about Japan's political economy since World War II.

In Chapter 12, Takatsugu Akaishi focuses on the failure of the Japanese government to adopt the administrative reforms necessary to enforce the personal income tax, particularly its self-assessed component. He places this failure in the context of the history of Japanese taxation since the Meiji Restoration, and suggests that the Japanese government has never replaced the system of "public-private trust" that it had abandoned in 1940, during wartime conditions. Without the thoroughgoing reform of the personal income tax, and the adoption of the comprehensive taxation of income that Shoup had recommended, taxpayers – particularly those who paid their taxes through a limited withholding system – became cynical about the fairness of the income tax system. In response, they demanded compensatory tax cuts. Akaishi suggests that the Shoup mission had a crucial effect – albeit one that was precisely the opposite of what was intended. This unintentional consequence was a weakening of the Japanese tax system by strengthening an already powerful tax-cutting political culture. The Japanese government, Akaishi argues, made tax cuts under the banner of the Shoup recommendations at the same time as cynically undermining the principles of horizontal equity and administrative rationality that the mission had sought to promote. This argument may help in understanding the high esteem that the Shoup mission has

continued to command in Japan for more than six decades, despite the
early abandonment of most of its central recommendations. Akaishi sees
the quasiofficial history of the Shoup mission – the self-serving historical
reconstruction of the Shoup mission by the Japanese government – as having had the purpose of deliberately obscuring the social realities behind
the Japanese tax system, and the strong elements of continuity between
the contemporary tax system and the wartime tax system created in
1940.

Eisaku Ide, in Chapter 13, analyzes Shoup's proposal to create a "Local
Public Finance Equalization Grant" that a new commission, largely independent of the central government, would administer. Although the scale
of local governments varied widely in postwar Japan, and huge horizontal fiscal gaps existed among them, both the per-capita levels of local tax
burdens and public services were truly uniform. The equalization grant
system represented an effort by Shoup and his colleagues to establish
greater financial accountability for local government, to provide adequate resources for the poorer prefectures, and, thereby, to promote a
more egalitarian fiscal system at the local level. Ide is the first scholar to
untangle the complex story of how the Japanese government, aided by
elements of the American occupation, first adopted and then transmo-
grified Shoup's democratizing reform into an instrument of central fiscal
control. In the process, Ide reminds us that the Shoup mission understood that tax and spending issues were inextricably linked, and that the
mission thought deeply about the expenditure side of Japanese budgets,
despite the admonitions by Dodge to limit its analysis to narrow matters
of taxation.

In an earlier essay, Ide discussed the impact of the Shoup mission
on another important element of budgetary policy in a similar vein.[17]
This was the "macrobudgeting" or "Treasury control" that the MOF
developed as it coordinated policy among the national government, the
Bank of Japan, and local government. This system had emerged in the
1930s and the wartime period to control the price of goods and concentrate fiscal resources on military expenditures. This coordination led
to the creation of institutions such as the National Financing Plan and
the Fiscal Investment and Loan Program (FILP). Macrobudgeting by the
MOF, such as national tax policy and local finance, largely survived the
occupation intact. As in the aspects of tax administration discussed by
Akaishi in this volume, however, the Japanese government pragmatically
absorbed the democratic ideals and practices that the Shoup mission had
promoted. The result was not only the survival of the "macrobudgeting"

of the 1930s, but also the enhancement of the legitimacy of its control of public finance at both national and local levels.

In Chapter 14, Satoshi Sekiguchi examines the collapse of another important component of the Shoup recommendations – the reform of corporate taxation. Shoup and his colleagues pressed for the integration of personal and corporate income taxation, and were disappointed by the failure to undertake this program. This failure stemmed from the commitment of Japanese business and government to a financial system supported in part by the favored treatment of interest income. Although corporations profited from low costs of capital, they additionally profited from labor's low share of national income. Meanwhile, in the period just after the Shoup reforms, corporate employees faced relatively high taxes because the individual income tax focused on withholding of taxes on wages and salaries. The success of this withholding system, Sekiguchi argued in an earlier essay, was to a large extent a result of the Shoup recommendations.[18] To keep this system afloat politically, the Japanese government subsequently cut personal income taxation to reduce the fiscal burdens carried by the middle class and maintained relatively high corporate taxes, which the corporations could tolerate because of low labor costs.

The chapters by Akaishi, Ide, and Sekiguchi consider the Shoup recommendations as sources of guidance for tax reformers in contemporary Japan. Ide sees potential in Japan for Shoup's program for local taxation to build both fiscal responsibility and capacity at the local level within an expanded welfare state. Sekiguchi regards both corporate tax reform, along Shoup's lines of base-broadening and rate reduction, and value-added taxation, which Shoup recommended for Japan in 1949, as promising vehicles for creating a balanced tax system in Japan. Akaishi believes that returning to and embracing Shoup's fundamental goal of establishing the faith of the Japanese people in a democratic tax system might hold the key to restoring their faith in government.

On the basis of their long-term perspective, the authors of Chapters 12 to 14 discern promise for the Shoup recommendations, recast in terms appropriate for the early twenty-first century, in helping to solve Japan's contemporary fiscal problems. Thus, even though these three scholars agree with Tsuru, Ito, Miyajima, and others that the Japanese government blunted or reversed some of the most democratizing elements of Shoup's recommendations, they argue that the Shoup mission still has the potential – through its ideas and democratic idealism – to influence the fiscal development of Japan today. They suggest that Shoup's message planted powerful ideas in Japanese political culture, and that these ideas provided a pragmatic foundation for later scholars and reformers such as Ishi, Kaneko, and Jinno. They found inspiration in Shoup's idealism, just as Ide, Sekiguchi, and Akaishi do now in their search for a resolution of the contemporary fiscal crisis in Japan.

Notes

1. Ikeda H. to John W. Snyder, July 10, 1941, copy in the possession of Douglas M. Moss, and used with his permission.
2. Suzuki, T., "Shaupu Kankoku to Sihon Chikuseki no Mondai" (Shoup Recommendations and the Issue of Capital Formation), *Keizaigaku Ronshu* 1950, vol. 19 (6–7) pp. 1–35.
3. Hayashi, Y., *Sengo Nihon no Sozei Kouzo* [*The Tax Structure in Postwar Japan*] (Tokyo: Yuhikaku, 1958), and Shima, Y., *Zaiseigaku Gairon* [*Introduction to Public Finance*] (Tokyo: Iwanami Shoten, 1963).
4. Shoup, C. S., Blough, R., Newcomer, M., *Facing the Tax Problem: A Survey of Taxation in the United States and a Program for the Future* (New York: The Twentieth Century Fund, 1937).
5. Miyajima, H., "'Shaupu Kankoku' no Saikento: 1930nendai no America Sozei Seisaku to no Kanren de" [Reexamination of Shoup Recommendations in Relation to U.S. Tax Policy in the 1930s], in *Keizai Hyoron* (Tokyo: Nihon Hyouronsha, 1972), 21.
6. See, for example, Hayashi, T., "Shaupu Kankoku to Zeisei Kaikaku" [Shoup Recommendations and Tax Reform], in Institute of Social Science of the University of Tokyo, ed., *Sengo Kaikaku 7kan, Keizi Kaikaku* (*The Postwar Reform: Volume 7, Economic Reform*) (Tokyo: Tokyo Daigaku Shuppankai, 1974); and Sekiguchi, S., "Shaupu Kankoku no Fukakachi-zei no Genryu: America Zaimusho Houkoku no Seisaku Ito to Genjitsu" [Origin of Value Added Taxation in the Shoup Recommendations: Policy Intention in the U.S. Treasury Report and its Actuality], *Local Public Finance* 1998, vol. 49–9, pp. 107–45.
7. S. Tsuru to C. S. Shoup, August 2, 1951, Mission Papers, Tsuru Series, Shoup Papers. About the same time, in almost the same words, Martin Bronfenbrenner told Shoup the same thing. Bronfenbrenner wrote to Shoup, alerting him to a review of *The Report* he had just written for the *American Economic Review*. Bronfenbrenner explained that because of lack of space he had said "nothing whatever about the nature of the forces whittling away at your recommendations." M. Bronfenbrenner to C. S. Shoup, September 12, 1951, 1, No. 1, Bronfenbrenner Series, Shoup Papers.
8. Ito, H., "Direct Taxes in Japan and the Shoup Report," *Public Finance* 1953, vol. 8, pp. 358 and 382–3.
9. Ishi, H. "The Impact of the Shoup Mission," in van de Kar, H. W., Wolf, B., eds., *The Relevance of Public Finance for Policy-Making* (Detroit: Wayne State University, 1987), 237; and Ishi, H., *The Japanese Tax System* (Oxford:

Oxford University Press, 1989), 27–37. In addition, see Ishi, H., "Historical Background of the Japanese Tax System," *Hitotsubashi Journal of Economics* 1988, vol. 29, especially pp. 10–19.

10. For a survey and discussion of Kaneko's career, see Nakazato, M., Ramseyer, J. M., "Hiroshi Kaneko and the Transformation of Japanese Jurisprudence," *American Journal of Comparative Law* 2010, vol. 58, pp. 721–36, and the historical survey in Nakazato, M., Ramseyer, J. M., Nishikori, T., "Japan," in Ault, H. J., Arnold, B. J., eds., *Comparative Income Taxation: A Structural Analysis* (The Hague: Kluwer Law International, 2004), 74–5. In addition, see Kaneko, H. "Shoup Kankoku to Shotoku-zei" [The Shoup Report and the Individual Income Tax], in Nihon Sozei Kenkyu Kyôkai [The Japanese Tax Association] ed., *Shoup Kankoku to Waga Kuni no Zeisei* [*The Shoup Report and the Japanese Tax System*] (Tokyo: Nihon Sozei Kenkyu Kyôkai, 1983).

11. Kaneko Hiroshi quoted in translation by Nakazato, M., "The Impact of the Shoup Report on Japanese Economic Development," in Eden, L., ed., *Retrospectives on Public Finance* (Durham, NC: Duke University Press, 1991), 64–5.

12. "New Tax Law Chair Endowed," *Harvard Crimson*, February 27, 1995.

13. Nakazato, M, "The Impact of the Shoup Report on Japanese Economic Development," 64.

14. Ishi, H., *The Japanese Tax System*, 33–4.

15. Jinno, N., "The 'Japanese-Model' Fiscal System," in Okazaki, T., Okuno-Fujiwara, M., *The Japanese Economic System and its Historical Origins* (Oxford: Oxford University Press, 1999), 208–38.

16. Ibid., 233.

17. Ide, E., "The Origins of Macro-Budgeting and the Foundations of Japanese Public Finance: Drastic Fiscal Reform in Occupation Era," *Keio Economic Studies* 2011, vol. 47, pp. 123–51. This essay was originally presented in December 2009 at "The Political Economy of Taxation in Japan and the United States: A Symposium on the Occasion of the 60th Anniversary of the 1949 Mission of Carl S. Shoup in Japan," Keio University and Yokohama National University.

18. Sekiguchi, S., "Sengo Nihon no Zeisei to Kaikei no Kousho Katei" [The Post-War Tax System and the Process of Accounting Negotiations: From the Perspectives of the Shoup Recommendations and the Ministry of Finance], in Shibuya, H., Maruyama, M., and Ito O., eds., *Sijyoka to America no Impacuto* [*Marketization and the Impact of America*] (Tokyo: Tokyo Daigaku Shuppankai, 2001).

Avoiding the Aid Curse? Taxation and Development in Japan

Monica Prasad

Just as failed laboratory experiments can be as informative as successful ones – pointing out flaws with the assumptions that led us to formulate the experiment and warning others away from the path – failed policies always teach us something about the world. One of the Shoup Mission's lasting contributions is to show us some things that can and cannot be done to engineer economic development. Carl Shoup wanted to give Japan a state-of-the-art tax system. Although many parts of that system broke down or were swept aside, some remained intact, and Japan went on to become the first non-Western nation to reach Western levels of development, pulling South Korea and the "little tigers" in its economic wake. The role that the Japanese tax system – both pre- and post-Shoup – played in Japan's sudden rise can offer us some small but important insights into economic development.

One of these is on how to avoid what scholars have come to call the "aid curse." Countries with abundant natural resources are able to avoid extending democratic rights to their citizens, a phenomenon labeled the "natural resources curse." Oil, gas, diamonds, timber, and narcotics undermine democracy by fostering insurgencies, by making countries vulnerable to trade shocks, and by limiting female participation in the labor force and in politics.[1] Recently, some scholars have begun to wonder whether foreign aid flows are analogous to natural resources in their developmental effects – whether countries that receive foreign aid can use it to avoid extending democratic rights to their citizens, in what they call "the aid curse." Djankov, Montalvo, and Reynal-Querol make the strongest version of this argument, pointing out that foreign aid is a larger proportion of the budget in many countries than natural resources.

Analyzing 108 countries over the period from 1960 to 1999, they conclude that countries at the seventy-fifth percentile in receipts of foreign aid fell one half to one point on a ten-point democracy scale. They write that "aid is a bigger curse than oil."[2]

A central mechanism through which foreign aid might undermine domestic institutions is by compromising the collection of tax revenue: "Taxation can stimulate calls for more representative and accountable governments, while the need to increase revenues can stimulate institution-building. . . . state expenditures primarily through resources that are raised without much effort (foreign aid or revenues derived from oil and other natural resources) does little to stimulate the development of state capacity."[3] Bräutigam and Knack assess this hypothesis for African countries, and find that aid is negatively correlated with tax revenues.[4] Chaudhry shows both the resource curse and the aid curse in action through a detailed reconstruction of the histories of Saudi Arabia and Yemen: the rise of a petroleum-based economy in Saudia Arabia and an aid- and remittance-dependent economy in Yemen in the 1970s led both countries to dismantle their tax institutions, and thereby halt the process of bargaining and capacity-building that taxation propels.[5]

This line of research descends from arguments about the centrality of taxation to the development of democracy and state capacity, a thesis developed through historical analysis of the development of democracy in Europe. As Charles Tilly has summed up the history, the initial impetus for democracy came when the state began to depend on tax revenue from economically independent citizens, and citizens in turn demanded a measure of control over how that revenue would be spent.[6] Moreover, the development of state agencies with the capacity to tax catalyzed infrastructural capacity more generally: "the stimulus for state capacity and the institutions of a modern economy lies in the revenue imperative, but as the professionalisation of taxation proceeds, it pushes additional changes that build states, as a response to legislative demands for accountability, as a way to nurture sectors of the economy with tax potential and as a way to make revenue raising more efficient and effective."[7]

The claim that aid undermines development and democracy was a central concern of dependency theorists in the 1970s and 1980s,[8] and the recent return to the topic has important practical implications. If it is true that the vast quantities of aid that have flowed to the developing world since the 1960s have been not only ineffective, as many have argued,[9] but have actually been destructive, we will need to rethink how to proceed with foreign aid. There is evidence that aid agencies are aware of this hypothesis,[10] and given the difficulty of sustaining political support for foreign aid, opponents may seize on this argument as a reason to reduce aid.

Given the high stakes of the question, it is surprising that scholars in this tradition have ignored the original reason for the launch of aid programs in the 1960s: the perception that aid worked. This perception was fed by the stunning success of the Marshall Plan, as well as of aid to Japan, Taiwan, and Korea. Although there is much debate among economic historians about whether postwar aid to Europe and Asia facilitated development, there has been no attention to the question of whether it actually *hindered* development and democracy in the ways that scholars of the "aid curse" are suggesting.

Between 1945 and 1952, Japan received over $2 billion in foreign aid from the United States, the equivalent of $16 billion today.[11] In the 1950s and 1960s, Japan further received a series of loans from the World Bank that it did not fully repay until the 1990s, and it was the recipient of the second-largest volume of aid from the World Bank throughout the 1960s.[12] The loans from the World Bank complicate a point that the recent scholarship has made about the need for an "exit strategy": Bräutigam and Knack argue that one solution to the problem of aid is "that large-scale aid programs be explicitly seen as a temporary (albeit medium-term) development tool" and they note that the Taiwanese experience of aid with an explicit deadline has been invoked in recent cases.[13] In Japan, however, as soon as the United States "exited," the World Bank entered, making Japan a recipient of aid for over two decades, from the end of the Second World War to the last loan from the World Bank in 1966.

Foreign aid was used in Japan to rebuild an economy that had been destroyed by the war. By the end of the Second World War, "A quarter of [Japan's] buildings were destroyed, a third of its industrial machinery ruined, 80% of its ships sunk, and a quarter of total assets simply lost. Three million Japanese had been killed during the war, and on surrender 17% of the population was without work."[14] Over 8 million people were homeless.[15] Industrial production was at one-third prewar levels, its merchant fleet was destroyed, trade with other Asian nations was blocked, and – as if the direct consequences of the war were not bad enough – the emergence of new synthetic fibers had killed its silk export industry.[16] Fearing economic collapse and a turn to Communism, American policymakers focused on the economic recovery of Japan, and the World Bank followed suit. One-third of the aid from the United States was used for industrial materials, oil, transportation, and the like; over half went into agricultural materials, and the remainder was used for medical supplies and direct payments to civilians.[17] The loans from the World Bank over the following decades were used to finance the development of electricity and water utilities, highways, railways, and even Toyota – reaching a total of $862 million altogether.[18]

The ease with which the aid given to Japan was used productively is striking compared to the difficulties of foreign aid in other contexts. In retrospect, it is the Japanese case, which was one reason for the development of the worldwide aid complex in the first place, that turns out to have been the exception.

If the foreign aid helped, or at least did not hinder, democracy and development in Japan, what lessons can we draw about the underlying reasons for this? Most contemporary studies of the effects of foreign aid focus on countries that failed to develop. Examining the role that foreign aid may have played in the economic and political development of a successful case can therefore clarify contemporary debates about the effectiveness of aid.

Of course, post-war Japan was attempting to restore rather than build from scratch its political and economic institutions. Japan had already established a basic tax collection bureaucracy that kept deficits manageable before the war, for example, and even during the war deficits kept pace with other belligerent countries. The country was already undergoing reform and industrialization, and had managed several decades of economic growth.

So Japan then was not the equivalent of Congo or Zimbabwe today. But most contemporary developing countries are not the equivalent of Congo or Zimbabwe, either. Many of them are in situations analogous to Japan at the time it received foreign aid: several African countries have a higher per-capita gross domestic product today than Japan did at its prewar peak, including Algeria, Botswana, Egypt, Morocco, Namibia, South Africa, and Tunisia. All of these countries have established some level of institutional capacity. Moreover, we know that the problems of the "resource curse" and the "aid curse" do not affect only the poorest countries: as Chaudhry notes, Saudi Arabia and Yemen both had tax institutions in place when the oil boom and the rise of foreign aid caused those institutions to fall into disuse and wither away.

Thus, the lessons of postwar Japan may apply to developing countries that have some level of institutional capacity. As one of the few countries to have moved "from aid recipient to aid donor,"[19] Japan may help explain how other countries can follow the same path.

THE MECHANISMS OF THE AID CURSE

The aid curse scholarship is stronger at showing correlations between aid and the absence of development than it is at explaining the reasons for that correlation, but analysts have suggested several plausible mechanisms. Bräutigam and Knack suggest that the coordination and administration of aid itself takes away institutional capacity, as government attention and resources are moved away from tax administration and into aid administration. They also suggest that aid allows the maintenance of soft budget constraints that allow policymakers to avoid the unpleasant task of tax collection: a main reason the aid curse occurs is that taxation is unpopular, and anything that helps a government avoid it will help that government stay in power. In seeking ways to stay in power, politicians turn to aid as a way to avoid the opprobrium arising from taxation.[20]

Although these may not be the only mechanisms through which aid affects taxation,[21] until we have a better understanding of the relationship between aid and development these two mechanisms provide a useful starting point. In Japan, then, we need to examine (1) the process of tax administration, and what happened to it during the period of foreign aid, and (2) budgets, budget-making, and the soft budget constraint during the period of foreign aid.

Tax Administration

Because of Carl Shoup, the period of foreign aid coincided with a strengthening of tax administration in Japan. Scholars, including many of the contributors to this volume, have shown that the Shoup tax recommendations were mostly scaled back, and taxation after the end of the Occupation returned in many ways to the 1940 tax system. Nevertheless, historians also believe that Shoup left a legacy of important administrative benchmarks for the Japanese tax system.

Perhaps the most important of these was the "blue return." The blue return was an attempt to encourage small shopkeepers to keep good records of their incomes and expenses. A small business owner who followed the administration's instructions on how to keep records was eligible to file a tax form on a distinct blue paper, and the tax office could not then reassess the tax amount without conducting an actual audit, effectively ending the practice of informal negotiations. Those businesses that did not keep records could not claim depreciations and losses and could not file the blue return. The blue return was only available to corporations and businesses, including small businesses and farms. Half of those eligible for the blue return used it, thus rapidly improving record-keeping and ameliorating the problems that poor recordkeeping led to, including reassessment and negotiations.[22]

Regardless of their overall assessment of the Shoup reforms, scholars agree on the role of the blue returns. In 1957, two scholars wrote:

Regardless of the outcome in terms of legislation ... two major administrative improvements seem to have caught hold and thereby increased the rule of law in income tax practice. One of these is the reduction of the scope of individual and especially collective bargaining on tax liabilities between taxpayers and tax offices. The other is the "blue return" with its encouragement of record-keeping and its safeguards against arbitrary reassessment.[23]

Several decades later an economist's judgment was similar: "even though one must admit that the system maintained since the mid-1950's is different from the system proposed by the Shoup Mission, this fact probably should not be emphasized too much. . . . The emphasis on tax administration has prompted changes from archaic to more efficient procedures."[24] Shoup himself said in the late 1980s that "I think perhaps of all our recommendations, the blue return proved to be the most useful."[25]

Although it is often cited, the secret of the blue return's success has not often been investigated. At the extreme, the language seems to suggest that all tax administrators need to do is rub indigo dye onto their tax forms and taxpayers will dutifully pay their taxes.

The main reason for the blue return's success was the contrast with what came before it. In the early years of the Occupation, Supreme Commander for the Allied Powers (SCAP) had introduced an extremely onerous income tax whose administration was overseen by the Eighth Army. The aim was to increase tax revenues, but the result was widespread dissatisfaction with the process of tax collection. In July 1949 the Shoup Mission commissioned a report on the attitudes of small business taxpayers in Tokyo.[26] The list of the private enterprises represented in this document conjures up a picture of the specialized stores and street markets of postwar Tokyo:

food stuff stores such as vegetables, fishes, meat, candy or wine; fuel shops such as coal and charcoal; various stores selling clothes, personal effects, foot wears and toilet articles; small factories and repair shops such as candy and beancurd makers, small machine makers and bicycle shops; proprietors of tea-rooms, cafes and amusement houses; and small subcontractors such as carpenters, stone cutters, 'tatami' (mat) makers, gardeners and furniture makers [and] such small income earners as stall-keepers and day labor[e]rs.[27]

The survey asked questions about every stage of the taxpaying process. It allows us to watch the success – or the lack thereof – of the tax administration of the early Occupation. In theory, the process proceeded as follows:

every taxpayer has a right to declare the amount of income decided by his own will, but the tax office has an authority to revise the declared amount according to its own investigation. When the declared amount of a taxpayer and the amount decided by the tax office are in conflict, the lat[t]er's revised amount overcomes the former. When a taxpayer was dissatisfied with the revised assessment and made a formal appeal of objection in written form, the case will be studied and the final decision is made by the tax office.[28]

But the survey immediately revealed widespread perceptions of dishonesty in tax declarations, to a level that had begun to seem natural to respondents. Of the 530 interviewees, 87 percent agreed that most taxpayers underreported their true income. The problem was twofold. First, most small businesses did not keep good records of their income and profit.[29] Second, because of this underlying problem, a prisoner's dilemma had arisen between taxpayers and the tax office: taxpayers underreported income because they expected the tax office to revise their declarations upwards, and the tax office revised declarations upwards because they expected taxpayers to underreport income. "The decision of one's income tax is, therefore, commonly made in such a negotiation as popular saying 'mutual trickery between the fox and the badger.'"[30]

These problems had led to a process of negotiation between taxpayers and the tax office that was generally perceived to be unpleasant. One taxpayer responded: "The official whom I met listened to me, but he asked my special favour of accepting the revised amount, because he had to accomplish the total amount which has been assigned to him."[31] Another noted "Since I had no reliable account book, I was obliged to accept the final decision of the tax office."[32] The worst cases were those in which the officials were not even respectful: "While I was earnestly explaining my circumstance, the young official who [w]aited on me did not pay much attention to me. He did not even put down his pen on the desk. When I finished my explanations, he said to me with bored attitude that I shall receive a decision from the tax office soon. I am back home in very blue mood." Another said "He (a young tax official) did not pay any attention to me, but finally he emphatically said that if the things which I have explained were true, I could not keep my every day living. He was furious."[33]

The report comments: "From every angle, the tax office is not a pleasant place to go for taxpayers. Previously, the police was thought of as a representative who menaces the people with the power of authority, but at present, there seems to be a general feeling among people that such an authority had been transferred to the tax officials."[34]

A form of tax farming had also developed. Despite the goal of self-determination of taxes by taxpayers "independent from all outside influences,"[35] the lack of reliable data with which to estimate income led many taxpayers to turn to trade associations for help, and the lack of sufficient staff led the tax offices to turn to the trade associations as well. This gave trade associations a powerful brokerage role that sometimes became a quasi tax-farming role in which the association would be given a quota by the tax agency and in turn set payments for individual taxpayers.[36] As the Shoup report later noted, a system that sets goals of certain amounts of tax to be collected is almost by definition iniquitous, as:

> If collections are behind the estimate for the local area in question, there is temptation to assess fairly heavily those taxpayers who are not stubborn and who happen to have the cash on hand, and to press for immediate payment. Once the end of the fiscal year was passed, and it was again twelve months before another local-area estimate had to be justified, the pressure of the goal is off, and the tax office is tempted to relax and not push so hard to collect the full tax from taxpayers who had somehow or other avoided making payment.[37]

This picture of tax administration pre-Shoup explains the success of the blue returns, which were avidly adopted by taxpayers seeking to escape the onerous surveillance, damaged tax morale, inequitable tax farming, and widespread dishonesty of the prior system of tax administration. It is the problems caused by the early Occupation's own attempts to implement a progressive tax that explains the blue returns' success. The introduction of the blue return changed the incentives for the players and, specifically, the value of being audited. Before the blue return, the slight chance of an audit was not enough to encourage taxpayers to report honestly because of the certainty that what they reported would be revised upwards even without an audit, and because the process was already as bad as an audit would be. Reporting honestly would lead to a loss; underreporting and being audited could provide no additional loss. This made the logic of the situation a prisoners' dilemma: even if the taxpayer reports truthfully, it is still optimal for the tax collector to revise upward (the tax collector always gains by revising upward); and even if the tax collector does not revise upward, it is still optimal for the taxpayer to underreport (the taxpayer always gains by underreporting). But after the introduction of the blue return, the chance of an audit could outweigh any incentive to underreport because in the absence of the automatic, harassing negotiations and the automatic upward-revision, the threat of an audit (the odds of which were not known to the taxpayer) now meant the taxpayer could actually lose something by underreporting. Reporting honestly would lead to no loss but underreporting and being audited would set in motion a harassing process that would otherwise have been avoided completely. The costs of being audited could now outweigh the gains from underreporting, and therefore it was no longer always optimal for the taxpayer to underreport. Before the blue return, the taxpayer's logic was "they are going to harass me anyway, so I might as well underreport." After the blue return the logic became "they are going to harass me only if I underreport." By binding the tax collector, the blue return changed the nature of the game. It is a remarkable example of an institutional innovation solving a prisoners' dilemma.

It is important not to overstate the importance of the blue return, which applied after all to only one component of the tax system, the self-assessed tax on enterprises. This proved to be a minor part of the whole system that, post-Shoup, developed according to the two pillars of corporate taxation and withheld personal income taxes that had characterized the 1940 tax system.

But the point here is not that the blue return *enhanced* administrative capacity – it is that the blue return *prevented the destruction of administrative capacity* at a time when Japan was receiving a large volume of foreign aid. As such, it allowed Japan to avoid one of the ways in which the aid curse is thought to operate, as all those beancurd sellers and tatami-mat makers of postwar Tokyo were slowly trained into recordkeeping and transparent tax assessment.

Soft Budget Constraint

A key reason for the undermining of tax capacity in the presence of foreign aid is simply that taxes are unpopular, and aid allows governments to avoid asking citizens to make unpleasant sacrifices. Taxes were certainly unpopular in Japan at this time: Prime Minister Yoshida had been elected on a promise to cut taxes. As other chapters in this volume have amply demonstrated, however, tax cuts were simply not possible in the context of the Occupation because of Joseph Dodge's insistence on balancing the budget.

Dodge was a banker from Detroit, a Republican and a strong anti-communist with the fervent belief in balanced budgets that character-ized the entire American political world in that pre-Keynesian time. He had helped in the reconstruction of Germany, and President Truman talked him into aiding General Douglas MacArthur in the economic recovery of Japan. Dodge was duly endowed with a hefty title and sole power to determine economic policy for a short but consequential moment: "for 3 crucial months Dodge's command of Japan's economy exceeded that of General MacArthur, Prime Minister Yoshida, and the Diet."[38]

Dodge's main approach to a balanced budget was to focus on cutting spending, which he did unapologetically:

I think what is most important in rebuilding the Japanese economy is to balance the budget. In order to balance the budget, you have to cut spending. Of course, people will lose jobs and suffer if the government does not spend enough money. However, the Japanese people who lost the war while living in misery cannot reconstruct without some suffering. What is most important for the Japanese people now is "taibo seikatsu," bear a hard life.[39]

His comments about losing the war suggest that the Occupation was not so far from the earlier, "punitive" stage that it had supposedly aban-doned in favor of the attempt to see Japan as an ally in the fight against Communism.

Dodge's enforcement of a balanced budget also affected tax collection, however, and this became the central struggle during his time with SCAP. Prime Minister Yoshida's campaign promise led to Finance Minister Ikeda meeting with Dodge in a series of budget meetings and begging him to allow tax cuts to go through. Ikeda promised that this would be the only concession granted against the balanced budget, and that its effect would be a "sedative" that would help the populace to absorb the shock of the spending cuts.[40] Dodge replied that doing so would be the thin edge of the wedge – it would make it seem that SCAP was susceptible to political pressure, and was bound to lead to more pleading for exceptions to budget balance.[41] This rigidity did not make Japanese politicians happy. As one said, "Dodge really wiped out in one stroke [these campaign pledges] which as finance minister Ikeda had to honor . . . [Ikeda] scrapped all party pledges in his negotiations with Dodge. Ikeda [was seen] as a stooge of Dodge and not faithful to the party platform. So Ikeda was in a very difficult position with Yoshida."[42]

Dodge's intransigence established what has come to be known as the "Dodge Line," the norm of budget balance. Immediately after the war, much government spending had gone toward "veterans pensions, occupation costs, and compensation to wartime contractors."[43] United States aid on top of this spending began to fuel substantial inflation from 1946 to 1948. The finance minister doubled spending from 1946 to 1947,[44] and the resulting inflation led to price volatility, government controls, and black markets.

Dodge's medicine was so strong, and seemed to have such clear effects in controlling this inflation (although the exact reasons for the decline in inflation remain subjects for debate), that some scholars believe it managed to single-handedly establish a balanced budget norm in Japan that lasted several decades: "It was Dodge who brought the balanced budget norm to Japan, which had not balanced its budget in the prior 50 years; promulgated it; bureaucratically institutionalized it; and who made it an influential, long-term factor in Japanese budgetary policy ... the presence of charismatic-like leadership with extra bureaucratic authority imposed a budgetary value system that became institutionalized in the [Ministry of Finance]."[45]

For Dodge, budget balance was in service to the overarching aim of promoting the export industries, and his policies of reducing social spending, curtailing government employment, and dampening consumption had the effect of making it easier for export-oriented enterprises to find loans. Dodge's influence is particularly noticeable in his unilateral rejection of the Economic Stabilization Board's suggestion to continue current credit policies: "the record reveals that careless and large-scale credit extension has encouraged speculative activity, black market transactions, rapidly rising wages and prices, ineffective management and unsound business practice ... the strictest emphasis should be on investment in capital outlay which contributes quickly and directly to increased output and productivity."[46] To coordinate the reconstruction of export industry, Dodge encouraged the establishment of the Ministry of International Trade and Industry, the central node of the Japanese developmental state, and one scholar even argues that "Japan's government-guided, export-driven economy, later described as a 'capitalist developmental state' or, less charitably, 'Japan, Inc.,' was nurtured by American directives."[47]

Scholars have debated whether the Dodge Line was itself responsible for the decline in inflation, whether it would have occurred anyway, and whether it was really the Korean War that prevented Dodge's bitter medicine from pulling Japan into recession.[48] The point we are interested in, however, is not the Dodge Line's macroeconomic consequences – it is whether the Dodge Line helped Japan to avoid the possibility of a soft budget constraint. Although the counterfactual of what would have happened in the absence of Joseph Dodge can never be confirmed, it is hard to avoid the sense that the immediate result without Dodge would have been a tax cut, even at the expense of a rise in the deficit, as Japanese politicians would have felt the need to fulfill their electoral promises. As one observer wrote, "What is striking about the Dodge plan . . . is the intense rebellion against it by the Japanese" and the State Department noted that "every major power element in the Japanese body politic considers itself injured and its interests jeopardized" by the Dodge Line.[49] Yoshida remembered that parts of the Dodge plan, such as the reduction in the number of government employees, "provoked the almost physical opposition of the parties of the Left in the Diet and even more violent appeals to direct action outside parliament."[50] In this scenario it is hard to imagine a successful internal policy of budget balance as draconian as the one Dodge imposed. Dodge's source of power – President Truman's approval – insulated him from the Japanese political context. He could therefore blithely ignore the mounting opposition, as no Japanese politician, even one predisposed to balanced budgets, could have done.

Of course, the limited tax cuts favored by many Japanese politicians immediately after the war might well have been a better policy, easing the situation of desperate households at the cost of a small deficit. Such a deficit might have been manageable and the budget could have come under control in the long run. Or, as Dodge feared, this one exception might have led to further exceptions, and to the substitution of foreign aid for taxation that we see in other aid contexts. What is clear is that if the specific question is why there was no soft budget constraint during the moment of the arrival of foreign aid in Japan, the answer is Joseph Dodge.

LESSONS FROM THE JAPANESE EXPERIENCE

Japan first received large-scale aid at a time when it was under foreign military occupation. As other chapters in this volume have demonstrated, the different elements of the Occupation did not always work in harmony, and the tax policies and preferences of Shoup were constrained by the vision of economic reconstruction that Dodge brought.

On the question of the aid curse, however, Shoup and Dodge pulled in the same direction – without collaboration, and certainly without explicit awareness of the problems related to aid administration that several decades of foreign aid have brought to our awareness. By focusing on tax collection to begin with, and then by implementing taxes in a manner that prevented the formation of soft budget constraints and that left a legacy of accurate recordkeeping and reduction of tax negotiation, the Occupation efforts regarding taxation prevented the vast amounts of aid flowing into Japan between 1945 and 1966 from undermining the collection of tax revenue through withered tax administration and soft budget constraints. Shoup's recommendations prevented tax administration from atrophying. As for Dodge, without his insistence on high taxes Japan might have gone the way of other countries unable to establish successful tax collection in the presence of foreign aid. Thorsten and Sugita note that Dodge was a lightning rod for the Occupation, taking the blame for painful policies so that MacArthur could come out smelling like a rose.[51] If the aid curse scholarship is right, then he may have performed the same lightning rod function for Japanese politicians. His presence gave Japanese politicians a way to avoid the soft budget constraint without having to take the blame for it.

Again, the point here is not that Shoup's attention to tax administration or Dodge's preference for high taxes actually *increased* tax revenue, nor is the aim of this chapter an evaluation of the macroeconomic effects of these policies. Rather, the specific point being made here is that these measures prevented the *decrease* in tax revenue that, according to the aid curse scholarship, can follow the introduction of foreign aid. The high taxes that Dodge single-handedly imposed on Japan are implausible in more democratic contexts, but the example of Shoup and his patient attention to tax administration suggests a way forward. The scholars of the "aid curse" often imply that if aid undermines taxation, then aid should be scaled back. But perhaps the ultimate legacy of Carl Shoup is to have shown us that aid simply needs to be coupled with explicit attention to taxation in order to contribute to economic development.

Finally, there is a more difficult question that is beyond the scope of this chapter but is worth considering: is it possible that Japan did *not* completely avoid the aid curse – that the stagnation that began in the 1990s can be traced to steps that were taken during the period of foreign aid, and because of the foreign aid? It may be, as some argue, that the tax resistance unleashed during the Occupation developed a life of its own, and prevented Japan from increasing tax revenue beyond the comparatively low levels for which it is known. But taxation is unpopular everywhere, at all times, and some scholars have argued that the success of revenue generation is instead dependent on the ability of the tax system to hide the amounts of revenue it is generating.[52] Taxes were unpopular before the Occupation and they remained unpopular after it, making it difficult to argue that the Occupation was an inflection point on tax popularity. It was the Japanese rejection of Shoup's value-added tax, the kind of national sales tax that has underwritten the development of the state in all European countries, that was more consequential – and this was a decision made by Japanese politicians precisely because of the unpopularity of taxation. As Junko Kato has argued, the introduction of value-added tax in 1989 came too late to allow it to become a successful revenue-raising instrument.[53]

A more serious problem introduced by the occupation is the severe restriction of consumption, Dodge's *taibo seikatsu*, "bear a hard life." Although economic austerity and a focus on the supply side of the economy may have been sensible policies during the early years of postwar reconstruction, Japan was not able to move away from that model in subsequent decades. It has developed neither the model of extensive private consumption found in the United States nor the public consumption of a well-developed welfare state as in Europe.[54] According to some theories, Japan is therefore more prone to Keynesian liquidity traps, and found itself in one such trap in the 1990s; moreover, the accumulation of savings caused by this liquidity trap led to indiscriminate lending by banks, a credit bubble, and consequent crisis. Gene Park has shown that the Fiscal Investment and Loan Program that was so central to the unique Japanese model of economic development, and that has been central to its recent credit crisis and economic malaise, was a direct response to the austerity policies implemented under the Occupation, and that Japanese politicians later embraced austerity themselves.[55] Of course, Japan's recent slowdown is only disappointing in comparison with its rapid earlier growth, as Japan remains a comparatively strong performer in the world economy. Nevertheless, the predominance of nonperforming loans remains problematic, and can be traced to the harsh measures imposed by the Occupation. If the Japanese case has positive lessons to offer on how to manage the short-term consequences of aid, it also suggests that the policies that best utilize aid in the short run may not be the policies that can keep an economy growing in the long run.

Notes

1. Ross, M. R. L., "Does Taxation Lead to Representation?" *British Journal of Political Science* 2004, vol. 34 (2), pp. 229–49.
2. Djankov, S., Montalvo, J. G., Reynal-Querol, M., "The Curse of Aid," *Journal of Economic Growth*, 2008, vol. 13 (3), pp. 169–94; 169.
3. Bräutigam, D., Knack, S., "Foreign Aid, Institutions and Governance in Sub-Saharan Africa," *Economic Development and Cultural Change* 2004, vol. 52 (2), pp. 255–86.
4. Ibid.
5. Chaudhry, K. A., *The Price of Wealth: Economies and Institutions in the Middle East* (New York: Cornell University Press, 1997).
6. Tilly, C., *Coercion, Capital, and European States, AD 990–1992*, Revised edition (New York: Wiley-Blackwell, 1992); Tilly, C., "Extraction and Democracy," in Martin, I., Mehrotra, A., Prasad, M., eds., *The New Fiscal Sociology* (New York: Cambridge University Press, 2009).
7. Bräutigam, D. A., "Introduction: Taxation and State-Building in Developing Countries," in Bräutigam, D., Fjeldstad, O.-H., Moore, M., eds., *Taxation and State-Building in Developing Countries* (New York: Cambridge University Press, 2009), 9.
8. For example, Bornschier, V., Chase-Dunn, C., Rubinson, R., "Cross-National Evidence of the Effects of Foreign Investment and Aid on Economic Growth and Inequality: A Survey of Findings and a Reanalysis," *American Journal of Sociology* 1978, vol. 84 (3), pp. 651–83.
9. For example, Easterly, W., *The White Man's Burden* (Oxford: Oxford University Press, 2006).
10. Harford, T., Klein, M., "Aid and the Resource Curse," *Public Policy for the Private Sector* 2005, World Bank Group Note 291.
11. Serafino, N., Tarnoff, C., Nanto, R. K., "U.S. Occupation Assistance: Iraq, Germany and Japan Compared," Congressional Report ADA458270 (Washington, DC: Congressional Research Service, 2006).
12. Furuoka, F., Oishi, M., Kato, I., "From Aid Recipient to Aid Donor: Tracing the Historical Transformation of Japan's Foreign Aid Policy," *Electronic Journal of Contemporary Japanese Studies* 2010, vol. 10 (3); Yoshida, T., "Japan's Experience in Infrastructure Development and Development Cooperation," *Japan Bank for International Cooperation Review* 2000, no. 3, pp. 62–92.
13. Bräutigam, D., Knack, S., "Foreign Aid, Institutions and Governance in Sub-Saharan Africa," *Economic Development and Cultural Change* 2004, vol. 52 (2), pp. 255–86.
14. Savage, J. D., "The Origins of Budgetary Preferences: The Dodge Line and the Balanced Budget Norm in Japan." *Administration & Society* 2002, vol. 34 (3), pp. 261–84, 261.

15. Ferguson, N., *The Ascent of Money: A Financial History of the World* (London: Penguin Press, 2008), 206.
16. Schaller, M., *Altered States: The United States and Japan Since the Occupation* (Oxford: Oxford University Press, 1997), 393.
17. Serafino, N., Tarnoff, T., Nanto, R. K., "U.S. Occupation Assistance: Iraq, Germany and Japan Compared."
18. Yoshida, T., "Japan's Experience in Infrastructure Development and Development Cooperation."
19. Furuoka, F., Oishi, M., Kato, I., "From Aid Recipient to Aid Donor: Tracing the Historical Transformation of Japan's Foreign Aid Policy."
20. Bräutigam, D., Knack, S., "Foreign Aid, Institutions and Governance in Sub-Saharan Africa," 278.
21. See, for example, Rajan, R., Subramanian, A., "Aid, Dutch Disease, and Manufacturing Growth," *Journal of Development Economics* 2009, vol. 94 (1), pp. 106–18.
22. Beyer, V., "Tax Administration in Japan," *Revenue Law Journal* 1994, vol. 4 (2), pp. 144–59; Gillis, M., "Legacies from the Shoup Tax Missions," in Eden, L., ed., *Retrospectives on Public Finance* (Durham, NC: Duke University Press, 1991), 31–50.
23. Bronfenbrenner, M., Kogiku, K., "The Aftermath of the Shoup Tax Reforms Part I," *National Tax Journal* 1957, vol. 10 (3), pp. 236–54, 243. In addition, see Bronfenbrenner, M., Kogiku, K., "The Aftermath of the Shoup Tax Reforms Part II," *National Tax Journal* 1957, vol. 10 (4), pp. 345–60.
24. Kaizuka, K., "The Shoup Tax System and the Postwar Development of the Japanese Economy," *American Economic Review* 1992, vol. 82 (2), pp. 221–5, 222.
25. Quoted in Beyer, V., "The Legacy of the Shoup Mission: Taxation Inequities and Tax Reform in Japan," *Pacific Basin Law Journal* 1992, vol. 10 (2), pp. 388–408, 395.
26. "Personal Declaration System of Income Tax and Private Enterprisers [sic], August 1949," Shoup Mission, Mission Correspondence, Box 3, No. 3, 355, Envelope 198, Yokohama National University, 1. Although the provenance of the report is unclear, it seems to have been prepared under the direction of Kazuya Matsumiya, a sociologist trained at Columbia with a specialty in attitude measurement and opinion surveys, who was now working for the Public Opinion and Sociological Research Division of the Civil Information and Education of the SCAP; see Matsumiya, K., "Family Organization in Present-Day Japan," *American Journal of Sociology* 1947, vol. 53 (2), pp. 105–10; "News and Notes," *American Journal of Sociology* 1946, vol. 52 (2), pp. 150–5; K. Matsumiya to C. S. Shoup, Shoup Mission, Mission Correspondence, Box 3, No. 3, 355, Envelope 198, Yokohama National University.
27. Ibid., 1.
28. Ibid., 31.
29. Ibid., 12–14.
30. Ibid., 6.
31. Ibid., 26.

32. Ibid., 27.
33. Ibid., 27.
34. Ibid., 27–8.
35. Ibid., 18.
36. Ibid., 21–2.
37. Supreme Commander for the Allied Powers, *Report on Japanese Taxation by the Shoup Mission* (General Headquarters, Supreme Commander for the Allied Powers, Tokyo, 1949), Chapter 14, p. 213.
38. Savage, J. D., "The Origins of Budgetary Preferences: The Dodge Line and the Balanced Budget Norm in Japan," 267.
39. Joseph Dodge, quoted in ibid., 271.
40. Ibid., 275.
41. Ibid., 275.
42. Ibid., 275.
43. Ibid., 266.
44. Ibid., 266.
45. Ibid., 264, 281.
46. Thorsten, M., Sugita, Y., "Joseph Dodge and the Geometry of Power in US–Japan Relations," *Japanese Studies* 1999, vol. 19 (3), pp. 297–314, 300–1.
47. Schaller, M., *Altered States: The United States and Japan since the Occupation*, 18.
48. Thorsten, M., Sugita, Y., "Joseph Dodge and the Geometry of Power in US–Japan Relations," 297–314, 300–1, 301.
49. Quoted in ibid., 302.
50. Yoshida, S., *Yoshida Shigeru: Last Meiji Man* (Lanham, MD: Rowman & Littlefield Publishers, 2007 [1961]), 75–6.
51. Thorsten, M., Sugita, Y., "Joseph Dodge and the Geometry of Power in US–Japan Relations."
52. Wilensky, H., *Rich Democracies: Political Economy, Public Policy, and Performance* (Berkeley: University of California Press, 2002); Kato, J., *Regressive Taxation and the Welfare State: Path Dependence and Policy Diffusion* (New York: Cambridge University Press, 2003).
53. Kato, J., *Regressive Taxation and the Welfare State: Path Dependence and Policy Diffusion*.
54. Logemann, J., *Trams or Tailfins?: Public and Private Prosperity in Postwar West Germany and the United States* (Chicago: University Of Chicago Press, 2012); Prasad, M., *The Land of Too Much: American Abundance and the Paradox of Poverty* (Cambridge: Harvard University Press, 2012).
55. Park, G., *Spending Without Taxation: FILP and the Politics of Public Finance in Japan* (Stanford, CA: Stanford University Press, 2011).

12

The Shoup Recommendations and Japan's Tax-Cutting Culture

Why Has Japan Failed to Reestablish the Personal Income Tax as a Key Tax?

Takatsugu Akaishi

"The great majority of Japanese are astonishingly capable of really fooling themselves.... Their mental processes and methods of reaching conclusions are radically different from ours.... It merely means that when that obligation runs counter to his own interests, as he conceives them, he will interpret the obligation to suit himself and, according to his own lights and mentality, he will very likely be perfectly honest in so doing so."[1]

(Joseph C. Grew)

INTRODUCTION

Since the end of the American occupation, the Japanese government has reduced the level of income taxation more significantly than in any other advanced nation. In the process, the government has concentrated the income tax on earned income, relieving what was seen as an overtaxed middle-working-class by providing annual tax cuts, at the same time as fine-tuning the total tax burden by manipulating indirect taxes and corporate taxes. During the entire period since the enactment of the Shoup recommendations, the government has considered tax bills in positive-sum terms, seeking to make everyone winners to some extent and constructing majorities by bargaining for amendments designed to secure group support, or at least acquiescence. In the post-Shoup environment, taxation becomes a positive-sum game of distributive politics constrained primarily by sensitivity to the middle class.[2]

From the perspectives of current structural changes in Japan's socio-economy, including the declining birthrate, aging society, and globalization, the Japanese government faces difficulties in continuing the postwar tax system and will find it necessary to review its taxation system in a fundamental way in order to establish the key taxes that will be suitable for the twenty-first century. In doing so, Japan will continue to participate in the international effort, which began in the 1980s, to reconstruct the world's tax system. Thus far, however, Japan, along with the United States, has diverged significantly from the international trends. Both countries have failed to incorporate a national general consumption tax as one of their key taxes, whereas European countries have succeeded in securing and improving social security benefits by increasing dependence on earned income and consumption taxes as the main sources of revenue.

There is also a large difference between the situation in Japan and that in the United States. Taking the Tax Reform Act of 1986 as a turning point, the United States succeeded in shifting from a positive-sum game of distributive politics to a zero-sum game in which the advantages accruing to one class became considered disadvantages to another. Through this shift, at least throughout the 1990s, the United States insisted on combining cuts in marginal tax rates with a broadening of the base of personal income taxation.

As Table 1 shows, Japan failed to switch from a positive-sum game to a zero-sum game during the 1990s. The Japanese government continued its policy of cutting the marginal income tax rate in addition to reducing the income tax base. In other words, Japan satisfied popular demands for both increased spending and reduced taxation, even after the end of the era of easy finance. Consequently, the Japanese government was forced to secure increased funds for public services through public deficits. This policy mix has prevailed up to the present day.

In this chapter, I attempt to explore why the Japanese government has failed to establish a high-yielding and stable tax system to finance increased needs for public services, despite facing structural changes in the socioeconomy, including the declining birthrate, aging society, and globalization. In doing so, I focus on the "refraction"[3] between the provisions of the tax code and how taxes are actually assessed and collected. I conclude that, ironically, the Shoup recommendations paved the way for instituting the tax-cutting culture in Japan. In this chapter, I define tax culture as "the entirety of all relevant formal and informal institutions connected with the national tax system and its practical execution, which are historically embedded within the country's culture, including the dependencies and ties caused by their ongoing interaction."[4]

TABLE I. *Main Taxes as a Percentage of Potential Total Tax Burdens*

Country	Japan		United States		Sweden		Denmark	
Year	1993	2000	1993	2000	1993	2000	1993	2000
1. Public deficits as a percentage of gross domestic product	2.4	7.5	4.8	−1.7	11.4	−5.1	2.2	−2.5
2. Total tax revenues as a percentage of gross domestic product	28.0	27.1	26.9	29.6	48.4	54.2	48.6	50.1
3. Personal income tax revenues as a percentage of gross domestic product	7.2	5.6	9.7	12.6	17.6	19.3	25.7	25.7
4. Social security contributions as a percentage of gross domestic product	9.4	9.9	6.9	6.9	13.2	15.2	1.6	2.2
5. Taxes on goods and services as a percentage of gross domestic product	4.0	5.1	4.8	4.7	13.2	11.2	15.3	16.1
6. Corporate tax revenues as a percentage of gross domestic product	4.2	3.6	2.2	2.5	2.1	4.1	2.1	4.1
7. Potential total tax burden (=1+2)	30.4	34.6	31.7	27.9	59.8	49.1	50.8	47.6
8. 3/7	23.7	16.2	30.6	45.2	29.4	39.3	50.6	54.0
9. 4/7	30.9	28.6	21.8	24.7	22.1	31.0	3.1	4.6
10. (3+4)/7	54.6	44.8	52.4	69.9	51.5	70.3	53.7	58.6
11. 5/7	13.2	14.7	15.1	16.8	22.1	22.8	30.1	33.8
12. (3+4+5)/7	67.8	59.5	67.5	86.7	73.6	93.1	83.9	92.4
13. 6/7	13.8	10.4	6.9	9.0	3.5	8.4	4.1	8.6
14. 1/7	7.9	21.7	15.1	−6.1	19.1	−10.4	4.3	−5.3

	France		Italy		Germany		United Kingdom	
	1993	2000	1993	2000	1993	2000	1993	2000
1. Public deficits as a percentage of gross domestic product	6.0	1.4	10.3	0.7	3.1	−1.3	7.9	−1.5
2. Total tax revenues as a percentage of gross domestic product	43.3	45.3	43.4	42.0	37.9	37.9	33.1	37.4

(*continued*)

TABLE I *(continued)*

	France		Italy		Germany		United Kingdom	
	1993	2000	1993	2000	1993	2000	1993	2000
3. Personal income tax revenues as a percentage of gross domestic product	5.0	8.2	11.8	10.8	10.3	9.6	9.1	10.9
4. Social Security contributions as a percentage of gross domestic product	19.1	16.4	13.7	11.9	14.5	14.8	5.9	6.1
5. Taxes on goods and services as a percentage of gross domestic product	11.5	11.7	11.3	11.9	10.6	10.7	11.8	12.1
6. Corporate tax revenues as a percentage of gross domestic product	2.0	3.1	4.0	3.2	1.4	1.8	2.4	3.7
7. Potential total tax burden (=1+2)	49.3	46.7	53.7	42.7	41.0	36.6	41.0	35.9
8. 3/7	10.1	17.6	22.0	25.3	25.1	26.2	22.2	30.4
9. 4/7	38.7	35.1	25.5	27.9	35.4	40.4	14.4	17.0
10. (3+4)/7	48.9	52.7	47.5	53.2	60.5	66.7	36.6	47.4
11. 5/7	23.3	25.1	21.0	27.9	25.9	29.2	28.8	33.7
12. (3+4+5)/7	72.2	77.7	68.5	81.0	86.3	95.9	65.4	81.1
13. 6/7	4.1	6.6	7.4	7.5	3.4	4.9	5.9	10.3
14. 1/7	12.2	3.0	19.2	1.6	7.6	−3.6	19.3	−4.2

Source: OECD, *Statistical Compendium 2004, #1, Central Government Accounts*, Vol. IV, 1992–2003.

The Public-Private Mutual Trust Atmosphere and Prewar Japanese Tax Culture

In the period immediately after Japan emerged as a modern state following the Meiji Restoration of 1868, more than 80 percent of the total tax revenue of the national government came from land tax. During this period of rapid national development, Japan believed it had to expand its naval forces. At the same time, from an industrial policy perspective, the government was under pressure to alleviate the tax on certain products from Hokkaido. In 1884, against a background of the rapidly increasing wealth of landlords and stockholders caused by urbanization and the swift growth of corporations, the Genrôin (the Council of Elders) proposed an income tax bill. The Meiji Restoration government drafted a bill in the Ministry of Finance (MOF) and pushed it through the Council of Elders, with the intention of enacting it, as well as other controversial reforms, before the establishment of the Imperial Diet in 1890. In 1887, the income tax was promulgated as a national tax.[5] Japan thus became a pioneer in the permanent use of income tax, although the revenue from this tax was insignificant. The income tax was exclusively a tax on the rich.

In accord with the traditional Japanese unit of the family, the income of all "co-living" family members was required to be aggregated for the purposes of applying graduated income-tax rates, which ranged from 1 percent to 3 percent on annual income of 300 yen and over. In calculating incomes, the government adopted the principle of averaging three years' actual income. For the sake of convenience of administration, payment of tax on the income in a given year was made during the following year. An assessment and collection system was in operation from the start of income tax. Taxpayers had the obligation to declare their income to their county manager or mayor's office (and then, after 1896, the county/city taxation office[6]). This office (or the taxation office) assessed a taxpayer's income on the tax return on the basis of its own independent investigation, and then notified the taxpayer of tax owed, formalized by the action of a County District/City Income Investigation Commission. The office was more interested in how smoothly it could get permission from the commission about the income assessed than how successful it was in achieving tax equity. In Japan, the government gave the impression that it respected taxpayers' declarations before the final assessments in order to avoid friction.[7] In cases where the negotiation on incomes between the commission and taxation office broke down, the taxation office itself made the final decision. In doing so, its decision on incomes was made within upper and lower limits that had already been decided in the taxation office circles.

The investigation commissions were established in each county/city taxation office jurisdiction in 1887 in order to gain the active cooperation of the high-income class, rather than to implement democratic taxpaying. The county manager or mayor chaired the commission, which consisted of no more than six members, who were indirectly elected from well-funded taxpayers in the county/city. Commission members were therefore men held in fairly high esteem within the region.[8] All in all, the system functioned as a cushion between the tax authority and taxpayers by relieving heavy tax burdens.[9]

Under the official assessment system, the office did not rigorously verify the accuracy of the tax returns, and did not fully investigate all tax materials that the taxpayers had submitted to the office. Part of the reason for this was that in those days, Japanese entrepreneurs with small- and medium-sized enterprises did not keep adequate books. Thus, the tax office could only assess income by making a crude approximation of net income. For example, in determining standard rates of profit for various types of enterprises, the tax offices relied on a sampling process. If the tax office could not understand the expenses of a business, it might estimate net income by multiplying receipts by the standard rates of profits.[10] Although the tax office might inspect the premises and books, it would wind up using the standard enterprise model, coupled with common sense, to determine the taxable income of an enterprise.[11]

Before World War II, wealthy entrepreneurs enjoyed extremely generous treatment under this system, especially when compared with wage and salary earners, whose income taxes were captured in the withholding system adopted in the wartime tax reforms of 1940. For one thing, tax authorities, in assessing the incomes of prosperous entrepreneurs, emphasized achieving a rough equality across a region and type of industry rather than seeking progressive equity among individual taxpayers. In addition, tax authorities applied some special rules and conventions to reduce assessments for wealthy entrepreneurs. For example, tax authorities eased the assessments of affluent taxpayers who cooperated in an income investigation, or those whose assessed income had rapidly increased since the previous year. There were criminal penalties for tax evasion; however, tolerance of a certain level of hidden income and the operation of the investigation commission system meant that prosecutions and convictions with prison sentences were rare.

In 1899, the Japanese government began taxing corporate income and maintained this system of assessment and collection until 1946. Corporations with tax liabilities had an obligation to submit their books (including a list of property, a balance sheet, a profit and loss statement, income amounts, and capital statements) to the district director of a taxation office within the jurisdiction. The district director investigated the books and determined the taxable income.

Tax administration for indirect taxation was quite different from that for direct taxation. Taxation offices made a point of enforcing the payment of indirect tax liabilities with far greater rigor, because those who paid the tax could usually pass on the burden of the taxes to others. For example, the government, under the Indirect Tax Violations Injunction

Law that was enacted in 1900, strictly taxed licensed sake brewers and retailers.[12] As in other countries, the government relied heavily on indirect taxes, in part because they enabled the government to pass on the cost of administration to private parties.

The Japanese government expanded indirect taxation during World War II. In the face of difficulties in financing the war with China in the late 1930s, it introduced new commodity taxes under the slogan "luxurious life is a hostile act." The government initially introduced the taxes as temporary taxes on ten luxury goods; however, it greatly expanded the number of taxable items and either decreased or abolished levels of exemption. As a result, most final consumer goods – except for those regarded as absolute necessities – were entered as taxable items under the commodity tax law. The continued protection of everyday necessities reflected the popular strength of the views that it was unfair to tax basic items that consumers needed. Consumers believed that it would be far more equitable to tax luxuries heavily and leave the average person's money in his or her pocket.[13]

During the early years of its income tax system, the Japanese government did not establish an independent tax collection structure. Instead, the government placed the responsibility for the investigation and assessment of income and the collection of income taxes with local governments. In 1896, the government transferred the investigation and assessment of income taxation to twelve Tax Affairs Supervision Bureaus (reorganized into the Local Finance Bureau in 1941), and shifted ultimate responsibility for income tax collection to 504 taxation offices throughout Japan. These offices only took action in cases of tax delinquency. According to a national tax bureau survey in 1977, the annual average rate of delinquency during the 1930s was only 5–7 percent of tax assessments, substantially lower than the levels after World War II.[14] At first glance, this result seems to be what we would expect in an era in which taxpayers lacked legal rights. I would argue, however, that the prewar tax system for both excise and income taxation fostered an atmosphere of "public-private mutual trust" by grouping taxpayers. In excise taxation, as I have discussed, the government had attempted to resolve public criticism by incorporating redistributive ideology into tax code design. In income taxation, the tax authority had mitigated tax burdens by establishing a buffer system that included devices such as an Income Investigation Commission, assessment adjustments, and lenient punishment for tax evasion. In local areas, the reputation of the head of the taxation office could have a great influence on the tax delinquency rate. In order to collect taxes smoothly, it was important for him to have a reputation both for being strict in carrying out his duties and for having an agreeable personality.[15] In addition, village chiefs not only encouraged taxpaying but played a buffering role by often advancing the unpaid tax liabilities of villagers on their behalf.

During World War II, the fact that income tax became a mass tax, accompanied by a gradual increase in the diversity of taxpayers, undermined traditional public-private mutual trust. To restore this trust and to make the mass income tax system workable, just before the end of the war the MOF created a committee that consisted of high-ranking bureaucrats from the MOF, the Ministry of Education, and the Ministy of Internal Affairs. It attempted to rebuild the *raison d'être* of taxation by setting forth *Kôkoku Sozei Rinen* – a tax ethic formed on the basis of emperor-centered historiography within traditional Shinto doctrine. The government loudly trumpeted the idea that tax delinquency would disappear "like dewdrops under the morning sun" if citizens recognized their taxes as the first rice offered to the gods. This committee was abolished just after World War II, but most of the high-ranking officers from the MOF who were in charge of the committee were still in influential positions when the Shoup recommendations were implemented.[16]

During wartime, the Japanese enacted the last two tax reforms of the period, both of which attempted to place greater reliance on self-assessment. The government created a self-assessment system for corporation income tax and established a system in which individuals would pay estimated income taxes during the current year. The goal of these reforms was to increase revenue by more effectively taxing the vastly increased income of individuals made rich by the war. These two measures laid down a foundation on which the self-assessment system of the postwar period would be built.

In 1947, during the second year of the American occupation, the Japanese government transformed the income tax, eliminating the distinction between classified income and aggregate income, and applying progressive tax rates to consolidated individual incomes as noted in the next section. At the same time, the Japanese government adopted a self-assessment system for the current year for all incomes, doing away with the old method of assessing taxes on income for the preceding year. Introducing a self-assessment system in the harsh economic and political conditions of 1947, however, meant that the Japanese government had to try to cultivate a new tax atmosphere.

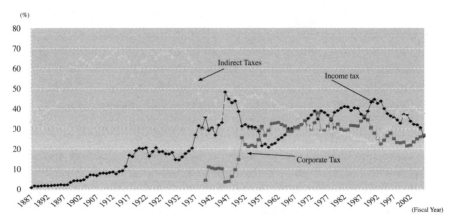

FIGURE 1. Tax as a percentage of total taxes. *Source:* Ministry of Finance, *Okura Sho She* [*The History of the Ministry of Finance*], vol. 4 (MOF, 1998); and Ministry of Finance, *MOF Statistics Monthly*, various years.

DISSOLVING A TRADITIONAL PUBLIC-PRIVATE MUTUAL TRUST ATMOSPHERE

The income tax law of 1887 was a copy of the German income tax. In 1899, however, the Japanese government departed from the German system in a major way by amending its tax to become a schedular tax, and applying it to corporate as well as individual income. This schedular income tax fundamentally endured until 1939.

In the twentieth century, the Japanese tax system underwent revision in response to political, social, and economic forces. As Figure 1 shows, until World War I indirect taxes, which were mainly on alcoholic beverages and tobacco, accounted for about two-thirds of tax revenues. It was after World War I, when the pace of economic growth accelerated, that the income tax became more important in the Japanese tax system and began to compete against the liquor tax for the top place in national revenue.

In this context, the Japanese government amended the income tax in various ways. In 1913, simple progressive rates were replaced by complex progressive rates on excess profits. The new rates ranged between 2.5 percent and 22.0 percent over fourteen brackets. A fixed deduction was allowed for earned income, the first instance of the kind in Japan. In 1920, the principle of aggregate income taxation was applied more thoroughly, with the rates on consolidated income ranging between 0.5 percent and 36.0 percent over twenty-one brackets. A special reduction was provided for the first time in Japan for each dependent. As a result of the series of tax reforms, the number of taxpayers on the income tax rolls increased from 120,000 in 1888 to more than 12 million in 1935, although most citizens fell outside the net of income tax. In that year, income tax became the most important single source of tax revenues.

Despite the reforms, the Japanese government faced growing demands to reduce the burden of the income tax on the old middle class (that is, farmers and small- and medium-sized businesses), and to make the income tax system fairer, taking into account rapid increases in corporate profits, wages, and salaries. In response to these pressures, and to meet the revenue demands of the war effort, the Japanese government instigated major income tax reforms in 1940.

As a result of the 1940 reforms, the old income tax system of three categories was abolished and a new personal income tax, which can be characterized as bipolar in structure, and a corporation tax were introduced. The creation of a distinction between personal income tax and corporation tax followed the pattern the United States and Germany had adopted. The establishment of the bipolar income tax system, which employed both a schedular income tax and an aggregated income tax, resembled the system that Britain and France had adopted.[17] The intention was to adopt something from each of the most advanced income tax systems elsewhere in the world.[18] This system remained in force with some amendments until 1947, when the Japanese government followed the recommendations of the American occupation government under General Douglas MacArthur, who was designated the Supreme Commander for the Allied Powers (SCAP), by adopting another major set of reforms. By the end of World War II, under the 1940 reforms, the schedular income tax accounted for most income-tax revenues, and the tax on earned income accounted for most of the schedular-tax revenues. By lowering the tax threshold on earned income, the 1940 reforms had tripled the number of taxpayers, creating a mass tax.[19]

In the schedular income tax system of 1940, taxes on business income, real estate income, and forestry income were calculated on the basis of net income from the previous year. By contrast, earned income was taxed on the basis of estimated incomes for the current year under the withholding-at-source method. During inflationary conditions, these methods of calculating income caused serious problems. The fact that a business was taxed on the lower income of the previous year, even if the current income far exceeded that from the previous year, meant that a business's tax burden would be much lower than that applied to current earned income under the withholding method. In the hyperinflationary experience of the years immediately following the end of the war, the tax inequity between business income and earned income became a matter of intense concern for the Japanese public.²⁰ Compounding the inequity, corporate net income sharply declined in this period on account of wartime damage. During this difficult period, the Japanese government had to deal with imbalance in the tax burden between business and the working masses, and with the need to raise revenues. In response, tax experts within the government became very enthusiastic about shifting taxation to a prepaid, current basis. They were not yet prepared to support a fully fledged self-assessment system, however they did realize that the shift to payment on a current basis could be a step toward the introduction of such a system.

SCAP, rather than the Japanese tax authority, was decisive in pushing the Japanese government into the adoption of a self-assessment system. SCAP believed that the U.S. tax system, which included a smoothly running self-assessment system, was the best one in the entire world.²¹ In 1947, SCAP therefore pressed the Japanese government to replace the official assessment system with a self-assessment system. Part of SCAP's interest in this was in promoting democracy. SCAP was critical of Japan's system of tax assessment because it seemed to give excessive power to local bosses, enabling them to intervene in, and corrupt, tax administration. SCAP had other motives as well. For example, Henry Shavell, who had responsibility for coordinating SCAP's tax policies, suggested that Japan's tax system should have more in common with the American one because of the need for a tax treaty between the two countries.²²

The tax experts within the Japanese government actually regarded a self-assessment system as an ideal form of tax administration but they were negative about its immediate adoption. They believed that considerable time and effort would be required to realize the system's ideal potential. Meanwhile, management of the tax system would be chaotic and confusing.²³ The Japanese government did, however, recognize the importance of the problems related to the imbalance of tax burden between salaried employees and business income earners. They also acknowledged the problem of inadequate tax revenue. Accordingly, the tax experts and the Japanese government as a whole adopted the self-assessment system in the spirit of cooperation. In a real sense, adoption of self-assessment reflected a consensus between both countries.

Under the traditional Japanese assessment system, although tax payers were obliged to report their incomes to tax offices, their actual tax amounts were not settled until the tax authorities had reached their decisions on tax liabilities. In contrast, under the self-assessment system that was introduced as part of the tax reforms of 1947, a taxpayer independently calculated taxable income and taxes owed based on tax laws, and then reported and paid the tax amount to tax office. The tax office would review the return for mistakes, relying on a "third person report system" based on the American model. The 1947 reforms abolished the Income Investigation Committee, which had played an advisory role in settling tax assessments by the chief of the taxation office. Other components of the 1947 reforms included elimination of the distinction between the classified, or scheduled, income and aggregate income; the introduction of twelve brackets of steeply progressive tax rates ranging from 20 percent on income over 1,000 yen to 75 percent for income over 1 million yen; and increased adjustments for lower-income taxpayers. These adjustments included a standard deduction that was set at 4,800 yen, a tax allowance for dependents of 240 yen a year per person, and an allowance of 20 percent for earned income up to 6,000 yen.

During the 1947 fiscal year, the new tax system encountered several major problems. First, as a consequence of the broadening of the tax base and the high progressive rates, the tax burden of the nation increased greatly over the previous year. Although the reforms had increased the adjustments for low-income earners, they had not sufficiently increased the adjustments to keep up – let alone catch up – with the rapid postwar inflation. The portion of tax burden on national income increased from 11.4 percent in the 1946 fiscal year to 21.7 percent in the 1947 fiscal year –increasing the overall tax rate by roughly 10 percentage points in one year. Moreover, between 1946 and 1947, the number of taxpayers increased by 7.5 millions. The tax thus became even more of a mass taxation. In addition, because of the shift to a current basis, taxpayers had to make their first tax payments by the end of March 1947.[24] Second, many middle-income taxpayers missed the "public-private mutual trust atmosphere" of the traditional system, particularly the Income Investigation Committees, which had acted as buffers between taxpayers and the tax authority. Wealthy entrepreneurs missed the special rules and conventions that had reduced their assessment. Across the spectrum of taxpayers, tax administration seemed "cold and inhuman."[25] Third, the efficiency of the tax administration had deteriorated. Although the Japanese government increased the number of tax officials in order to implement the new system, it had great difficulty in recruiting new employees. The burden of recruitment was especially heavy for the national government, because the responsibility for collecting national taxes was transferred to it from municipalities. The percentage of tax officials under thirty years of age grew to 80 percent, and those with job experience of fewer than three years reached 70 percent.[26] The public viewed many of these officials as lacking the will to work, basic competence, and honesty. In addition, taxpayers proved to be too conscientious, flooding tax offices with detailed paperwork. They were uncertain as to how tax officials would behave under the new system, and concluded that they should report all income, regardless of how small the amounts, to avoid the possibility that they would be punished for dishonesty.[27]

In late 1947, the Japanese government, through a "White Paper on Public Finance" published by the MOF on December 7, explained the severe fiscal problems to the nation, and urged the public's cooperation with the new tax system. The cabinet, however, decided not to take strong measures to enforce the new self-assessment system. It concluded that it was impossible to expect taxpayers to report their incomes honestly because of the aggravation of inflation, the rampancy of black markets, and the deterioration of tax administration.[28] The cabinet decided to try and informally revert to the traditional cooperation between tax authority and taxpayers that had prevailed since the introduction of income tax.

SCAP, however, was displeased with this approach and decided, over the strong objections of the Tax Bureau and its chief, Maeo Shigesaburô, to implement a target, or quota, system for enforcing the self-assessed tax system. Under this system, the Japanese government, consulting with SCAP, would allot quotas for tax collection to each tax office, and would collect the taxes under the surveillance of SCAP and the Eighth Army.

The quota system operated in practice as a combination of the traditional investigation system, on one hand, and top-down coercion provided by SCAP, on the other. There was a large degree of correction of tax returns under the system, but the correction was usually based not on the investigation of individual returns or taxpayers, but on estimations of the traditional kind. The arbitrary nature of this process, coupled with the large increases in rates of taxation, produced taxpayer complaints and demands that tax offices review and explain their corrections. Added to this, many taxpayers refused to pay their taxes, or were unable to pay, creating a huge increase in tax arrears.[29] Wealthy entrepreneurs accounted for a large share of the arrears. As a result, in the fiscal year of 1949, taxpayers who earned salaries and wages (and paid their taxes through withholding), and who received modest business incomes, accounted for most income tax revenues.[30]

In 1949, the Japanese government sought to find ways of restoring the trust of the Japanese people by removing what had come to be seen as an excess tax burden and by making the administration of the tax system more rational. The traditional Japanese tax collection system had broken down during the period toward the end of World War II, and Japanese tax experts had recognized the potential of a self-assessment system.[31] The shift toward that system in 1947 was epoch-making. The system was in principle democratic, calling on taxpayers to report their incomes and settle their tax liabilities themselves. In practice, however, the quota system that SCAP imposed for its administration created a vicious circle of tax avoidance; arbitrary examination, determination, and correction; and loss of public faith in the tax authority. To the Japanese people, it appeared that the government was interested in acquiring revenue not by encouraging tax consciousness but by strengthening the penal regulations with the help of SCAP and the police. When revenue-raising became the dominant priority within the self-assessment system, democratization of the tax system suffered, the construction of a new public-private trust collapsed, and the tax system became crippled. By 1949, the Japanese government was faced with the difficult problem of how to deal with "refraction" between the tax laws on paper and the ways in which taxes are actually assessed and collected. The government needed to establish a new relationship of mutual trust; one that would resolve the contradiction between the democratic goals of the new tax system created in 1947 and the undemocratic, economic harshness of its reality.[32] In so doing, the government sought to rebuild the tax system to alleviate friction between tax authorities and taxpayers as well as trading on *Okami no Ishiki* (the Japanese consciousness that idealized the authorities).

The Shoup Recommendations: Toward a New Relationship of Mutual Trust

The idea at the core of the Shoup recommendations was that tax collection should be carried out strictly but the system should be rational, commanding respect and voluntary compliance. The goal was to enable Japan to break out of the vicious cycle of dependence on tax arrears, reliance on a large force of officials for correcting returns and enforcing collection, and intense public distrust and demands for tax reform. In the recommendations, the income tax would remain at the core of the tax system and continue to be a mass-based tax, but would feature lower tax rates, increased allowances for earned income, and improved tax administration. The Shoup mission believed that these reforms would improve cooperation on the part of taxpayers.

In addition to these long-term goals, the recommendations had a short-term goal – to raise enough tax revenue to balance the budget according to the strict "line," or directive, imposed by Detroit banker Joseph Dodge on behalf of the occupation. The Shoup mission began its work with the goal of raising 250 billion yen from the income tax for the 1950 fiscal year. The mission estimated that the total expenditures of the Japanese government would reach 646 billion yen in that year.[33]

To devise a table of rates for the income tax, the Shoup mission had to estimate the size and distribution of income. For this estimate, the mission used data provided by the MOF, which estimated that national income in 1950 would be 3,200 billion yen, reflecting an increase of 65–70 percent over 1,900 billion yen in 1948. The calculation incorporated an estimated increase in effective prices of 40 percent and a growth in total production of nearly 25 percent, including 50 percent growth in industrial production but no growth in agricultural output. The mission's own estimate, however, was more optimistic. Shoup and his colleagues believed that national income had already reached 4 trillion yen in 1949. This higher estimate conveniently enabled the Shoup mission to more easily conform to the Dodge Line for budget balancing. Although the MOF estimate of national income would mean that the aggregate rate of income taxation would be 7.8 percent, Shoup's estimate would produce the much lower overall rate of 6.3 percent.

In deriving its tables of income-tax distribution, the Shoup mission estimated conservatively that taxable income in the fiscal year of 1950 would be 2.2 trillion yen, and that the distribution of income would be concentrated on low- and middle-income earners. (Shoup believed that the MOF's underestimate of national income was most significant for the upper-income brackets.) In fact, according to an investigation by the MOF to which Shoup referred in the mission's recommendations, in 1950 taxable incomes of below 50,000 yen a year would account for 53 percent of total taxable income and those below 300,000 yen would account for 93 percent. The MOF also estimated that income of middle- and low-income earners accounted for 63 percent of the taxable income in the fiscal year of 1949. In light of these estimates, it is clear that the intention of the Shoup mission was to establish the income tax as a mass tax primarily on earned income. In its report, the mission wrote: "Whereas there is little room for controlling tax rates, it is necessary to increase revenue, to lighten the tax burden on all the people to some extent, and to reduce the gap between earned income and the other incomes to 10 per-cent."[34] More specifically, the mission recommended that the Japanese government create a new income tax system that would provide a lower tax threshold, increase the rate of taxation for the lowest bracket, create more tax brackets for middle- and low-income earners, and lower the highest marginal rate. In the recommendation, it was estimated that the reformed income tax, on the basis of the 2.2 trillion yen of taxable income, would yield 320,000 million yen – more than the 250,000 million yen the mission had first considered as its revenue goal. The reformed tax would have eight brackets ranging from 20 percent (for earnings below 50,000 yen) to 55 percent (for earnings of more than 300,000 yen).

This set of proposals implied that the mission intended to build a tax system that would be focused even more heavily on incomes that were withheld or easily verified, and whose success would rest more heavily on voluntary compliance with the taxation of unearned income. Within this rationalized tax system, taxation offices would exercise much less discretion. Shoup and his mission colleagues sought to more closely align the reality of income taxation with its theoretical principles by stressing the importance of a dependable, rational connection between taxable income and the tax table rates, and deemphasizing the role of the MOF's intuition of what taxpayers ought to be paying. In effect, Shoup sought to eliminate the "refraction" that had intensified following the 1947 reforms. MOF officials, however, were pessimistic about the revenue potential of the Shoup reforms. They believed that under the new system it would receive returns from only about 65 percent of all the self-assessed taxpayers and, without the ability to correct tax returns and engage in vigorous collection, would have to assume that the rest were not tax evaders. As a consequence, the MOF concluded, the new system would yield 250,000 million yen, rather than the 320,000 million yen predicted by Shoup.[35]

The Shoup mission also recommended reducing the tax credit for earned income (from 25 percent to 10 percent) on the grounds that the mission was proposing an effort to reduce the gap between the high rate of capture of earned income and the low rate of capture of unearned income.[36] The mission also recommended that with the funds raised through designing such a mechanism, the government should increase the amount of the basic deduction from 15,000 yen to 24,000 yen and increase the tax exemption for dependents from 1,800 yen per person to 12,000 yen. The strategy was to move away from favoritism of any form of income. In the same spirit of providing horizontal equity, Shoup recommended abolition of the separate taxation of interest income. At the same time, however, Shoup recommended adding an important new element of progressive taxation. Although proposing a reduction in the top income tax rate (from 85 percent to 55 percent), Shoup recommended creating an offsetting tax on aggregate wealth.

Finally, in the field of tax administration, the Shoup mission proposed numerous reforms to design a strict and rational tax system, thereby enhancing the effectiveness of the self-assessed income tax, and reducing the gap between the capture of earned income and that of unearned income. These reforms included:

- abolition of the quota system;
- the introduction of provisional declarations on the basis of tax returns for the previous year;
- the simplification of tax return forms;
- the requirements of high-income earners to proclaim their income and submit their detailed statements of assets and debts;
- the introduction of the blue-form return system;
- the prohibition of anonymous and pseudonymous bank accounts;
- the implementation of a system for registering bond sales and stock transfers;
- the opening of tax affairs to certified public accountants;
- the opening of intra-agency directives (circulars) to the public; and,
- in general, the improvement of communications between tax administrators and the general public, including their tax advisors.

To sum up, it can be said that the Shoup recommendations sought to establish tax principles and administrative procedures that could win the trust of the Japanese people. The recommendations sought to correct the distortions that inflation had created in the tax system, widening the gap between the tax laws as written and how they were actually assessed and collected.[37] Compounding the way in which this gap undermined public faith in the tax system was the huge discretion that the tax offices had in manipulating the tax base as a consequence of lack of clarity in the tax law and lack of transparency in tax administration (including, for example, the confidentiality of circulars). At the same that the Shoup mission recommended the creation of a rational and transparent tax system, it proposed measures designed to promote fairness, which it defined as "the idea that people with a similar ability to pay taxes should pay similar amounts."[38]

The Shoup mission compromised, however, by accepting the MOF's deliberately underestimated level of national income. Tacitly, Shoup permitted the MOF to set the income-catching rate for all taxpayers except salaried employees at 65 percent. In other words, the Shoup mission postponed addressing the most practical and serious problem facing tax administration – namely, unfairness between taxpayers whose income is subject to withholding tax and self-assessed taxpayers.[39] The mission did so in order to deal with other issues, among them the rationalization of tax administration.[40] The MOF had succeeded, however, in establishing a pattern of behavior that would persist after 1950, undermining the spirit of the Shoup recommendations. In underestimating the revenues that it expected the income tax to produce, the MOF accomplished two goals. First, it relieved the pressure to tax more heavily higher-income individuals, most of whom filed self-assessed returns. Second, it ensured that economic growth and inflation would produce an increase in revenue that the Japanese government could use to expand the scope of government or to provide generous tax cuts. These tax cuts quickly became a permanent part of the post-Shoup tax culture, and obscured the dramatic ways in which the Japanese government proceeded to abandon the principles of taxation that the Shoup mission had sought to advance.

Institutionalizing a Tax-Cutting Culture

In 1950, the Japanese government undertook tax major reforms that were based on the Shoup recommendations. In these reforms, the government pursued Shoup's goal of establishing a stable, long-lasting tax system on the basis of principles of tax fairness and a rationalized system of tax administration. Among the reforms were significant tax cuts, most of which – such as the reductions in top marginal rates – had been recommended by Shoup. The government implemented these measures under the banner of the Shoup recommendations but intended in the future to carry the tax cuts well beyond the intentions or formal recommendations of the Shoup mission. As it turned out in subsequent years, in the process of cutting taxes the Japanese government quickly moved away from some of the key principles of the Shoup recommendations, at the same time praising the work of the Shoup mission, particularly its emphasis on the central importance of income taxation. These tax cuts became key elements in Japan's strategy for economic growth and in its incomes policy during the postwar period.

Even in crafting the 1950 reforms, the Japanese government ignored important elements of the Shoup recommendations. There were already signs that the Shoup tax system would collapse. Before the enactment of the formal issuance of the Shoup recommendations, the Japanese government had negotiated a significant increase in the income allowance, raising it to 15 percent from the 10 percent that Shoup had recommended. This weakened the horizontal equity of the tax from what Shoup had proposed. In addition, in enacting the 1950 reforms, the government ignored recommendations that would have required the registration of securities, reports on depositors by banks, the submission of balance sheets by high-income earners, and the investigation of banks' internal documents by tax auditors. All of these were devices that the Shoup mission was convinced were necessary for self-assessed income taxation to capture interest and dividend payments, and to ensure its horizontal and vertical equity. The effects of the tax cuts implemented in 1950, the lax enforcement of the self-assessed income tax, and the pessimistic projection for income growth all appeared immediately. In the 1949 fiscal year, the burden of all taxes had been 28.5 percent of national income, and the burden of national taxes 23.3 percent. The comparable ratios declined to 22.4 percent and 16.9 percent, respectively, in the 1950 fiscal year. Meanwhile, the number of income taxpayers fell from 21.06 million (including 9.45 million self-assessed taxpayers) in 1949 to 14.25 million (including just 4.32 million self-assessed taxpayers) in 1950.[41] These results reflected a strategic incomes policy that the Japanese government had adopted and continued with throughout the era of rapid economic growth. The reductions in the burden of the income tax, advertised under the banner of the Shoup recommendations, enabled the Japanese government to deflect criticism that the current tax system was designed primarily to benefit high-income earners and promote capital accumulation.[42]

In 1951, the Japanese government began to revise the Shoup system of 1950, enjoying the rapid growth of tax revenue that the Korean War Special Procurement had produced. Director General of Tax Bureau Hirata Keiichiro had returned from an inspection of Western countries convinced that government should give first priority to economic recovery – even if it sacrificed the rationality of the tax system.[43] In addition, Hirata and the other leaders of the Tax Bureau were economic liberals in the context of Japanese thinking about government in that they believed that it was more efficient to pursue industrial policy through tax cuts and tax expenditures than through direct subsidies.[44] Consequently, the Tax Bureau increasingly emphasized the need to sacrifice the principle of the horizontally equitable taxation of consolidated income in order to promote capital formation and economic recovery.[45] Among the reforms the government enacted was the institutionalization of various special measures for depreciation that the Ministry of International Trade and Industry demanded.[46] In addition, the government raised the basic deduction and the deduction for dependents on the basis that income tax burden was still excessive, particularly on low-income taxpayers. This marked the formal beginning of the post-Shoup tax history, which has been called the "income-tax-cut history." In every year except 1960, the government implemented a tax cut, increasing the effective threshold for income taxation.[47] The rate structure that Shoup had proposed in his recommendation, made on the basis of the MOF's unrealistically low estimates of national income, had created the basis for this ongoing process.

The conclusion of the peace treaty in 1952, and the restoration of Japan's sovereignty at the end of the occupied era, accelerated the collapse of the Shoup system.[48] In 1952, the government provided another major tax cut by allowing, for the first time, deduction of the compensation of family employees to taxpayers who filed blue returns. Scholars have suggested that the allowance of this deduction led to "the beginning of subsequent endless repetition of tax cuts to adjust imbalance of tax burden among taxpayers, including blue return taxpayers, white return taxpayers, family corporations, salaried employees."[49] This process had, in fact, begun with the increases in the taxpaying thresholds enacted in 1949 and 1950. But the 1952 revisions no doubt significantly accelerated the shift away from self-assessed taxpaying toward even greater reliance on the withholding of taxes.

In 1953, in the first major tax reforms following the peace treaty, the government gutted crucial elements of the Shoup system by the wholesale abandonment of the principle of consolidated income taxation. The government excluded capital gains from income taxation and restored separate withholding tax on interest income. Although it increased the top income tax rate, it did not seek to make the tax effective for self-filers. At the same time it abolished the wealth tax, which had the potential to be more effectively enforced.[50]

The abolition of the wealth tax revealed the reluctance of the Japanese government to make a significant effort to tax wealthy or high-income individuals. One of the key reasons the Shoup mission had recommended the tax was as a practical mechanism to gather information that could be used to enforce the income tax. The Japanese government justified the abolition of the tax on the grounds that it was impractical from an administrative point of view. One of the most significant features of the collapse of Shoup's tax system was that it was abolished mainly for administrative reasons. The MOF claimed that it would be extremely difficult to acquire information regarding bank accounts and bearer bonds, that the evaluation of such assets was difficult, and that the tax revenues would not be great enough to justify the costs of collection. At the same time, however, the Japanese government made no real effort to make the self-assessed income tax an administrative success. The government neglected the recommendation of the Shoup mission to collect precise information on individuals' incomes, deliberately weakening its effectiveness, and reestablishing former relations between the tax authority and taxpayers by grouping the blue-return taxpayers into blue-return taxpayers associations, and rendering the increase in the highest marginal tax rate rather meaningless.[51] The reform was a blatant effort to reduce the tax burden on high-income individuals and small businesses. The government refused to discuss this failure, which would have involved admitting the existence of significant "refraction" between the principled design of the Shoup income tax and its actual operation.

Between 1952 and 1955, the tax cuts absorbed the vast majority (about 86 percent) of the "natural" increase in income tax revenues resulting from the expansion of national income.[52] As a consequence of these cuts, over the same period the number of taxpayers (primarily salaried employees, business income earners, and earners of agricultural income) fell as a percentage of the population. After 1950, Japan's taxes as a percentage of national income fell below that of other advanced countries as a result of this and the cuts. The result was no different, even after deducting the cost of food and drink from national income.[53] This means that referring to an "excessive tax burden" – which the MOF began doing to justify tax cuts as early as 1949, and even more intently from 1951 – made sense only if comparisons were drawn with the prewar tax burden. This tax-share outcome reflected the fundamental strategy of the government to promote savings and investment. As one scholar has written, "From a structural viewpoint, the conditions which generated Japan's high economic growth before the beginning of its industrial policy were a tax cut and the balanced budget policy of the budgetary authorities."[54] Although the overall tax burden fell as a consequence of the tax cuts, the contributions of salaried workers to income tax revenues grew, and the income tax moved ever closer to purely being a tax on labor.[55] The government came to focus on taxing salaried employees, who fell largely within the low- and middle-income classes. Meanwhile, the income tax, as applied to high-income individuals, focused heavily on well-paid managers.[56]

In 1955, the Hatoyama cabinet appointed the Temporary Ad Hoc Tax Advisory Commission of the prime minister to address issues that various components of Japanese public opinion had raised. In December 1957, in its last report, the commission, which the MOF's Tax Bureau had heavily influenced, summarized the income tax policy that had prevailed in the first half of the 1950s, and tried to orient the future of that policy. Through the commission, the MOF insisted that the government should return the unexpected "natural" increase in tax revenue caused by economic growth to low- and middle-income employees instead of using it to finance government programs.[57] In making this recommendation, the MOF reflected a view that was also held by Nippon Keidanren (the Japan Business Federation), representing large corporations that faced cries to raise wages, the Ministry of Labor, which also wanted to relieve the relative tax burden of salaried employees, and Prime Minister Hatoyama, who wanted tax reductions for salaried employees in order to stabilize the relationship between labor and capital.

Within Hatoyama's Liberal Democratic Party (LDP), however, there were powerful conflicting demands. The prevailing strategy of the LDP for distributing political favors consisted, on the one hand, of providing tax expenditures to well-defined regional and industrial pressure groups, and, on the other hand, through making public works expenditures in developing areas and sectors that were declining economically or socially. The strength of these traditional demands had forced Hatoyama to accept a compromise in the previous fiscal year.[58] Within the LDP there was no path by which salaried employees could directly bring their political favors. The only organized support was within the Social Democratic Party of Japan, which advanced the interest of the labor unions within large corporations. These unions, whose workers faced high levels of tax withholding, enthusiastically supported tax cuts.[59]

Despite division within the LDP, Hatoyama and the Tax Bureau launched an effort to focus the anger of salary earners on tax reform. The final report of the commission contributed to this mobilization, declaring that "we have to resolve the problem of tax burden of low and middle class."[60] The commission and the Tax Bureau appealed to public opinion to embrace a tax cut of 100 billion yen that would be targeted at the middle class. Following the report, Hatoyama gathered popular support and finally won the consent of the LDP for the large cut.

In the resulting tax cut during 1957, the government took a major new departure. Rather than raising exemptions or deductions, it emphasized rate reductions, thus marking a major shift in the cut policy.[61] In this reform, the lowest tax rate was reduced from 15 percent to 10 percent, the top marginal rate was raised from 65 percent to 70 percent, and the remarkable progressivity within the low- and middle-income range was drastically eased.[62] As a consequence of increasing the income-tax threshold during the early 1950s, the Japanese government had narrowed the tax brackets and tax schedules above the tax threshold, creating a kind of camel-back-shaped distribution of tax burden. In the 1957 rate reductions, the Tax Bureau and the MOF smoothed the progression of taxes as well as reducing their overall burden on middle income taxpayers.[63]

The "excessive tax burden" that the MOF had emphasized in reducing income taxes during the 1950s and 1960s was a subjective sense of the tax burden that Japanese governments had fostered during the period of the Shoup reforms through intentional comparisons with pre-war Japan.[64] Later governments tried to ease this sense of burden and thereby maintain popular support for the income tax. In particular, governments had to correct periodically the imbalances among various types of income and taxpayers that resulted from various factors: the government's favoritism for certain powerful groups of taxpayers, its reluctance to enforce the self-assessed income tax, and the bracket creep and rising minimum taxable income that inflation and economic growth produced. Under the progressive income tax, rapid increases in personal income during the high economic growth era generated huge amounts of tax revenue, but also strengthened popular demand to reduce tax burdens and reinforced the popular idea that "tax reform means income tax reduction."[65]

The 1957 reforms effectively institutionalized tax cutting as a central strategy of postwar Japanese governments to maintain economic and political stability. The commission's report revealed the economic motive, asserting that it was essential to stimulate popular will to work for the advancement of productivity because a "high income tax rate and steep progressivity would disturb popular will to work and to improve productivity."[66] The commission, the Tax Bureau, and the Hatoyama government all shared faith in the effectiveness of a private investment-led economic growth strategy, and believed in using tax policy to cement public support for this strategy. The goal was "developing the middle class which would support the society."[67] To enable labor to participate more fully in the fruits of economic growth, the Hatoyama government incorporated income tax cuts into interest-group politics. That is to say, the government placed income tax reduction into the core of its mechanism to maintain a small government and to achieve political stability. Tax cutting became on permanent part of the effort to engender mutual trust between the government and the people.

SUMMARY AND CONCLUSION

Before World War II, the Japanese government did not place importance on the legal rights of taxpayers. In order to ease popular discontent with the tax burden, however, the government adopted various mitigating measures. With regard to taxes on consumption, the government incorporated a philosophy of redistribution into the tax code. For taxes on income, it established the Income Investigation Committee, adopted generous penal regulations, and underrated income assessments. Through these efforts, and others, the government successfully built tax practices within a "public-private mutual trust atmosphere."[68]

The new income tax system of 1940 introduced a withholding system, and because radical revenue increases were required for the war effort, the government transformed the individual income tax into mass taxation based on labor income. This deterioration gradually undermined the "refraction effect," the conventional way of dissolving popular complaints against tax burdens. The top executives of the MOF, such as Matsukuma and Ikeda, were forced to collect tax, emphasizing "the Japanese empire tax history view" that regarded tax as a compulsory contribution to the Emperor. Hyperinflation after the Second World War further confused the tax collection system and caused a serious shortfall in tax revenue. In 1947, the government introduced consolidated income taxation and self-assessed taxpaying, but because the government did not raise tax exemptions and deductions sufficiently, this new income tax further expanded mass taxation. To make matters worse, SCAP ordered the abolition of the Income Investigation Committee, which had played an important role in mitigating popular complaints, and suspended generous tax treatments of enterprise income. Tax administration became a scene characterized by high friction and discord.

The Shoup recommendations embraced the income tax-centric system as the best basis for rebuilding Japanese taxation, which was on the verge of collapse, and emphasized the importance of adopting rational and strict tax collection. Finance Minister Ikeda, however, believed that "there is nothing to learn from the Shoup Mission in Japan," and it was dubious as to whether the government would really accept Shoup's recommendations.[69] Although the Japanese government superficially paid its respects to the Shoup recommendations, it exploited a political atmosphere shaped by the expectations of the Japanese people that the Shoup mission would be an envoy on behalf of tax cuts. The government stressed the tax-cutting aspects of the Shoup recommendations, even to the point of distorting reality. In addition to this, the government skillfully incorporated a mechanism in the tax code to produce a "natural" increase in revenue. This mechanism provided a stable structure for absorbing tax revenue from the group targeted by the withholding system – the low- and medium-income laboring class. The government did, at least initially, adopt some of the key elements of the Shoup recommendations – democratic and rational aspects, such as consolidated progressive taxation and provisions for taxpayers' rights. The government appealed to the Japanese public to support these measures as transitional steps to a modern tax system. It is quite significant that Ikeda Hayato, Matsukuma Hideo, and Hirata Keiichiro, all of whom had sought a tax system built on the basis of the "Japanese empire tax history view," led in advancing the Shoup reforms. First they respected the Shoup mission, then they took advantage of it, and finally they ignored it.

The Shoup mission had correctly perceived that Japanese taxpayers had not developed a modern sense of tax awareness. There were substantial differences between prescriptions in the tax code and the realities of tax collection. The Shoup mission sought to close this gap. With the exception of the blue-return system, however, the Japanese government never institutionalized the methods that the Shoup mission had recommended for reinforcing the self-assessed income tax. Instead, it tried to reestablish prewar relations between the tax authorities and taxpayers through grouping the blue-return taxpayers. It focused on utilizing the withholding system with a year-end adjustment to make tax administration effective and able to secure stable tax revenues from low- and middle-class labor income.

The success of the withholding tax system in tapping the "natural" increase in income meant that during the high economic growth era the Japanese government could maintain fiscal soundness and expand the scale of government. Sustained reliance on this system, however, meant an inevitable increase in the tax burden of labor income. Consequently, as the Tax Advisory Commission report of 1961 pointed out, the Japanese government "set a basic goal to control the ratio of tax burden of national income below about 20% which is equal to the current level of the burden."[70] To maintain this ratio, the government continued relentless tax cuts at the same time as it was increasing the funding for public works. Under the cover of its interpretation of the Shoup recommendations, the government used tax cuts and public works expenditures to build popular trust.

The Japanese revenue system, which the government built by skillfully and politically exploiting the Shoup recommendations, relied on the "refraction effect." The resulting tax-cutting culture forced the tax authority and the government to continue to implement tax cuts even after the "natural" increase in tax revenue had weakened. This necessity had emerged as early as the mid-1960s. The Tax Advisory Commission report of 1965 justified the first public bond issuance after the peace treaty, declaring that "the government should make fiscal management elastic through the introduction of public bond policy." The commission added that the government "does not necessarily stick to manage fiscal policy under the constraint of natural increase in tax revenue."[71] The commission took the same position a year later, and beginning in the fiscal year of 1966, the government began to borrow funds for public works. This resort to fiscal drugs was necessary in the face of the political requirement to continue to provide tax cuts while funding the "construction state," despite the weakening of tax revenues.

Today, for the purpose of rebuilding Japanese taxation in the twenty-first century, the Japanese government should swiftly reexamine the Shoup recommendations, which it has largely ignored since 1950. It should use these recommendations as the basis on which to build genuine broad-based support for the taxation required to wean Japan from its addiction to deficit spending and public debt.

Notes

1. Grew, J. C., *Ten Years in Japan – A Contemporary Record Drawn from the Diaries and Private and Official Papers of JOSEPH C. GREW United States Ambassador to Japan 1932–1942* (New York: Simon and Schuster, 1944), 84.
2. The same observation is also made in the United States before the introduction of the Tax Reform Act of 1986; see Witte, J. F., *The Politics and Development of the Federal Income Tax* (Madison: University of Wisconsin Press, 1985), 242–3.
3. Tsuru Shigeto established this term. This implies the difference between the ideal situation that the government presumed existed and the situation that actually prevailed in the field of tax collection. Tsuru, S., "Dai 7 kai Kokkai Ôkuraiinkai Kôchôkai Dai 1gô" [A testimony before the hearing on the Committee of Finance in the 7th Diet, part 1], *Syûgiin Kaigiroku Jyôhô* [*The Proceedings of the House of Representatives*], vol. 9 (Tokyô: House of Representatives, 1950), 5 Available at: http://kokkai.ndl.go.jp/SENTAKU/syugiin/007/0624/00703020624001c.html, accessed on July 8, 2010.
4. Nerré, B., "Tax Culture: A Basic Concept for Tax Politics," *Economic Analysis and Policy*, 2008, vol. 38 (1), 155.
5. For a brief summary in English, see Itô, H., "Direct Taxes in Japan and the Shoup Report," *Public Finance*, 1953, vol. 8 (1), pp. 361–2; Shiomi, S. (translated by Hasegawa, S.), *Japan's Finance and Taxation, 1940–1956* (New York: Columbia University Press, 1957), 115–9.

6. A county in Japan, *or Gun*, is a kind of jurisdiction between villages or towns and prefectures that was established in 1878. Its mayor and staff were dispatched by the national government ministries.

7. Satô, S., *Bungaku ni arawareta Nihonjin no Nôzei Ishiki [Japanese Taxpaying Consciousness in Literary Works]* (Tôkyô: University of Tôkyô Press, 1987), 236–7.

8. The members were mainly merchants of long-established shops, presidents of banks, or wealthy individuals in the region. Available at: http://www.nta.go. jp/ntc/sozei/tokubetsu/h18shiryoukan/03.htm, accessed on August 10, 2010.

9. Takahashi, M., "Shoki Shotokuzei no keisei to kôzô" [The formation and structure of the early income tax system], *Keizai Shirin*, 1958, vol. 26 (1), 77.

10. Ôkurasyô Zaiseishi Shitsu [The Ministry of Finance Public Finance History Compilation Section], *Shôwa zaisei-shi-shûsen kara kôwa made [Public Finance History in Shôwa era – From the end of WW II to San Francisco Peace Treaty]*, vol. 8, (Tôkyô: Tôyô Keizai Shinpô sha 1977), 319.

11. In addition, tax was levied on an estimate of income made on the basis of the standard amount of income in the trade and pro forma variables, such as the number of employees and business assets.

12. Inoue, I., *Zeimu gyôsei shi-Shûsen kara senryôshoki made [The History of Tax Administration from the End of War to the early time of Occupation]* (Tôkyô: Chûôkeizai-sha, 1980), 166–7.

13. Ozaki, M., *Zaisei seisaku eno shiten [A Viewpoint to Fiscal Policy]* (Tôkyô: Ôkura zaimu Kyôkai, 2001), 309–11. Ozaki, ex-director general of the Tax Bureau, in looking back on this episode, suggests that it laid the basis for hostility to general consumption taxation in Japan.

14. National Tax Bureau, *Kokuzei Chô Tôkei Nenpôsho – Dai 100 kai Kinen gô [National Tax Bureau Statistics Almanac – 100th Memorial Version]* (Tôkyô: National Tax Bureau, 1977).

15. A banquet with Geisha girls could play an important role. In local towns at that time, popularity among Geisha girls could shape the reputation of local figures. Ex-director-general of the Tax Bureau and ex-member of the Lower House, Maeo Shigesabuô, recalled the time he headed a local tax office: "It was impossible to collect tax smoothly unless I had a good reputation among Geisha Girls. It took a year after I assumed the post for them to recognize me. After that, the delinquency rate abruptly dropped off." Maeo, S., *Watashi no Rirekisho [My Personal History]* (Tôkyô: Nihon keizai Shinbun-sha, 1974), 182. See also Satô, S., *Nihon no Nôzei Bunka [Tax Culture in Japan]* (Tôkyô: Gyôsei, 1990), 195–6.

16. It is very interesting that these leading members, Matsukuma Hideo, Hirata Keiichirô, and Ikeda Hayato, took responsibility for rebuilding a postwar Japanese tax system as a director general of the Tax Bureau or minister of finance.

17. The schedular income tax was imposed on incomes in six groups: earned income, income from business, dividends and interest, income from real estate, forestry income, and retirement-allowance income. The first four types – referred to as regular incomes – were taxed at flat rates, although the

rate varied according to the type of incomes. The latter two – called irregular incomes – were taxed at progressive rates, but they were excluded from the general income aggregate income tax base. See Shiomi, S. (translated by Hasegawasa, S.), *Japan's Finance and Taxation, 1940–1956*, 128–9; Itô, H. (1953), "Direct Taxes in Japan and the Shoup Report," 362–3.

18. Shiomi, S. (translated by Hasegawa, S.), *Japan's Finance and Taxation, 1940–1956*, 127.

19. Hayashi, Y., *Sengo Nihon no Sozei Kôzô* [*The Tax Structure in the Post-World War II*] (Tokyô: Yûhikaku, 1957), 75.

20. The wholesale prices rose by 2.15 times, whereas retail prices increased by 2.37 times in the period from July 1945 to January 1946.

21. Chû, S., "Shinkoku Nouzei Seido no Hatten" [The development of the Self-Assessment System], *Finance*, 1975, vol. 11 (8), 76.

22. Inoue, I., *Zeimu gyôsei shi-Shûsen kara senryôshoki made*, 214.

23. Ôkurasyô Zaiseishi Shitsu, *Shôwa zaisei-shi-shûsen kara kôwa made*, 390.

24. Inoue, I., *Zeimu gyôsei shi-Shûsen kara senryôshoki made*, 238.

25. Chû, S., "Shinkoku Nouzei Seido no Hatten," 78.

26. Kokuzeichô [National Tax Agency], *Kokuzeichô 30 nen shi* [*National Tax Agency's 30 years history*] (Tokyô: National Tax Agency, 1979), 22.

27. Inoue, I., *Zeimu gyôsei shi-Shûsen kara senryôshoki made*, 192.

28. Ôkurasyô Zaiseishi Shitsu, *Shôwa zaisei-shi-shûsen kara kôwa made*, 393.

29. Another reason for tax arrears was that the national tax collection administration was not created quickly enough after the system of tax collection entrusted to municipalities was abolished.

30. Hayashi, Y., *Sengo Nihon no Sozei Kôzô*, 84–104.

31. Ôtake, H., "Hatoyama, Kishi jidai ni okeru chiisana seihuron" in *Nenpô Seijigaku 1991* (Tokyô: Iwanami shoten, 1992), 182.

32. Tsuru, S., Dai 7 kai Kokkai Ôkuraiinkai Kôchôkai Dai 1gô," 5. See also, Shoup, C. S. (1989), "The Tax Mission to Japan, 1949–50," in Gillis, M., ed., *Tax Reform in Developing Countries* (Durham, NC: Duke University Press, 1989), 177–232.

33. Tsuru, S., "Dai 7 kai Kokkai Ôkuraiinkai Kôchôkai Dai 1gô," 5–6. Kimura, K., "The criticism of effective demand policy," *Keizaihyôron*, November 1950, 24–5; Andô, M. "Shoup Zeiseikaikau no Tokuchô" [Features of Shoup Tax Reform], *Keizai* 1988, vol. 292, 159–60.

34. Shoup Mission, *Report on Japanese Taxation by the Shoup Mission* (Tokyô: Supreme Commander for the Allied Forces, 1949), vol. 1, 65.

35. Tsuru, S., "Dai 7 kai Kokkai Ôkuraiinkai Kôchôkai Dai 1gô," 6.

36. Itô, H. "Dai 7 Kai Kokkai Ôkuraiinkai Kôchôkai Dai 1gô" [A testimony before the hearing on the Committee of Finance in the 7th Diet, part 1], *Syûgiin Kaigiroku Jyôhô* [*The Proceedings of the House of Representatives*], vol. 2 (Tokyô: House of Representatives, 1950), Available at: http://kokkai .ndl.go.jp/SENTAKU/syugiin/007/0624/00703020624001c.html, accessed on August 2, 2010.

37. Izumi, M., *Zeihô no Kiso–Wagakuni Zeisei no Kiso Chishiki* [Fundamentals of Tax Law – Basic Knowledge of Tax System in Japan] (Tokyô: Zeimu Keiri Kyôkai, 1979), 194.

38. Suzuki, T. *Sengo Nihon Zaiseishi*, vol. 3 (Tokyô: Daigaku Syuppankai, 1960), 275.
39. Satô, S. and Miyajima H., *Sengo Zeiseishi, Zouhoban* [Post-War Public Finance History, enlarged edition] (Tokyô: Zeimu Keiri Kyôkai, 1982) 14.
40. Miyajima, H., "Zeisei Kaikaku Rongi no Pointo" [Issues of Arguments for Tax Reform], *Keizai Seminar*, October 1985, 44.
41. Hirata, K., Chû, S., and Izumi, M., *Shôwa Zeisei no Kaiko to Tenbô Jyôkan* [*Memoirs and Prospect of Taxation in Shôwa Era*, vol. 1], (Tokyô: Ôkuraa Zaimu Kyôkai, 1979), 506.
42. Itô, M. and Ekonomisuto Henshubu, eds., *Sengo Sangyô-shi eno Shôgen – Sangyô Seisaku* [*Testimony on Postwar Industrial History I – Industrial Policy*] (Tokyô: Mainichi-Shinbunsha 1977), 18–19.
43. Hirata, K., Chû, S., Izumi, M., *Shôwa Zeisei no Kaiko to Tenbô Jyôkan*, 517.
44. Hirata, K., Chû, S., and Izumi, M., *Shôwa Zeisei no Kaiko to Tenbô Gekan* [*Memoirs and Prospect of Taxation in Showa Era*, vol. 2], (Tokyô: Ôkura Zaimu Kyôkai, 1979), 273.
45. Hirata, K., Chû, S., Izumi, M., *Shôwa Zeisei no Kaiko to Tenbô Gekan*, 44–5, 274.
46. Hirata, K., Chû, S., Izumi, M., *Shôwa Zeisei no Kaiko to Tenbô Jyôkan*, 521–2.
47. Kokuritsu Kokkai Toshokan Chôsa Rippô Kôsa Kyoku [Research and Legislative Reference Bureau], *Wagakuni Shotokuzei no Hensen* [*Transition of Income Tax in Japan*] (Tokyô: Kokuritsu Kokkai Toshokan, 1972), 18–19.
48. Ishi, H., *The Japanese Tax System*, 3rd. ed. (Oxford and New York: Clarenton Press, 2001), 26.
49. Satô, S., Miyajima, H., *Sengo Zeiseishi, Zouhoban*, 36–7.
50. Satô, S., Miyajima, H., *Sengo Zeiseishi, Zouhoban*, 35–53.
51. Satô, S., Miyajima, H., *Sengo Zeiseishi, Zouhoban*, 41.
52. Satô, S., Miyajima, H., *Sengo Zeiseishi, Zouhoban*, 60.
53. Ôkurasyô Zaiseishi Shitsu [The Ministry of Finance Public Finance History Compilation Section], *Shôwa zaisei-shi-Shôwa 27 nen kara Shôwa 47 nen made* [*Public Finance History in Shôwa era – From 1952 to1973*], vol. 6 (Tokyô: Tôyô Keizai Shinpô sha 1990), 3–4.
54. Itô, M. and Ekonomisuto Henshubu, eds., *Sengo Sangyô-shi eno Shôgen ISangyô Seisaku* [*Testimony on Postwar Industrial History I – Industrial Policy*], 32.
55. Satô, S., Miyajima, H., *Sengo Zeiseishi, Zouhoban*, 60–1.
56. Hayashi, Y., *Sengo Nihon no Sozei Kôzô*, 88–9.
57. Ôkurasyô Zaiseishi Shitsu, *Shôwa zaisei-shi-shûsen kara kôwa made*, 128–32.
58. Otake, H., "Hatoyama, Kishi jidai ni okeru chiisana seihuron," 168.
59. Komiya, R., *Gendai Nihon Keizai Kenkyu* [A Study on Modern Japanese Economy] (Tokyô: Tôkyo Daigaku Shuppankai, 1975) 120–1.
60. Ôkurasyô Zaiseishi Shitsu, *Shôwa zaisei-shi-Shôwa 27 nen kara Shôwa 47 nen made*, 130.
61. Satô S., Miyajima H., *Sengo Zeiseishi, Zouhoban*, 76–7.

62. Satô S., Miyajima H., *Sengo Zeiseishi, Zouhoban,* 77.
63. Itô, M. and Ekonomisuto Henshubu, eds., *Sengo Sangyô-shi eno Shôgen ISangyô Seisaku,* 46–7.
64. Ôtake, H., "Hatoyama, Kishi jidai ni okeru chiisana seihuron," 176.
65. Kokuritsu Kokkai Toshokan Chôsa Rippô Kôsa Kyoku, *Wagakuni Shotokuzei no Hensen,* 1.
66. Ôkurasyô Zaiseishi Shitsu, *Shôwa zaisei-shi-shûsen kara kôwa made,* 129; Hideo, O. "Hatoyama, Kishi jidai ni okeru chiisana seihuron," 177–8.
67. Tanami, K., "San nin no Ôkuradaijin" [Three Ministers of Finance I worked as their secretary], *Nihon Keizai Shinbun Morning edition,* (Tokyô: Nihon Keizai Shinbun Honsha August 7, 1997). 36. This is a response by Murayama Tatsuo, Tanami's senior at the Ministry of Finance and ex-Minister of Finance, to the question of Tanami, ex-director general of the Ministry of Finance: What was the goal of the postwar Japanese tax policy?
68. Chû, S., "Shinkoku Nouzei Seido no Hatten," 78.
69. Ikeda, H., *Kinkô Zaisei [Balanced Finance]* (Tokyô: Cyûkô Bunko 1999), 256.
70. Seihu Zeisei Chôsakai [Government Tax Advisory Commission], *Seifu Zeisei Chôsakai Chôki Tôshin [Tax Advisory Commission Report of Long Term Tax System]* (Ôkurasyô Insatsukyoku: The MOF Printing Office, 1961), 2.
71. Seihu Zeisei Chosakai [Government Tax Advisory Commission], *Shôwa 41 nendo Zeiseikaisei nikansuru Zeiseicyousakai Tôshin [Report of the Tax Advisory Commission on for FY1966 Tax Reform]* (Tokyô: Ôkurasyô Insatsukyoku: The MOF Printing Office, 1965), 2.

13

A Political Dispute over the Local Public Finance Equalization Grant

The Legacy of Shoup's Policy Choices

Eisaku Ide

INTRODUCTION

The first report of the Shoup mission to Japan proposed a fundamental reform of the national taxation system centered on direct taxation.[1] In addition, it offered a comprehensive plan for reforming local fiscal and administrative systems.[2] This chapter will examine the Shoup mission's role in the democratic fiscal reform in Japan, and pay particular attention to the impact of the mission on the political, institutional, and philosophical dimensions of postwar intergovernmental relations in Japan.

Through the first report, Shoup wanted to strengthen dramatically local autonomy and Japanese democracy. For example, he proposed:

- establishing local taxation at levels that would be adequate to meet popular demands for government services;
- creating local fiscal plans that would be largely independent from those of the central government;
- reinforcing the responsibility of local authorities and the awareness of citizens of local fiscal burden;
- introducing a system of fiscal equalization to ensure a minimum level of public services at the same time as protecting local autonomy; and
- establishing a council composed of local representatives to management negotiations with the central government on behalf of local governments.

In the process of proposing these innovations, Shoup introduced the groundbreaking concept of what is now called the "principle of subsidiarity," which is the idea that fiscal resources should be allocated as closely

336

as possible to the citizens and that the higher-level governments should not take action unless doing so would be more effective than action taken by municipalities.

After the release of the first report, the government sought to pass legislation to implement the mission's proposals. In March 1950, the government submitted the Local Tax Act to the seventh Diet. The focal point of the Local Tax Act was the establishment of a value-added tax (VAT) at the prefectural level. The new tax, which had never been adopted anywhere, not even in the victorious nations of World War II, stimulated a great deal of criticism within Japan. This was largely because of the relatively heavy tax burden it would have imposed on labor-intensive industries, and because of ambiguity in the concept of the value added. Although the Diet approved the VAT in 1950, the government never implemented the tax, and four years later the Diet put it on the shelf, where it remained until 1997.

The first Shoup report also proposed the local public finance equalization grant, and the seventh Diet approved it. This grant is often regarded as having been the model for the local allocation tax grant that Japan employs today. Notable innovations that Shoup proposed, and that the Diet included in the equalization grant, were the concepts of basic fiscal demand and basic fiscal revenue for calculating local grants, and a local public finance committee (LPFC) that would make this calculation. The Diet, however, changed Shoup's recommendations in a significant way. Under the legislation, the equalization grant as calculated by the LPFC was only a "basic estimation" (Article 6–1 of the Local Public Finance Equalization Grant Act), and the Ministry of Finance (MOF) had the power to make the final determination of local grants. In practice, much political effort, and often conflict, between the MOF and the LPFC would be required before reaching an agreement on the size of the grants.

In this way, and in the abandonment of a VAT, the Japanese government amended the local public finance reform recommended by the Shoup mission.[3] We would be hasty, however, in rendering a negative evaluation of these modifications.[4] It would be more fruitful to suggest that these experiences in the occupied era were part of an ongoing learning process in which the Japanese government struggled to understand and solve an important set of social problems. It is important to understand that in making decisions to *adopt or reject* Shoup's recommendations, the Japanese government, including its fiscal experts, tried to *connect* the essence of recommendations to preexisting institutions from the

prewar and war periods. Through various political conflicts, people were
learning how to adapt both traditional institutions and new ideas to contemporary reality. In the process, they impressed the stamp of Japanese
characteristics on the new intergovernmental fiscal relations.

In this chapter, I will focus on the political conflicts involved in the
budgetary process launched by the creation of the equalization grant
system. The system has had considerable historical significance. First, it
played a crucial role in improving the conditions of local finance in prewar Japan. Abuses of the household tax (*Kosuwari*) at that time were
rampant, and local authorities often had to face fiscal bankruptcy. But
taking advantage of the equalization grant system, Japan developed what
has been described as an "egalitarian local tax system."[5] Second, after a
serious confrontation between the MOF and the LPFC, the new system
institutionalized control of local fiscal resources by the central government.

In its first report, the Shoup mission touted the equalization grant as
"the kind of grant which minimizes detailed national control of local
bodies." The way in which the Japanese government transformed the
equalization grant into the local allocation tax grant, however, may have
had just the opposite effect to what Shoup had intended. In this chapter,
taking account of the reactions of both the Supreme Commander for the
Allied Powers (SCAP) and the Japanese public to the Shoup recommendations, I will attempt to clarify the meaning of the political confrontations
between the Shoup mission, the MOF, the LPFC, and a coalition called
the Organizations Related to Local Authorities (ORLA), and describe the
transformation process of Japanese local public finance.

Fiscal Issues during the Shoup Mission's Visits

*Political Context of the Mission and the Fiscal Problems of the Japanese
Government.* In 1949, as a result of the general election held in January,
the Democratic Liberal Party won an absolute majority by 264 seats in
the Diet. The number of successful candidates won by the second party,
the Democratic Party, was just 86, so the victory by the Democratic
Liberal Party was apparently overwhelming.[6] Despite such a landslide
victory, the Yoshida cabinet faced political difficulties. On one hand, the
Japanese government had to impose a strict retrenchment policy defined
by the "Nine Principles for Economic Stabilization" (the "Dodge Line").
On the other hand, the Democratic Liberal Party had won the election by
making public commitments to reduce income tax and abolish the general

consumption tax (the "turnover tax"). If, as the Dodge Line required, the government reduced the subsidies that it had provided to offset price differentials, living expenses would rise. To Yoshida and the Democratic Liberal Party, this would, in turn, require tax reductions to mitigate the burden of the cost of living. Joseph Dodge, whose policies led to the Dodge Line, vigorously opposed such tax cuts. Thus, the Yoshida cabinet found itself forced into a tight corner.[7]

Salvation for the cabinet arrived, however, when Dodge admitted that he did not have sufficient knowledge to evaluate major tax reform in Japan, and when SCAP indicated that it wanted to sponsor an expert mission – the Shoup mission – to develop a concrete plan for tax reform. Seizing this opportunity, the Democratic Liberal Party appealed to the public to maintain its support of the cabinet, and declared that the Yoshida government would be able to reduce the tax burden with the help of the Shoup mission.[8] This tactic was well-grounded. Harold Moss, who had taken up the post of chief of the Internal Revenue Division (IRD) of the Economic and Scientific Section (ESS) of SCAP, had emerged as a powerful rival of Eugene M. Reed, who was the chief of the Public Finance branch within the Finance Division. Reed was a proponent of high taxes, and an ally of high-tax supporters within the MOF. Moss adopted a positive attitude toward the tax reduction, in part to win the Japanese government's favor.[9] Moss honestly admitted his difficulty in changing the policy direction of SCAP, and he maintained that what might bring about tax reductions was the advice of tax specialists from the United States. Finance Minister Ikeda Hayato adroitly took advantage of this political situation.[10]

The Shoup mission had been appointed by General Douglas MacArthur. Dodge, in contrast, held a personal appointment from President Harry Truman and operated under the authority of a directive issued by the President and the Joint Chiefs of Staff. Dodge therefore had more power over Japanese economic policy than Shoup. This posed a problem because Dodge was far tougher on tax cuts than Shoup, and Dodge's retrenchment policy restricted the work of the Shoup mission in significant ways.[11] Shoup, however, had the advantage of becoming much better informed with regard to Japan's fiscal situation. He spent a great deal of time investigating local conditions. He became keenly aware of the serious tax burden carried by inhabitants in rural areas, and recognized the necessity for significant tax reduction. He negotiated by teleconference with Dodge, who had returned to Washington from Japan. Shoup finally made a recommendation suggesting a tax reduction of about

5 billion yen in the 1949–50 fiscal year (FY) and 59 billion yen in the 1950–1 FY.[12]

Finance Minister Ikeda was unhappy with this recommendation for a tax reduction, regarding it as far too small. Even more importantly, Ikeda did not trust the tax reform plan proposed by foreign scholars. He did not believe that they could understand Japanese tax culture or institutions, and he had no interest in the theoretical justification that Shoup and his colleagues provided for their proposals. Ikeda only cared about the whether or not the aggregate tax reduction proposed by the mission was large enough to serve his political purposes. If it was, he would have a basis from which to negotiate with the SCAP. In addition, he might be able to increase the effective size of the cut through various fiscal management techniques. At the conclusion of the Shoup mission, Ikeda participated in a press conference and declared that the Japanese government would reduce income tax by 100 billion yen in FY 1950–1.[13]

The Japanese government adopted the practice of distributing the fruits of the high economic growth every year through tax expenditures and raising tax exemptions.[14] In 1949 and 1950, however, just before the onset of the era of high economic growth, Ikeda and the MOF proposed making an attempt to raise funds for tax reduction partially by administrative curtailment. This curtailment would come through cutting the expenditures of local governments. Various reasons lay behind this focus on local cuts, the dominant ones being Ikeda's and the MOF's strong suspicion of local autonomy in Japan, and their unhappiness over the shouldering of local government expenditures by the central government.

In his correspondence with Shoup, Ikeda presented his criticism of the local authorities: "I cannot tolerate fiscal decentralization because the current local administration is restricted by the decision-making of the central government, and the local authorities should curtail excessive public works expenses and personnel expenses." In addition, Ikeda asserted that the function of the local distribution tax grant, which was the predecessor of the local public finance equalization grant, should not be defined as a fiscal-guarantee system but as a fiscal-equalization system, and that the total financial commitment for equalization should be lower.[15] The MOF made similar points, insisting that local authorities had responsibilities set by the national government, and could not expect to exercise complete local autonomy. It added that local governments had engaged in reckless spending and needed to be restrained. The MOF proposed simplifying the distribution formula of the local distribution tax grant. It agreed with Ikeda, however, on the need to weaken the function of the fiscal-guarantee system.[16]

In this way, Ikeda and the MOF assumed that they could find the fiscal resources for tax reduction through the radical reduction of local expenditures. The government's approach conflicted with Shoup's approach, which he based on his strong belief in the need for local autonomy.[17] The stage was set for potential conflict between the Japanese government and the Shoup mission.

The Local Public Finance Equalization Grant and the Local Public Finance Committee. With the imposition of the Dodge Line, SCAP had required the Japanese government to reduce radically the allocation to the local distribution tax grant in the FY 1949–50 budget. Under the local distribution tax grant, which had been enacted in 1940, each FY the government allocated a certain portion of national income tax and corporate income tax revenues to local governments. Following the Dodge Line, SCAP suddenly ordered a dramatic reduction of the grant from 33.14 percent to 16.29 percent of income tax revenues, causing serious trouble for local authorities.

SCAP's decision decisively undermined the ORLA's trust in the local distribution tax grant system.[18] The ORLA included the National Governors' (prefectural governors) Association, the Japan Association of City Mayors, and the National Association of Towns and Villages, and each of them drafted opinions and representations to criticize this reduction. They argued that it would inevitably destroy local public finance, and demanded restoration of the transfer rate to 33.14 percent, the adoption of institutional guarantees of local fiscal management, and permission for local authorities to cope with the shortage in fiscal resources by imposing surtaxes on income and corporate taxation.[19]

The ORLA brought its complaints to the mission as well, and Shoup and his colleagues agreed that the arbitrary change in the local distribution tax grant by SCAP and the central government would have an undesirable effect on the stability of local fiscal management.[20] In response, the mission proposed the equalization grant in its first report.[21]

The equalization grant, which was implemented in 1950 to comply with the recommendations of the first report, had two central elements. The first element was a lumping of the distribution tax grant and other subsidies to local government into a single block grant. The intent was to establish the political independence of local authorities. In its first report, the mission proposed appropriating 120 billion yen for this consolidated grant, and including all subsidies except funding for public works in it. Some divisions in SCAP had a strong desire to preserve earmarked subsidies, however, so the government decided to maintain the subsidies for the Ministry of Health and Welfare, and finally appropriated 105 billion yen for the equalization grant budget. The total of the old distribution tax grant in 1949 was only 57.7 billion yen, so the 1950 reform was quite broad in scope.[22] The second central element was the introduction of the concepts of basic fiscal demand and basic fiscal revenue for calculating the total size of the equalization grant.

Basic fiscal demand was a measure of the standard fiscal demands of the local authorities. To obtain the basic fiscal demand, the law defined two factors for each category of public service: a "unit of measurement" and a "unit cost" (for example, cost per student) taken as the average cost per unit across all localities. The basic fiscal demand of each local authority would be calculated as follows. For each category of service, the unit cost would be multiplied by the number of units (for example, students) in that locality. The demands would be summed across all categories of public service and then adjusted by a coefficient that took into account special factors (such as natural conditions) in each local area.

Derivation of the basic fiscal revenue began simply with the calculation of the average rate of taxation. This was determined by dividing all expenditures of local tax revenues by the tax base (which the Local Tax Act defined). Then, for each locality, the nationwide tax rate would be multiplied by each locality's tax base. Finally, 70 percent of this product would be regarded as each locality's basic fiscal revenue.[23] The amount of each grant allocated to a locality would be the difference between its basic fiscal demand and its basic fiscal revenue.

The equalization grant system as designed by the Shoup mission seemed to be a reasonably straightforward way of achieving fiscal equalization across Japan's localities. Its aim was similar to what has become the local allocation tax grant today. Even from the outset, however, implementation of the equalization grant system was more complicated and contentious than the Shoup mission had expected.[24]

First, a serious problem emerged with regard to determining the institution that would calculate the equalization grant. The Local Autonomy Agency, with jurisdiction over local public finance issues, already existed. But, for the purpose of reinforcement of local autonomy, Shoup insisted on establishing a new committee. In May 1950, the Japanese government therefore created the LPFC, which was composed of representatives of the local authorities, with the responsibility for calculating the equalization grant.[25]

The allocation of responsibilities between the two committees immediately became very controversial.[26] The dispute focused on the issue of whether it should be an agency attached to the cabinet or should be independent, reporting directly to the Diet. The dispute became very complex, involving arguments between the MOF and the Local Autonomy Agency, between ESS and the Government Section (GS) of SCAP, and even within the ESS.[27] Howard G. Bradshaw, a staff member of the local tax subsection of the IRD, reported to Shoup that he had proposed revisions to a LPFC bill, however the MOF and the cabinet had modified them, and the GS had opposed a proposal by the Japanese government to allow the continuation of the Local Autonomy Agency. The GS argued that the government proposal did not sufficiently reflect the spirit of the Shoup recommendation. Bradshaw and Moss agreed with this. The Public Finance Division of the ESS, however, strongly supported the Japanese proposal.[28] Finally, MacArthur intervened. He insisted on making the LPFC an agency that was independent of the cabinet; however he accepted the view of the Public Finance Division that the Local Autonomy Agency should continue. This meant, however, that the Local Autonomy Agency, which was a component of the national bureaucratic organizations, might prove to be very influential in the decision-making process of intergovernmental fiscal relations.[29] A particularly difficult problem would result if the MOF disagreed with the LPFC, as the Local Autonomy Agency had to report to the cabinet, meaning that the MOF might be able to use the agency to prevail over the LPFC in any disagreements between the two local entities.[30] This problem did, in fact, emerge.

The second, and related, problem that emerged regarded the calculation of the grant. Under Shoup's recommendation and the 1950 reforms, the LPFC took responsibility for calculating the excess of the basic fiscal demand over the basic fiscal revenue in each local authority and then adding up the figures for all the local authorities to arrive at the estimate of the total grant. This was called the "piling-up" method. It became enormously important because this system gave local authorities an objective basis on which to claim fiscal assistance from the central government, particularly in cases where the local fiscal burden was generated by the projects initiated, but only partly funded, by the central government.[31] As a practical matter, however, negotiations among the MOF, the Local Autonomy Agency and the LPFC would play an important role in determining the equalization grant budget on a top-down basis, despite the result the "piling-up" method produced. As Bradshaw pointed out, the Local Autonomy Agency and its secretary was a constituent of the central government and cabinet, increasing the possibility that the government might chose to ignore a determination by the LPFC's "piling-up" methodology. Some supporters of the cause of local governments worried that Shoup had not gone far enough by way of providing guarantees, and expressed a preference for reliance on the kind of fixed rates of national tax revenue that the local distribution tax grant system had employed. After reading the mission's first report, one member of the LPFC declared: "I was astonished to know that Shoup recommended determining the amount of the Equalization Grant not through a fixed rate of national tax revenue, but through a way like prefectural budget compilation."[32]

The third problem involved institutionalizing the block-grant concept. Cabinet ministries and other government offices feared situations in which the local authorities would not carry out the policies set by the central government. In response, the ministries sought to complicate the definition of basic fiscal demand.[33] At the first stage of the debate over basic fiscal demand, the MOF insisted on simple classifications of service functions and units of measurement. The other ministries strongly opposed the MOF, however, wishing to move back toward a system that earmarked funds for specific purposes and restrained local governments from developing programs of purely local interest. These ministries sought to subdivide the unit of measurement of the basic fiscal demand by as much as possible, and the Diet cooperated, resulting in serious administrative burdens for the LPFC.

Thus, in the context of the severe economic troubles of the occupation period and in conjunction with the imposition of the Dodge Line, the victory of the Yoshida government, and the arrival of the Shoup mission combined to produce a crisis of local government in Japan. The discord that ensued over local budgets was a significant break in the history of intergovernmental fiscal relations in Japan. Centralization had prevailed since the Meiji Restoration; serious local challenges to central authority had been quite exceptional. It is true that a chain of democratizing steps during the American occupation, such as the election, rather than appointment, of prefectural governors, and the enactment of the Local Autonomy Act and Local Public Finance Act, had preceded the disputes over the equalization grant. In 1949, however, the economic priorities of both the American occupation and the Japanese government had shifted and were now a long way from those of local officials, who increasingly harbored a sense of impending crisis and a need to defend their interests.

Political Support for the Organizations Related to Local Authorities in the Second Report of the Shoup Mission. Political conflict over the equalization grant between central and local government continued throughout the Shoup mission's second visit to Japan in the summer of 1950. In its second report, the mission noted that "the problem of a local financial system adequate to support local autonomy in Japan is on the road to solution, but is still some distance from the end of the journey." Among the central objectives of the second mission was a resolution of the remaining structural issues relating to local finance and the production of advice regarding the local budgets for FY 1951–2.[34]

The ORLA welcomed Shoup's strong interest in the matter. The coalition was unhappy about the heavy influence that the MOF seemed to have had over the writing of Shoup's first report. One ORLA official looked back on the mission's first visit and recalled that the mission had not seemed to recognize the existence of the Local Autonomy Agency, despite the fact that it had submitted all sorts of documents to the mission through the MOF. In addition, this official complained that Shoup's inspection tours relating to local taxation had been managed by officials from the Tax Bureau of the MOF.[35] Excited by the prospect that Shoup would pay more attention to local conditions on his second visit, the ORLA prepared thoroughly for it, developing various papers documenting the severity of local fiscal problems.[36] One of the most important issues that the ORLA highlighted was the question of whether or not the Japanese government should increase the equalization grant.[37]

The National Governors' Association led the way in this lobbying effort, submitting a document that set forth this issue quite clearly.[38] The governors asserted that the importance of local autonomy required the reinforcement of independent fiscal resources, which were primarily local taxes. In addition to this, the association requested an expansion of the equalization grant on the grounds that the level of public services within fiscally poor prefectures should be raised to that of average prefectures. To accomplish this, the National Governors' Association proposed the following: (1) determination of the equalization grant by adding the increase in obligatory expenditures prescribed by law and the local share of the national public-works expenses to the equalization grant made in the previous year, (2) raising the unit costs used for calculating the basic fiscal demand sufficiently to allow fiscally poor prefectures to maintain public services, and (3) calculating the basic fiscal revenue as 60 percent, rather than 70 percent of the standard tax revenue.

During his second visit, Shoup welcomed the ORLA's assistance, and worked particularly closely with the new LPFC. Tamotsu Ogita, head of a secretariat of the LPFC, later recalled: "At the beginning Shoup mission referred to various points in the draft of second report. But Mr. Shoup showed us a draft in advance and if we pointed out problems, he kindly reduced disadvantageous points for us."[39]

Although the Shoup mission was conducting its investigations, including the extensive consultation with the new LPFC, the Japanese government actively worked on the national budget for FY 1951–2. On July 11, 1950, before Shoup's arrival, the government had held a cabinet meeting and settled on the guidelines for the budget. In the eighth item, "Tax Revisions and Establishment of Local Public Finance," the cabinet stated the need for a reduction in income taxation and called on local authorities to rationalize public services as directed by the central government, and to clarify the classification of expenses between the central and local governments. Then, on the basis of this guideline, the MOF embarked on a close assessment of local public finance.

The MOF submitted its first draft of the budget to the cabinet meeting held on September 5, before Shoup had completed his second report. This bill incorporated revenues of 654.9 billion yen and expenditures of 586.9 billion yen. Under this budget, the surplus would reach almost 70 billion yen. Ikeda declared that the government was going to cease inflation according to the Dodge Line and implement the Liberal Party's campaign promise by reducing taxes by 70 billion yen.[40] The LPFC requested 145.6 billion yen for the equalization grant – a 40.6 billion yen increase from the previous fiscal year, but the MOF approved only a 3 billion yen increase, making the new grant 108 billion yen.

The LPFC was prepared to react. On September 5, on the same day that the MOF submitted its first draft of the budget to the cabinet, the LPFC submitted a document titled "Relations between Rough Estimate of FY1951–2 National Budget and Local Public Finance" to the Shoup mission. The document indicated that the costs of public services were rising, that a fixed rate of assistance for the national public works would inevitably create greater burdens for local authorities, and that increases in population were generating new fiscal demands. All of these circumstances pointed to the need to increase local taxes or increase the equalization grant.[41] At the cabinet meeting three days later, on September 8, Okano, the director of the Local Autonomy Agency, criticized Ikeda and his colleagues who insisted on a tax reduction. He said, "from the view point of LPFC, local tax should be preferably increased and if current situation continues, local governments will go bankrupt."[42] He then submitted a document titled "Requests for the Local Public Finance on the Occasion of FY 1951–2 National Budgetary Process" to the MOF.[43]

Two weeks later, on September 21, SCAP released the second report of the Shoup mission. In it, Shoup took a position that was clearly in support of the LPFC and the ORLA. He argued that if the FY 1951–2 budget was in surplus, the surplus ought to be used for both the reduction of the national-level taxes and increases in the equalization grant. One of the mission's scenarios was a budget surplus of about 25 billion yen in FY 1951–2, of which at least 12 billion yen would be devoted to an increase in the equalization grant. A second scenario was a 60 billion yen surplus and a 22 billion yen equalization grant accompanied by reductions in the income tax rate, increased exemptions, and the repeal of various commodity taxes. The 22 billion yen that the Shoup mission proposed was far larger than the 3 billion that the MOF had approved.

The mission anticipated that the local fiscal burden would increase by 60 billion yen as a consequence of national policies favoring increases in public works and welfare, a reduction in fiscal assistance for disaster recovery efforts, and a revision of public officials' salaries. The mission knew that an increase in the equalization grant of this magnitude would be opposed by the Japanese government, which sought even larger cuts in national taxes. The heart of the mission's response was an assertion that if a person compared the larger cuts in national taxes with a larger increase in local fiscal burden, the latter would be found to be more harmful than the former. Thus, the Shoup mission had accepted almost all of the recommendations by the LPFC and the ORLA and, in effect, intervened in the early stages of the budgetary process in FY 1951–2.

Local Autonomy under Assault: The Beginning of the End?

Confrontation between the Ministry of Finance and the Organizations Related to Local Authorities on the 1951–2 Fiscal Year Budget. Finance Minister Ikeda was no doubt aware of the drift of the updated Shoup recommendations on intergovernmental relations. At the cabinet meeting on September 20 – the day before the release of the second report – the cabinet diplomatically reaffirmed its intention to discuss the problem of local fiscal burden extensively and to pay serious attention to the Shoup mission's proposals. In the wake of Shoup's second report, however, the MOF stiffened its attitudes toward the proposals that the ORLA had advanced. The Budget Bureau and Tax Bureau of the MOF drafted numerous documents advancing vigorous criticisms of the Shoup recommendations.[44] First, the MOF critiqued the methodology that the first Shoup report had used to calculate the local budget for FY 1950–1, projecting a 10 billion yen increase. The MOF pointed out that the second report's projection of a 60 billion yen increase was made on the basis of the flawed assumptions of the first report. Second, on the basis of an investigation of actual conditions in localities, the MOF argued that the personnel costs per capita were excessive – higher than those of the central government – and that other expenses at the local level also were unnecessary. Thus, the MOF claimed, local authorities had much more room for reducing expenditures than did the central government. The MOF even suggested that local tax reduction might be possible. Third, the MOF insisted that the equalization grant it had recommended was sufficient, and added that any fiscal inequality was being caused not by the shortage of the amount but mainly by an excessive distribution of grants to urban areas. Fourth, the MOF claimed that local authorities would have money to spare because local revenues from tax and bonds would increase by 10 billion yen from FY 1950–1, and in addition non-tax revenues (royalties, for example) would increase. Consequently, the MOF contended that local authorities would be able to reduce taxes by 30 billion yen rather than require additional fiscal resources of 60 billion yen. The MOF declared: "There isn't the slightest reason for an increase in the Equalization Grant."[45]

The LPFC promptly registered its strong opposition to the MOF's position by issuing a document titled "Local Public Finance Problems."[46] The LPFC defended the methodology of the first Shoup report and pointed to difficulties in comparing local expenditures in the postwar era with those in the prewar era. The committee pointed out that new demand for public services had emerged after World War II as a consequence of the expansion of compulsory education and increases in the relative size of local police forces. In the committee's view, the MOF had made arbitrary and incorrect assumptions. Next, the committee argued that if the local expenditures were excessive, the main reason was the huge fiscal burden caused by the projects imposed by the central government. Indeed, the LPFC declared, when taking into account the rapid postwar decline in national defense expenditures, the central government could afford to reduce its spending. The committee went on to criticize the MOF for using biased samples in its investigation of local government. In response to the MOF's criticism of the high personnel cost of local governments, the committee warned of the possibility of a brain drain from rural to urban areas if salaries for local public servants were reduced. The LPFC added that the need to offer higher wages to local officials had prevailed since before the war.

Unfortunately for the ORLA, during the ongoing discussion of the national budget for FY 1951–2 Shoup's political influence was far weaker than it had been during his first visit. The Japanese government was no doubt well aware of that fact long before the Shoup mission submitted its second report.[47] Both the imminent peace treaty with Japan and the intensification of the Korean War weakened MacArthur's willingness to resist the Japanese government or to insist on continuing his program of local democratization. This enabled Dodge's power over occupation policy to grow, and he – along with Reed, the head of SCAP's Public Finance division, and William Marquat, the chief of the ESS – shared the MOF's belief in the profligacy of Japan's local government. In addition, they shared a dislike for the work of the Shoup mission, particularly its interventions in expenditure issues. Moss and IRD officials interested in local finance shared Shoup's viewpoints on this topic, but they put a lower priority on the equalization grant program than Shoup and his colleagues.[48] In any case, without support from MacArthur, Moss lacked the power to offset the influence of Dodge and his key allies within SCAP, Reed and Marquat. Similarly, the GS, which had supported the ORLA's cause, had lost its leverage.

Consequently, SCAP abandoned any serious interest in following through on the failures of the Japanese government to implement the recommendations in Shoup's first report, including those in the realm of local finance. SCAP largely accepted the critical position that the Japanese government took in responding to the second report. Reed recommended that "While careful consideration and study should be given to all recommendations contained in the recent report of the Shoup mission, such recommendations are not to be considered as necessarily representing the position of ESS and that in developing its financial policy the Japanese Government is not bound by them."[49] In addition, SCAP severely edited Shoup's report before its circulation, declaring that it was just a guideline and would not constrain the budget process in any fashion.[50] In effect, SCAP buried the second report. Consequently, the ORLA could do little more than gesture to the reputation of the Shoup mission and insist on the theoretical strength of the second report in continuing its argument with the central government in the process of formulating the FY 1951–2 budget. The Shoup mission had ceased to be a valuable political ally.

The hard line of the Japanese government in opposition to increasing the equalization grant and the underwhelming impact of the second Shoup report disappointed the ORLA. Nonetheless, the ORLA fought back. On October 4, the prefectural governors held an emergency meeting regarding a supplementary budget of FY 1950–1 that had been drawn up in parallel with the FY 1951–2 budget. The governors reached an agreement to request an increase in the equalization grant. Meanwhile, on October 6, both the MOF and the LPFC discussed the position papers of the various contending parties. On October 17, representatives of prefectural governors and Ikeda exchanged opinions. The governors emphasized the fiscal distress of local governments, and insisted on the necessity of an increase in the equalization grant by 38.9 billion yen in the supplementary budget. Ikeda turned down this request, however, commenting that: "Each prefecture asserts shortage of fiscal resources, but we need to dig into problems more and investigate the actual situation at the local level" and he required governors to submit the documents on the basis of fiscal requirements.[51]

On November 15, the LPFC sent its recommendation for an increase in the equalization grant in the FY 1951–2 budget to Okano, the director of the Local Autonomy Agency. On November 24, the committee submitted the same recommendation to the prime minister. The recommendation was for an equalization grant of 135.9 billion yen.[52] The MOF rejected the proposal, suggesting 105 billion yen instead (which was the same level as the previous FY).[53] The LPFC, whose opinion the government consistently ignored, offered stubborn resistance by submitting its written opinion again to the speaker and the president.[54] Finally, the government, with Ikeda consulting closely with Dodge, approved an equalization grant of 110 billion yen – an increase of only 5 billion yen over the previous year.[55] The fiscal shortage, according to the estimate by the LPFC, remained unresolved in the FY 1951–2 budget.[56]

Disarray among Supporters of Local Autonomy. The Japanese government had approved the FY 1951–2 budget despite the thrust of Shoup's second report and the complaints of LPFC. The force of the Dodge Line, Ikeda's tax reduction policy, and the MOF's distrust had been overwhelming. Contributing as well to the defeat of the ORLA and the LPFC were internal divisions within local governments and the fact that the Japanese public was rather disinterested in the complexities of intergovernmental finance and extremely interested in tax cuts.

In representing the fiscal interests of local governments, the ORLA was far from monolithic.[57] For example, there was a split between large and small cities. On the one hand, the five biggest cities believed that from the standpoint of improving their own fiscal standing it would be desirable to minimize the equalization grant and avoid contributing, indirectly, to the strengthening of fiscally weak governments. On the other hand, the other cities complained of an insufficiency of fiscal assistance from the central government. The five biggest cities also demanded that special unit costs be defined in ways that reflected the fiscal demands peculiar to their cities, whereas the other cities emphasized the need to calculate basic fiscal demand in a way that paid primary attention to the fiscal instability of small municipalities.

Another important set of conflicts divided prefectures from municipalities. These conflicts all had to do with the problem of distributing funds – both equalization grant funds and new local tax sources – between prefectures and municipalities. The prefectures claimed that the equalization grant process would not fully address their problems, and that even if the government increased the equalization grant in line with the second report, a fiscal shortage of 43.7 billion yen would remain.[58] The prefectures raised important issues. Although Shoup's first report recommended increasing local tax revenues by 40 billion yen, the proposed increase would be allotted wholly to municipalities.[59] In addition, the value-added tax that the Shoup mission had proposed for the prefectures (and that the government had put on the books in 1950 but not implemented) would have exempted agriculture, but the newly enacted municipal property tax applied to farmland. Consequently, prefectures that depended on tax revenues from agriculture would suffer from the rapid fall in tax revenues under the 1950 reforms. This issue caused sharp confrontations not only between prefectures and municipalities, but also among prefectures.[60] On the basis of this situation, which should be called "cohabiting but living in different worlds," it was very difficult for the LPFC to demonstrate the unity of local governments in opposition to the MOF. It is hardly surprising that the MOF took a consistently unyielding line and refused political concessions to the committee on the budgetary process. Further weakening the cause of local autonomy and fiscal decentralization was the fact that Japanese public opinion failed to attach much importance to these issues. An important part of the background of the public discussion of local public finance was the widespread expectation

TABLE 1. *The Local and National Tax Burden in Japan between 1934 and 1951*

Year	National Income	Tax Burden (million yen)			Ratio of Tax Burden (%)		
		National	Local	Sum	National	Local	Sum
1934–6	13,465	1,226	634	1,860	9.1%	4.7%	13.8%
1941	30,813	4,931	879	5,810	16.0%	2.9%	18.9%
1947	1,128,700	189,165	20,198	209,363	16.8%	1.8%	18.5%
1948	2,165,300	445,956	76,998	522,954	20.6%	3.5%	24.2%
1949	2,874,700	636,068	152,464	788,532	22.1%	5.3%	27.4%
1950	3,314,000	557,116	190,849	747,965	16.8%	5.8%	22.6%
1951	3,804,000	557,590	208,722	766,312	14.7%	5.5%	20.1%

Source: Ministry of Finance, "National Income and Tax Burden in the pre-post war era," MOF Overall Co-ordination Division Documents, 16–15.

in 1949 that the Shoup mission would bring about significant tax reduction.

During the occupation era, the tax burden had grown remarkably over the levels of the prewar period. During the FY 1949–50, when the Dodge Line was implemented and Shoup first arrived in Japan, the burden was at its postwar peak. Table 1 shows this, and that the tax burden in that year was roughly twice as large as it had been before the war – compounding the severe difficulties people faced because of wartime destruction and postwar inflation. In addition, the public distrusted tax authorities, especially after the occupation undertook strict tax collection under the surveillance of the Eighth Army. Under this pressure, small businesses went into bankruptcy.[61] Scandals concerning bribery and the corruption of tax officials, most notably the incident of the Urawa tax authority, came to light, one after another, prompting a nationwide anti-tax movement.[62] Thus, the Shoup mission visited Japan when its people harbored a widespread desire for lightening the tax burden and increasing the fairness of taxation.

Just before the arrival of the Shoup mission, a questionnaire aimed at independent businesses in Tokyo revealed that 80 percent of respondents knew about the mission's visit to Japan and 41 percent could correctly identify Shoup's name. The share of the respondents desiring tax reductions, such as raising the basic deduction, reached 41 percent, and 17 percent of respondents expressed a desire for fair tax collection by tax authorities.[63] The overwhelming victory of the Yoshida cabinet in a general election early in 1949 both reflected and stimulated the extensive desire for tax relief.

The desire for local autonomy figured only marginally in the public's understanding of tax burden. In another public opinion poll, 67 percent of respondents answered that they had never heard of the words "centralization" or "decentralization." Almost two-thirds (63 percent) of respondents expressed an interest in the municipalities' budgets; however, 87 percent had never participated in the public discussion of these budgets.[64] It seems clear that there was little popular support for, or interest in, strengthening local autonomy, despite the second report of the Shoup mission and the ORLA's political offensive against the MOF. The lack of public interest in and local government consensus behind this issue no doubt strengthened the resolve of the central government in resisting the Shoup recommendation for the equalization grant and thus contributed to its ultimate failure.

The Calm after the Storm. The central political problem of the equalization grant system was the inherent conflict between Shoup's "piling-up" process, which produced a fine-tuned value for the equalization grant, and the calculation of the central government, which was largely able to ignore the "piling-up" methodology. Political confrontation was almost inevitable between the "bottom-up" calculation of one set of stakeholders and the "top-down" calculation of the other.

Local governments and the central government had discovered the difficult political implications of the equalization grant system. In preparation for the FY 1952–3 budget, the MOF decided to try to bring an end to the confrontational negotiations. The MOF proposed a return to the system of local budgeting that the Japanese government had employed during World War II. It turned out that local governments and their representatives were in a receptive frame of mind. They had grown tired of the stressful clashes of 1950, had discovered the issues dividing local governments, and – perhaps most important – had learned that the technical challenges relating to calculation were often daunting and beyond their technical capability. Consequently, the community of local governments decided to accept the MOF's offer.[65]

To understand the mutual interest of central and local governments in the MOF's solution, it is necessary to understand the wartime system of local finance. In the wartime situation, the Japanese government undertook "macrofiscal assurance" for relieving local fiscal shortages. In the crucial tax reforms of 1940, the government introduced the distribution tax grant, which can be regarded as a predecessor of the equalization grant or local allocation tax grant.[66] In this system for local finance, the central government first determined the total funds of all kinds required for financing local governments. Next, it estimated local fiscal revenues based on the tax revenues from the previous year. To provide the additional funds required to meet local needs, the central government then allocated the additional revenues to be used by issuing bonds and creating the local distribution tax grant. The central government would grant permission to local authorities to borrow money from the national postal-savings fund. During wartime, however, the central government used the vast majority of available postal savings to buy bonds for national purposes. Local authorities could not expect much borrowing from this source to cover fiscal shortages. Consequently, the government appropriated additional funds through the local distribution tax grant. The total of this grant was determined by multiplying national income tax and cooperate tax revenues by a rate that the government could vary after a negotiation between the MOF and the Ministry of Interior, which was the predecessor of the Local Autonomy Agency. In other words, the MOF could strongly influence local fiscal needs; this obliged the MOF, however, to undertake macroassurance for relieving local fiscal shortages.

In following the World War II model when developing the budget for FY 1952–3, the Japanese government calculated the equalization grant as follows. First, the LPFC estimated local expenditures by adding new fiscal demands to the previous year's budget. Second, assuming the same level of equalization grant and bond issuance as the previous year, the LPFC calculated local fiscal revenues by estimating the increase in local tax revenues and predetermined subsidies from the government.

The difference between expenditures and revenues was called the "macrofiscal shortage of local public finance" and was the target of negotiation. The amount of bond issuance was decided according to the availability of postal savings. Then the MOF proceeded to negotiate with the LPFC, attempting to eliminate the fiscal shortage by increasing the equalization grant. In so doing, the MOF considered fiscal conditions in the nation as a whole and consulted with the LPFC over the level of local tax increase. This process was called "the macrolevel national assurance of local fiscal resources," and it was implemented under the rubric of the "local public finance plan" outlined in Table 2.

With respect to general fiscal issues, the LPFC found itself in sharp opposition to the MOF. As a result of the agreement to use the World War II model, however, the development of the plan for the equalization grant in FY 1952–3 became much smoother. As is shown in Table 2, the LPFC required a 130 billion yen equalization grant, an increase of 10 billion yen from the previous year. On January 18, 1952, the cabinet decided

TABLE 2. *Calculation of Local Public Finance by the Local Government in 1952 (Million Yen)*

Revenue in 1951	606,977
New fiscal demands in 1952	93,599
Sum	700,576
Tax	277,692
Equalization grant	120,000
Subsidies	150,376
Bond	40,500
Others	77,264
Sum	665,832
Revenue and expenditure	− 34,744
Way of compensation	
Increase in equalization grant	10,000
Increase in bond	15,000
Increase in tax	9,744

Source: *Wagakuni chiho zeizaisei seido no saikento* [*Reexamination of Japan's Local Tax-fiscal System*] (Tokyo: Kokkai Toshokan Chosa Rippo Kosa Kyoku, 1952), 46.

that it would impossible to appropriate an equalization grant of over 125 billion yen, and the cabinet conveyed this news to the LPFC. Within only five days, the committee and the cabinet had reached a compromise in which the committee accepted an equalization grant of 125 billion yen (an increase of 5 billion from the year before) and adjusted its estimates of local tax revenues upward by 5 billion yen, from 9.7 billion yen to 14.7 billion yen.[67] The two positions were quite close and agreement was reached within a very short period of time. We can trace this cooperative relationship to the prior budgetary agreement on compensation for the local macrofiscal shortage.

The budgeting of local government had suddenly become free of the kind of intense conflict that had characterized the determination of the FY 1951–2 budget. In 1953, after the formulation of the FY 1952–3 budget, the government, with the agreement of local authorities, dissolved the LPFC and turned over its responsibilities to the Home Affairs Agency, which had just been established in the national government. Many local governments had lost confidence in the LPFC, and felt they would probably be more effectively represented by a fully fledged cabinet-level agency. A year later, the government abandoned the label "equalization grant" and reinstated the term "local allocation tax grant," along with the formal practice of determining it by multiplying national tax revenues and a fixed rate. The Home Affairs Agency reserved the right to calculate basic fiscal demand and basic fiscal revenue, however, and regarded this right as an important tool for negotiating over the local allocation tax grant. Moreover, the total of this grant continued to be determined initially by calculating the macrofiscal shortage of local authorities in the local public finance plan. But the MOF continued to play the decisive role in the budgetary process. In other words, the Home Affairs Agency and later the Ministry of Home Affairs (currently the Ministry of Internal Affairs and Communications) had to negotiate with the MOF in determining the total of the local allocation tax grant. The size of this grant had been determined in advance by negotiation between central agencies, and the process that Shoup had regarded as ideal had been shattered.

CONCLUDING REMARKS

In the second report of his mission to Japan, Shoup wrote that "1951–52 will be a critical year for local finance," and "the way in which the problem is met will in large part determine whether local autonomy will develop." His prediction was eerily correct, but in a sense that was the opposite of what he had hoped. Ironically, the system of local finance that Shoup had proposed as a means of enhancing the rationality and stability of Japan's public finances actually intensified, rather than ameliorated, political conflict over taxation. Even more ironically, Shoup's recommendations prompted the Japanese government, supported initially by Dodge and his allies within SCAP, to reinforce and restore the system of intergovernmental finance that had been introduced during World War II.

We should note, however, that the adoption of the Shoup recommendation regarding local finance did not simply mean a return to the wartime intergovernmental fiscal system. The Shoup recommendation rationalized and codified at the macrolevel national assurance of local fiscal resources that had originated in the wartime period.

Japan's system of intergovernmental finance, as modified during the Shoup era and the period of reaction that followed, has survived to the present day, and has important implications for the contemporary fiscal situation. Since the wartime period, the central government has conducted a fiscal retrenchment policy at the local level. Without the Shoup modifications, the wartime fiscal system that allowed the central government to decide – unilaterally and often arbitrarily – the amount of local fiscal expenditures through the local distribution tax grant would not have maintained its legitimacy during the postwar regime. By following the democratic procedures, such as the requirement that the central government calculate local fiscal demands precisely, which Shoup had proposed in the local public finance equalization grant, fiscal control by the central government acquired legitimacy, enabling local public finance to become integrated into national economic policy.[68]

In addition, we should note the fact that, despite the canyon tragically dividing Shoup's idealism from Japanese reality, almost all of the points Shoup made have reemerged recently as highly salient within the contemporary discussion of fiscal issues in Japan. Among other issues that Shoup raised, the expansion of the value-added base of business taxation, the integration of personal and corporate income taxation, the assurance of local fiscal resources through the fiscal equalization system, the creation of an organization for effective negotiation between the central government and local authorities, and the principle of subsidiarity have once again become central matters of political concern. Does this mean that the public finance community of Japan is now caught up in a learning process that involves revisiting the experiences of the occupation era and reexamining Shoup's idea? The answer is "no." The Japanese government took advantage of Shoup's ideas and successfully built a democratically fashioned system of intergovernmental finance. In a different historical context, however, politicians may have tried to utilize Shoup's idealistic message for their own ends. No-one can predict whether or not Japan will follow the reform path Shoup laid out more than sixty years ago, but there is no doubt that study of the legacy of Shoup's policy choices will inform Japan's future choice of fiscal road.

Notes

1. Suzuki, T., *Sengo nihon zaisei shi* [*Postwar Fiscal History*], vol. 3–1 (Tokyo: Tokyo Daigaku Shuppankai, 1960); Miyajima, H., "Shoup kankoku no saikento" [Reexamination of the Shoup Recommendation], *Keizai Hyouron* 1972, vol. 21 (4), pp. 176–91; Hayashi, T., "Shoup kankoku to zeisei kaikaku" [Shoup Recommendation and Tax Reform] in Institute of Social Science, eds., *Sengo Kaikaku* [*Postwar Reform*], vol. 7 (Tokyo: Tokyo Daigaku Shuppankai, 1974), pp. 205–259; Jinno, N., "Shoup kankoku ni okeru shisan kazei" [Property Tax in the Shoup Recommendation], *Sozei ho kenkyu* 1984, vol. 12, pp. 26–65; Sekiguchi, S., "Shoup kankoku ni okeru hukakachi zei no genryu" [The Origin of the Value Added Tax in the Shoup Recommendation], *Local Tax* 1998, vol. 49 (9), pp. 107–45; Sekiguchi, S., "Gendai kigyo zaisei kaikaku no genryu" [The Origin of the Modern Corporate Tax Reform], *Shoken keizai kenkyu*, 2000, vol. 23, pp. 175–97.

2. Okurasho Zaiseishi Shitsu, *Showa zaisei shi* [*Fiscal History in the Showa Period*], vol. 16 (Tokyo: Toyo Keizai Shinposha, 1978); Hayashi, T., "Chiho zaisei iinkai" [Local Public Finance Committee], in Hidaka, H.i and Ouchi, T. eds., *Marx keizaigaku*[*Marx Economics*] (Tokyo: Tokyo Daigaku Shuppankai, 1978); Sekiguchi, S., "Shoup kankoku ni okeru zaisei chosei system" [Fiscal Equalization System in the Shoup Recommendation], *Chiho zaisei* 2005, vol. 44 (4), pp. 195–215.

3. Sato, S. and Miyajima, H., *Sengo zeisei shi* [*The Postwar Tax History*] (Tokyo: Zeimu Keiri Kyokai, 1979).

4. Since the 1970s, in the context of criticizing a Marxist historical view, Japanese researchers have regarded the Shoup recommendations as "exogenous variables" and discussed paying attention to the distinction between Shoup's theoretical consistency and its unreality. Basically this view overemphasized a return to the pre-Shoup era, however, and cannot concretely explain the relations in the wartime and postwar fiscal system. This view would not sufficiently describe policy makers' efforts to improve defects of the wartime fiscal system.

5. In the tax reforms of 1940, the government transformed the household tax into the inhabitant's tax, but the local tax rates in each municipality still varied greatly. By around 1965, local tax rates had converged more or less on the local standard rate prescribed in the Local Tax Act. Fumio Kanazawa argued that during this period the Japanese people had come to focus on equalizing the tax burden level rather than equalizing benefits from expenditures, and correctly cited this change as the key element in the formation of Japan's "egalitarian local tax system" (Kanazawa, F., "Byodo shiko gata kokka no sozei kozo" [Tax structure in the equality-oriented state], in Kanazawa, F., *Jichi to bunken no rekisiteki bunmyaku* [*Local Autonomy and Decentralization in Historical Context*] (Tokyo: Aoki Shoten, 2010), 61–2). The fiscal equalization system created in 1950 provided the institutional basis for making local tax rates consistent.

6. Imamura, T., *Showa okurasho gaishi* [*The Unofficial History of the Ministry of Finance in the Showa Period*] (Tokyo: Showa Okurasho Gaishi Kankokai, 1968).

7. Ikeda, H., *Kinko zaisei* [*Balanced Finance*] (Tokyo: Chuo Koron Shinsha, 1999), 221–5. In the general public, some voices praised the political responsibility of the Yoshida cabinet whereas others criticized the Democratic Liberal Party's populism and the making of unrealistic commitments. *Asahi shinbun* [*Asahi newspaper*], March 27, 1949.

8. Local Autonomy College, *Sengo jichi shi* [*Postwar History of the Local Autonomy*], vol. 13 (Tokyo: Jichisho Jichi Daigakko, 1988), 4.

9. *Sengo kojyutsu shiryo* [*Oral Documents on the Postwar Fiscal History*], vol. 8–3 (Tokyo: The Library of Institute of Social Science, University of Tokyo).

10. Ikeda asserted that he and Moss had invited the Shoup mission on the spur of the moment (Ikeda, H., *Kinko zaisei*, 259). Brownlee, on the other hand, has clarified that the appointment of the Shoup mission was part of a long-term plan devised by MacArthur and Moss to democratize the Japanese

tax and political systems. They both believed that democratization would not be inconsistent with increasing revenue. Much earlier, in the fall of 1948, they crystallized plans for the mission, and MacArthur shared his power with Moss, entrusting to him the selection of the members of the tax mission, which became the Shoup mission. Brownlee, W. E., "Shoup vs. Dodge: Conflict over Tax Reform in Japan, 1947–1951," *Keio Economic Studies* 2011, vol. 47, pp. 91–122.

11. Hayashi has pointed out that the details of Shoup's first report were highly theoretical, and many of the key ideas were original, with the result that Dodge had difficulty intervening in the process of tax reform (Hayashi, T., "Shoup kankoku to zeisei kaikaku"). In addition, see Brownlee, W. E., "Shoup vs. Dodge: Conflict over Tax Reform in Japan, 1947–1951."

12. Local Autonomy College, *Sengo jichi shi*, vol. 13, 90. The conscientious fact-finding tour of the Shoup mission strengthened popular expectations of a tax reduction, making it difficult for Dodge to ignore the first report (Ikeda, H., *Kinko zaisei.*)

13. *Yomiuri shinbun* [*Yomiuri Newspaper*], August 27, 1949. Why were the official estimates of Shoup and Ikeda so different? In calculating the reduction in tax revenues that was likely to occur in FY 1950–1, both Shoup and Ikeda tried to take account of the adoption of the Shoup recommendations as well as the economic conditions, such as the growth of national income, which would affect tax collections. They disagreed on some of their economic assumptions; however the main difference between the two in their reporting of tax reductions was simply their point of reference. Shoup compared the projected reduction in tax revenues between FY 1949–50 and FY 1950–1 with tax revenues in FY 1949–50. Ikeda, however, took the projected reduction in tax revenues and compared them with the tax revenues that he believed would be collected if the Shoup recommendations were *not* adopted. This way of calculation was repeatedly adopted during the high economic growth era by the Ikeda cabinet and this was called the "tax reduction based on the tax law." In the late summer of 1949, when analyzing Shoup's draft recommendations, the Internal Revenue Division (IRD) of SCAP decided that it actually preferred Ikeda's way of understanding the size of the tax cut. The IRD believed that "the revenue 'cost' of the adoption of the Shoup recommendations will be in the order of 100–150 billion yen," and worried that Shoup's 20 billion yen figure might lead to "popular misconception." On Ikeda's methodology, see *Asahi shinbun*, September 6, 1950; Local Autonomy College, *Sengo jichi shi* 1988, vol. 13, pp. 98. On the IRD's approach, see "Summary of the Shoup Taxation Mission Report By Chapters," September 10, 1949, pp. 3, and a more detailed analysis in H. Moss to W. Marquat, "ESS/IRD Analysis of Shoup Tax Mission Final Report," August 23, 1949, in File Folder 9 TR-60 Shoup Tax Mission, Box 7637, Record Group 331, National Archives and Record Service, Washington D.C.

14. Akaishi, T., "Nihon gata shohizei seisaku no shin seiji keizaigaku" [New Political Economy of Japanese Consumption Tax Policy], in Japan Public Finance Association, eds., *Zaisei Kenkyu* vol. 1 (Tokyo: Yuhikaku, 2005).

15. "Correspondence from Finance Minister Ikeda to Dr. Shoup," Local Autonomy College Documents 54–15, Local Autonomy Materials Room, Local Autonomy College, Tokyo.
16. "A Study of Local Tax Problem" and "On the Coordination between National Public Finance and Local Public Finance and the Revision of Local Taxation," Local Autonomy College Documents 54–15.
17. On the thinking behind Shoup's recommendation and the importance of the ideas of another mission member, Howard Bowen, see Chapter 8 of this volume.
18. Ishihara, N., *Shin chiho zaisei chosei seido ron* [*An Essay on the New Fiscal Equalization System*] (Tokyo: Gyousei, 2000), 41.
19. "Memoirs for Shoup Taxation," Local Autonomy College Documents 54–14, and "Written Representation on Tax Reform," Local Autonomy College Documents 54–10.
20. In its first report, the mission sharply criticized the central government for too frequently changing the percentage of tax revenues devoted to the distribution tax grant. Shoup may have assumed that the changes in percentage resulted from variations in the fiscal circumstances of the central government; however, as I will explain later – from a theoretical point of view – the central government could also vary the rate according to local fiscal demands. There is no evidence that Shoup understood the extent to which this might have been the case.
21. According to Genichi Akaiwa, who was an official of the Ministry of Foreign Affairs and an interpreter for the Shoup mission, Shoup requested that the Information Division of the General Headquarters (GHQ) translate all of the many thousands of written representations into English ("My Cooperation with the Shoup Mission," Local Autonomy College Documents 32–02). The LPFC submitted documents on various topics, including the distribution tax grants problem, to Shoup on May 16 (*Jiji shinpo* [*Jiji News*], May 16, 1949).
22. Okurasho Zaiseishi Shitsu, *Showa zaisei shi*, vol. 16, 404–5.
23. Multiplying the total by 70 percent, rather than 100 percent, reflected the preference of Japanese bureaucrats. Shoup approved this revision of his original proposal. "Shoup kankoku no koro no omoide" [Memories around Shoup Recommendation's Period], Local Autonomy Materials Room, Local Autonomy College.
24. In the following discussion, I rely extensively on "Current Situation of Public Finance and its issues – How was the Shoup Recommendation realized?" Local Autonomy College Documents 32–18.
25. Although its character was quite different, there was already a Local Public Finance Committee whose legislation had been established in January 1948. Thus the new committee, which supervised the equalization grant, was formally called the Second Local Finance Committee.
26. Personnel exchanges in these two organizations were, however, very close. For example, the section chief of the LPFC concurrently held the portfolio for the Local Autonomy Agency, and an executive of the Local Autonomy Agency played crucial role in negotiating with the LPFC. See Shibata, M.,

Jichi no Nagare no Nakade [*In the Trend of Local Autonomy*] (Tokyo: Gyosei, 1975), 69–70.

27. For details of this, see Local Autonomy College, *Sengo jichi shi* vol. 13, 342–8.

28. "Correspondence from Howard G. Bradshaw to C. S. Shoup, April 4, 1950," Suitland papers, vol. 3, no. 22, Policy Research Institute, Ministry of Finance, Tokyo.

29. "Correspondence from H. G. Bradshaw to C. S. Shoup, 5 May 1950," Suitland papers, vol. 3, no. 28. The fact that the Local Autonomy Agency officials went on loan to the secretariat of the LPFC, and the latter was almost occupied by the former, suggested this danger.

30. The MOF succeeded in insisting on the key technical requirement that the total of equalization grant would be determined in the annual budget ("Institution of Local Public Finance Equalization Grant," Aoki Papers 1–17, Policy Research Institute, Ministry of Finance, Tokyo). This secured the power of the government to reduce any "basic estimation" that the LPFC might recommend.

31. The total of the local distribution tax grant was determined by a certain proportion of national tax revenue, and by raising this rate in proportion to the increasing fiscal demands of local authorities the central government could compensate for a shortage of local revenue sources. In contrast, in the equalization grant, Shoup asked the central government to remove this link and take responsibility for guaranteeing fiscal resources to local governments through the "piling-up" method.

32. "Shoup kankoku no koro no omoide," Local Autonomy College, 27. The National Governors' Association submitted a written opinion to the Shoup mission complaining that the Shoup recommendation did not address the issue of how to guarantee that the powerful central government would actually accept, in practice, the outcome of the "piling-up" methodology used in deriving the equalization grant. August 1950, "Written Opinion on the Local Public Finance Reform (Written Opinion to the Shoup Mission)," Local Autonomy College Documents 54–18.

33. "Institution of Local Public Finance Equalization Grant," Aoki Papers 1–17.

34. In preparing for the second visit to Japan, Shoup displayed a particularly strong interest in prefectural conditions. On May 11, Shoup asked the staff of the IRD of SCAP to provide: (1) detailed information on eleven topics regarding local public finance including, for example gains or losses in tax revenues of individual prefectures in 1950–1 compared with 1949–50, (2) an examination of the finances of three or four poorer prefectures in different areas of the nation, and (3) the classification of prefectures with regard to their economic structure (in other words their agricultural and industrial characteristics). "Status of Shoup Projects as of 19 July 1950." File Folder: Shoup Projects, Box 7631, RG331, National Archives and Record Service.

35. This is the reminiscence of Ogita Tamotsu and Okuno Seisuke. Local Autonomy College "Local Tax and Local Public Finance under the Occupation," Local Autonomy Materials Room, Local Autonomy College. Both

were executive officials of the Local Autonomy Agency and they were in charge of the secretariat of the LPFC.

36. For example, on August 1, the LPFC submitted "Issues and Requests of Local Public Finance and Local Taxation," to the mission. Later that month, it submitted "Current Situation of Local Public Finance and its Issues – How was the Shoup Recommendation Realized?" On August 21, the National Governors' Association submitted its "Written Opinion on the Local Public Finance Reform (Written Opinion to the Shoup Mission)," Local Autonomy College Documents 54–18.

37. Okuno remembered that the "focus of the second Shoup mission for us was whether Shoup would permit us to improve the way of calculating the total of the Equalization Grant" ("Memories around Shoup Recommendation Period," Local Autonomy Materials Room, Local Autonomy College).

38. "August 1950, Written Opinion on the Local Public Finance Reform (Written Opinion to the Shoup Mission)," Local Autonomy College Documents 54–18.

39. Local Autonomy College "Local Tax and Local Public Finance under the Occupation."

40. The Democratic Liberal Party and Democratic Party had merged, founding the Liberal Party on March 1, 1950.

41. Local Autonomy College, *Sengo jichi shi* [*Postwar History of the Local Autonomy*], vol. 14 (Tokyo: Jichisho Jichi Daigakko, 1978), 155–9.

42. *Jichi Nippo* [*Jichi News*], September 15, 1950. Okano was a cabinet member, however, and he finally said that he had to follow cabinet policy.

43. This paper emphasized the irrationality of the MOF's policy, which would require local authorities to generate local fiscal resources by raising taxes and issuing local bonds. The paper called for an increase in the equalization grant by 24.3 billion yen (Local Autonomy College, *Sengo jichi shi* vol. 14, 205–7).

44. See "On FY 1951–52 Local Public Finance," Showa Okurasho Zaiseishi Shitsu, *Showa zaisei shi* vol. 16, 483–5; "Written Opinion on FY1951–52 Local Public Finance," Tax Bureau Papers 122–1, Policy Research Institute, Ministry of Finance; "On Local Public Finance Problems," Tax Bureau Papers 122–1; and "Local Public Finance Problems," Local Autonomy College, *Sengo jichi shi* vol. 14, 209–13.

45. "Local Public Finance Problems," Local Autonomy College, *Sengo jichi shi*, 209–13.

46. Local Autonomy College, *Sengo jichi shi* vol. 14, 214–7.

47. On the political circumstances in September 1950, see Brownlee, W. E., "Shoup vs. Dodge: Conflict over Tax Reform in Japan, 1947–1951," 114–20, and Murai, T., *Sengo seiji taisei no kigen* [*The Origin of Post War Political Regime*] (Tokyo: Fujiwara Shoten, 2008), 241–4, 289–93.

48. On October 18, Moss explained to Shoup some of SCAP's views on his second report, including his recommendations on local finance and the equalization grant. "Tax – Shoup Report," Box No. 10, File Folder: JAPAN 1950, The Joseph M. Dodge Papers in the Burton Historical Collection of the Detroit Public Library, Detroit.

49. E. Reed to W. Marquat, September 29, 1950, Japan 1950, Box 2, Joseph M. Dodge Papers, Detroit Public Library.
50. *Asahi shinbun*, September 29, 1950.
51. *Jichi Nippo*, October 24, 1950.
52. "Prime Minister's Office, Collection of Public Documents 85," Policy Research Institute, Ministry of Finance.
53. "Report on the Local Fiscal Situations of FY1951," Local Autonomy College Documents 39–3, 32. The case for the 105 billion yen grant is explained in "Documents on Local Public Finance of FY1950–51 and 1951–52," Tax Bureau Papers 105–31.
54. After this, the committee advised the prime minister and the Diet that it had reduced its recommendation from 135.9 billion yen to 121 billion yen. See "Reply on the Equalization Grant in FY1951–52," Local Autonomy College Documents 39–11; Local Autonomy College, *Sengo jichi shi*, vol. 14, 217–8.
55. In the correspondence from Dodge to Marquat on November 28, 1950, Dodge mentioned that the discussions with Japanese government officials on the FY 1950–1 supplementary budget and FY 1951–2 budget were extremely time consuming. Dodge explained that he put up with this at the request of Finance Minister Ikeda, who said that it would be helpful to him in his work with the cabinet and Diet. "Budget Negotiations," Dodge Papers, Vol. 12–17, Policy Research Institute, Ministry of Finance.
56. "Report on Local Public Finance in FY1951–52," Local Autonomy College Documents 39–3.
57. "Opinion on the Equalization Grant," Tax Bureau Papers 106–12.
58. "Resolution on Demanding the Central Government's Budgetary Provision for Local Public Finance," Tax Bureau Papers 106–24.
59. Okuno mentioned the lack of a rigorous base for this number. "We told Mr. Shoup about the forced donation and unreasonable taxation by local governments and then he asked us how much they totaled. Mr. Ogita suddenly said it would reach 40 billion yen and the Shoup Mission accepted this amount in the first report" ("Local Public Finance under Occupation").
60. Local Autonomy College, *Sengo jichi shi*, vol. 13, 209–11.
61. In the round-table talk of *Mainichi shinbun*, one participant pointed out that in assessing taxes for FY 1949–50, tax officers did not trust taxpayers' accounts and insisted that they had arbitrarily increased their reported incomes by 50 percent over what they had reported the previous year (*Mainichi shinbun*, July 19, 1949).
62. According to poll conducted by *Mainichi shinbun*, just 8.6 percent of the respondents believed that the government was able to expose tax evasion. *Mainichi shinbun*, July 10, 1949.
63. "Second Poll on the Tax Reform," Prime Minister's Office, http://www8.cao.go.jp/survey/s24/S24-07-24-03.html.
64. "First Poll on the Local Autonomy in 1951" and "Poll on the Local Autonomy in 1952," Prime Minister's Office, http://www8.cao.go.jp/survey/s25/S26-03-25-19.html, http://www8.cao.go.jp/survey/s26/S27-01-26-16.html.
65. Ishihara, N., *Shin zaisei chosei seido ron*, 65.

66. Correctly speaking, in 1940 the local distribution tax grant was introduced and contained both the return tax grant and the local distribution tax grant. The former returned tax revenues – that the central government collected for convenience – to local authorities, and the latter distributed a fixed rate of national tax revenue to local authorities for the purpose of fiscal equalization. In this sense, the distribution tax grant became the institutional basis for the postwar fiscal equalization system.
67. Regarding above exchanges between LPFC and the Cabinet, see "Binding for Local Public Finance in FY1952–53," *Local Autonomy College Documents* 39–75.
68. This relationship between national and local finance contributed to growing deficits during the 1990s, as the central government used the local government to finance public works projects and to take on greater debt. See Jinno, N. and Kaneko, M., *Chiho ni zeigen wo* [*Transfer Tax Resources to the Local Government*] (Tokyo: Toyo Keizai Shinposha, 1998).

14

Corporate Income Tax in Postwar Japan and the Shoup Recommendations

Why Did the Corporate Income Tax Become So High?

Satoshi Sekiguchi

INTRODUCTION

In framing tax reform in 2011, the Japanese business community and the Ministry of Economy, Trade and Industry (METI) negotiated with the Ministry of Finance (MOF) in the hope of reducing the effective corporate tax rate. The business community and METI argued that a rate reduction was necessary to ensure the international competitiveness of Japanese industry. The MOF was willing to consider such a reduction; however, it sought to secure alternative resources by enlarging the tax base. Finally, the Japanese government adopted a 5 percent reduction in the effective rate of corporate taxation.[1]

This was not the first reduction in the rate of corporate income tax during the postwar era. Considerable reductions took place during both the high economic growth era (1955–75) and the period from the latter half of 1980s to the present. During the first period, however, the government reduced the rates of both personal and corporate income taxation. It was not until the late 1980s that the government reduced the rate of corporate taxation relative to the rate of personal taxation, and thereby sought to increase the ability of Japanese corporations to compete in global markets. During the second period, however, the government accompanied the cuts in corporate tax rates with offsetting base-broadening measures. Thus, the reform in 2011, which involved no base-broadening, was unique in the post-World War II history of corporate taxation in Japan.

Behind the demand for corporate tax reductions was the wide recognition that Japan's legal effective tax rate and the ratio of corporate income tax to its national income or to its gross domestic product (GDP) are higher than in other major industrial nations. The relatively high ratio of corporate income tax to GDP was a long-standing trend. The corporate income tax was not relatively high in Japan during the 1950s, but has been so since 1960. Despite the high level of corporate taxation in Japan, the ratio of tax and social security contributions to its national income or GDP is lower than in other major nations. This chapter will explore the reasons why the ratio of corporate income tax to GDP became relatively high after the Japanese government adopted many of the Shoup recommendations.

SURVEY OF POSTWAR TAX REFORM AND THE CORPORATE INCOME TAX

The Shoup Recommendations: The Starting Point

The Shoup recommendations comprised the most comprehensive analysis and proposal for tax reform in the history of postwar Japan's tax system, and the enactment of most of the recommendations in 1950 represented a drastic tax reform.[2] Among the recommendations were proposals for revising the corporate income tax.[3] On the basis of the fictional theory of a corporation that holds that "fundamentally, a corporation is but a kind of aggregation of individuals, formed for the purpose of carrying on given business," and on the related assumption that capital gains will be fully taxed to those individuals, the Shoup mission made four central recommendations. The first was for a basic tax rate of 35 percent on corporate net income. Shoup assumed that this rate, which was at the level currently in force, was essentially a prepayment, or the withholding, of taxes owed by corporate stockholders. Accordingly, the second Shoup recommendation was that individual stockholders receive a credit against personal income taxes of an amount equal to 25 percent of the dividends received from corporations. Shoup intended that, under the tax code for individuals, individual taxpayers with marginal rates above 53 percent would be only slightly better off than if they had earned their profits through an unincorporated business, and those with a lower marginal rate would be only slightly worse off. In the mission's *Report on Japanese Taxation*, Shoup wrote: "There will still be some tax discrimination between businesses that are incorporated and unincorporated, but the amount seems to be tolerably small, and at least is not always in the same direction." Further, Shoup suggested that if the reformed system turned out to work smoothly, the Japanese government should consider adopting something similar to the more complex British system for equalizing the burdens on incorporated and unincorporated businesses. The third recommendation was the imposition of a 1 percent (6 percent in the case of family corporations) surcharge on the aggregate earned reserves of corporations. This was a kind of interest charge to those corporations that deferred dividend payments to the government and thus caused the deferral of individual tax payments on those dividends. Shoup hoped that this would reduce the discrimination against unincorporated businesses in their efforts to attract investment from the wealthiest taxpayers. Fourth, the Shoup mission recommended excluding from the net taxable income of corporations all dividends received from other taxable domestic corporations. The goal was to prevent the double taxation of intercorporate dividends, and thereby avoid discouraging the use of holding companies, subsidiary companies, or intercorporate stockholding. In offering these recommendations, the Shoup mission made two major assumptions. One was that the corporate income tax was would not be shifted forward to consumers. If this assumption turned out to be incorrect, Shoup favored repeal of the corporate income tax and the discontinuance of dividend credits.[4] The second was that Japanese corporations and the MOF would develop appropriate accounting and bookkeeping methodologies for the assessment of corporate income taxes.[5]

As Shiozaki Jun, who served as an official in the Tax Bureau of the MOF at that time, testified later, the ministry and the Japanese government accepted nearly all of the Shoup recommendations, and did not engage in any systematic examination of the operations and effects of a system of corporate income tax on the basis of the fictional theory of corporation.[6] In accord with the Shoup mission, the Japanese government sought to stabilize the corporate tax system and reduce its economic drag. At the same time, the government, also following the recommendations of the mission, sought to strengthen other parts of the tax system, particularly the self-assessed personal income tax. The mission wished to strengthen the personal income tax at the same time as turning the corporate income tax into a kind of back-stop for the personal tax. In light of these intentions, it is surprising how important the corporate income tax became within the Japanese revenue structure.

Table 1 shows that immediately after the adoption of the Shoup reforms, the corporate income tax accounted for 9.2 percent of total tax revenue and took 2.1 percent of GDP. The personal income tax, in contrast, accounted for nearly half (46.5 percent) of total tax revenue and more than 10 percent of GDP. Even as early as 1955, the corporate share

TABLE 1. *Trend in Tax Shares: Each Tax as a Percentage of Total Tax and as a Percentage of Gross Domestic Product (GDP)*

(Unit %)

		Shoup	1955	1960	1965	1970	1975	1980	1985	1990	1995	2000	2005
Tax	Individual income tax	46.5	28.6	20.0	28.4	28.0	35.0	35.6	36.8	38.9	34.7	34.1	30.3
	Corporate income tax	9.2	21.1	32.9	28.4	34.7	30.1	31.6	30.8	31.3	24.9	22.2	25.5
	Value–added tax	–	–	–	–	–	–	–	–	6.3	8.7	14.4	15.8
	Excise tax	36.8	38.8	36.1	32.6	27.3	21.7	20.7	17.8	10.6	12.7	12.6	12.7
	Property tax	7.5	11.6	11.0	10.6	10.0	13.3	12.1	14.6	13.0	19.1	16.8	15.8
GDP	Individual income tax	10.6	4.2	3.1	4.0	4.2	5.0	6.2	6.8	8.1	6.0	5.7	5.0
	Corporate income tax	2.1	3.1	5.1	4.0	5.2	4.3	5.5	5.7	6.5	4.3	3.7	4.2
	Value–added tax	–	–	–	–	–	–	–	–	1.3	1.5	2.4	2.6
	Excise tax	8.4	5.7	5.6	4.6	4.1	3.1	3.6	3.3	2.2	2.2	2.1	2.1
	Property tax	1.7	1.7	1.7	1.5	1.5	1.9	2.1	2.7	2.7	3.3	2.8	2.6

Note 1. Total tax is the total of national and local tax.
Note 2. Value–added tax, which the Shoup recommendations substituted for the business tax, is included in the corporate income tax.
Note 3. The Shoup column is based on the recommendation and not the Tax Reform of 1950.
Source: Author's calculations from the Shoup mission (1949) and *Fiscal and Financial Statistics Monthly*, various annual editions.

of tax revenues had more than doubled (to 21.1 percent) and took a larger (3.1 percent) share of GDP. Meanwhile, the importance of the personal income tax plummeted. Its revenue share declined to 28.6 percent, and it took only 4.2 percent of GDP. Table 1 reveals this shift even more dramatically.

Why did the corporation income tax as a share of total tax and GDP increase so dramatically, and remain high until the present day? Why did the corporate income tax in Japan develop so differently from the way in which the Shoup mission expected? To answer these questions, the remainder of this chapter analyzes the position of the corporate income tax within the whole tax system, and especially its relationship to personal income tax and consumption taxes.

General Survey of Postwar Tax Reform in Japan

The history of income tax reforms in Japan since World War II can be roughly divided into three periods. The period from the tax reforms in 1950, which were made on the basis of the Shoup recommendations, to 1965 constitutes the first period. During this time, economic growth caused continuous "natural" increases in tax revenue (revenues were growing because of the growth of national income and the upward movement of individuals through the progressive income brackets). During this period, the main issue for tax reformers was how much of this natural increase in tax revenue should be distributed to reduce income taxes. The period from 1965, when the Japanese government began issuing national bonds (also called construction bonds, reflecting their exclusive purpose) to 1975 comprises the second period. In this period, which was the latter half of Japan's era of high economic growth, the central objective of tax reform was still the reduction of income taxation. Several successive crises – the stock market crisis of 1965, the so-called "Nixon shock" in 1972, and the oil crisis in 1973 – increased the cumulative pressure on the issuance of national bonds, however, and consequently the emphasis of corporate tax reform moved from reducing the tax to increasing it.[7] The period from 1975 until the passage of a general consumption tax bill in 1988 constitutes the third period, and was marked by a complete change in key aspects of tax reform. This occurred because in 1975 the Japanese government began the issue of deficit-financing bonds to finance ordinary expenditures, and the MOF responded by paying less attention to providing tax cuts and more to developing general consumption taxation as a source of revenue.[8] In other words, the MOF adopted a strategy

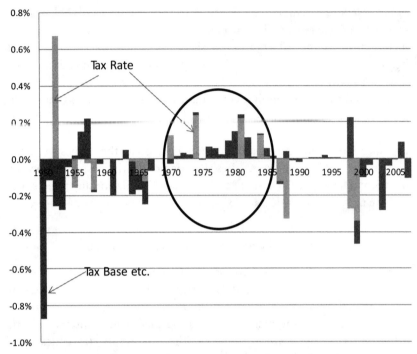

FIGURE 1. Estimated corporate income tax revenue by tax reform (as a percentage of gross domestic product). Note 1. Based on a normal year. Note 2. Local tax not included. Note 3. Corporate special surtaxes from 1992 to 1994 are excluded. *Source:* Author's calculations from various annual editions of the *Fiscal and Financial Statistics Monthly*.

of increasing corporate tax rates in order to persuade business leaders to accept a value-added tax (VAT).

Reform of Corporation Taxation: The Details

I now turn to the ways in which the Japanese government reformed the corporation income tax within its larger strategies of tax reform. Figure 1 suggests the relative importance of changes in tax rate and changes in the tax base within the corporate-tax reforms.

During the first period (from 1950 to 1965), the Japanese government reduced the corporate income tax along with income taxes in general. The most common method of reducing corporate taxes was through reductions in the tax base that were designed to stimulate investment in targeted industries. On these occasions, which usually resulted from initiatives led by the Ministry of International Trade and Industry (MITI), which became the Ministry of Economy, Trade and Industry in 2001, the usual pattern was for the government not to reduce tax rates at the same time as it shrunk the tax base. Conversely, in the less numerous instances of reductions in tax achieved through rate cuts, the government did not change the corporate tax base. The only exceptions to the tax cutting that characterized this period were a hike in the tax rate in 1952, and a gradual expansion of the tax base during the second half of the 1950s.

During the second period (from 1965 to 1975), the government sometimes attempted to increase revenues garnered by the corporate income tax by increasing its rates. This meant that corporate income tax rates moved in a different direction from the rates on personal income.

During the third period (from 1975 to 1988), the government halted the cuts in income taxes. In fact, it expanded the base of corporate taxation during the second half of the 1970s and then raised corporate tax rates during the 1980s. Interestingly, although the government did not increase the personal income tax after the beginning of the issuance of either the construction bonds in 1965 or the deficit-financing bonds in 1975, it attempted to increase the corporate tax in every year except one (1975) in the eighteen-year period from 1969 to 1988.

In the next section, I examine the reasons that explain why, during the period 1975–85, the government could increase the corporate income tax, and why the business community accepted the increasing dependence of the government on corporate taxes.

JAPANESE CORPORATE STRUCTURE AND ITS EFFECTS ON CORPORATE INCOME TAX REVENUES

International Comparisons

The amount of corporate income tax paid by corporations in any nation is determined not only by the structure of the tax code but also by the interactions between the corporate tax system of each country and the structural characteristics of corporations in those countries. For this reason, when discussing trends in corporate income tax revenues, it is necessary to examine the tax code and to have an awareness of the structural characteristics of corporations. To begin, I identify a few key elements of Japanese corporations by making international comparisons. To assist with this, Figure 2 shows direct corporate taxes (as a percentage of GDP) on the horizontal axis and internal reserves (as a percentage of GDP) on the vertical axis and indicates changes over time in various countries.

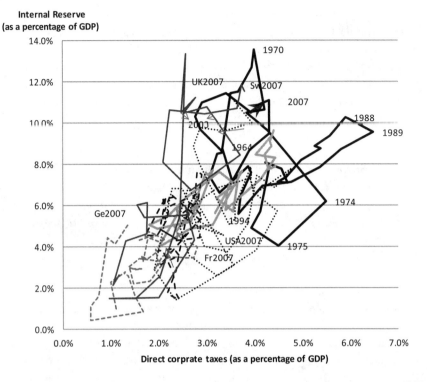

Internal Reserve
(as a percentage of GDP)

FIGURE 2. Trend of direct corporate taxes and internal reserves between 1960 and 2007. Note 1. Internal reserve = operating surplus + property income (received) − property income (paid). Note 2. 1960–95: System of National Accounts of 1968; 1995–2007: System of National Accounts of 1993. Note 3. Both calculations from the United States from 1995 to 1998 and Japan in 1995 are based on System of National Accounts of 1968. *Source:* Author's calculation from various annual editions of OECD, *National Accounts.*

It is immediately apparent that in the postwar period, Japanese corporations have paid relatively high corporate income taxes and consistently maintained relatively high internal reserves (with the exception of 1974 and 1975). In other words, postwar Japanese corporations have been subject to corporate income tax burdens at the same time as they maintained high internal reserves.[9] The high level of internal reserves was a major factor in the difference between the projected corporate income tax revenues in the Shoup mission's *Report on Japanese Taxation* and the corporate income tax revenues that actually materialized after the

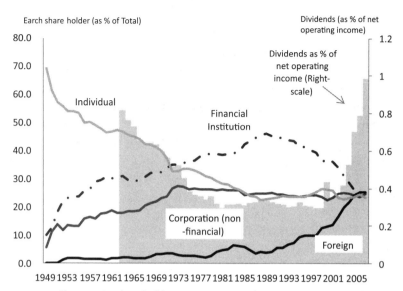

FIGURE 3. Changes in shareholder composition of Japanese corporations in the postwar period. Note 1. Data of net operating income and dividend are not available before 1963. *Source:* Author's calculations from the Features of Corporations from the *Perspective of Tax Statistics* (various annual editions) and the 2008 *Share Ownership Survey.*

adoption of the Shoup recommendations. The mission assumed that retained earnings would be far lower, and that tax payments in the form of taxes on dividends (instead of corporate taxes on profits) would be much higher than turned out to be the case. The ways in which corporations managed capital emerged as very different from those that Shoup expected. These differences were particularly prominent during the period on which this chapter focuses – from the late 1970s, when high-rate economic growth ended, until the mid-1980s. These differences turn out to be critical in explaining Japan's high, and increasing, levels of corporate taxation. In this section I discuss six of those key structural characteristics.

Cross Holdings among Japanese Corporations. The first characteristic factor that made the increase in corporate income tax possible is the pattern of cross-holdings among Japanese corporations. From the late 1970s through the mid-1980s, Japanese corporations made collective decisions to maintain extensive cross-holdings of shares. These decisions, in turn, limited the payment of dividends and increased corporate income taxes. Figure 3 shows changes in the shareholder composition of Japanese corporations in the postwar period.

Immediately after the war, the breakup of the *zaibatsu* (corporate conglomerates) under occupation reforms resulted in a large increase in the number of individual shareholders, however this number declined swiftly and steadily. The decline in individual shareholders intensified when it became possible, under a 1969 change in commercial law, to raise capital by issuing shares at market price (rather than book value). In spite of this change, even though the amount of capital paid in by shareholders was greater than the book value of their shares, corporations continued to pay dividends on the basis of the par value of shares.[10] At the same time, ownership of shares by banks and incorporated enterprises (business corporations) increased.

Three shifts in public policy advanced the process of increasing cross-holdings. The first was the introduction of a system that separated banking and securities. This system, adopted during the occupation, was created on the basis of America's Glass-Steagall Act. Under Japan's system of separating banking and securities, however, the ownership of shares by banks was not prohibited. The second policy shift was the 1965 adoption by the Security Bureau of the MOF of the practice of requesting corporations to acquire shares from individual investors during a market downturn. The third policy shift was the promotion of capital liberalization that began during the 1960s. This liberalization led corporations to respond by using cross-holdings of shares as a defense against hostile takeovers.[11]

To connect these patterns of cross-holding with changes in tax policy, we must first examine what impact the increase in corporate shareholders (caused by cross-holding shares among corporations) had on the payment of corporate dividends. To begin with, I examine changes in the ratio of dividends paid to net operating income; see Figure 4. Data concerning the ratio of dividends paid to net operating income are available only from 1963, however the ratio – that was initially high – declined in step with the drop in the number of individual shareholders. It remained steady, at low levels, when corporate shareholders remained stable from the mid-1970s through the 1990s, and then rose again in the 2000s. In other words, during the period of cross-holdings of shares among business corporations from the mid-1970s to the 1990s, dividends remained steady at low levels. Looking at these data alone, it appears that there is a relationship between high share cross-holdings and low dividend payments.

To draw clear conclusions regarding the relationship between the amount of dividends and the tax system, I turn to Figure 4. The bar graph (left scale) reproduces the percentage of corporate net operating

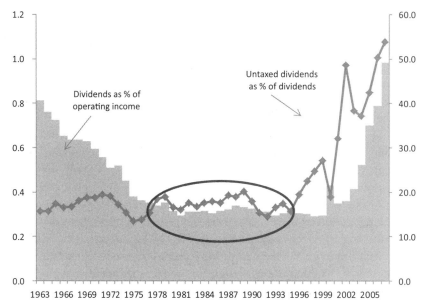

FIGURE 4. Dividends as a percentage of net operating income and untaxed dividends as a percentage of dividends. Note 1. Sales dividends ratio = dividends paid/sales × 100. Note 2. Untaxed dividend ratio untaxed dividends received/dividends paid × 100. *Source:* Author's cCalculations from the Features of Corporations from the *Perspective of Tax Statistics* (various annual editions).

income accounted for by dividend payments from Figure 3. The line graph (right scale) shows the percentage of total dividends accounted for by the dividends that corporations received that were not subject to taxation (the "untaxed dividend ratio"). It is apparent at a glance that the untaxed dividend ratio remained stable at low levels from the post-war period until the late 1990s, and then began rising.

The provision exempting 100 percent of dividends (excluding them from gross revenue) paid between corporations that the Japanese government introduced pursuant to the Shoup *Report* remained in place until the late 1980s.[12] Previous scholars have claimed that the tax burdens of large corporations that held the shares of other corporations had been reduced because of the provisions, introduced pursuant to the Shoup recommendations, which excluded the payment of dividends among corporations from taxable income. These scholars claimed that cross-holdings of shares among corporations facilitated the payment of dividends among corporations, and dividend payments that made use of the provisions excluding these dividends from total revenue increased. Despite this, the untaxed dividend ratio reveals no trend in which corporations made greater use of the Shoup reform provisions from the mid-1970s to the early 1990s, when cross-holdings of shares by corporations were stable.[13] These observations are in agreement with empirical research by Kunieda and Hotei, who pointed out that changes within the tax system between 1971 and 2001 had almost no impact on the dividend policies of Japanese corporations.[14]

There is a strong likelihood that the increase in corporate shareholders and decrease in individual shareholders, in conjunction with cross-holding of shares, led corporations to reduce dividend payments. It is difficult to conclude, however, with respect to the tax system and dividend policies, that there was a major impact on dividend policies in the form of higher dividend payments among corporations. In other words, during the period from the mid-1970s to the early 1990s, when corporate shareholders remained stable as a result of cross-holdings, it is more likely that cross-holdings of shares restrained the payment of dividends among corporations than that the tax system worked to encourage such payment of dividends. This conclusion has important implications for contemporary tax reform. Because outflows of capital from Japanese corporations in the form of dividends are low, corporations have sufficient margin to withstand modest increases in corporate taxes.

Methods by which Japanese Corporations Raise Capital. A second factor that contributed to the increase in corporate income tax payments from the late 1970s through the mid-1980s was the heavy reliance of Japanese corporations on bank loans for raising capital.

The primary method by which Japanese corporations raised external capital in the postwar period has been loans rather than the sales of securities. Loans had become the primary method of raising capital well before World War II. During the war, in order to impose capital controls in the wartime economy, the Japanese government imposed restrictions on dividends and limited the scope of securities markets. Concurrently, the wartime government maintained prewar policies of encouraging savings by keeping the tax burdens on interest income low. Meanwhile, the government encouraged the merger of banks, and the newly merged banks were exempt from the Act for Elimination of Excessive Concentration of Economic Power enacted during the occupation. These banks were the primary source for the provision of capital during the postwar period. As we know from Chapter 10, the Shoup mission wished to remove the privileged treatment of interest income, and proposed introducing the consolidated taxation of all income, including interest payments.

At the time, and even a decade later, some observers believed that the mission wanted to replace the banking-dominated capital system with a capital market focused on American-style security exchanges.[15] These observers noted Shoup's assertion: "The full taxation of bank deposits would have the beneficial effect of driving the wealthy investor out of bank deposits and into types of investment, such as the purchase of stocks and other equities, which the banks cannot well undertake themselves."[16] The intent of the mission was not to subsidize the development of stock exchanges, however, but to establish an even-handed approach to the taxation of capital markets, which would include both indirect and direct modes of finance.[17]

In any event, in 1953 the Japanese government returned to the prewar preferential treatment of interest income in the form of separate taxation without adopting any special policies at the time to promote the shift towards direct financing. (For details of this major departure from the Shoup recommendations, see Chapter 10.) It should be kept in mind that the restoration of preferential treatment for interest income under the income tax tended to keep interest rates artificially low, thereby contributing to the heavy reliance of corporations on raising capital via borrowing. The source of funds for such corporate borrowing was primarily individuals' savings in bank accounts and postal savings accounts.[18] The relatively low levels of interest paid, which the tax policy helped establish, meant that the amount of interest on payments included in losses for the purpose of calculating the corporate taxes of borrower corporations was relatively low. In addition, it meant that the corporate tax base was, correspondingly, relatively broad. The policy of promoting capital procurement through borrowing remained attractive during the period of high inflation in the 1970s.[19] Inflation reduced effective capital costs to corporations, and in addition provided benefits to corporate creditors. The benefits to creditors can be seen as an indicator of corporate strength in the form of unrealized income that is not reflected in corporate earnings.

The Employment Practices and Wage Systems of Japanese Corporations.
A third factor that made the increase in corporate income taxes from the mid-1970s through the mid-1980s possible was the ability of Japanese corporations to keep labor costs relatively low through hiring practices and wage systems. A characteristic feature of labor-management relationships in Japanese corporations during this period was a powerful role for company unions. Company labor unions helped to guarantee long-term employment for workers at the same time as enabling management

to control wages in a range that did not impact capital investment. In addition, it enabled management to exercise flexibility in the assignment of labor within the company.[20] Company labor unions engaged in fierce labor disputes during the 1940s and 1950s, and by the early 1960s – in exchange for recognizing basic management policies and management's right to control personnel assignments and wage determinations – secured wage increases in proportion to productivity increases and guarantees of lifetime, or long-term, employment.[21]

The practice of guaranteeing long-term employment provided benefits to both labor and management. Many Japanese corporations required worker proficiencies and work-related knowledge that were unique to each corporation, and wages, retirement benefits, and corporate pension payments were determined by the length of employment. As a result, long-term employment offered the benefit of stable wages to workers, and management could secure skilled labor that was loyal to the company and did not need to consider costs for midcareer recruiting and retraining.

In other words, the relatively low labor costs of Japanese corporations tended to expand the tax base for the corporate income tax.[22] For the corporate controls used to keep labor costs relatively low to be effective, they must be supplemented by lower personal income taxes. This issue will be addressed in the conclusion to this chapter.

Overseas Business Expansion by Japanese Corporations. A fourth factor that made the increase in corporate income taxes possible from the late 1970s through the mid-1980s was the relatively low level of foreign tax credit. Figure 5 shows the change in the ratio of foreign tax credits to corporate taxes owed before the deduction of tax credits. The foreign tax credit ratio shown here expresses the percentage of total corporate income taxes on worldwide income accounted for by tax payments to foreign governments.[23] It can be seen that although the foreign tax credit ratio in Japan averages 5 percent or lower from the early 1970s, it was substantially and consistently higher in the United States and United Kingdom; the ratios in these countries have been in the 30 percent range at their peak and in the 15 percent range more recently.

This result indicates that Japanese corporations pay a relatively low percentage of corporate income taxes to foreign governments and, consequently, pay a high percentage of taxes to the government in Japan, where the parent companies are based. To put it differently, Japanese corporations are characterized by relatively low levels of overseas business

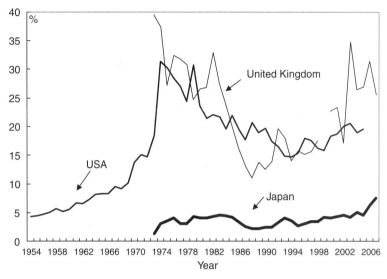

FIGURE 5. Trend of foreign tax credit ratio. Note 1. Foreign tax credit ratio = foreign tax credit/calculated corporate tax × 100. Note 2. Data before 1973 are not available in Japan. Note 3. Data before 1970 are not available and the item of foreign tax credit had became independent after 1988. *Source:* Author's calculations from various annual editions of *the Features of Corporations from the Perspective of Tax Statistics* (Japan), *Inland Revenue Statistics* (United Kingdom), and *Statistics of Income: Corporation Income Tax Returns* (United States).

operations in the form of foreign subsidiaries and branches compared to companies from the United States and United Kingdom.[24]

Unrealized Income from Corporate Assets. A fifth factor that made the increase in corporate income taxes possible from the late 1970s through the mid-1980s is high unrealized income (latent income) from corporate assets. Corporate income taxes on taxable income appear to be nominally high; however unrealized income, which is hidden behind the taxable income, is very high. As a result, it is possible that the effective tax burdens on corporations were low. The data in Figure 6 permit examination of this point.

In every year from 1970 to 1990 (with the exception of 1974), assets (land and shares, including cross holdings) in which corporations invested using some capital raised through internal reserves included unrealized income (latent income) and exceeded internal reserves. These data must be used with care.[25] Nonetheless, during the period covered in this chapter – from the end of rapid economic growth in the late 1970s to the

As a percentage of GDP

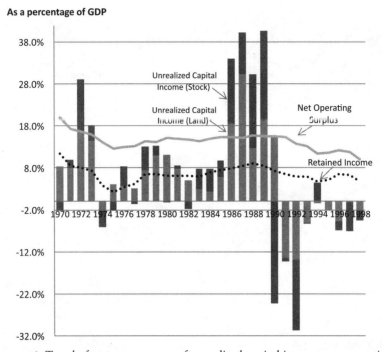

FIGURE 6. Trend of corporate sector of unrealized capital income, net operating surplus, retained income. *Note:* Data are 68SNA (benchmark year = 1990). *Source:* Author's calculations from the national accounts for 1998.

mid-1980s – the fact that unrealized gains exceeded internal reserves makes it certain that unrealized gains should be taken into consideration as an indicator of corporate strength. Put somewhat differently, the effective tax rate aggregated for the entire corporate sector would be much lower if unrealized income was taken into account.

The Relationship between Small Business Enterprises and Large Corporations. The interest large corporations had in securing excess profits through protective policies on behalf of small- and medium-sized enterprises (SMEs) was a sixth factor that helps account for the increase in corporate income taxes from the late 1970s through the mid-1980s.[26] Under the Japanese corporate system, the government adopted protective policies, such as tax cuts and regulatory requirements (especially import and price regulations), to enable SMEs to do business in otherwise unviable lines of activity. Originally, the main purpose of adopting these policies was to ensure employment, and the SMEs that were the immediate beneficiaries often developed strong cross-holding stock relationships as subcontractors to large companies, which were their partners in corporate conglomerates. The SMEs benefitted from reduced transaction costs through engagements in the long-term, ongoing, direct transactions with large corporations, and the large corporations benefitted from being able to use SMEs to absorb excess labor (including retirees) and to act as cushions during periodic downturns.[27] As part of this social contract, through the corporate income tax large corporations were willing to support the expansion of economically inefficient SMEs and related social welfare measures.[28] In other words, through the corporate income tax, large corporations accepted the burdens of that tax as a type of guarantee of the excess profits generated from the protective regulations concerning SMEs.[29]

THE MINISTRY OF FINANCE'S TAX REFORM STRATEGY: THE SEVENTH FACTOR BEHIND CORPORATE TAX REVENUES

The final factor that produced high levels of corporate income tax revenue between the late 1970s and early 1980s was a political strategy on the part of the MOF rather than an element of corporate structure. To understand the reasons for the adoption of this strategy by the MOF, it is necessary to explore further some characteristics of corporate structure in Japan – characteristics that tax policy helped create. More specifically, we need to examine the relationship between personal income taxation and corporate income taxation, because dividends to stockholders (which include corporations) and salaries and wages to employees are distribution income from corporations and, as such, are taxed by the withholding of personal income taxes.

The Personal Income Tax: A Tax on the Distribution Income from Corporations

Income Tax Trends. Table #2 shows two distributions for the period 1950–2007. The first is that of all income tax revenues between those collected by the self-assessed income tax and those collected by the withholding income tax. The second distribution is that of withholding-tax revenue by tax base (employment income, retirement income, miscellaneous income, capital income [interest and dividends], capital gains, and the income of non-residents).

One of the most striking trends that the table reveals is the decline in revenues from the self-assessed income tax following the Shoup reforms

TABLE 2. *Trends in Individual Income Tax between 1948 and 2005*

(Unit %)

	1948	1949	1950	1955	1960	1965	1970	1975	1980	1985	1990	1995	2000	2005
Self-assessment income tax	67.6	56.7	39.5	21.7	23.6	23.8	26.8	27.3	23.5	20.1	27.4	17.5	14.6	15.9
Withholding income tax	32.4	43.3	60.5	78.3	76.4	76.2	73.2	72.7	76.5	79.9	72.6	82.5	85.4	84.1
Employment income	31.6	41.4	57.8	68.1	56.8	55.8	49.3	52.7	59.1	62.7	46.8	58.0	55.7	60.3
Retirement income	0.3	1.0	1.3	1.4	1.3	1.4	0.8	0.7	1.0	1.5	0.7	1.2	1.6	1.8
Remuneration, fee, etc.	0.2	0.3	0.5	3.0	3.9	4.2	4.0	4.8	4.4	4.7	4.4	5.7	6.0	7.8
Interest and dividend income	0.4	0.7	0.9	5.2	13.0	13.1	17.8	13.5	11.3	10.1	17.9	15.6	18.1	11.0
Interest income	0.3	0.5	0.9	0.9	3.9	6.8	10.3	15.5	13.7	13.2	20.3	15.5	17.3	3.7
Dividend income	0.1	0.2	0.1	4.3	9.1	6.3	7.4	5.2	4.8	4.4	4.6	3.9	5.6	14.3
Δ in corporation receipts	n/a	n/a	n/a	n/a.	n/a	n/a.	n/a	-7.3	-7.2	-7.4	-7.0	-3.9	-4.8	-6.9
Capital gain of listed stock, etc.	n/a	n/a	n/a	n/a	n/a	n/a	n/a	n/a	n/a	n/a	1.9	0.8	2.1	1.5
Income of non-residents, etc.	n/a	n/a	n/a	n/a	1.4	1.6	1.4	0.9	0.7	0.9	0.8	1.1	1.8	1.7
Total revenue (unit: 100 million yen)	2,359	3,316	2,100	2,761	3,962	9,690	24,468	51,694	100,580	143,277	241,015	198,039	182,716	168,173

Note: Interest and dividend income tax withheld by corporations can be excluded after 1972.
Source: Author's calculations from the *National Tax Agency Statistical Annual* and *Features of Corporations from the Perspective of Tax Statistics* (various annual editions).

of 1950. In that year, the self-assessed income tax accounted for 39.5 percent of all income tax revenues. Although Shoup had wanted to strengthen the self-assessed personal income tax, ten years later the self-assessment system accounted for only 23.6 percent of all income tax revenues, and by 1995 this share had fallen to less than 20 percent. The decline of self-assessed revenues resulted from two trends: the increased reliance on separate withholding (separate in the sense of not requiring final tax returns) as a means of taxing capital income, and the decline in the number of self-employed owners of small farm businesses. Conversely, withholding accounted for 60.5 percent of income tax revenues immediately after the enactment of the Shoup reforms and then rose to 76.4 percent by 1960, and to 85.4 percent by 2000. This trend resulted from the increasing reliance on withholding for the taxation of capital income and the relative increase of employees compared to the number of the self-employed.

Organization of the system of accounting and bookkeeping, which the Shoup mission *Report* had suggested would be crucial, enabled the Japanese government to turn the withholding system into a success.[30] Let me take up the analysis of these trends in terms of the taxation of capital income, and then the taxation of earned income.

Reduction in Taxation of Capital Income. Other contributors to this volume have noted that the introduction of tax incentives for capital income immediately after the Shoup reforms represented an effort by the Japanese government to promote the development of financial and capital markets (see Chapter 10). This effort led to the collapse of not only the self-assessed, broad-based personal income tax but also the structure of corporate income tax that the Shoup reforms had introduced. In this section, I consider a key issue in this dual collapse: the relationship between the reduction of taxation on capital income and the use of external financing by Japanese corporations.

One component of capital income is, of course, interest income. Immediately after the Shoup recommendations, the Japanese government reformed the taxation of interest income by introducing a system of optional assessment (at a level of 50 percent in 1950) and separate withholding taxation (at 10 percent in 1953, 15 percent in 1967, and 20 percent in 1989). Perhaps surprisingly, despite the tax relief that this system of incentives provided for capital income, the portion of income tax revenues produced by withholding taxes on interest income (including that received by corporations) actually increased from 0.9 percent in 1950 to 13.7 percent in 1980, and then to 20.3 percent in 1990.[31]

It should be noted that most Japanese families hold their savings in the form of bank deposits, and consequently interest income is mainly earned by individuals through deposits in commercial banks and postal banks. In addition, however, these deposits can represent loans from banks to corporations. The restoration of preferential treatment for interest income under the individual income tax in the early 1950s lowered the cost to banks of acquiring deposits, thus "indirectly" encouraging corporations to raise capital through borrowing from banks.[32] To describe the basic situation differently, the increasing proportion of taxes raised from withholding interest income "indirectly" reflects a key fact about Japanese corporations: they raise capital mainly from loans from banks.

The other side of the coin is that after 1960 the importance of dividend income within capital income and tax revenues declined. Withholding taxation was applied to dividends (including dividends received by corporations) as well as to interest income. Immediately after the Shoup reform, the Japanese government restored a withholding system for taxation of dividends (20 percent in 1952, 15 percent in 1967, and 20 percent in 1978). In addition, the government introduced a system of optional assessment at a level of 15 percent in 1965, and separate withholding (final tax returns unnecessary) at the level of 10 percent in the same year. The ratio of withheld taxes on dividend income to total income tax revenues increased sharply between 1950 and 1960, but it then fell from 9.1 percent in the 1960 year to 7.4 percent in 1970. It remained relatively constant, at about 5 percent, between 1975 and 2000. This trend is consistent with the trend of dividends as a percentage of corporate operating income, which was discussed in the section on Japanese corporate structure and its effects on corporate income tax revenues.

The Reduction of Earned Income. It is well established that the transformation of Japan's employment system after World War II produced an increase in the number of recipients of employment income (salaries and wages). This alone should have led to an increase in the share of income tax revenues accounted for by earned income. The proportion of withholding of taxes on earned income (as a percentage of total personal income tax revenues) actually declined, however, from 57.8 percent in 1950 to 49.3 percent in 1970. It then increased only slowly, to 52.7 percent in 1975, before increasing more rapidly to 62.7 percent in 1985.

The decrease in the proportion of withholding of taxes on earned income from 1950 to 1970 reflects two changes: the shift from self-assessment to withholding in capital income, and cuts in income taxes on the wage income of middle-level salaried employees through increases in their deductions and decreases in their rates. This continued a pattern that the Japanese government had successfully established as early as 1950, in opposition to the thinking of the Shoup mission, by enacting a special deduction for employment income. The Shoup mission originally opposed such a deduction, but, according to Izumi Minomatu, who served in the Tax Bureau of the MOF at that time, Finance Minister Ikeda "petitioned Mr. Moss that it should be approved and [General] Marquat finally approved it. The United States has no employment income deduction and Dr Shoup did not want to introduce it in Japan; consequently, he was reluctant to accept the rate of 10%. However . . . Ikeda did not accept the severe rate and negotiated to increase the rate to 15%."[33]

The increase between 1975 and 1985 in the relative tax burden carried by employment income, which broke the trend that began in 1950, reflected a halt in tax cuts for earners of employment income coupled with the unlegislated tax increases associated with inflation-driven bracket-creep. Meanwhile, recipients of capital income not taxed by progressive rates escaped bracket-creep, thus raising the relative tax burden on earners of employment income.[34] Figure 7 shows the relationship between labor's relative share and the changing levels of the taxation of individual incomes over time.

It is obvious that the labor's relative share of GDP on the horizontal axis started at a relatively low level and increased gradually. Meanwhile, this relative share of GDP increases on the vertical axis, after income and social security taxes are deducted, reflecting the efforts of the Japanese government from 1950 to the mid-1970s to ease the burden of taxation on middle-income households.[35]

A desire to protect and enhance take-home earnings by reducing the burden of personal income tax therefore led to reductions of the income tax on labor income. The tax reductions for the middle class (mainly comprised of salaried workers) took the primary form of larger employment-income deductions and personal deductions. The Japanese government designed such reductions during the high economic growth period to enable taxpayers, especially members of the middle class, to experience the fruits of economic growth. Nevertheless, beginning in the latter half of the 1970s and continuing into the early 1980s, the Japanese government ceased its efforts to secure take-home earnings. The results of this policy shift appear clearly in Figure 7 as the sharp downward shift in labor's relative share on the vertical axis. It appears that the rising proportion of

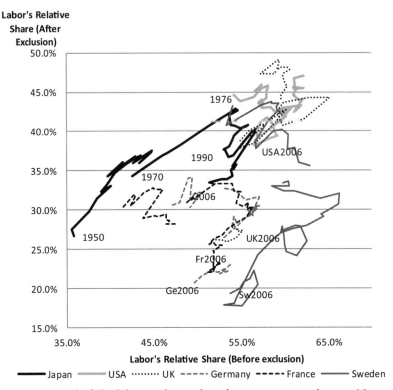

FIGURE 7. Trend of the labor's relative share between 1950 and 2006. Note 1. Labor's relative share (before exclusion) = compensation of employees/GDP. Note 2. Labor's relative share (after exclusion) = (compensation of employees − income tax and social security contribution in households)/GDP. Note 3. From 1950 to 1969: old SNA; from 1970 to 1995: 68SNA; from 1996 to 2006: 93SNA. *Source:* Author's calculation from various annual editions of the OECD, *National Accounts* and United Nations, *Yearbook of National Accounts Statistics*.

capital income increased the relative tax burden of employment income earners.[36] For the first time since 1950, labor's share of GDP before taxes stopped growing, and its share after taxes declined significantly. In other words, during this period it became increasingly difficult for corporations to contain personnel costs through the conventional mechanism of cutting personal income taxes.

The Tax Bureau of the Ministry of Finance and the Business Community

The seventh, and final, factor that made the increase in corporate income taxes from the late 1970s through the mid-1980s possible was the political strategy of the Tax Bureau of the MOF concerning the adoption of a general consumption tax.

As discussed in the section on the reform of corporation taxation, reforms of corporate income tax were implemented in conjunction with increases in the tax rate in 1952 (¥19.1 billion), 1970 (¥75.2 billion), 1974 (¥352 billion), 1981 (¥640 billion), and 1984 (¥414 billion). One feature of the tax increases since 1974 was the expansion of the tax base through the abolition of special taxation measures when the tax rates were raised. Another feature was the tax increase following the issuance of deficit-financing bonds in 1975. Below, I examine the intentions of the Tax Bureau from the 1970s through the mid-1980s with regard to raising corporate income taxes, and the reaction of the business community.

Increasing the Corporate Income Tax versus Imposing a General Consumption Tax. Even during the period of high-rate economic growth, the business community opposed increases in the corporate income tax. This was the case in 1970, during one of the major efforts to reform corporate taxation following the Shoup era. During this reform episode, a great deal of popular support emerged for raising tax rates to acquire funds for public investment.[37] The Tax Bureau favored the accomplishment of this by lowering personal income taxes while raising corporate income taxes. Hosomi Takashi, then head of the Taxation Bureau (August 1968 to June 1971), described the hostility of the large corporations, represented by the Japanese Federation of Economic Organizations:

Vice Minister Sumita and I were constantly attacked by the Japan Federation of Economic Organizations . . . and were told things like "You have no feelings" and "You're biting the hand that fed you." This was the first tax increase since [the 1952 tax increase by] Finance Minister Ikeda. We went on to explain that it was necessary to prevent the private economy from overheating and to supplement lagging social capital from public finances, and this was a necessary source of funds for maintaining sound finances. Eventually, the Federation – after all, they were adults – agreed that we might have been right, and the tax increase passed.[38]

What is noteworthy about the process of tax reform in 1970 is that this was the first time since the Shoup reforms that leaders of the Japanese government considered adopting a general consumption tax as an alternative to the corporate income tax. In fact, in March 1970, Prime Minister Fukuda Takeo declared: "We want to increase indirect taxes in response to the decrease in direct taxes and the demand for funding." Hosomi explained the background to this as follows:

At the time of the corporate income tax increase, I was spoken very poorly of by Tanaka Kakuei, the secretary-general of the Liberal Democratic Party. I was encouraged on by the Chairman of the Policy Research Council Mizuta [Mikio], [a former Minister of Finance], who was by my side and said, "It's time you gave up on taxes that are going to anger to secretary-general, such as the corporate tax, and use something like the value added tax in France." When I asked him if he was for the value added tax, he said, "Sure, if you propose it, I will support it." When we spoke about it to [Prime Minister] Fukuda, he adopted it as a way out.[39]

Despite this, there was no significant support among the general public or the business community to carry forward the idea of introducing VAT.

Changes in the Tax Bureau's Thinking.[40] While Hosomi was willing to entertain the idea of a VAT, few others within the Tax Bureau supported it. The dominant thinking within the Tax Bureau was to maintain, or even enhance, the role of the income tax at the core of the national tax system. Even in the 1970s, however, other bureaus within the MOF, such as the Budget Bureau, found a general consumption tax appealing. Following the issuance of deficit-financing bonds in 1975, even experts within the Tax Bureau began to consider seriously the possibility of creating a national revenue system that had two primary taxes – the income tax and a general consumption tax. In January 1979, the cabinet adopted an outline of a plan for tax reform that featured the introduction of a general consumption tax in fiscal 1980. Hostility towards the idea of a general consumption tax emerged during the general election in the fall of 1979, however, and toward the end of the year the Diet, in a special fiscal-reform session, ended it. Having been defeated, the Tax Bureau turned to base-broadening reform of the income tax, and especially the corporate income tax, in an effort to promote horizontal equity and to raise revenues.

The Tax Reform of 1981. In 1981, the Tax Bureau sought to raise taxes by as much as possible within the existing framework of income taxation and special consumption taxes. Through base-broadening, it hoped to make up for a 2 trillion yen reduction in government bonds. The Bureau concluded that if the base-broadening was not sufficient, adopting a general consumption tax was the only practical alternative.[41] The government's proposal was an increase in the corporate income tax rate from 40 percent to 42 percent and, similar to the 1970 and 1974 tax reforms, the government hoped to accomplish the increase without any wide-ranging discussion regarding its purpose. The government described the purpose of the act as simply "reconstructing public finances," by which it meant reducing deficits and deficit bonds.[42] In the middle of

March 1981, however, as the tax reform bill – which was of unprecedented scale – made its way through the Diet and seemed likely to pass, a movement in direct opposition to the tax increases suddenly emerged. For the first time in the postwar era, all of the major organizations representing Japanese corporations joined together.[43] The Japan Federation of Economic Organizations, the Japan Federation of Employers' Associations, Japan Association of Corporate Executives, and the Japan Chamber of Commerce and Industry all requested that the government drop its plans for corporate tax increases. They insisted on "fiscal reconstruction without tax increases."[44]

The Tax Reform of 1984. Calls for reconstruction of public finances – that is to say, budget balancing – without tax increases continued into the early 1980s. These calls were joined by contradictory calls for tax relief for wage and salary earners, who faced the problem of unlegislated tax increases produced by inflation eroding the value of exemptions and causing bracket-creep. The result, in 1984, was the reduction of taxes by 760 billion yen. The Diet increased the standard deduction, the spousal exemption, and the dependent exemption by 40,000 yen each.[45] In addition, the deduction for employment income was raised for the first time in ten years.

The Tax Bureau believed that the 1981 reforms had exhausted the only practical ways of raising revenue through increases in specific consumption taxes. To provide the funds for personal income tax reductions, therefore, the Tax Bureau instead decided to rely on increases in the corporate income tax. The Tax Bureau was confident that corporations had the capacity to pay the additional taxes.[46] Umezawa Setsuo, then head of the Tax Bureau (June 1982 to June 1985), made the following comment regarding this point:

> It's true that the result was the highest corporate income in the post-war period, but the mid-term proposal by the Tax Commission in 1983 implied that corporate tax rates were at appropriate levels, but in the midst of severe fiscal circumstances, there was still a margin to increase them further. The Tax Bureau used this as a starting point. And another thing, I talked with Japan Federation of Economic Organizations personnel at the time. At that time – let me emphasize, at that time – we claimed that even if tax rates were raised by one or two points, based on the status of Japanese businesses, there would be no impact on their international competitiveness or capital investment.[47]

The business community, however, led by the Japan Federation of Economic Organizations, mounted fierce opposition, arguing for "fiscal reconstruction without tax increases." Umezawa explained: "The business community was strongly opposed, but the reasons for the opposition, more than the effects on competitiveness or capital investment...had to do with...a sense of crisis concerning future tax increases."[48] The Tax Bureau insisted that the business sector accept some increase in the corporate income tax but in the end agreed to only a temporary (two-year) increase in the rate.[49] The Tax Bureau took its firm stand on the need to rely heavily on corporate income taxation in order to convince the business community that in the long run it would have to accept a tax increase it did not like. Umezawa later wrote that "We sought the understanding of the business community to show that the current tax system was beyond hope. This is why the Tax Bureau didn't agree to these financing measures until the end."[50]

The Tax Bureau political strategy succeeded. In July 1985, as an alternative to raising the corporate income tax, the business community decided to support the general consumption tax proposed by the Nakasone administration. Three years later, in 1988, in exchange for the introduction of the value-added tax, the business community achieved a reduction in the corporation income tax.

CONCLUSION: REFLECTIONS ON THE SHOUP LEGACY

This chapter has discussed the factors that contributed to the large, and often increasing, size of the corporate income tax in post-World War II Japan as a percentage of GDP (and of total taxation). At the same time, it elucidated the differences between actual conditions and the assumptions of the Shoup recommendations concerning corporate income taxes. Particular consideration was given to the features of Japanese corporations, the political and economic relationships involved in the reform of personal income taxes, the reform of corporate income taxes, and the introduction of a general consumption tax. Shoup regarded corporate income taxes as primarily a withholding mechanism for capital income owed under the personal income tax. The reality, however, was that the personal income tax collapsed as a means of taxing capital income, that the rates at which Japanese corporations have accumulated internal reserve have far exceeded the rates experienced in other modern nations, and that corporate income taxation in Japan has become a central instrument in the larger search for social stability within the political economy. In the process, the discussion within Japan of reform of the taxation of corporations has become detached from discussion of the reform of personal income tax.

The core of Japan's post-World War II financial system has been the dependence, sustained by public policy, of Japan's corporations on internal reserves and bank loans, rather than equity shares, for their capital needs. The main banks have been at the center of power within this system, leading in the coordination of the operations of the corporate system. The main banks have exercised their oversight through the process of lending capital to affiliated corporations, and large corporations among those borrowers have, in turn, coordinated the conduct of business by smaller corporations through a complex process of cross-holding shares.

Some aspects of the tax system may have played major roles in maintaining this financial system. The favored treatment of interest income within the Japanese system of personal income tax strengthened the central position within capital markets of individual savings and the banks that held those savings and loaned them to, or invested them in, other corporations. Under uncertain circumstances, the tax exemption of intercorporate dividends may have encouraged the cross-holding of shares.

At the same time that corporations profited from relatively low capital costs, they profited from the relatively low wages and salaries they paid their employees. These employees, however, faced relatively high levels of taxes under the personal income tax, which since the period of the Shoup reforms had turned into a tax focused on labor income. To sustain this system politically, the Japanese government compensated for the low taxation of capital income under the personal income tax by imposing relatively low taxes on labor income and relatively high taxes on corporate income.

Following the 1950 adoption of the Shoup recommendations, tax reform turned to providing favors for capital income under the personal income tax. The success in doing so then spurred reforms focused on balancing the tax burdens between capital income and property income, on one hand, and labor income, on the other. In other words, after the Japanese government separated personal income tax from corporate income tax, an effort to balance the tax burden between wage earners and the recipients of capital income became a staple of income tax reform. Thus, there has been an intimate relationship, within Japan's political economy, between two of its most distinctive features – the highest rates of corporate internal reserves among the advanced industrial nations, and the highest rate of taxation of corporate income among those nations.

It hardly needs saying that the process of securing a balance between capital income and labor income differs dramatically from what the architects of the Shoup recommendations envisaged.[51] Under the Shoup recommendations for the personal income tax, all types of income – capital income, capital gains, and labor income – would be taxed at the same rate providing horizontal equity. And, there would be an ongoing effort to integrate the taxation of dividends under the personal income tax with the corporate income tax.

The post-Shoup method of securing a balance will, however, be increasingly difficult to sustain in the future as a consequence of the weakening of the base of the personal income tax resulting from Japan's low birthrate and aging population, and the weakening of the base of the corporate income tax resulting from globalization pressures. Perhaps some new way of seeking tax balance will be required. Perhaps the base-broadening ideals that lay behind the Shoup recommendations might rise to again serve as a standard.[52] One thing that is clear concerning the impact of the Shoup recommendations, however, is that throughout the postwar period Japanese tax experts have constantly employed them in evaluating the Japanese tax system. In this sense, the Shoup recommendations have reigned as a landmark achievement.

In its 2011 tax reforms, the Japanese government lowered the corporate income tax rate while encouraging business leaders to use the resulting benefits to support national investment and increase employment. This tax reduction might be seen as contributing to the process of returning to the corporate income tax revenue structure contemplated by the Shoup recommendations. The lower corporate rates are more in line with what Shoup recommended, and a decrease in corporate income tax revenues may be reflected in higher personal income tax revenues in conjunction with wage increases. To date, however, the debate over corporate tax reform has not revealed a serious concern with the relationship between corporate income taxation and personal income taxation in either a technical sense or in the sense of its role in the Japanese social contract. Instead, debates have focused on the general consumption tax versus personal and corporate income tax from the perspective of securing revenue sources. This chapter has sought to contribute to a broadening of the debate over contemporary tax options to the larger issues surrounding the development of Japan's political economy since World War II.

Notes

1. The corporation tax rate was reduced from 30 percent to 25.5 percent for the fiscal years beginning on or after April, 1 2012, so the effective tax rate (including the local tax rate) was changed from 40.69 percent to 35.64 percent. At the same time, however, in order to increase tax revenue for financing post-earthquake reconstruction, the special reconstruction corporation tax

was imposed for three years. Consequently, until March 31, 2015, the corporation income tax will increase from 25.5 percent to 28.05 percent and the effective tax rate (including the local tax rate) will increase – from 35.64 percent to 38.01 percent.

2. Sato, S. and Miyajima, H., *Sengo zeisei shi* [*History of the Post-war Tax System*] (Tokyo: Zeimu Keiri Kyōkai, 1990), 1–2.; Kaneko, H., *Sozei hō* [*Tax Law*] (Tokyo: Kōbundō, 2010), 54–60.

3. Shoup Mission, *Report on Japanese Taxation* (Tokyo: General Headquarters Supreme Commander for the Allied Powers, 1949), 105–114.

4. Shoup, C. S., "Tax Reform in Japan", in National Tax Association, ed., *Proceedings of the National Tax Association* (New York: National Tax Association, 1949), 410. In the *Report*, Shoup did not present any argument regarding the shifting of corporate income tax. On September 21, 1949, however, just after he came back to United States, he delineated his views on this issue at the annual meetings of the National Tax Association.

5. Author has discussed the impact of the Shoup recommendations on the accounting system of Japan. See Sekiguchi, S., "Sengo nihon no zeisei to kaikei no kosyo katei" [The Post-war Japanese Tax System and the Process of Accounting Negotiations: From the Perspectives of the Shoup Recommendations and the Ministry of Finance], in Shibuya, H., Maruyama, M., and Ito, O., eds., *Shijōka to amerika no impact* [*Marketization and the Impact of America*] (Tokyo: University of Tokyo Press, 2001).

6. Yoshikuni, J., ed., *Sengo hōjin zeisei shi* [*History of Post-war Corporate Taxation*] (Tokyo: Zeimu Kenkyūkai, 1996), 812. Shiozaki was later (1965–7) director of the Tax Bureau.

7. The policy of liberalizing stock market regulations, which expanded gradually from July 1967 until May 1973, also played a role in those tax reform debates.

8. Mizuno, M., *Zeisei kaisei gojūnen* [*Fifty Years of Tax Reform*] (Tokyo: Ōkura Zaimu Kyōkai, 2006), 299.

9. In this comparison, it is necessary to take into consideration the statistical limitations of national accounts. In other words, we need to consider the facts that profitable and unprofitable businesses are totaled when corporate income is calculated, that "enterprise taxes" (local Japanese taxes on business income) are not included in direct corporate taxes, and that my calculations are based only on data from 1973 and later.

10. Yoshikuni, J., ed., *Sengo hōjin zeisei shi*, 822, 825.

11. The introduction of shares with restrictions on transfers imposed in the articles of association in accordance with revisions to the Commercial Code in 1966 is another reflection of this era.

12. In 1989, the government reduced the percentage of intercorporate dividends not subject to taxation to 80 percent. In 2002 the government further reduced this to 50 percent. These were significant tax reforms designed to expand the taxation base of corporate income tax.

13. A tendency for the amount of dividends received – excluded from gross revenue – to increase as the scale of capital increases can be seen. More detailed empirical research is therefore needed. It is noteworthy that the payment of dividends became more active in the late 1990s, when the tax system was

reformed to include the payment of dividends among corporations in the tax base.

14. Kunieda, S. and Hotei, M., "Nihon Kigyō no haitō seisaku to zeisei" [Dividend Policies of Japanese Corporations and the Tax System], in Nihon zaisei gakukai [Japan Institute of Public Finance], ed., *Zaisei saiken to zeisei kaikaku* [*Fiscal Reconstruction and Tax Reform*] (Tokyo: Yuhikaku, 2008).

15. Suzuki, T., "Shoup kankoku to shihon chikuseki no mondai" [The Shoup Recommendations and Issue of Capital Accumulation], *Keizaigaku Ronshū* [*Collected Essays in Economics*] 1950, vol. 19 (3–4), pp. 22; Ide, F., *Kindai nihon zeisei shi* [*History of Japan's Modern Tax System*] (Tokyo: Seikei dokuhon sha, 1961), 161.

16. Shoup Mission, *Report on Japanese Taxation*, 71.

17. Miyajima, H., "Shoup kankoku no saikentō" [Re-examination of the Shoup Recommendations], *Keizai Hyōron* [*Economic Critic*] 1972, vol. 21 (4), pp. 189–190, 191; Hayashi, T., "Shoup kankoku to zeisei kaikaku" [The Shoup Recommendations and Tax Reform], in Tokyo daigaku shakai kagaku Kenkyūjyo [University of Tokyo, Institute of Social Science], ed., *Sengo kaikaku 7: Keizai kaikaku* [*Post-War Reform No. 7: Economic Reform*] (Tokyo: University of Tokyo Press); Hayashi, T. and Jinno, N., *Nihon zeisei no hensen* [*Changes in the Japanese Tax System*] (Tokyo: Ministry of Finance Fiscal and Financial Institute, 1986).

18. Ikeo Kazuto states, "It appears that a portion of the rent generated as a result of deposit interest rate regulations spilled over from bank departments to corporate departments." (Ikeo Kazuto, "Sengo nihon no kinyu system no keisei to tenkai, soshite retsuka" [Formation, Development, and Decline of the Post-War Japanese Financial System], *Financial Review*, 2001, vol. 54, p. 9.

19. Atoda, Hashimoto, Maekawa, and Yoshida state: "during the period of rapid economic growth, price factors had a greater impact on investment costs than tax or interest rate related factors. But as markets were liberalized and globalized, the effect of interest rates, which more easily reflect developments in capital markets than prices, became greater." (Atoda, N., Hashimoto, K., Maekawa S., and Yoshida, Y., "Nihon no Syotokukazei wo furikaeru" [Looking Back on the Japanese Income Tax], *Financial Review*, 1999, no. 50, p. 60).

20. Tsunekawa, K., *Kigyō to kokka* [*Corporations and the State*] (Tokyo: University of Tokyo Press, 1996), 185.

21. Tsunekawa, *K. to kokka*, 204.

22. In conjunction with the tendency for large corporations to keep labor costs relatively low, it is necessary to take fringe benefits into consideration.

23. In Japan, tax reform in 2009 introduced the foreign dividend exclusion system, which is called "the territorial system." See Masui, Y., Yuko, M., *Kokusai sozei hō* [International tax Law] (Tokyo: University of Tokyo Press, 2010).

24. Points that must be kept in mind when drawing conclusions on the basis of these data are that investment formats, such as direct overseas investment and

indirect investment, and methods of income transfers, such as the return of income from foreign subsidiaries, are ignored. In addition, it is possible that in some cases Japanese corporations operating abroad may have understated their overseas profits. Although the foreign tax credit was established in 1953, Japanese tax statistics are only available from 1973, and data from the United Kingdom are lacking prior to 1970. Nonetheless, these reservations probably should not change the conclusion that the expansion of overseas business by Japanese corporations was relatively low, resulting in the relatively low payment of corporate income taxes to foreign governments, and therefore the amounts of corporate income tax payments to the Japanese government were high.

25. The amounts of unrealized income shown here are from national economic accounting, not tax statistics. As a result, there are various limitations including the facts that unrealized income is not the difference between the acquisition price of an asset and the market value at the end of the fiscal term, but the difference between the market values at the end of the prior fiscal term and the end of the current fiscal term; that not all assets are readily salable; and that the distribution of unrealized income according to business scale and industry within the corporate sector is uncertain.

26. Miyajima, H., "Hōjin zei kaikaku no hōkō sei" [The Direction of Corporate Tax Reform], in Nihon sozei Kenkyū Kyōkai [Japan Tax Association], ed., *Sozei Kenkyū taikai: dai 46 kai taikai [Records of the Taxation Study Group: Conference No. 46]* (Tokyo: Japan Tax Association, 1995).

27. Calder, K. E., *Crisis and Compensation-Public Policy and Political Stability in Japan* (Princeton: Princeton University Press, 1988), 314–15.

28. Calder, K. E., *Crisis and Compensation-Public Policy and Political Stability in Japan*, 200–2.

29. Calder, K. E., *Crisis and Compensation-Public Policy and Political Stability in Japan*, 465–6.

30. Sekiguchi, S., "Sengo nihon no zeisei to kaikei no kōsyō katei".

31. According to the estimate by Miyajima, the tax relief was substantial during the late 1970s and early 1980s. The untaxed interest income received by individuals produced by interest and dividend income received by that individual was 61.1 percent of their total interest and dividend income in 1978, and rose to 68.3 percent in 1983. Miyajima, H., *Sozeiron no tenkai to nihon no zeisei [Development of Tax Theory and the Japanese Tax System]* (Tokyo: Nihon Hyoron sha, 1986), 146.

32. The taxing of interest is a bit more complicated in reality because in Japan interest payments and dividends received by corporations are taxed initially by withholding income tax but taxed finally by the corporation income tax, with corporations receiving a tax credit for taxes previously withheld. The line labeled "△ in corporation receipts" in Table 2 reveals the size of the tax credits given for withheld taxes on interest and dividends.

33. Izumi, M., Yoshikuni, J., and Takagi, F., "Sengo sangyō shi e no syōgen (Dai 39 kai)" [*Post-war Industrial History Evidence (No. 39)*], *Economist*, September 21, 1976, p. 80.

34. Miyajima, H., *Sozeiron no tenkai to nihon no zeisei*, 155.

35. It must be noted, however, that this graph does not take into account the beneficial side of public spending. The benefits to labor from spending generated by personal and social security taxes may well have offset some of the burdens of taxation on labor income.

36. Ishi, H., *Gendai zeisei kaikaku shi* [*The History of Modern Tax Reforms: From the End of the War to the Collapse of the Financial Bubble*] (Tokyo: Toyo Keizai, Inc., 2008).

37. Sato, S., and Miyajima, H., *Sengo zeisei shi*, 201.

38. Yoshikuni, J., ed., *Sengo hojin zeisei shi*, 827.

39. Yoshikuni, J., ed., *Sengo hōjin zeisei shi*, 831–2.

40. This section relies heavily on Mizuno, M., *Zeisei kaisei gojūnen*, 175–7 and 260–1.

41. Yoshikuni, J., ed., *Sengo hōjin zeisei shi*, 854.

42. Susumu, S., Hiroshi, M., *Sengo zeisei shi*, 356.

43. Shindo, M., *Zaisei hatan to zeisei kaikaku* [*Fiscal Collapse and Tax System Reform*] (Tokyo: Iwanami Shoten, 1989), 77.

44. Mizuno, M., *Zeisei kaisei gojūnen*, 275.

45. Ishi, H., *Gendai zeisei kaikaku shi*, 384.

46. Yoshikuni, J., ed., *Sengo hōjin zeisei shi*, 862.

47. Yoshikuni, J., ed., *Sengo hōjin zeisei shi*, 861.

48. Yoshikuni, J., ed., *Sengo hōjin zeisei shi*, 862.

49. Mizuno, M., *Zeisei kaisei gojūnen*, 316–17.

50. Yoshikuni, J., ed., *Sengo hōjin zeisei shi*, 862.

51. The current corporate income tax is somewhat chaotic, with some theorists seeing it as "a bare framework of the Shoup tax system" and others believing that "there hasn't been any movement in the basis of the tax system since the Shoup recommendations, but it does not have a unifying concept."

52. We should remember, too, that value-added taxation (VAT) – another form of broad-based taxation that ultimately reaches all forms of income – was a central element of the Shoup recommendations, and the tax might become a more vital part of the revenue system, relieving corporate tax burdens on one hand and financing welfare-state services on the other. Author has already compared the VAT proposed in the Shoup recommendations with the VAT in U.S. history. See Sekiguchi, S., "*Shoup kankoku no fukakachi zei no genryū*" [The Origin of Value added Tax in the Report on Japanese Taxation by Shoup Mission], *Chihou zei* [Local Taxation] 1998, vol. 49 (10), pp. 107–45.

PART FOUR

GLOBAL SIGNIFICANCE

Introduction to Part Four

Parts One to Three have discussed the Shoup mission, using it to reflect on the political economy of tax reform in Japan and, indirectly, the United States during the second half of the twentieth century. The Shoup mission was also significant in terms of its setting within a larger context of global fiscal and financial reform after World War II. Now, in Part Four, we turn to that topic.

In Chapter 15, Martin Daunton emphasizes that the Shoup mission's discussion of taxation ought to be seen as part of a larger discussion of how to create economic institutions and policies that would maximize employment, stabilize prices, promote growth, and advance development. Such questions were hotly contested in the post-World War II era and, as earlier chapters in the volume point out, they prompted sharp debates within both the American occupation and the Japanese government over taxing, spending, and borrowing. Carl Shoup and Joseph Dodge disagreed, for example, on the role of fiscal policy in controlling Japanese inflation and stimulating Japanese export industries at the same time as addressing unemployment and depressed real incomes. Daunton reminds us that such debates during the American occupation of Japan formed one segment of what was a global conversation. The creation of the Shoup mission was mainly to do with implementing the democratic goals of the first phase of the American occupation and, as such, the mission's intellectual basis was largely the "embedded progressivism" of prewar tax missions. The shifting of occupation goals during the "reverse course" of the occupation, however, forced the Shoup mission into debates with the Dodge mission that resembled those surrounding other international financial missions during the immediate post-World War II years.

Following Daunton's lead, scholars of tax history might usefully consider whether the international transfer of tax ideas was an important aspect not only of the reconstruction of Japan, but also of the larger reconfiguration of economic institutions and programs that the United States and other victorious powers undertook in the wake of World War II (and the Great Depression). Although there is a great deal of important historical scholarship on the origins and significance of the International Monetary Fund (IMF), the General Agreement on Tariffs and Trade, the World Bank, and the Marshall Plan, no historians have systematically examined whether, how, and to what effect the efforts at institutional globalization during the postwar era extended into the realm of taxation and public finance. Public finance specialists, as we noted above, have suggested the significance that the Shoup mission to Japan had on later tax missions, but historians have not yet undertaken a comprehensive history of those missions (including the tax missions ensconced within financial missions) or set that history in the context of the creation of new international economic institutions following World War II. Both projects ought to go hand in hand, and together they would expand on this volume and perhaps yield further insights into both the promise and the risk of global tax reform in the twenty-first century.

In the last chapter in this book, "Shoup and International Tax Reform after the Japan Mission," W. Elliot Brownlee and Eisaku Ide observe that after World War II, specialists in international finance intensified their study of the tax systems of other nations. Between Shoup's presidential address to the National Tax Association (NTA) in 1949 and 1951, when Shoup reported for a second time on his mission to Japan, other missions had completed their work and were also ready to report to the NTA. Among them were various projects run by the United Nations (Fiscal Division, Department of Economic Affairs), the American Mission for Aid to Greece, IMF Missions (including one to Bolivia conducted by public finance economist Richard Goode), four American missions to Turkey, and a study of the fiscal problems of West Germany conducted by Alvin Hansen (at the time perhaps the Dean of American Keynesians) and Richard Musgrave.[1] Of all of these missions and others that followed during the 1950s and 1960s, the Shoup mission to Japan was the most visible. Despite this, the extent to which these "tax assistance" efforts profited from Shoup's Japanese adventure remains unclear; extensive analysis of this question lies beyond the scope of this volume, but Chapter 16, by Brownlee and Ide, explores it in a preliminary fashion.

Chapter 16 takes up the question of what Shoup learned from the Japan mission as he reflected on its history, and as he planned and executed the other important foreign missions he conducted over the next two decades in Venezuela, Brazil, and Liberia. In addition, the chapter explores how recent international tax assistance programs have compared with Shoup's international work, beginning with the mission to Japan. Through this comparison, Brownlee and Ide offer some suggestions as to how the Shoup mission to Japan might inspire contemporary tax reformers in the international arena.

Shoup was not the only member or associate of the 1949 mission to Japan who went on to play a leading role in international tax reform. Harold Moss, William Vickrey, and Stanley Surrey, as well as Shoup, all believed that they had learned from their work in Japan. Throughout the rest of their careers they attempted to apply lessons learned in Japan to tax reform projects around the world. In the 1960s, Moss created and then directed the Foreign Assistance Office of the U.S. Treasury. In 1962, when the Office was first created, it assisted the nations within the Alliance for Progress of the Americas in improving the efficiency and management of fiscal systems and by the time Moss retired in 1970 he had sent its consulting teams around the world, reaching more than 30 nations during the 1960s.[2] Vickrey collaborated with Shoup in a mission to Liberia, as well as in a mission to study the federal district of Venezuela.[3] Surrey served with Shoup on a mission to Venezuela, became a pioneer in designing tax treaties between developing and developed nations, and played the central role in establishing the Harvard Law School's program in international tax law. Both Shoup and Surrey influenced a number of their students and colleagues to undertake significant roles in tax assistance. In light of the tax reform issues facing the United States in 2013, it should be noted that Surrey's commitment to the principles of Robert Murray Haig led him to become a pioneer in defining the concept of tax expenditures and a significant reformer of the American tax system. As assistant secretary of the U.S. Treasury for Tax Policy during the John F. Kennedy and Lyndon Johnson administrations, Surrey advocated powerfully for base-broadening reform in the United States as well as elsewhere. Domestically, his work helped strengthen a tradition within the U.S. Treasury that contributed in a crucial way to the base-broadening accomplishments of the Tax Reform Act of 1986. Shoup's *Report on Japanese Taxation* and "Treasury I," the 1984 document that established the intellectual basis for the 1986 act, may well be, to date, the most influential policy documents ever written on behalf of comprehensive income taxation, and

Surrey's career formed a significant link between the two.[4] In December 2010, echoes of Surrey's approach were heard in the report by the bipartisan fiscal commission (the "Simpson-Bowles" commission) appointed by President Barack Obama.[5] The echoes were heard again during 2012 and 2013, when the closing of tax "loopholes" gained some bipartisan support, at least in principle, as a means of long-term deficit and debt reduction.

The concluding chapter of the book employs Shoup's later career as a prism through which to view the history of international tax reform since 1950. For now, however, comprehensive analysis of the influence and effectiveness of Shoup and his like-minded colleagues and students on global tax reform after the Japan mission will have to remain a subject for future research.

Notes

1. "Round Table: Reconstruction of Tax Systems of Foreign Countries by United States Missions," in *Proceedings of the 44th Annual Conference on Taxation, National Tax Association, November 26–29, 1951* (Sacramento, CA: National Tax Association, 1952), 202–31.

2. Harold Moss, "Biographical Sketch," copy in the possession of Douglas M. Moss, and used with his permission.

3. See Shoup, C. S., Harriss, C. L., and Vickrey, W. S., eds., *The Fiscal System of the Federal District of Venezuela* (Baltimore: Garamond Press, 1960). C. Lowell Harriss, another former graduate student and Columbia colleague of Shoup's, joined Shoup and Vickrey on this urban tax mission. Harriss was a specialist in land economics and property taxation who had his own distinguished career in international tax assistance. "C. Lowell Harriss (1912–2009): Columbia University Educator, Economist, and Advocate of Land Reform Dies," Department of Economics, Columbia University, http://econ.columbia.edu/c-lowell-harriss-1912–2009.

4. See Surrey, S., *Pathways to Tax Reform: The Concept of Tax Expenditures* (Cambridge, MA: Harvard University Press, 1973) and Brownlee, W. E., *Federal Taxation in America: A Short History*, 2nd ed. (Cambridge and Washington, D.C.: Cambridge University Press and the Wilson Center Press, 2004), 130–2.

5. The National Commission on Fiscal Responsibility and Reform, "The Moment of Truth: Report of the National Commission on Fiscal Responsibility and Reform," http://www.fiscalcommission.gov/sites/fiscalcommission.gov/files/documents/TheMomentofTruth12_1_2010.pdf.

15

The Shoup Mission

The Context of Post–World War II Debates over International Economic Policy

Martin Daunton

When Carl Shoup visited Japan in 1949 and 1950, debates over postwar reconstruction of the world economy were at a critical point. Shoup's debates with Joseph Dodge need to be placed within the wider international context of the Bretton Woods agreement of 1944 and the Charter of the International Trade Organization (ITO) negotiated at Havana in 1947–8. Neither the monetary nor the trade policies evolved as expected during the period of idealism about the postwar international order; and by 1949 matters were being reassessed in a fundamental way. Shoup's mission to Japan coincided with the much wider contestation over international economic policy.

The international monetary regime created at Bretton Woods in 1944 rested on exchange rates pegged to the dollar, with the ability to devalue under certain conditions to prevent the need for deflationary policies harmful to domestic welfare and political stability, with a possible return to economic nationalism. For its part, the dollar was pegged to gold at $35 per ounce. Once rates were fixed, the next stage was to make all currencies fully convertible, after a relatively short period of transition. The operation of this new regime was then to be overseen by the International Monetary Fund (IMF).[1] The other major institution created at Bretton Woods, the International Bank for Recovery and Development (IBRD), faced the question of what policies to adopt to stimulate recovery and development in countries devastated by war, in underdeveloped countries in Latin America, and other parts of the world.

The failure of a speedy resumption of convertibility posed serious questions related to how the transition was to be handled. American insistence that sterling – the world's second major currency – should be convertible came to grief in 1947 and a new, more pragmatic, approach was needed to rebuild economies prior to convertibility. In pursuit of this ambition, Marshall Aid was announced in 1947 and the European Recovery Program (ERP) started in 1948. At this time, American policy toward Germany changed to a realization that its prosperity was essential to the recovery of Europe. The huge overhang of debt from the Nazi regime, and the accumulated spending power of personal savings, created the danger of a drain on the economy and the threat of inflation. In 1948, existing Reich marks were converted into new Deutsche marks, most of which were then "blocked" to prevent inflation. They were, however, available as credit for business. Dodge was deeply involved in these currency reforms before his move to Japan. The currency reform was "one of the greatest confiscations of wealth in history," wiping out 93 percent of pre-1948 savings, whereas corporations retained 96 percent of their real assets. This change in policy toward Germany meant that the economy started to recover and, more than the ERP, provided the basis for the growth of the European economy.[2]

It was obvious that American assistance could not continue indefinitely. Instead, attention turned to policies designed to stimulate the recovery of intra-European trade through the European Payments Union (EPU) of 1950. After the war, each country settled its balances with each of its trading partners; in the EPU, all eighteen members "cleared" their balances as a whole. As a result, it was hoped that trade within Europe would recover as a precondition for the convertibility that eventually came in 1958.[3] The discussions in Japan in 1949–50 between Dodge and Shoup were therefore part of a much wider reassessment of the unrealistic ambitions of the wartime conference on international monetary policy at Bretton Woods.

By 1949, greater realism was also apparent in the grandiose plans for a postwar world of multilateral trade. These plans emerged from the conviction of Secretary of State Cordell Hull that a return to multilateral trade would secure peace and prosperity, and after Hull retired in 1944 his approach was continued by Assistant Secretary Will Clayton, the chief American negotiator at Havana. In the view of Hull and Clayton, the reduction of trade barriers and the replacement of the bilateral trading systems of the 1930s (exemplified by British Imperial preference, German Schachtianism, and the Japanese coprosperity zone) by multilateral trade, would lead to economic growth and prosperity, and tie nations together in comparative advantage and peaceable exchange. In December 1945, the American and British governments issued their "Proposals for Consideration by an International Conference on Trade and Employment." An extended series of conferences was duly held, culminating in the meetings at Havana in 1947–8 that produced a Charter for an ITO (hereafter referred to as the charter). By 1949–50, it was clear that such ambitions were naïve and unrealistic. The American government had no intention of proceeding with ratification of the charter, and the more modest (and, as it turned out, realistic) interim General Agreements on Tariffs and Trade signed during the conference held at Geneva in 1947 provided a mechanism to restore multilateral trade in stages.[4]

The idealism of the wartime and the postwar periods was tempered by reality. The drive for multilateral trade was constrained by the economic plight of victors such as Britain and defeated nations such as Japan, who simply could not open up their markets, given their parlous balance of payments and the shortage of dollars to buy goods from the United States. The Cold War and outbreak of the Korean War led to another shift in American policies, as laid out in April 1950 in NSC-68 on "United States Objectives and Programs for National Security."[5] The debates between Shoup and Dodge over economic policies in Japan in 1949–50 should therefore be set in the context of wider discussions over the nature of the postwar world economy and strategic considerations.

RECREATING THE POSTWAR ECONOMY

The Shoup mission to Japan came soon after the resolution of the rate at which the yen was to be fixed to the dollar in April 1949. After the war, the price of trade goods was established by American officials, and there was a discrepancy between international and domestic price levels. The policy initially adopted was to set multiple exchange rates for the yen – a low rate for exports to increase their competitiveness and a high rate for imports to make them expensive. In March 1948, George Kennan and William Draper of the U.S. State Department visited Japan and concluded that a single rate was desirable but premature. A few months later, a delegation to Japan led by Ralph Young of the U.S. Federal Reserve's research and statistics division concluded that multiple rates were leading to inflation, and recommended a single rate of 300 yen to the dollar, with a 10 percent margin either way.

The American administration in Washington agreed that a single rate was desirable; however, the Japanese Ministry of Finance was wary, fearing that a single rate would hit Japanese industries. In addition, there was considerable uncertainty about the correct rate. The Supreme

Command for the Allied Powers initially proposed a rate of 330 yen to the dollar, which Dodge recommended to the American government. The National Advisory Council, however, felt that inflation meant the rate should be set at 360 yen to the dollar. Dodge concurred, and the new rate was established in April 1949. Although the devaluation of the pound sterling in September 1949 hit Japanese exports, the rate was held. Obviously, Japanese goods would have been less competitive if the yen had been pegged at 300 or 330 to the dollar; the yen was arguably somewhat undervalued, thus providing support for recovery. The rate was held until 1971, by which time the American government was strongly of the view that the yen was heavily undervalued.[6]

At the same time as the yen was being pegged to the dollar, the Charter of the ITO faced serious tensions over the exact relationship between trade and employment, as set out in the proposals of December 1945. Their relationship was a matter of considerable dispute, both within the United States and with the other participants at the successive conferences in London, Geneva, and Havana held between 1946 and 1948. As far as Clayton was concerned, multilateral trade came first and created the conditions for a prosperous, dynamic world economy that would lead to full employment in a free market. Others were less sure of the logic of his argument.

In 1945, the United States Congress was considering a Full Employment Bill, a radical progressive proposal that drew on the argument of Vice President Henry Wallace that federal "compensatory finance" was needed in order to ensure that "all Americans able to work and desiring to work are entitled to an opportunity for useful, remunerative, regular, and full-time employment." The bill aroused powerful opposition from critics, who argued that the economy usually tended to full employment, and that business cycles allowed economic adjustment in response to changing consumer demand. Economists such as Henry Simons of the University of Chicago stressed that budget deficits would lead to inflation, which was not an acceptable price to pay for full employment. The counterargument of economists such as J. K. Galbraith, a leading figure in the wartime Office of Price Administration – that inflation could be contained by price and wage controls – was not widely accepted. The promise to end controls was a central element in the Republican success in the congressional elections of 1946. The outcome was the Employment Act of 1946 that expressed an intention and not a requirement to achieve maximum employment (that is, what was actually feasible) rather than full employment.[7]

The defeat of the more radical Full Employment Bill did not mean the end of pressure for full employment because compensatory finance could be achieved in other ways. A key figure in this was Leon Keyserling, who, similar to Shoup, studied economics at Columbia. After reading law at Harvard, he returned to Columbia to start on a doctorate in economics. From 1933, he became deeply involved in the New Deal, working with Robert Wagner on legislation to allow union recognition and collective bargaining. We might note here that another feature of American policy in Japan at the end of the war was the Trade Union Law of 1945, which gave workers the right to organize, strike, and engage in collective bargaining. This was a reflection of a strand in the New Deal policy that was not entirely to the liking of businessmen such as Dodge, and that came under attack from Republicans in the U.S. Congress with the Taft-Hartley Act of 1947. Keyserling became vice chairman of Truman's Council of Economic Advisers and he served as chairman from 1949 to 1953. Keyserling was committed to full employment and welfare, and he had retained strong links with the American Federation of Labor since his involvement in the New Deal labor legislation. Keyserling and the American Federation of Labor under George Meany turned to military spending as a way of securing full employment through anti-Communist "military Keynesianism," in a policy of guns (a high level of defense expenditure) and butter (the provision of welfare benefits).[8]

The response of the British government to the proposals and subsequent conferences took a different line from that of the American administration and Congress. The wartime white paper published by the coalition government in 1944 contained a pledge to maintain "a high and stable level of employment after the war."[9] The postwar Labour government was committed to full employment, and realized that the restoration of multilateral trade had serious implications. The British economy was highly dependent on trade, and needed to expand its exports after the war to correct the serious payment deficit that had arisen. American negotiators at the postwar conferences argued that freer trade would lead to economic growth and hence to more employment. Labour politicians and many U.K. Treasury officials feared that freer trade posed the dangers of national bankruptcy and depression, unless there was a prior commitment to domestic policies of full employment – above all in the United States, which was prone to boom and bust.

The approach adopted by the Labour government was not so much Keynesian demand management as planning of the domestic economy. This could only be combined with multilateralism in foreign trade by a program of international economic planning to ensure that American recessions did not pull down the rest of the world.[10] Such an approach was far removed from the wishes of the American negotiators of the charter of the ITO who were wary about a commitment to full employment and international planning, and felt that the real need was for Britain to remove Imperial preference.

The Attlee and Truman administrations placed multilateral trade within different ideological contexts. Even more marked divergences were to appear when the Australians took the lead on behalf of other undeveloped countries and primary producers, pressing for a commitment on the use of international resources to their fullest extent in order to maintain international demand and employment.[11] Matters took a still more alarming turn from the point of view of both American and British negotiators as other primary-producing or underdeveloped countries took an even more radical position on employment issues that pushed policy towards a concern for economic development. In 1946, the Colombian representatives argued that full employment was inseparable from a variety of production and manufacturing industries that paid higher wages than extractive industries and helped to create "a mentally and morally superior working class." The Colombians argued that the Economic and Social Council (ECOSOC) of the United Nations "should ask itself if such an evolution can be got by depriving young industries of all protection, and if it is not more natural that a policy of trade freedom should be developed in harmony with the peculiar conditions prevailing in industrially-backward countries."[12]

When Shoup and Dodge proposed their own solutions to the reconstruction of the Japanese economy, they were enmeshed in these contested approaches to postwar reconstruction. Such was the dissension over the charter that it is not surprising it was never ratified. Despite the failure of the ITO, the case for international full employment did not disappear. The Attlee government was anxious to pursue plans for full employment through the ECOSOC of the United Nations, not least with the prospect of recession in the United States.

In 1949, the British secured a resolution to appoint a group of experts to produce the *National and International Measures for Full Employment* report that was largely the work of the British economist, Nicholas Kaldor. The report was ambitious, calling for each country to announce employment targets that would be assured through international coordination: any country that allowed its imports to fall below the level consistent with full employment would deposit funds with the IMF equivalent to the deflationary impact on the world economy. Further, an international conference should be held to scrutinize each country's trade plans. Full employment required concomitant economic development of poor countries through planned capital movements from advanced economies through the IBRD. Such proposals were anathema to most American politicians and businessmen. They were directed against the Hull-Clayton stress on trade liberalization as the precondition for full employment; they rejected Republican hostility to planning and deficits; and they were designed to force corrective action on the United States as the world's major creditor.

The report ran into opposition from the IMF and IBRD, as well as from the American representatives at ECOSOC in 1950. American opposition was formulated by Jacob Viner, the economist and former adviser to the U.S. Treasury, who saw a socialist threat and an impractical desire to pursue full employment at the expense of economic freedom, inflation, and efficiency. Opposition came from another direction as well, along the lines of some of the approaches of the Colombian delegates at the ITO conferences. The problem was not the stabilization of the economies of developed countries through demand management, but the removal of underemployment in less developed countries through a program of economic development.

In 1950, the American representative at ECOSOC proposed a new group to consider underemployment in underdeveloped countries. Their 1951 report on *Measures for the Economic Development of Under-Developed Countries* was heavily influenced by one of their members, the development economist W. Arthur Lewis. In Lewis's view, the scarcity of capital in underdeveloped countries meant that capital had a high marginal productivity, whereas agricultural labor was underemployed with negative marginal productivity. Consequently, workers could be moved from agriculture without any reduction in output and employed in industry, where cheap labor was combined with capital to produce industrial commodities for export and to generate profits for reinvestment in the further growth of industry. The report moved attention away from the transmission of recession to a concern for economic development by means of industrialization and planning for capital investment.[13]

The debates over trade and employment were giving way to debates over development. Concerns about full employment in advanced countries became less pressing with their continued growth and prosperity. At the same time, "underdeveloped" countries, such as Colombia and

Cuba, demanded policies that differed from Hull's and Clayton's vision of free trade as beneficial to all parties in a world of comparative advantage. These tensions were soon to appear within the fledging IBRD. The debates between Shoup and Dodge in Japan were occurring at a time of considerable controversy over the nature of economic policy to be adopted by the new international organizations of ECOSOC and the IBRD. Let us turn now to the debates over development within the IBRD, which provide a context for the different approaches of Shoup and Dodge.

DEVELOPMENT: BALANCED AND UNBALANCED GROWTH

The initial role of the IBRD was to assist in the reconstruction of Western Europe. With the arrival of Marshall Aid, however, it refocused on economic development. Economists were soon in conflict over the policy to be adopted, as they had been in conflict over the policies of the ITO relating to full employment and economic development. One of the most significant disputes arose over the advice offered to Colombia.[14]

In 1949, the IBRD dispatched its first general mission to Colombia – at the same time as Shoup was sent to Japan by the American government. The aim was to devise a development program to raise the standard of living of the people of Colombia. This posed a major question for the IBRD: just what should it finance, and on what grounds? The head of the mission was Lauchlin Currie (1902–1993), a Canadian who studied at the London School of Economics before moving to Harvard to study for his PhD on banking and monetary policy. He was a critic of the U.S. Federal Reserve's tight money policy in 1929 and in the Great Depression, anticipating the later critique of Milton Friedman – but in addition he argued strongly for budget deficits and public spending. In 1934, he joined the U.S. Treasury as a member of Viner's "freshman's brain trust," where he worked on reform of the monetary system. He soon moved to the Federal Reserve with Marriner Eccles, where he helped to draft the Banking Act of 1935, as well as arguing for monetary expansion and a more active fiscal policy on the basis high consumption and low savings to be created by progressive taxation and redistribution in support of welfare – policies that meshed with the proposals of Keyserling and Wallace to create postwar employment. His approach toward deficit finance was more radical than that of Secretary of the Treasury Morgenthau in response to the check in recovery after 1937. Although Roosevelt initially agreed with the more cautious response of Morgenthau, the subsequent downturn in the economy led to a shift toward the more expansionist policies of Eccles and Currie. In 1939, he moved to the White House as economic adviser to Roosevelt, and with his long-time friend Harry Dexter White – another member of Viner's brain trust – he played a major role in developing American international monetary policy.[15]

In 1949, Currie was invited to head the IBRD mission to Colombia. Although he took personal responsibility for the reports, he was supported by a group of officials from the bank, and by Richard Musgrave, an academic economist who specialized in public finance and banking who was, along with Shoup, the most important player in tax missions for the twenty years after the war.[16] The report on *The Basis of a Development Program for Colombia* appeared in 1950, setting out policies to increase productivity ahead of the rapidly growing population. Agriculture was the largest sector of the economy and was crucial to success. Currie felt that land should be used more productively by imposing a regressive tax on farmers whose productivity was below the norm for a particular quality of soil so as to encourage efficient cultivation – a proposal developed by a somewhat skeptical Musgrave. The question of land tenure, and how to divide the produce of the soil between the cultivator, landlord, and state, is one of the most important considerations in understanding patterns of economic development, and was central to debates over economic development. Many economists and political commentators in the past have debated the virtues of large-scale landownership versus peasant cultivation or small family farms for productive efficiency. In addition, tenure connects with taxation, for a major issue in any agrarian society is the division of the surplus between the cultivator, landlord, and tax collector.

The debates were given a radical edge at the end of the nineteenth and early twentieth centuries by Henry George, including in Japan where his work inspired Kahei Nikaido in the general election of 1902 (see Chapter 6). George's extreme "single tax" position – the claim that the only tax needed was on the unearned increment from land – was not widely accepted in any country. What was much more electorally feasible was a tax on the unearned increment as part of a wider mix of taxes, with a desire to break up great estates on the grounds of social justice and economic efficiency. These debates over land tenure continued after the Second World War, including in Japan where land reform was a major element in American policy. Fukagai notes that the Shoup mission was linked with a major change in landlord-peasant relations. Farmers comprised about half of the workforce, and about two-thirds of the land was rented, very often in small units with about half of the output going to landlords in rent. After the war, the American administration redistributed property from landlords to tenants in the hope that making them owner-occupiers would create incentives and raise productivity. Whether the policy worked in Japan has been the subject of debate: farms remained small and agriculture was protected, slowing down the release of labor. What it did achieve was political support for the ruling Conservative Party.[17]

Above all, Currie argued for a policy of balanced growth. He followed Paul Rosenstein-Rodan's work of 1943 on Eastern and South-Eastern Europe, which stressed the existence of excess rural population and disguised unemployment – a view that strongly influenced Lewis.[18] Labor should be moved from the land into a series of industries that would assist in creating a market, providing incentives to invest, and delivering a "big push" to power the economy into self-sustaining growth. Balanced growth required program loans and an integrated development plan, as well as investment in social overhead capital. This position was pressed by Currie and by Rosenstein-Rodan, who was a leading economist at the IBRD between 1947 and 1952.

Tensions soon appeared between the IBRD and Currie over the implementation of his proposals. The IBRD turned to another economist, Albert Hirschman, for advice. As in Japan, there were now two economists advising on the policy to be followed. Hirschman argued for unbalanced growth, claiming that growth depended on inducements to use existing underutilized resources. Rather than a short "big push," he argued for smaller steps concentrating on processes designed to stimulate investment, and project loans for directly productive activities rather than social purposes. In his view, a wide program would benefit some groups and harm others, so generating internal political opposition; by contrast, a single, defined project would be easier to implement. Furthermore, a wide program rested on an attempt to create virtue that was harder than the realistic aims of specific projects.

Rosenstein-Rodan was skeptical about Hirschman's argument. As he pointed out, the IBRD might be providing funds for a project that would have happened anyway, and the money set aside by the government for that project could be released for some marginal purpose. Hence "the bank thought it financed an electric power station, but in fact financed a brothel."[19] Currie and Rosenstein-Rodan faced serious challenge within the IBRD from those who favored project loans of a productive type and believed that the correct path to development was by means of investment in industrialization that would raise the standard of living, with spending on social capital coming later. The first presidents of the IBRD – John McCloy, Robert Garner, and Eugene Black – came from Republican financial backgrounds and were unsympathetic to the more radical and progressive policies associated with the New Deal. Dodge had much in common with them as a Detroit banker who played an important role in the Eisenhower administration as director of the Bureau of the Budget and chairman of the Council on Foreign Economic Policy. Yet again, the debates between Shoup and Dodge over Japan need to be viewed as part of a wider debate within the IBRD concerning policies for economic development in other areas of the world economy.

The victory of project loans was not complete, and debate continued in the 1950s. Part of the explanation was the evidence from the IBRD's own missions and staff. One staff member thought it "ridiculous" that loans could be given for irrigation projects and not for urban water supplies because they were not "productive." Reports from missions pointed to wider social issues of poverty and inequality, reinforced by the demands of poor countries, and of activists in the advanced economies. There were also political reasons for taking a wider view. John Foster Dulles, Secretary of State from 1953 to 1959, saw the dangers of a rigid stance on self-financing loans. "It might be good banking to put South America through the wringer, but it will come out red." East and West were engaged in a battle for development, and he remarked that defeat "could be as disastrous as defeat in the arms race." In 1960 a new organization, the International Development Association, was created to offer soft loans or "credits" for wider programs of poverty alleviation, and regional development banks were set up, starting with the Inter-American Development Bank in 1959. Although the IBRD focused on project loans, it evaluated the overall development program of borrowers, which allowed it to move toward wider approaches to economic development in the future.[20]

The debates over economic development did not only involve land tenure and taxation, for disagreements within the IBRD over Colombia also entailed different policies toward investment and aid. One danger of loans for development, whether through specific projects or a general program, was default or dependence. The matter troubled Shoup in the 1930s, and was a concern in postwar reconstruction. Investors feared that borrowers might default or expropriate assets in order to prevent economic and political dependence.

DEBT, EXPROPRIATION AND CAPITAL

Shoup had experience in dealing with debt default resulting from ill-considered investment programs, for his mission to Cuba in 1931 arose from the prospect of sovereign debt default. The Cuban government embarked on an expensive program of public works in the 1920s in order to secure electoral support, but a fall in commodity prices made debt service difficult, and the attempt to secure revenue to cover interest payments resulted in political unrest. By the time Shoup returned on his second mission in 1938–9, Cuba had defaulted. The Cuban problems posed questions that had arisen in the past and would again in the future: could the creditors look to their own government to intervene or should they be left to their own devices, paying the penalty for their ill-considered investment decisions?

After the defeat of Spain in the war of 1898, the United States occupied Cuba. In 1901, Congress passed an act to define future relations with Cuba, which was incorporated in a treaty with the newly independent Cuba in 1903. The second clause of the act and treaty laid down that the government of Cuba "shall not assume or contract any public debt, to pay the interest on which, and to make reasonable sinking fund provision for the ultimate discharge of which, the ordinary revenues of the island, after defraying the current expenses of government shall be inadequate." In the next clause, the government of Cuba "consents that the United States may exercise the right to intervene for the preservation of Cuban independence, the maintenance of a government adequate for the protection of life, property and individual liberty."[21] In effect, these clauses gave the United States powers to intervene in Cuba in defense of American investments that potentially encouraged over-lending. Wall Street financiers, such as J. P. Morgan, pressed for American control over Cuban finances (see Chapter 4). The American administration was wary of providing guarantees, although it did wish to be informed of loans to ensure that they did not act against American policy.

The American delegation at the ITO conference at Havana in 1947–8 was anxious to stimulate overseas investment as a way of encouraging recovery of the international economy. Businessmen wished to insert a chapter into the Charter of the ITO to stimulate American foreign investment for "economically desirable purposes" as a way to assist recovery and deal with the balance of trade surplus by injecting funds back into the world economy. They argued that the chapter needed to provide security for investment, for it was one thing to deal with the ordinary risks of business, but quite another to deal with "the hazards of debt repudiation, property confiscation, foreign exchange blockages, and discriminatory practices."[22] In the absence of security, American overseas investment would come to a halt and the costs of stimulating recovery would instead fall on the American government and taxpayer through initiatives such as Marshall Aid.

More cautious voices in the administration were wary about the overexpansion of foreign investment. Might it lead to hostility toward America as a result of exploitation of natural resources, special privileges given to American corporations, or manipulation of local support? These fears were not just theoretical, for congressional investigations exposed irresponsible actions in the 1920s, when large commissions were paid to American financiers, with onerous terms, a wasteful use of loans, and defaults. The result was poor relations with the debtor countries and the danger of a backlash of tariff protection. Such concerns led to a working group of the National Advisory Council and the Executive Committee on Economic Foreign Policy in 1946 recommending registration and administrative controls over foreign loans.[23] Clearly, not everyone in the administration would accept such limits on free enterprise, but the recommendations reflected the problems that arose in the case of Cuba in the 1920s and 1930s.

There was a careful balance to be struck. If the chapter was strengthened to offer more security for American investment, it might be criticized as being no more than a disguised form of imperialism. If the chapter was not sufficiently strengthened, American businessmen would denounce the ITO as inadequate. Meanwhile, less developed countries pressed for changes to allow expropriation of foreign investment with compensation. Consequently, businesses criticized the charter for offering inadequate protection and making the world safe for socialistic planning. In 1949, the National Association of Manufacturers expressed a common view of major corporations that the charter had failed to "establish a climate favorable to the revival of abundant and sustained private foreign investments, which are indispensable for promoting economic advance throughout the world."[24] These concerns about the potential threat to American overseas investments were another reason for doubts about the ratification of the charter.

Although American businessmen argued that foreign direct investment after the Second World War would be an important element in the reconstruction of the world economy, the architects of the Bretton Woods regime were not entirely enthusiastic about the restoration of free capital flows such as those that characterized the world economy before 1914, when Britain invested such a massive amount in Argentina, Canada, and other areas of recent settlement. Their concern was not the creation of domination and dependency that troubled less developed countries at Havana; it was that capital flows in the interwar period were destabilizing, speculative reactions to uncertainty around the world, contributing to pressure on currency, and to the collapse of the international financial order.[25]

The architects of the Bretton Woods system wished to combine domestic prosperity with a commitment to multilateral trade so that there was not, as between the wars, a nationalistic backlash against external policies that were seen as detrimental to domestic welfare. The answer was stable exchange rates that would stimulate trade, but with capital controls that would allow interest rates to be fixed for domestic reasons, without provoking an outflow or inflow of capital or putting pressure on the exchange rates. Keynes realized that "the whole management of the domestic economy depends upon being free to have the appropriate rate of interest without reference to the rates prevailing elsewhere in the world. Capital control is a corollary to this." Similarly, Bertil Ohlin remarked that the movement of goods "is a prerequisite of prosperity and economic growth" whereas the movement of capital was not. Article VI section 3 of the IMF agreement specified that "members may exercise such controls as are necessary to regulate international capital movements."[26] Although Wall Street and city of London financiers were not entirely happy, these powers were used extensively in the decades after 1945, including by the Kennedy and Johnson administrations, in order to encourage domestic investment and remove pressure on the dollar from an outflow of funds. They were also used in Japan to limit inward investment.

One of the major problems of foreign assistance was that it lessened the need to collect tax revenues, and so weakened representative and accountable governments. Chapter 11 shows that Japan avoided this "aid curse." It also avoided high levels of inward investment after the war. The Foreign Investment Law of 1950 prevented the inflow of foreign capital, excepting specified cases where it was considered desirable. The result was to limit American purchases of Japanese assets so that Ford or General Motors, for example, did not buy Japanese motor manufacturers. The Japanese policy of investment from domestic savings in banks had, as its corollary, a low level of foreign direct investment.[27]

The criticism of capital movements as either destabilizing or as an agent for domination was countered by another, more positive, interpretation. Arguably, capital exports from Britain before 1914 were a source of stability in the international economy. British capital exports were countercyclical: when Britain was experiencing prosperity, its open market meant that the goods of the world had an outlet and previous loans could be serviced; when Britain was less prosperous, it invested overseas and so helped to stabilize the international economy. Furthermore, overseas investment was largely in social overhead capital – above all, railways – in temperate zones of recent settlement that produced food and raw materials for the developed economies, with general benefit to the recipients of the loans. In the opinion of Ragnar Nurkse and Hans Singer, American foreign direct investment was different in character and less beneficial. It went largely into the production of raw materials for the advanced countries through direct ownership of capital linked with the employment of low-waged local labor, unlike before 1914 when capital exports were associated with European migration. The result was an export-oriented sector in the borrowing country with limited connection with the rest of the domestic economy. Nurkse and Singer felt that investment in social overhead capital with a more beneficial impact on the domestic economy required the recreation of something similar to British portfolio investment in government and utility bonds – and this could only be done through the intervention of governments or international institutions.[28] As we have seen, the terms on which aid should be given was itself the subject of considerable debate – and it could lead to a curse of dependency and a weakening of institutional capacity.

The Shoup and Dodge missions to Japan should be placed within these wider debates over capital flows and aid that troubled economists and politicians after the Second World War. Capital movements did not recover to the level experienced before 1914 until the end of the century – although by the 1960s, capital flows were already proving more difficult to control, with consequential pressure on the fixed exchange rate regime of Bretton Woods. The emergence of balance of payments surpluses in West Germany and Japan, and the shift of the United States into deficit, meant that pegged exchange rates were under pressure. This eventually led to depreciation of the dollar and appreciation of the Deutsche mark and yen in 1971. Furthermore, an increase in capital flows led to greater problems in maintaining stable exchanges alongside an active domestic economic policy. Any attempt to use interest rates to stabilize the domestic economy could now lead to a greater inflow or outflow of funds, which created problems in maintaining the fixed exchange rate. The Bretton Woods system came under serious pressure, and the trade-off between policy goals that had been agreed in 1944 was reassessed.

Loans in the form of government bonds needed tax capacity to service interest payments – and aid might be at the expense of securing revenue from local taxpayers. Shoup was eager to avoid the "aid curse" in Japan, and his approach in both Cuba and Japan was to resolve the structural tax issues. If a country is to borrow, it needs a strong tax base on which to service the debt and to ensure that the costs of borrowing are held down; a steady flow of tax revenue would reduce the need for borrowing to fund the actions of the government. Unlike many developing countries, Japan did have tax capacity and an institutional structure, so aid was less likely to lead to problems: it was more akin to a European country in receipt of Marshall Aid. The insistence of Dodge on balancing the budget at this time meant that it was more difficult for the Japanese government to cut taxes, however, and the American administration was anxious to improve the administration of revenue collection to create greater compliance and legitimacy.

Shoup's views on taxation in Japan reflect earlier debates within the United States going back to the New Deal (see Chapter 5). Secretary of the U.S. Treasury Morgenthau wished to reform the tax system, and in 1934 Shoup joined Viner in this task. Similar to Morgenthau and in contrast with Currie at the Federal Reserve, Shoup was cautious about debt and deficit funding. He argued on the same lines as William Gladstone in mid- and late-Victorian Britain that debt was "hidden" taxation, passing costs onto future generations who had no voice. Debt encouraged feckless behavior, leading taxpayers to believe they could secure benefits from the state without paying, and so undermining tax morale. In Gladstone's mind, loans also led to militarism, for bellicose taxpayers did not need to pay for their adventures. In his view, debt should be minimized and taxpayers made to pay the cost of their policies. Of course, when war did come for whatever reason, borrowing might be necessary, and at this point interest rates were lower because of confidence in the ability of the government to service the debt.[29]

The difference was striking in the First World War. The French only introduced an income tax at the outbreak of the war, and had become more dependent on sales taxes in the previous fifty years. Their taxing capacity was lower: Shoup estimated that taxes covered 15–18 percent of the cost of the First World War in France, and the interest rate was higher. In Britain, taxation covered 28 percent of the cost of the war, and loans were cheaper. Even so, the costs of servicing debt were high and the burden was a major political issue in all the combatant countries, leading to hostility toward "parasitical" rentiers. In the case of Britain, the greater sense of equity in the tax system meant that the difficulties were successfully overcome, and government spending remained at the new higher levels, supported by a legitimated income tax and without a general sales tax. In France, the debt burden was greater and the income tax was not legitimated, and as Shoup showed in his doctoral thesis, the government turned to a sales tax which was itself unpopular and divisive. Similar problems arose in other European states, where debt service led to political instability in the absence of agreement on the tax system.[30]

Shoup, similar to Gladstone, believed that taxation was preferable to debt, which threatened to become addictive. This is not to say that he always wanted a balanced budget, for he was willing to accept a counter-cyclical use of tax policy in some conditions. Making recommendations on the active use of fiscal policy was outside the scope of his mission to Japan. Shoup wanted a tax system that was fair between classes without harming investment and growth by distorting economic decision-making. He therefore argued that the taxation system should not seek to alter preferences for expenditure to promote capital investment, which might not be economically efficient and might well reduce the revenue capacity of the state. In his view, the structure of taxation reflected the level of economic development, which in turn influenced the legal and administrative framework. Shoup's approach harked back to the policies adopted in Britain after the reintroduction of the income tax by Robert Peel in 1842, as laid down in Gladstone's great budget of 1853. The tax system should be "disinterested" in the differences between classes and occupations. The payment of taxes would be more legitimate and remove hostility toward the state, which had been so marked in the second quarter of the nineteenth century.[31] Such an approach had many similarities with the stress of the Columbia school (especially Robert Murray Haig) on "horizontal equity" in taxation. Gladstone believed that payment of income tax should be linked with the vote, so that decisions were responsible and prudent. The British Treasury and Inland Revenue insisted that the tax system should not seek to "engineer" the economy or society; their concern was administrative acceptability. This was very much in line with

Shoup's thinking: more people should come into the income tax by reducing exemptions, consumption taxes that "concealed the average citizen's role as a taxpayer" should be reduced so that taxpayers came into closer contact with the state, and taxes on higher incomes should be increased. He supported progressive taxation, although he did not feel that economics had much to say about the optimal level of progressivity that was more a matter of politics and the need to avoid encouraging evasion and avoidance, with a loss of legitimacy. The result would be greater interest in government through the broadening and democratizing of the tax base. Once popular confidence was created in the tax system, democratic government would have more fiscal capacity and it might be possible to use the income tax as a Keynesian tool.

Shoup, as Gladstone had, accepted the case for the taxation of estates at death, for reasons that connect with his stance on debt. The problem with debt was that it passed burdens onto future generations who had no say in the matter. The problem with inheritance was that future generations received assets for which they had not worked, and that would therefore stifle energy and enterprise. In the same way that government debt created passive recipients of interest, so did inheritance. Economists such as Arthur Pigou argued that collective spending was more efficient than private spending by heirs, so the taxation of estates at death was beneficial.[32] Furthermore, the accumulation of large estates was a threat to the democratic ordering of society by leading to the growth of oligarchic politics rather than the democratic engagement of many modest property owners. A similar line was taken in the Viner reports on American taxation, which departed from the policy of cutting inheritance taxes pursued by Andrew Mellon as secretary of the U.S. Treasury.

The recommendations of the Viner reports were not accepted in the United States prior to the Second World War. Most Democrats preferred a narrow income tax with higher rates on the rich and on corporations, whereas most Republicans were opposed to corporation taxation and the income tax. Shoup was able to press for the adoption of his policies in the different political circumstances of Cuba, where he recommended the creation of a tax system that would encourage compliance and create support for democracy. As the tax system stood, the absence of land and income taxation allowed the wealthy to escape payment and undermined consent. Nevertheless, his detailed analysis of Cuba led him to accept that conditions were not suitable for the adoption of an income tax, and he accepted a dwelling tax as a presumptive tax on income. His approach differed from that of Edwin Kemmerer, an economist from Princeton who had a more conservative, Wall Street orientation: he recommended a set package of policies based on the gold standard, an independent central bank, and balanced budgets rather than empirical studies of the particular country and its circumstances. Kemmerer, similar to Dodge in postwar Japan, was a "money doctor" who argued for deflation and balanced budgets in response to sovereign debt crises.

The debate between Kemmerer and Shoup in Cuba was repeated between Dodge and Shoup in Japan. Shoup stressed tax equity, with uniform taxation of all forms of income to avoid distortions in the allocation of resources. He proposed a reduction of the special treatment of income from savings in bank accounts. He hoped that these reforms would lead to acceptance of the income tax as fair, avoiding the need for deficit finance and ensuring that the public sector was not starved of funds. Rather than encouraging capital formation through tax breaks on savings, he argued that neutrality of taxation would remove barriers to growth. He was also anxious to ensure that the collection of taxes was fair and transparent. By contrast, Dodge was not interested in horizontal equity or in democratization. He preferred to encourage savings in banks that could be invested in private business. The outcome was a strategy of capital formation that had been followed since the Meiji Restoration.

The outcome was not entirely what either Dodge or Shoup wished. The Japanese government did not follow Shoup's recommendations to create broad-based support for taxes, and instead turned to tax-cutting as a way of securing popular support. The tax breaks on savings gave the government access to funds on cheap terms, and led to the use of public works for electoral reasons, with a very high ratio of debt to gross domestic product – precisely what Shoup did not want to happen. The reduction in personal income tax meant that the government was more dependent on corporate taxation, which was only possible as a result of the structure of Japanese business. The limited use of equity markets meant that dividends were low, and intercorporate dividends on extensive cross-holdings were exempt from tax. As a result, there was a margin created that could be used to pay corporate taxation. Further, the existence of tax breaks on savings in banks meant that firms could borrow from banks on favorable terms that led to sufficient profits to pay corporate tax. Large corporations were able to secure reasonable profits by using small- and medium-sized enterprises as a cushion over the trade cycle. The Japanese tax system and corporate structure were thus interconnected: a reliance on corporate taxation was linked with a fall in income taxation, tax breaks on personal savings, a lack of consent to taxation, and a high dependence on debt to fund the state (see Chapters 12 and 14). These were not the outcomes desired by Shoup.

The discussion of tax policy in 1949–50 should be linked to a further element of American policy in Japan at the end of the war: the attempt to move corporate structure away from the *zaibatsu* or family controlled, vertically integrated firms, with interlocking directorships. Hostility to trusts and monopolies was a powerful element in American economic policy, and in 1947 the American administration took steps to break up the *zaibatsu* as undemocratic monopolies. Such attacks on cartels and monopolies constituted another element in the Charter of the ITO, for the American negotiators wished to break up international agreements over market sharing and pricing that emerged in the 1920s and 1930s as a response to the Great Depression. The British were more wary, seeing the cartels as a way of stabilizing the international economy, maintaining British export markets, and allowing more rational planning. Much the same applied in Japan, where there was much less concern about competition and a greater emphasis on order and stability. Despite American attempts to break up the *zaibatsu*, they were able to evolve into *keiretsu* – a horizontal rather than vertical structure – which complemented the system of taxation that evolved after the failure of Shoup's proposals.[33]

CONCLUSION

My aim in this chapter has been to place the Shoup mission in a number of different contexts. First, the debates between Shoup and Dodge should be set in the wider framework of the New Deal and the different approaches that flourished in the Roosevelt administration, with their competing proposals for recovery and reform. Second, the Shoup and Dodge responses to Japanese economic recovery should be located in the context of varying policies for postwar reconstruction of the world economy, which grew out of the tensions within the New Deal as well as the divergences between American, British and less developed countries. Third, Shoup's policies toward debt, development, and taxation can be located in the different approaches toward the role of taxation and its connection with economic development and democracy. The Shoup mission to Japan was just one of many such missions that attempted to create a legitimate tax regime that would provide the basis for a democratic society, and prevent an overreliance on external aid and internal debt. As in other cases, the outcome was shaped as much by domestic politics as by external advice.

As subsequent events were to show, the Japanese tax regime encouraged high levels of personal saving. These savings were diverted into business investment, with a high level of public debt that was used both for infrastructure and for political patronage. The distinctive pattern of low personal and high public debt in modern Japan has its origins in the shaping of the postwar financial regime.

Notes

1. James, H., *International Monetary Cooperation since Bretton Woods* (Oxford: Oxford University Press, 1996).
2. Hughes, M. L., "Hard heads, soft money? West German ambivalence about currency reform, 1944–1948," *German Studies Review* 1998, vol. 21, pp. 309–27.
3. Kaplan, J. J., Schleiminger, G., *The European Payments Union: Financial Diplomacy in the 1950s* (Oxford: Oxford University Press, 1989).
4. See Diebold, W., *The End of the ITO: Essays in International Finance* (Princeton, NJ: International Finance Section, Dept. of Economics and Social Institutions, Princeton University, 1952); Brown, W. A., *The United States and the Restoration of World Trade: An Analysis and Appraisal of the ITO Charter and the General Agreements on Tariffs and Trade* (Washington, DC: Brookings Institute, 1950). For the general background, see Zeiler, T. W., *Free Trade, Free World: The Advent of GATT* (Chapel Hill: University of North Carolina Press, 1999).
5. Available at http://www.fas.org/irp/offdocs/nsc-hst/nsc-68.htm; Gaddis, J. L., *Strategies of Containment: A Critical Appraisal of American National Security Policy during the Cold War*, revised edition (Oxford: Oxford University Press, 2005); Caldwell, C., *NSC-68 and the Political Economy of the Early Cold War* (Cambridge: Cambridge University Press, 2011).
6. Tsuchiya, T., Asai, Y., eds., *Nihon Kinyushi Shiryo [Materials on Japanese Monetary History]*, vol. 25 (Tokyo: Bank of Japan Research Department Tokyo, Okurasho Insatsukyoku, 1996). Thanks to Dr. Hiroki Shin.
7. Wallace, H. A., *The Century of the Common Man* (London: Hutchinson, 1943) and *Sixty Million Jobs*, (London: Heinemann, 1945); Santoni, G. J., *The Employment Act of 1946: Some History Notes* (St. Louis: Federal Reserve of St. Louis, 1986), available at: http://research.stlouisfed.org/publications/review/86/11/Employment_Nov1986.pdf, accessed October 4, 2012; United States Senate, Committee on Banking and Currency, Assuring Full Employment in a Free Competitive Economy: Report from the Committee on Banking and Currency 79th Congress, first session, September 1945 and Sub-Committee on Banking and Currency, Full Employment Act of 1945: Hearings Before a Sub-Committee on Banking and Currency 79th Congress, first session, September 1945; Leeson, R., "The political economy of the inflation-unemployment trade-off," *History of Political Economy* 1997, vol. 29, pp. 117–56.

8. Pickens, D. K., "Keyserling, Leon," *American National Biography Online*, http://anb.org/articles/07/07--00155 and "Truman's Council of Economic Advisers and the legacy of the New Deal," in Levantrosser, W. F., ed., *Harry S. Truman: The Man from Independence* (Westport, CT: Greenwood Press, 1986). On unions and guns and butter, see Wehrle, E. F., *Between a River and a Mountain: The AFL-CIO and the Vietnam War* (Ann Arbor: University of Michigan Press, 2005), 3, 24–5, 59–60. On labor policies in Japan, see Harari, E., *The Politics of Labor Legislation in Japan* (Berkeley: University of California Press, 1973).

9. Parliamentary Papers, Employment Policy, Cmd. 6257; Beveridge, W. H., *Full Employment in a Free Society: A Report* (London: Allen and Unwin, 1944), 18–19.

10. Toye, R., "The Labour Party's external economic policy in the 1940s," *Historical Journal* 2000, vol. 43, pp. 190, 195, 204, 215.

11. Rowse, T., "Full employment and the discipline of labour: a chapter in the history of Australian social democracy," *The Drawing Board: An Australian Review of Public Affairs* 2000, vol. 1, pp. 1–13, available at: http://www.australianreview.net/journal/v1/n1/rowse.pdf, accessed October 4, 2012; Jenkins, S., "Australia plans full employment," *Far Eastern Survey* 1945, vol. 14 (17), pp. 240–2.

12. TNA, 236/704, United Nations, Economic and Social Council, "Preparatory committee of the international conference of trade and employment: memorandum on the objectives of the international trade organization in respect to employment (submitted by the secretariat), London E/PC/T/W.18," October 19, 1946; "Committee I, summary record of meetings, second meeting, part two," October 21, 1946.

13. Toye, J., Toye, R., "How the UN moved from full employment to economic development," *Commonwealth and Comparative Politics* 2006, vol. 44, 16–40. On Lewis, see Tignor, R. L., *W. Arthur Lewis and the Birth of Development Economics* (Princeton, NJ: Princeton University Press, 2005).

14. The following discussion of Columbia and the IBRD rests on Alacevich, M., *The Political Economy of the World Bank: The Early Years* (Palo Alto, CA: Stanford University Press, 2009).

15. Sandilands, R. J., "Currie, Lachlan," *American National Biography Online*, April 2002 update, http://www.anb.org/articles/14/14–01124.html.

16. Ibid., and *The Life and Political Economy of Lauchlin Currie: New Dealer, Presidential Adviser, and Development Economist* (Durham, NC and London: Duke University Press, 1990).

17. Dore, R. P., "Land reform and Japan's economic development" and Kawagoe, T., "Agricultural land reform in postwar Japan: experiences and issues," World Bank Policy Research Working Papers no. 2111, Nov. 1999.

18. See Tignor, R. L., *W. Arthur Lewis and the Birth of Development Economics*.

19. Quoted in Alacevich, M., *Political Economy of the World Bank*, 80.

20. Kapur, D, Lewis, J. P., Webb, R., eds., *The World Bank: Its First Half Century*, vol. 1 (Washington, DC: Brookings Institution, 1997), 110, 117, 130–8.

21. Bevans, C. I., ed., *Treaties and other International Agreements of the United States of America, 1776–1949*, vol. 8 (Washington, DC: U.S. Government Printing Office, 1971); "The Platt amendment," pp. 1116–7.

22. National Archives and Records Administration, College Park, RG43, International Trade Files, Box 14, Folder: trade Habana, Chapter III economic development, articles 8 through 15, "Investment clauses in Geneva draft Charter, 21 Nov 1947, appendix D: memorandum on importance of encouraging foreign investments;" Box 38, folder: foreign investment policy documents: United States foreign investment policy July 18, 1946.

23. NARA, RG43, International Trade Files, Box 38, folder: foreign investment policy documents: "Control over American private foreign investment, working draft 14 Feb 1946;" "US policy toward control and disclosure of American private foreign investment, 13 Dec 1945" and "Committee on foreign economic investment policy and NAC D-103, 24 April 1946."

24. NARA, RG 43 International Trade Files, Box 7, "The Havana Charter for an International Trade Organization: An Appraisal. National Association of Manufacturers, Economic Policy Division Series No. 9, April 1949."

25. United Nations Department of Economic Affairs, *International Capital Movements during the Inter-War Period Lake Success* (New York: United Nations, Department of Economic Affairs, 1949).

26. Moggridge, D. E., ed., *The Collected Writings of John Maynard Keynes*, vol. 26 (London: Macmillan, St. Martin's Press for the Royal Economic Society, 1980): Activities 1943–46; *Shaping the Postwar World. Bretton Woods and Reparations* (London: Macmillan, 1980); Helleiner, E., *States and the Re-emergence of Global Finance from Bretton Woods to the 1990s* (Ithaca: Cornell University Press, 1994); Horsefield, J. K., *The International Monetary Fund, 1945–65*, III: Documents (Washington, DC: IMF, 1969).

27. Komiya, R., "Direct foreign investment in postwar Japan," in Drysdale, P., ed., *Direct Foreign Investment in Asia and the Pacific* (Canberra: Australian National University Press, 1972).

28. Nurkse, R., "'International investment today in the light of nineteenth-century experience," *Economic Journal* 1954, vol. 64, pp. 744–58; Singer, H. W., "The distribution of gains between investing and borrowing countries," *American Economic Review* 1950, vol. 40, pp. 473–85.

29. Daunton, M., *Trusting Leviathan: The Politics of Taxation in Britain, 1799–1914* (Cambridge: Cambridge University Press, 2011), chapter 5, pp. 109–135.

30. On the higher yield on French and German bonds compared with British, see Ferguson, N., *The Pity of War* (London: Penguin, 1998), 126–35; and for a comparison with the handling of postwar debt, see Daunton, M., "How to pay for the war: state, society and taxation in Britain, 1917–24," *English Historical Review* 1996, vol. 111, pp. 882–919; Shoup, C. S., *The Sales Tax in France* (New York: Columbia University Press, 1930).

31. Daunton, M., *Trusting Leviathan: The Politics of Taxation in Britain, 1799–1914*, see chapters, 2, 3, 4, 6 and 7 for a detailed analysis of the shift from hostility to acceptance of the fiscal state.

32. For Gladstone on inheritance, see Daunton, M., *Trusting Leviathan: The Politics of Taxation in Britain, 1799–1914*, chapter 8, pp. 224–255; Collard, D., "Pigou and future generations: a Cambridge tradition," *Cambridge Journal of Economics* 1996, vol. 20, pp. 589–91.
33. See Bissell, T. A., *Zaibatsu Dissolution in Japan* (Berkeley: University of California Press, 1954); and Morikawa, H., *Zaibatsu: The Rise and Fall of Family Enterprise Groups in Japan* (Tokyo: University of Tokyo Press, 1992).

16

Shoup and International Tax Reform after the Japan Mission

W. Elliot Brownlee and Eisaku Ide

As the introduction to this volume noted, various international tax experts have testified eloquently as to the ongoing significance and influence of the Shoup mission on global tax reform. Expanding on their comments to provide a detailed and in-depth assessment of exactly how the experience of the Shoup mission influenced the hundreds of missions that have promoted international tax reform since 1950 lies beyond the scope of this volume. It is possible, however, to move toward such an assessment by doing three things: (1) suggesting some of the key elements of the Shoup mission to Japan that shaped his other missions, (2) considering what Shoup learned from his experiences in Japan and how this learning influenced his subsequent missions, and (3) examining, albeit briefly, how recent international tax assistance has compared with the work of Shoup's supposedly prototypical missions.

REPORT ON JAPANESE TAXATION: AN INSTANT CLASSIC

At the heart of the Shoup's international legacy is the mission's formal report – the four-volume *Report on Japanese Taxation*.[1] Tens of thousands of copies of the report and an elaborate summary were printed, and were distributed widely to libraries around the world and the global community of tax experts as well as within Japan. Shoup and his colleagues had written the *Report* to be read easily by the Japanese public (then, as now, voracious readers of books on public affairs). The authors of the *Report* handled technical tax issues in a graceful, clear fashion and set their technical discussions within commentary on the larger issues of Japanese institutions and political economy. They grounded their recommendations both in public finance theory and in analysis of political and economic reality in Japan. Thus, the tax architecture they recommended seemed democratic in sprit, aesthetically pleasing, and eminently functional.

The intellectual and stylistic strengths of the *Report* resulted in part from the interdisciplinary collaboration that had produced it. Broad-gauged economists, attorneys, and administrators wrote or contributed to it. With Shoup leading the way, they and the mission's admirers followed up its publication by promoting its dissemination and discussion through their professional societies and universities. Japanese professors, economists, and legal scholars joined the vanguard, using the *Report* as a textbook on Japanese taxation. Thus, the *Report* functioned as a kind of networking tool for Shoup, serving as the intellectual foundation for his efforts to build up organized tax scholarship, create bridges between scholars and tax practitioners, and reinforce the development of an international community of tax experts.

Shoup, meanwhile, stayed in touch with his expert friends in Japan, especially Hara Sumio, Tsuru Shigeto, Ito Hanya, and Shiomi Saburo, who became the first president of the Japan Tax Association, and provided them with professional assistance.[2] Even before the conclusion of the Japan mission, Shiomi discussed with Shoup his ambition to publish "a little book in English entitled 'Japan's Finance 10 years,'" putting all my study in the past together." With Shoup's considerable help, that ambition produced *Japan's Finance and Taxation 1940–1956*.[3] Thus, in a sense, Shoup and his colleagues in the United States and Japan institutionalized the knowledge base that the mission had created.

In 1962, Martin Bronfenbrenner cited the *Report* as conforming to his "Sixth Commandment" for "visiting economists": "Thou shalt content thyself with serious consideration of thine opinions and recommendations, and thou shalt not anticipate complete acceptance." The *Report*, Bronfenbrenner suggested, "remains a major statement of the principles of fiscal equity applied to a society concerned on the Right primarily with capital formation, and on the Left primarily with thorough-going social revolution."[4] In 1971, more than twenty years after the appearance of the *Report*, Oliver Oldman and Stanley Surrey expressed their agreement with Bronfenbrenner's stress on its importance. They wrote that Shoup's "publications dominate the field of tax technical assistance," and that the *Report*, along with Shoup's 1959 report on Venezuela's tax system, "are still of the two most important and best documented works" in the field.[5] In 2008, Roy Bahl and Richard Bird concluded: "In the long run, undoubtedly the most valuable contributions of scholars such as Shoup and Musgrave... was that by publishing their policy studies they helped to train a generation of scholars, from both developed and developing countries, who influenced tax policy discussions and design for years to come."[6]

Further contributing to the influence of the *Report* was its seemingly immediate success in shaping legislation. Shoup himself trumpeted this accomplishment, perhaps a bit nervously, in his presidential address, titled "Tax Reform in Japan," at the 1949 annual meeting of the National Tax Association. "As of the present moment," he wrote, "it appears likely the recommendations of the tax mission will be enacted into law in a special session of the Japanese Diet scheduled for the end of October or sometime in November."[7] Even without proof of concrete, long-term results in Japan, however, American promoters of financial and tax assistance missions had good reason to turn to the *Report* as a useful model during the 1950s and 1960s. They found its combination of democratic idealism, market sensitivity, Keynesian economics, and institutional awareness appealing.

SHOUP'S EARLY RETROSPECTIVES

In the immediate wake of the mission, Shoup seemed most euphoric about his success in promoting a democratic "tax atmosphere." He found encouragement in those views even from members of the Japanese government. In September 1949, Hara Sumio, a close collaborator in the Tax Bureau of the Japanese Ministry of Finance (MOF), wrote to Shoup that he had some disagreements over "inessential and technical matters;" however, he was "a whole-hearted follower" of "what I deem are your most basic principles...: that taxation must be the very field where the people should learn the truly democratic welfare of the community through comparisons between the impact of taxation and the benefit of governmental activity."[8]

After Shoup's pronouncement of the mission's victory at the annual meeting of the National Tax Association in 1949, he soon became more cautious in staking out claims for having produced shifts in tax policy. The concrete results of the "second mission" in 1950 disappointed him, as did subsequent policy reversals. Despite this, he still remained convinced that the mission had democratized the tax atmosphere in Japan. The new complexity of Shoup's assessment of the mission appeared clearly in a long, and uncharacteristically emotional, letter to General Douglas MacArthur more than a year later, in April 1951, just after President Truman fired MacArthur. On the one hand, Shoup associated his mission with the democratizing accomplishments of the occupation. "When the record of the post-war period comes to be written in proper perspective," Shoup told MacArthur, "your achievement in transforming the attitude of the Japanese people toward the goals of civic life will stand out as one of the most remarkable feats of which history has any record." That transformation included changes in attitudes toward taxation, Shoup explained. "The fact that taxation is everybody's business, a fact that we take for granted in the United States, has been accepted by the Japanese people, and the importance of this mental transformation can be fully recognized only by those who saw what the attitude was before you decided to set in motion the steps leading to reform." On the other hand, Shoup gave MacArthur, as if he were still Supreme Commander for the Allied Powers (SCAP), a detailed rendition of the problems Shoup's mission encountered and stressed during its second visit to Japan. These were the problems of compliance with the self-assessed income tax, the excessive dependence on tax and budget policy for controlling inflation, and the lack of commitment to reform local taxation and intergovernmental fiscal relations.[9]

In November of the same year, Shoup gave a second follow-up report on the Japan mission to the National Tax Association. By then he had become guarded, even with regard to his democratizing accomplishments. He made no grand statements about raising the tax consciousness of the Japanese public, and advanced a much more modest claim relating to the improvement in the tax atmosphere. Although he asserted that "Whatever the ultimate fate of our recommendations," he and his colleagues "like to believe that on at least one front the mission has achieved success," he went on to explain that he referred "to an intelligent interest in, and growth of skill in analyzing, tax problems on the part of lawyers, accountants, government officials, scholars and others." He cited the creation of two chairs in tax law at the universities of Tokyo and Kyoto and the active work of the Japan Tax (Research) Association, whose formation the mission had promoted. "Over the long-run, currents like those, which our group helped to some extent to set in motion, may prove more useful than any of the specific proposals that were adopted."[10]

The next point that assists in charting Shoup's reassessment of the mission came in May 1957, when Martin Bronfenbrenner asked Shoup to review a substantial manuscript on "The Aftermath of the Shoup Tax Reforms" written with Kogiku Kiichiro.[11] In the manuscript, Bronfenbrenner provided the first systematic evaluation in English of the results of the Shoup mission. Bronfenbrenner was rather dubious with regard to the sustained accomplishments of the mission. He noted that significant departures from Shoup's framework had occurred "in the direction not of further experimentation but of return to pre-war Japanese traditions and practices."[12] He expressed some technical quibbles with certain aspects of the Shoup recommendations, particularly in the realm of local finance, and suggested that the mission had neglected to take into account certain folk prejudices.[13] Despite this, Bronfenbrenner placed little blame on the mission itself for the major reversals. He put the onus on a wide variety of factors outside of the control of the mission and concluded, overall: "The wonder is less that the Shoup program was modified drastically than that it has survived at all."[14] Bronfenbrenner, however, suggested that a different political strategy might have improved the mission's chances of success. Following a suggestion that Harold Groves had offered, he wrote that "Had time permitted, the *Shoup Report* might have been more palatable if presented in the form of *alternatives* among which the Japanese themselves might choose (perhaps within limits)." He went on to elaborate: "Only one of the alternatives need have been so revolutionary as the actual proposal, and the Japanese might have been left not only a choice between them but also a good deal of leeway in combining elements from two or more of them."[15]

Shoup responded to Bronfenbrenner with three pages of commentary, none of which was defensive. He called the article an "excellent job, one that badly needed doing," described it as reflecting "a judicious, scholarly state of mind in a field where that is difficult to attain – and maintain," and asked for five to ten copies for "my tax seminar next fall." Shoup made no comments on Bronfenbrenner's extended discussion of the reasons for reversals of the mission's recommendations, and mainly raised minor technical issues regarding Bronfenbrenner's data. Shoup proposed another way of assessing "the success or failure of a tax mission." He declared: "Theoretically" it should be "measured by a comparison of what the system is now compared with what it would have been if the mission had not visited the country." He admitted "this we shall never know;" however, "speculation on the point might be worthwhile." Despite the risks of hypothetical counter-factual speculation, Shoup was firm on one mark of success derived through this procedure. He revived the theme of democratization, telling Bronfenbrenner that "one accomplishment cannot be undone: tax policy has been pulled out into the daylight, for wide public discussion" as a consequence of the publication and dissemination of the *Report*. A related accomplishment was in advancing the "rule of law" in tax policy. "I get the impression," Shoup wrote, "that pre-war taxation was in large part a thing of bargaining between individual firm and tax office without too much reference to the laws and regulations." In addition, he suggested that "the inclusion of depreciable assets in the local real estate tax base – one of the most important elements in the strengthening of local finance – has stuck." He was more tentative on the contribution of the "blue-return" system, asking Bronfenbrenner what he really thought and commenting that "We had considerable hopes for it." Shoup raised questions about Bronfenbrenner's warning that the income tax was on the way to becoming "little more than a disguised payroll tax;" however, he acknowledged both the collapse of the system of local tax reform and the narrowing of the base of personal income taxation. On the whole, in this letter Shoup adopted a tone that was relaxed, detached, and very much open to a serious reexamination of the mission's work.

Shoup sent a copy of his comments to Surrey, to whom Bronfenbrenner had also posted his manuscript. Surrey seconded Shoup's comments. "I have the impression as Carl does," he told Bronfenbrenner, "that there is a good deal more discussion, especially in Japanese academic circles, about tax matters than existed formerly. Perhaps out of this all this discussion will come a desire for continued improvement of the system." He did not, however, provide any explicit agreement with Shoup's larger democratization theme. He did, however, end by reinforcing Shoup's main point: "One wonders, given the conservative nature of the Japanese government, what the tax system would have looked like without a mission's ever having been made."[16]

NEW VENUES FOR REFORM: VENEZUELA, BRAZIL, COMMON MARKETS, AND LIBERIA

Shoup soon had an opportunity to demonstrate in action the nature and extent of his learning from reflection on the mission to Japan and accomplishments that had fallen short of his aspirations. In May 1958, Shoup agreed to conduct a comprehensive study of the tax system of Venezuela for that nation's minister of finance. The Venezuela mission, along with the two that followed in Brazil and Liberia, are especially important points of reference because, after Japan, they were his most substantial and influential missions within the history of international tax assistance.[17] The mission to Venezuela was, moreover, interesting because it was his first to what was clearly a developing nation. Although Japan had presented some characteristics of a developing nation, it had already dramatically demonstrated its capacity for a high level of economic performance.

In the Venezuela mission, Shoup replicated some of the elements of his mission to Japan that he believed had worked well.[18] As in Japan, the disciplinary mix of colleagues he assembled included economists (himself, John Due, whom he had unsuccessfully tried to recruit for the Japan mission, and Sir Donald MacDougall, an Oxford economist), law professors (Surrey, now at Harvard, and Oliver S. Oldman, also at the Harvard Law School in its international tax program), and a tax administrator (Lyle C. Fitch, first deputy administrator for the city of New York). As in Japan, the group included two trusted friends and colleagues, Due and Surrey, the latter being a veteran of the Japan mission. As in Japan, the inner circle took primary responsibility for writing the final report.[19] The inclusion of MacDougall provided the mission with a European member, just as Shoup had wished to do to in order to broaden the comparative scope of the Japan mission. The appointment of Fitch indicated Shoup's continuing interest in local taxation within a program of national reform. The appointment of members from Venezuela was never an issue because the Venezuelan government sponsored and paid for the mission and had appointed a Fiscal Reform Commission to assist it. A crucial consideration to Shoup was an agreement for the publication and wide dissemination of the report. Shoup made sure the report would be translated into Spanish, and arranged for The Johns Hopkins University Press to publish it in 1959.[20]

In making recommendations to the Venezuelan government, Shoup followed in outline much of the plan he had proposed for Japan. At the same time, however, he adapted his recommendations to conditions in Venezuela, and to the lessons he had learned from the Japan mission. In Venezuela, Shoup demonstrated that his extended encounter with Japan had made a marked impact on not only the Japanese tax system but his own approaches to tax reform as well.

On the Venezuelan mission, as in Japan, Shoup stayed true to the principles of Robert Murray Haig by focusing on the introduction of a comprehensive income tax for the purposes of both enhancing equity (vertical as well as horizontal) and increasing revenues. The new system would replace a complex income tax having nine schedules. As in Japan, Shoup placed a great deal of emphasis on improved income tax administration, including enhanced training in tax law and accounting. The overall thrust of Shoup's recommendations for Venezuela, however, was more progressive than had been the case in Japan. Shoup seems to have concluded that his recommendations for income tax reform in Japan had not been sufficiently progressive; however, he was additionally taking into account the more concentrated distribution of income and more significant underinvestment in education in Venezuela. "There is room," Shoup wrote, "for a tax system that is more progressive, less erratic in its distribution of the tax bill, and less burdensome at the very lowest levels of income, than the one now in force."[21] To increase progressivity Shoup recommended the abolition of a cascading sales tax, which in Venezuela applied to gross receipts, in addition to income tax reforms. Shoup and his colleagues complained that the cascading sales tax was inefficient and "results in an unjustifiable burden on the large numbers of persons in Venezuela at bare subsistence levels, and checks increases in the standards of living of the lower income groups." In contrast with the Japan *Report*, however, Shoup recommended against replacing it with any form of general sales tax, including a value-added tax (VAT). This was another instance of Shoup's learning from his work in Japan. "The revenue lost by repeal," Shoup wrote, "can be obtained more equitably and with less administrative trouble by an increase in the income tax."[22] Shoup recognized, however, that increased revenue needs or possible opposition to increases in income taxation might lead to the adoption of a general sales tax. In preparation for that possibility, Shoup provided a discussion of alternatives, including a VAT. His preference, on the basis of conditions in Venezuela, was for a wholesale sales tax rather than a VAT. Although the VAT had the advantage of spreading "the impact of the tax over a larger number of firms," thus lessening "the incentive to evade," a VAT would be "more complicated, especially if exemptions are granted."[23] Shoup's qualified views regarding the tax emerged from sustained research after returning from Japan. In 1955 he published an influential article clarifying issues surrounding the various alternatives within a VAT, and throughout the 1950s he mentored a PhD student, Clara K. Sullivan, who published a book Shoup described as "the standard reference for a history and analysis of the value-added tax."[24]

In recommending a progressive turn in Venezuela's tax policy, Shoup explicitly addressed, and then dismissed, the possibility that it might decrease capital accumulation. Shoup did so through an extended analysis of the expenditure side of public budgets – something he had not been given permission to do in Japan. He coupled this analysis with an extensive discussion of both the distribution of income and Venezuela's economic structure, including its social budgeting.[25] Shoup concluded that "government expenditure probably tends to benefit disproportionately the larger – more prosperous – towns rather than the smaller ones and the countryside; and expenditure on trunk roads, hotels and the like probably tends to benefit particularly the richer classes."[26] He noted that the nation's "level of education relative to income is one of the lowest in the world" and offered cost-benefit computations showing the high rates of return to additional educational investments. Shoup stressed, in countering the implications of increasing tax progressivity for capital formation, that "education is in itself a form of investment" and that in Venezuela "education is one of the highest yielding investments."[27] In contrast with Japan, Shoup regarded expansion of the fiscal capacity of the national government as the highest priority. "If a frontal attack is to be made within a short period of time on the great problem of educating the growing numbers of children (not to speak of the not far from half of the adult population who are said to be illiterate), it cannot very well be left to the states and municipalities."[28] Under Shoup's plan, the reform of taxation at the national level would both promote tax equity and establish the basis for the badly needed creation of social capital.[29]

The Venezuela mission enjoyed less success than the mission to Japan. As with the Japan report, Shoup's Venezuela study received high marks from the international community of tax experts. Despite this praise, however, the policy results were disappointing. Public finance economist Charles McLure, Jr. has suggested that this resulted in part from "the abundance of petroleum reserves" and the consequent lack of any pressure to undertake fundamental reform.[30] Thirty years later, Shoup agreed with McClure's explanation but additionally reflected that his mission may have failed to provide adequate follow-through in the process of implementing its recommendations. To have done so, he noted, would have required a much larger reform project.[31]

Shoup's next major foray came in 1964, when he traveled to Brazil.[32] In some ways that mission differed significantly from the one to Japan. Shoup worked alone; he was the entire mission. As in Venezuela, no fiscal or economic crisis prompted the study. The early 1960s was a relatively tranquil period for the Brazilian government, which had decided that the calm offered an opportunity for tax rationalization. In addition to this, Brazil had a very specific operational objective: it wanted an outsider to review a proposal by the Getúlio Vargas Foundation for a new income tax system. The Brazil mission was, however, similar in fundamental ways to its Japan counterpart. Shoup once again applied Haig's principles. He recommended the abolition of schedular income taxes and excess-profits taxation, and their replacement by a reformed income tax. The only new tax he suggested was a VAT for the states, which they would use to replace a cascading turnover tax. In addition, Shoup proposed a system of grants-in-aid to replace a tax-sharing program. On one hand, these recommendations for value-added taxation and grants-in-aid paralleled those he had made for Japanese prefectures. On the other hand, he recommended the VAT to Brazil with what he described in 1989 as "some diffidence."[33] Again, he revealed the caution that he had learned in Japan. His specific language in Brazil was that "If the states are to retain the sales tax, consideration could be given to a VAT."[34] If he had decided, he explained later, to discuss "the problems and possibilities of the VAT" at any length, his "report would have had to depend largely on introspection and speculation, since no country in 1964 imposed a value-added tax that extended through the retail stage."[35] Overall, in making recommendations to Brazil, Shoup had adopted a more conditional approach than he had in Japan. He settled for publication of his relatively brief report only in Brazil (in both English and Portuguese), thus moderating any claim for its contributions to tax scholarship in the United States and Europe.[36] In 1987 Shoup found it very difficult to connect subsequent reforms in Brazilian taxation with his recommendations. He consequently declined to render a verdict on the effects of his single-handed study, except to note that the Brazilian tax system "has improved," and to imply that that his report had influenced at least some of the positive changes.[37] At the same time, Malcolm Gillis noted that although Brazil did subsequently enact a VAT, "it has adopted only small bits and pieces of the rest of the Shoup program in the last twenty-three years."[38]

Shortly before Shoup conducted his study of the Brazilian tax system, he had turned to the study of tax reform within nations, both developed and developing, that sought to form or expand common markets. He launched this project in the wake of the 1962 report of the Fiscal and Financial Committee of the Commission of the European Economic Community. Fritz Neumark, who had returned to Germany from Turkey in 1952 after playing a central role in tax reform there, chaired the committee, and the resulting "Neumark Report" became the framework for the common market tax policy.[39] Shoup, who had wanted to appoint Neumark to his Japan team in 1949, was finally able to collaborate with him in 1963–4 at Columbia. The large project was reminiscent of Shoup's major efforts during the 1930s. With substantial support from Columbia and the Ford Foundation, Shoup gathered a broad array of interdisciplinary scholars to improve the theoretical and practical understanding of coordinating tax policy within common markets not only in Europe but in Central and Latin America, East Africa, and "Soviet-type" economies. In addition to Neumark, he attracted John Due, Peggy Musgrave, Hirofumi Shibata (a student of William Vickrey's), and Shoup's students Clara Sullivan and Richard Bird, among others, to the project. The group worked for three years, between 1962 and 1965, and a massive two-volume report emerged in 1967. At the intellectual core of the project was Shoup's preference for the coordination of national fiscal and tax systems (the meaning of "harmonization") rather than crude homogenizing that disrespected national traditions and the legitimacy of social choices made within individual nations.[40]

A year later, in 1968, Shoup conducted another international mission – this one in Liberia. It was much more elaborate than his Brazilian effort.[41] Harold Moss figured once again in Shoup's work. During the 1960s, Moss, who had returned to the Internal Revenue Service after his stint in Japan, initiated and ran the Foreign Assistance Office, which he modeled on his service to SCAP. With this program, funded heavily by the United States Agency for International Development, the Internal Revenue Service loaned personnel, often on a long-term basis, to developing nations.[42] When the Liberian government sought assistance from the U.S. Treasury in increasing the revenues required to fund education, infrastructure, and protective services without overburdening the formal economy or overrelying on foreign aid and loans, Moss proposed a technical tax mission with Shoup as its director. Shoup met with Liberia's President William Tubman in London and agreed to take on the project. As before, he obtained the ability to appoint his colleagues, who included Vickrey and two new members to a Shoup mission: Rudolph G. Penner of the University of Pennsylvania and Douglas Dosser of York University, who worked with Shoup on the fiscal harmonization project. Dosser's appointment reflected the desire of both the Liberian government and Shoup to include a member from outside the United States. In contrast with the missions to Japan and Venezuela, all of the team members were public finance economists. As in Japan and Venezuela, an inner group – just Shoup and Vickrey in Liberia – drafted the final report.[43]

The goals of the Liberian mission were to increase the income elasticity of Liberia's tax revenues, "to remove some of the tax burden that now rests on low-income families," and "to facilitate the economic development of Liberia."[44] A central goal of the Liberian mission was to provide advice on how to develop rules for computing the taxable profits of foreign-owned corporations, particularly the iron-ore mining companies.

The efforts of Shoup and his colleagues, he recalled, represented "probably the first attempt in taxation literature to develop systematically the issues" surrounding those rules. He explained that "Although the tone of the report was restrained . . . the inference was clear: sophisticated foreign investors may well have taken advantage of the government's lack of expertise in the tax field in the drawing up of the concession agreements, and if the concessions could be reopened, these tax anomalies should be rectified."[45] Beyond that task, Shoup and his colleagues did not push too hard. Shoup displayed the same caution in rendering advice to foreign governments that he had displayed following the mission to Japan. Moreover, he was aware of that "the power of the tax system in Liberia to sustain the Government is endangered by . . . multifarious informal contributions," and he did not want to add to disincentives "to enter the monetary economy permanently."[46] Finally, Shoup recognized that the Liberian government had little interest in new taxes. The mission considered national real estate taxation; however, in the report Vickrey – who had the tax as his special assignment – and Shoup wrote: "This form of taxation appears to be deeply involved with the social and political character of the country, and we have not been in Liberia long enough to explore the problem to the depth that it would require if definite recommendations were made."[47] The mission did not recommend the enactment of a VAT. Its report weighed the tax against alternatives and came down on the side of a tax on inventories. It would be, the mission reported, "a desirable, if crude, substitute for a retail sales or value-added tax, because it is relatively easy to administer even where the establishment keeps no records or keeps multiple records for tax and other purposes."[48]

Twenty years later, Shoup wrote that because none of the recommendations of the Liberian tax mission were adopted, it "must be considered a failure." He had no success in reforming income taxation, and "the mission's warning against attempting a general sales tax has apparently been ignored." Shoup said he was willing to accept responsibility; however, he went on to suggest other factors at play: lack of pressure for new revenues, too few resources committed to the mission, and a huge cultural gap that the mission had identified by pointing to problems of corruption and informal economies but had not been able to surmount in its recommendations.[49]

None of Shoup's major post-World War II missions, with the possible exception of the Brazilian mission, was as successful as the one to Japan. A comparative analysis of the complex question of their relative lack of success is beyond the scope of this chapter; however, it is safe to say that it would probably be a mistake to blame an overreliance on the reform model that Shoup had developed for the Japan mission. As noted above, one of the most likely reasons for the failures of the Venezuela and Liberia missions was the availability of nontax revenue sources that had the kind of debilitating effect on the development of the "tax state" discussed by Monica Prasad in Chapter 11.[50] If there was also a common pattern in those two nations of political resistance to the progressive dimensions of Shoup's recommendations, it was hardly a commentary on the value of Shoup's reform model. In any case, even before he went to Venezuela, Shoup had begun to reevaluate his work in Japan and develop a more flexible application of the principles of the "Shoup recommendations." He had demonstrated significant flexibility even earlier that this. When preparing for the mission to Japan, Shoup had regarded the components of his reform model – expanding state capacity by shifting to moderately progressive and broad-based taxation, strengthening tax administration, and energizing local government – as guidelines that he intended to adapt to institutional realities. In fact, describing these elements as comprising a "model" risks overstating the coherence of Shoup's rather eclectic approach to the practicalities of reform. In all his missions, beginning with the one to France and including the one to Japan, Shoup demonstrated his commitment to social learning in the process of tax reform. In 1967, he told political scientist Samuel P. Huntington that "in many countries" the study of "the problems of political reform and social change ... deserves research priority over the issues of tax policy problems."[51] As a consequence of his recognition of the need to develop a deep understanding of fiscal institutions and their social context, his policy prescriptions differed in significant ways across the four nations that he studied.

SHOUP'S REASSESSMENTS, 1989–91

Shoup's encounter with Japan had a major influence on his subsequent tax missions; however, he waited forty years to publish his first systematic reevaluation of the mission to Japan. In 1989, he wrote his own history of the mission for a celebratory conference in Japan, and two years later he added a paper that addressed the question of how tax missions ought to allocate their time among the tasks of "tax architecture, tax engineering, and tax administration." As Ajay Mehrotra discussed in Chapter 2, by tax architecture Shoup meant the overall structure of the tax system; by tax engineering, the structure of each particular tax; and by tax administration, the implementation of the mission's recommendations in tax law. In both these retrospective evaluations, Shoup evaluated his work in Japan in the context of international tax reform since 1949–50.[52]

In this retrospective view, Shoup ducked the question of how to develop a rigorous measure of the success of tax missions. He did, however, propose a *prima facie* test for identifying obvious failure. In 1989, he declared that a tax mission should be judged a failure if a country either failed to adopt any of its recommendations or succeeded in adopting all of them. The former outcome meant that the authors had "misunderstood the environment." The latter meant that the mission had failed "in is educational aim" and had not "taught the country to think for itself, and think clearly, on tax matters." In 1989 Shoup claimed that he had applied the same standard four decades earlier. He recalled that he "was not only surprised, but somewhat uneasy, when, shortly after returning to the United States in 1949," he "learned that almost all the mission's recommendations had, it was said, been put into law." He added: "As it turned out, I need not have been quite so uneasy."[53]

Although Shoup was not prepared to advance a precise standard for success, he was willing to discuss, in context, the specific accomplishments of his major missions, often invoking the hypothetical counter-factual test he had proposed to Bronfenbrenner in 1957. In the discussion three decades later, Shoup took particularly seriously the charge that his ambitions for the Japan mission, and the elaborate one that followed soon after in Venezuela, had been too ambitious. In doing so, he declared his strong, principled belief in the importance of the "foreign expert" making recommendations on the fundamental issues of "tax architecture." He sharply criticized the opposing view, which he attributed to Ikeda Hayato, Japan's finance minister in 1949, and to Enrique F. Gittes, a tax researcher at Harvard Law School's international tax program, who commented in 1968 on Shoup's mission to Venezuela. Shoup had just discovered that Ikeda had written that in 1949 the Japanese "tax system as such was based on a fairly careful study of various European systems, and its theoretical underpinnings were well developed, so there was no particular need to seek the guidance of foreigners on the system itself. But there was a lot of confusion in the operation of the tax laws, that is, in tax administration."[54] In addition, Gittes had asserted that "foreign technicians will not be the first persons in the host countries to suggest broad policy changes." Shoup retorted: "It is the foreign experts who are likely to have the broad view of what is going on in the world at large, in taxation, and what styles of tax architecture have proved successful for what types of country." Shoup emphasized the importance of foreign experts in providing a comparative approach: "The reasoning supporting one or another kind of tax architecture for a particular country involves sophisticated analyses of social and political influences, and hence the mission expert who has had occasion to study several tax systems has an advantage." He acknowledged that the Liberian report had not addressed questions of tax architecture, but this reflected "Liberia's comfortable budget condition and the general acceptability of the existing tax structure." The focus there, instead, was on engineering issues "common to many less developed countries": concession agreements with foreign-owned mining companies (iron ore in the case of Liberia) that provided the concessionaires with income tax breaks; and problems with the "network of taxes on imports and exports."[55]

On the specific accomplishments of the Japan mission Shoup emphasized two primary achievements of the mission, just as he had in 1951 and 1957. These were improving the administration of the income tax and enhancing the general tax "atmosphere." With regard to the first accomplishment, Shoup detailed the success of the blue-return system (including the formation of the Blue Return Taxpayers' Association), the expansion of the National Tax Administration Agency, whose creation Harold Moss had overseen in early 1949, and the government sponsorship of the Japanese Federation of Certified Public Tax Accountants' Associations (which the National Tax Administration Agency supervised).[56] In discussing the inherently vague category of tax "atmosphere," Shoup remained as modest as he had been in 1951 (but perhaps not in 1957), focusing only on his contributions to tax education. He emphasized the creation of other associations – the Japan Tax Association, which he had envisioned as an interdisciplinary organization that would be similar in its structure and functions to the National Tax Association in the United States, and the separate Japan Tax Law Association, which had a more narrow disciplinary and professional focus. He added that tax law professorships had increased from the two established by 1951, and now included five in the major national universities and thirty in various private universities.[57]

By 1989 Shoup had concluded that the mission could have modified its recommendations to make the whole package more effective. He acknowledged that it had not achieved all of its objectives, and he went on to identify what he had come to regard as three major problems with the mission's recommendations. The first problem was the heavy reliance on the recommendation of a VAT. This, he said, "Now seems at least dubious." He explained that the mission's fears that three levels of income taxation would have unduly burdened business had turned out to be "unwarranted." In addition, he noted, administrators and taxpayers understandably feared the "great unknown" of a VAT. Shoup admitted that "Even the pure theory of the value-added tax had not yet been worked out completely." In summary, he reflected, the practical matter of allocating a VAT among prefectures "was not seriously addressed" in 1949–50. Shoup was somewhat more tentative with regard to the two other problems. The second problem was that the mission had failed to reduce the dependence of the collection of personal income taxation on "simple withholding without any filing of a personal return by wage earners and salaried persons." He quickly added, however, that "what else might have been recommended . . . is by no means evident." The third problem regarded timing. He wrote that the "minor innovations" of the net wealth tax, the tax on undistributed profits, and the accessions tax "might have been recommended only for some future year when these novelties could have been accommodated more readily than in the chaotic days of 1949–1950." These innovations "were minor," Shoup recalled, "not in the sense of principles at stake, but in the revenue implications, and might have been postponed" even though that "would probably have meant negation."[58]

Shoup went on to suggest that he thought a major limitation that his missions had faced, and that future missions would have to address, was in "the growing problems of the underground economy (illegal sector, informal economy) in certain developing countries." Shoup singled out, in particular, his mission to Liberia for its failure to address issues of informal economy, although his Liberian report had, in fact, commented at length on its significance. The Japan mission, he volunteered, had a similar failing. It had not really addressed "the extralegal, quasi taxes in the Japan of 1949." In fairness to Shoup, however, he wrote in the Japan *Report* that "In every municipality the members of our mission visited on our field trips, we encountered evidence of substantial amounts of money being raised for municipal purposes by means of the so-called voluntary contributions."[59] In 1989 he added that the problem of "socioeconomic payments, or voluntary contributions" is "primarily an administrative problem, one which is linked to an architectural policy that depends heavily on the kinds of tax that the taxpayer does not view as being in close competition with the informational requirements: the sales tax, for example, compared with the income tax." Dealing with these problems "calls not only for special measures in tax administration, but also for special provisions in . . . the tax law, to specify the details of a tax base that is suitable for the informal economy." He suggested that the size of missions ought to be increased to deal with such difficulties, and that their composition should shift. Missions, he suggested, might profitably shift somewhat away from economists and tax lawyers to "sociologists or social psychologists" who could help "fit the tax engineering as precisely as possible to social patterns in the particular country's household and business environments" and to political scientists, "who could have a special understanding of the political limitations surrounding any tax proposal."[60]

SHOUP AND LESSONS FOR INTERNATIONAL FINANCIAL AGENCIES

The Shoup mission influenced the subsequent mobilization of technical expertise from the developed world. The reputed success of the Shoup mission to Japan helped to inspire other missions by Richard Musgrave, and the students and disciples of Shoup and Musgrave. Their influence remained significant throughout the 1980s; however, during that decade marked shifts began to occur in the scale and purpose of tax assistance activity, in its organization, and in the reform messages embedded in the assistance. Although some of Shoup's and Musgrave's institutional DNA remained evident, the new wave of technical assistance departed in major ways from the approaches that Shoup had crafted in his four prototypical missions. Ironically, the new wave seemed more consistent with the objectives, methods, and results of Joseph Dodge's 1949–52 mission to Japan than that of Carl Shoup.[61]

International financial agencies, especially the International Monetary Fund (IMF) and the World Bank, through its main arm the International Bank for Reconstruction and Development, as well as the Organization for Economic and Community Development, the World Trade Organization, and regional development banks, drove the postwar acceleration in the number of tax assistance missions. Along with the increasing activity of these international agencies came greater external, top-down pressure from these institutions, and their creditors, for tax reform within developing economies. This activity represented a continuation of the kind of financial and fiscal mission that Dodge had led, shifting the approach from the one Shoup had taken in his major tax missions. None of Shoup's four major missions were sponsored by international agencies, and two – the missions to Japan in 1949 and Liberia in 1968 – were sponsored by American agencies (SCAP and the U.S. Treasury). With the exception of the one to Japan, none of his missions was set in an economic crisis. Only the mission to Japan operated under threats of financial sanctions, and even these threats turned out to be remote. Throughout his career as international reformer, his central goal was to promote social and political development along democratic lines rather than to damp down financial crises.

At the time of Shoup's mission to Japan, the IMF had only just begun to be a force in the international economy and had not yet turned its attention to tax reform. The IMF, organized under the 1944 Bretton Woods agreement, began financial operations in 1947 and focused its work on the stabilizing role of establishing and maintaining a fixed exchange-rate, or par value, system. In these early years, the IMF mainly served the major industrial nations, whereas the World Bank, on behalf of a wider range of client nations, took under its purview the issues of fiscal capacity, good government, and institutional strength. These issues were necessarily bound up in the World Bank's lending activities, and so the organization moved somewhat more quickly into the role of international tax reformer. In 1949, as Martin Daunton mentioned in Chapter 15, the World Bank employed Musgrave to conduct a pioneering in-depth study of taxation in Colombia as part of a larger financial reform project led by Lauchlin Currie.[62] Despite this, the IMF soon got into the act as well. Developing nations faced problems in adopting and managing fixed exchange rates, and this led the IMF to become increasingly involved in shaping their economic policies and, in particular, pressing for more vigorous anti-inflationary actions in those nations as well as those that were more industrialized. During the early postwar years, as Margaret Garritson de Vries, the official historian of the IMF, has written, "Fund officials... believed that it was the inflationary impact of domestic fiscal and monetary policies that was by far the most important cause of continued and recurrent payments deficits." In the view of the IMF, within most of the member nations "excessive demand existed that weakened incentives to undertake the transfers of productive resources necessary for long-term external equilibrium."[63] Just as Shoup discovered in Japan, when an agency or a mission, such as the one that Dodge led, with prime responsibility for exchange-rate stability, turned to issues of stabilization, it was difficult to keep them away from deep involvement in issues of institutional structure, particularly in a zone of policy, such as taxation, that had closely bound implications for both stabilization and development. Margaret de Vries has described the IMF staff as favoring what amounted to roughly the same perspective as Dodge. The staff embraced "a policy of financial stability" as "the best way to attain balanced growth" at the same time as it rejected approaches that meant increased public investment and a higher risk of inflation.[64] Although during the 1950s the IMF paid increasing attention to monetary variables, it continued to emphasize "a member's reducing fiscal imbalance so as to help correct external payments equilibria."[65]

In 1962, at a significant turning point, the IMF began to work with the Colombian government to devise a multiyear investment plan and an implementation program that included tax reforms.[66] The IMF now led the efforts of international agencies in that country, despite the longer-standing involvement of the World Bank. In 1964, the IMF created a Fiscal Affairs Department to provide technical assistance to developing nations, including the training of personnel. In its 1965 annual report, the IMF stressed the importance of tax reform that enhanced revenues and reduced deficits.[67] With this expanded involvement in fiscal reform, their different missions meant that collaboration between the IMF and the World Bank often proved difficult.[68] Consequently, in 1966 they struck an agreement that established the primary responsibilities for each and set procedures for the coordination of their work in policy areas of potential conflict.[69] In the late 1960s and early 1970s, with this agreement in place, the IMF accelerated its technical assistance efforts, sending staff members to dozens of developing nations in Asia, Latin America, and Africa, including Liberia at the same time Shoup, sponsored by the Treasury, conducted his mission to that country.[70]

The rough division of labor between the IMF and the World Bank began to break down during the mid-1970s following the collapse of fixed exchange rates and the first oil crisis. Since this time, the IMF has been under especially great pressure from its creditor nations to deepen and expand its involvement in tax reform, using its financial support as leverage. The World Bank, with its own array of debtor nations, has tended to follow the lead of the IMF with regard to tax reform. During the international recession and associated financial crises of the 1980s, both agencies pressed for reductions in mounting deficit spending and inflation within developing nations, especially those in Latin America. In the 1990s, the two agencies shifted attention to Southeast Asia and Korea during financial crises. Amid the aftermath of the collapse of Communism, when the United States seized on the opportunity to accelerate the transition from centrally planned to market economies, the IMF and World Bank also paid close attention to the "transition" nations. Similar to the state-building that Dodge sought, the kind of reform often favored by the

IMF and the World Bank has been designed to increase the capacity to repay debt rather than expand social services. The top-down pressure for reform served to reduce the problem of lack of follow-through on recommendations that often frustrated Shoup and the other experts who were financed by the countries they studied. However, the top-down pressure tended to be for the kind of economic stabilization program that Dodge had pushed – strict retrenchment through tax increases and lower government spending – rather than the kind state-building program that Carl Shoup had advanced.[71]

Odd-Helge Fjeldstad and Mick Moore believe that it is reasonable to pose "a strong hypothesis: that the global tax reform agenda has been set by the international financial institutions... in pursuit of the same kinds of objectives that they have putatively been advancing worldwide by other means, notably the neo-liberal agenda of strengthening markets and weakening states, trade unions, popular political movements and other loci of organized political power." Fjeldstad and Moore step back from this hypothesis, however, by asserting that it is "hard to sustain the argument that the global tax reform agenda constitutes a significant neo-liberal project to weaken the state," noting that the IMF often puts heavy pressure on "poor countries to increase their tax revenues."[72] In-depth exploration of the political and economic motives behind the "neo-liberal" wave of tax reform lies beyond the scope of this chapter. It seems reasonable to agree with Miranda Stewart, however, that in recent years the IMF and World Bank have "through the sheer scale of their operations... mass-produced tax reform" and that this reform project has been "shaped by the historical context of imperial influence in the past two centuries."[73]

As the key international agencies have intensified top-down tax reform, the public finance specialists involved in designing and serving in international missions seem to have become more technocratic than was the case in the several decades immediately following World War II. Bahl and Bird point out that although Shoup and his mission colleagues tended to be "scholars who studied the tax system in question, usually doing much of the work in the field while drawing on their analytical knowledge and accumulated experience," the new specialists, despite sometimes being scholars, have been drawn more heavily from the ranks of the "staff or consultants" of the international agencies.[74] Fjeldstad and Moore describe this emerging group of experts as an "epistemic community of taxation professionals" who are "employed in national tax administrations, in consultancy companies and in international financial institutions, and organized in regional and global professional associations."[75] The members of the new wave of experts, similar to Shoup and Musgrave before them, have believed that their recommendations would "help countries achieve a more sustainable growth path." Despite this, the recommendations of many have tended to be narrower in scope and more united around a rigid reform model than was the case in the decades immediately following World War II. These experts have often displayed a hard ideological edge that is reminiscent of the attitudes of Dodge and the pre-World War II "money doctors." Bahl and Bird perhaps allude to this when they describe some of the new advisors as "driven to a much greater extent" than before "by such goals as reducing the fiscal deficit or promoting the private sector, in part at least in response to the political imperatives under which they operated."[76]

The technocratic reformers have embraced an increasingly homogeneous program of reform. They often believed that a major source of the fiscal difficulty was poorly administered income taxes with rates that were too high and bases that were too low.[77] In response, the primary proposals within the "mass-produced" reform program became improved tax administration, tax simplification, and the introduction or expansion of VATs.

The "mass-produced" reform agenda shares some similarities with elements that were important at various times to Shoup's program. Certainly a concern with improving tax administration, in at least a general sense, is one of the most important points of commonality. Although Shoup called out the need to take corruption and informal economies into account in proposing administrative reform, and freely admitted his own failure in addressing this problem, the outside advisers staffing the "neo-liberal" wave, as Joseph Stiglitz has pointed out, "often lecture moralistically on the need to improve tax administration and reduce corruption," at the same time as "they seldom address corruption as part of tax design."[78]

Simplification, other things being equal, was something Shoup favored. He recognized its virtues, particularly when simplicity meant broadening the base of income taxation. However, he never pushed blindly in that direction. Even in Japan, he qualified his base-broadening recommendations to take account, for example, of the special needs of Japanese corporations. Shoup never just replicated the simplifying recommendations from his last report or attempted to develop a template that he could transfer from one study to the next. His recommendations in Japan, for example, often introduced new complexities while trying to clean up old ones.

The VAT has certainly played a prominent role in the new and what may well be correctly described as a "neo-liberal" wave of tax reform. The VAT has often been a prominent feature of IMF prescriptions for developing nations. A signal element of that convergence of the IMF and the World Bank during the 1990s was the World Bank's abandonment of its earlier reservations about the fairness and practicality of the VAT and its embrace of the tax as a means of promoting fiscal consolidation and liberalization of trade.[79] Regardless of the source of reform impetus, in the process of liberalizing trade, developing nations have tended to reduce complex indirect taxes on exports and imports while attempting to replace the foregone revenues with VATs rather than income taxes or property taxes. In a 2010 study of the tax systems of six countries (Argentina, Brazil, India, Kenya, Korea, and Russia), economist Roger Gordon reported that they collected between one-fifth and one-fourth of their tax revenue with a VAT, while relying far less on personal income taxation (as little as 5 percent of tax revenue in Russia and 10 percent in Brazil and India).[80] At the same time, property tax revenues have contributed relatively little to recent state-building projects in developing nations. Roy Bahl and Jorge Martinez Vazquez estimate that in 2000–1 developing countries' property taxes accounted for only 0.6 percent of gross domestic product, and only 0.68 percent in "transition" countries – less than one-third of the level in industrialized nations.[81]

The fiscal results from increasing reliance on VATs have sometimes disappointed. Various observers have noted some of the reasons for this: difficulties in capturing undocumented transactions, the creation of incentives for the shift of transactions into the informal economy, and the lack of adequate income tax systems for offsetting the regressive effects of VATs.[82] Ironically, perhaps, given Shoup's pioneering role in advancing the popularity of VATs, over the past few decades some tax reformers have lost sight of the reservations that weighed increasingly on Shoup's mind after the mission to Japan. These informed his later analysis of the VAT. Just as the VAT was beginning to catch the wave of international neoliberalism, Shoup wrote: "No generalization seems justified on the suitability of the value-added tax for developing countries as a group."[83] In addition to this, in their preoccupation with VATs, reformers have at times lost sight of the potential Shoup identified and seized on for using both income and property taxation to enhance social equity and inspire trust in government. We should make it clear, however, that there are members of the current generation of VAT advocates who still take Shoup's reservations about VATs to heart and express support for taxes on income and wealth. Prominent among them is economist Richard Bird, a student of Shoup's who was first exposed to issues of public finance in developing economies while assisting Shoup on his Venezuela volume. Bird has presented arguments for the inclusion of income, property, and other wealth taxes in the mix for developing nations. In addition, he has written that "the level, structure, and effectiveness of taxation – including VAT – vary enormously from country to country and over time within countries." In the spirit of Shoup, Bird has called for more research on tailoring the tax mix to the needs of individual nations. For example, he has asked for improved knowledge regarding "whether there is a taxonomy within which countries can be placed in designing VAT." In addition, he has declared that "distributional issues lie at the core of the discipline" of public finance. "Given the centrality of the incidence question in all public finance analysis in developing and transitional countries, there must, one has to hope, be more that can be done than we have so far demonstrated."[84]

The primary point of contrast between Shoup and more recent reform enthusiasms is that in each of his post-World War II missions Shoup labored to adapt his proposals, however strong the principles driving them, to local conditions – institutional, political, and economic. Shoup expressed this respect for social diversity in his harmonizing prescriptions for both developing and high-income societies that sought to align in common markets. An intimately related difference between recent international tax reformers and Shoup is a contemporary lack of concern, similar to that revealed by Dodge during the occupation of Japan, for fostering broad and deep social support for the revenue systems required to fund modern welfare states. Shoup recognized that international tax reform would require not only the exportation of what he regarded as the best new ideas in tax theory and practice but also the respect of historically based distinctions among national fiscal systems. It was important, Shoup maintained, to recognize these differences if governments were to accomplish the dual goals of increasing tax consciousness and winning public confidence in government.

Shoup's ideals, and his sustained capacity for social learning, could provide useful inspiration to those reformers who would attempt to understand the potential for taxation to ease the contemporary fiscal crisis as well as to create governments that are able to meet the social needs of a globalizing world. In fact, we would argue that this crisis is two-fold. A structural deficiency in key types of public investment and social service expenditure is as much a part of the contemporary fiscal crisis as the large scale of public deficit and debts. Further, two key elements of the current fiscal crisis in the United States, Japan, and other nations – deficit spending and low levels of public investment – are mainly a consequence of a failure to raise tax revenues adequate to cover expenditures rather than a result of depressed economies or profligate spending and inefficiency. To resolve this dual crisis, the arguments on behalf of both revenue and the public sector must be made simultaneously, in an integrated fashion, and include what might be described as fundamental tax reform. Governments will have to argue not only that new social programs require significant new tax revenues – "the price of civilization" – but that the increased taxes will be accompanied by substantial reforms that make tax systems much better, that is to say much fairer, more efficient, and more transparent. Perhaps it is time to reconsider Haig and Shoup's tax reform program and take inspiration from their proposals for linking fundamental tax reform to the building of tax consciousness and the enhancement of the modern state.

Notes

1. Shoup, C. S., the Shoup Mission, *Report on Japanese Taxation by the Shoup Mission* (Tokyo: Supreme Command Allied Powers, 1949).

2. See, for example, S. Hara to C. S. Shoup, September 12, 1949 and November 14, 1949; C. S. Shoup to S. Shiomi, February 28, 1951, August 2, 1951; S. Tsuru to C. S. Shoup, August 2, 1951; H. Ito to C. S. Shoup, October 3, 1950, July 21, 1951, and August 9, 1951, Mission Series, Shoup Papers, Yokohama National University, YNU.

3. Shiomi, S., *Japan's Finance and Taxation, 1940–1956* (New York: Columbia University Press, 1957). See Shiomi, S. to C. S. Shoup, August 12, 1949, C. S. Shoup to S. Shiomi, August 24, 1949, S. Shiomi, to C. S. Shoup, August 25, 1952; and many letters between C. S. Shoup and S. Shiomi, in 1955 and 1956. Shiomi File, Box #1, Japan Series, Shoup Papers, Yokohama National University (YNU).

4. Bronfenbrenner, M., "Balm for the Visiting Economist," *The Journal of Political Economy* 1963, vol. 71, pp. 293–7.

5. Oldman, O., Surrey, S. S., "Technical Assistance in Taxation in Developing Countries," in Bird, R. M., Head, J. G., eds., *Modern Fiscal Issues: Essays in Honor of Carl S. Shoup*, (Toronto: University of Toronto, 1972), 278; Commission to Study the Fiscal System of Venezuela, Shoup, C. S., *The Fiscal System of Venezuela: A Report* (Baltimore: The Johns Hopkins University, 1959).

6. Bahl, R., Bird, R., "Tax Policy in Developing Countries: Looking Back – and Forward," *National Tax Journal* 2008, vol. 61, pp. 285.

7. Shoup, C. S., "Tax Reform in Japan," Presidential Address, National Tax Association, Wednesday, September 21, 1949, in *Proceedings of the*

Forty-second Annual Conference on Taxation Held under the Auspices of the National Tax Association (Sacramento, CA: National Tax Association, 1950), 400–13.

8. S. Hara to C. S. Shoup, September 12, 1949, All No. 7, Shoup Papers, YNU.

9. C. S. Shoup to D. MacArthur, April 12, 1951, Mission Correspondence Series 3, Box No. 3, MacArthur Series, Shoup Papers, YNU.

10. Shoup, C. S., "The Tax Mission to Japan," in "Round Table: Reconstruction of Tax Systems of Foreign Countries by United States Missions," in *Proceedings of the 44th Annual Conference on Taxation, National Tax Association, November 26–29, 1951.* (Sacramento, CA: National Tax Association, 1952), 231.

11. Later that year the manuscript would appear in two parts: Bronfenbrenner, M., Kogiku, K., "The Aftermath of the Shoup Tax Reforms: Part I," *National Tax Journal* 1957, vol. 10, pp. 236–54; and " . . . Part II," Ibid., 1957, pp. 345–60.

12. Bronfenbrenner, M., Kogiku, K., "The Aftermath of the Shoup Tax Reforms: Part I," 241.

13. Bronfenbrenner, M., Kogiku, K., "The Aftermath of the Shoup Tax Reforms: Part II," 353, 356–7.

14. Ibid., 358.

15. Ibid., 359. It is not clear when Groves made this suggestion to Bronfenbrenner. Groves did not make it after his first readings of Shoup's preliminary memos and final report. Groves made some criticisms, however he said that "in general the mission seems to have done a good job." Later he replaced the adjective "good" with "thoughtful and courageous." H. M. Groves to M. Bronfenbrenner, September 2 and November 15, 1949, Folder 21, Box 2, Harold M. Groves Papers, State Historical Society of Wisconsin.

16. C. S. Shoup to M. Bronfenbrenner, May 27, 1957, File: "Tax Mission 1950 (1)," Box 27 and S. Surrey to M. Bronfenbrenner, June 4, 1957, File: "Tax Mission 1949 (1)," Box 27, Stanley Surrey Papers, Special Collections, Harvard University Law Library.

17. His other studies of national tax systems came mainly after his retirement from Columbia University in 1971, when he served for three years as an advisor under the auspices of the Center for United Nations Development Programs Policy and Planning. In that role, he submitted reports on taxation in various nations, including Bahrain (1971), Turkey (1972), Israel (1972), and Swaziland (1974). Each of these reports, however, was far more limited in scope than the reports on Venezuela, Brazil, and Liberia. "Shoup" files under S-Files, Shoup Papers, YNU.

18. For Shoup's retrospective assessment of the Venezuelan mission, see Shoup, C. S., "Retrospectives on Tax Missions to Venezuela (1959), Brazil (1964), and Liberia (1970)," in Gillis, M., ed., *Tax Reform in Developing Countries* (Durham, NC: Duke University Press, 1989), 254–77.

19. At the end of the process Shoup wrote to Surrey: "I still can't realize that the job is done. And it certainly never would have been done, without your support, advice, and encouragement every step of the way." C.S. Shoup to

S. Surrey, December 21, 1959, "Venezuela" file, Box 27, Stanley Surrey Papers, Harvard University Law Library.

20. Commission to Study the Fiscal System of Venezuela, Shoup, C. S., *The Fiscal System of Venezuela: A Report.*

21. Ibid., 7.

22. Ibid., 300–1.

23. Ibid., 308.

24. See Shoup, C. S., "Theory and Background of the Value-Added Tax," in *Proceedings of the Forty-eighth Conference on Taxation* (Sacramento, CA: National Tax Association, 1955). Shoup first suggested the VAT as a dissertation topic to Clara Sullivan in January 1950 as a follow-up to the Japan mission's recommendation, and in April the topic gained momentum in the collaboration between advisor and advisee when Shoup learned that France had adopted a VAT-style tax. She completed her dissertation in 1959. C. S. Shoup to C. Sullivan, January 5, 1950 and April 12, 1950; C. S. Shoup to C. Sullivan, June 1, 1959, S-file, Shoup Papers. Sullivan's dissertation became a book the year after the subsequent Brazilian mission. See Sullivan, C. K., *The Tax on Value Added* (New York: Columbia University Press, 1965). For Shoup's quotation describing Sullivan's book, see Shoup, C. S., *Public Finance* (Chicago: Aldine, 1969), 251, n. 12; and, see Ibid., 250–69, for Shoup's survey analysis of the VAT. For analysis of Shoup's contributions to the VAT, see Thirsk, W., "Intellectual Foundations of the VAT in North America and Japan," in Eden, L., ed., *Retrospectives on Public Finance*, 133–48.

25. The report contained full chapters on the distribution of income (21–42), "general economic considerations relevant to public finance" (43–86), national accounts and accounting reports (365–405), and the costs of education and health (406–24).

26. Commission to Study the Fiscal System of Venezuela, Shoup, C. S., *The Fiscal System of Venezuela: A Report*, 42.

27. Ibid., 409 and 8.

28. Ibid., 20.

29. One of the reasons Shoup stressed the primacy of national tax reform may have been his belief that significant increases in property taxes within wealthy communities was politically impossible. A few years later, Shoup observed that in Caracas there was "a rich land and buildings base on which a substantial real estate could be, but is not, imposed." Shoup, C. S., *Public Finance* (Chicago: Aldine Publishing Company, 1969), 384, n. 3.

30. McLure, C. E. Jr., "Income Tax Reform in Venezuela: Thirty Years after the Shoup Mission," in Eden, L., ed., *Retrospectives on Public Finance* (Durham, NC: Duke University Press, 1991), 82–3.

31. Shoup, C. S., "Retrospectives on Tax Missions to Venezuela (1959), Brazil (1964), and Liberia (1970)," 277.

32. For his retrospective assessment, see Ibid., 277–88.

33. Ibid., 281.

34. Shoup, C. S., *The Tax System of Brazil* (Rio de Janeiro: Fundacãó Getúlio Vargas, 1965), 79.

35. Shoup, C. S., "Retrospectives on Tax Missions to Venezuela (1959), Brazil (1964), and Liberia (1970)," 287–8.
36. Shoup, C. S., *The Tax System of Brazil*.
37. Shoup, C. S., "Retrospectives on Tax Missions to Venezuela (1959), Brazil (1964), and Liberia (1970)," 284–8.
38. Gillis, M., "Introduction" to Shoup, C.S., "Retrospectives on Tax Missions to Venezuela (1959), Brazil (1964), and Liberia (1970)," 253.
39. On Neumark's role in Turkey, see Andic, F. M., Andic, S., "Fritz Neumark, Teacher and Reformer: A Turkish View," *FinanzArchiv / Public Finance Analysis* 1981, vol. 39, pp. 11–19.
40. Shoup, C. S., ed., *Fiscal Harmonization in Common Markets, Volume I: Theory and Volume II: Practice* (New York: Columbia University Press, 1967). On the organization of the project, see Volume I, vii–ix and xv–xx. For Shoup's own conclusions regarding harmonization, see Volume II, xi–xxi and Shoup, C. S., *Public Finance*, 640–51. The volumes included extensive analysis of value-added taxation.
41. Shoup, C. S., "Retrospectives on Tax Missions to Venezuela (1959), Brazil (1964), and Liberia (1970)," 289–312.
42. In 1972, Oliver Oldman and Stanley Surrey noted the importance of this IRS effort. They observed that during the second half of the 1960s it had been responsible for "the largest group providing tax technical assistance," serving primarily in South America and Asia, including Vietnam. Oldman, O., Surrey, S.S., "Technical Assistance in Taxation in Developing Nations," 279–280.
43. Shoup, C. S., *The Tax System of Liberia: Report of the Tax Mission* (New York: Columbia University Press, 1970).
44. Ibid., 1.
45. Shoup, C. S., "Retrospectives on Tax Missions to Venezuela (1959), Brazil (1964), and Liberia (1970)," 293–4.
46. Shoup, C. S., *The Tax System of Liberia*, 6.
47. Ibid., 95.
48. Ibid., 129.
49. Ibid., 310–11.
50. Marc Leroy usefully describes national governments that rely on rents from either natural resources or "geostrategic resources generating foreign aid" as "'rentier' states" rather than tax states. See Leroy, M., *Taxation, the State and Society: The Fiscal Sociology of Interventionist Democracy* (Brussels: Peter Lang, 2011), 163–5.
51. C.S. Shoup to S. P. Huntington, October 9, 1967. Shoup's made his remarks to Huntington during a discussion of the possibility of Shoup doing a study "of the politics of tax reform in modernizing countries" for Harvard's Center for International Affairs. See, also, Huntington to Shoup, March 24, 1967, Shoup to Huntington, March 29, 1967, and Huntington, to Shoup, June 8, 1967. "Huntington" files under H-Files, Shoup Papers, YNU.
52. Shoup, C. S., "The Tax Mission to Japan, 1949–50," 177–232; Shoup, C. S., "Melding Architecture and Engineering: A Personal Retrospective on

Designing Tax Systems," in Eden, L., ed., *Retrospectives on Public Finance*, 19–30.

53. Shoup, C. S., "The Tax Mission to Japan, 1949–50," 218–19.

54. Shoup, C. S., "Melding Architecture and Engineering: A Personal Retrospective on Designing Tax Systems," 23. In July 1951 Ikeda presented a different point of view in July 1951 when he wrote to Secretary of the Treasury John Snyder to praise Harold Moss on the occasion of Moss's return to the United States. Ikeda lauded Moss for his "magnificent and outstanding job in reforming and modernizing the Japanese tax system and its administration." He went on to declare that "the basic concepts and principles of taxation as laid down by his assistance will have their eternal place in the tax history of Japan." H. Ikeda to J. Snyder, July 10, 1951, copy in possession of Douglas M. Moss, and used with his permission.

55. Shoup, C. S., "Melding Architecture and Engineering: A Personal Retrospective on Designing Tax Systems," 23–5.

56. The Japanese Federation of Certified Public Tax Accountants' Associations (JFCPTAA), and the Japan Tax Research Institute, which the JFCPTAA created, jointly sponsored the celebratory occasion in 1989 where Shoup presented his retrospective history.

57. Shoup, C. S., "The Tax Mission to Japan, 1949–50," 202–7. In this discussion, Shoup heavily cited his 1985 correspondence with Kaneko Hiroshi.

58. Ibid., 221–2.

59. Shoup, C. S., "Melding Architecture and Engineering: A Personal Retrospective on Designing Tax Systems," 27–8; Shoup, C. S., *The Tax System of Liberia: Report of the Tax Mission*, 5–7; and Shoup, C. S., *Report on Japanese Taxation by the Shoup Mission, Volume II* (Tokyo: SCAP, 1949), 210.

60. Shoup, C. S., "Melding Architecture and Engineering: A Personal Retrospective on Designing Tax Systems," 27 and 29.

61. See the introduction to Part Two; Chapter 10 of this volume; and Brownlee, "Shoup vs. Dodge: Conflict over Tax Reform in Japan, 1947–1951," *Keio Economic Studies* 2011, vol., 91–122.

62. See also Alacevich, M., *The Political Economy of the World Bank: The Early Years* (Palo Alto, CA and Washington, DC: Stanford University Press and The World Bank, 2009), 32, 37, 48, and 65. Alacevich does not mention the work of the Currie mission and Musgrave (who was its chief economist) on taxation.

63. Garritson de Vries, M., *Balance of Payments Adjustment, 1945 to 1986: The IMF Experience* (Washington, D.C.: International Monetary Fund, 1987), 21.

64. Ibid., 23.

65. Ibid., 29–30.

66. On the IMF's work in Colombia in 1962, see ibid., 70–6.

67. On the intensified technical assistance program of the IMF, see Ibid., 102–5.

68. On the background of tension between the IMF and the World Bank over their overlapping zones of interest, see Woods, N., *The Globalizers: The IMF,*

the *World Bank, and Their Borrowers* (Ithaca, NY and London: Cornell University Press, 2006), 6–9.

69. Garritsen de Vries, M., *The International Monetary Fund, 1966–1971: The System under Stress, Volume I: Narrative* (Washington, D.C.: International Monetary Fund, 1976), 363–4.

70. For details, see Ibid., 582–4.

71. Marc Flandreau suggests that these policy shifts represented "the emergence of a regime which by many aspects brings memories of pre-1914 operations." Flandreau, M., "Introduction: Money and Doctors," in Flaundreau, M., ed., *Money Doctors: The Experience of Financial Advising 1850–2000* (London: Routledge, 2003), 6–7.

72. Fjeldstad, O.-H., Moore, M., "Tax Reform and State-Building in a Globalized World," in Bräutigam, D., Fjedstad, O.-H., Moore, M., eds., *Taxation and State-Building in Developing Countries* (Cambridge: Cambridge University Press, 2008), 238–9.

73. Stewart, M., "Global Trajectories of Tax Reform: The Discourse of Tax Reform in Developing and Transition Countries," in Lindsey, T., *Law Reform in Developing and Transitional States* (London: Routledge, 2007), 378; see also Stewart, M., "Tax Policy Transfers to Developing Countries: Politics, Institutions and Experts," in Nehring, H., Schui, F., eds., *Global Debates about Taxation* (Houndmills, England: Palgrave Macmillan, 2007), 182–200, especially 182–8.

74. Bahl, R. W., Bird, R. M., "Tax Policy in Developing Countries: Looking Back – and Forward," *National Tax Journal* 2008, vol. 61, 285–6.

75. Fjeldstad, O.-H., Moore, M., "Tax Reform and State-Building in a Globalized World," 285.

76. Bahl, R. W., Bird, R. M., "Tax Policy in Developing Countries: Looking Back – and Forward," 285–6.

77. For a good summary of the shift of international tax reform in the 1980s, see Thirsk, W. R., "Recent Experience with Tax Reform in Developing Countries," in Faini, R., de Melo, J., *Fiscal Issues in Adjustment in Developing Countries* (New York: St. Martin's Press, 1993), 169–95.

78. Stiglitz, J. E., "Development–Oriented Tax Policy," in Gordon, R. H., ed., *Taxation in Developing Countries: Six Case Studies and Policy Implications* (New York: Columbia University Press, 2010), 11.

79. Stewart, M., "Global Trajectories of Tax Reform: The Discourse of Tax Reform in Developing and Transition Countries," *Harvard International Law Journal* 2003, vol. 44, pp. 169. For evidence of the shift in assessment of the VAT, see World Bank, *Lessons of Tax Reform* (Washington, D.C.: The World Bank, 1991), 29–35. The Public Economics Division produced this book under the supervision of Lawrence H. Summers, who was then vice president for development economics at the World Bank; see ibid., v.

80. Gordon, R. H., "Introduction," in Gordon, R. H., ed., *Taxation in Developing Countries: Six Case Studies and Policy Implications*, 1–3. For a comprehensive analysis of the failure of developing nations to rely heavily on income taxation, see Bird, R., Zolt, E., "Redistribution via Taxation: The

Limited Role of the Personal Income Taxation in Developing Countries," *UCLA Law Review* 2005, vol. 52, pp. 1627–95.

81. For citation of the Bahl and Martinez-Vasquez data, see Bahl, R., Wallace, S., "A New Paradigm for Property Taxation in Developing Countries," in Bahl, R., Martinez-Vazquez, J., Youngman, J., *Challenging the Conventional Wisdom on the Property Tax* (Cambridge, MA: Lincoln Institute of Land Policy, 2010), 169. For discussions of the status of property tax reform within programs for international tax reform, also see Ibid., 165–201; Bird, R. M., Slack, E., eds., *International Handbook of Land and Property Taxation* (Cheltenham, UK: Edward Elgar, 2004), especially 1–66; and Bird, R. M., Slack, E., "Property Tax and Rural Local Finance, in Bahl, R., Martinez-Vasquez, J., Youngman, J., eds., *Making the Property Tax Work: Experiences in Developing and Transitional Countries* (Cambridge, Massachusetts: Lincoln Institute of Land Policy, 2008), 103–26.

82. On the limitations and problems associated with the VAT, see Bird, R., Gendron, P.-P., *The VAT in Developing and Transitional Countries* (New York: Cambridge University Press, 2007); Stiglitz, J. E., "Development – Oriented Tax Policy," 11–36; and Fjeldstad, O.-H., Moore, M., "Tax reform and State-Building in a Globalized World," 258–9.

83. Shoup, C. S., "The Value-Added Tax and Developing Countries," *World Bank Research Observer* 1988, vol. 3, pp. 156. Shoup held even stronger reservations about adopting a VAT in the United States. In 1979 he expressed the view that a national VAT would put great revenue pressure on state and local governments, which would not have much leeway to expand taxes on payrolls, incomes, and profits even if the federal government reduced those taxes. "It would be a dubious distinction for the United States," Shoup wrote, for the nation to be "the only country in the world where this regressive taxation of retail values was being carried on, virtually nationwide, by two – in some places three – levels of government." Letter to the *New York Times*, October 23, 1979.

84. Bird, R. M., "Taking the Low Road," in Martinez-Vasquez, J., Alm, J., eds., *Public Finance in Development and Transitional Countries: Essays in Honor of Richard Bird* (Cheltenham, UK: Edward Elgar), 336 and 345; Bird, R. M., *Tax Policy and Economic Development* (Baltimore: The Johns Hopkins University Press, 1992), 85–118 and 130–41; Bird, R. M., Gendron, P.-P., *The VAT in Developing and Transitional Countries*, 219 and 221; and citations in footnote 56.

Index

economic efficiency, 248
Economic Interpretation of History
    (Seligman), 50
Economic Journal of Tokyo, 146
Economic Stabilization Board, 180–181
Economic White Paper of 1947 (Tsuru),
    214
economics, historical approaches to, 36–37
Economics for Ladies (Ouchi), 184
ECOSOC. *See* Economic and Social
    Council
education, 188, 434
Eheberg, Karl Theodor, 158
*Elements of Liberty: On the Average of
    Property, The* (Sen), 147
Elements of Political Economy (Wayland),
    146
Elements of Public Finance (Ouchi), 159
Ellis, William, 144
Ely, Richard T., 148–156
empirical methods, 51, 53, 82
employment
    British policies, post-WWII, 406–407
    Columbia policies, 407
    Cuba and, 100
    currency markets and, 89
    income revenues and, 382
    public works programs, 89, 100
    rural, 411
    trade and, 405–407
Employment Act of 1946 (U.S.), 405
enterprise tax, 268
EPU. *See* European Payments Union
equality principle, 96
ERP. *See* European Recovery Program
Essays in Taxation (Seligman), 152
estate taxes, 119, 203, 419
European common market tax policy,
    435–436
European Payments Union (EPU), 403
European Recovery Program (ERP), 403
excess-profits taxation, 128, 435
    capital formation goals, 268
    Shoup on, 249
excise taxes
    administration problems and, 123
    demand elasticity and, 120
    fairness and, 119, 122
    four groups of, 121
    Great Depression and, 120
    piecemeal approaches to, 122
    regressivity issues, 122, 185, 312

revenues from, 368t
sales taxes compared, 123–124
Exim bank, 99, 100, 103–104
export policies, 299, 378–379

Facing the Tax Problem (Shoup), 44, 46,
    101, 215, 279
faculty theory, of taxation, 44. *See also* tax
    capacity
Feldstein, Martin, 15, 58n62, 221n9
Fenollosa, Ernest Francisco, 147
feudal systems, 143
financial missions and "embedded
    liberalism" and "embedded
    progressivism," 5
Finanzwissenshaft (Cohn), 156
fiscal consciousness, 49, 111, 113, 184,
    186–189
fiscal harmonization, 436
Fiscal Investment and Loan Program
    (FILP), 302
fiscal sociology, 73–78
fiscal stimulus, investment/consumption,
    127–128
Fisher, Irving, 60n75
Fitch, Lyle C., 432
Fjeldstad, Odd-Helge, 444
foreign aid. *See* aid curse; *specific countries*
Foreign Assistance Office, U.S. Treasury,
    400, 436
foreign direct investment, 414–415
Foreign Investment Law of 1950 (Japan),
    415
foreign tax credits, 378–379
France
    American view of, 62–66
    currency market collapse, 61
    debts, 62, 70
    estimated taxes, 69
    Haig-Shoup mission and, 61–82, 66–67
    income tax and, 66, 69
    Japan influenced by, 144
    Japan mission and, 228, 232
    sales taxes, 63–65, 72–79
    Shoup on, 71
    small-scale production and, 66
    tax reform history, 66, 67–68, 71, 74,
        81, 418
    tax revenues, 67–68, 71, 74–75,
        308–309, 418
    war reparations and, 62
Friedman, Milton, 77, 128, 209

Galbraith, J. K., 405
Garst, Charles E., 155–156
gasoline taxes, 115, 119
General Agreements on Tariffs and Trade,
    399, 404
George, Henry, 149, 410. *See also* single
    tax movement
Germany
    currency reforms, 403
    Dodge and, 403
    Historical School and, 36, 37
    hyperinflation and, 170, 171
    income tax law, 314
    Japan influenced by, 144, 145, 149, 156,
        158
    monetary reforms, 180
    tax revenues, 308–309
    war debts and, 62, 70–71, 72
Getúlio Vargas Foundation
Gide, Charles, 70–71
Gillis, Malcolm, 6, 435
Gittes, Enrique F., 439
Gladstone, William, 417–418
Glass-Steagall Act, 374
Goode, Richard, 399
Gordon, Roger, 447
governmental size issue, 183–185, 434
Great Depression, 43, 115–116, 120
Grew, Joseph C., 306
Groves, Harold, ix, 199–200, 210, 430,
    450n15
Guggenheim, Harry F., 23, 86, 91–93

Haig, Robert Murray, 15, 21–22, 34, 63,
    92, 400
    Puerto Rico mission and, 202–203
    sales taxes and, 43, 71
    Seligman and, 39
    Shoup and, 20, 26, 31, 43, 54, 199,
        235
    Simons and, 199, 202–203
Hansen, Alvin, 399
Hara Sumio, 229–230, 427–428
Harada Sen, 147
Harriss, C. Lowell, 47, 58n51, 401n3
Hashimoto Masajiro, 156
Hatfield, Rolland, 208–209, 225n49, 230,
    232, 235
Hatoyama cabinet, 326–328
Hawley-Smoot Tariff Act, 86, 90
Hayashi Takehisa, 279

Hayashi Yoshio, 279
Hayes, Carlton J. H., 61
Hirata Keiichiro, 263–265, 324
Hirschman, Albert, 411
historical contingency
    Cuba mission and, 87
    political context and, 37
    sales taxes and, 78–79
    social order and, 206
    tax reform and, 206
History of Civilisation in England (Buckle),
    155
History of Fiscal Science (Seligman), 50
Holdren, Hale
Hoover, Herbert, 19–20, 27n5, 64
Horie Kiichi, 157
horizontal equity
    capital formation and, 248, 268, 324
    capital gains taxation and, 247–248
    consumption taxes and, 82, 281
    definition by Shoup, 136
    economic development and, 41–42
    economic efficiency and, 248
    interest income and, 263, 321
    Korean war and, 324
    labor income and, 247
    sales taxes and, 75
    secret accounts and, 252
    tax equity and. *See* tax equity
    tax neutrality and. *See* tax neutrality
    vertical equity and, 82
horizontal firm integration, 421
household tax, 338
Hull, Cordell, 403
Huntington, Samuel P., 438

IBRD. *See* International Bank for Recovery
    and Development
Ichimada Hisato, 262, 265
Ikeda Hayato
    Dodge Line and, 298–299
    general background of, 171–173
    local autonomy and, 338
    policies of, 169, 179, 182–185, 187
    secret accounts and, 265
    Shoup mission and, 212–213, 229, 329,
        358n10, 358n13, 439, 453n54
    tax burden and, 178–179
    Tsuru Shigeto and, 214
IMF. *See* International Monetary Fund
income averaging, 48

Organizations Related to Local Authorities
(ORLA), 338
Ouchi Hyoe, 158, 282
background of, 169–170
Shoup mission and, 173–176, 179, 180,
184–188
Outlines of Social Economy (Ellis), 146

Park, Gene, 302
peacetime dividend, 199
Penner, Rudolph G., 436
Personal Income Taxation (Simons), 51
personal income taxes
corporate income tax and, 389
corporation distribution income,
381–383
deductions and, 321, 325, 385
democratic values and, 97
revenues from, 115–118, 368, 382
Platt Amendment, 88–89, 91
political economics, institutionalism and,
34, 42–54. *See also specific countries,
topics*
*Political History of the Federal Income
Tax, The* (Ratner), 50
*Political Science and Comparative
Constitutional Law* (Burgess), 35
Political Science Quarterly, 36
Post, Louis P., 152
postal savings banks, 243, 247, 253, 258,
260, 266, 269
Primi Elementi di Scienza delle Finanze
(Cossa), 148
Principles of National Income Analysis
(Shoup), 198
Principles of Political Economy (Mill),
146
prisoner's dilemma, 295–297
production taxes, 80
Progress and Poverty (George), 151
progressive income taxation
ability-to-pay argument, 116
capital accumulation and, 433
democracy and, 184
progressivity comparisons, 74–75
public perceptions of, 69
Puerto Rico tax mission, 203
socialism and, 158
tax avoidance and, 246, 269
tax burdens and. *See* tax burden
distribution

taxpaying capacity and, 38
Venezuela mission and, 433
progressivism, 5, 20, 200. *See also*
insitutionalism
property taxes, 185, 447
local fiscal autonomy, 185
revenues from, 368t
Proposal of Land Tax Reform (Kanda),
146
public finance
comparative study of, 36
debt versus taxation and, 63
deficit financing and, 331
national bonds, 369
political economy of, 42–54
social justice and, 86
Public Finance (Sagane), 148–149
Public Finance (Shoup), 53–54
Public Finances of Post-War France, The
(Haig), 72–73
Public Information Office, 238
public opinion polls, 294–295, 352
public works programs, 89, 100
public-private partnerships. *See* dollar
diplomacy
Puerto Rico mission, 202–203
Purdy & Henderson, 99

Rathgen, Karl, 147
rational tax system, 322
Ratner, Sidney, 50
real estate income, 315
Recent American Socialism (Ely), 153
Reconstruction Finance Bank, 181
record-keeping
accountant associations, 440
blue returns. *See* blue returns
corporate income taxation, 366
Cuba tax mission, 97
excessive income reporting, 318
income taxation and, 79
inquisitorial state and, 79
as learning process, 297
multiple books, 228
pre-WWI Japan and, 311
sales taxation and, 79
security transactions, 260
self-assessment systems, 232, 324
withholding systems. *See* withholding
systems
Reed, Eugene, 256–257, 261, 263

educational role of, 439
foreign experts and, 439–440
historical overview, 4–5, 438–440
international institutions and, 444
post-war increase, 442
success criteria for, 52, 439
tailoring to specific countries, 439,
448
See also specific countries, missions
tax neutrality, 41–42, 279, 418, 420. *See
also* tax equity
Tax Policy League survey, 115
tax reform
in 2011, 365
budget requirments and, 320–321
economic development and, 289
French history of, 67
historical contingency and, 206
post-Occupation, 426–429
successfulness of, 430, 437–438
wars and, 67
*See also specific reforms, tax missions,
taxes*
Tax Reform of 1981 (Japan), 388–389
Tax Reform of 1984 (Japan), 389–390
Tax Reform Act of 1986, 307, 400
tax revenues, international comparisons,
308–309, 367–369
tax simplification, 178, 183, 446
democracy and, 184
tax compliance and, 71
transparency and, 297
Viner studies and, 111
taxable income
ability-to-pay and, 45–46
definitions of, 39–42, 44, 202, 247
horizontal equity and, 45
as living mutable concept, 40
Simons on, 51
taxable units and, 51
taxation
definitions of, 157–158
democracy and, 183–189
development and, 38, 41
distributive politics and, 306–307
economic structures and, 66, 420
inflation and, 174–177, 177, 181
middle class and, 306–307
professionalization of, 290
wars and, 143, 175
See also specific countries, topics

Taxation Investigating Committee,
212–213
teleological methods, 37–38
Tentearo Makato, 152
Thierry, Joseph, 69–70
Tilly, Charles, 290
tobacco taxes, 119–121, 314
Tolstoy, Leo, 152
Toward Social Economy (Bowen),
205–206
trade, employment and, 405–407
trade globalization, 306–307
Trade Union Law of 1945 (Japan), 406
Traite de la science des finances
(Leroy-Beaulieu), 146
transparency, democracy and, 184
Treasury I (1984), 400
Truman administration, 6, 196, 199
trust. *See* tax culture
Tsuru Shigeto, 2, 169, 212–216,
427
Bronfenbrenner and, 237–238
Ikeda and, 214
policy and, 182, 189
Shoup mission and, 182, 189
Willoughby surveillance list, 238
Tubman, William, 436
Turkey missions, 399
turnover tax, 42, 71–72
administrative capacity and, 79–81
agricultural/urban groups and, 78–82
Brazil mission and, 435
currency markets and, 77
horizontal equity and, 82
inflation and, 76–77
point of collection, 76
revenues from, 81t
sales taxes and. *See* sales taxes
tax evasion and, 78
value-added taxes and, 42, 435
vertical equity and, 82
yield from, 81
Twentieth Century Fund, 25, 44, 46, 101,
215

Umezawa Setsuo, 389
underground economies, 441
self-assessment system and, 318
value-added taxes and, 447
unearned income, 115, 311
United Nations, 399